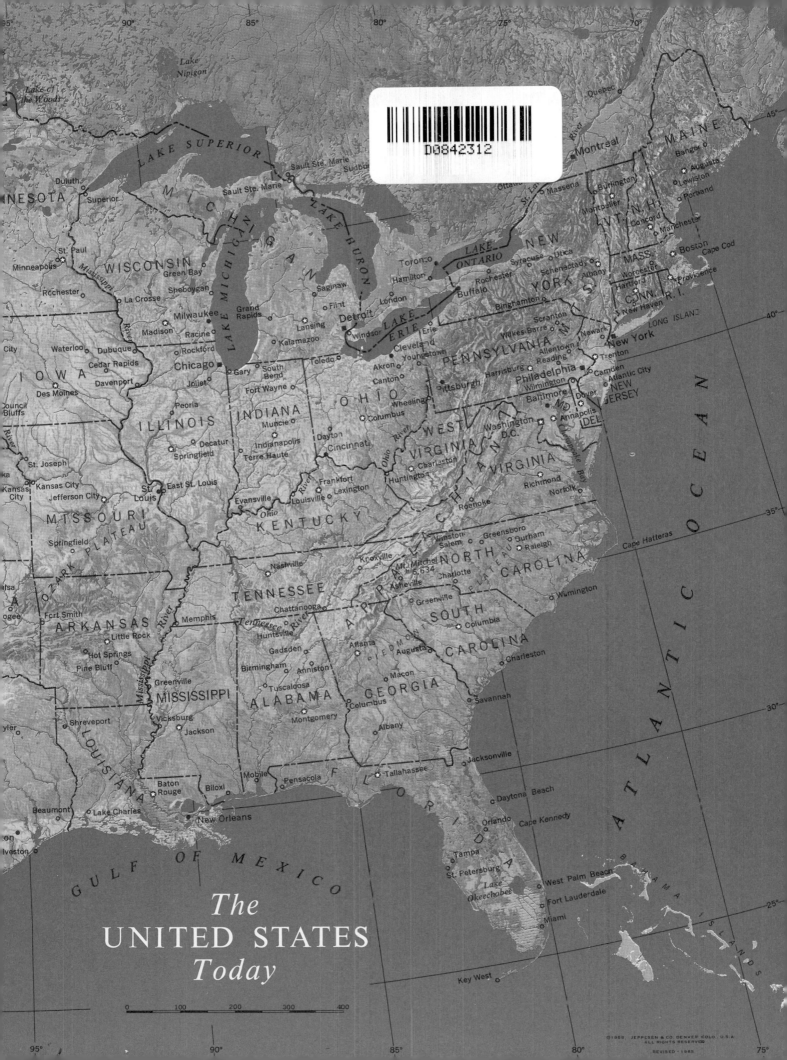

The UNITED STATES Today

The AMERICAN HERITAGE

By the Editors of
AMERICAN HERITAGE
The Magazine of History

Editor in Charge
HILDE HEUN KAGAN

Chapter Texts by
ROGER BUTTERFIELD

BRUCE CATTON

JOHN A. GARRATY

ALVIN M. JOSEPHY, JR.

STEPHEN W. SEARS

Consultant
RICHARD B. MORRIS

Published by
AMERICAN HERITAGE PUBLISHING CO., INC., New York

Book Trade Distribution by
McGRAW-HILL BOOK COMPANY

PICTORIAL Atlas

of

UNITED STATES HISTORY

CARTOUCHE FROM FIRST MAP OF U.S. BY ABEL BUELL, 1783, BY PERMISSION OF NEW JERSEY STATE HISTORICAL SOCIETY

AMERICAN HERITAGE
The Magazine of History

Publisher: James Parton
Editor in Chief: Joseph J. Thorndike
Senior Editor: Bruce Catton
Editor: Oliver Jensen
Editorial Director, Book Division: Richard M. Ketchum
Senior Art Director: Irwin Glusker
Editor, American Heritage Books: Alvin M. Josephy, Jr.

Staff for this Book

Editor: Hilde Heun Kagan
Art Director: Murray V. Belsky
Associate Editor: Beverley Hilowitz
Assistant Editors: Caroline Backlund, Nancy Kelly,
        Mary Zuazua
Contributing Editors: Joseph L. Gardner,
        Kenneth W. Leish
Research: Susan L. Beckwith, Karen Curtin,
        Angelica Peale White
Copy Editor: Brenda Savard Bennerup
Picture Editors: Wesley Day, Alice D. Watson
Map Compilation: Margo L. Dryden
Assistant Art Director: John J. Conley
Pictorial Maps: David Greenspan
Cartographic Director: Duncan M. Fitchet

01503

TABLE *of* CONTENTS

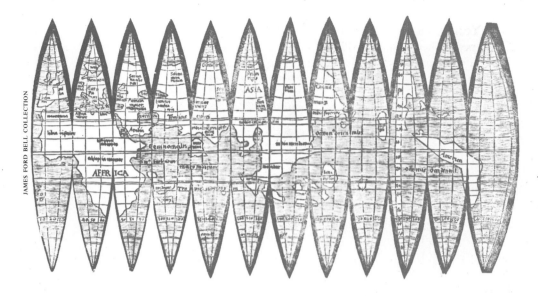

This 1507 map of the earth by Martin Waldseemüller of the Academy of Saint-Dié in Lorraine christened the New World. On South America, shown as an island (right), appeared for the first time the name America, *to honor Amerigo Vespucci, explorer and Pilot Major of Spain.*

LIST *of* MAPS

Benjamin Franklin was perhaps the first scientist to study the Gulf Stream. Using information supplied him by Nantucket whalers, he prepared a chart in 1769 that was engraved "for the benefit of navigators." Later, he conducted his studies of the Gulf Stream during transatlantic crossings.

AMERICAN PHILOSOPHICAL SOCIETY

NATIONAL ARCHIVES

Mappers of the great mountains of the West are shown at work among the peaks in the superb panoramic view below of Colorado's La Plata range. It was drawn by William H. Holmes, a remarkably talented artist-topographer with Ferdinand V. Hayden's Colorado Survey, 1873–76.

INTRODUCTION

Historic personages, so the poet reminds us, leave behind them "foot-prints on the sands of time," and great events are etched in the memory of a people. Alas, the foot-prints blur and the memory fades. That is why the historian is enlisted to place *who,* and *when,* and sometimes *why* in a chronological framework. Too often the historian takes for granted that the reader comprehends *where* the events he is narrating transpired. Here is where the historical atlas is needed to pin down the chronological record in space and thereby make it more meaningful, to show the reader down what streams the fur traders paddled their canoes, on what plain the Indians made their stand, through what mountain pass the pioneers proceeded on their westward course. Designed as a cartographic guide to the history of the immense American empire, this atlas seeks to answer the question *where.* Providing an essential reference tool for those who would understand American history, this volume, by means of its maps and its accompanying narrative text, may be read as well as studied.

Every generation demands a fresh and up-to-date cartographic record of the American past, and ours has more reasons than earlier ones for taking a backward look through a new set of spectacles. Consider just a few of the modifications of our knowledge of the American past which recent discoveries have dictated. There is, for example, the effect of the atomic clock: physical tests based on the half cycle of carbon 14, which is present in all organic matter and which disappears at a known rate, have documented the settlement of early man in America even prior to the end of the Ice Age. Such tests place man's appearance here as early as 35,000 B.C., entirely revising the view of the prehistoric period that prevailed until the early 1950's. Another example of the way our ideas of American history have altered may be seen in the recent and fortuitous uncovering of the Vinland Map—a map that provides additional confirmation of the early Norse voyages to the New World.

Even at the time of the Federal Convention, much of the interior of the United States—for which the Founding Fathers had such splendid plans—remained to be discovered, surveyed, and mapped. A number of the maps in this atlas show how much was added to our geographical knowledge of the American West by the explorations and surveys of the nineteenth century, and how important that information was for the rapid development of transportation systems spanning the nation. In the twentieth century the Arctic and Antarctica were mapped, and aerial and space photography in our own generation have given us a new and exciting look at the contours of our continent and have added still another dimension to map making.

In certain respects this atlas departs from conventional treatments. Instead of lumping all such material together, consideration is given at appropriate periodic intervals to the ethnic and religious composition of American society, to its changing economic characteristics, and to the key role of natural resources in the dynamics of our industrial society. And the enormous broadening of our nation's geographical horizon brought about by World War II and the coming of the Nuclear Space Age is reported in these pages.

The student will find in this volume answers to a variety of problems in American history, including the confrontation of white man and Indian at various stages in time. In a curious way, certain of these maps raise their own questions, and careful scrutiny of these pages will provide many fascinating answers. What, for example, were the stakes of empire in the four great Intercolonial Wars waged by England and her colonies against France and Spain? How rigid was the Proclamation Line of 1763 and how seriously did it hamper westward settlement and land speculation? How did the Federal government obtain the Northwest Territory? What were the issues in diplomacy over the northern boundary of Maine and the fisheries off the Grand Bank? Why was the western boundary of Louisiana a matter of dispute between Spain and the United States after the Louisiana Purchase? Why was the United States so eager to effect the Gadsden Purchase from Mexico? What does the map of railroads on the eve of the Civil War suggest about the nature of East-West ties as compared with North-South communication lines?

There was a time when environmental determinism held American geography in its iron grip. Now we know, as an abundance of these maps conclusively demonstrate, that, while environment does affect civilization, man himself can, and frequently does, refashion his environment. He can tunnel through mountains, connect separate water systems by a network of canals, bypass falls and rapids, irrigate deserts, and turn primeval forests into concrete thruways. Indeed, technological change, the population explosion, and the unchecked march of urban civilization have upset the balance of nature and created new environmental problems, such as those posed by impure air and polluted streams, problems unimagined by the pioneers who settled the nation. It is a special virtue of this atlas that it has been conceived and created not only as a collection of historical maps but as a visual recording of the physical wonders that once made up this America. The volume is a reminder that our past is around us still. To those with historical perception, it can never be consumed.   *Richard B. Morris*

CHAPTER 1

PREHISTORIC NORTH AMERICA

During eons of geological time, totaling perhaps half a billion years, lighter kinds of rock in the earth's cooling crust were buoyed up by the denser materials below, and became fused in a rigid block—known as the Canadian Shield—which is now the hard core of North America. This platform of very ancient rock underlies northern and eastern Canada, and reaches down beneath Lake Superior to bolster Wisconsin and Minnesota. Anchored to it is another big region, the so-called "stable interior," comprising the central provinces of Canada, the intermountain United States, and the northern two-thirds of Mexico. This segment, like the Canadian Shield, is firmly based on primeval rock. But it subsided a little after it coalesced. So for millions of years at a time it was flooded by inland seas, which deposited sediment—now layers of rock—on top of its original foundations.

The mountain chains of the East and West, and the coastlines with most of their islands, were formed by the crumbling and earth-flexing actions that occur on the edges of all great continents. Enormous deposits of eroded matter press down on the continental shelf, causing the ocean floor to buckle. This produces corresponding upward thrusts (geanticlines) in nearby, or distant, locations. The Appalachian Mountains were thus created four times in 400 million years; three times they were worn away into troughs. The Rocky Mountains are younger; they were marine sediment during most of their history, and were elevated to their present grandeur some 30 million years ago.

The majestic rivers and lakes, game-filled forests, and fertile prairies that have made the continent so attractive to man, are, compared with the mountains, brand new. Their extent and location were largely determined during the latest retreat of the glaciers, beginning about 9000 B.C. At that date three major ice sheets still occupied most of the surface from the Arctic Ocean to Cincinnati, and from Long Island to Puget Sound (see pages 16–17). The melting glaciers filled the Great Lakes and rearranged river systems; they also dropped boulders and masses of gravel that became hills and low mountains. The land rose as the weight of ice disappeared; trees took root in the warmer soil. In some areas the climate dried permanently, causing lakes to evaporate and turn into deserts, a process that still goes on in and around the Great Salt Lake of Utah, and at Pyramid Lake, Nevada.

Before the present landscape existed, the first human discoverers of North America arrived. They came—almost certainly—while glaciers still covered half the continent, and much of Europe and Asia as well. So much of the world's water was then imprisoned in ice that ocean levels fell hundreds of feet, and a land bridge, believed to have been as much as 1,300 miles wide, extended across the present Bering Sea and Strait, connecting Siberia and Alaska. Oddly enough (or so it seems today) most of Alaska remained ice-free, with a climate favorable to animal life. Anthropologists believe the entire area—northeastern Siberia, the broad land bridge, and western Alaska—was an Ice Age game preserve, and the obvious route by which primitive hunters first reached any part of the Western Hemisphere.

The first immigrants were few and nomadic, as were their descendants who wandered across North and South America. Their bones are not easy to find; less than 20 really ancient skulls have been uncovered so far on both continents. Like their contemporaries in the Old World they hunted and ate big animals—giant sloth, mammoth, long-horned bison—that flourished until the glaciers vanished, and then became extinct. Their most enduring achievement was shaping handsome projectile points (stone tips for their wooden spears), of which a great many have been collected. The varied designs of these small works of art are used to trace the cultural progress that preceded Indian nations and tribes known in historic times.

Between the unknown date of the first arrivals and the coming of Columbus in A.D. 1492, there was an interval of at least 25,000 years, perhaps even 50,000. It was during this period that primitive men in Asia, North Africa, and Europe formalized their religion and art, invented agriculture and writing, began living in villages and cities, studied astronomy, organized kingdoms and castes, and employed scribes to make historical records. The same developments took place in the Americas—independently, and generally later—so the civilizations the Spaniards found were behind the times in important respects. Yet they were mightily impressive. The Aztec capital of Tenochtitlán (Place of the Cactus), which became Mexico City, was more populous than Paris or Rome when the conquistadors saw it. It was built on lakes and approached by four causeways, the main one being three miles long and broad enough for eight lanes of traffic. Two of the causeways were also aqueducts, equipped with ceramic pipes and troughs, that carried water from mountain springs to fountains throughout the city. The Aztec system of public sanitation was more advanced than the Europeans were used to, and they paused to admire it. But they were annoyed by fastidious Aztec diplomats who "fumigated" Cortés and his officers (sprayed them with sweet-smelling incense) before engaging in close conversation.

In 1519 Cortés sent Charles V of Spain a sampling of Aztec handiwork. "The first article presented was a wheel like a sun, as big as a cartwheel, with many sorts of pictures on it, the whole of fine gold . . . Then another wheel . . . of greater size made of silver of great brilliancy in imitation of the moon, with other pictures

shown on it . . . twenty golden ducks, beautifully worked and very natural looking . . . many articles of gold worked in the shape of tigers and lions and monkeys . . . and two rods like staffs of justice, five palms long, all in beautiful hollow work of fine gold." These treasures and many like them were shown to the king at Brussels, where they were seen and ecstatically praised by the artist Albrecht Dürer. Then they were melted and minted into coin. The same fate came to all items of gold, regardless of artistic appeal, that the Spaniards could find in Mexico or Peru. Cortés himself collected rare gems. When he returned to Spain to marry, he gave his bride five big emeralds carved by Aztec craftsmen, "one in the form of a rose, one like a bell with a pearl for a tongue, one like a fish, one like a trumpet, and one like a cup."

Mexico's several Indian civilizations were based on the cultivation of maize, which was tamed from its wild grass state by prehistoric Mexican seedsmen. As corn, it is still North America's most abundant food. In ancient Peru corn was also a staple, but the native potato (called *papa* by the Incas) was the indispensable crop. The Peruvians had 40 kinds of white and sweet potatoes, some of which thrived at 15,000-foot heights. To preserve them Inca farmers left them out to freeze, and then trampled the water out of them by foot. The resulting product was a dry, long-lasting flour, *chuñu,* the earliest form of dehydrated mashed potato.

Unlike the mystical Aztecs, whose religious practices made them poor administrators, the Incas from their base in Peru put together the only real empire in pre-Columbian America. Their 10,000 miles of government roads reached from Quito in Ecuador to central Chile, and far into the mountainous interior, where they suspended bridges from fiber cables to get across rivers and chasms. (An Inca bridge was in continuous service from A.D. 1350 to 1890.) When the Incas conquered a neighboring people, they brought home promising youths to educate them as colonial officials; the Aztecs tied their captives to slabs and cut out their hearts for sacrifice. The Incas' *quipu,* a kind of abacus with knots tied in strings, made them masters of decimal arithmetic and accounting. In a few respects they lagged behind Mexico; their calendar was not so exact as the Mayan, and they never had paper like the Aztecs, whose subjects made it in long yellow rolls, out of wild fig bark fibers.

Yet with all their inventions and splendors, and their long experience in war, the civilized nations were speedily subjugated by a few shiploads of Spaniards. This was partly because they lacked iron and gunpowder, partly because they mistook the white men for gods, and mostly because their populations were trained to obey. Farther north, in the present United States, where Stone Age hunters still roamed, Indian tribes retained their identity for centuries.

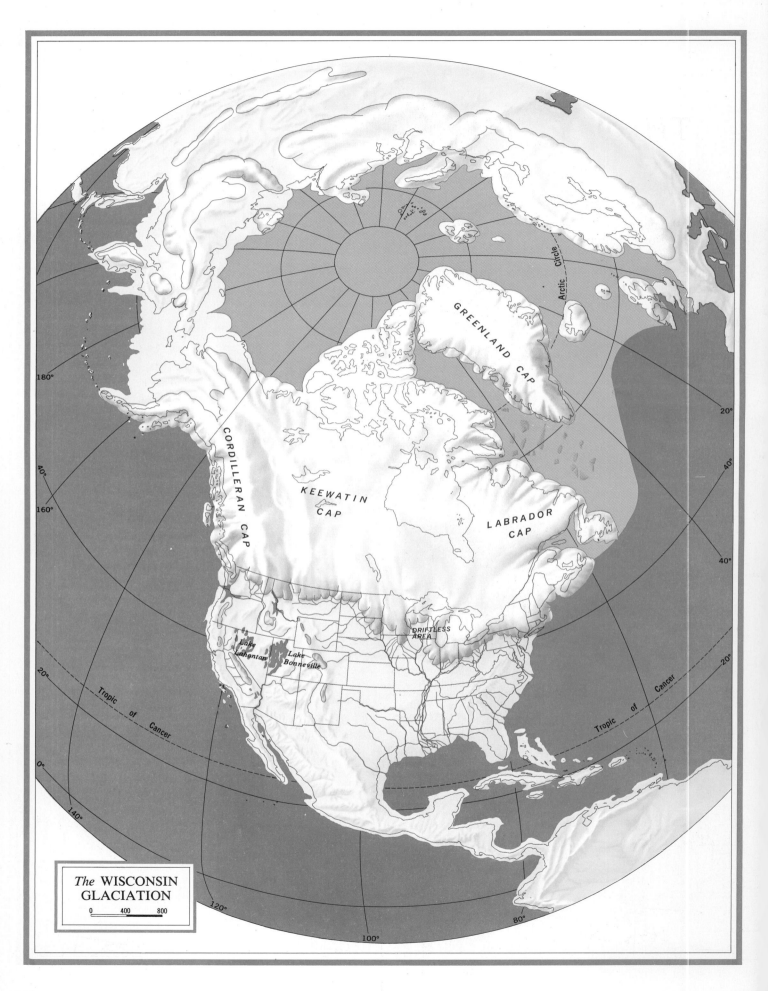

The **WISCONSIN GLACIATION**

0   400   800

CORDILLERAN CAP

KEEWATIN CAP

GREENLAND CAP

LABRADOR CAP

Arctic Circle

DRIFTLESS AREA

Lake Lahontan

Lake Bonneville

Tropic of Cancer

Tropic of Cancer

180°

160°

140°

120°

100°

80°

0°

20°

40°

20°

20°

40°

40°

THE ICE AGE

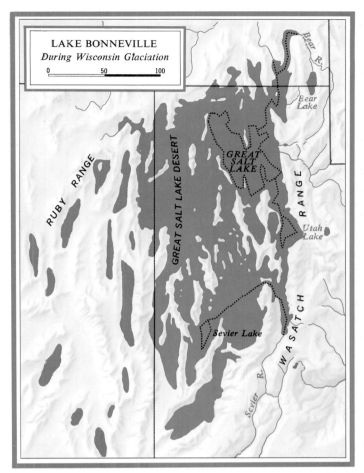

Four lengthy periods of glacial activity have shaped the landscape of North America during the last million years. They are named for the states where their drift deposits (unstratified mixtures of rocks, sand, and clay) were first identified by geologists. The earliest was the Nebraskan, then the Kansan, the Illinoian (which reached to St. Louis), and the Wisconsin, the latest. As shown on the large map, opposite, the Wisconsin glaciation extended into southern Ohio and Indiana, but did not cover a "driftless area," mostly in Wisconsin itself, which was virtually surrounded by glacial ice. While the Wisconsin period was at its peak, regions south of the glaciers were drenched by rain, and vast pluvial lakes, Lahontan and Bonneville, filled basin areas in present-day Nevada and Utah.

Any mass of ice that fails to melt in summer can grow and become a glacier. In the Wisconsin era, which lasted about 80,000 years, the summers were short and cold, and ice built up a mile or two high in three extensive Canadian caps: the Labrador, Keewatin, and Cordilleran. The glaciers' weight supplied the pressure that started them flowing in all directions, at the rate of a few feet a year, until they buried half the continent. A fourth cap covered all of Greenland then, and it is not much smaller today.

The glaciers affected human history in myriad ways. The rocks and gravel they dumped at their edges created Long Island, Cape Cod, and Nantucket; their grinding action converted old river beds into the Great Lakes. The ice front prevented two ancient rivers from flowing north, as they did originally, and forced them to find central outlets. They became the Ohio and the Missouri —main routes which led white men into the West.

Lake Bonneville once covered nearly half of Utah; its waters were fresh and drained north through Red Rock Pass into the Snake and Columbia rivers. When this channel was blocked, and the climate warmed in postglacial times, nine-tenths of Bonneville evaporated. The biggest remnant, Great Salt Lake, is drying up rapidly today.

Lake Arkona, (left, below) was one of many transitional lakes that collected at edges of melting ice sheets. In the later Two Creeks interval (named for a Wisconsin forest buried by ice about 9500 B.C.) the present Great Lakes began to take form. The St. Lawrence, with Lake Champlain and the northern Hudson, was then an inland sea.

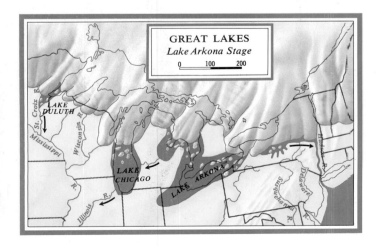

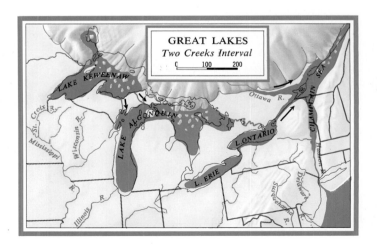

ARCHAIC STAGE
Begins approximately 7,000–6,000 years ago

PROTOARCHAIC STAGE
Approximately 10,000–6,000 years ago,
but continuing longer in some areas
—food grinding implements
—unfluted, lanceolate points,
parallel flaking by pressure

Desert Culture
Gypsum Cave, Nevada
Cochise Complexes, Arizona
Ventana Cave, Arizona
Topanga Complex, California
Danger Cave, Utah
Frightful Cave, Mexico

Plano Culture
Russell Cave, Alabama
Modoc Rockshelter, Illinois
Starved Rock Site, Illinois
Graham Cave, Missouri
Scottsbluff Site, Nebraska
Eden Site, Wyoming
Plainview Site, Texas

Other Sites
Lind Coulee Site, Washington
Wilson Butte Cave, Idaho
Denbigh Flint Complex, Alaska
Kayuk Complex, Alaska

PALEO-INDIAN STAGE
Approximately 20,000–10,000 years ago
—thin and flat percussion-chipped artifacts
—stone projectile points, lanceolate or
leaf-shaped, usually fluted

Old Cordilleran Culture
Five-Mile Rapids Site, Oregon
Fort Rock Cave, Oregon
Yale Site, British Columbia
Fort Liard Complex, Yukon
Flint Creek Complex, Yukon

Lindenmeier Culture
Lindenmeier Site, Colorado
Folsom Site, New Mexico

Llano Culture
Dent Site, Colorado
Naco Site, Arizona
Lehner Site, Arizona
Blackwater Draw Site, New Mexico
Scharbauer ("Midland") Site, Texas

Lucy Site, New Mexico
Sandia Cave, New Mexico

PRE-PROJECTILE POINT STAGE
More than 20,000 years ago,
perhaps more recent in some areas
—bone implements; crude stone tools

Kogruk Complex (Anaktuvuk Pass), Alaska
Santa Rosa Island Sites, California
La Jolla Site, California
American Falls Site, Idaho
Tule Springs Site, Nevada
Malakoff Site, Texas
Friesenhahn Cave, Texas
Lewisville Site, Texas
Valsequillo Site, Mexico
Tequixquiác Site, Mexico

MILLING STONE

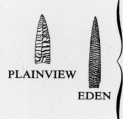

PLAINVIEW

EDEN

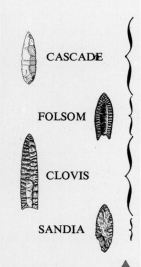

CASCADE

FOLSOM

CLOVIS

SANDIA

THE COMING *of* MAN

Near Folsom, New Mexico, in 1927, a carefully shaped and pointed stone object was found lodged between the buried ribs of an extinct breed of long-horned bison. The circumstances convinced all scientists, for the first time, that Ice Age hunters like the cave men of Europe were the original discoverers of North America. Their weapons and tools have been identified at scores of sites from northern Alaska to southern Mexico (and at many others in South America, down to the tip of Patagonia). Their first point of entry was western Alaska, which was linked to Siberia by a land bridge during glacial times. In later migrations they may have used dugouts or skin craft to island-hop along the Aleutians, and also to cross postglacial Lake Agassiz, which once covered much of Manitoba and North Dakota.

The chart at left lists 41 of the places where ancient people left proof, or possible proof, of their passing. Sites are grouped to show technological progress, leading up to the Archaic Stage, when Indian societies known to history began to evolve. (The arrangement of cultural stages here is based on published suggestions of archaeologist Alex D. Krieger.) In the oldest stage the hunters had hand axes—chunks of stone with chipped edges —but they must have relied also on wood spears. In the next stage, the Paleo-Indian, they improved their spears by attaching stone points, which were distinctively and purposefully shaped in specific areas and periods. Clovis and Folsom fluted points would have been effective when driven by hand, like bayonets; later needle-shaped points were designed for weapons hurled like lances, or projected by notched throwing sticks. The significant artifacts of the Protoarchaic Stage were milling stones, which showed that men (or more likely, women) were collecting and grinding wild grain. Agriculture, pottery jars for storage, and the bow and arrow were introduced during the Archaic Stage.

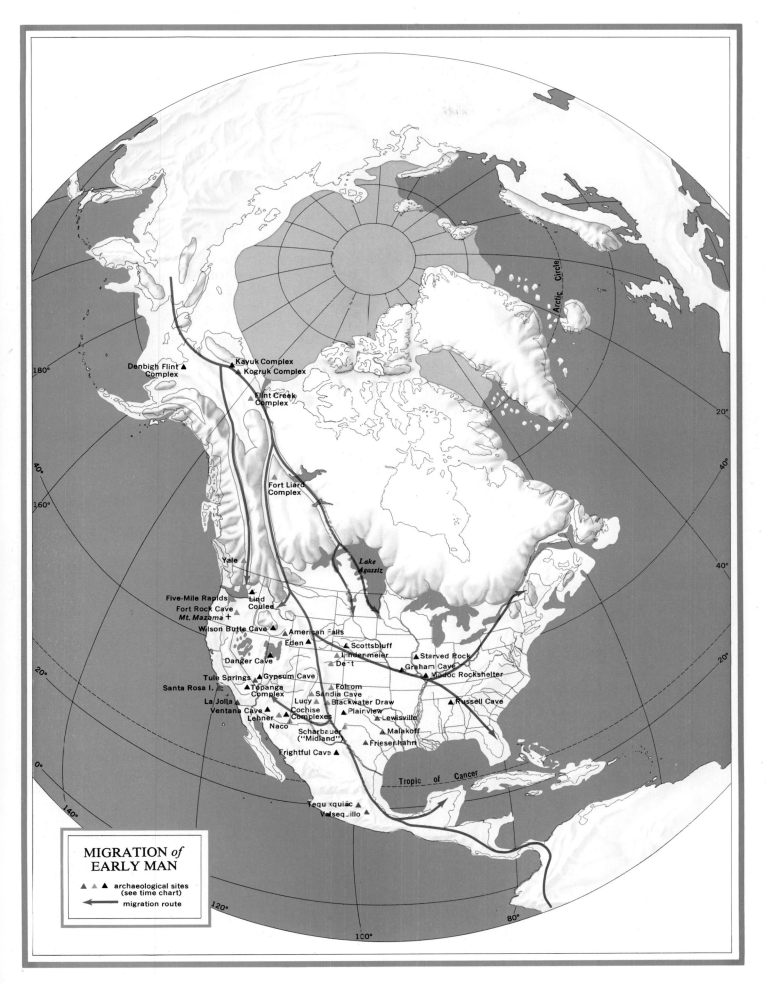

MIGRATION of EARLY MAN

▲ ▲ ▲ archaeological sites (see time chart)

⟵ migration route

Denbigh Flint Complex ▲

Kayuk Complex ▲
Kogruk Complex

Flint Creek Complex ▲

Fort Liard Complex ▲

Lake Agassiz

Yale

Five-Mile Rapids ▲
Fort Rock Cave
Mt. Mazama +
Wilson Butte Cave ▲

Lind Coulee ▲

American Falls

Eden ▲

Scottsbluff ▲

Lindenmeier ▲

Starved Rock ▲

Danger Cave ▲

Dent ▲

Graham Cave ▲
Modoc Rockshelter ▲

Tule Springs ▲ Gypsum Cave ▲

Santa Rosa I. ▲

Topanga Complex ▲

La Jolla ▲

Ventana Cave ▲
Lehner ▲

Cochise Complexes ▲

Naco

Folsom ▲
Sandia Cave ▲
Lucy ▲
Blackwater Draw ▲
Plainview ▲

Lewisville ▲

Russell Cave ▲

Scharbauer ("Midland") ▲

Malakoff ▲

Frieser hahn ▲

Frightful Cave ▲

Tropic of Cancer

Tequixquiac ▲
Valsequillo ▲

180°

160°

140°

120°

100°

80°

20°

40°

40°

20°

0°

Arctic Circle

19

THE RISE *of* CULTURES

Seeds of cultivated pumpkins and chili peppers have been unearthed in Mexican cave shelters that were inhabited before 5000 B.C. Beans, squashes, and corn were developed later; agriculture as a steady occupation began in the central valley of Mexico around 3000 B.C. Surplus food that lasted over the winter gave men a sense of security they never knew in their hunting days. They settled down and built houses, at first of wattle (stick frames) daubed with mud, later of adobe brick. Pottery, baskets, woven cloth (from fibers of the maguey plant), the working of softer metals (copper and gold), and intricate systems of religion and government marked stages of their growing prosperity. But the best evidence of the civilization they achieved was in their great temple towns and cities, of which 47 are located on the two maps below.

People who lived near modern Veracruz and spread a style called Olmec were among the early builders of ceremonial towns. Teotihuacán, in the valley of Mexico, and Monte Albán, in Oaxaca, were the first true cities north of the Mayan region. At Teotihuacán's peak (*c.* A.D. 500), its pyramids, temples, and huge public buildings covered 2,000 acres, and the homes of its 60,000 people extended into numerous suburbs. Cholollan, Tajín, Mitla, and the Toltecs' Tula were other large cities. The Zapotecs and Mixtecs were among many peoples subjected by the Aztecs, who reached central Mexico from somewhere in the north during the thirteenth century. The Aztecs created their impressive capital by building a new lake city, Tenochtitlán, and linking it with conquered and allied cities on the mainland by causeways and water routes.

The Mayas of Yucatan and Guatemala built their biggest cities after A.D. 200, and abandoned them about A.D. 900—today no one knows why. The Mayas were still a busy, seafaring people when the Spaniards came; Columbus met one of their large trading parties on an island off Honduras in 1502. The Inca Empire in South America was a consolidation of earlier groups that developed separately along the coast and in the highlands of Peru (see the maps and chart on the opposite page). It reached its peak with the conquests of Huayna Capac, in 1525, only eight years before the last native ruler, Atahualpa, was strangled by Pizarro's order. North of Mexico, before white men arrived, the nearest approach to civilization was made by pueblo-building Indians in the American Southwest, and by "mound builders" of Archaic times, whose elaborate ornaments, tools, and cemeteries are found in the midwestern and eastern U.S.

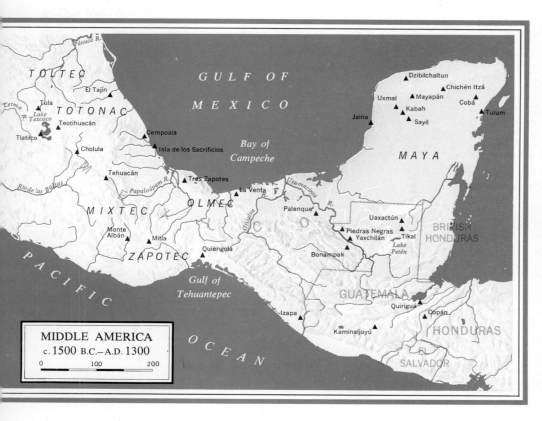

MIDDLE AMERICA
c. 1500 B.C.–A.D. 1300
0   100   200

AZTEC HOMELAND
c. A.D. 1520
———— causeway   – – dike
◉ capitals of Triple Alliance
0   10

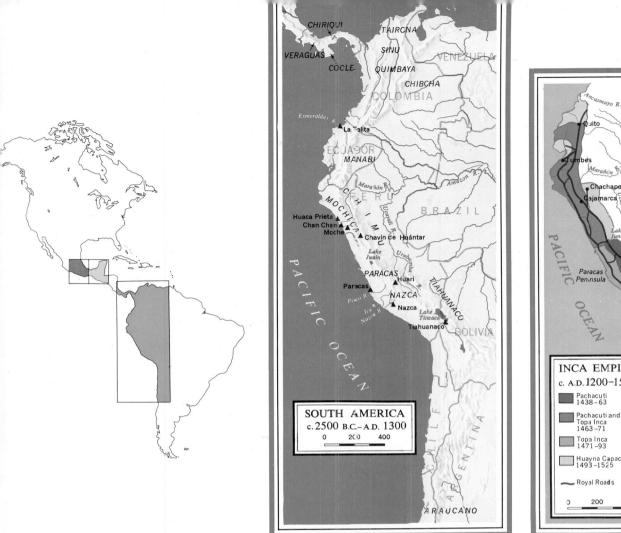

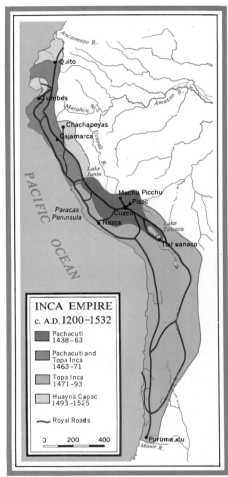

SOUTH AMERICA
c. 2500 B.C.–A.D. 1300

0   200   400

INCA EMPIRE
c. A.D. 1200–1532

Pachacuti
1438–63

Pachacuti and
Topa Inca
1463–71

Topa Inca
1471–93

Huayna Capac
1493–1525

Royal Roads

0   200   400

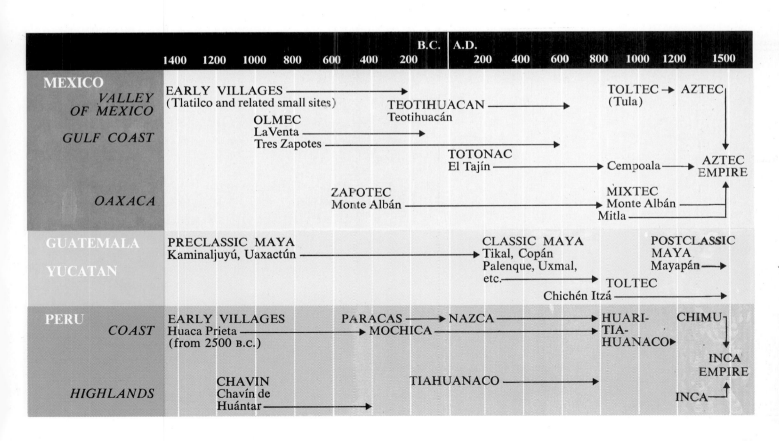

		B.C.	A.D.		
	1400 1200 1000 800 600 400 200		200 400 600 800 1000 1200 1500		

MEXICO

VALLEY OF MEXICO — EARLY VILLAGES (Tlatilco and related small sites) → TEOTIHUACAN → TOLTEC → AZTEC (Tula)

GULF COAST — OLMEC LaVenta Tres Zapotes → Teotihuacán

TOTONAC El Tajín → Cempoala → AZTEC EMPIRE

OAXACA — ZAPOTEC Monte Albán → MIXTEC Monte Albán Mitla

GUATEMALA / **YUCATAN** — PRECLASSIC MAYA Kaminaljuyú, Uaxactún → CLASSIC MAYA Tikal, Copán Palenque, Uxmal, etc. → POSTCLASSIC MAYA Mayapán → TOLTEC Chichén Itzá →

PERU

COAST — EARLY VILLAGES Huaca Prieta (from 2500 B.C.) → PARACAS → NAZCA → HUARI-TIA-HUANACO → CHIMU → INCA EMPIRE
MOCHICA →

HIGHLANDS — CHAVIN Chavín de Huántar → TIAHUANACO → INCA →

21

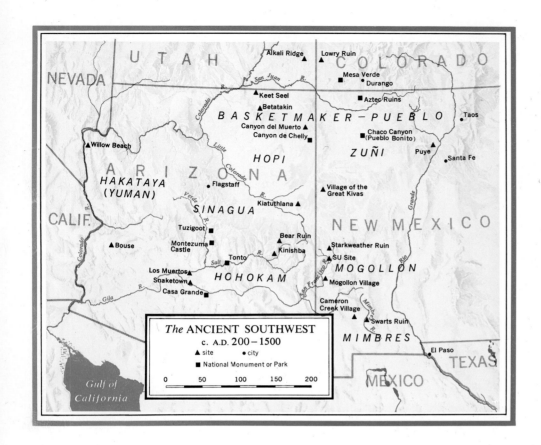

The ANCIENT SOUTHWEST
c. A.D. 200–1500
▲ site   ● city
■ National Monument or Park
0   50   100   150   200

NATIVES
of
NORTH
AMERICA

Pueblo Bonito, in Chaco Canyon, New Mexico, was the largest apartment house in prehistoric America. It is pictured here, from a Smithsonian Institution report, as it looked when 1,200 people lived in it, about A.D. 1067. Its 800 rooms rose in horseshoe-shaped tiers, one to four stories high, around a court that contained several community halls, or kivas. The stone walls were set in adobe cement; interior partitions were marked off by poles, and screens of woven willow and cedar. The building was abandoned before A.D. 1300, probably because of a disastrous drought in the area. Its ruins are now a protected national monument.

The copper-skinned, black-haired people who were called Indians by the Europeans, but who knew each other by many tribal names, varied considerably in their physique and features, and were probably descended from several different strains of Asiatic ancestors. On the opposite page their tribes are labeled showing the areas where white explorers first found them; the map thus covers a long span of time, from about A.D. 1250, when the Norsemen encountered Eskimos in Greenland, to the findings of American mountain men in the nineteenth century. The native population was densest in Mexico, which had between four and five million inhabitants when the Spanish conquest began. Indians within the present United States, including Alaska, are believed to have totaled 900,000 before European settlement, with another 200,000 scattered thinly across Canada. Their economic status ranged all the way from the poverty-stricken Paiutes of the Great Basin deserts, who ate anything edible, including rodents and certain insects, to the Aztec Montezuma of Mexico, who washed down his *tortillas* with vanilla-flavored hot chocolate, out of a solid gold cup.

The Eastern Woodland and Southeast regions abounded with game and fish, and agriculture varied the local diet. The tribes of the Plains enjoyed their most affluent years after they obtained horses from the Spaniards, making buffalo hunting a romp. The only Indians north of the Rio Grande addicted to urban-style living were corn-raising tribes who built multiple dwellings, wove handsome baskets, and created magnificent turquoise jewelry, in the present "Four Corners" of New Mexico, Arizona, Utah, and Colorado (map above).

INDIAN TRIBES
of
NORTH AMERICA

0   200   400   600

23

THE NATIONS
and
THEIR LANGUAGES

Indian tribal kinships are traced through their languages, of which 200 distinct varieties were spoken in North America, above the Rio Grande, just prior to contact with Europeans. In Mexico and Central America another 350 languages existed, and there were 1,450 more in South America; the 2,000 native American languages were one third of all the languages of the world. Groups that spoke the same or similar languages often banded together in nations and leagues, such as the Sioux, Iroquois, and Creek. But they could also be deadly enemies. The New York State Iroquois, for example, annihilated their language kinsmen, the Erie, Neutral, Susquehanna, and Tobacco tribes.

The geographical distribution of Indian languages suggests ancient migrations and/or conquests of which no other record survives. Siouan languages were spoken by the Catawbas in North Carolina, and the Biloxi of Mississippi, as well as by the courageous Dakotas (a Sioux word that means "allies") who were the well-known Sioux of the American West. The Iroquois language was closely related to Caddoan dialects used by Arikaras in South Dakota, Pawnees in Kansas, and Wacos in Texas. The civilized Aztecs and nomadic Comanches belonged to the same language family, along with the pueblo-building Hopis, and Utes, Shoshonis, and Bannocks, who lived among the mountains and arid lands of the Great Basin.

Pre-European Indian writing, even in Mexico and Peru, did not advance beyond pictorial glyphs, or symbols. The first true Indian alphabet was created by a Cherokee scholar, Sequoyah, who reduced his tribe's Iroquoian language to 85 characters, that could be cast into type, at Echota, Georgia, in 1821.

The Ojibwas (Chippewa) of Minnesota were sketched by George Catlin near present-day St. Paul in 1835. They spoke an Algonquian language.

24

INDIAN LANGUAGES
(North America including Northern Mexico)

ESKIMO-ALEUT: Aleut, Eskimo

NA-DENE
  ATHAPASCAN: Ahtena, Apache (Jicarilla, Kiowa Apache, Lipan, Mescalero, Western Apache), Bear Lake, Beaver, Carrier, Chilcotin, Chipewyan, Dogrib, Han, Hare, Hupa, Ingalik, Kaska, Koyukon, Kutchin, Mattole, Nabesna, Navaho, Sarsi, Sekani, Slave, Tahltan, Tanaina, Tanana, Tuchone, Umpqua, Yellowknife
  OTHER: Haida, Tlingit

ALGONQUIAN: Abnaki, Arapaho, Atsina (Gros Ventre), *Blackfeet:* Kaigani (Blood), Piegan, Siksika (Blackfoot); Cheyenne, Chickahominy, Cree, Delaware (Leni Lenape), Illinois (Kaskaskia, Peoria, Piankashaw, Wea), Kickapoo, Mahican, Malecite, Massachuset, Mattapony, Menomini, Miami, Micmac, Mohegan, Montagnais, Nanticoke, Narraganset, Naskapi, Nipmuc, Ojibwa (Chippewa), Ottawa, Pamlico, Pamunkey, Passamaquoddy, Pennacook, Penobscot, Pequot, Potawatomi, Powhatan, Sauk and Fox, Shawnee, Wampanoag, Wappinger

RITWAN: Wiyot, Yurok

KUTENAI: Kutenai

IROQUOIAN: Cherokee, Erie, Huron, *Iroquois:* Cayuga, Mohawk, Oneida, Onondaga, Seneca; Neutral, Nottoway, Susquehanna (Conestoga), Tobacco, Tuscarora

CADDOAN: Arikara, Caddo, Kichai, Pawnee, Tawakoni, Waco, Wichita

GULF
  MUSKOGEAN: Alabama, Apalachee, Chickasaw, Choctaw, Creek, Guale, Hichiti, Mobile, Seminole, Tuskegee, Yamasee
  OTHER: Atakapa, Calusa, Chitimacha, Natchez, Timucua, Tunica

SIOUAN: Assiniboin, Biloxi, Catawba, Crow, Hidatsa, Iowa, Kansa, Mandan, Missouri, Omaha, Osage, Oto, Ponca, Quapaw, *Sioux:* Santee, Teton, and Yankton Dakotas; Tutelo, Winnebago

YUCHI: Yuchi

UTO-AZTECAN: Acaxee, Aztec, Bannock, Cáhita, Cahuilla, Chemehuevi, Comanche, Concho, Gosiute, Hopi, Huichol, Kawaiisu, Mono, Opata, Paiute, Panamint, Papago, Paviotso, Pima, Serrano, Shoshoni (Snake), Tarahumara, Tlaxcala, Toltec, Ute, Yaqui

TANOAN: Pueblo (Isleta, Jémez, Nambé, Picurís, Piro, San Ildefonso, San Juan, Sandía, Santa Clara, Taos)

KIOWA: Kiowa

MOSAN
  SALISHAN: Bella Coola, Chehalis, Coeur d'Alêne, Colville, Cowlitz, Flathead, Kalispel, Lillooet, Nisqually, Okanagan, Puyallup, Salish, Sanpoil, Shuswap, Spokane, Thompson, Tillamook
  WAKASHAN: Bella Bella, Kwakiutl, Makah, Nootka

PENUTIAN: Cayuse, Chinook, Coos, Costanoan, Kalapuya, Klamath, Klikitat, Maidu, Miwok, Modoc, Molala, Nez Perce, Palouse, Takelma, Tsimshian, Wallawalla, Wintun, Yakima, Yokuts

YUKIAN: Yuki

HOKAN: Achomawi, Atsugewi, Chontal, Chumash, Cochimi, Havasupai, Karok, Maricopa, Mohave, Pericu, Pomo, Salinan, Seri, Shasta, Waicuri, Walapai, Washo, Yana, Yavapai, Yuma

COAHUILTECAN: Coahuiltec, Karankawa, Tamaulipec, Tonkawa

KERES: Pueblo (Acoma, Cochiti, Laguna, San Felipe, Santa Ana, Santo Domingo, Sia)

ZUÑI: Zuñi

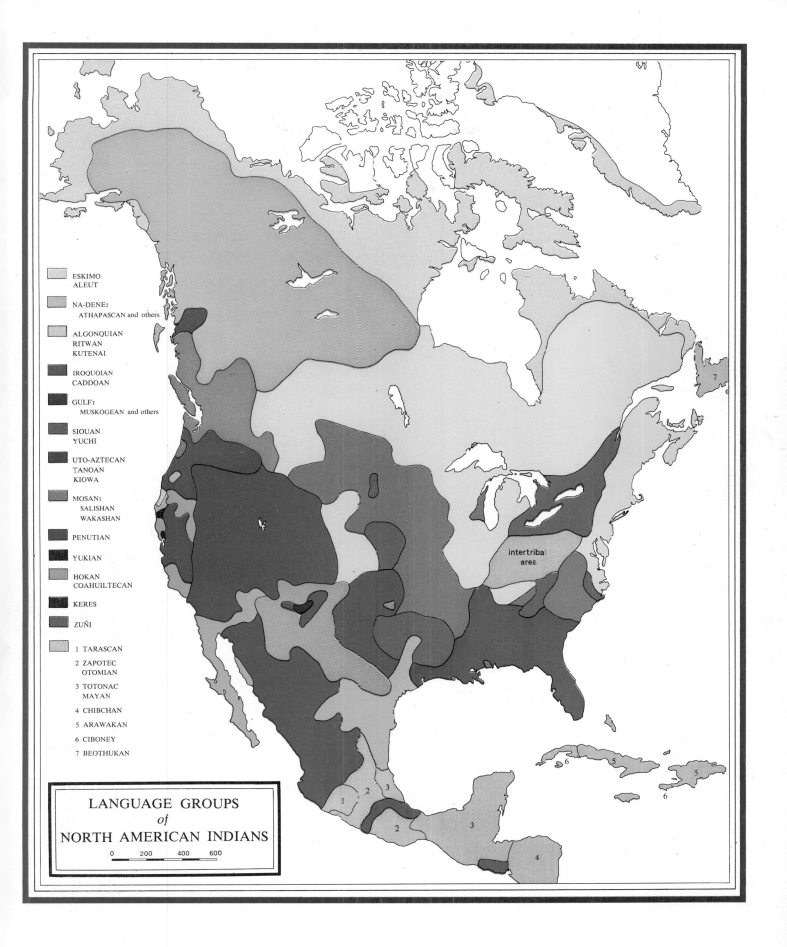

ESKIMO
ALEUT

NA-DENE:
ATHAPASCAN and others

ALGONQUIAN
RITWAN
KUTENAI

IROQUOIAN
CADDOAN

GULF:
MUSKOGEAN and others

SIOUAN
YUCHI

UTO-AZTECAN
TANOAN
KIOWA

MOSAN:
SALISHAN
WAKASHAN

PENUTIAN

YUKIAN

HOKAN
COAHUILTECAN

KERES

ZUÑI

1 TARASCAN

2 ZAPOTEC
OTOMIAN

3 TOTONAC
MAYAN

4 CHIBCHAN

5 ARAWAKAN

6 CIBONEY

7 BEOTHUKAN

intertribal
area

LANGUAGE GROUPS
of
NORTH AMERICAN INDIANS

0   200   400   600

25

In 1541 Coronado, seeking the wealth of legendary Quivira, found instead grass huts of Wichita Indians in present-day Kansas. The Wichita lodges, seen above in an 1852 engraving, typified homes of some tribes of the eastern border of the plains. At right is a Seminole settlement in Florida, and farther right is a 1580 John White painting of a North Carolina Algonquian Indian town. The Zuñi dwelling, below, was drawn by H. B. Möllhausen in New Mexico in the 1850's, and to its right is George Catlin's view of a Comanche tipi village on the Texas plains in 1834.

VILLAGES

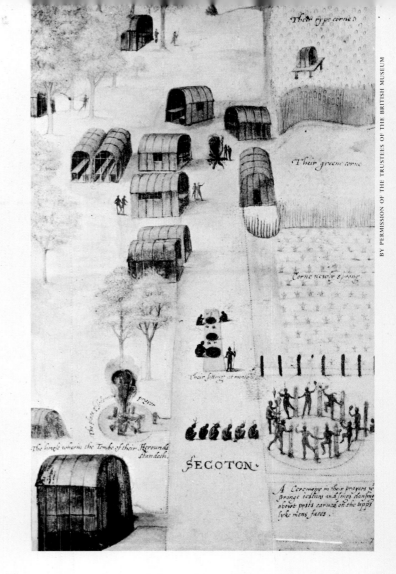

Early man in America lived in rock shelters, caves, brush wickiups, or in the open. As societies became more organized, dwellings evolved into more sophisticated structures—differing in all parts of both continents, as natives made use of local materials and found the most functional forms for their ways of life. Southwestern Indians, using stones or adobe, developed rooms which in time they joined together contiguously in clusters of apartmentlike buildings, sometimes terraced several stories high. When the Spaniards came on them, they called them and their occupants pueblos, the Spanish word for towns. In the woodlands of the Northeast and Great Lakes, Algonquian tribes and Iroquois developed bark- and skin-covered wigwams and long houses which they erected in palisaded villages near their gardens. Southeastern Indians, needing less protection from the elements, raised platforms without walls above marshy land where reptiles were common. And on the plains, the various bands of nomadic hunters used the efficient portable tipi of buffalo hide covers, which they could tie to lodgepoles and drag behind dogs and horses as they followed the game herds.

27

CHAPTER 2

DISCOVERERS
AND
POSSESSORS

"Tierra! tierra!" cried a Spanish sailor, at about 2 A.M. on October 12, 1492. The fragment of land he saw was a coral island in the eastern Bahamas—which one is disputed by experts, and probably always will be. (Watling Island, also called San Salvador, is the choice of modern historians; East Caicos, Grand Turk, Mayaguana, Samana, Rum Cay, Conception, and Cat islands have, or have had, their advocates.) The commander of the little discovery fleet, the Admiral Christopher Columbus, was sure his first landfall was just off the coast of Asia. So Columbus called the people he found there *Indios,* or Indians, and he referred always to the islands and shores of the Caribbean as *las Indias* —the Indies.

As an adventure, and as an enlargement of man's terrestrial knowledge, Columbus's first westward voyage can never be surpassed. That it was based on a huge geographical mistake only made it more wonderful. Cristoforo Colombo (or, in Spanish, Cristóbal Colón), the son of a wool weaver of Genoa, was a sailor, expirate, and sugar merchant who visited the Azores, England, and probably Iceland; swam ashore in Portugal after his ship was sunk in a battle; and shared the conviction, common among the philosophers of his time, that the earth was round. A contemporary who knew him in Spain remembered also that Columbus was once "a hawker of printed books . . . very skilled in the art of cosmography and the mapping of the world."

An expert draftsman of charts and maps Columbus undoubtedly was. But he was also a man who relied much on his hunches. By misconstruing the distances on old Arabic and classical maps, and by believing the guesses of Marco Polo (who in his writings wildly overestimated the eastward thrust of China and Japan), Columbus persuaded himself that the earth was a much smaller globe than it is, and that the eastern fringes of Asia were no more than 3,000 miles west of the coast of Europe. For 15 years Columbus tried to find someone who would give him ships and men to sail in that direction. In 1492 the royal couple of Spain, Fernando and Ysabel, agreed to finance his expedition.

In its strictly technical details, the voyage was almost uneventful. Columbus with his three tiny ships first headed south some 800 miles, from Palos in Spain to the Canary Islands off Africa. (Columbus made this preliminary detour to avoid the strong westerly winds that prevailed in the northern Atlantic.) From Hierro, the most western of the Canaries, he set his course almost due west, and pushed out at once onto a route that had never been followed to its end by any previous navigator (see map on pages 32–33). It was one of the smoothest crossings on record. The weather, Columbus wrote in his journal, was "like April in Andalusia . . . the Sea was like a river . . . the air sweet and very soft." A dove and a whale, both signs of land, caused the admiral to change course once, but briefly, halfway in the 32-day journey. The distance was more than he had anticipated: 3,409 nautical miles from Hierro to the Bahamas. His sailors were tense and sometimes panicky; Columbus was serene. He believed Asia was straight ahead, and in that he was correct. What he had no way of knowing (and what was left to others to prove) was that two unrecorded continents, teeming with natural riches and wonders, alive with organized human activity, and comprising a fourth of the world's habitable surface, lay squarely in his path.

On his first day in the New World, Columbus performed a ceremony which had a serious meaning to the 90 Europeans who watched him. The admiral carried the Spanish flag on shore, and his captains brought banners embroidered with crosses, and the initials F and Y, representing the Spanish monarchs. Columbus instructed his assembled officers to "bear faithful witness that he . . . now took possession of said island for the King and Queen his Lords, making the declarations that are required." That was the start of colonial sovereignty, and of all legal land titles to the present day, in North and South America. The Supreme Court of the United States has upheld and restated "the original fundamental principle," asserted in Columbus's time by all the seafaring nations, that "discovery gave exclusive title to those who made it." As applied to islands, this meant that the discoverer of one shore of an island was entitled to claim it all. The discovery of a large mainland river, and the navigation of some part of its length, was assumed to give the discovering nation possession of all the land that drained into it. The native inhabitants were left with a vague legal claim to continue to occupy as much of the soil as they needed to live on. But they were rarely able to maintain this right, and not at all when their possessions attracted invading armies of white men, equipped with superior weapons.

Columbus's contract with the rulers of Spain made him the sole viceroy and governor-general over all the islands and mainlands he could discover. It also gave him a one-tenth share of all the gold, gems, spices, or other precious commodities he could collect and bring back to Spain. The naked Taino Indians on the first island he found had nothing to offer except skeins of cotton, pet parrots, and the darts they used for hunting. Columbus noted, however, that some of them wore little pieces of gold "in a hole they have in their nose." By means of signs, he learned of other islands to the south where there was a bigger supply of gold, and "a king who had great cups full."

Setting out in that direction he coasted along the north shore of Cuba (which he identified at first as Marco Polo's "Zipangu," or Japan), and finally settled on Hispaniola (comprising the future Dominican Republic and Haiti) as a headquarters for more explora-

tions. On Christmas Eve a careless pilot let his flagship *Santa Maria* run onto a sandbar, where it had to be abandoned. To relieve Columbus's distress, a local cacique, or Indian chief, brought him many presents, including large nuggets of gold and a mask of fine beaten gold which covered the admiral's face. In this way the Spaniards learned that there were gold-bearing streams in the vicinity.

Columbus sailed back to Spain, and was equipped with 17 ships and 1,200 men to found a colony on Hispaniola. When he returned to the island (November, 1493), he found that the 39 men he had left as a garrison were dead, and their remains bore evidence of cannibalism. Presumably they mistreated the Indians, but the incident gave the Spaniards an excuse for their tough Indian policy. While Columbus cruised in the Caribbean, discovering and naming new places, his brother Bartholomew, a ruthless administrator, laid out villages and plantations, and established stern rules for the gold-mining industry. The natives were conscripted for labor at first, and then kidnapped outright as slaves. Sickness and political dissension undermined Columbus's authority; in 1500 he was arrested by a new governor, and was shipped to Spain in chains. By then scores of aggressive adventurers from Spain, Portugal, and even England, had reached, or were on their way to, the New World. Ponce de León, who came with Columbus in 1493, conquered Puerto Rico, and reaped a fortune from slave hunting. Diego Velásquez founded the first settlement on Cuba, whose natives fought until 1519, but were eventually annihilated. Vasco Núñez de Balboa, a hardy character, came to Hispaniola in 1501, and had himself nailed in a cask in order to reach the restricted pearl fisheries on the coast of South America. At the head of a gang of cutthroats he slaughtered Indians and hacked his way across the Isthmus of Panama, where he glimpsed the Pacific—"silent upon a peak in Darien"—in 1513. He immediately claimed the entire Pacific Ocean and all the lands it touched for Spain. With him was Francisco Pizarro, who later destroyed the Inca civilization of Peru. Hernán Cortés, who helped subdue Cuba, landed in Mexico in 1519, and completed his conquest of the Aztecs in 1521.

Meanwhile, a forgotten map, copied into a handwritten book at Basel in Switzerland, about the year 1440, proved that Viking sailors from Iceland and Greenland had reached the coast of North America almost 500 years before Columbus's first voyage. Columbus could have heard old rumors of the Vikings' exploits; but he never saw the map, which was acquired by Yale University, and first published there, in 1965. It is reproduced on the next two pages, and purports to show the whole world. The indented coastline at farthest left is labeled (in Latin) "Vinland Island, discovered by Bjarni [Herjolfsson] and Leif [Eiriksson] in company."

Uolunt hic post longitudines de insulis Groudlanda et meridiem ad
els in tres continuatas partes occidentales oceani maris reis... circa ad
... ...glacies hyemus et leuibus estiuis ... ...
uidelicet hec eis innenierunt quam Vinlandia insula appellauerunt ... ...
translande conuenunc primarum sedis apostolice consequo leuanui in hac terra
spaciose uero et epulenissima insulas uiue possunt Balale ... ... nomine de
mignoris eodem tempore mundi citius et Vinlandia postea Vinlandia trimiliarulo ...
ad ... breuiall ... limitibus debitum sui ... ...
latius ... ...

Groudlia

Vinlandia Insula
a Bruno repa
et leubo sociis

Islanda
formai

Rex
Noriceorum

Mare oceanum

Islanda insula

Ibernia

Say
rex Sach

Bergla

Insula
terra insula

Ipsia

Magne
Insule
Beati Brandam
Branzilie
Siete

Desiderate
insule

Rex
francorum

hispanorum rex

alben

Mare Oceanum

Tunesis
rex

Belo
con

Loaci

Re
Thari

Phaz

Beata insule
fortune

brecume

magnus

Unre

THE NEW WORLD

On this map are depicted the principal voyages which disclosed the existence and general contours of the two American continents, from 1492 to 1616. The much earlier Viking route, shown as a white line, is necessarily hypothetical. Leif Eiriksson and his fellow navigators had neither maps nor compass, and made no written record of their discoveries. Helluland, Markland, and Vinland are names in the Viking sagas. Their locations are not yet identified, though excavations at L'Anse aux Meadows, in northern Newfoundland, may have uncovered the site of Vinland.

Columbus kept such careful records that his first voyage can still be traced on a day-by-day basis. On his second voyage Columbus discovered Dominica, Puerto Rico, and many of the Leeward and Virgin Islands; then from Hispaniola, in 1494, he discovered Jamaica, and explored the south coast of Cuba. His third voyage from Spain made him the discoverer of South America, where he found pearl fisheries in the Gulf of Paria, and identified Trinidad. On his fourth voyage he skirted Central America, and then was wrecked and marooned eight months on a beach on Jamaica.

Amerigo Vespucci, an Italian businessman and astronomer, helped lead a Spanish expedition of 1499 to the mouths of the Amazon. His name was attached to the New World because he widely propagandized his theory that South America was a separate continent, distinct and distant from Asia. This was proved by Ferdinand Magellan, who found the southern strait in 1519, and then sailed to the Philippines, where he was killed by natives. Magellan had been in the Philippines before, after sailing in an eastward direction, on the route around Africa which was opened up by Vasco da Gama for Portugal. Pedro Cabral, a pupil of da Gama, detoured to the west in 1500 and established Portugal's "right of discovery" to Brazil. (The Treaty of Tordesillas in Spain had already awarded Portugal this region.) Gaspar and Miguel Corte-Real, Portuguese brothers from the Azores, searched vainly for a northern route to Asia, as did several later English explorers: Frobisher, Davis, Hudson, and Baffin. John Cabot (who like Columbus was born in Genoa) made two early voyages, in 1497 and 1498, on which England's later colonial claims were based. Giovanni da Verrazano, an Italian who sailed in behalf of France, kept a meticulous record of his important discoveries, including the harbor of New York, where he arrived 85 years before Henry Hudson. Francis Drake, Queen Elizabeth's favorite, raided Spain's colonial cities, and gave England a shadowy claim to ownership of San Francisco Bay.

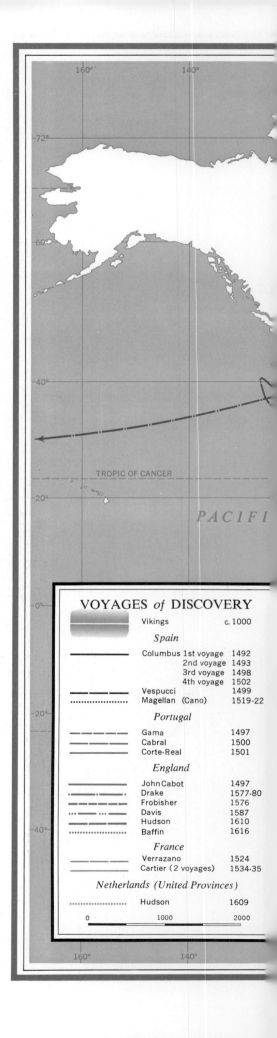

TROPIC OF CANCER

PACIFI

VOYAGES of DISCOVERY

	Vikings	c. 1000

Spain

	Columbus 1st voyage	1492
	2nd voyage	1493
	3rd voyage	1498
	4th voyage	1502
	Vespucci	1499
	Magellan (Cano)	1519-22

Portugal

	Gama	1497
	Cabral	1500
	Corte-Real	1501

England

	John Cabot	1497
	Drake	1577-80
	Frobisher	1576
	Davis	1587
	Hudson	1610
	Baffin	1616

France

	Verrazano	1524
	Cartier (2 voyages)	1534-35

Netherlands (United Provinces)

	Hudson	1609

0	1000	2000

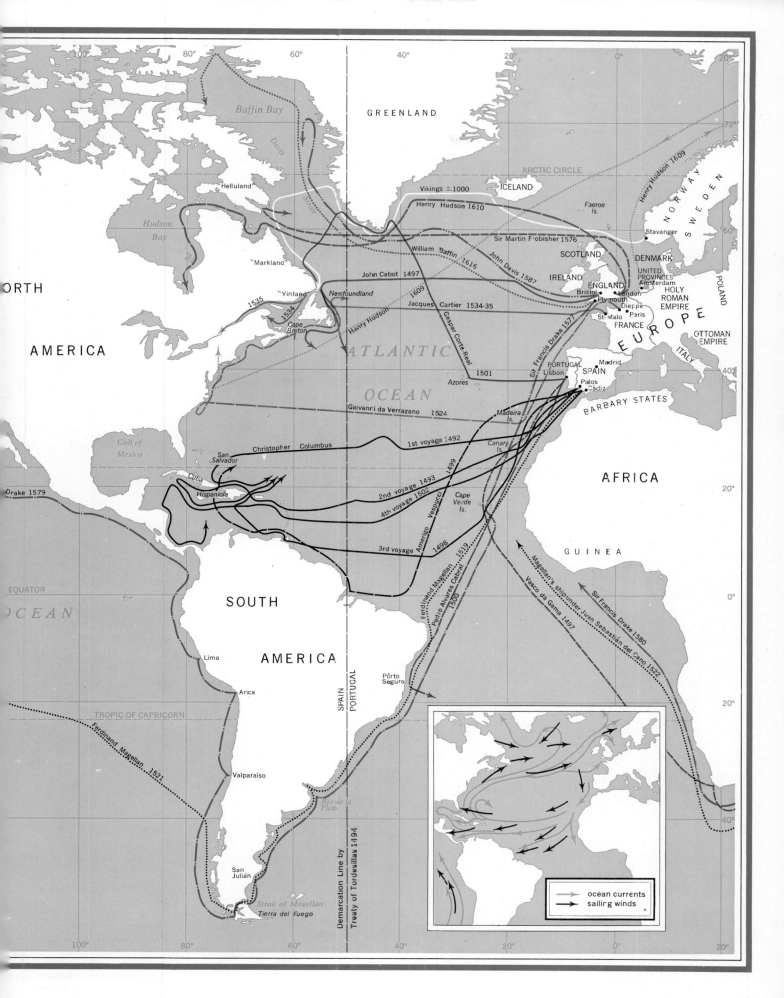

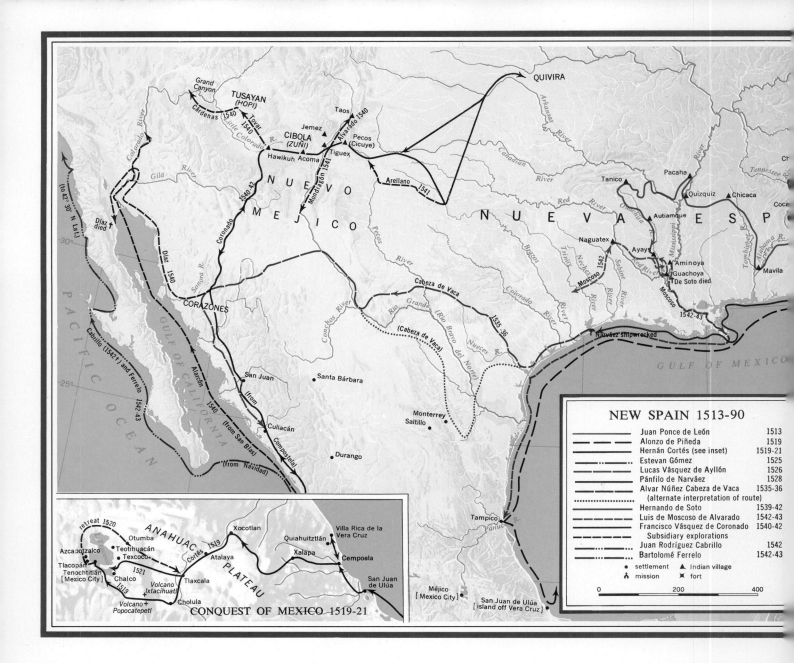

Columbus's discoveries in the Caribbean—and especially the gold and pearls he found—touched off great feats of exploration and empire building. In less than fifty years Spain's naval commanders traced the coastlines of North and South America from Newfoundland around to Oregon. In the same time Spanish soldiers, priests, slave raiders, and land pirates took possession of two colonial "kingdoms" that stretched across both continents. New Spain, above, was even larger than appears on this map: it included also Central America, much of modern Venezuela, and all the Caribbean islands. A second realm, officially named Peru, comprised most of South America.

Juan Ponce de León, the conqueror of Puerto Rico, was the first Spanish leader to see any part of what is now the United States. In March, 1513, he sighted a sandy shore backed by dense tropical greenery which he named *La Florida*, after *Pascua Florida*, the Spanish Easter feast. Perhaps he was seeking a fountain of youth, as legend says; what he found was death at the hands of Indians who re-sisted his efforts to kidnap them as slaves. His two voyages suggested that Florida was a peninsula. Other Spanish captains soon filled in the rest of the Gulf and Atlantic coasts. The news of Cortés's victories in Mexico, and the riches he and Pizarro derived from sacking Indian civilizations, sent other less lucky Spaniards on a hunt for cities and gold farther north. Narváez was last seen in a leaky boat on the Gulf, but one of his men, Cabeza de Vaca, survived by walking all the way across Texas and into northwest Mexico. De Soto discovered the Mississippi, and was buried in its waters. Coronado found only Zuñi pueblos and the plains of central Kansas. Other Spaniards reached the Grand Canyon and the mouth of the Colorado, and sailed up the West coast past the 42d parallel, but failed to notice San Francisco Bay.

In the East a thin string of forts and missions asserted Spain's claim to all of North America. By 1590 this claim had been challenged by France (in Canada, South Carolina, and Florida) and England (on Roanoke Island).

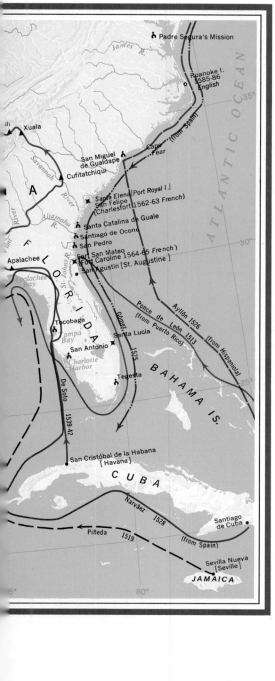

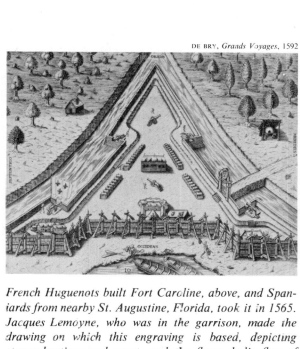

DE BRY, *Graads Voyages*, 1592

French Huguenots built Fort Caroline, above, and Spaniards from nearby St. Augustine, Florida, took it in 1565. Jacques Lemoyne, who was in the garrison, made the drawing on which this engraving is based, depicting strong bastions and moat, and the fleurs-de-lis flag of France. Below is the Aztec capital of Tenochtitlán, built on lakes and causeways, which became Mexico City after Cortés seized it in 1519. The flames and peaks at the top of this 1556 woodcut represent the volcanic ridge of Popocatepetl, across which the 400 Spaniards came.

SPANISH
CONQUESTS

RAMUSIO, *Delle Navigatione et Viaggi*, 1606

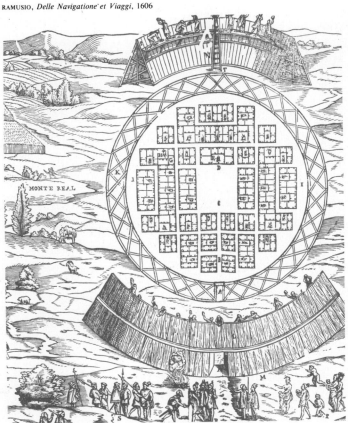

In 1535 the circular village of Hochelaga was guarded by a palisade "in three tiers like a pyramid," Cartier reported. In each of its fifty wood and bark houses several Huron families lived and shared a common fire. "Monte Real," left, locates the future city.

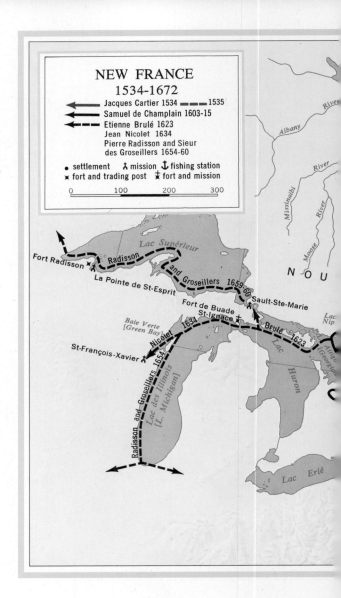

NEW FRANCE
1534-1672

Jacques Cartier 1534 — 1535
Samuel de Champlain 1603-15
Etienne Brulé 1623
Jean Nicolet 1634
Pierre Radisson and Sieur des Groseillers 1654-60

● settlement   ⚓ mission   ⚓ fishing station
✕ fort and trading post   ✝ fort and mission

0   100   200   300

FRENCH FOOTHOLD *in the* NORTH

John Cabot's report that the ocean near Newfoundland was "swarming with fish, which can be taken not only with the net, but in baskets let down with a stone," opened up regular traffic between the Old World and the New. From 1500 on the Grand Bank and its neighbors—shown above as shaded areas off the coast—supplied Catholic Europe with much of its diet. In order to dry and preserve their catch, anonymous fishermen from various nations went ashore as far south as Maine, and so preceded the official "discoverers."

Jacques Cartier, from the fishing port of St-Malo in Brittany, made the first systematic exploration of the region in behalf of Francis I of France. In 1535, on his second voyage, Cartier found the entrance to the St. Lawrence and ascended the river to Hochelaga, the Indian stronghold that became Montreal. His praise of the country he saw led to a short-lived French colony near Quebec. This was abandoned in 1543 after "gold ore" and "diamonds" Cartier took to France proved to be iron pyrites and quartz.

It was the insatiable curiosity of Samuel de

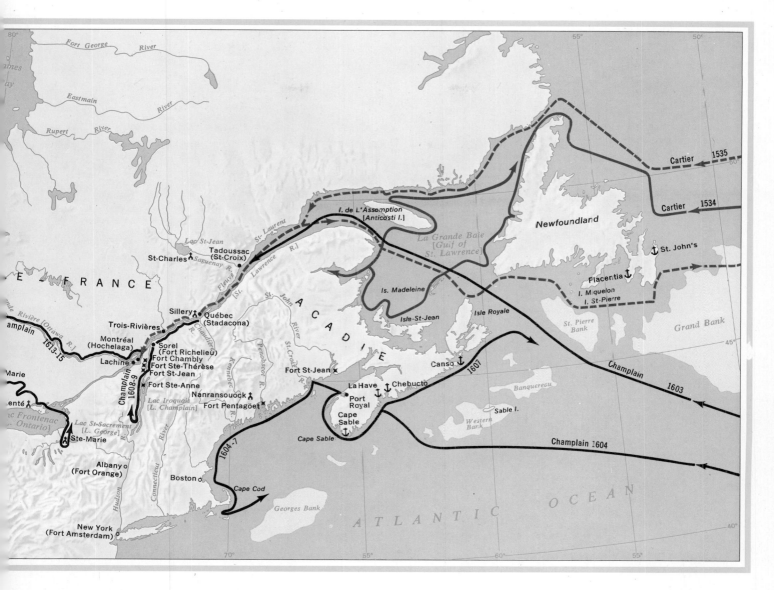

Champlain that gave France a firm foothold in North America. By the time he arrived, in 1603, the demand in Europe for American furs—particularly for making beaver felt hats—had created a trade more profitable than fish. Champlain represented French fur monopolists and established a headquarters at Quebec. But his passions were exploration and map making. He charted the New England coast in detail, discovered the lake that bears his name, and in 1615 journeyed 20 days by canoe and portage to stand on the Georgian Bay shore of Lake Huron. Champlain sent young Frenchmen to live with the Indians and learn their languages, and assigned them to reconnoiter the wilderness as far west as Wisconsin and Illinois.

To help the Hurons in their wars Champlain invaded what is now upstate New York and took part in two fights with the Iroquois (on Lake Champlain and near Syracuse). This gave the vengeful Five Nations a motive to harass and hem in New France in the east. But his alliances with other tribes unlocked the heart of the continent to French traders and missionary priests.

CHAMPLAIN, *Voyages*, 1613

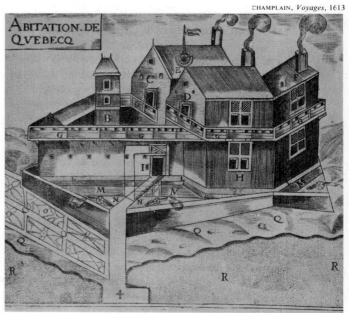

Champlain's Quebec headquarters, pictured in his 1613 Voyages, *had a fur storehouse, platforms for cannon (N), pigeon loft (B), and sundial (E). It was entered by a drawbridge leading to the main door (I). Champlain died in his official residence (H) in 1635.*

Champlain drew this decorative map of New France for publication in 1613, before he himself had explored beyond the St. Lawrence. In the legend (top right) he explained it was made "according to the compasses of France, which vary to the northeast"—so what is here shown as due north is closer to northwest. The outline of Newfoundland and the Gulf region (right) is generally accurate, while Quebec, Montreal, and the Thousand Islands are properly placed along the river. Farther west Champlain relied on Indian descriptions for his misshapen

Lake Ontario and swollen Lake Huron (grand lac contenant), and he knew nothing yet about Lake Erie. South of Lake Champlain, where he killed two Iroquois with one shot of his arquebus in 1609, the explorer gave a foreshortened version of the coast to about Chesapeake Bay. Of the more than 50 French place names located on the map only three—Quebec, Port Royal, and Île de Sable—are marked with flags to show they were actual settlements in 1613. Square forests, rounded mountains, and fanciful streams fill in the unexplored regions.

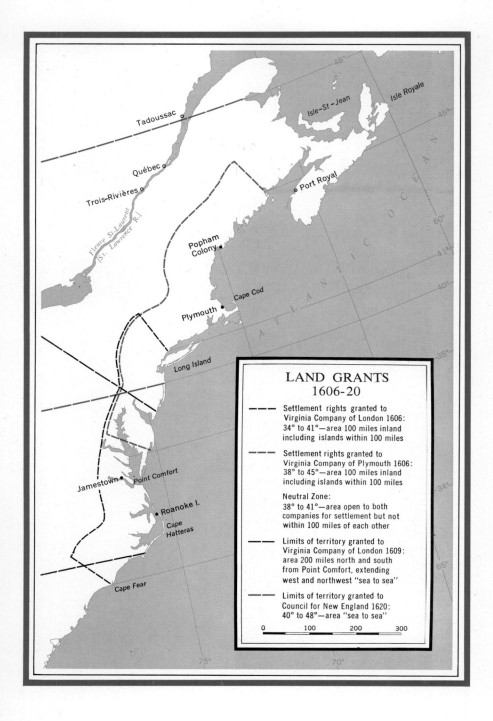

LAND GRANTS
1606-20

- - - - Settlement rights granted to
Virginia Company of London 1606:
34° to 41°—area 100 miles inland
including islands within 100 miles

– – – Settlement rights granted to
Virginia Company of Plymouth 1606:
38° to 45°—area 100 miles inland
including islands within 100 miles

Neutral Zone:
38° to 41°—area open to both
companies for settlement but not
within 100 miles of each other

—— Limits of territory granted to
Virginia Company of London 1609:
area 200 miles north and south
from Point Comfort, extending
west and northwest "sea to sea"

—— Limits of territory granted to
Council for New England 1620:
40° to 48°—area "sea to sea"

0   100   200   300

THE FIRST
ENGLISH
SETTLEMENTS

Virginia, explained Captain John Smith, in 1612, "is a Country in America, that lyeth betweene the degrees of 34 and 44 of the north latitude [from South Carolina to the middle of Maine]. The bounds thereof on the East side are the great *Ocean*. On the South lyeth Florida: on the North nova Francia. As for the West thereof, the limits are unknowne."

Sir Walter Raleigh gave the name Virginia to this large but vague slice of North America to honor his Virgin Queen, Elizabeth. But the two colonies Raleigh sent over did not reach what is now Virginia. They stopped at Roanoke Island, at the confluence of Albemarle and Pamlico sounds, on the coast of North Carolina. The first group stayed less than a year (1585–86), and then returned to England with Sir Francis Drake. The second Roanoke colony (1587–91) disappeared mysteriously while its governor, John White, the artist and map maker, was in England obtaining supplies.

The real beginning of English settlement came in 1606 when James I gave a businesslike charter to two co-operating groups of merchant investors: the Virginia Company of London, and the Virginia Company of Plymouth. As shown at the left, each company had rights to plant colonies and exploit inland resources along a broad strip of the Atlantic coast. In 1607 the London Company landed 105 male settlers on a marshy James River site that became the Virginia capital of Jamestown. After 1614, when the first shipment of Virginia tobacco reached England, the success of this colony was assured. The company encouraged its wealthy members to bring over laborers and operate plantations for private profit; these large landholdings were called "hundreds," an old English administrative term for districts smaller than a county. The map on the opposite page shows how rapidly they spread westward on both sides of the James River.

In the north the Virginia Company of Plymouth lost large sums on a short-lived coast of Maine colony commanded by George Popham. In 1620 the Plymouth Company's rights were enlarged and transferred to another group of private investors, the Council for New England. But before they could start any new colonies, a small band of English religious dissenters sailed for New England on their own.

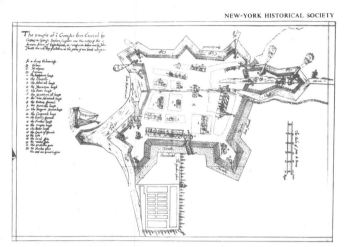

This 1607 "draught of st. Georges fort," by an unknown artist, depicts a grandiose scheme for defending the Popham colony at the mouth of the Kennebec River in Maine. It is likely the fort was never built, for the colony was abandoned in 1608.

The arrival of the first English colonists at Roanoke Island was drawn by John White in 1585 and engraved in Germany by Théodore de Bry. Secotan and Weapemeoc were mainland Indian towns. Wrecks of earlier expeditions line the Outer Banks.

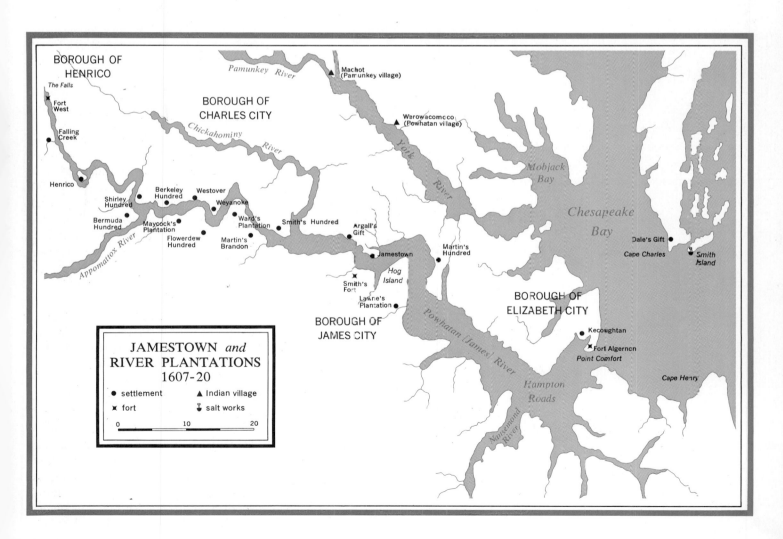

JAMESTOWN *and*
RIVER PLANTATIONS
1607-20

- settlement ▲ Indian village
- ✗ fort ⛏ salt works

0   10   20

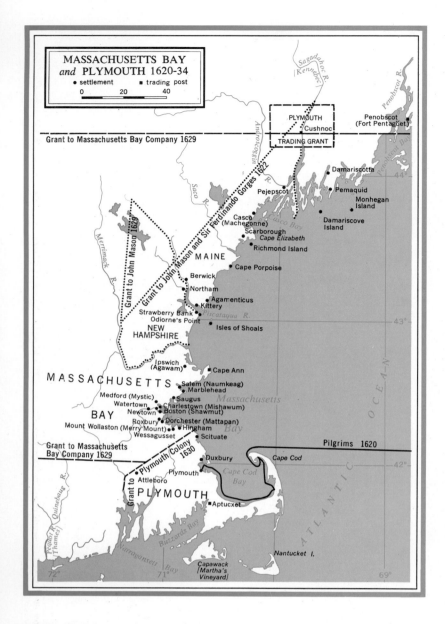

**MASSACHUSETTS BAY
and PLYMOUTH 1620-34**
• settlement   ▪ trading post
0   20   40

Grant to Massachusetts Bay Company 1629

Sagadahoc (Kennebec) R.

PLYMOUTH
Cushnoc
TRADING GRANT

Penobscot (Fort Pentagöet)

Penobscot Bay

Damariscotta
Pemaquid
Monhegan Island

44°

Androscoggin R.

Saco R.

Pejepscot

Casco (Machegonne)
Scarborough
Cape Elizabeth
Richmond Island

Damariscove Island

Casco Bay

MAINE

Cape Porpoise

Grant to John Mason and Sir Ferdinando Gorges 1622

Berwick
Northam
Agamenticus
Kittery
Strawberry Bank
Odiorne's Point

Piscataqua R.

43°

NEW HAMPSHIRE

Isles of Shoals

Grant to John Mason 1629

Merrimack R.

Ipswich (Agawam)

Cape Ann

MASSACHUSETTS

Salem (Naumkeag)
Marblehead
Medford (Mystic)
Watertown
Saugus
Charlestown (Mishawum)
Newtown Boston (Shawmut)
Roxbury Dorchester (Mattapan)
Mount Wollaston (Merry Mount) Hingham
Wessagusset Scituate

BAY

Massachusetts Bay

Pilgrims 1620

42°

Grant to Massachusetts Bay Company 1629

Pequot R. (Thames)

Quinebaug R.

Plymouth Colony 1630
Duxbury
Plymouth
Attleboro

Grant to Plymouth

PLYMOUTH

Aptucxet

Cape Cod

Cape Cod Bay

ATLANTIC OCEAN

Buzzards Bay

Narragansett Bay

Nantucket I.

Capawack [Martha's Vineyard]

72°   71°   69°

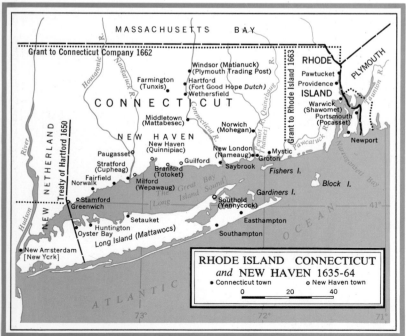

MASSACHUSETTS   BAY

Grant to Connecticut Company 1662

Windsor (Matianuck)
(Plymouth Trading Post)

RHODE
Pawtucket
Providence

PLYMOUTH

Farmington (Tunxis)
Hartford (Fort Good Hope Dutch)
Wethersfield

Housatonic R.
Naugatuck R.

CONNECTICUT

ISLAND

Warwick (Shawomet)
Portsmouth (Pocasset)

Grant to Rhode Island 1663

Taunton R.

Middletown (Mattabesec)

Norwich (Mohegan)

NEW HAVEN

Connecticut R.

Paugasset
Stratford (Cupheag)
Fairfield
Norwalk

New Haven (Quinnipiac)
Guilford
Branford (Totoket)
Milford (Wepawaug)

New London (Nameaug)
Mystic
Groton
Saybrook

Pequot R. (Thames)

Quinebaug R.

Pawcatuck R.

Newport

Narragansett Bay

Treaty of Hartford 1650

NEW NETHERLAND

Stamford
Greenwich

Setauket
Huntington
Oyster Bay
Long Island (Mattawocs)

Southold (Yennycock)

Easthampton
Southampton

Fishers I.
Block I.
Gardiners I.

The Great Bay
(Long) Island Sound

Hudson River

New Amsterdam [New York]

ATLANTIC OCEAN

41°

**RHODE ISLAND   CONNECTICUT
and NEW HAVEN 1635-64**
• Connecticut town   ○ New Haven town
0   20   40

73°   72°   71°

NEW ENGLAND

"They knew they were pilgrimes," wrote William Bradford of the congregation of English Puritans that left its snug exile in Holland and arrived in the "hidious and desolate wilderness" of Massachusetts in December, 1620. The Pilgrims chose New England deliberately—and landed there in violation of their arrangements with London officials—so they could worship God in a land where no other churches competed. They were soon followed by many more Puritans—perhaps 10,000 by 1634—who founded towns all along the coast. The Puritan-dominated Massachusetts Bay Company had a royal charter that conflicted with other claims (map at top left). But in the mid-17th century, while civil war raged in England, possession made the laws in America.

The first overland migration occurred in 1635-36 when several churches from the Boston area moved to form a Connecticut colony near Hartford. The men walked and drove cattle along 80 miles of Indian paths; the women and children rode horses. Household goods were shipped around by water. New Haven was started in 1637 as a separate colony. By treaty with the New Amsterdam Dutch both Connecticut colonies settled towns on Long Island. In 1664 New Haven and Connecticut became one colony, and Long Island was joined to New York.

Roger Williams, a dissenter among dissenters, founded Rhode Island in 1636 as a haven of total religious freedom. The original Pilgrim Plymouth Colony remained independent—with fur-trading privileges in Maine and Connecticut—until it was merged in 1691 with Massachusetts Bay. New Hampshire grew out of private grants to Captain John Mason and Sir Ferdinando Gorges.

By 1750 the four New England colonies had a population of 360,000, mostly living along the coast and the more navigable rivers. Vermont was still a disputed wilderness, and Maine was ruled by Massachusetts, which purchased the claims of the Gorges family in 1677.

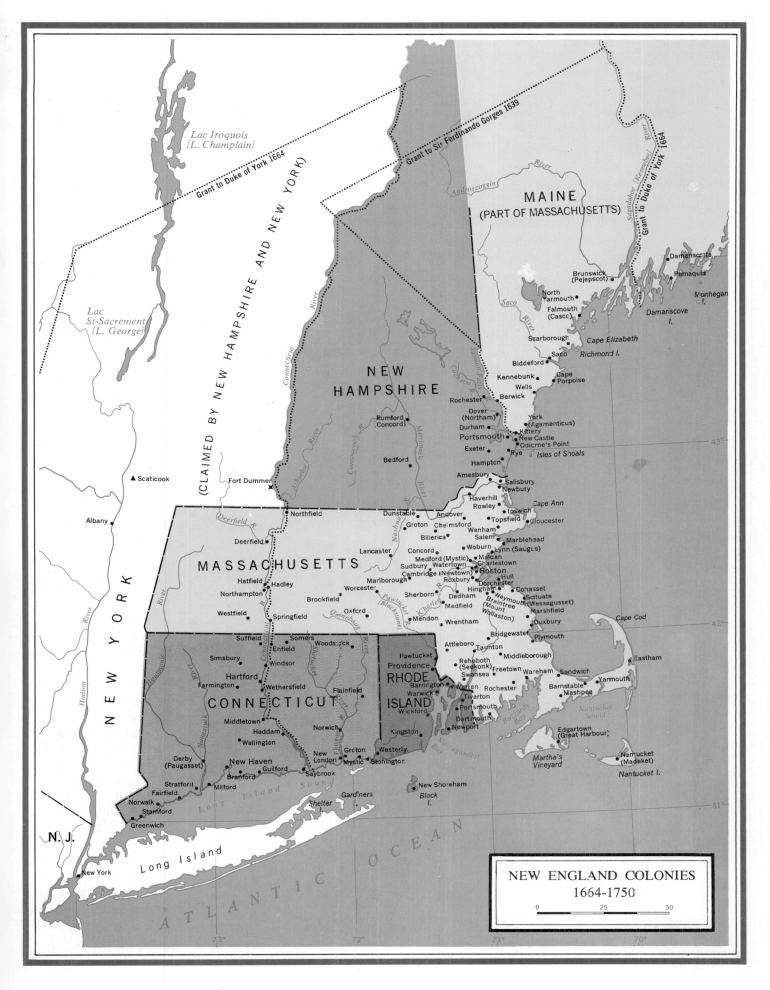

Lac Iroquois
[L. Champlain]

Lac
St-Sacrement
[L. George]

Grant to Duke of York 1664

Grant to Sir Ferdinando Gorges 1639

Grant to Duke of York 1664

MAINE
(PART OF MASSACHUSETTS)

Androscoggin River

Saco River

Damariscotta
Brunswick (Pejepscot)
Pemaquid
North Yarmouth
Falmouth (Casco)
Monhegan I.
Damariscove I.
Scarborough
Cape Elizabeth
Saco
Richmond I.
Biddeford
Kennebunk
Cape Porpoise
Wells
Berwick
Rochester
York (Agamenticus)
Dover (Northam)
Kittery
Durham
New Castle
Portsmouth
Odierne's Point
Exeter
Rye
Isles of Shoals
Hampton
Amesbury
Salisbury
Newbury

NEW HAMPSHIRE

(CLAIMED BY NEW HAMPSHIRE AND NEW YORK)

Connecticut River
Salmon Falls River
Cocheco R.
Contoocook R.
Merrimack River
Ashuelot R.

Rumford [Concord]
Bedford

▲ Scaticook

Fort Dummer ★

Albany

Deerfield R.
Northfield
Deerfield

Hatfield
Hadley
Northampton
Westfield

MASSACHUSETTS

Haverhill
Rowley
Dunstable
Andover
Topsfield
Cape Ann
Groton
Chelmsford
Ipswich
Gloucester
Billerica
Wenham
Lancaster
Woburn
Salem
Marblehead
Concord
Lynn (Saugus)
Medford (Mystic)
Malden
Sudbury
Watertown
Charlestown
Marlborough
Cambridge (Newtown)
Boston
Hull
Worcester
Roxbury
Dorchester
Brockfield
Sherborn
Hingham
Cohasset
Oxford
Dedham
Weymouth
Scituate (Wessagusset)
Medfield
Braintree (Mount Wollaston)
Marshfield
Mendon
Wrentham
Duxbury
Bridgewater
Cape Cod

NEW YORK

Hudson River
Housatonic River

Nashua R.
Quinebaug River
Pawtucket (Blackstone) R.
Charles R.

Suffield
Somers
Simsbury
Enfield
Woodstock
Windsor
Hartford
Farmington
Wethersfield
Plainfield

CONNECTICUT

Middletown
Haddam
Wallington
Norwich
Derby (Paugasset)
New Haven
New London
Branford
Guilford
Groton
Stratford
Milford
Saybrook
Fairfield
Norwalk
Stamford
Greenwich

N.J.

Naugatuck River
Shetucket River
Thames River

Attleboro
Taunton
Middleborough
Eastham
Pawtucket
Rehoboth (Seekonk)
Freetown
Wareham
Sandwich
Providence
Swansea
Rochester
Barnstable
Yarmouth
RHODE ISLAND
Barrington
Warren
Mashpee
Warwick
Tiverton
Wickford
Portsmouth
Dartmouth
Nantucket Sound
Kingston
Newport
Buzzards Bay
Westerly
Edgartown (Great Harbour)
Stonington
Nantucket (Madeket)
Mystic
Kingston
Martha's Vineyard
Nantucket I.

New Shoreham
Block I.

Long Island Sound
Gardiners
Shelter I.

Long Island

New York

ATLANTIC OCEAN

NEW ENGLAND COLONIES
1664–1750

0   25   50

43

The first map printed in what is now the United States shows Puritan New England at the end of King Philip's War (see page 59); the Atlantic coast is at the bottom and Long Island Sound at left. This was engraved on wood by John Foster, a young Harvard graduate, to illustrate Rev. William Hubbard's A Narrative of the Troubles with the Indians in New-England, *which Foster printed on the first press in Boston in 1677. At top right the cartographer apologizes for defects in his pioneer effort, but insists "yet doth it sufficiently shew the Scituation of the Countrey, and conveniently well the distance of Places." At the right are New Hampshire's White Mountains (downgraded to "Hills") and an island-studded Lake Winnipesaukee (unnamed). The ships at the bottom seem generally headed toward Boston, which is shown in the center, mostly surrounded by water. Nantucket and Martha's (here called "Martins") Vineyard are left of Cape Cod, whose precise contour and relation to Rhode Island were obviously not well known to the artist. The clusters of settlements along the lower Merrimack and Connecticut rivers (center and top) show how much the early New Englanders depended on water transportation. Foster also engraved the first seal of Massachusetts and the first American woodcut portrait (of Richard Mather, about 1670). His gravestone at Dorchester is inscribed: "The Ingenious Mathematician & printer Mr. John Foster Aged 33 Years Dyed Septr. 9th, 1681."*

44

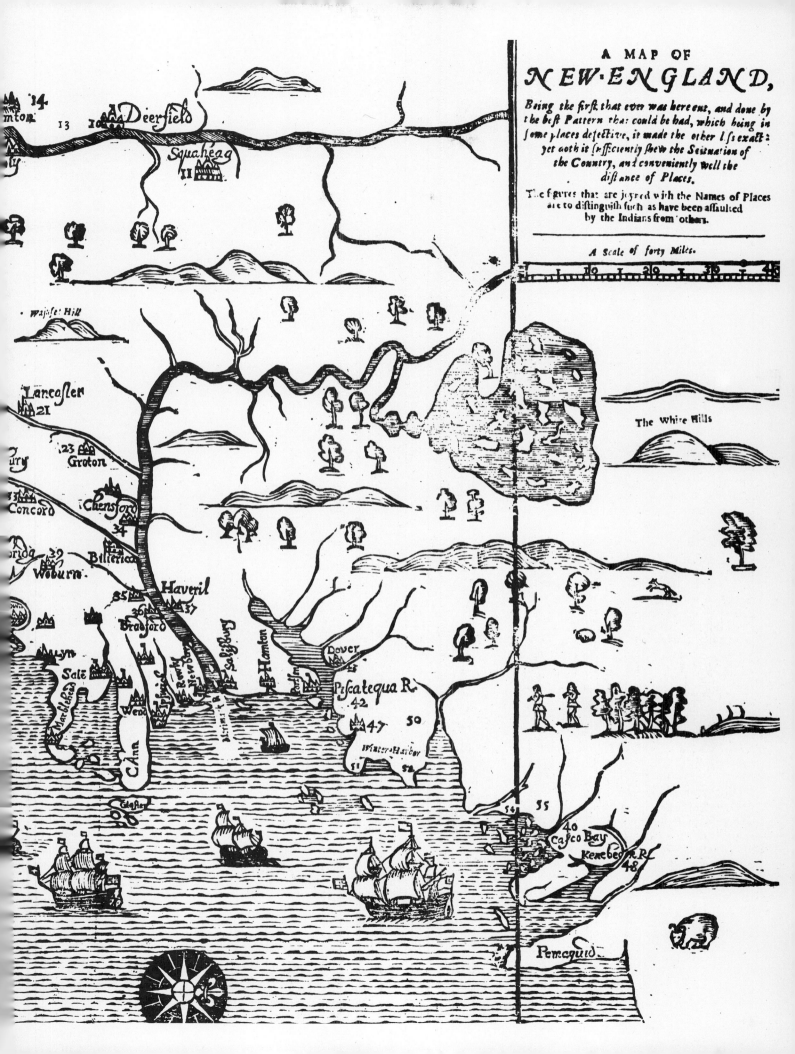

A MAP OF NEW-ENGLAND,

Being the first that ever was here cut, and done by the best Pattern that could be had, which being in some places defective, it made the other less exact: yet doth it sufficiently shew the Scituation of the Country, and conveniently well the distance of Places.

The figures that are joyned with the Names of Places are to distinguish such as have been assaulted by the Indians from others.

A Scale of forty Miles.

10   20   30   40

The White Hills

Deerfield

Squaheag
11

Wajafet Hill

Lancaster
21

Groton 23

Concord

Chensford
34

Billerica 39

Woburn

Haveril
35   37
36
Bradford

Lyn

Sale

Marblehead

Wen

C. Ann

Chester

Dover

Piscatequa R.
42

47   50

Winters Harbor

54   55

40
Casco Bay
Kenebeck R.
48

Pemaquid

THE MIDDLE COLONIES

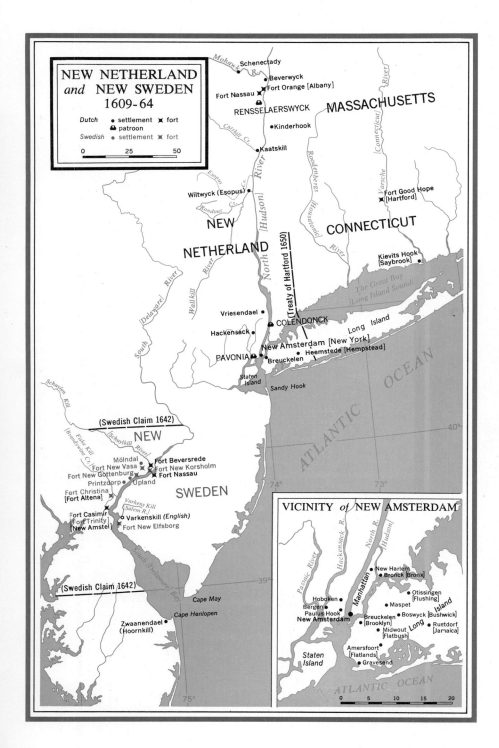

NEW NETHERLAND *and* **NEW SWEDEN** 1609-64

Dutch ● settlement ✕ fort
🏰 patroon
Swedish ● settlement ✕ fort

0   25   50

Schenectady
Mohawk R.
Beverwyck
Fort Nassau ✕ Fort Orange [Albany]
RENSSELAERSWYCK
MASSACHUSETTS
● Kinderhook
Catskill Cr.
● Kaatskill
Esopus
Wiltwyck (Esopus) ●
NEW
NETHERLAND
Rondout Cr.
North (Hudson) River
(Treaty of Hartford 1650)
Roodenbergs
Housatonic River
Varsche (Connecticut) River
✕ Fort Good Hope [Hartford]
CONNECTICUT
Kievits Hook [Saybrook] ●
The Great Bay [Long Island Sound]
Delaware River
Wallkill River
Vriesendael ●
COLENDONCK
Hackensack ●
Long Island
New Amsterdam [New York]
PAVONIA ● Heemstede [Hempstead]
Breuckelen ●
Staten Island
Sandy Hook
ATLANTIC OCEAN
40°

Schuylen Kill
NEW
(Swedish Claim 1642)
Fiske Kill
Brandywine Cr.
Schuylkill River
Mölndal ● ✕ Fort Beversrede
Fort New Vasa ✕ ✕ Fort New Korsholm
Fort New Gottenburg ✕ ✕ Fort Nassau
Printzdorp ● ● Upland
Fort Christina [Fort Altena] ✕
SWEDEN
Varkens Kill [Salem R.]
Fort Casimir [Fort Trinity] [New Amstel] ✕ ○ Varkenskill (English)
Fort New Elfsborg
South (Delaware) Bay
(Swedish Claim 1642)
Cape May
Cape Henlopen
Zwaanendael (Hoornkill) ●
74°   73°

VICINITY of NEW AMSTERDAM

Passaic River
Hackensack R.
North R. (Hudson)
New Harlem ●
● Bronck [Bronx]
Hoboken ●
Bergen ●
Paulus Hook ●
New Amsterdam ●
Manhattan
Otissingen [Flushing] ●
Maspet ●
Breuckelen [Brooklyn] ●
Boswyck [Bushwick] ●
Midwout [Flatbush] ●
Long Island
Rustdorf [Jamaica] ●
Amersfoort [Flatlands] ●
Gravesend ●
Staten Island
ATLANTIC OCEAN
0   5   10   15   20

Dutchmen, Belgians, Swedes, and Finns were the first settlers in the middle colonies, followed by Welsh and English Quakers and Mennonites from Germany. Dutch fur traders plied the Hudson River one year after Hudson was there, and built a post (Fort Nassau) near Albany in 1614. Peter Minuit bought Manhattan Island from "the wild men" for trade goods worth $24, in 1626, and made New Amsterdam the capital of the colony.

Many "Dutch" colonists, including Governor Minuit, were French-speaking Walloons from what is now Belgium. In 1638 Minuit and other seceders from New Netherland encouraged two shiploads of Swedes and Finns to build Fort Christina (Wilmington) and claim Delaware Bay and River for the 12-year-old Swedish Queen. New Sweden was never much more than a glorified trading post, with a capital at Fort New Gottenburg (southwest of Philadelphia). In 1655 a Dutch expedition overpowered the Swedes and retook what they called the South River.

By the Treaty of Hartford in 1650 Governor Peter Stuyvesant tried to fix a firm boundary between New Netherland and fast-growing New England. But after the Stuart monarchy was restored, the Dutch wedge between England's Atlantic colonies was doomed. Charles II "gave" New Netherland to his brother James, the Duke of York, who sent four frigates to awe the Dutch and was acknowledged as proprietor of New York in 1664. The Duke's grant also included New Jersey, which he presented to friends. This colony was split into East and West Jersey and divided among conflicting proprietorships until it was united in 1702.

New York's English governors allowed the Dutch patroons—big landholders on the Hudson River—to retain their semi-feudal rights and made similar grants ("manors" and "patents") to Britishers. The pattern was different in Pennsylvania, which Charles gave to the Quaker William Penn to settle a royal debt. Penn opened his broad and fertile colony to small farmers of all nationalities and creeds. He paid the Indians for lands they had previously "sold" to the Dutch and the Swedes. Penn's heirs staged the "walking purchase"—a bargain for as much land as a man could walk around in a day and a half, but which was actually paced off by fast runners. Delaware, also granted to Penn, had its own assembly, but shared Pennsylvania's governor.

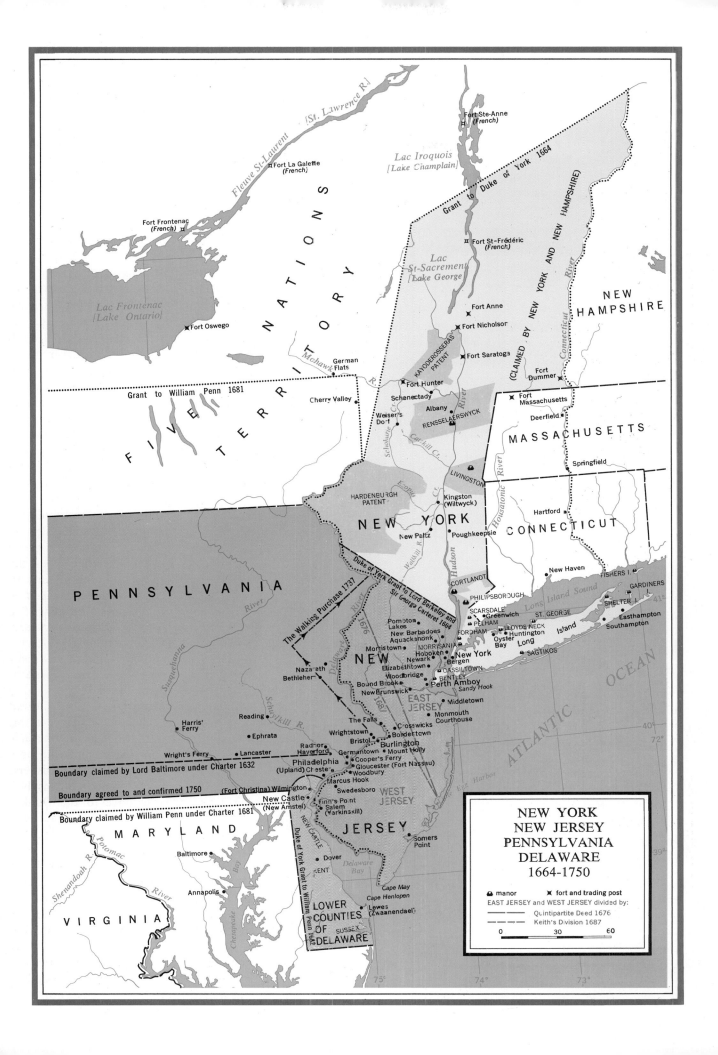

Fleuve St-Laurent (St. Lawrence R.)

Fort La Galette (French)

Fort Ste-Anne (French)

Lac Iroquois (Lake Champlain)

Grant to Duke of York 1664

NEW HAMPSHIRE

Fort Frontenac (French)

F I V E   N A T I O N S   T E R R I T O R Y

Fort St-Frédéric (French)

Lac St-Sacrement (Lake George)

(CLAIMED BY NEW YORK AND NEW HAMPSHIRE)

Connecticut River

Lac Frontenac (Lake Ontario)

Fort Oswego

Fort Anne

Fort Nicholsor

Fort Saratoga

Mohawk R.

German Flats

KAYODEROSSERAS PATENT

Fort Dummer

Fort Hunter

Fort Massachusetts

Grant to William Penn 1681

Cherry Valley

Schenectady

Weiser's Do-f

Albany

RENSSELAERSWYCK

Schoharie Cr.

Cat-kill Cr.

Deerfield

MASSACHUSETTS

Springfield

LIVINGSTON

Housatonic River

Esopus Cr.

HARDENBURGH PATENT

Kingston (Wiltwyck)

Walkill R.

NEW YORK

New Paltz

Poughkeepsie

Hartford

CONNECTICUT

PENNSYLVANIA

Hudson River

CORTLANDT

New Haven

FISHERS I.

Long Island Sound

GARDINERS

PHILIPSBOROUGH

SCARSDALE

Greenwich

ST. GEORGE

SHELTER I.

41°

Duke of York Grant to Lord Berkeley and Sir George Carteret 1664

Pompton Lakes

PELHAM

FORDHAM

LLOYDS NECK

Oyster Bay

Huntington

Easthampton

The Walking Purchase 1737

Delaware River

1676

NEW

New Barbadoes

Aquackanonk

MORRISANIA

Long

Island

Southampton

Susquehanna River

Nazareth

Bethlehem

Morristown

Newark

Hoboken

Bergen

New York

SAGTIKOS

Schuylkill R.

Elizabethtown

Woodbridge

CASSILTOWN

BENTLEY

ATLANTIC

Bound Brook

Perth Amboy

Sandy Hook

Harris' Ferry

Reading

The Falls

New Brunswick

EAST JERSEY

Middletown

Monmouth Courthouse

OCEAN

Wrightstown

Crosswicks

40°

Ephrata

Bristol

Bordentown

Wright's Ferry

Lancaster

Radnor

Haverford

Germantown

Mount Holly

Burlington

72°

Boundary claimed by Lord Baltimore under Charter 1632

Philadelphia (Upland) Chester

Cooper's Ferry

Gloucester (Fort Nassau)

Woodbury

Little Egg Harbor

Marcus Hook

Boundary agreed to and confirmed 1750

(Fort Christina) Wilmington

Swedesboro

WEST JERSEY

Boundary claimed by William Penn under Charter 1681

New Castle (New Amstel)

Finn's Point

Salem (Yarkinskill)

NEW CASTLE

JERSEY

Somers Point

MARYLAND

Potomac River

Baltimore

Shenandoah R.

Duke of York Grant to William Penn 1682

Dover

KENT

Delaware Bay

Chesapeake Bay

Annapolis

River

VIRGINIA

LOWER COUNTIES OF DELAWARE

SUSSEX

Cape May

Cape Henlopen

Lewes (Zwaanendael)

39°

75°

74°

73°

NEW YORK
NEW JERSEY
PENNSYLVANIA
DELAWARE
1664-1750

⌂ manor   ✕ fort and trading post

EAST JERSEY and WEST JERSEY divided by:
——— Quintipartite Deed 1676
– – – Keith's Division 1687

0   30   60

THE SOUTHERN COLONIES

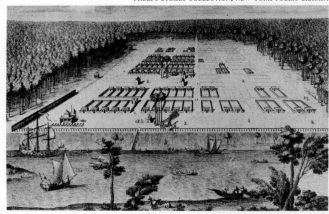

This view of Savannah, Georgia's new capital, was done in 1734.

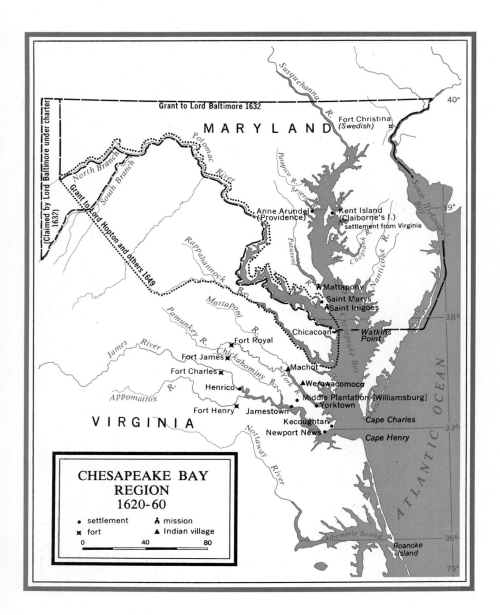

CHESAPEAKE BAY REGION 1620-60

- settlement
- × fort
- ⋔ mission
- ▲ Indian village

0   40   80

English kings carved big chunks from Virginia to form the other four southern colonies. Maryland, north of the Potomac, went to Cecilius Calvert, Lord Baltimore, whose brother Leonard, aged 28, brought over Catholic and Protestant settlers and founded a capital at St. Marys in 1634. Maryland thrived on tobacco planting but was embroiled in small wars with Virginia over oyster-bed rights in Chesapeake Bay and a Virginia fur post on Kent Island that was established three years before Calvert arrived.

Virginians also moved into Albemarle County, the starting point of North Carolina, before the whole region of the Carolinas was granted to eight noble Englishmen in 1663. Charles Town (now Charleston, S.C.) prospered from trade in furs, deerskins, and slaves, and was capital of both Carolinas until 1712. Georgia was taken from South Carolina and given to James Oglethorpe and other trustees as a refuge for worthy debtors in 1732. The first settlers planted mulberry trees and raised silkworms, but soon switched to rice and turpentine.

Virginia, even after its territorial losses, led all the colonies in population (231,000) in 1750. Its "first families" mostly began with hard-working farmers who collected "head rights"—warrants for 50 free acres of land—for each person, including children and servants, whom they brought to the colony at any time. A notable exception was Thomas, Baron Fairfax, who inherited more than five million acres from a grant above the Rappahannock. In North Carolina, too, the heirs of Lord Granville, an original proprietor, still owned most of the northern half of the colony in the mid 1700's.

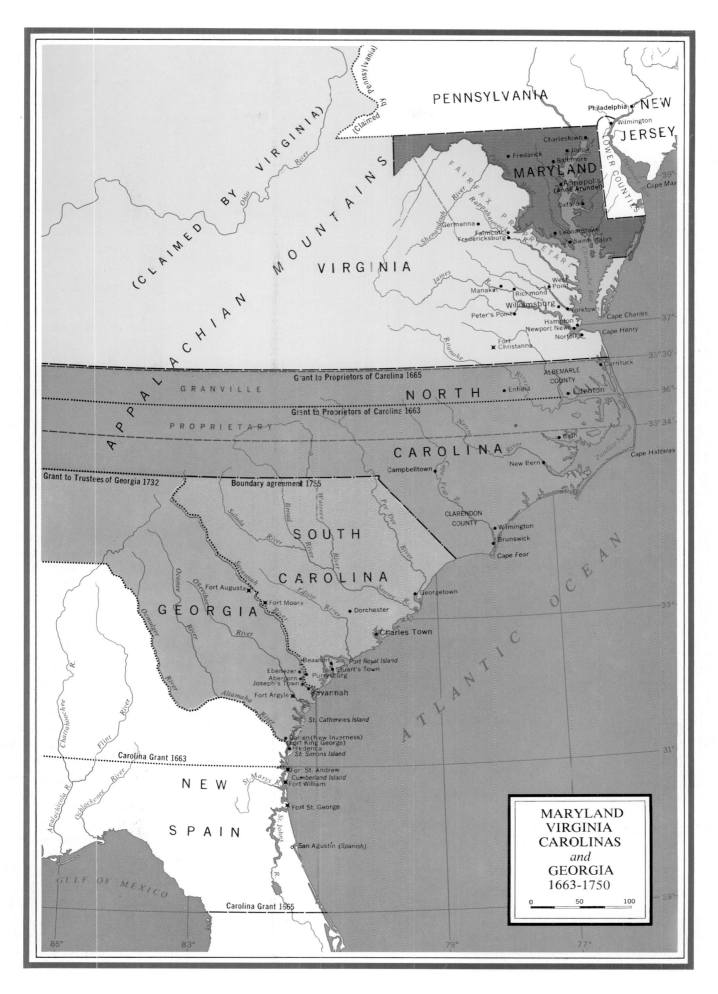

MARYLAND
VIRGINIA
CAROLINAS
and
GEORGIA
1663-1750

NEW SPAIN
and the
PACIFIC COAST

Hive-shaped huts of the Caddo Indians of east Texas, and fences to hold their livestock, appear in this 1691 drawing, said to have been made by the first Spanish governor, Domingo de Terán.

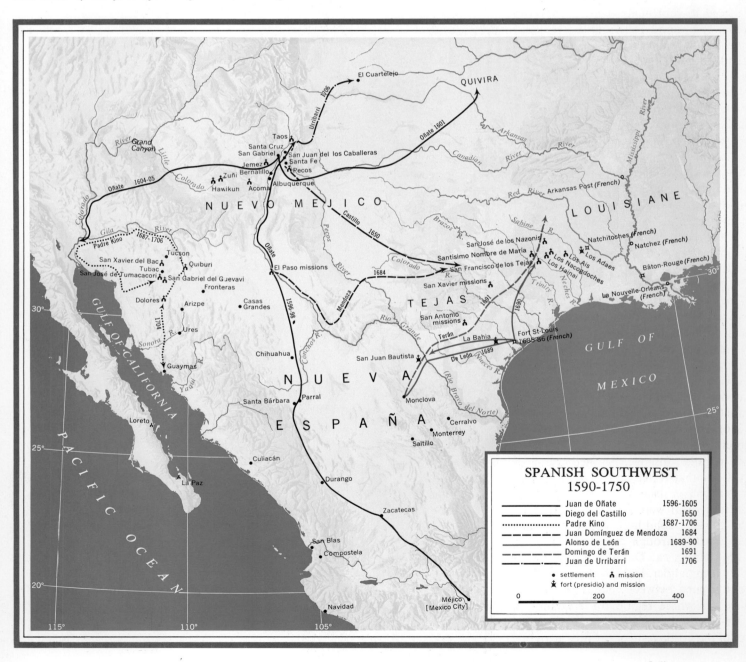

SPANISH SOUTHWEST
1590-1750

Juan de Oñate	1596-1605
Diego del Castillo	1650
Padre Kino	1687-1706
Juan Domínguez de Mendoza	1684
Alonso de León	1689-90
Domingo de Terán	1691
Juan de Urribarri	1706

● settlement   ⚲ mission
✶ fort (presidio) and mission

0   200   400

"All this district is filled with pueblos," wrote Juan de Oñate, the Mexican-born general who led 130 soldiers up the Rio Grande and took possession of New Mexico for Spain in 1598. Oñate brought with him 7,000 cattle and horses in the first big livestock drive in what is now the United States. With him also were Franciscan friars who won converts and built missions in Indian villages around the capital at Santa Fe. In 1680 the Pueblo tribes revolted and wiped out the colony, which was restored with difficulty a dozen years later. Refugees from this uprising founded the first Spanish settlement in modern Texas: Ysleta mission, near El Paso.

New Spain's expansion after 1600 resulted mostly from missionary zeal and the need to protect its treasure ships on homeward bound routes to Spain. Galleons from Manila sailed due east to Cape Mendocino in northern California, then down the coast to Acapulco, where their spices and gems were packed on mules and freighted to eastern ports. In 1602 Sebastián Vizcaíno chose Monterey Bay as the main Spanish base for guarding the California coast. In east Texas Spain reacted sharply when a French colony (Fort St-Louis) appeared at Matagorda Bay, threatening the main treasure fleet route. Spanish generals converged on the area to find that Indians and shipwrecks had already eliminated the French. In 1691 Texas became a Spanish province.

A Jesuit mathematician, Father Eusebio Kino, was the first Spanish administrator in Arizona, starting missions near Nogales and Tucson (San Xavier del Bac) and mapping the region on more than 50 exploring trips. In Alta (Upper) California the Franciscan Junípero Serra founded the famous string of missions from San Diego (1769) to San Francisco (1776). Spanish naval captains Pérez and Heceta pushed on up the coast to the 55th parallel, discovering the mouth of the Columbia River and Nootka Sound on Vancouver Island. Pushing south to confront them were Russian fur traders, who gained a solid hold in the Aleutians and Alaska through the discoveries of Vitus Bering, a Danish-born Russian Navy commander. In 1778 Captain James Cook slipped between these rivals to explore the whole region for England. A three-cornered race was now on for control of the northwest coast (map at right).

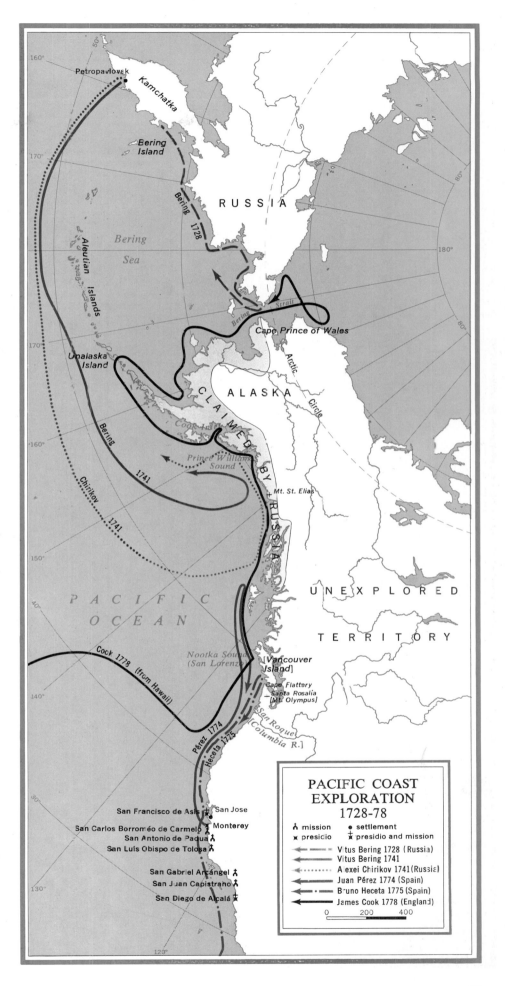

PACIFIC COAST
EXPLORATION
1728-78

⋏ mission   ● settlement
✕ presidio   ⛫ presidio and mission

Vitus Bering 1728 (Russia)
Vitus Bering 1741
Alexei Chirikov 1741 (Russia)
Juan Pérez 1774 (Spain)
Bruno Heceta 1775 (Spain)
James Cook 1778 (England)

0   200   400

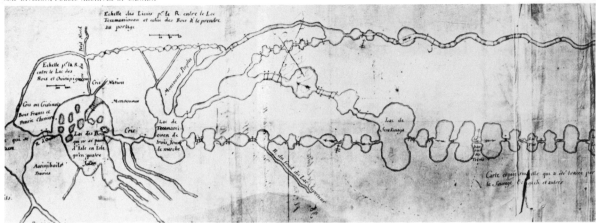

This surviving fragment of a map, drawn by an Indian guide on birch bark in 1728, helped Pierre de la Vérendrye follow the canoe and portage route between Lake Superior (off map at right) and the Lake of the Woods (left).

FRENCH EXPANSION
and the
FUR TRADE

While Spain and England concentrated on the coasts, amphibious Frenchmen in light Indian canoes mastered the continent's central waterways. Louis Jolliet, a successful young fur trader, and Jacques Marquette, an experienced missionary, were the first to traverse the Mississippi over more than 1,000 miles of its length, from Fort St-Nicolas (Prairie du Chien) to the mouth of the Arkansas. "The joy that we felt at being selected for this expedition," wrote the middle-aged Père Marquette, "animated our courage, and rendered the labor of paddling from morning to night more agreeable to us." Their journey opened a practical trade route between the Great Lakes and the Gulf of Mexico, using either one of two short portages: between the Fox and Wisconsin rivers (only 2,700 paces), or the more direct Chicaou (Chicago) portage between the Illinois River and Lake Michigan.

Robert Cavelier, Sieur de La Salle, inaugurated sailboat travel on the lakes in 1679, in the 60-ton *Griffon*. Then he and his brilliant Italian lieutenant, Henry de Tonti, descended the Mississippi in canoes, noting just south of the Illinois "a great river that comes in from the west" (the Missouri). When he reached the Gulf, in April, 1682, La Salle claimed for Louis XIV all lands drained by the Mississippi and its tributaries. Out of this grew, in the next 70 years, the vast wedge-shaped province of Louisiana, occupying roughly half the territory that is now the United States. La Salle led a colony, directly from France, to the Gulf coast of Texas

in 1684 (Fort St-Louis; see page 50). Three years later the great explorer was murdered by mutineers near present-day Navasota, Texas, while trying to reach Illinois by land.

Biloxi, first permanent French post on the Gulf, was established in 1699 by Pierre Lemoyne, Sieur d'Iberville. His brother Jean Baptiste, Sieur de Bienville, founded New Orleans in 1718, giving Louisiana a capital secure from Spanish raids, and one of the world's great seaports. French missionary and colonizing efforts converted the Illinois River country into "the garden of New France," exporting grain and tobacco to the north and south. By building forts to hold the Iroquois in check, and developing portage routes to the Wabash, Ohio, and Tennessee rivers, Frenchmen dominated the Indian fur trade west of the Appalachians. The lead mines of Missouri were worked by 700 men in the 1720's. Fanning out westward from Mississippi river towns, French explorers probed the plains of Nebraska, Kansas, and Colorado, and opened trade with Spanish Santa Fe.

In the north Pierre Gaultier de Varennes, Sieur de la Vérendrye, erected a chain of forts from Lake Superior to Lake Winnipeg, tapping the fur resources of central Canada, and pointing toward the Pacific northwest. On a swing south and west in 1742–43, Vérendrye's sons, Louis Joseph and Francois, reached the Black Hills of South Dakota, but failed to find the way to the Pacific, as they had hoped to do.

FRENCH MISSISSIPPI-MISSOURI EXPLORATION 1673-1750

Louis Jolliet and Père Marquette	1673
Sieur de La Salle	1679-82
Sieur de La Salle	1684-87
Louis Juchereau de Saint-Denis	1714
Bernard de la Harpe	1719
Claude Charles du Tisné	1719
Etienne Veniard de Bourgmont	1724
Sieur de la Vérendrye and sons	1731-43
Pierre and Paul Mallet	1739-41

• settlement   ⚲ mission
⪤ portage   ✳ fort

0   200   400

Map labels

NOUVELLE—FRANCE

Lac Ouinipique [L. Winnipeg]
(to mouth of Saskatchewan R.)
Fort Dauphin
La Prairie Portage
Fort Maurepas
Fort La Reine
Fort Rouge
Fort St-Charles
Fort St-Pierre
Lac des Bois [L. of the Woods]
La Vérendrye and sons 1731-38
Grand Portage
Lac Nipigon
Fort La Tourette
Fort Nipigon
Fort Kaministiquia
Lac Supérieur
Abitibi R.
La Grande Rivière (Ottawa R.)
St-Laurent
Montréal
Lachine
Sorel

Fort La Butte
Red River of the North
Fort Chequamegon
Duluth Portage
Fort Ste-Croix
Sault-Ste-Marie
St-Ignace
Fort Michilimackinac
L'Arbre Croche
Lac Huron
Fort La Galette (La Présentation)
Fort Frontenac
Fort Rouille
Lac Frontenac [Ontario]
Fort Oswego (English)
Fort Niagara (Fort Conti)

Yellowstone River
1742-43
Mandan villages
La Vérendrye sons
BLACK HILLS
Missouri River
Fort La Baye
St-François-Xavier
Fort St-Antoine
Fort Beauharnais
Fort Trempealeau
Fort St-Nicolas
Wisconsin Portage
Wisconsin R.
Fox R.
Lac des Illinois [L. Michigan]
Fort St-Joseph
Fort Pontchartrain du Détroit
Fort Miami
Fort St-Joseph
Fort Miami
Maumee R.
Niagara Portage
Chautauqua Portage
French Creek Portage
Cuyahoga Portage
Sandusky Portage
Lac Erié
Scioto R.
APPALACHIAN MOUNTAINS
Baltimore

ROCKY MOUNTAINS
N. Platte R.
S. Platte R.
Platte River
Mallet brothers 1739
Platte River
Fort Orleans
1724
Bourgmont
Fort Cavagnolle
Du Tisné 1719
Ange Guardien
Chicago Portage
Fort St-Louis
Fort Crèvecoeur
Illinois R.
Wabash Portage
Fort Ouiatanon
Wabash R.
[Ohio R.]
Vincennes
Rivière Ohio
La Belle Rivière
Williamsburg

1673
1679-82
Cahokia
Fort de Chartres
Kaskaskia
Ste-Geneviève
La Salle
Jolliet and Marquette
Fort L' Assomption (Fort Prudhomme)
Tennessee R.
Tombigbee R.

North Canadian River
Canadian River
Mallet brothers 1740-41
Arkansas River
La Harpe 1719
Arkansas Post
Mississippi R.
Fort Tombecbe

Santa Fé (Spanish)
Red River
Sebine R.
Brazos R.
Trinity R.
Neches R.
Natchitoches
Los Adaes (Spanish)
Natchez (Fort Rosalie)
Fort St-Louis
Mobile (Fort Condé)
Bâton-Rouge
Lac Maurepas
Biloxi
30°

El Paso del Norte (Spanish)
Rio Grande (Rio Bravo del Norte)
Pecos River
Colorado River
Saint-Denis 1714
La Salle killed 1687
San Antonio (Spanish)
Fort St-Louis
La Nouvelle-Orléans
90°

San Juan Bautista (Spanish)
Nueces R.
La Salle 1684 (from France)
Matagorda Bay
GULF OF MEXICO

CHAPTER 3

STRUGGLE FOR THE CONTINENT

A promoter's vision of the American future appears in the published *Voyages* of Pierre Esprit Radisson, a young soldier of fortune and fur hunter who journeyed through the upper Great Lakes and was one of the first two white men to enter present-day Minnesota, in 1659–60. The country was so beautiful, he wrote, that it grieved him to see it so uninhabited. "This I say," he added, "because that the Europeans fight for a rock in the sea against one another, or for a sterill land or horrid country . . . Contrarywise those [American] kingdoms are so delicious & under so temperat a climat, plentifull of all things . . . What conquest would that bee at little or no cost; what laborinth of pleasure should millions of people have [there], instead that millions complaine of misery & poverty!"

During the first century after Columbus the North American continent above Mexico was either an obstacle on the route to Asia, or a wilderness to ransack for quick profits. After another 100 years, by 1700, it was well understood to be a gigantic prize in itself. The three major European powers—Spain, France, and England—were deeply committed, by national pride and commercial interest, to maintaining possessions there. Arrayed at times, against, or with, any one or all of them, was another important force: the power of the Indian tribes that still controlled at least nine-tenths of the choicest land.

Spain, with the oldest American empire, and the biggest and richest, used Florida, Texas, and New Mexico as military buffer lands to ward off encroachment from the north. The silver mines of northern Mexico, and the great cattle ranches that grew up alongside them, gave New Spain dependable sources of wealth to support its ruling class. This consisted (in both Americas) of what were counted as 32,000 "Spanish families," numbering about 160,000 persons. However, as one traveler observed, not even one-tenth of the European-born Spaniards in Mexico were women, suggesting that many "Spanish families" must have had Indian wives and mothers. The natives numbered about five million in a census taken 50 years after the conquest. Patient priests turned them into Catholics, and landholders organized them in self-supporting villages, providing tools and seeds. Much has been said of the agricultural novelties that the New World gave the Old: potatoes, Indian corn, tomatoes, tobacco, cacao, vanilla, rubber trees, and some others. But the exchange was one-sidedly to the advantage of the Americas. The Spaniards brought over wheat, barley, rice, rye, lentils, flax, alfalfa, apples, cherries, almonds, walnuts, olives, pears, and—important in their semi-tropical colonies—sugar cane, oranges, lemons, limes, mangoes, and varieties of bananas and grapefruit. They also imported the first horses, mules, cattle, sheep, and domestic hogs. And they did not forget their flowers; in 1552 a mass was said at Lima, Peru, with a seed on the altar, to celebrate the arrival of the first rose seeds from Castille.

New France during the 17th century was served by the ablest governors, the most successful explorers, the most daring and skilled frontiersmen (coureurs de bois and voyageurs) who had yet appeared on the continent. But the French domain was far overextended, in proportion to its manpower. In 1700 almost all the 15,000 habitants (colonist-farmers) lived in the St. Lawrence Valley; their number rose only to 60,000 in the next 60 years. Illinois had about 1,500 French residents, New Orleans only 1,900 (plus 1,200 Negro and Indian slaves) as late as 1763. In a campaign to produce more families the intendant Talon brought to Quebec shiploads of "women of ordinary reputation . . . some fair, some brown, some fat, and some meager," and gave to each man who selected a bride "an ox, a cow, a hog, a sow, a cock, a hen, two barrels of salt meat, and eleven crowns." Bachelors who evaded the summons were punished by having their hunting licenses revoked.

Yet New France remained to its end a thinly peopled frontier—a land of scanty clearings and crops, occasional villages, and hewn timber churches, surrounded by silent forests. Its priests and nuns worked as faithfully as their Spanish counterparts to convert and educate the Indians. But with escape to the woods so easy, their charges rarely became steady workers. Not a few French missionaries found a reward like that of Père Marquette: a deathbed on the forest floor, and a birch bark box to carry his bones back to his mission at Michilimackinac.

The colony's only important export was fur, which involved the best of its male population in arduous commerce with the wilderness Indians. Beginning in 1670 the tribes north of the Great Lakes learned that English wool blankets and Sheffield steel knives were better than what the French had to offer. This information spread from new British posts on Hudson Bay, which shipped home cargoes of Canadian furs, and paid 75 per cent dividends to London stockholders. The English claim to this northern region was based on Henry Hudson's 1610 voyage, and earlier ones by Cabot and Frobisher.

New France was unlucky because its years of greatest potential coincided with the 72-year reign of Louis XIV (an all-time record for European monarchs). The Sun King was pleased when Louisiana was named for him, but he never grasped its significance: his way of building an empire was to marry his grandson to the throne of Spain. In spite of his disasters in war he remained absolute—"L'état, c'est moi"—and his will was law for all Frenchmen, from the fur compound that became Detroit to the mirrored throne room at Versailles. Two of his obvious mistakes were his persecution of French Protestants—the Huguenots—and his refusal to let them colonize Louisiana. So thousands of them came instead to add their considerable talents and wealth to the resources of English America.

On the Atlantic seaboard the English colonies formed a compact column that pressed against New France like an army. After 1732 there were 14 of them, including Nova Scotia and Georgia. Separately the English possessions were small, compared with Louisiana and Canada, or the vast Spanish borderlands. Their terrain was not America's most productive, though it had fine seaports, fertile river valleys, and tidelands. Their population in 1700 was 250,000, including 27,000 Negro slaves. During the French and Indian wars these numbers increased amazingly, to about 1,400,000 whites and 350,000 Negroes in 1763. Immigration from England, Scotland, Ireland, Germany, France, and Switzerland was certainly a major factor, but the local birth rate should not be underestimated. "Marriages in America are more general, and more generally early, than in Europe," wrote Benjamin Franklin, who reckoned that the average colonial couple produced eight children, who were likely to marry again at 20, so that "if one half grow up . . . our People must be at least doubled every 20 Years."

In booming English America, kings were accorded distant respect, but only limited obedience. As was definitely not true in New Spain or New France, the English colonies that were well established took a firm part in governing themselves, through elected assemblies or advisory councils. Their self-reliance was thrust upon them early; neither king nor Parliament lifted a hand to help Jamestown or Plymouth in their starving years. Only two originated through royal initiative: New York, a take-over from the Dutch, and Nova Scotia, a military conquest. The others were founded by private investors, proprietors, churches, and one incorrigible nonconformist (Rhode Island, by Roger Williams). In New England, a 1745 French-Canadian writer observed, the people "have their own laws and administration, and their governor plays the sovereign . . . No nation but the English is capable of such bizarreries,—which, nevertheless, are a part of the precious liberty of which they show themselves so jealous."

English settlement in the 17th century stopped short of the Appalachian Mountains and the Iroquois strongholds in upper New York. But English claims and charter grants ran across the mountains and beyond; even, in some cases, to the "East Indian [Pacific] Sea." It was not likely that nine-tenths of North America's white inhabitants (above the Rio Grande) would remain cooped up for long in one-tenth of its living space. So the wars that began in 1689 in Europe, with French conquest of a few square miles of the Rhenish Palatinate, became in America the means of deciding who would rule a continent.

THE WILDERNESS FEDERATION

Fort La Tourette
Lac Nipigon
O J I B W A
Fort Kaministiquia
Lac Supérieur
Fort des Abitibis
M O N T A G N A I S   Tadoussac
Saguenay R.
Lac St-Jean
St. John
River
M I C M A C
Penobscot R.
St. Croix
A B N A K I
Kennebec
R.
NOUVELLE - FRANCE
Québec
Fort Richelieu
OTTAWA
La Grande Rivière
[Ottawa R.]
Lac
Nipissing
Sault-Ste-Marie
Fort de Buade
Baie Verte
[Green Bay]
Lac Attigouantan
Georgian Bay
Montréal
Lachine
St-Laurent Fleuve
Connecticut River
M A H I C A N
Lac Iroquois
[L. Champlain]
H U R O N
Lac
Huron
TOBACCO
Fort Frontenac
Lac Frontenac
[L. Ontario]
MOHAWK
ONEIDA
ONONDAGA
CAYUGA
SENECA
Mohawk
R.
C O L O N I E S
Albany (Fort Orange)
Boston
Cape Cod
NEUTRAL
Fort Conti
Hudson
R.
SAUK
Wisconsin
R.
POTAWATOMI
Fort St-Joseph
Lac des Illinois
[L. Michigan]
Mississippi
River
FOX
ERIE
Lac Erié
Maumee R.
MIAMI
Delaware
R.
New York (New Amsterdam)
Long Island
40°
Fort St-Louis
Fort Crèvecoeur
Illinois
River
I L L I N O I S
River
[Ohio R.]
Allegheny
Susquehanna R.
S U S Q U E H A N N A
DELAWARE
Delaware Bay
E N G L I S H
A T L A N T I C
O C E A N
La Belle
Rivière
S H A W N E E
Wabash
River
Potomac
Chesapeake
Bay
James
River
Jamestown
P O W H A T A N
Norfolk
Cumberland
River
River
Roanoke
Pee Dee River
T U S C A R O R A
Cape Hatteras
35°
Tennessee
River
C H E R O K E E
C A T A W B A
Santee
L O U I S I A N E
Fort
Prudhomme
River
C H I C K A S A W
Tombigbee
River
Chattahoochee River
Savannah River
Y A M A S E E
Charles Town
Arkansas Post
Alabama River
C R E E K
Flint
Altamaha R.
C H O C T A W
S P A N I S H
Mississippi
A P A L A C H E E
St. Marys R.
T I M U C U A
San Agustín
GULF OF MEXICO
F L A.
30°

IROQUOIS WARS
1642-89

Five Nations of the Iroquois

● settlement   ✕ fort or trading post

0   100   200

90°   85°   80°   75°   70°

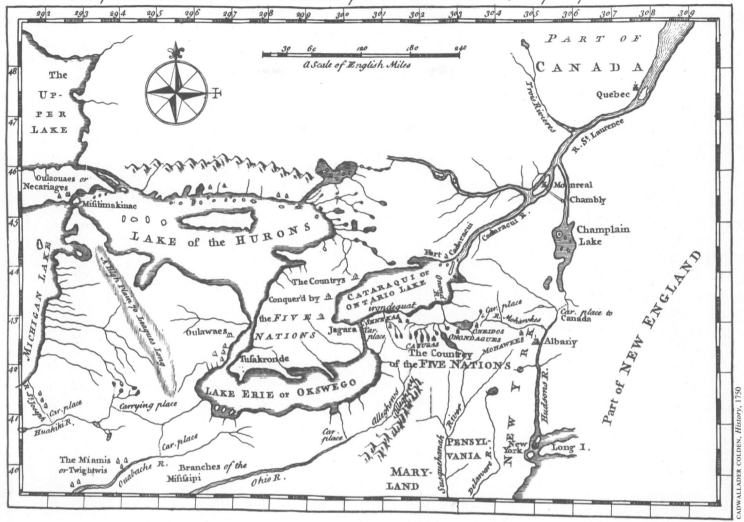

A MAP of the Country of the FIVE NATIONS, belonging to the Province of NEW YORK; and of the LAKES near which the Nations of FAR INDIANS live, with part of CANADA.

Cadwallader Colden of New York published a History of the Five Indian Nations *in 1727. This map is from a later London edition, at which time an adopted sixth nation, the Tuscaroras, driven from North Carolina by English settlers, lived between the Oneidas and Onondagas.*

The key to military control of the continent was England's alliance with the Five Nations of Iroquois, whose narrow, deep-trodden paths provided the fastest communication between the Atlantic and the interior. The Iroquois were among the first Indians to obtain guns for their warfare (from Dutch "free traders"—i.e., bootleggers—on the Hudson River). But their conquests were won less by firepower than by their commando-style tactics. "They come like foxes," wrote a French priest. "They attack like lions . . . They take flight like birds."

The Iroquois had to strike hard when they struck, for they never had more than 2,300 warriors. The main thrust of their wars was against other Indians; their purpose was to be absolute lords of the fur trade. Beginning in 1642 their murderous raids demoralized and dispersed four groups of their neighbors: the 35,000 Hurons of southeastern Canada, friends and allies of the French, who had grown rich and lazy on middlemen's profits from furs; the 15,000 Petuns, or Tobacco Nation; the 12,000 "Neutrals,"

who also lived by agriculture; and the 10,000 Eries, who made the mistake of sheltering Huron refugees. The Mohawks, keepers of the Iroquois' "eastern fire," drove the Mahicans from the Adirondack fur grounds and into exile in Massachusetts. Senecas and Cayugas destroyed their southern kinsmen, the Susquehannas, who were unable to save themselves with firearms, including cannon, obtained from the Delaware Swedes.

To the west Iroquois war bands traveled 800 miles to attack France's forts and Indian allies on the Illinois River. In revenge French armies from Canada burned the towns of the Onondagas and Senecas. That only made the Iroquois more dangerous than ever to New France: in the colonial wars that began in 1689 they were likely at any time to swoop down on French settlements, or cut the French life line to the west. To the English, who bought their furs at Albany, the Iroquois remained allies—on equal and independent terms—for 140 years, and through the American Revolution.

NEW ENGLAND'S INDIAN WARS

This 1638 woodcut shows Pequots besieged in their circular fort.

Just before the *Mayflower* came to Plymouth, an epidemic, perhaps introduced by white seamen, had decimated the Algonquian tribes on the New England coast. So the Pilgrims planted their first crops in deserted Indian cornfields. One day in March, 1621, Samoset, a visiting Pemaquid from Maine, strode into the Plymouth settlement and addressed the colonists in the broken English he had learned from fishermen. He arranged a meeting between the Pilgrim leaders and the grand sachem of the nearby Wampanoags, Massasoit, who signed a treaty of peace, and later attended (with 90 of his braves) the first Thanksgiving dinner. Another helpful Indian, Squanto, who had lived in London for several years after being kidnapped by an English captain, moved in with the Pilgrims as interpreter, guide, and instructor in agriculture.

This happy state of affairs lasted a dozen years. After the great Puritan migration began, the small and divided New England tribes were caught in a desperate squeeze. Settlers pushed them off the best land; overbearing white traders, armed with muskets, gave them many bad bargains. There was no refuge farther west, where the Mohawks along the Hudson River were the merciless foes of the New England Algonquians.

The Pequot War of the 1630's was really an organized massacre to revenge scattered killings of whites and the burning of Wethersfield in the new Connecticut colony. It began when John Oldham, a well-known trader, was killed on his boat by hatchet-wielding Pequots from Block Island. A Massachusetts force led by John Endecott went after the murderers, but the Pequots hid them. On May 26, 1637, Major John Mason and 90 Connecticut soldiers set fire to a fort near the Mystic River where 600 Pequot men, women, and children were penned up with no chance for escape. "It was a fearfull sight to see them thus frying in the fyer, and the streams of blood quenching the same,

and horrible was the stinck and sente ther of," wrote Governor Bradford of Plymouth, who noted also that hundreds of Narraganset Indians—then the allies of the colonists—"stood round aboute . . . and left the whole execution to the English, except it were the stoping of any that broke away." More fleeing Pequots were caught and killed near Fairfield, Connecticut, and a small band that reached Mohawk territory—including their principal sachem Sassacus—were immediately put to death by those Indians.

A son of Massasoit named Metacom—known to the whites as King Philip—endeavored from 1662 on to unite the New England tribes in a league like that of the Iroquois. In 1675 some of Philip's men murdered a Christian ("Praying") Indian who had informed the English of this activity. Colonial officials demanded that Philip's warriors surrender their flintlock muskets. Instead, Philip struck at Swansea, Massachusetts—the signal for a general war that briefly threatened New England's existence. Of 90 towns in the four colonies, 52 were attacked and 12 destroyed; the Connecticut Valley was overrun (map on opposite page). The decisive battle was fought in Rhode Island between a 1,000-man New England army and 3,000 Narragansets, who were strongly entrenched, with plenty of guns, behind palisades and blockhouses. The Great Swamp Fight of 1675, according to Samuel Eliot Morison, "was the toughest battle, not excepting Bunker Hill, ever fought on New England soil." It cost the New Englanders 80 dead, including eight company commanders; 2,000 Narragansets were killed in battle or burned to death later. The war lasted eight more months, until Philip's last followers lost the battle of Bridgewater Swamp. Philip himself was shot down in the woods near his home base at Mount Hope; his head was displayed on a pole at Plymouth for the next 20 years. It took Massachusetts the same length of time to repair the damage done by King Philip's War.

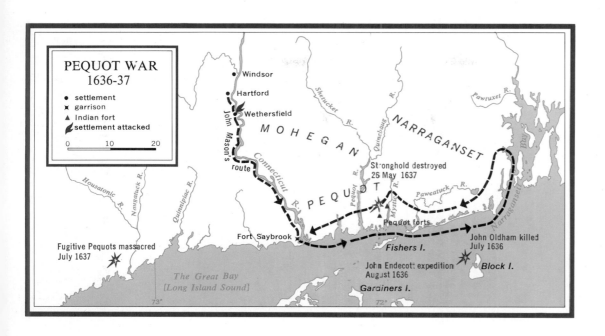

PEQUOT WAR
1636-37

● settlement
✕ garrison
▲ Indian fort
⚑ settlement attacked

0   10   20

Windsor

Hartford

Wethersfield

John Mason's route

Sherucket R.

MOHEGAN

NARRAGANSET

Pawtuxet R.

Quinebaug R.

Narraganset Bay

PEQUOT

Stronghold destroyed
25 May 1637

Connecticut R.

Pequot R.

Mystic R.

Paweatuck R.

Pequot forts

Housatonic R.

Naugatuck R.

Quinnipiac R.

Fort Saybrook

Fugitive Pequots massacred
July 1637

Fishers I.

John Oldham killed
July 1636

John Endecott expedition
August 1636

Block I.

*The Great Bay
[Long Island Sound]*

Gardiners I.

73°   72°

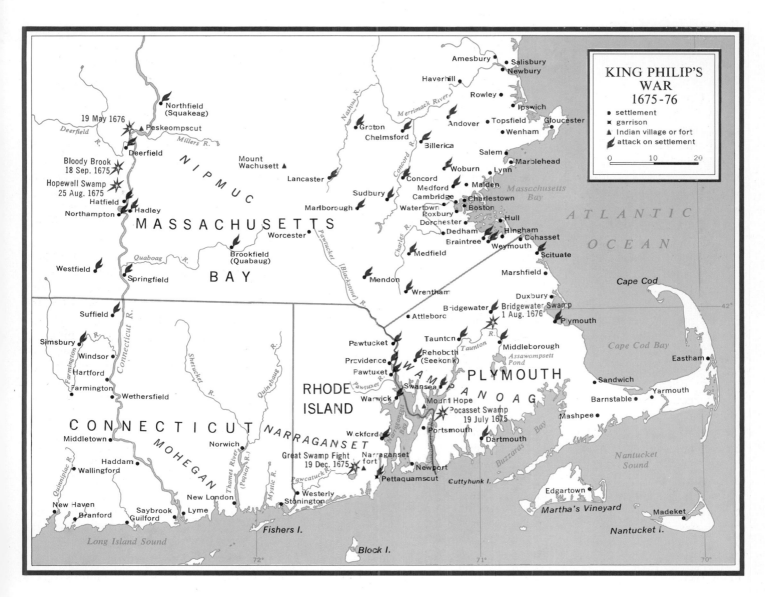

KING PHILIP'S
WAR
1675-76

● settlement
✕ garrison
▲ Indian village or fort
⚑ attack on settlement

0   10   20

Amesbury

Salisbury
Newbury

Haverhill

Rowley

Ipswich

Merrimack River

Nashua R.

Northfield
(Squakeag)

19 May 1676

Deerfield R.

Peskeompscut

Millers R.

Groton

Chelmsford

Andover

Topsfield

Wenham

Gloucester

Billerica

Salem

Marblehead

Deerfield

NIPMUC

Mount
Wachusett ▲

Lancaster

Concord R.

Woburn

Lynn

Bloody Brook
18 Sep. 1675

Hopewell Swamp
25 Aug. 1675

Hatfield

Concord

Medford

Malden

Charlestown

*Massachusetts
Bay*

Northampton

Hadley

MASSACHUSETTS

Sudbury

Cambridge

Watertown

Boston

Roxbury

Hull

ATLANTIC

Worcester

Marlborough

Dorchester

Dedham

Hingham

Braintree

Cohasset

OCEAN

Quaboag R.

BAY

Brookfield
(Quabaug)

Weymouth

Scituate

Westfield

Springfield

Mendon

Medfield

Marshfield

Cape Cod

Connecticut R.

Wrentham

Duxbury

Suffield

Bridgewater

Bridgewater Swamp
1 Aug. 1676

42°

Simsbury

Sheruckel R.

Pawtucket (Blackstone) R.

Attleboro

Plymouth

Cape Cod Bay

Windsor

Quinebaug R.

Pawtucket

Taunton

Taunton R.

Middleborough

Hartford

Providence

Rehoboth
(Seekonk)

*Assawompsett
Pond*

Eastham

Farmington

Wethersfield

Pawtuxet

WAMPANOAG

PLYMOUTH

Sandwich

Yarmouth

CONNECTICUT

NARRAGANSET

RHODE
ISLAND

Swansea

Warwick

Mount Hope

Portsmouth

Pocasset Swamp
19 July 1675

Dartmouth

Buzzards Bay

Mashpee

Barnstable

*Nantucket
Sound*

Middletown

MOHEGAN

Norwich

Wickford

Narraganset
fort

Newport

*Thames River
(Pequot R.)*

Great Swamp Fight
19 Dec. 1675

Haddam

Wallingford

Mystic R.

Pettaquamscut

Cuttyhunk I.

New Haven

Branford

Saybrook

Guilford

Lyme

New London

Pawcatuck R.

Westerly

Stonington

Edgartown

Martha's Vineyard

Madeket

Quinnipiac R.

Long Island Sound

Fishers I.

Block I.

Nantucket I.

72°   71°   70°

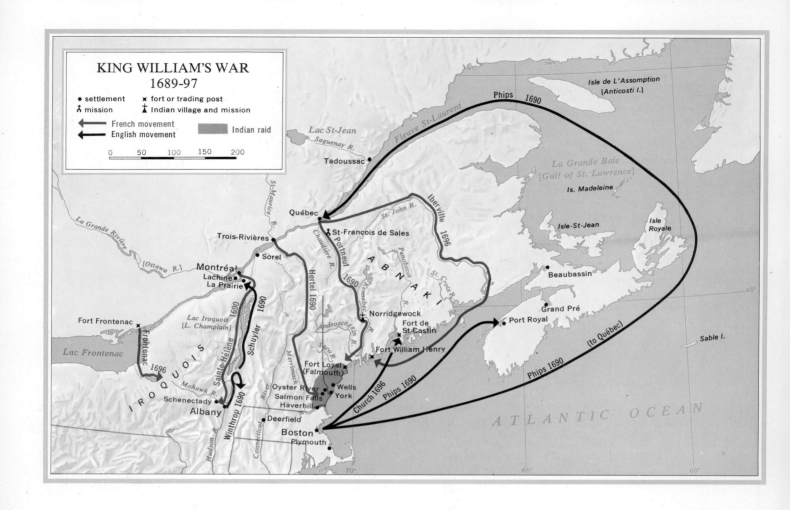

THE CONFLICT BEGINS

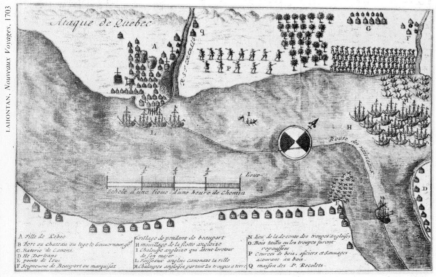

A New England navy of merchant ships, manned by volunteer fishermen, demanded Quebec's surrender in October, 1690. The French drove off a landing party (right, above), and the Yankees sailed away. This print is from a 1703 French history.

The five wars that spanned 75 years and gave seafaring England the world's greatest empire are often grouped in American minds as the French and Indian wars. In fact, they were global wars that settled India's fate as much as Canada's; they included Marlborough's victory at Blenheim, English seizure of Gibraltar, naval battles from Manila to Cuba, the downgrading of Spain and Portugal, the rise of militaristic Prussia, and the first intrusion of Russia into Europe's power politics. In North America they erased New France from the map.

For the northern colonists King William's War and Queen Anne's War (which both had different names in Europe) were virtually one continuous struggle. They opened with a typical frontier incident: an Iroquois raiding party surprised Lachine, westernmost French village on the St. Lawrence, in August, 1689. They "kidnapped 120 persons, men, women, and children, after having slaughtered more than 200, whom they clubbed, burned, and roasted," reported Governor Frontenac. The next massacre was on English territory; French-Canadian woodsmen

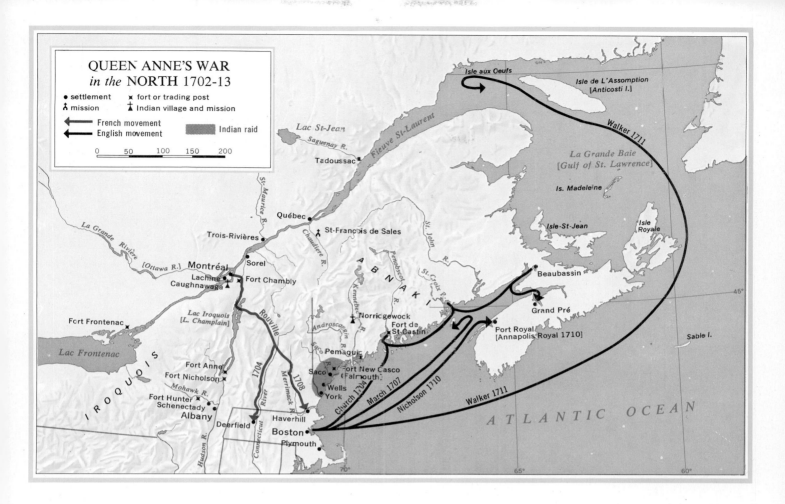

QUEEN ANNE'S WAR
in the NORTH 1702-13

and mission Indians found Schenectady guarded by two Dutch snowmen, and tomahawked 60 young and old inhabitants. Other sneak attacks through the wilderness ravaged English towns in northern New England, and French La Prairie, near Montreal.

The big English achievement of both wars was the conquest of Port Royal and Nova Scotia (French L'Acadie). But two naval expeditions against Quebec ended in dismal failure. The first was led by Sir William Phips, one of 26 children of a Maine fisherman, who won his fortune and English knighthood by raising gold and silver from a sunken Spanish galleon. His ships reached Quebec, but were driven away by French cannon. In Queen Anne's War an English admiral, Sir Hovenden Walker, wrecked his fleet at the mouth of the St. Lawrence, losing 1,600 lives.

A Franco-Spanish alliance enlarged Queen Anne's War in the South. Carolina militia and Indian allies plundered St. Augustine and destroyed Spanish missions among the Apalachees of Florida. A small Franco-Spanish fleet demanded the surrender of Charles Town, but was repulsed.

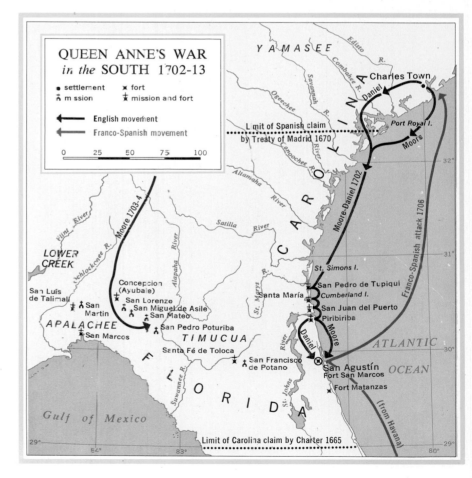

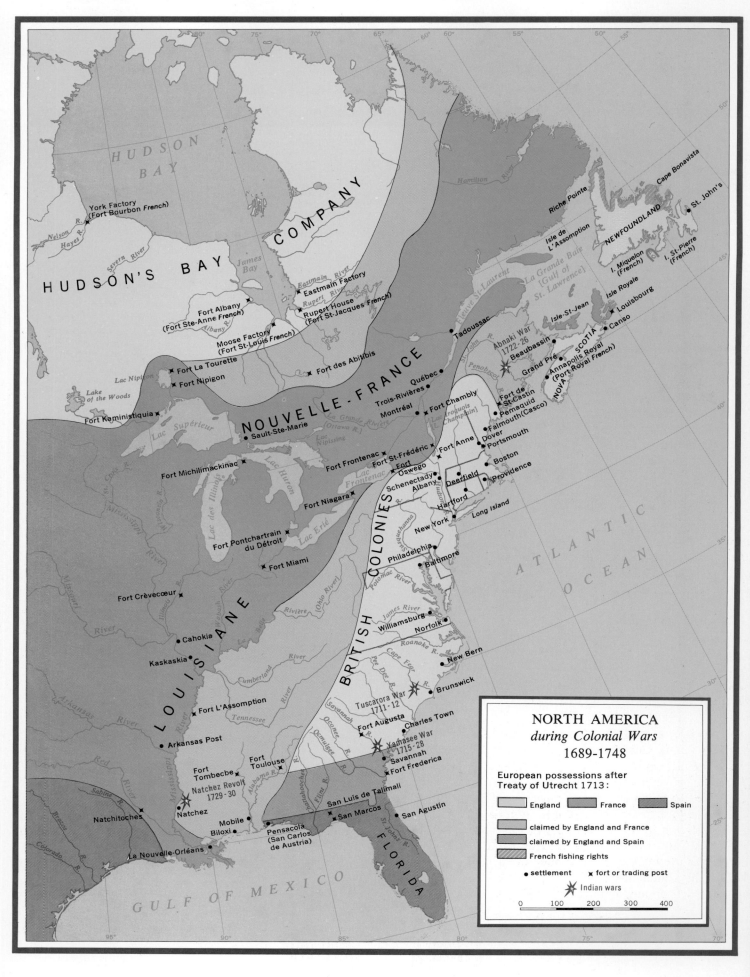

HUDSON BAY

HUDSON'S BAY COMPANY

York Factory
(Fort Bourbon *French*)

Nelson R.
Hayes R.
Severn River

James Bay

Eastmain River
Eastmain Factory
Rupert House
(Fort St-Jacques *French*)
Rupert River

Fort Albany
(Fort Ste-Anne *French*)
Albany R.

Moose Factory
(Fort St-Louis *French*)

Fort des Abitibis

Fort La Tourette
Fort Nipigon

Lac Nipigon

Lake of the Woods

Fort Kaministiquia

Lac Supérieur

NOUVELLE - FRANCE

Sault-Ste-Marie

Lac Nipissing

Fort Michilimackinac

Lac Huron

Lac des Illinois

La Grande Rivière (Ottawa R.)

Tadoussac

Québec
Trois-Rivières
Montréal
Fort Chambly
Fort Frontenac
Fort St-Frédéric
Fort Lac Frontenac
Oswego
Fort Niagara

Lac Erié

Fort Pontchartrain du Détroit

Fort Miami

Fort Crèvecœur

LOUISIANE

Cahokia

Kaskaskia

Fort L'Assomption

Arkansas Post

Fort Tombecbe
Natchez Revolt 1729-30
Natchez

Natchitoches

Mobile
Biloxi
Pensacola
(San Carlos de Austria)

La Nouvelle-Orléans

Fleuve St-Laurent

St-Jean
Penobscot

Fort de St-Castin
Pemaquid
Falmouth (Casco)
Dover
Portsmouth
Fort Anne
Boston
Schenectady
Albany
Deerfield
Providence
Hartford

Hudson R.

New York
Long Island

Philadelphia
Baltimore

Susquehanna River

Potomac River

James River
Williamsburg
Norfolk

Roanoke R.

BRITISH COLONIES

Cape Fear
New Bern

Pee Dee R.
Brunswick

Tuscarora War 1711-12

Savannah R.
Fort Augusta
Charles Town

Oconee R.
Ocmulgee R.
Yamasee War 1715-28
Savannah
Fort Frederica

Fort Toulouse
Alabama R.
Flint R.
Chattahoochee R.

San Luis de Talimali
San Marcos
St. Johns R.
San Agustin

FLORIDA

GULF OF MEXICO

Red River
Sabine R.
Brazos R.
Colorado R.

Missouri River
Mississippi River
Riviere (Ohio River)
Cumberland
Tennessee

Iroquois
(Lac Champlain)

Abnaki War 1722-26
Beaubassin
Grand Pré
Annapolis Royal
(Port-Royal *French*)
NOVA SCOTIA
Canso

Riche Pointe
Isle de L'Assomption
La Grande Baie (Gulf of St. Lawrence)
Isle-St-Jean
Isle Royale
Louisbourg

NEWFOUNDLAND
Cape Bonavista
St. John's
I. Miquelon (French)
I. St-Pierre (French)

Hamilton River

ATLANTIC OCEAN

NORTH AMERICA
during Colonial Wars
1689-1748

European possessions after
Treaty of Utrecht 1713:

England   France   Spain

claimed by England and France

claimed by England and Spain

French fishing rights

• settlement   ✕ fort or trading post

✳ Indian wars

0   100   200   300   400

62

YEARS *of* TRUCE *and* TROUBLE

The Treaty of Utrecht, which ended Queen Anne's War, severely curtailed France's American empire. Louis XIV, who lost the war in Europe, surrendered to England all French claims to Nova Scotia, Newfoundland, and the vast Hudson's Bay Company trading area. France, however, retained for its fishermen the right to land and dry their catch on part of the Newfoundland coast.

The treaty failed to draw precise boundaries between the British and remaining French colonies, or between the Carolinas and Florida. Nor did the cease-fire in Europe end grudge fights on American frontiers. In 1715 the Yamasee Indians were stirred by trade grievances and Spanish intrigue to begin a war against their old ally South Carolina. Militia from three southern colonies eventually drove the Yamasees into Florida, and appropriated the Yamasee lands for the new colony of Georgia. In the north the Abnaki Indians of Maine, converts to French Catholicism, continued to raid the farms and settlements of the Protestant Yankees. Frenchmen fought Spaniards for Pensacola, wiped out the dissatisfied Natchez Indians, and established Mobile and the future Montgomery (Fort Toulouse) on territory claimed by England.

The weakness of Spanish Florida invited aggression from all sides. In 1738 an English mariner named Robert Jenkins displayed to a House of Commons committee an ear which he said had been cut from his head by a Spanish captain in the Caribbean. He swore he had kept the ear in a box, wrapped in cotton, for seven years, after his ship was stopped and searched as a suspected slave smuggler. The incident started a cry for war, which was declared by England in 1739, and led to a futile invasion of Florida by General James Oglethorpe, founder and governor of Georgia. In 1742 Governor Montiano of Florida landed in Georgia with 3,000 men, but was beaten back with heavy losses at the battle of Bloody Marsh.

Meanwhile, a great British expedition, including hundreds of young colonial volunteers, attacked Cartagena in South America. It was driven away with terrible bloodshed, and worse losses from yellow fever. Among the Americans present was Captain Lawrence Washington of Virginia, who returned home broken in health, but a hero and inspiration to his ten-year-old half brother, George. Soon afterward, Lawrence Washington named his plantation house Mount Vernon, in honor of Admiral Edward Vernon, his commander at Cartagena. The name is about all that is left on any map from the War of Jenkins' Ear.

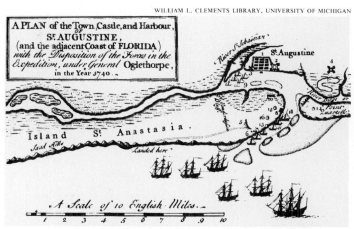

This detail from a contemporary British map shows the siege of St. Augustine in 1740 by the troops of General James Oglethorpe in the War of Jenkins' Ear. Despite the blockade which is suggested here, relief ships from Cuba slipped by and supplied the fort's defenders.

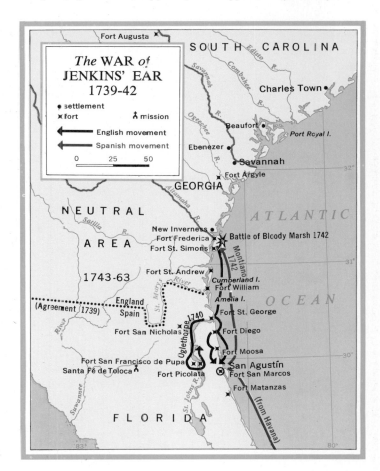

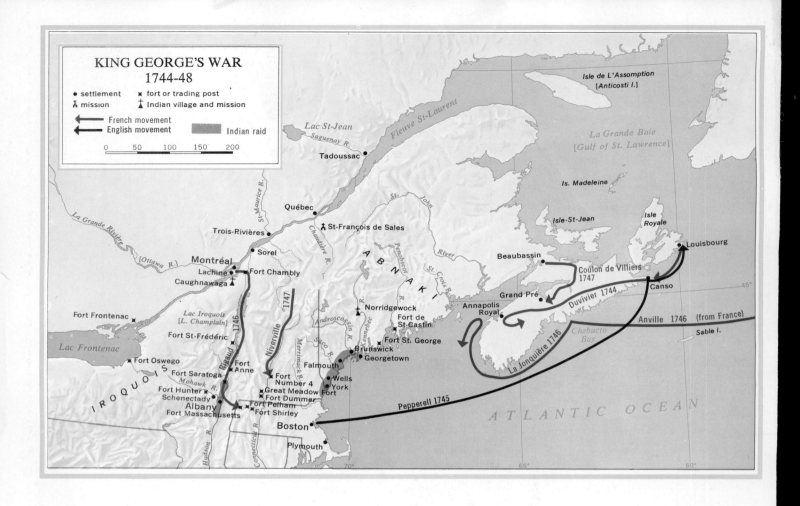

settlement • fort or trading post ✗
mission ⚡ Indian village and mission ✝

◀— French movement
◀— English movement   Indian raid

0   50   100   150   200

FIGHT *for a* FORTRESS

To compensate for its territorial losses France spent decades of work and 30 million livres (about six million dollars) to build the fortress city of Louisbourg, on Isle Royale (Cape Breton Island). Louisbourg was a full-scale naval base, with a harbor ringed by seven batteries, and the strongest concentration of cannon (including 36-pounders) on the North American continent. Frowning out on the Atlantic approaches to New England and Canada, Louisbourg was a nest of French privateers, a standing affront to British sea power, and a Maginot Line-like symbol of France's burning desire for revenge.

In 1744 Louisbourg was the first to learn that France and England were once more at war in Europe. The French general Duvivier promptly ferried his garrison troops to Nova Scotia, but failed to recapture Port Royal (Annapolis Royal to the English). In Massachusetts the next year Governor William Shirley assembled an army of 4,200 New Englanders and sent them on what one chronicler called a "mad frolic" against Louisbourg. The invaders were mostly undisciplined farm boys who got wildly drunk on captured brandy, and were happy to find "2 pritty gurls" in a deserted French camp. They hauled their siege

guns through miles of bogs, chased after French cannon balls and fired them back, and turned a captured French battery (opposite page, below) on the inner citadel with deadly effect. After two months of heavy siege, Louisbourg surrendered. "Never was a place more mal'd [mauled]," wrote the winning general, William Pepperell, a merchant and politician from Kittery Point in Maine. "We gave them about nine thousand cannon-balls and six hundred bombs."

Half the French navy, 66 ships, sailed out of Brest in 1746 to repair this blow to French pride. Storms and wrecks on the fogbound Nova Scotia coast so riddled the fleet that the Duc d'Anville, its commander, either died of apoplexy or swallowed poison on his flagship in Chebucto Bay. Vice Admiral d'Estournel, named to succeed him, fell on his sword and died instead. The Marquis de La Jonquière led the remaining French ships to Annapolis Royal, but found it too strongly held to attack. In 1747 Coulon de Villiers, in a daring raid through blinding snow, took the British fort at Grand Pré. Other French forces overran tiny Fort Massachusetts, on New England's western frontier, but failed to capture Fort Number 4 (now Charlestown, New Hampshire), defended by 30 militiamen.

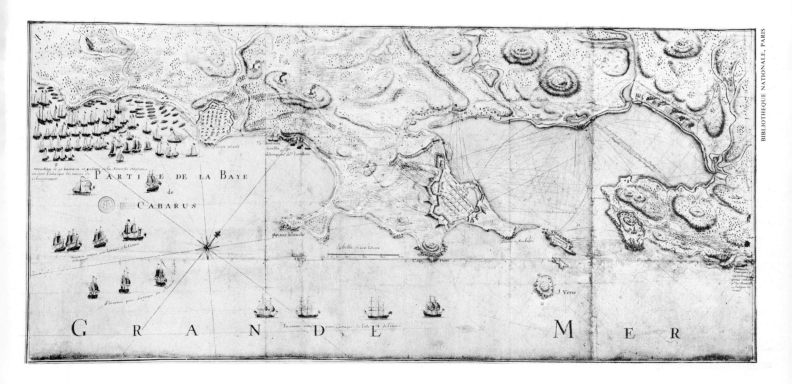

Louisbourg's formidable Batterie Royalle is depicted below in profile and plan in a French military drawing. Above, in another French view, it appears in small scale at the center of the upper shore of the harbor (right). Its defenders in 1745 fled to the main fort, on the peninsula jutting right at center, when the New Englanders landed (far left) and circled around to attack from the rear. The 36 big cannon were spiked, but Yankee gunsmiths repaired them overnight and began using them in the morning.

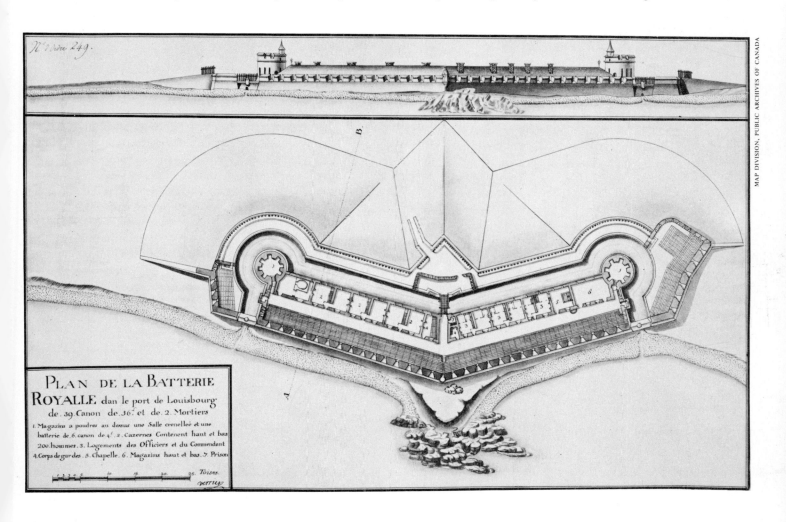

PLAN DE LA BATTERIE
ROYALLE dan le port de Louisbourg
de 39 Canon de 36.et de 2 Mortiers

1. Magazins a poudres au dessus une Salle crenelleé et une
batterie de 6. canon de 4. 2. Cazernes Contenent haut et bas
200. hommes. 3. Logemens des Officiers et du Commendant
4. Corps de gardes. 5. Chapelle. 6. Magazins haut et bas. 7. Prison

RIVAL CLAIMS *to the* OHIO

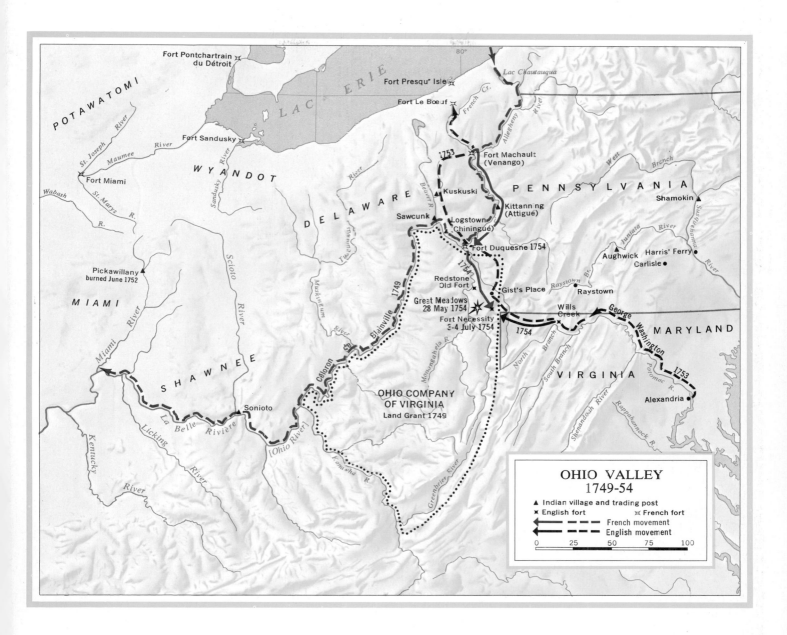

Autumn's brilliance in the Virginia mountains was dissolving in cold November rains as Major George Washington, aged 21, pointed his horse toward a disputed wilderness in 1753. The map he drew of his 26-day journey from the Alleghenies to Fort Le Bœuf, near Lake Erie, is reproduced on the opposite page. Above, in a modern cartographer's version, his route is shown by a broken black line.

Washington rode into the area to deliver an official warning to the French commander at Fort Le Bœuf: "The lands upon the Ohio River in the western parts of the colony of Virginia are . . . the property of the Crown of Great Britain." The Frenchman replied that he was instructed to maintain "the rights of the King, my Master . . . and to contest the pretensions of the King of Great Britain." The two monarchs were at peace, temporarily, but their subjects

were waging a small cold war to possess the lush Ohio valley. Virginia speculators, by royal grant, received title in 1749 to half a million acres between the Kanawha and the Ohio. The French sent an armed force down the main river that year (solid red line above), and raced to build forts, southward from Canada, to seal off the region. Washington, in 1754, hurried back over the mountains with 300 Virginia militiamen, expecting to find a Virginia fort at the great fork of the Ohio (now downtown Pittsburgh), a site he himself had selected. Instead, he learned the French already had built Fort Duquesne there. His men turned off to Great Meadows (solid black line above), where they wiped out a French scouting party. Then they were forced to surrender after an all-day battle with 1,000 French and Indians at Fort Necessity (near modern Uniontown, Pennsylvania).

THE FINAL CONTEST

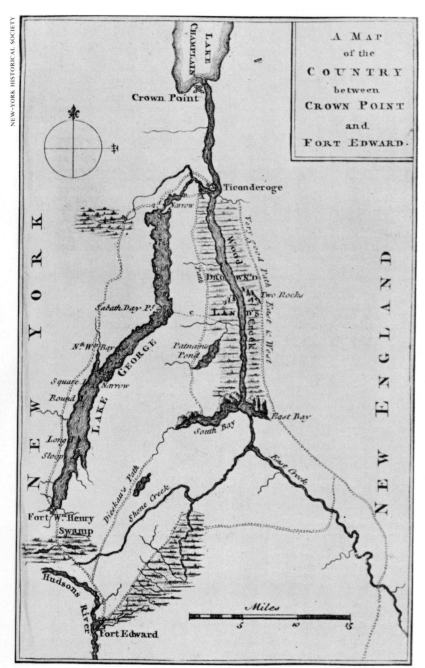

"A Map of the Country between Crown Point and Fort Edward," an engraving published in the Gentleman's *Magazine of London for May, 1759, shows the terrain between southern Lake Champlain and the Hudson River which became the principal battleground in the last of the French and Indian wars.*

Frontier skirmishes became all-out war with the arrival, in 1755, of Major General Edward Braddock as Britain's commander in chief in North America. Braddock, a bulldog in personal bravery, was determined to prove that British regulars had nothing to fear from "naked Indians . . . [or] Canadians in their shirts." In June he moved out of Fort Cumberland, Maryland, at the head of 2,500 men, to oust the French from Fort Duquesne. With 300 axmen clearing the way, Braddock's army and its awkward wagons averaged better than three miles a day over the mountainous Indian trail that Washington had followed in the two previous years. In a dense forest (now replaced by factories) Braddock's advance "flying column"—English redcoats, and Virginia militia in blue—was ambushed and cut to pieces in a classic Indian trap. Of 1,459 English troops engaged, 977 were killed or wounded; Braddock soon died from wounds; and his successor in command fled all the way to Philadelphia, leaving the western frontier wide open to Indian massacres.

Other English operations in 1755 were also botched, though they were not so bloody. Governor William Shirley of Massachusetts collected armed galleys at Fort Oswego, but never got started on his plan to attack French Fort Niagara, at the other end of Lake Ontario. Sir William Johnson, the colorful Irishman who was England's resident agent among the Iroquois, won a fight against French invaders at Fort William Henry, near Lake George, then let his victory slip away by marching his men back to Albany.

The next two years, 1756–57, saw the start of a new general war in Europe, with France and England on opposing sides, and a series of stunning French victories on the Canadian-New York frontier. The Marquis de Montcalm, a brilliant French commander, destroyed the British posts on Lake Ontario, overran Fort Bull at the "Great Carrying Place" between the Mohawk and Oswego Rivers, and wiped out the settlement of German Flats. In 1757 Montcalm struck from another direction, taking Fort William Henry and 2,000 prisoners, of whom 200 were slaughtered in an Indian orgy. In 1758 an army of English, German, and Swiss colonists, with 1,200 kilted Highlanders, under Brigadier General John Forbes, avenged Braddock's defeat by cutting a great new road through Pennsylvania and finally capturing Fort Duquesne.

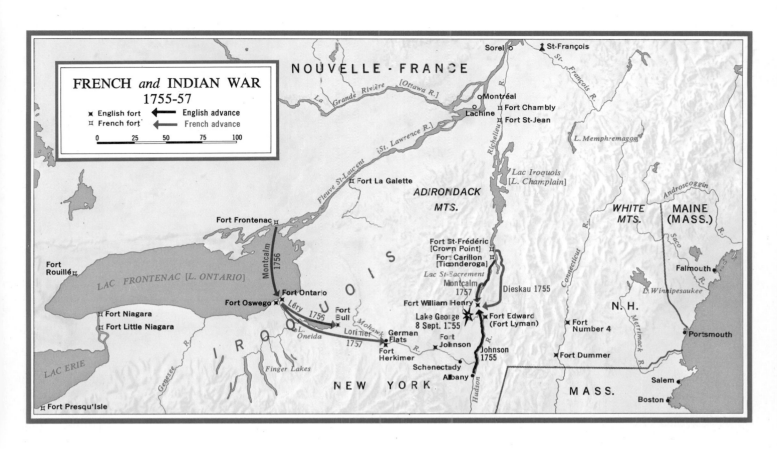

FRENCH and INDIAN WAR
1755-57

× English fort   ⟵ English advance
⊭ French fort   ⟵ French advance

0   25   50   75   100

NOUVELLE · FRANCE

Sorel   St-François

La Grande Rivière [Ottawa R.]

St-François R.

Montréal
Lachine
Fort Chambly
Fort St-Jean

Fleuve St-Laurent [St. Lawrence R.]

Fort La Galette

ADIRONDACK MTS.

L. Memphremagog

Richelieu R.

Lac Iroquois [L. Champlain]

WHITE MTS.

MAINE (MASS.)

Androscoggin R.

Fort Frontenac

Montcalm 1756

Fort St-Frédéric [Crown Point]
Fort Carillon [Ticonderoga]

Lac St-Sacrement

Falmouth

Fort Rouillé

LAC FRONTENAC [L. ONTARIO]

Fort Ontario
Fort Oswego

Léry 1755

Fort Bull

Montcalm 1757
Fort William Henry

Dieskau 1755

Connecticut R.

Saco R.

L. Winnipesaukee

N. H.

Portsmouth

Fort Niagara
Fort Little Niagara

I R O Q U O I S

L. Oneida

Lorimer 1757

Mohawk R.

German Flats

Fort Herkimer

Lake George 8 Sept. 1755

Fort Johnson

Fort Edward (Fort Lyman)

Johnson 1755

Fort Number 4

Merrimack R.

Fort Dummer

LAC ERIE

Genesee R.

Finger Lakes

Schenectady
Albany

Hudson R.

Salem

MASS.

Boston

Fort Presqu'Isle

NEW YORK

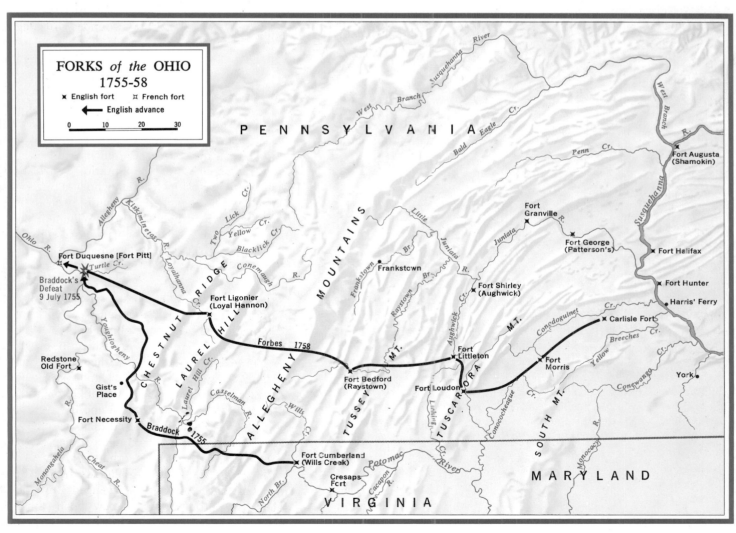

FORKS of the OHIO
1755-58

× English fort   ⊭ French fort

⟵ English advance

0   10   20   30

P E N N S Y L V A N I A

Susquehanna River

West Branch

Branch

Bald Eagle Cr.

Penn Cr.

West Branch

Fort Augusta (Shamokin)

Allegheny R.

Kiskiminetas R.

Two Lick Cr.
Yellow Cr.
Blacklick Cr.

Loyalhanna R.

Conemaugh R.

C H E S T N U T   R I D G E

L A U R E L   H I L L

M O U N T A I N S

Little Juniata R.

Frankstown Br.

Frankstown

Juniata R.

Raystown Br.

Fort Granville

Juniata R.

Fort George (Patterson's)

Fort Halifax

Susquehanna R.

Ohio R.

Fort Duquesne [Fort Pitt]
Turtle Cr.

Braddock's Defeat 9 July 1755

Fort Ligonier (Loyal Hannon)

Forbes 1758

A L L E G H E N Y

T U S S E Y   M T.

Fort Shirley (Aughwick)

Aughwick Cr.

T U S C A R O R A   M T.

Fort Littleton

Fort Hunter

Harris' Ferry

Carlisle Fort

Conodoguinet Cr.

Redstone Old Fort

Youghiogheny R.

Gist's Place

Laurel Hill Cr.

Casselman R.

Wills Cr.

Fort Bedford (Raystown)

Fort Loudon

Fort Morris

S O U T H   M T.

Yellow Br. Cr.

Breeches Cr.

Conewago Cr.

York

Fort Necessity

Braddock 1755

Cheat R.

Monongahela R.

North Br.

Fort Cumberland (Wills Creek)

Cresaps Fort

Potomac R.

Cacapon R.

Licking Cr.

Conococheague Cr.

Monocacy R.

M A R Y L A N D

V I R G I N I A

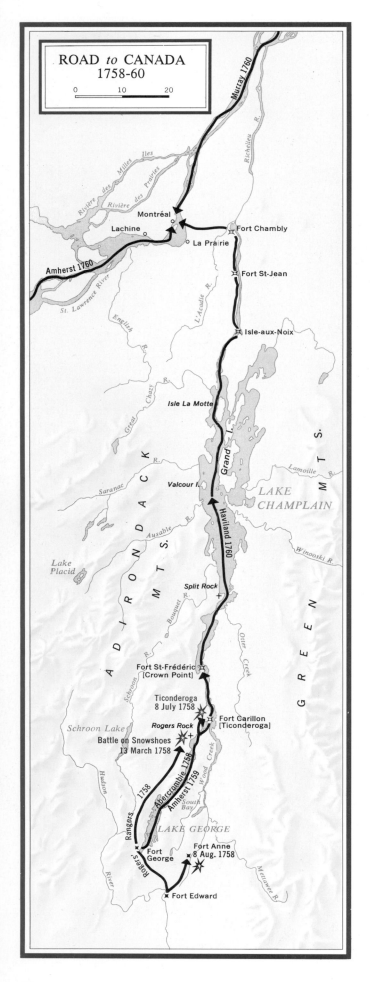

ROAD *to* CANADA
1758-60

0   10   20

TICONDEROGA

The Iroquois gave Ticonderoga its name, which means the place between big waters. White men in all the colonial wars camped or fought at the rocky point where Lake George spills down a twisting ravine to become part of Lake Champlain. In 1755 the French built bristling Fort Carillon atop the promontory of Ticonderoga (opposite page). This strong advance base, together with the older French fort at Crown Point, ten miles north, gave the Marquis de Montcalm command of the best invasion route between New York and Canada. The English replied with a cluster of forts at the south end of Lake George.

In 1758 the British home government and the northern colonies mustered the biggest army—12,200 men—yet seen in North America, equipped it with plenty of cannon, and floated it on 800 flat-bottomed bateaux up the 33-mile length of Lake George. The English commander, General James Abercrombie, was a heavy, slow-witted man who suffered from stomach cramps; he ordered an immediate frontal assault on Fort Carillon, without artillery support, when he might have starved and bombarded the 3,500 defenders into early surrender. In a six-hour battle on July 8 the attackers lost 1,944 men (killed, wounded, and missing) under point-blank musket fire, which was directed by Montcalm himself. At the end of the day Abercrombie hurried back to his boats and retreated, though he still had a big advantage in men and weapons. The disgusted New England soldiers nicknamed him "Mrs. Nabbycrombie."

In this campaign the English had little help from the Iroquois, who were thoroughly cowed by Montcalm. The deficiency was partly made up by a tough band of forest-wise scouts (Rogers' Rangers) led by Major Robert Rogers of New Hampshire. In a fight in which both sides wore snowshoes, early in 1758, Rogers lost most of the 181 men he had taken north to spy on Fort Carillon. Later that year he salvaged his reputation by rescuing British regulars from a French ambush at Fort Anne.

By 1759 the weight of English numbers, attacking from several directions, was wearing down the great Montcalm. Major General Jeffery Amherst returned with 8,000 men to Fort Carillon, whose garrison had dwindled to 400. The French blew up and abandoned the fort July 26, 1759. Five days later they pulled out of Fort St-Frédéric at Crown Point. The central route to Canada was now open, but the English scarcely needed it. In December, 1759, Quebec was taken (see pages 72–73), and in 1760 three British armies converged on New France's last stronghold, Montreal. The map shows this movement: Haviland north via Lake Champlain, Amherst east from Fort Oswego, and Murray up the St. Lawrence from English-held Quebec. Montreal —and with it all Canada—capitulated September 8, 1760.

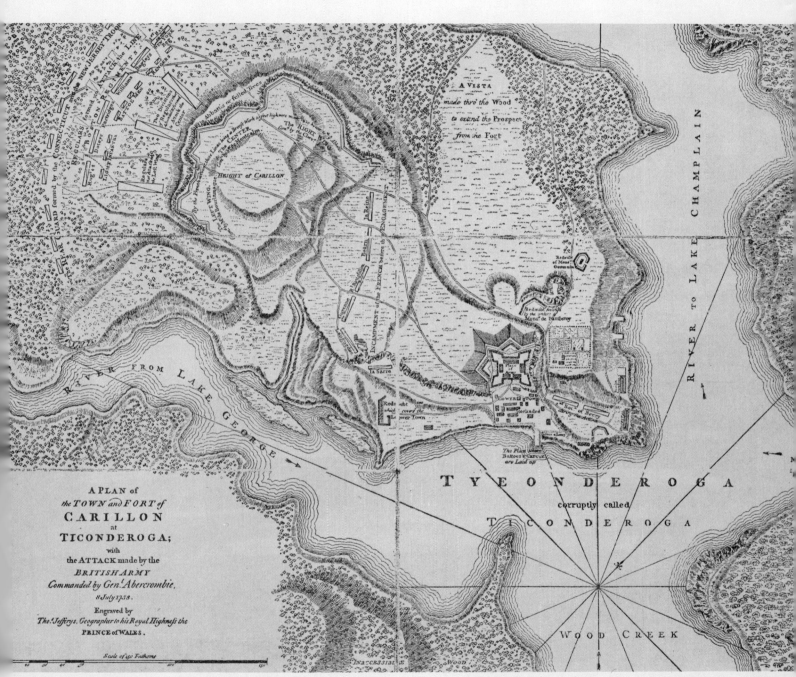

*This English engraving of French Fort Carillon shows the main
citadel on Ticonderoga point, center right, and the scene of the
British defeat under Abercrombie on July 8, 1758, upper left.
The English and colonial troops attacked in an arc from the
woods; the French behind breastworks around the height blasted
the oncoming lines with close-range musket fire. Brigadier Lord
Howe, the ablest officer on the English side, was shot dead in
the first few minutes. Montcalm, who held the French center,
wrote home exultantly to a friend: "The army, the too-small
army of the King, has beaten the enemy. What a day for France!"*

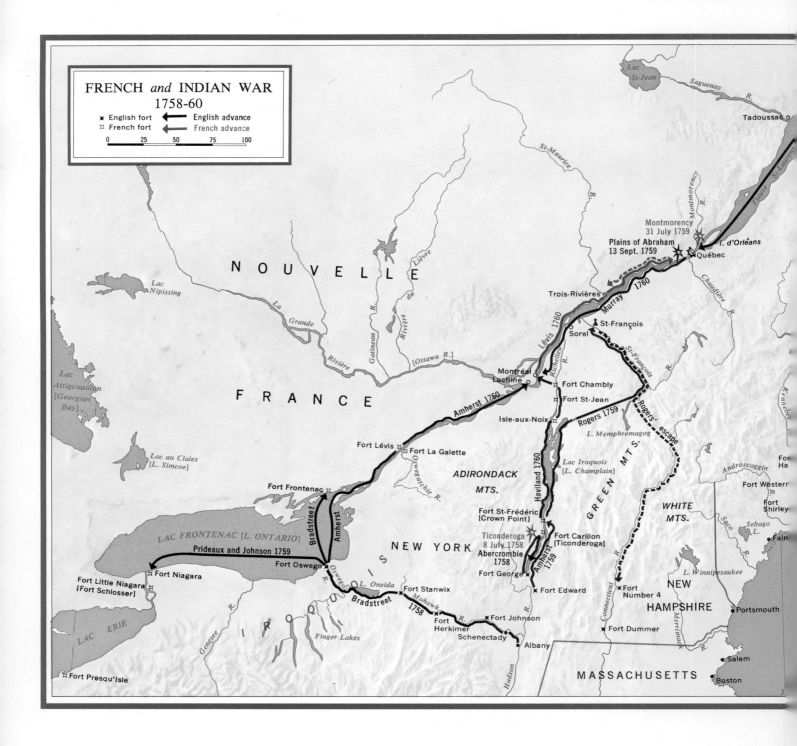

THE FALL
of NEW FRANCE

In England the management of the war was transferred to the hands of a forceful genius when William Pitt, the Earl of Chatham, became secretary of state and prime minister in 1757. This "Winston Churchill of the eighteenth century" made the winning of Canada and the American West the principal aim of his government. He achieved it in a series of assaults that crumpled and pierced New France's defenses across an expanse of 1,100 miles (above).

On Lake Ontario Fort Frontenac, a French stronghold for 85 years, fell to Lieutenant Colonel Bradstreet in 1758. The next year Fort Niagara was taken by General Prideaux and Sir William Johnson's reactivated Iroquois. These victories severed Canada from Louisiana and forced abandon-

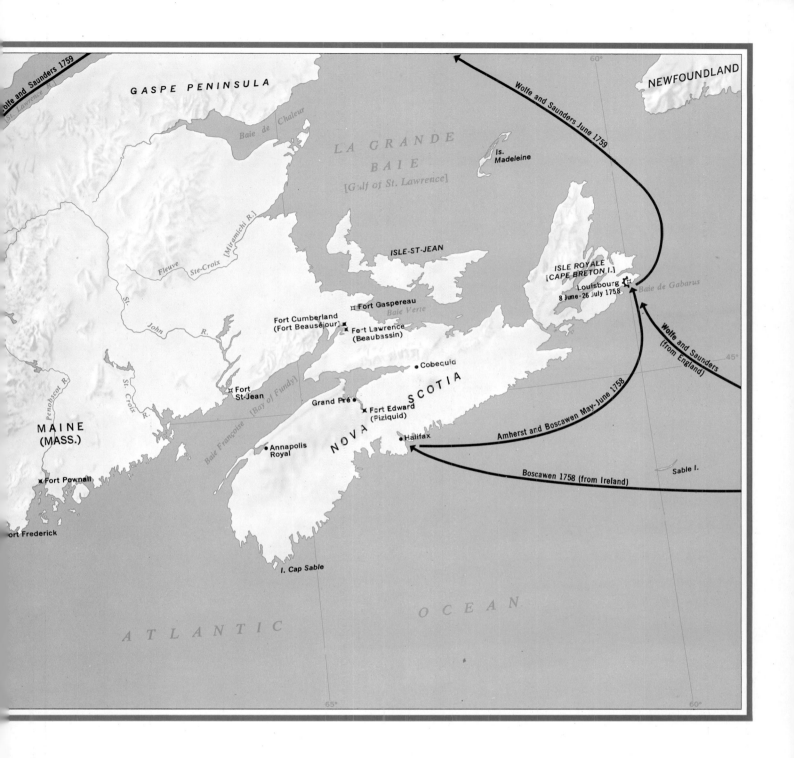

ment of the French forts from Lake Erie into the Ohio country. Captured Ticonderoga was used by Rogers' Rangers as a base for guerrilla raids to the north. In Nova Scotia, even before a formal declaration of war, the English seized French forts near the border and on the Bay of Fundy.

On the Atlantic side France began the war in possession of its great fortress of Louisbourg (which England gave back, after King George's War, in exchange for Madras in India). As an offset the British built Halifax. From this port, in 1758, an expedition under Amherst and Admiral Boscawen sailed to take Louisbourg again. A skinny, impatient, precocious brigadier, James Wolfe, aged 31, who wore his flaming red hair in a queue, directed the seven-week siege.

Louisbourg gave up July 26, and Wolfe wrote at once to Amherst: "What I most wish to do is to go to Quebec." In 1759 he got his wish, as a major general with 4,500 men, and 200 ships under Vice Admiral Saunders. Montcalm at Quebec had an army of 14,000, but he left a path up the cliffs poorly guarded. On September 13 he awoke to find Wolfe's whole army deployed for combat on the Plains of Abraham. In the climactic battle of the colonial wars the two commanders were mortally wounded; Wolfe lived long enough to know the French were beaten. Most of Montcalm's army surrendered. From Montreal, in 1760, the Chevalier de Lévis tried to retake Quebec; then he too was surrounded by ships and armies, and forced to surrender.

To the Right Honourable WILLIAM PITT Esq.
One of His Majesties most Honourable Privy Council
AND PRINCIPAL SECRETARY OF STATE &c

This Plan is most Humbly Inscribed
By his most Obliged and
most Obedient Humble Serv.
Tho. Jefferys.

DEFENCES of QUEBEC.

Batteries	N.° of Gus.	Mort.ᵗ
A. The Citadel	9	0
B. The Clergy en Barbette	28	5
C. Sailors leap	7	0
D. The Hospital	2	0
E. A New Battery over the jetty pointed thro Pickets	2	0
F. Queens Battery no G. mounted		0
G. New Battery at the upper part of the Kings yard	3	0
H. New Battery at the lower part of the Kings yard	3	0
I. Royal Battery	12	0
K. Dauphin Battery	10	0
L. M.} New Battery	{7 13}	a

Charlebour
le Petit V

Larrey R.

FRENCH INCAMPMEN

Notre Dame des Anges

Place of Arms to Defend the Head of the Bridge

R. S .t CHARLES

Bridge of Boats

Hospital General

les Islets

of 3 Guns Each

New Battery of 3 Gun

a Floating Battery

The Place where a Feint was made by the Boats of the Fleet during the whole night, whilst the Troops landed at Sillery

les Batures de Beauport a Shoal Dry at Lou

FRENCH BRITISH ARMY

Sillery

New Battery with a Mortar

Landing Place

THE LITTLE R.

a French Wreck

Buoys that deceiv'd the Enemy, Into which the Boats Moored that protected the Fleet from the Rafts of Fire Stages

THE ADMIRA

FRIGATES

Stores

Small Vessels with Artillery

LOWER TOWN

Cape Diamond

ADMIRAL HOLMES'S

Squirrel

DIVISION

Transports with the Troops ready for Landing after the First Battalion had gained the Heights

RIVER S.t LAURENCE

Point des Peres

Redoubt

POINT

BRIG. GEN. MONCTONS CAMP

St. Joseph

Road from St. Nicholas

Road to

Etchemin R.

An AUTHENTIC PLAN
of the
RIVER S.t LAURENCE
from
Sillery, to the Fall of Montmorenci,
with the Operations of the
SIEGE of QUEBEC
under the Command of
Vice-Adm.l Saunders & Major Gen.l Wolfe
down to the 5. Sep.r 1759.
Drawn by a CAPTAIN in his Majesties Navy

British Miles

The fall of Quebec set bells ringing in London and produced this triumphant 1760 engraving which shows how naval command of the river led to British victory. Wolfe feinted by landing some of his men at Montmorency

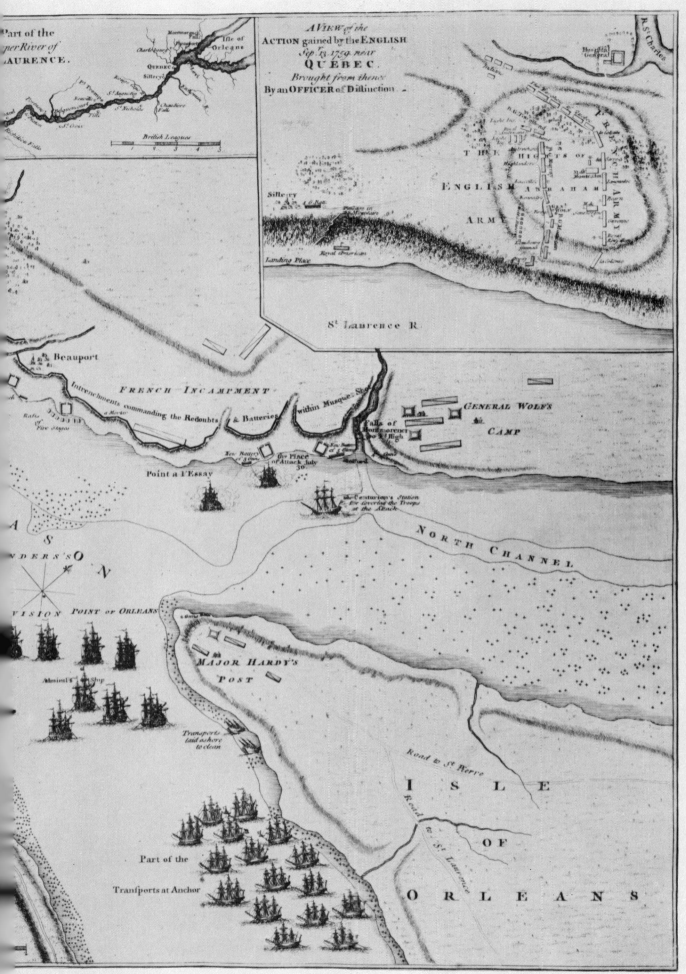

Falls (right center). Then English guns on the south shore (left center) pounded the city, while ships slipped by at night and landed Wolfe's army at Sillery (far left), where a narrow path led to the Plains of Abraham.

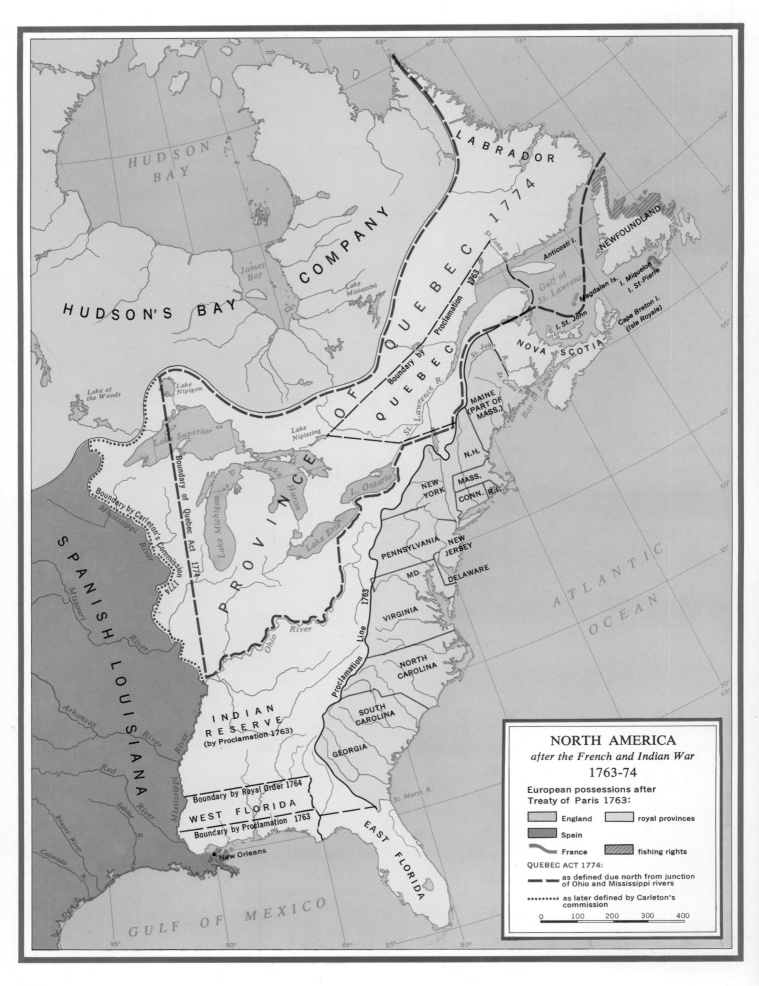

HUDSON BAY

HUDSON'S BAY COMPANY

James Bay

Lake Mistassini

Lake of the Woods

Lake Nipigon

Lake Superior

Lake Michigan

Lake Huron

Lake Nipissing

L. Ontario

Lake Erie

BOUNDARY OF QUEBEC ACT 1774

BOUNDARY BY CARLETON'S COMMISSION 1774

LABRADOR

QUEBEC 1774

PROVINCE OF QUEBEC

Boundary by Proclamation 1763

Boundary of Quebec R.

St. Lawrence R.

St. John R.

Gulf of St. Lawrence

Anticosti I.

NEWFOUNDLAND

Magdalen Is.

I. Miquelon
I. St-Pierre

I. St. John

Cape Breton I.
(Isle Royale)

NOVA SCOTIA

St. John R.

St. Croix R.

Bay of Fundy

MAINE (PART OF MASS.)

N.H.

MASS.

CONN. R.I.

NEW YORK

NEW JERSEY

PENNSYLVANIA

DELAWARE

MD.

VIRGINIA

NORTH CAROLINA

SOUTH CAROLINA

GEORGIA

Proclamation Line 1763

INDIAN RESERVE
(by Proclamation 1763)

SPANISH LOUISIANA

Missouri River

Mississippi River

Arkansas River

Red River

Sabine River

Brazos River

Colorado R.

Ohio River

WEST FLORIDA

Boundary by Royal Order 1764

Boundary by Proclamation 1763

New Orleans

EAST FLORIDA

St. Marys R.

GULF OF MEXICO

ATLANTIC OCEAN

NORTH AMERICA
after the French and Indian War
1763-74

European possessions after
Treaty of Paris 1763:

England   royal provinces

Spain

France   fishing rights

QUEBEC ACT 1774:

— — — as defined due north from junction
of Ohio and Mississippi rivers

········· as later defined by Carleton's
commission

0   100   200   300   400

THE NEW TERRITORIES

Every sign of French sovereignty was wiped from the map of the North American mainland after the British conquest of Canada. Only two tiny islands, St. Pierre and Miquelon, plus fishermen's rights on the Newfoundland coast, were left to France in the Gulf of St. Lawrence region. In an effort to save Louisiana, France secretly ceded that colony to Spain, expecting to get it back later. Victorious Britain allowed the arrangement to stand, in the 1763 Treaty of Paris, but stipulated that Louisiana's eastern boundary must be the Mississippi (except for New Orleans). Spain also was forced to hand over all of Florida to England.

This tremendous transfer of territory opened up tempting vistas to the colonial gentry, whose investments were usually in unsettled land. "Any person who neglects the present opportunity of hunting out good lands . . . will never regain it," advised George Washington, who was picking up western tracts from Pennsylvania to Florida. But immediately the British home government moved to restrict the older colonies. George III assumed by proclamation direct rule over all the areas obtained from France and Spain, and cre-

ated three new royal colonies: Quebec (limited at first to the St. Lawrence valley—broken black line on opposite page); East Florida; and West Florida (enlarged by royal order in 1764). All other lands to the west of "the sources of the rivers which fall into the sea" were reserved as hunting grounds for Britain's Indian allies.

The "Proclamation Line," if strictly enforced, would have barred white settlements beyond the Appalachians. But it was not intended to be permanent. Indian agents of the royal government, at Fort Stanwix in Iroquois territory (below), on Hard Labor Creek, and at Lochaber, in Cherokee country, negotiated treaties that threw open to settlers large parts of the "Indian reserve." Promoters organized temporary colonies—Vandalia and Transylvania—which were resented by older colonial governments and vanished in the American Revolution. A grievance that helped to bring on that revolt was the Quebec Act of Parliament, in 1774, extending the border of Quebec to the Ohio River (opposite page). That threatened to cut off the English seaboard colonists from the lands that became the American Midwest.

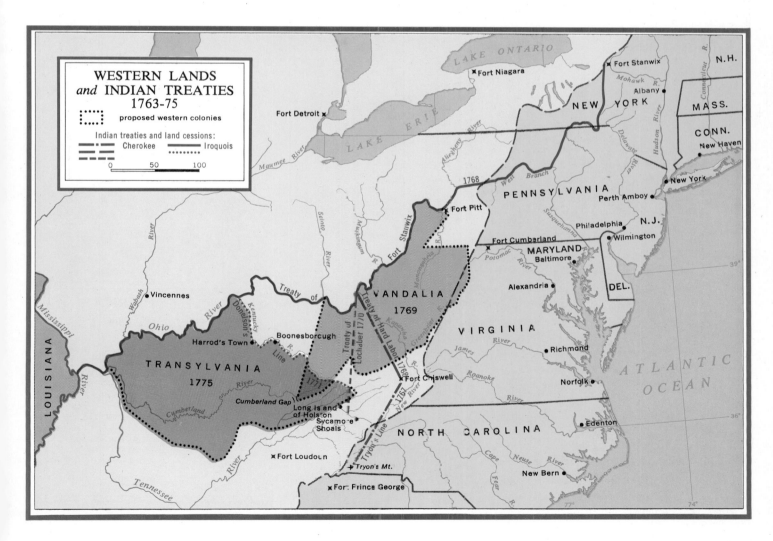

CROSSING *the* APPALACHIANS

Cumberland Gap, wrote Dr. Thomas Walker, "may be seen at a considerable distance. . . . On the South side is a plain Indian Road. On the top of the Ridge are Laurel Trees marked with crosses, others Blazed and several Figures on them." Buffalo, Indians, and some white hunters knew the notch in the mountains before Walker found it, on April 13, 1750. But he was the first to describe it, and he gave it a permanent name—in honor of the Duke of Cumberland, William Augustus, son of King George II, who defeated the Scots at Culloden Moor in 1746.

Scouting for a London land company, Walker and five other Virginians crossed the Gap from the south and east, on the route later known as Boone's Trail (lower center on the map). They built the first frame house—Walker's Cabin—in what is now Kentucky, then circled back to John Chiswell's lead mines through a rugged wilderness where they killed and ate "13 Buffaloes, 8 Elks, 53 Bears, 20 Deer, 4 Wild Geese, [and] about 150 Turkeys," in a four-month journey. Walker wrote in his diary that commercial hunters of skins were already slaughtering hordes of game animals that gathered at salt licks. To the pioneers of Appalachia these licks were important places. Some grew into cities (Roanoke and Nashville); others still appear on modern maps (Blue Licks and Big Bone Lick in Kentucky, the latter a mastodon bone yard).

Adventurers from the first Appalachian settlements—Drapers Meadows, Watauga, Nolichucky, Holston—made Cumberland Gap their gate to the west. Daniel Boone led the first big party of settlers through it, in March, 1775. Then he cut a road through "turrabel cainbrakes" to the site of his fort at Boonesborough. James Harrod, coming from Pennsylvania, had already founded Harrod's Town nearby. The "Long Hunters," free-lance frontiersmen, working down the Ohio and Cumberland rivers, matched forest skills with the Indians, and made fur-hunting trips often two or three years long—hence their nickname.

In 1763 the westward push was stalled by an uprising of Indian tribes—most of them recent allies of France—who were convinced by a wilderness statesman named Pontiac that the British planned to disarm and disperse them. Pontiac's followers seized eight British forts, but failed in attacks on Detroit and Fort Pitt. Regular troops under Colonel Henry Bouquet smashed the Indians at Bushy Run, Pennsylvania, then marched into Ohio and freed more than 200 captives. In 1774, in a similar war with the Shawnee, Virginia's Governor Dunmore and Colonel Andrew Lewis led converging forces to the Ohio River. Lewis defeated Cornstalk's warriors at present-day Point Pleasant, West Virginia. Dunmore forced them to sign a treaty, submitting to Virginia's rule, at Camp Charlotte, on Ohio's Scioto River.

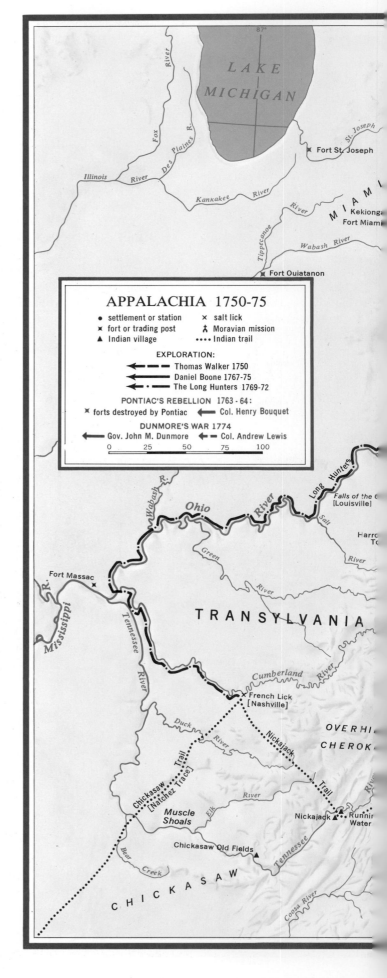

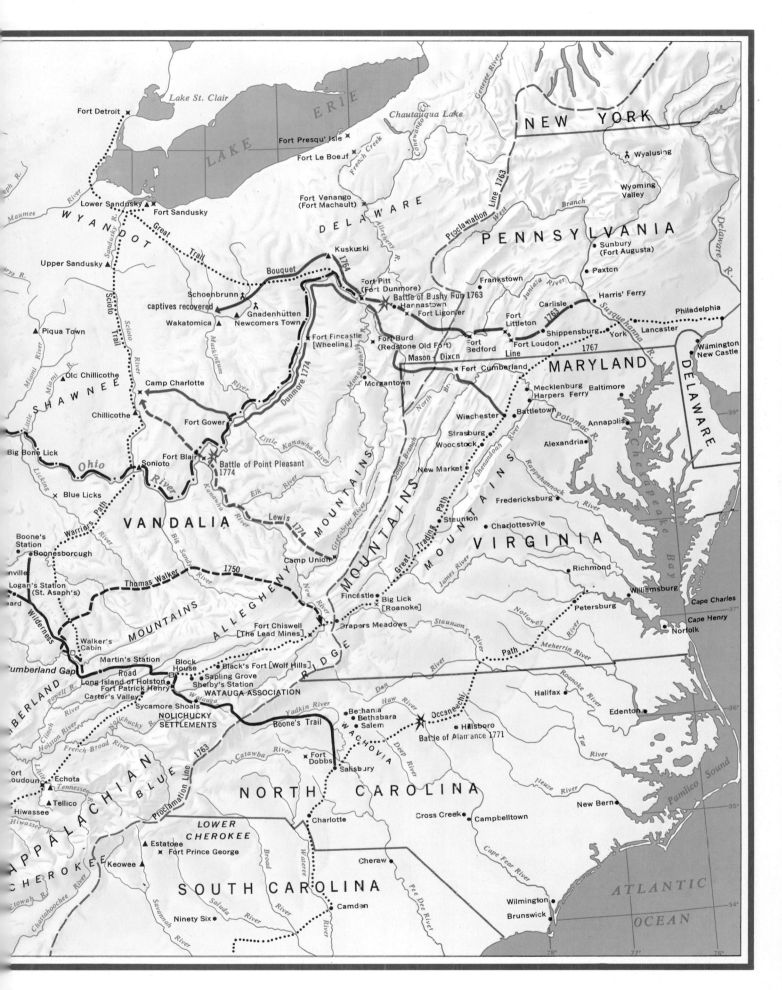

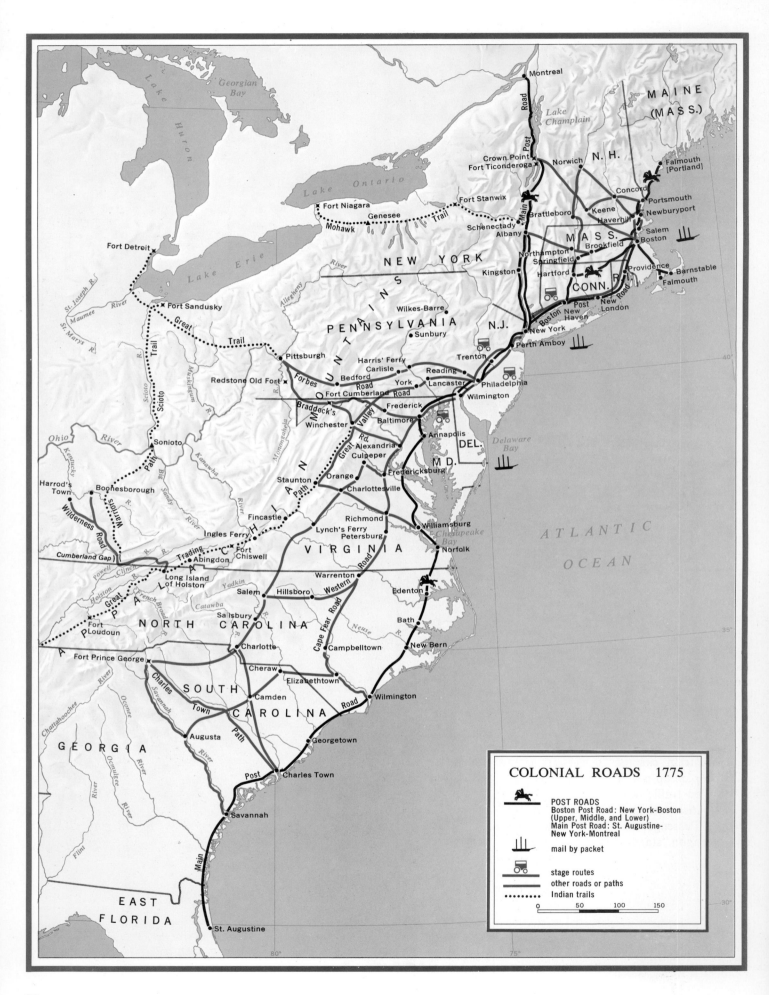

Georgian
Bay

Lake Huron

Lake Ontario

Lake Erie

MAINE
(MASS.)

Montreal
Road
Lake Champlain

Post
Road

Crown Point
Fort Ticonderoga
Norwich   N.H.   Falmouth [Portland]
Concord
Fort Stanwix   Brattleboro   Keene   Portsmouth
Fort Niagara   Genesee   Trail   Schenectady   Haverhill   Newburyport
Mohawk   Albany   MASS.   Salem
Northampton   Brookfield   Boston
Springfield
Kingston   Hartford   CONN. R.I.   Providence   Barnstable
Falmouth
Boston Post   New   New London
New Haven

Fort Detroit
Fort Sandusky
Great
Trail

NEW YORK

MOUNTAINS

PENNSYLVANIA

Wilkes-Barre

Sunbury

N.J.
New York
Perth Amboy

Trenton

St. Joseph R.
Maumee River
St. Marys R.
Scioto R.
Muskingum R.
Allegheny River

Pittsburgh
Forbes   Road
Redstone Old Fort   Bedford   Harris' Ferry   Carlisle   Reading
Fort Cumberland Road   York   Lancaster   Philadelphia
Braddock's   Frederick   Wilmington
Winchester   Valley   Baltimore
Sonioto   Rd.   Alexandria   Annapolis   DEL.
Scioto   Path   Great   Culpeper   MD.   Delaware Bay
Ohio   River   Orange   Fredericksburg
Harrod's   Staunton   Charlottesville
Town   Boonesborough   APPALACHIAN   Path
Kentucky R.   Fincastle   Richmond   Williamsburg
Wilderness   Ingles Ferry   Lynch's Ferry   Chesapeake
Road   Warriors   VIRGINIA   Petersburg   Bay   Norfolk
Cumberland Gap   Trading   Fort Chiswell
Abingdon
Powell R.   Long Island   Warrenton
Clinch R.   of Holston   Western   Road   Edenton
Holston R.   Salem   Hillsboro   Road
Fort   Great   Salisbury   Bath
Loudoun   NORTH   CAROLINA   New Bern
Yadkin
Fort Prince George   Charlotte   Cape Fear Road   Campbellton
Charles   Cheraw
Town   SOUTH   Elizabethtown
Camden   Wilmington
CAROLINA   Road
Augusta   Path   Georgetown

GEORGIA

ATLANTIC
OCEAN

40°

35°

Savannah

Post   Charles Town

Main

30°

EAST
FLORIDA

St. Augustine

80°   75°

COLONIAL ROADS 1775

POST ROADS
Boston Post Road: New York-Boston
(Upper, Middle, and Lower)
Main Post Road: St. Augustine-
New York-Montreal

mail by packet

stage routes

other roads or paths

.... Indian trails

0   50   100   150

INTERCOLONIAL COMMUNICATIONS

The first road-building tools in America were buffalo hooves and Indian feet in moccasins. "Buffalo streets" were broad swathes in the canebrakes, broken by four or five animals abreast. Boone followed one of them for miles in opening his Wilderness Road in Kentucky. Indian paths were narrow and deep; the colonists found some of them worn down 12 inches below the forest floor. Packhorses used by traders and settlers widened the Indian trails and trampled down the surrounding underbrush so they could be easily found and followed. Many colonial roads began this way; others were built for British armies, or to meet the needs of postal riders—the only means the British government had, aside from verbal proclamations, to make its decisions known in all the American colonies.

The postal service, a royal monopoly, tied the Atlantic colonies together in the beginnings of national unity. All mail was carried on horseback. The first riders, in 1673, between New York and Boston, were three weeks on the road each way. In the 1750's Benjamin Franklin, as deputy postmaster general, dispatched mails between Philadelphia and New York three times a week in good weather, and twice a week in winter; delivery in 36 hours was usual. Official mail went free; private letters, in 1765, cost two pennies per 100 miles, paid by those who received them. Franklin made sure of collecting by sending pedestrian carriers to persons who failed to pick up mail the day it came in.

Wheeled traffic was rare on colonial roads, which lacked bridges, paving, or grading. Passenger service could be had only in wagon "stages" like the one below.

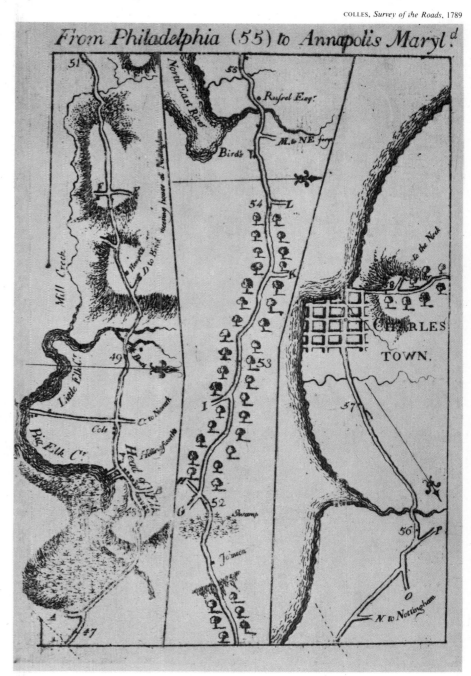

COLLES, *Survey of the Roads*, 1789

Above is one page from a survey of roads compiled by Christopher Colles in the 1780's. It shows the route in Maryland from Head of Elk (now Elkton) through the port of Charles Town; it is read from bottom to top of each of the three panels. At left is an advertising cut of John Mercereau's "Flying Machine," which in 1771 whisked passengers from Perth Amboy, across the bay from New York, to Philadelphia, via Trenton, in a day and a half. Travelers sat on benches under the linsey-woolsey top.

New York Gazette-Post Boy, JUNE 1787

British policy encouraged colonial businessmen to build ships and make money in maritime commerce. One of every four "English" merchant ships, at the start of the Revolution, was American owned and operated. A series of trade and navigation acts, beginning in 1660, had the effect of giving the colonists a virtual monopoly of trade between their own Atlantic ports, and also between the mainland and British islands in the West Indies (Jamaica, on the opposite page, and others in the Lesser Antilles, at right). These "sugar colonies" produced a commodity that was in great demand; in exchange they depended on the "bread colonies" (Pennsylvania, New Jersey, New York, New England) for the flour, barreled pork, and salt codfish they used to feed their hard-worked slaves.

The British laws allowed the colonists a share of the profits of the English mercantile system—but a definitely limited share. Many basic American exports—furs, tobacco, indigo, naval stores (pine tar, pitch, and turpentine)—could be shipped only to England, or to an English colony. And Americans were prohibited from importing textiles, hardware, or other manufactured goods from any country but England. (Madeira wine was one exception; it could be brought directly from the islands off Portugal.) Rice and fish could be exported anywhere; but generally, in their trade with Europe, the colonies bought more goods than they sold. Partly offsetting this adverse balance, the British treasury paid cash subsidies to shippers of favored products.

As these maps show, the West Indies in the 1700's were divided among five owners: Spain, Britain, France, Holland, and Denmark. In the old pirate haunts of the Lesser Antilles, Yankee captains made their biggest profits from illegal trade with the French islands, which supplied molasses to make New England rum. In 1713, by the Treaty of Utrecht, English and colonial shipowners acquired a 30-year monopoly for transporting Negro slaves to the Spanish islands.

Thus geography, politics, and private enterprise combined to create the cruel and lucrative "triangular trade." Rum and "African iron" (short bars used as currency in Africa) went out from America to the African coast. Shackled slaves and ounces of gold dust were carried to Jamaica or some other island, via the notorious "Middle Passage." Sugar, molasses, and barrels of Spanish dollars—the standard coins of the American colonies—came back to enrich investors in Marblehead, Newport, and Boston.

J. B. DU TERTRE, *Histoire des Antilles*, 1667–71

OVERSEAS TRADE

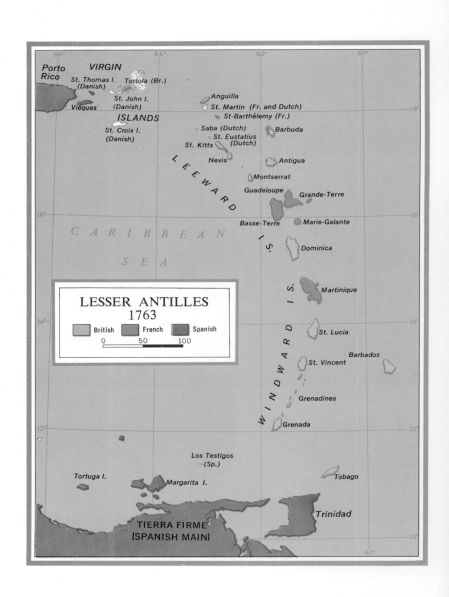

LESSER ANTILLES
1763

British French Spanish

0   50   100

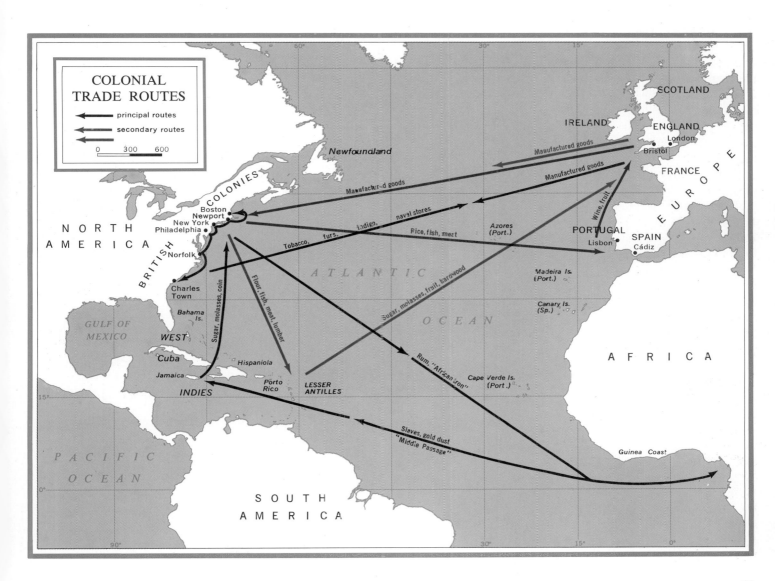

T. ASTLEY, *A New and General Collection of Voyages*, VOL. III, 1745–47

On the opposite page is a sugar plantation in the French West Indies, as pictured in a 1667 engraving. Slaves at left cut the stalks of cane; oxen power the press (1) at right. In the center the juice is boiled in open vats. The engraving at right shows the slave factories, or compounds, maintained for traders from four European nations by a native king on the Gulf of Guinea, in what is now Nigeria. This was published in 1747 in London.

with EUROPE *and* AFRICA

COLONIAL TRADE ROUTES

principal routes
secondary routes

0   300   600

SCOTLAND

IRELAND

ENGLAND
London
Bristol

FRANCE

E U R O P E

Newfoundland

Manufactured goods

Manufactured goods

COLONIES

Boston
Newport
New York
Philadelphia

Manufactured goods

indigo,   naval stores

Rice, fish, meat

Azores
(Port.)

Wine, fruit

PORTUGAL

SPAIN

Lisbon   Cádiz

N O R T H
A M E R I C A

Tobacco,   furs,

Norfolk

B R I T I S H

Charles
Town

A T L A N T I C

Madeira Is.
(Port.)

Bahama
Is.

Canary Is.
(Sp.)

GULF OF
MEXICO

WEST

O C E A N

Sugar, molasses, coin

Flour, fish, meat, lumber

Sugar, molasses, fruit, barwood

A F R I C A

Cuba

Hispaniola

Jamaica

Porto
Rico

LESSER
ANTILLES

Rum, "African iron"

Cape Verde Is.
(Port.)

INDIES

P A C I F I C
O C E A N

Slaves, gold dust
"Middle Passage"

Guinea Coast

S O U T H
A M E R I C A

A PLAN of the TOWN of BOSTON

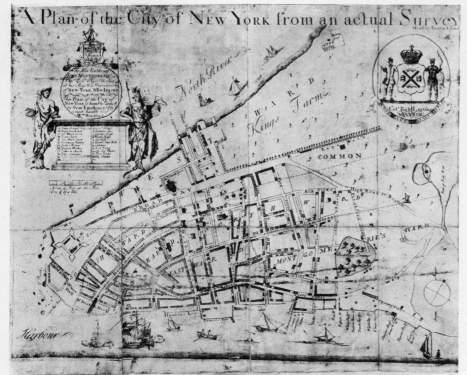

A Plan of the City of NEW YORK from an actual Survey

CITIES of

Boston was only four years old (in 1634) when a promoter boasted it had an ideal location, "being a necke [peninsula] and bare of wood," and thus free from "the three great annoyances of Woolves, Rattle-snakes and Musketoes." In 1774, when the plan at left was published, a few of Boston's 16,000 citizens had just defied the whole British Empire by dumping 342 chests of tea into the harbor. Contrary to popular myth, Boston's streets were not laid out by cows; they converged in a purposeful pattern at the main market place, where King (now State) Street, leading from the wharves, met the road from the mainland across Boston Neck, at lower left. (This later became Washington Street.) Mill Pond, at top, was converted into dry land and streets in the early 1800's.

New York, five years older than Boston, had about 25,000 people at the start of the Revolution. The 1730 engraving reproduced here shows the tip of Manhattan; as in Boston the densest network of streets led to and from the East River markets and wharves (bottom). Wall Street, originally a "curtain of planks" erected to keep out Indians in 1653, was the main crosstown artery. Broadway then, as now, began at the Battery (left), where the British Union Jack waved longer than in any other American city (until November 25, 1783).

Charles Town, South Carolina (opposite), was the first colonial town affected by city planning. Its checkerboard of regularly spaced streets was laid out in 1672; then its residents moved in from an earlier settlement seven miles away. Its population during the Revolution was about 12,000. The same rectangular grid design, recommended by English architects after the 1666 London fire, was used by William Penn's surveyor in plotting Philadelphia, in 1682. Youngest of the cities shown here, Philadelphia grew the fastest; 1775, with 40,000 people, it was larger than any city in England except London itself. Penn deeded the city a huge public square at the crossing of its two main streets (where City Hall now stands). The plan at the top of the opposite page shows the metropolis of the colonies a decade after the Revolution, when it had become the capital of the United States.

the EIGHTEENTH CENTURY

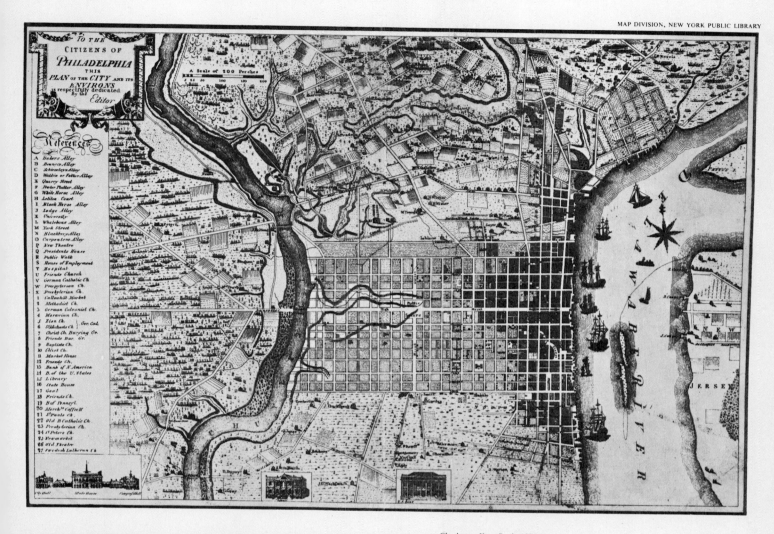

Charleston Year Book, 1884

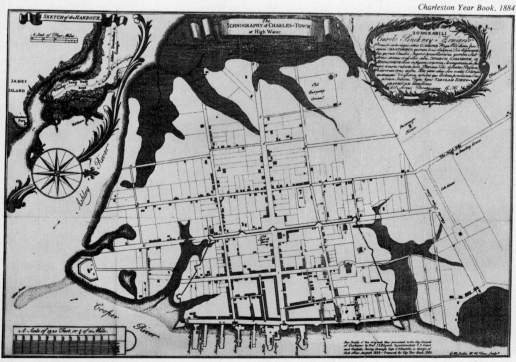

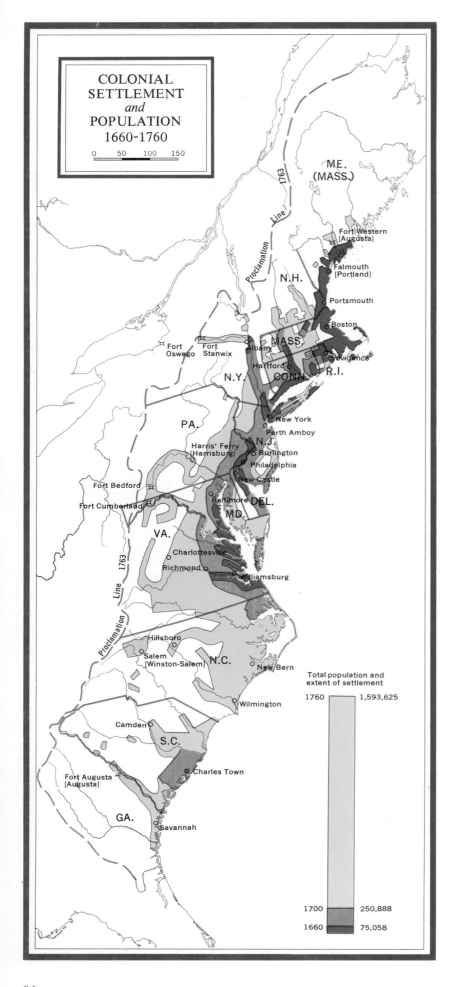

COLONIAL
SETTLEMENT
and
POPULATION
1660-1760

0   50   100   150

ME.
(MASS.)

Fort Western
[Augusta]

Falmouth
[Portland]

Portsmouth

N.H.

Boston

Fort   Fort
Oswego   Stanwix   Albany   MASS.

Hartford   Providence

N.Y.   CONN.   R.I.

PA.   New York

Perth Amboy

N.J.

Harris' Ferry   Burlington
[Harrisburg]   Philadelphia

New Castle

Fort Bedford

Fort Cumberland   Baltimore   DEL.

MD.

VA.

Charlottesville

Richmond   Williamsburg

Hillsboro

Salem   N.C.
[Winston-Salem]   New Bern

Total population and
extent of settlement

1760   1,593,625

Wilmington

Camden

S.C.

Fort Augusta
[Augusta]   Charles Town

GA.   Savannah

1700   250,888

1660   75,058

THE HUMAN

In the century that ended in 1760 the population of English America increased more than twentyfold, while its settled area quadrupled. In the next 15 years, leading up to the Revolution, another million inhabitants were added. The most rapid growth was in the Piedmont, or foothill, regions of the middle and southern colonies, where immigrants from Ireland and Germany could buy cheap land and begin at once to support large families by farming. The filling up of the Shenandoah Valley made Virginia the most populous colony; by 1770 it had more whites (260,000) than Pennsylvania (240,-000) or Massachusetts (235,000), and more Negroes (187,000) than South Carolina (75,000). In North Carolina, where back-country settlers received their first 50 acres free, the population during the Revolution was larger (270,000) than New York's (210,000).

"Whence came all these people?" asked Hector St. John de Crèvecœur, a Frenchman who fought in Montcalm's army, and then became a farmer in colonial New York. To answer his own question, Crèvecœur wrote that "the Americans were once scattered all over Europe," and two thirds left their native lands with nothing. In the English colonies they found liberal naturalization laws, an opportunity to acquire land of their own, and—if they went to the right places—an absence of social

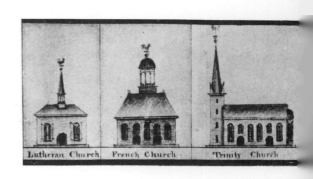

Lutheran Church   French Church   Trinity Church

ELEMENT

snobbery, and "indifference" toward their religion—or lack of it.

The map at right is based on statistics and family names collected in 1790 for the first United States census. Before that date there were no reliable figures relating to national origins. "English," as used in the upper key to the map, includes many Welsh; "Scotch-Irish" combines all arrivals from present-day Ireland and Northern Ireland. If the latter were divided on geographical lines, 5.9 per cent of the total would be true Scotch-Irish from Ulster, and 3.6 per cent would be Irish.

Crèvecœur wrote in 1782 that in America "all sects are mixed"; this is reflected on the map by symbols locating religious denominations in areas where they were strongest. By 1790 only two former colonies had "established"—i.e., tax-supported—churches. Connecticut abolished such favoritism in 1818; Massachusetts in 1833. The Puritan colonies, before 1700, granted tolerance to all Protestants, and began sharing tax funds with Anglicans and Baptists in 1727. Rhode Island and Pennsylvania allowed total freedom of worship from the start. Most other colonies, led by Virginia, did the same in their Revolutionary constitutions. New York, the melting pot city, had nine kinds of churches in 1742 (but none for Roman Catholics). Seven of these are depicted below in a panel from a contemporary print.

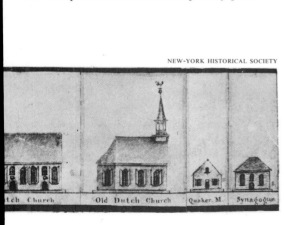

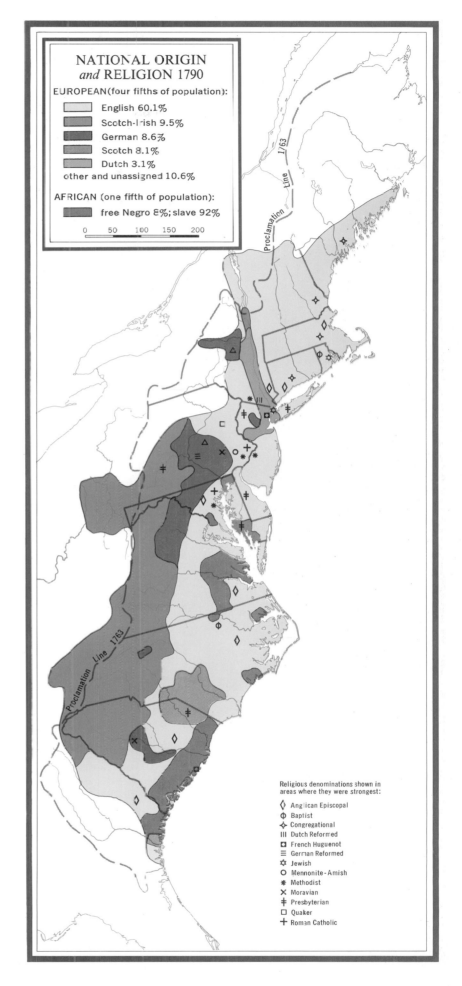

NATIONAL ORIGIN and RELIGION 1790

EUROPEAN (four fifths of population):

English 60.1%
Scotch-Irish 9.5%
German 8.6%
Scotch 8.1%
Dutch 3.1%
other and unassigned 10.6%

AFRICAN (one fifth of population):

free Negro 8%; slave 92%

0   50   100   150   200

Religious denominations shown in areas where they were strongest:

◊ Anglican Episcopal
Φ Baptist
✧ Congregational
III Dutch Reformed
▯ French Huguenot
≡ German Reformed
✡ Jewish
O Mennonite-Amish
✳ Methodist
X Moravian
‡ Presbyterian
□ Quaker
+ Roman Catholic

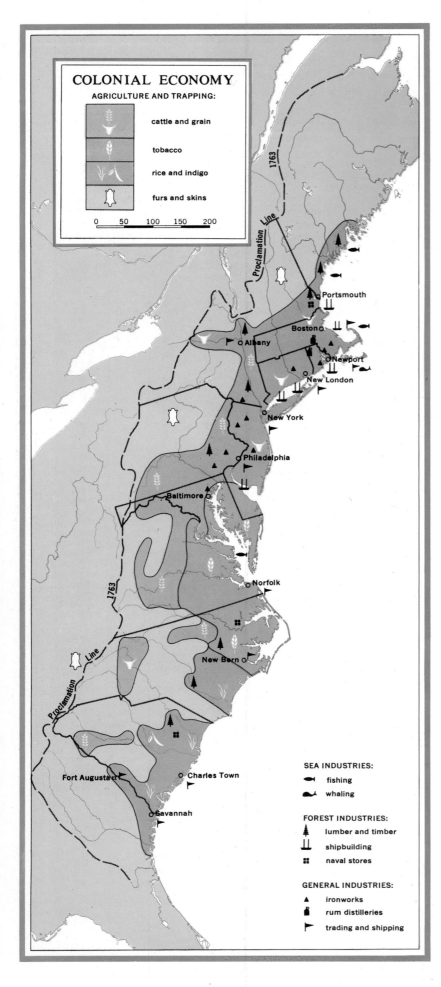

COLONIAL ECONOMY
AGRICULTURE AND TRAPPING:

cattle and grain

tobacco

rice and indigo

furs and skins

0 50 100 150 200

Portsmouth

Boston

Albany

Newport

New London

New York

Philadelphia

Baltimore

Norfolk

New Bern

Fort Augusta

Charles Town

Savannah

Proclamation Line

1763

SEA INDUSTRIES:

fishing

whaling

FOREST INDUSTRIES:

lumber and timber

shipbuilding

naval stores

GENERAL INDUSTRIES:

ironworks

rum distilleries

trading and shipping

CONFLICTS *of* INTEREST

The pine tree on the Massachusetts shilling, and the sculptured cod that hung in its council chamber, symbolized sources of colonial income, which had its ups and downs in the decades before the Revolution. Rising tobacco prices in the mid-18th century gave the landed gentry of Virginia and Maryland their golden age of prosperity. Tidewater planters in South Carolina and Georgia reaped large profits from subsidized indigo (much in demand for dyeing textiles in England). Charles Town merchants shipped to London as many as 160,000 deerskins a year; they were used to make buckskin breeches worn by English workmen.

The Southerners spent their profits for handsome mansions, imported furniture, wines, and carriages, and for educating their sons abroad. Their accounts were kept by London agents; when the price of tobacco slumped, in the 1760's, George Washington and other planters ran into debt each year. Their troubles were aggravated by a dearth of cash; the colonies produced no gold or silver, and were not allowed to import British currency. They were supposed to take payment for their exports in British goods instead.

Increasingly the mainland colonists ignored restrictions placed on their business enterprise, for the benefit of interests elsewhere in the empire. Maine loggers refused to obey the law which told them to leave their best white pines standing, as future masts for the royal navy. Pennsylvania ironmasters, required to send their pig iron to England to be made into finished products (nails, tools, and stoves), instead built an illegal fabricating industry as large and efficient as England's. British sugar planters in the West Indies pushed through the hated Molasses Act of 1733, which put a ninepence per gallon duty on cheap, French island molasses. Smuggling was always a colonial industry; after the Molasses Act was passed it became an entirely respectable one, so far as distillers and drinkers of New England rum were concerned.

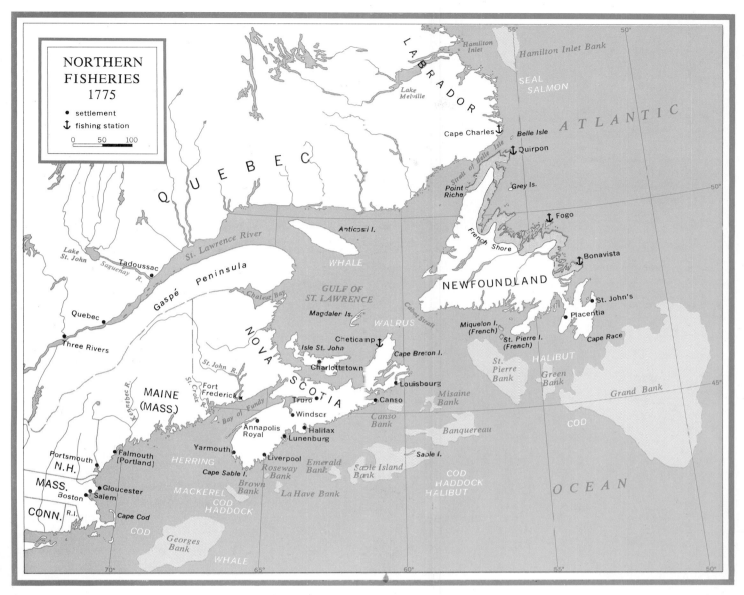

NORTHERN FISHERIES 1775

- settlement
- fishing station

0   50   100

QUEBEC

LABRADOR

Hamilton Inlet

Hamilton Inlet Bank

ATLANTIC

SEAL
SALMON

Cape Charles

Belle Isle

Quirpon

Strait of Belle Isle

Point Riche

Grey Is.

Lake Melville

Lake St. John

Tadoussac

Saguenay R.

St. Lawrence River

Anticosti I.

WHALE

French Shore

Fogo

Bonavista

Gaspé Peninsula

Chaleur Bay

GULF OF ST. LAWRENCE

NEWFOUNDLAND

Quebec

Magdalen Is.

WALRUS

Cabot Strait

St. John's

Three Rivers

NOVA SCOTIA

Chéticamp

Miquelon I. (French)

Placentia

St. John R.

Isle St. John

Cape Breton I.

St. Pierre I. (French)

Cape Race

St. Croix R.

MAINE (MASS.)

Fort Frederick

Charlottetown

Louisbourg

St. Pierre Bank

HALIBUT

Green Bank

Grand Bank

Kennebec R.

Bay of Fundy

Truro

Canso

Misaine Bank

Windsor

Canso Bank

Banquereau

COD

Portsmouth

N.H.

Annapolis Royal

Halifax

Lunenburg

Sable I.

Falmouth [Portland]

Yarmouth

Liverpool

HERRING

Emerald Bank

Sable Island Bank

COD HADDOCK HALIBUT

MASS.

Gloucester

Cape Sable I.

Roseway Bank

Brown Bank

La Have Bank

OCEAN

Boston

Salem

MACKEREL COD HADDOCK

CONN.

R.I.

Cape Cod

COD

Georges Bank

WHALE

The whalers of colonial New England (said Edmund Burke) led all the world's nations, including England, in pursuit of their gigantic game from both polar seas to the coasts of Africa and Brazil. Yankee fishermen extracted their living from the banks between Cape Cod and Newfoundland, where they arrived in large numbers each spring, weeks before boats from England could get there. They preserved their catch by drying and salting on stages erected on shore, as shown in the 1720 print at right.

CHAPTER 4

REVOLUTION AND A NEW NATION

Basic facts of geography were among the reasons for the American Revolution, and were decisive in making it a success. Separated from England by the Atlantic Ocean, facing west toward a thrilling prospect of expansion after helping win the French and Indian wars, and with 150 years of history behind them, the colonies in 1775 were too extensive, populous, and proud to be whipped into obedience by military means. Yet George III and his ministers decided to try it, from a distance of 3,000 miles.

The war began in eastern Massachusetts, the first part of North America to be thickly settled by Englishmen. It ended (so far as large-scale action was concerned) in tidewater Virginia, a few miles from the Jamestown site where permanent English colonization began. The fighting ranged from old French Quebec, which the Americans notably failed to capture, to the polyglot port of Pensacola, wrested from the British and their Creek Indian allies by a Spanish force from New Orleans and Havana. George Rogers Clark and his frontier riflemen took Kaskaskia on the Mississippi, below St. Louis, but were not able to oust the British from their principal western post at Detroit. In the east the British held on longest (until November, 1783) at Castine in Maine, and on Manhattan Island.

At first it was strictly a family fight. But following the pattern of earlier American wars, the other colonial powers of Europe joined in, all as allies of the United States, and all seeking revenge and territorial gains at the expense of England. France helped the Americans with money, guns, uniforms, and shoes; after the American victory at Saratoga (1777) Louis XVI's government opened formal hostilities, and sent an army and two large fleets to collaborate with George Washington. Spain entered the war in 1779, Holland in 1780. The fighting spread to the West Indies and South America, to Gibraltar (where a Virginia volunteer, Lewis Littlepage, was blown up on a floating French battery during an unsuccessful attack on the fortress), and to the coast of England itself, where John Paul Jones, with the small but heavily gunned *Bonhomme Richard,* captured the British man-of-war *Serapis,* in the most amazing naval feat of the war.

The main American theater stretched north and south for 1,000 miles along the Atlantic Coast, but rarely extended deep into the interior. In spite of previous colonial experience, the top British generals failed to solve problems of distance, lack of roads, and the perfect facilities for guerrilla warfare which characterized so much American terrain. The British occupied, at one time or another, all of the principal American cities. They overran large rural areas, especially in New Jersey, Georgia, and the two Carolinas. But they were not able to maintain a front, or even reliable communications, between their sea-based salients, which were harassed by

American partisans, and readily penetrated by American spies. As a result they tended to follow a rule—enunciated by Sir Henry Clinton—of not allowing large bodies of troops to fight farther than 40 miles from their ships.

Eight weeks was the shortest time in which orders and reports could pass between England and North America; storms and the menace of French naval action often made the interval longer. A snafu of enormous consequence came in 1777, when General Burgoyne invaded from Canada, with orders to "join" General Howe in New York. At the same time Howe, following an earlier plan, sailed from New York to Philadelphia. The cabinet minister in charge of the war, Lord George Germain, in London, never tried to make the two generals co-operate. Instead he expressed the hope, in a letter that came too late, that Howe would take Philadelphia and then return to the Hudson River, all in a few weeks' time. Any military map of America, of which the British had the best, would have shown this idea to be absurd.

The war gave lessons in topography to Americans as well. It was ironic that Washington, who knew Virginia's landscape intimately, and earned his reputation on the Pennsylvania frontier, fought his crucial battles in the suburbs of New York and Philadelphia, the streets of Trenton, and the vicinity of Princeton's Nassau Hall. Nathanael Greene, a Rhode Island Quaker, manager of a family-owned iron forge when the war began, became a daring and successful tactician among the pine woods and red dirt hills of the South. Henry Knox, the fat Boston bookseller, supervised the midnight crossing of the icy Delaware. Benedict Arnold, the New Haven druggist, was a patriot at Ticonderoga, Quebec, and Saratoga (where he left a leg); a traitor at Philadelphia (where he began correspondence with British headquarters) and at West Point (which he failed to betray); and a British general at New London and Richmond, both which he and his loyalist raiders burned, in 1781.

American weather fought on both sides. It saved Washington's army in 1776, after the British victory on Long Island. A sudden northeast storm, typical of late August, stopped British ships from coming up the East River; then a dense fog hid the fishermen's boats which ferried 9,500 men to Kip's Bay on Manhattan. A June heat wave, reaching 96 degrees, tormented the British in their heavy uniforms at Monmouth, killing 59 of their men by sunstroke. Heat and swarms of Adirondack gnats contributed also to Burgoyne's failure. The Americans suffered most from the winters: Valley Forge was the famous example. But the next winter at Morristown (1778–79) was, incredibly, even worse. An early snowfall piled up 12-foot drifts before the men could build huts; many slept in brushwood lean-tos in temperatures of zero and less. New York's harbor was frozen across. Lord Stirling (an American general who claimed to be a British peer) used the ice to lead a sleighborne attack against Staten Island. Both sides were too numb to do much fighting; the action cost six Americans dead, and 500 "slightly frozen."

"Revolutions are no trifles," wrote John Adams many years later. "They ought never to be undertaken rashly; nor without deliberate consideration and sober reflection; nor without a solid, immutable, eternal foundation of justice and humanity; nor without a people possessed of intelligence, fortitude, and integrity. . . ." The American Revolution, by and large, met these specifications. It was not a sudden uprising. The first aggression, in American eyes, was committed by the British government when it passed the Stamp Act in 1765. Benjamin Franklin, then living in London as agent for Pennsylvania, took the stand before the whole House of Commons, and calmly explained why his fellow Americans would "never, unless compelled by force," pay stamp taxes or any other taxes imposed on them directly by Parliament:

"They understand it thus . . . they are entitled to all the privileges and liberties of Englishmen; they find in the great charters, and the petition and declaration of rights, that one of the privileges of English subjects is, that they are not to be taxed but by their common consent; they have therefore relied upon it, from the first settlement . . . that the parliament never would, nor could . . . assume a right of taxing them, till it had qualified itself to exercise such right, by admitting representatives from the people to be taxed. . . ."

It was not that the Americans refused to pay any taxes at all. But they insisted, as Englishmen did, on being taxed by their own legislatures. Pennsylvania alone, according to Franklin, ran up a debt of a half million pounds during the French and Indian wars. Its citizens paid property taxes of 18 pence per pound, profits and other business taxes amounting to 25 per cent of net income, and a poll tax of 15 shillings per voter, all levied by the Pennsylvania assembly, and used to pay the colony's expenses. The same system prevailed from New Hampshire to Georgia. It was deeply rooted in colonial experience: the first meeting of the Virginia House of Burgesses (1619) imposed the first tax in English America—one pound of tobacco from every adult male. It was, in fact, a form of home rule, in which the colonies pledged allegiance to the crown; let Parliament govern their foreign relations and trade; but jealously managed their own local business, agriculture, schools, churches, roads, courts, militia, voting qualifications, and finance.

This kind of freedom the Americans fought to retain. Yet there were eleven years of sober debates and deliberate resistance—including seven years while British troops occupied Boston, and more than a year of organized war—before the thirteen colonies, in Congress assembled, agreed to dissolve their bonds with England, and be, henceforth, the United States.

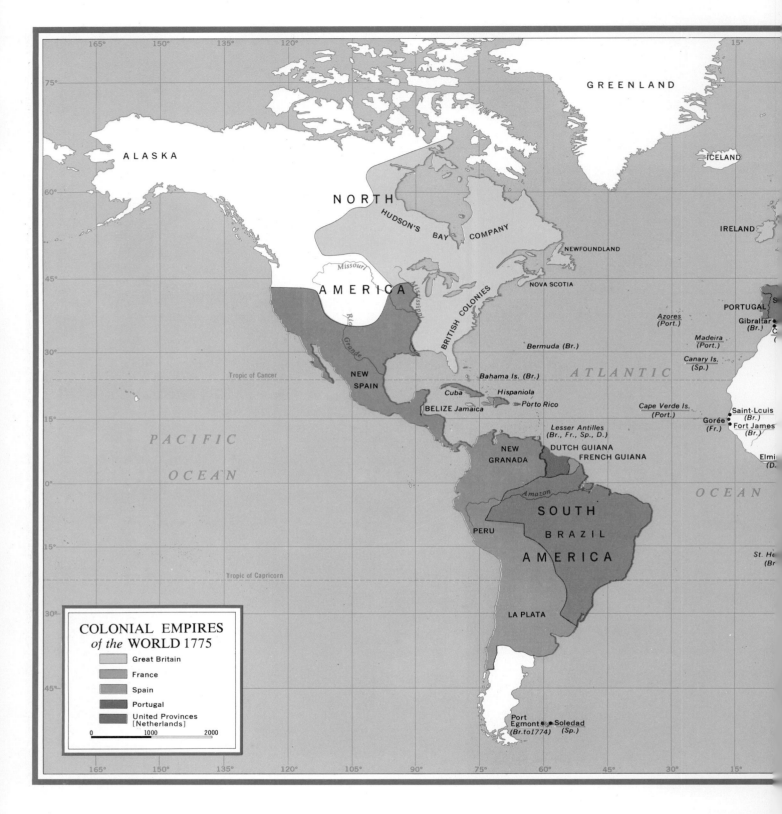

COLONIAL
EMPIRES

Great Britain, when the Revolution began, boasted 18 colonies on the North American mainland (including New-foundland, Nova Scotia, Quebec, East and West Florida). The Hudson's Bay Company administered an area as large as the others combined. These were Britain's most extensive possessions in the 18th century, and they had by far the largest English-speaking population existing outside the home islands. This proved no political asset; in the Revolutionary War all but two of the English colonies (Nova Scotia

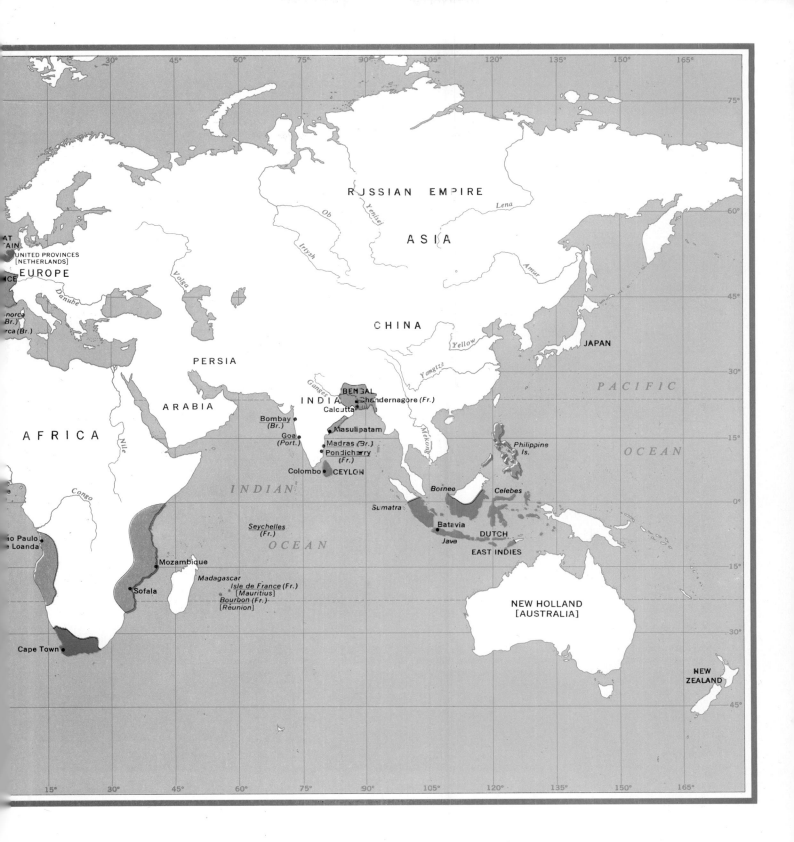

and Newfoundland) lined up against the king. The French in Canada refused invitations to join the revolt, even after France became an American ally.

The West Indies islands of Jamaica and Barbados, with their sugar crops, were profitable jewels in the British crown. So was Belize (later British Honduras) which supplied mahogany to the fashionable furniture makers of London. In the South Atlantic the Falkland Islands, important as whaling stops, were disputed by England and Spain. Africa was still owned mostly by the natives. The Portuguese, who explored it first, had colonies on the west and east coasts, but their early slaving posts on the Cape Verde bulge were now either British or French. The Dutch began settling the Cape Town area in 1652, and carved out an empire, at Portugal's expense, in Ceylon and the fabled East Indies. England secured a sure grip on India by the great victories of Sir Robert Clive over the French at Pondicherry (1748) and native armies at Calcutta (1756) and Plassey in Bengal (1756).

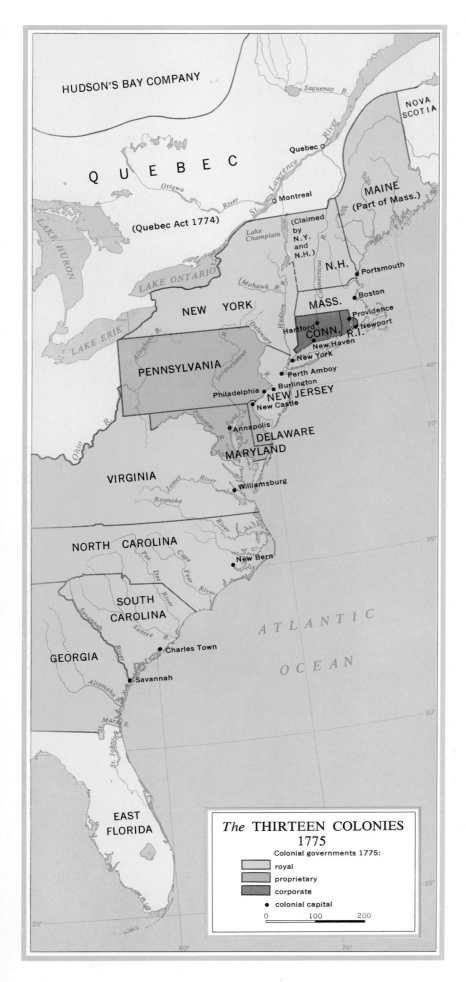

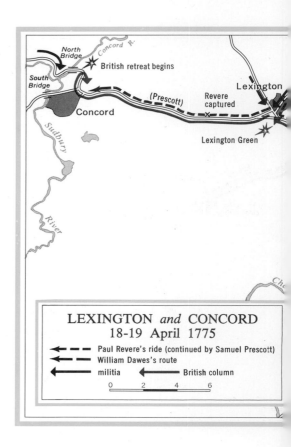

LEXINGTON and CONCORD
18-19 April 1775

- - → Paul Revere's ride (continued by Samuel Prescott)
- - → William Dawes's route
→ militia → British column

0   2   4   6

The THIRTEEN COLONIES
1775

Colonial governments 1775:

☐ royal
☐ proprietary
☐ corporate
● colonial capital

0   100   200

AMERICANS

Riders teemed on the roads around Boston on the night of April 18, 1775. British officers on slow-footed steeds intercepted Paul Revere between Charlestown and Cambridge, forcing him to detour through Medford (above). William Dawes, another patriot courier, slipped past sentries at Boston Neck, alarmed Roxbury and Brookline, and reached Lexington just behind Revere. They were stopped by more British riders on the road to Concord: Revere was captured, but Dawes escaped on foot. Samuel Prescott, a young Concord doctor who had been sparking a Lexington girl until after midnight, was with them by then; he jumped his horse across a fence and rode on with their message.

The message was that British regulars were on the way from Boston to seize the gunpowder, ammunition, and muskets the Massachusetts provincial congress had stockpiled in Concord. At Lexington, at sunrise on April 19, the 700 British saw 38 armed militiamen lined up across the common. Officers on both sides shouted

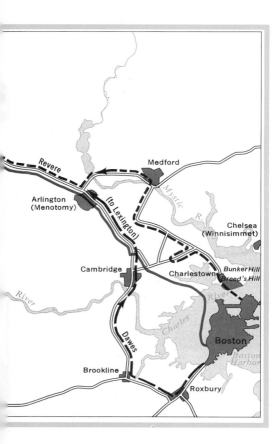

in REBELLION

"Don't shoot!" but someone (never identified) did. In the brief melee that followed the Americans had no chance; eight were killed, and nine wounded. The British column pushed on to Concord, where most of the valuable military supplies had already been safely hidden. Shooting that started at the North Bridge became a small battle, then a British retreat, and finally a 30-mile rout in which the swarming Americans, usually firing from ambush, killed or wounded 247 regulars.

News of this bloodshed brought militiamen on the run from all four New England colonies. And, for the first time, nine other colonies, from New York to Georgia, united in a solid front to aid the rebellious Yankees. On June 17 General William Howe led 2,300 troops across the Charles in boats, to where the Americans were entrenched at Charlestown (right, from a 1775 London engraving). The British took Breed's and Bunker hills, but their casualties were so painful they fought no more battles in Massachusetts.

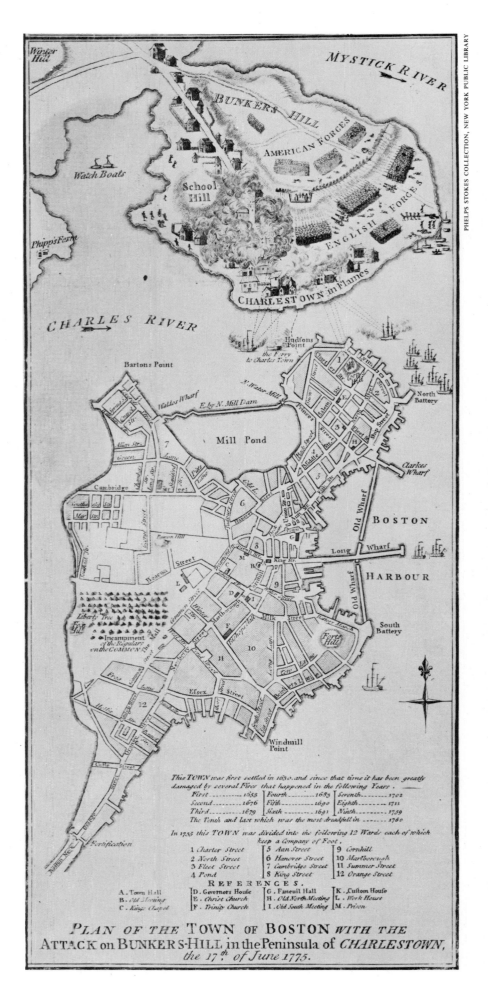

This TOWN was first settled in 1630. and since that time it has been greatly damaged by several Fires that happened in the following Years.

First	1653	Fourth	1683	Seventh	1702
Second	1676	Fifth	1690	Eighth	1711
Third	1679	Sixth	1691	Ninth	1759

The Tenth and last which was the most dreadful in 1760

In 1735 this TOWN was divided into the following 12 Wards each of which keep a Company of Foot.

1 Charter Street	5 Ann Street	9 Cornhill
2 North Street	6 Hanover Street	10 Marlborough
3 Fleet Street	7 Cambridge Street	11 Summer Street
4 Pond	8 King Street	12 Orange Street

REFERENCES.

A. Town Hall	D. Governors House	G. Faneuil Hall	K. Custom House
B. Old Stowing	E. Christ Church	H. Old North Meeting	L. Work House
C. Kings Chapel	F. Trinity Church	I. Old South Meeting	M. Prison

PLAN OF THE TOWN OF BOSTON WITH THE ATTACK on BUNKERS-HILL in the Peninsula of CHARLESTOWN, the 17th of June 1775.

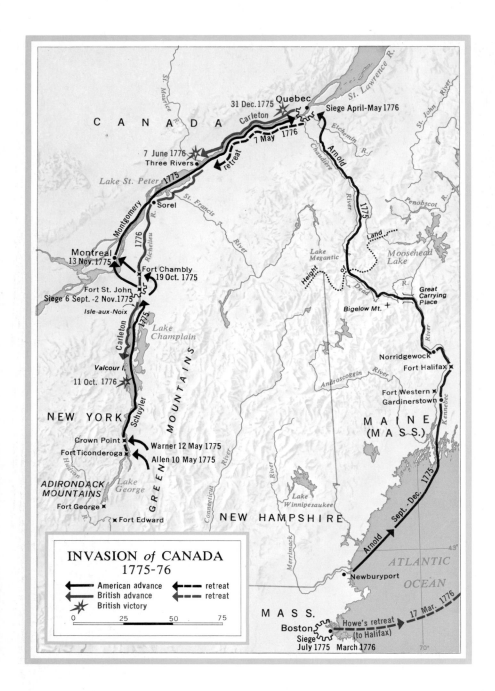

INVASION of CANADA
1775-76

American advance ← — ← **retreat**
British advance ⇐ -- ⇐ **retreat**
✦ **British victory**

0   25   50   75

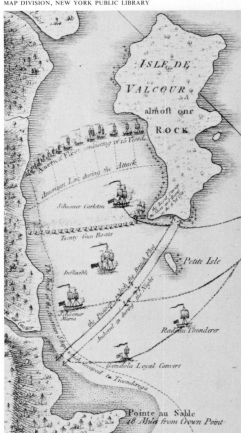

At Valcour Island on Lake Champlain, an outgunned American flotilla (upper left) stalled an invading British fleet, late in 1776. This view of the battle was published in London.

1775–77

After Lexington and Concord, and before Bunker Hill, the rebellion jumped to northern New York (above). British forts at Ticonderoga and Crown Point were surprised and captured by New Hampshire frontiersmen (Green Mountain Boys) led by Ethan Allen and Seth Warner. With these strong points in American hands, the Continental Congress, in the summer of 1775, ordered an invasion of Canada. An army commanded by Philip Schuyler, and later by Richard Montgomery, pushed up the Lake Champlain route, took Fort St. John after a lengthy siege, captured Montreal, and proceeded toward Quebec. A smaller force under Benedict Arnold hacked its way through woods and swamps to the St. Lawrence River. About 900 veterans of these two tough marches stormed Quebec in a New Year's Eve snowstorm; 1,800 defenders gave them a hot reception. Montgomery was killed in the first assault. The Americans were driven back, losing nearly 500 men, most of them as prisoners. In the spring both

sides were reinforced, and the Americans lost another battle, at Three Rivers. In July, 1776, they withdrew from Canada.

The map opposite shows the military problem that confronted the former colonies at the time they declared their independence and in the six months that followed. A British army of 32,000, the largest ever sent overseas, attended by an overpowering fleet, converged on New York Harbor. It included Howe's troops from Boston (evacuated in March, and refitted at Halifax), and Clinton's force, driven off from South Carolina's Charles Town (renamed Charleston in 1783). Against this, General George Washington, commander of the Continental army, had less than 20,000 men, most of them poorly trained militia. Unable to prevent the loss of New York, with its important forts on the Hudson River, Washington fell back across New Jersey. Then, in his Christmas surprise at Trenton (see pages 106–7), he gave the British a stinging notice that the war was not over.

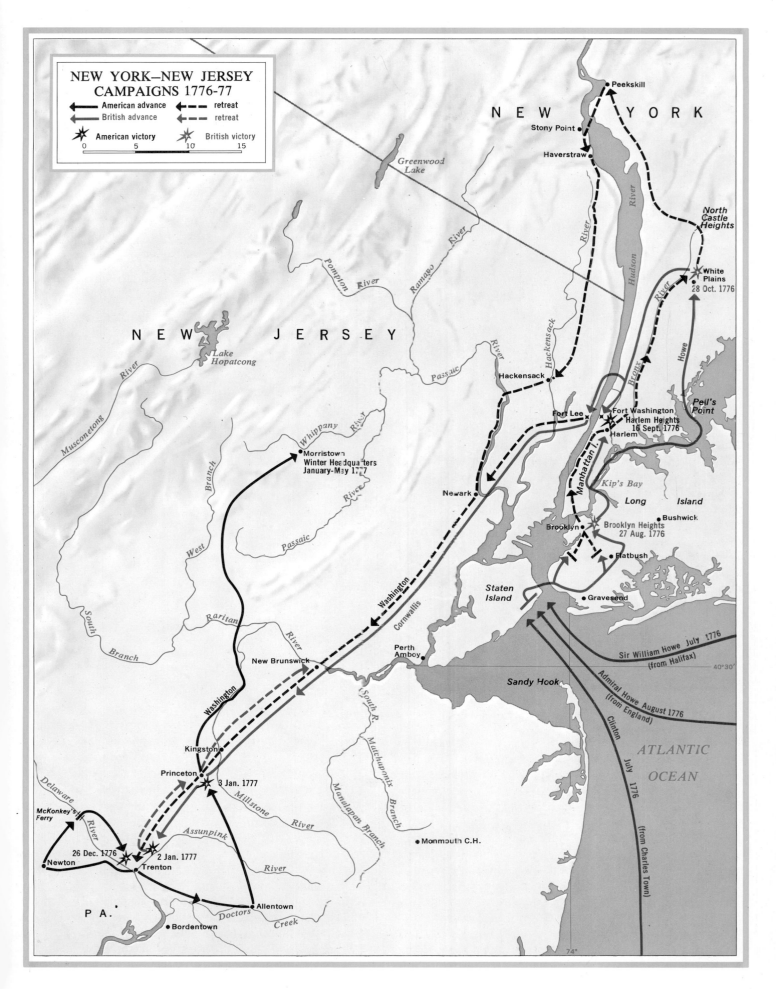

NEW YORK–NEW JERSEY CAMPAIGNS 1776-77

← American advance   ⇠ retreat
← British advance   ⇠ retreat
✦ American victory   ✧ British victory

0   5   10   15

Greenwood Lake

N E W   Y O R K

Peekskill

Stony Point

Haverstraw

North Castle Heights

Pompton River

Ramapo River

Hudson River

White Plains
28 Oct. 1776

N E W   J E R S E Y

Lake Hopatcong

Musconetong River

Whippany River

Passaic River

Hackensack River

Hackensack

Fort Lee

Fort Washington

Harlem Heights
16 Sept. 1776

Harlem

Bronx River

Howe River

Pell's Point

Morristown
Winter Headquarters
January-May 1777

West Branch

Raritan River

Newark

Manhattan I.

Kip's Bay

Long   Island

Bushwick

Brooklyn

Brooklyn Heights
27 Aug. 1776

Flatbush

South Branch

New Brunswick

Perth Amboy

South R.

Staten Island

Gravesend

Washington

Cornwallis

Sandy Hook

**ATLANTIC
OCEAN**

Sir William Howe July 1776
(from Halifax)

40°30′

Admiral Howe August 1776
(from England)

Kingston

Millstone River

Matchaponix Branch

Manalapan Branch

Clinton
July
1776

Princeton
3 Jan. 1777

Delaware River

McKonkey's
Ferry

26 Dec. 1776

Newton

Trenton

2 Jan. 1777

Assunpink River

Monmouth C.H.

(from Charles Town)

P A.

Allentown

Doctors Creek

Bordentown

74°

97

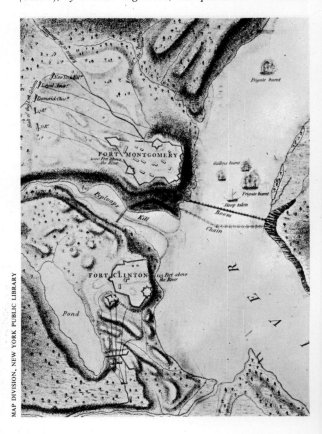

1777–78

In a last-minute effort to assist Burgoyne, a British force from New York, led by Sir Henry Clinton, stormed and captured the American forts Montgomery and Clinton (the latter named for New York's governor, no relation to Sir Henry), and removed the chain across the Hudson River, a few miles below West Point. The plan of attack (below), by British engineers, was published in London.

Map labels:

Ottawa River

Montreal • ✱ Fort Chambly

Richelieu R.

✱ Fort St. John

CANADA

Isle-aux-Noix

St. Lawrence River

St. Leger

Lake Champlain

Oswegatchie

ADIRONDACK MOUNTAINS

LAKE ONTARIO

Burgoyne

Crown Point

Fort Ticonderoga Fraser

★ Fort Oswego 25 July

Hubbardton

✱ 7 July

Skenesboro

Lake George

Siege 3-22 Aug. Fort Stanwix

Fort George

Fort Anne

Oswego R.

Oneida Lake

Oriskany

6 Aug. ✱

Fort Edward
Burgoyne surrenders
17 Oct. 1777

Manchester

Fort Herkimer

Herkimer

Mohawk R.

Arnold

19 Sept.
7 Oct. ✱
Stillwater

Saratoga

Baum

Stark

Cherry Valley •

Albany •

Gates

• Bennington
16 Aug. 1777

NEW YORK

River

MASS.

Susquehanna

Hudson River

Kingston •
15 Oct.

Hartford •

PENNSYLVANIA

Delaware R.

Vaughan

CONN.

Fort Montgomery
6 Oct.
Fort Clinton
Peekskill •

New Haven •

UPPER NEW YORK CAMPAIGNS 1777

→ American advance ⇢ retreat
→ British advance ⇢ retreat
✱ American victory ✱ British victory

0   25   50   75

• New York

Long Island

Plan of attack labels:

FORT MONTGOMERY

Frigate burnt

Galleys burnt

Frigate burnt

Poplopens Kill

Sloop taken

Boom

Chain

FORT CLINTON

Pond

At Quebec, British soldiers cut the tails from their red service coats, and trimmed their three-cornered hats to make practical caps, as they prepared to plunge into the American forest. British strategy for 1777 included a two-pronged invasion from Canada (above) to detach New England from the other new states. Brigadier General Barry St. Leger, with 1,700 regulars, Tories, and Indians, drove east from Fort Oswego to Fort Stanwix, whose defenders refused to surrender. About 800 Mohawk valley militiamen battled part of St. Leger's force to a standstill at Oriskany, near present-day Utica; the American general, Nicholas Herkimer, died of a wound, but the invasion went no further. Benedict Arnold, with reinforcements, reached Fort Stanwix, and St. Leger returned to Lake Ontario.

The main British thrust, down Lake Champlain and the Hudson valley, ended in total American victory. Lieuten-

ant General "Gentleman Johnny" Burgoyne started with 8,000 formidable troops, who drove the Americans from Ticonderoga, cut a 23-mile road through the woods from Skenesboro to Fort Edward, and won a preliminary fight at Hubbardton. Near Bennington, Vermont—but in what is now New York State—Burgoyne lost 900 of his German dragoons in a dramatic battle with Colonel John Stark's New Hampshire militiamen. More militia companies from northern states swelled the American army of Major General Horatio Gates and broke Burgoyne's supply lines from Canada. The brilliant field leadership of Benedict Arnold supplied the margin of victory at the final battles of Freeman Farm and Bemis Heights (see pages 108–9). On October 17, 1777, for the first time on North American soil, an entire British army—seven generals, 300 officers, and 5,600 noncoms and privates—surrendered at Saratoga.

While Burgoyne strove to break through to New York, the main British army, under Sir William Howe, left New York behind and headed toward Philadelphia. The reasons for this lack of co-ordination have never been satisfactorily explained; the results included Burgoyne's surrender, and eventual futility elsewhere. Instead of marching his men across New Jersey, 60 miles, Howe kept them on ships for 46 days, sailed around Cape Charles and up Chesapeake Bay to Head of Elk (Elkton) in Maryland—where he was still 50 miles from Philadelphia. "That route . . . to be sure . . . is a very strange one," wrote Washington to Israel Putnam, as he rallied 16,000 Continentals and militia to oppose Howe's march at Chadds Ford on Brandywine Creek. The British, with an equal force, outmaneuvered and al-most surrounded the Americans, who escaped just in time to open country in northern Chester county. In October Washington, in a surprise attack, broke part way through the British line at Germantown, then retired to the bleakness of Valley Forge to wait for another year.

General Howe wintered comfortably in Philadelphia; in the spring he was fired as British commander. His successor, Sir Henry Clinton, was ordered to abandon the city Howe had won, and bring the British troops back to New York. Clinton made the trip, overland, in only 12 days, speeded on his way by Washington's veterans, who came away from their drillgrounds at Valley Forge in an eager mood for a fight, and forced Clinton's army to give them one, at Monmouth Court House, New Jersey.

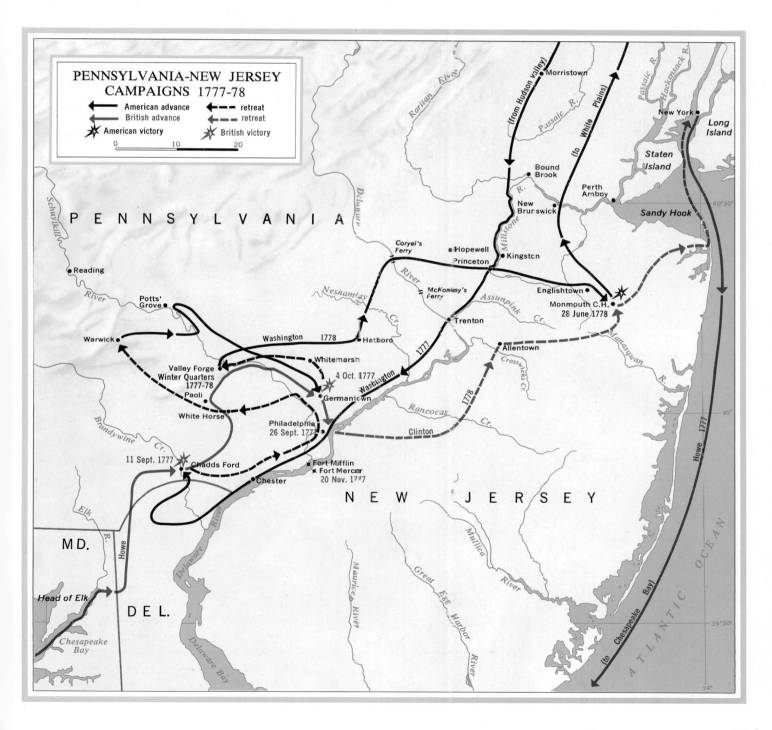

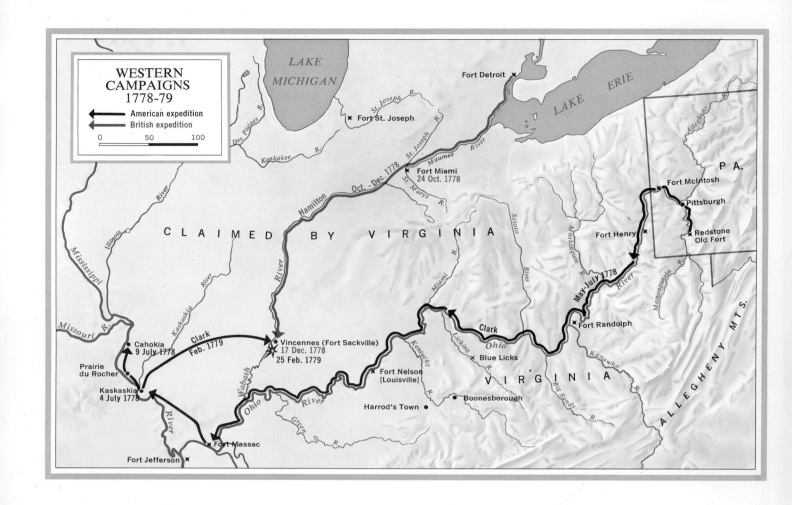

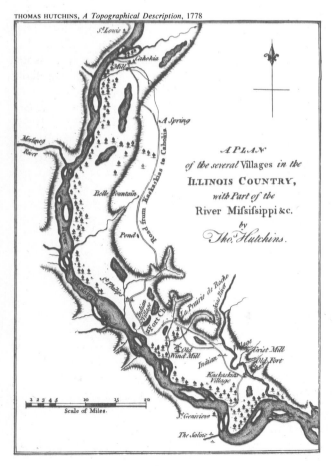

THOMAS HUTCHINS, *A Topographical Description*, 1778

WAR *in the* INDIAN COUNTRY

Clark's conquests on the Mississippi River are outlined at left on an English engraving of 1778. The French towns of Kaskaskia and Cahokia, founded in 1703 and 1699 respectively, and named after local Indian tribes, were ceded to England in 1763. St. Louis, at top, on the west bank of the river, belonged to neutral Spain when Clark arrived. Vincennes (not shown) on the Wabash River was then the most important town in what is now Indiana. It was named to honor the younger Sieur de Vincennes, who fortified it in the 1730's.

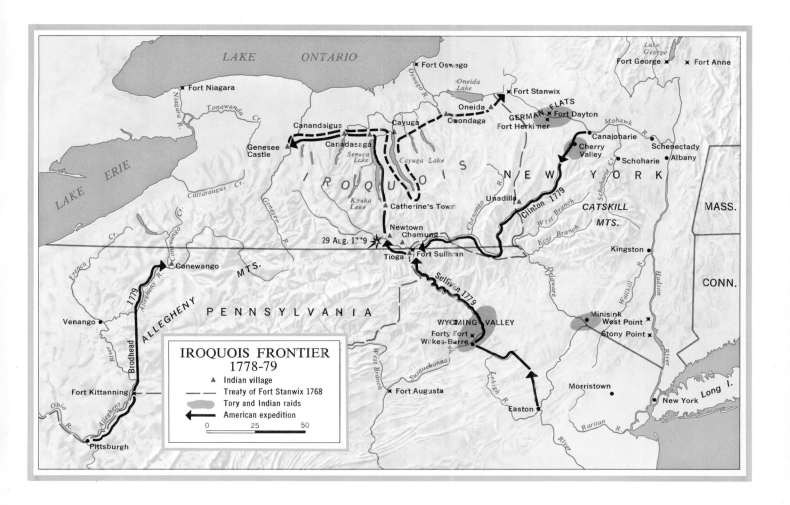

The following image shows a map titled:

IROQUOIS FRONTIER 1778-79
- ▲ Indian village
- – – – Treaty of Fort Stanwix 1768
- Tory and Indian raids
- ← American expedition

0 25 50

Lieutenant Colonel Henry Hamilton, commander of British Fort Detroit, earned the nickname the Americans gave him—"the Hair Buyer." Hamilton armed his Indian allies with 8,640 knives; the Indians brought him American prisoners and scalps, for which he gave them additional gifts. (During ten months of 1778, Hamilton listed 55 prisoners and 210 scalps in reports to headquarters at Quebec.)

Americans no doubt did some scalping too, especially in the savage fighting in Kentucky between white encroachers and red defenders, before and during the Revolution. It was George Rogers Clark, a rugged Virginia militia colonel (later brigadier general), who raised this frontier war to the level of statesmanship. With 175 men, all forest trained and expert shots, Clark cut the British West in two (map on opposite page). His expedition descended the Ohio River in flatboats, 900 miles, to abandoned Fort Massac, near the mouth of the Tennessee, then marched overland 120 miles to the Mississippi. The garrison at Kaskaskia (French militia under the British flag) tumbled out of bed and surrendered. Clark pushed on at once to Cahokia, then sent a detachment east to accept the surrender of Vincennes. The Indians in the region were much impressed; they promised to stop raiding American settlements.

Hamilton, with 500 British and Indians from Detroit, retook Vincennes in December, 1778, and settled down to starve out the Americans on the Mississippi. But Clark, in a famous winter march, led his tiny force 180 miles through frozen swamps and icy streams, stormed into Vincennes, and took strongly built Fort Sackville after an all-day battle and siege. "The Hair Buyer" was sent to a Williamsburg jail, and the United States controlled the Ohio-Indiana-Illinois country to the end of the war and ever after.

In New York and Pennsylvania (above) the war brought misery to frontier dwellers, and death to the Iroquois federation. Two Iroquois tribes—Oneidas and Tuscaroras—sided with the Americans. The others—Mohawks, Onondagas, Cayugas, and Senecas—honored their old alliance with England. Indians and loyalists from Fort Niagara burned every house in Wilkes-Barre, drove off 1,000 cattle, and harvested 227 scalps in raids on Wyoming Valley. In New York they destroyed German Flats and Cherry Valley, where 30 unarmed villagers were massacred. Americans based at Schoharie burned the Indian town of Unadilla in revenge. In 1779 a great expedition of 2,700 Continental troops, under Generals James Clinton and John Sullivan, converged from north and south on the Susquehanna River. The Senecas abandoned their towns, which the Americans systematically destroyed, along with flourishing apple orchards and 160,000 bushels of corn. U.S. regulars from Pittsburgh wreaked similar ruin along the Allegheny River. This deliberate devastation did not stop border raids in the area, which continued through 1781. But it ended the Iroquois' sway in New York. After the war their lands were divided among Revolutionary veterans and incoming settlers.

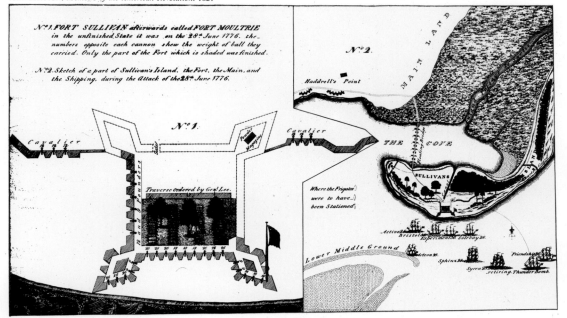

JOHN DRAYTON, *Memoirs of the American Revolution*. 1821

N.º 1. FORT SULLIVAN afterwards called FORT MOULTRIE in the unfinished State it was on the 28.ª June 1776. the numbers opposite each cannon shew the weight of ball they carried. Only the part of the Fort which is shaded was finished.

N.º 2. Sketch of a part of Sullivan's Island, the Fort, the Main, and the Shipping, during the Attack of the 28.ª June 1776.

Charles Town's unfinished harbor defenses beat back a 1776 attack by the British squadron of Sir Peter Parker, as shown in this American engraving. Four years later the British landed their army south of the city and cut it off from the interior (below). Their ships blockaded the harbor, and ran past Fort Moultrie without suffering damage.

WAR *in the* SOUTH

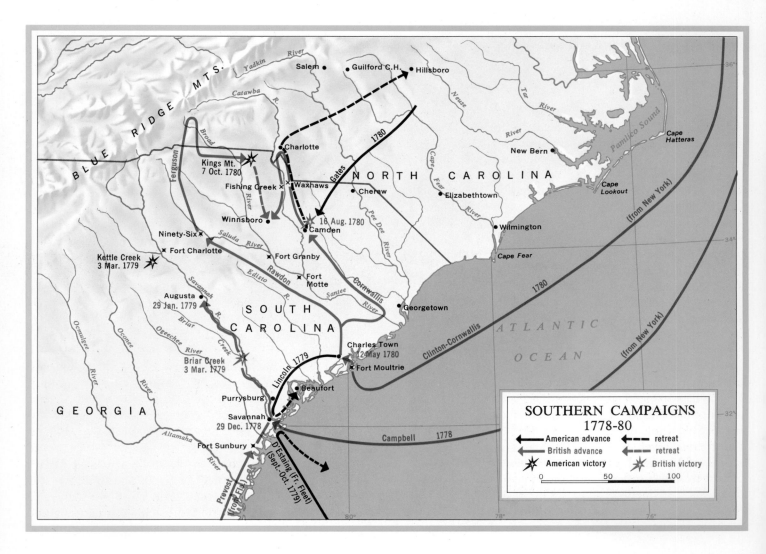

SOUTHERN CAMPAIGNS
1778-80
← American advance — ◄ - - retreat
← British advance — ◄ - - retreat
✴ American victory — ✴ British victory

0   50   100

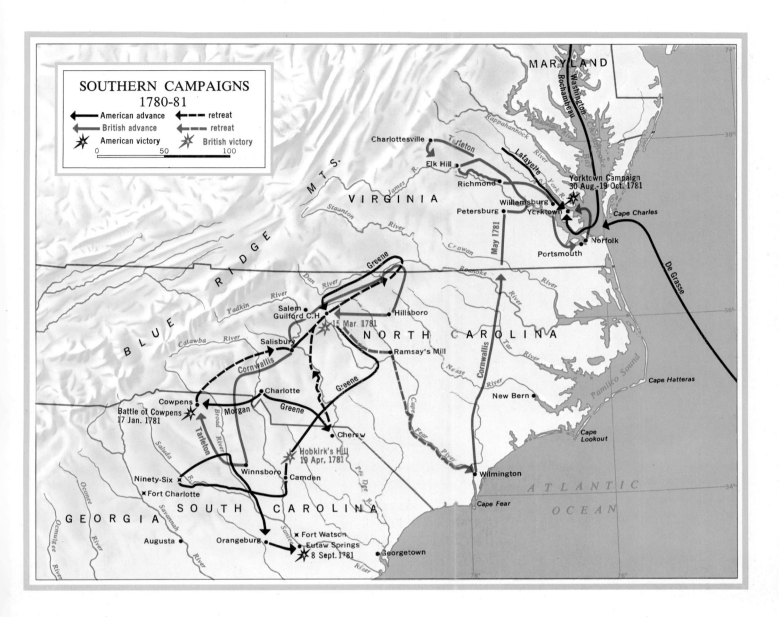

SOUTHERN CAMPAIGNS
1780-81
American advance ← retreat
British advance ← retreat
American victory ✦ British victory
0   50   100

In the South the British achieved their longest string of victories. Seaborne regulars from New York, joined by invaders from British East Florida, conquered Savannah and most of Georgia in the winter of 1778–79. A Franco-American attempt to retake Savannah, in October, 1779, became a Bunker Hill in reverse. The 4,500 attackers broke into the town's defenses, but were driven back in hand-to-hand combat. The defenders included about 500 Negroes (slaves who had run away, or been captured from patriot owners), and American Tories from as far away as New Jersey. Georgia became a secure British base for the rest of the war.

Charles Town and South Carolina were next. Sir Henry Clinton and Lord Charles Cornwallis besieged Charles Town with 8,500 soldiers, 200 cannon, and 5,000 sailors to man the guns. The American general Benjamin Lincoln surrendered his whole defending army: 5,500 men, with stores of munitions, seven generals, and three signers of the Declaration of Independence. British forces fanned out from the port to smash scattered militia and establish strong inland posts, at Ninety-Six and Camden. In August, 1780, Horatio Gates, commander of Continental troops in the South, was trounced by Cornwallis at Camden. The American defeat was complete: only 700 of 4,000 men escaped to Charlotte, North Carolina. Among the survivors was General Gates, who had the fastest horse in the army.

The British reverses began soon after. Frontier militia from both Carolinas stormed Kings Mountain and killed or captured (and in nine cases, hanged) 1,000 hard-fighting Tories. At Cowpens (see pages 110–11) Virginia's Daniel Morgan defeated "Bloody" Tarleton. Major General Nathanael Greene rebuilt the southern American army into an effective, and elusive, force. Cornwallis lunged after Greene in a twisting, back-country campaign (above) that wore down British strength and patience; at Guilford Court House, their biggest battle, neither was a decisive winner. Cornwallis returned to the coast, at Wilmington, to pick up supplies. "Now, my dear friend, what is our plan?" he wrote to ask the British general William Phillips. Without waiting for a reply he headed for the heart of Virginia, and fought his way to the coast again, at Yorktown. Only this time the sails that whitened the horizon belonged to the French ships of Admiral de Grasse. And the army that rushed down from the north consisted of Americans and Frenchmen, led by Washington and de Rochambeau.

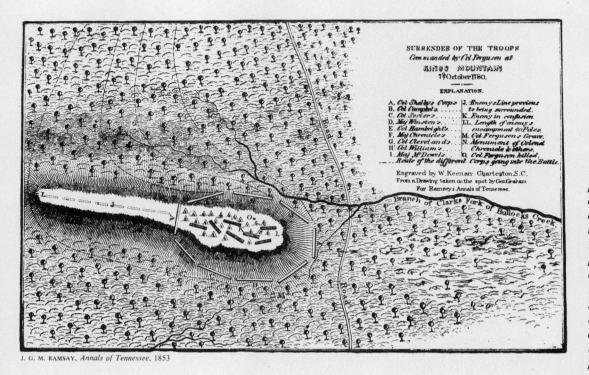

SURRENDER OF THE TROOPS
Commanded by Col Ferguson at
KINGS MOUNTAIN
7th October 1780.

EXPLANATION.

A. Col Shelby's Corps
B. Col Campbel's
C. Col Sevier's
D. Maj Winston's
E. Col Hambright's
F. Maj Chronicle's
G. Col Cleveland's
H. Col William's
I. Maj McDowl's
J. Enemy's Line previous to being surrounded.
K. Enemy in confusion.
LL. Length of enemy's encampment & Piles.
M. Col Ferguson's Grave.
N. Monument of Colonel Chronicle & others.
O. Col Ferguson killed.
— — — Route of the different Corps going into the Battle.

Engraved by W. Keenan Charleston S.C.
From a Drawing taken on the spot by Gen Graham
For Ramsey's Annals of Tennessee.

J. G. M. RAMSAY, *Annals of Tennessee*, 1853

The crude battle plans on this page were based on drawings and descriptions by participants, and published in American books many years after the war. Kings Mountain was fought between patriot militia and Tories; the only Britisher present, Colonel Patrick Ferguson, refused to surrender and went down fighting. At Eutaw Springs Nathanael Greene won his first victory over British regulars in his campaign to mop up the Carolinas, after Cornwallis was in Virginia.

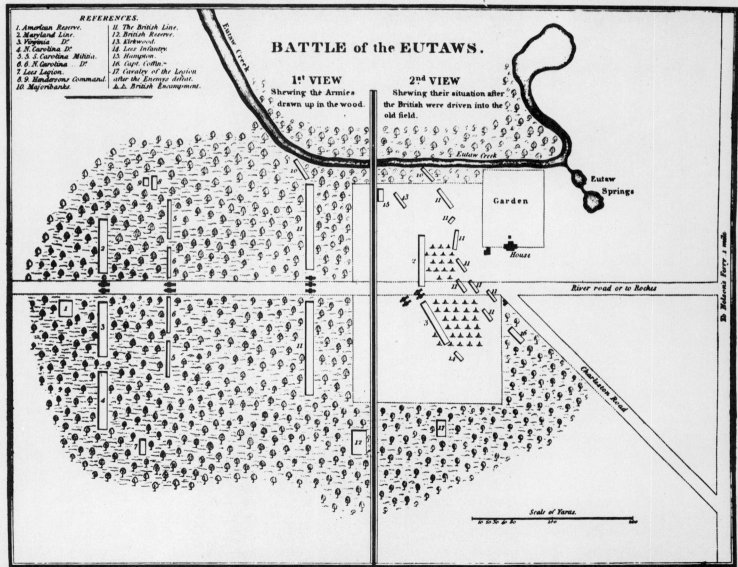

REFERENCES.

1. American Reserve.
2. Maryland Line.
3. Virginia Do.
4. N. Carolina Do.
5. S. S. Carolina Militia.
6. 6. N. Carolina Do.
7. Lees Legion.
8. 9. Hendersons Command.
10. Majoribanks.
11. The British Line.
12. British Reserve.
13. Kirkwood.
14. Lees Infantry.
15. Hampton.
16. Capt. Coffin.
17. Cavalry of the Legion after the Enemy's defeat.
△△ British Encampment.

BATTLE of the EUTAWS.

1st VIEW
Shewing the Armies drawn up in the wood.

2nd VIEW
Shewing their situation after the British were driven into the old field.

Eutaw Creek

Eutaw Creek

Eutaw Springs

Garden

House

River road or to Roches

To Nelsons Ferry 1 mile

Charleston Road

Scale of Yards.

WILLIAM JOHNSON, *Sketches of the Life and Correspondence of Nathanael Greene*, 1822

BATTLES
of the
REVOLUTION

A Portfolio of Pictorial Maps

On the following pages three key battles of the Revolutionary War have been re-created on panoramic maps, prepared for this volume by the artist David Greenspan. Each was an American success which helped change the course of the war. The Christmas night attack at Trenton, with its follow-up battle at Princeton, in 1776–77, established Washington as a skillful strategist who won praise from the military experts of Europe, and the lasting respect of his English foes. It proved also that defeated, retreating American soldiers had remarkable recuperative powers. Bemis Heights, in 1777, forced the surrender of Burgoyne's army, which in turn persuaded France to recognize openly American independence, and to send military aid. Cowpens, in 1781, was the turning point in the South. Southern troops who fought there had the satisfaction of defeating "Bloody" Tarleton, who had ordered the slaughter of 100 surrendering Virginia militia at the Waxhaws the year before.

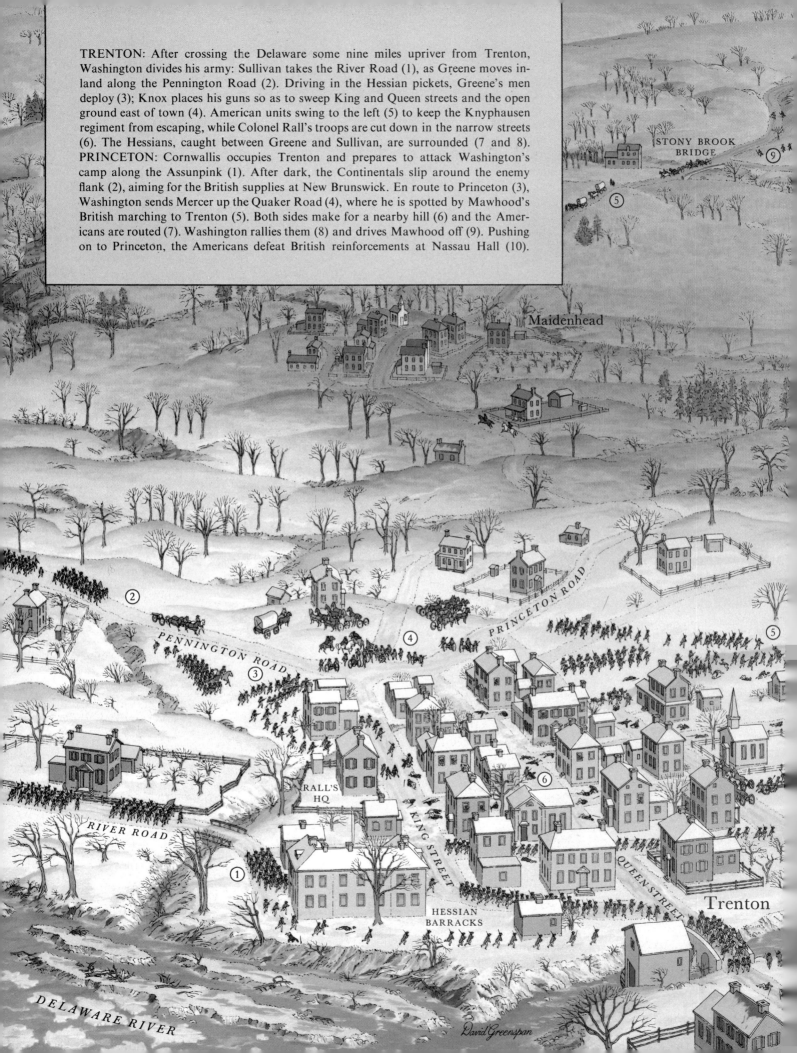

TRENTON: After crossing the Delaware some nine miles upriver from Trenton, Washington divides his army: Sullivan takes the River Road (1), as Greene moves inland along the Pennington Road (2). Driving in the Hessian pickets, Greene's men deploy (3); Knox places his guns so as to sweep King and Queen streets and the open ground east of town (4). American units swing to the left (5) to keep the Knyphausen regiment from escaping, while Colonel Rall's troops are cut down in the narrow streets (6). The Hessians, caught between Greene and Sullivan, are surrounded (7 and 8). PRINCETON: Cornwallis occupies Trenton and prepares to attack Washington's camp along the Assunpink (1). After dark, the Continentals slip around the enemy flank (2), aiming for the British supplies at New Brunswick. En route to Princeton (3), Washington sends Mercer up the Quaker Road (4), where he is spotted by Mawhood's British marching to Trenton (5). Both sides make for a nearby hill (6) and the Americans are routed (7). Washington rallies them (8) and drives Mawhood off (9). Pushing on to Princeton, the Americans defeat British reinforcements at Nassau Hall (10).

STONY BROOK BRIDGE

Maidenhead

PENNINGTON ROAD

PRINCETON ROAD

RALL'S HQ

KING STREET

QUEEN STREET

RIVER ROAD

HESSIAN BARRACKS

Trenton

DELAWARE RIVER

David Greenspan

TO NEW BRUNSWICK

PRINCETON ROAD

NASSAU HALL

Princeton

⑩

⑧

⑥

⑦

QUAKER ROAD

④

⑦

QUAKER MEETING
HOUSE

③

②

N

STONY BROOK

PRINCETON

January 3, 1777

QUAKER ROAD

TRENTON

December 26, 1776

⑦

⑧

SUNPINK CREEK

①

HUDSON RIVER

← TO SARATOGA

GREAT REDOUBT

⑫

BURGOYNE'S HQ

NORTH FORK

GREAT RAVINE

②

FREEMAN FARM

FREEMAN COTTAGE

⑪

⑨

⑩

BREYMANN'S REDOUBT

David Greenspan

BEMIS HEIGHTS: With the road to Albany blocked by a strong American position at Bemis Heights (1), Burgoyne sends out a reconnaissance in force from his lines near Freeman Farm (2). As they leave the high, open ground (3), the British and German troops are hit by Gates's force. Poor advances on the British left (4), Morgan's riflemen attack from a heigh on the enemy right (5), while Benedict Arnold, temporaril without a command, overtakes Learned's brigade and leads dramatically into the fray (6). As a bullet fells British Gen eral Fraser, the entire enemy line falters and withdraws unde

BEMIS HEIGHTS
October 7, 1777

ROAD TO ALBANY →

MILL CREEK

SOUTH FORK

MIDDLE RAVINE

BALCARRES'
REDOUBT
7

BEMIS
TAVERN

BEMIS
HEIGHTS
1

FORT
NEILSON

8

CHATFIELD
FARM

MUNGER
FARM

4

BARBER
FARM

WHEAT FIELD

3

6

5

great pressure to its fortifications in the rear. In pursuit of
the retreating army, Arnold leads an unsuccessful attack on
Balcarres' Redoubt (7). With reinforcements coming up (8),
Arnold sweeps to his left, routing the British from stockaded
log cabins between the redoubts (9). Snatching up Daniel
Morgan's troops, who have circled around to the right of
Breymann's Redoubt (10), Arnold captures the fortification
from behind (11), and is wounded. The defeated British withdraw to the Great Redoubt (12), and on October 17, near the
town of Saratoga, Burgoyne's 6,000 men lay down their arms.

TO BROAD RIVER↗

MORGAN'S HQ

⑦

⑧

⑥

⑤

⑨

GREEN RIVER ROAD

N

David Greenspan

COWPENS: Having chosen his battleground carefully, General Daniel Morgan deploys his troops in three lines, with his cavalry posted well in the rear, concealed behind a hill. Tarleton's British advance against Morgan's front line of skirmishers (1), who open fire with deadly effect and drop back as ordered. Tarle-

ton now pushes on against Pickens's militia in the second line (2). After firing two volleys, Pickens's men withdraw across the American left (3) to re-form out of sight in the rear. Taking this for a general retreat, the British pursue, encountering Howard's Continentals in the main American line (4). Tarleton calls on his

COWPENS
January 17, 1781

OLD MILL GAP ROAD

reserve (5) in a move to outflank the Continentals. As the American right (6) swings back to block the movement, the entire line begins a retreat and the British break ranks and give chase. At the strategic moment, Morgan directs the Americans to face about and fire (7). Meanwhile, Pickens's re-formed militia (8) and McCall's mounted reserve (9) strike the British left as William Washington's cavalry moves in to surprise the enemy right (10). Faced with a double envelopment, the British troops begin to surrender. Tarleton's attempt to rally his cavalry (11) is futile, and they flee from the field, with Washington in hot pursuit.

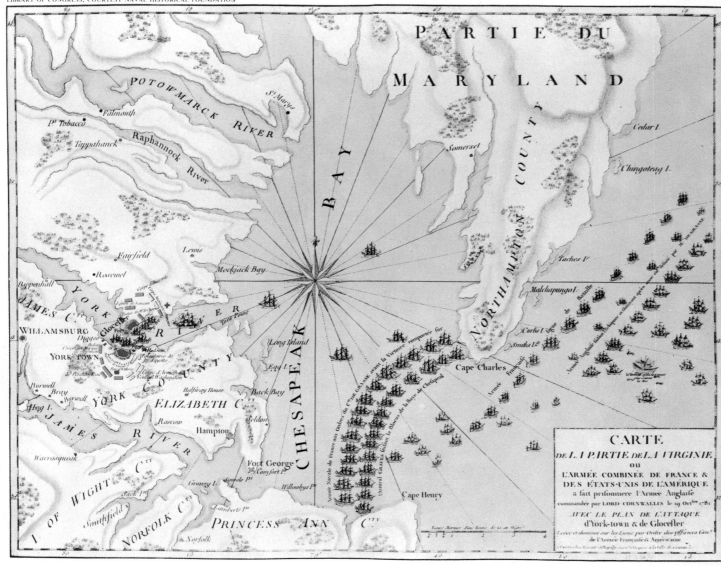

"*O God! It is all over!*" *exclaimed Lord North, the British prime minister, when the news reached him at 10 Downing Street that Cornwallis had surrendered at Yorktown. The French map above shows the lines of the siege, left, and the English-French naval battle, right, which sealed Cornwallis's fate. The superior French fleet of 30 ships and 1,700 guns blocked the entrance to Chesapeake Bay (lower center). The English ships got their signals mixed and were outmaneuvered by de Grasse, some of whose ships are pictured here in broadside formation lined up outside Cape Charles. The British Terrible, outlined in red, was set afire and abandoned; the rest escaped to New York. On land the British positions at Yorktown and Gloucester (across the York River) are marked in red; Washington's Continental regiments in yellow; the besieging French units in blue. Cut off from the sea and surrounded by 16,000 allied troops, Cornwallis sent out a white flag and surrendered 8,087 men of all ranks, on October 19, 1781. The war was not all over, however. There were more months of heavy fighting in the south and west, and protracted treaty negotiations, before peace was formally proclaimed by the Congress of the United States on April 19, 1783—the eighth anniversary of Lexington and Concord.*

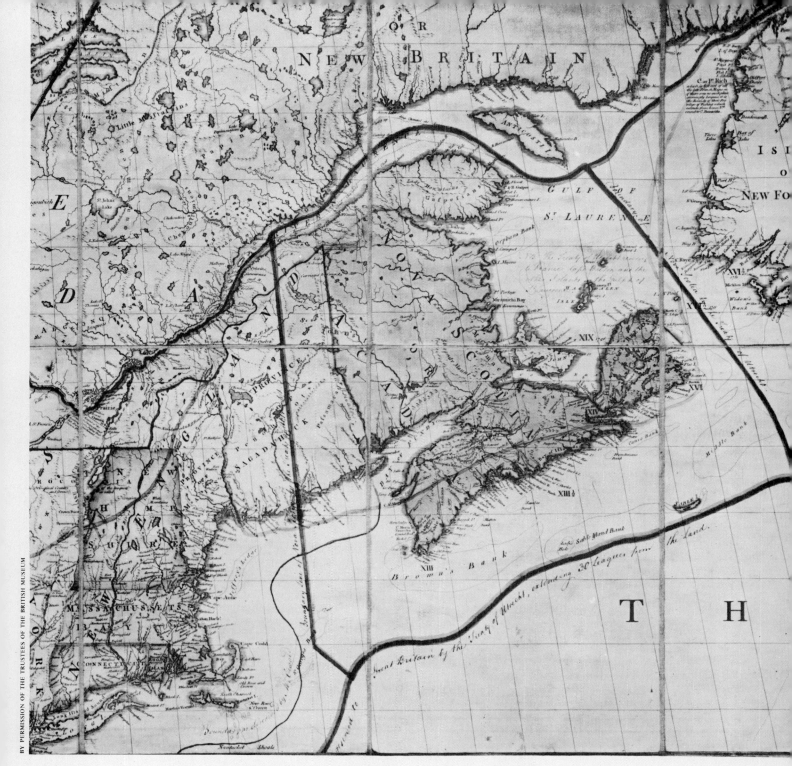

*Both armies used English-made maps during the Revolutionary War; the Americans had
a few trained cartographers, but lacked engraving and printing facilities to produce
their own maps. For the same reason, when diplomats sat down to draw for the first time
the boundaries of the United States, they began with an out-of-date map illustrating
"the British Colonies of North America," published by John Mitchell in London in
1755. Above is one corner of the copy of Mitchell's map that was owned and closely
studied by King George III. The heavy lines extending into the ocean are labeled "Line
expressing Exclusive Right of the Fishery Reserved to Great Britain . . ." and "Boundary
Line of Nova Scotia by the Treaty of Utrecht [1713]." Within these lines is another
line, drawn northward from the coast, and faintly marked in handwriting, "Boundary
described by Mr. Oswald." This in fact became part of the 1783 treaty boundary between Maine and what is now New Brunswick. And Richard Oswald, British peace ne-
gotiator, was here identified, in the mind of his king, with giving up a slice of 70-year-
old British territory. The line, however, did not settle the matter; because of mistakes
in Mitchell's map, the Maine-Canadian boundary remained in dispute until 1842.*

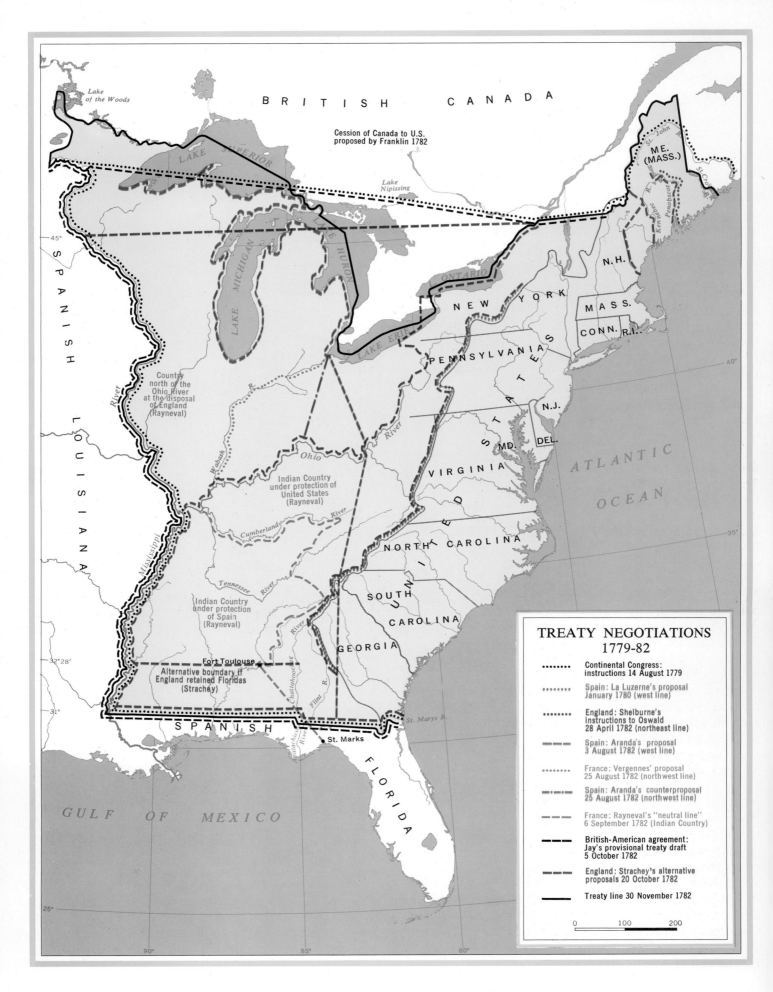

BRITISH CANADA

Cession of Canada to U.S.
proposed by Franklin 1782

Lake of the Woods

LAKE SUPERIOR

Lake Nipissing

SPANISH LOUISIANA

LAKE MICHIGAN

LAKE HURON

LAKE ONTARIO

LAKE ERIE

ME. (MASS.)

N.H.

NEW YORK

MASS.

CONN. R.I.

PENNSYLVANIA

N.J.

MD. DEL.

Country north of the Ohio River at the disposal of England (Rayneval)

Ohio

River

Wabash

Indian Country under protection of United States (Rayneval)

River

VIRGINIA

ATLANTIC OCEAN

Cumberland River

Mississippi

Tennessee River

Indian Country under protection of Spain (Rayneval)

NORTH CAROLINA

SOUTH CAROLINA

River

GEORGIA

Fort Toulouse

Alternative boundary if England retained Floridas (Strachey)

Chattahoochee River

Flint R.

St. Marys R.

SPANISH

St. Marks

FLORIDA

GULF OF MEXICO

UNITED STATES

St. John R.

St. Croix R.

Kennebec R.

Penobscot R.

TREATY NEGOTIATIONS
1779-82

Continental Congress: instructions 14 August 1779

Spain: La Luzerne's proposal January 1780 (west line)

England: Shelburne's instructions to Oswald 28 April 1782 (northeast line)

Spain: Aranda's proposal 3 August 1782 (west line)

France: Vergennes' proposal 25 August 1782 (northwest line)

Spain: Aranda's counterproposal 25 August 1782 (northwest line)

France: Rayneval's "neutral line" 6 September 1782 (Indian Country)

British-American agreement: Jay's provisional treaty draft 5 October 1782

England: Strachey's alternative proposals 20 October 1782

Treaty line 30 November 1782

0   100   200

NEGOTIATIONS *for* PEACE

"We have gone the utmost lengths to favor peace," wrote John Adams in November, 1782. "We have at last agreed to boundaries with the greatest moderation." Moderate or not, the three American peace commissioners—Adams, Benjamin Franklin, and John Jay—achieved a great victory for the United States at the bargaining tables in Paris and Versailles. The solid black line on the map, opposite, marks the boundary of the young nation as defined in the final 1783 treaty with England; it encloses an area roughly four times larger than the settled parts of the 13 states.

The most important American war aim, after independence, was a western boundary on the Mississippi River. This was insisted upon by Congress in the first instructions to the negotiators (1779). It was bitterly opposed, during most of three years, by America's allies, France and Spain. The French were eager to satisfy Spain with more land in North America in order to lessen Spain's demands elsewhere; they also expected to regain Louisiana themselves (which they did in 1800). At a time when Americans sorely needed French aid, the French minister in Philadelphia, La Luzerne, bribed one congressman and persuaded others that the United States should accept a boundary with Spain along the Allegheny Mountains (dotted brown line on map). La Luzerne also lobbied through Congress new instructions to the Americans in Paris, directing them to "undertake nothing" without French "knowledge and concurrence." Adams and Jay, determinedly, and Franklin somewhat reluctantly, declined to obey this instruction. The separate and (until it was signed) secret treaty which they negotiated with English diplomats enormously extended the American domain; it also included valuable advantages, territorial and otherwise, for England. (Henry Strachey's 1782 proposal, that England retain all lands north of the Ohio River—the future Northwest Territory—was a last-minute bargaining point that was not taken seriously by either side.)

On the southern border, the Americans failed in a devious game. They agreed secretly with the English that the boundary of West Florida should be 100 miles farther north if Britain retained that territory (broken red line on map). But England ceded both Floridas to Spain, as balm for retaining Gibraltar. The alternate boundaries soon became known, and Spain naturally claimed the one farther north. West Florida also gave Spain both sides of the Mississippi extend-ing more than 200 miles above the Gulf of Mexico. Spain was thus able, under international usage, to refuse free navigation of the river to flatboats loaded with American produce. This remained a sore point in the west until 1795, when the weakened Bourbon monarchy of Spain, left isolated by the French Revolution, agreed to a treaty that gave Americans free navigation to Spanish New Orleans, and the Florida boundary line they wanted.

The most disputed border, so far as the Americans and English were concerned, was in the northeast, between Maine and Nova Scotia (now New Brunswick). King George clung to the belief that the Treaty of Utrecht (1713) had given the Penobscot River valley to Britain. (For his reasons, see page 113.) The Americans insisted on a line farther east—"from the mouth of the St. Croix River to its source and thence due north to the southern boundary of Quebec." This was written into the final treaty. Unfortunately Mitchell's 1755 map did not locate the St. Croix River accurately. In later surveys the St. Croix was identified as either one of two Indian rivers—the Schoodiac or the Magaguadavic—which were close together at their mouths, but 50 miles apart at their sources. That left a vast expanse of north woods as territory still in dispute.

The principal northern boundary with Canada grew out of a sensible American proposal which followed the 1763 Quebec line, and gave the Canadians an equal share of four Great Lakes. It then extended to Lake of the Woods, and "from thence on a due western course to the Mississippi River." This last clause was based on Mitchell's map, which showed the Mississippi rising far north of its actual source. The mistake enlarged the whole northwest, and eventually added the Mesabi iron range to future American assets (see pages 158–59). It was slightly rectified in England's favor in 1818. But it provided the basis for the 49th parallel boundary with Canada that still stretches, in a broad arc, across the top of the western half of the United States.

In 1783 there were few Britons (besides King George) who begrudged the Americans their independence. At a dinner party after the preliminary treaty was signed, a Frenchman teasingly predicted that "the Thirteen United States" would become "the greatest empire in the world."

"Yes, sir," replied the secretary of the British delegation, "and they will *all* speak English, every one of 'em."

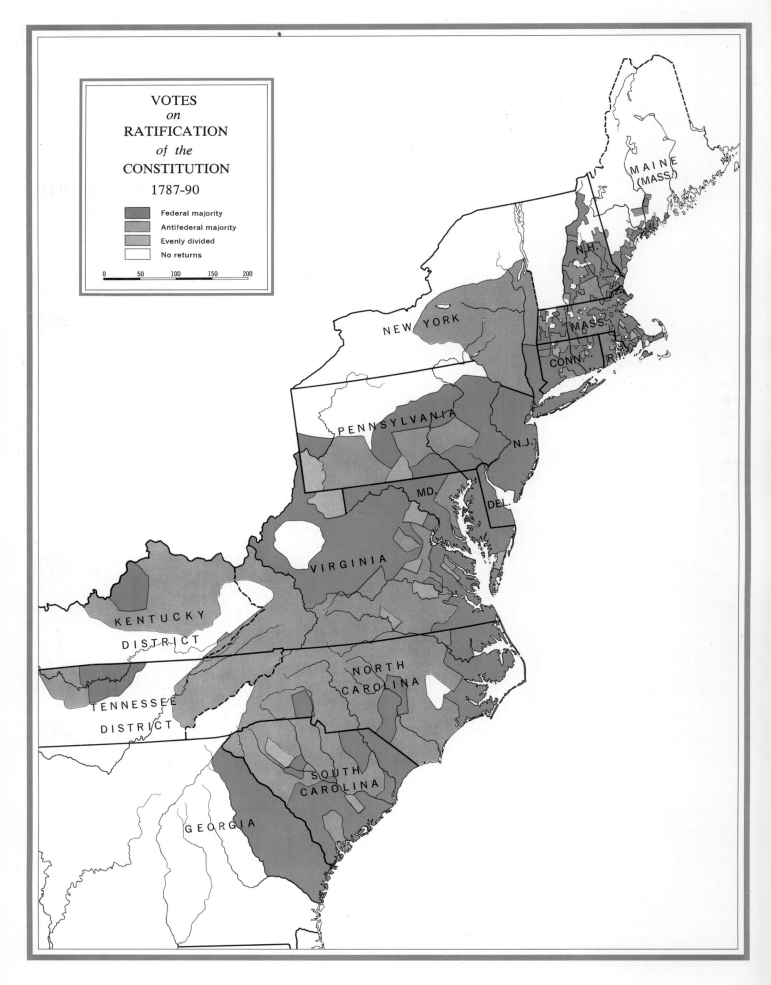

VOTES
on
RATIFICATION
of the
CONSTITUTION
1787-90

Federal majority
Antifederal majority
Evenly divided
No returns

0   50   100   150   200

MAINE
(MASS.)

N.H.

MASS.

CONN.   R.I.

NEW YORK

PENNSYLVANIA

N.J.

MD.

DEL.

VIRGINIA

KENTUCKY
DISTRICT

TENNESSEE
DISTRICT

NORTH
CAROLINA

SOUTH
CAROLINA

GEORGIA

THE STRUGGLE
for FEDERAL UNION

This 1790 American engraving shows President Washington being sworn in, April 30, 1789, at Federal Hall, facing Broad Street, New York.

The first nationwide clash between political factions can be traced in the map, opposite, which records pro and con votes on the Federal Constitution. Only three original states —Delaware, New Jersey, and Georgia—accepted the Constitution by unanimous vote in special ratifying conventions. In the others, 1,544 votes were cast by delegates elected for the purpose, and 577—more than 35 per cent— were against the Constitution. The contest was hottest in New York, where ratification squeaked through by 30-27, and in Virginia, where an 89-79 vote was obtained by assuring the delegates that George Washington (from Virginia) was sure to be the first Federal President.

The map is colored to show local sentiment in the counties or districts the delegates came from. Proponents of the Constitution (Federalists) were strongest in the big seaport cities and the old, established, tidewater plantations; they included most of the "rich and wellborn," along with the educated ministers, lawyers, and editors, and the more highly skilled urban workmen. There were also pockets of Federalist strength on the Ohio River and southern fron-

tiers, where the promise of a permanent United States army, to deal with the Indians, was a convincing argument.

The opposition, as the map shows, came largely from the rural areas where 90 per cent of Americans lived. The postwar hard times and depreciated currency hit small farmers and veterans the hardest; they were in no mood to approve a new central government with swarms of paid officials and tax collectors. The Antifederalists had powerful leaders— Patrick Henry in Virginia, George Clinton in New York— but they failed to become a united party, and they were no match for the well-organized Federalists.

Delaware was the first to ratify, on December 7, 1787, followed quickly by Pennsylvania, New Jersey, Georgia, and Connecticut. In Massachusetts the Antifederalists insisted on a group of amendments (which eventually became the Bill of Rights) as a condition for ratification. New Hampshire, in June, 1788, gave the ninth and decisive vote, which put the Constitution in operation. North Carolina and Rhode Island were holdouts (below); they finally joined the Union in November, 1789, and May, 1790, respectively.

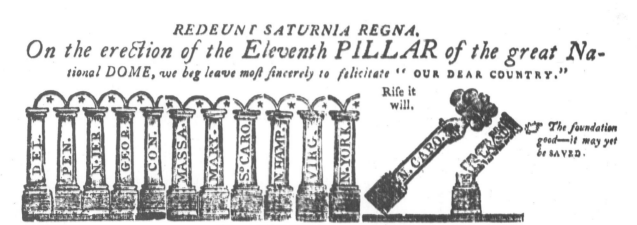

A 1788 cartoon from a Boston newspaper depicts the progress of ratification up to the day Washington became President.

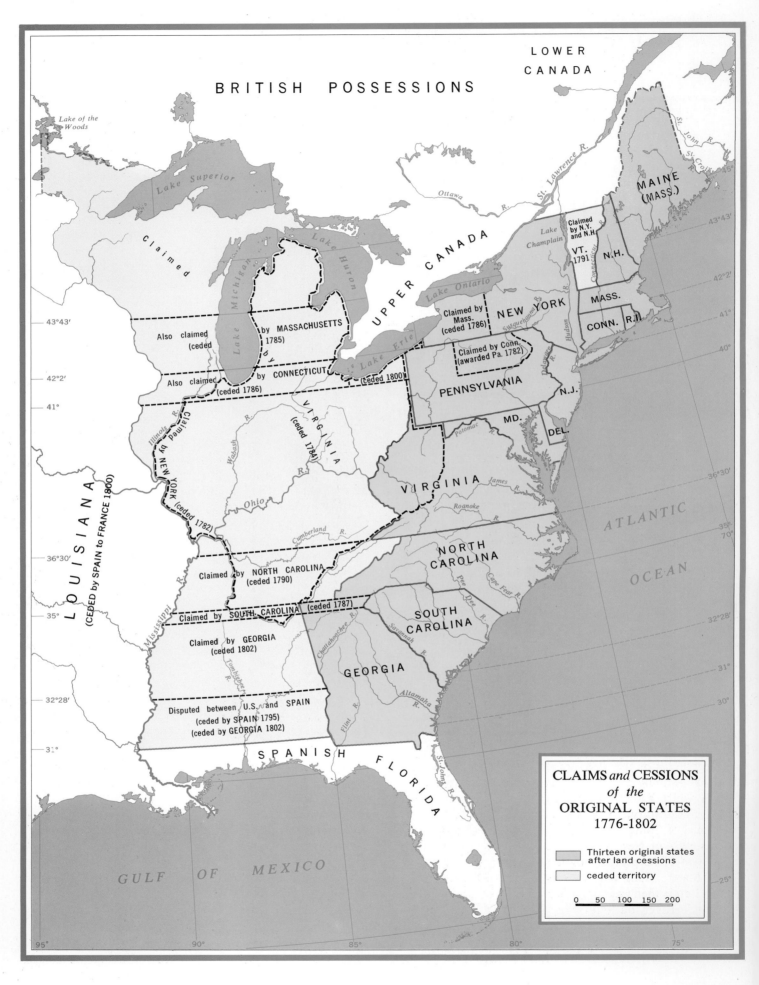

LOWER
CANADA

BRITISH POSSESSIONS

Lake of the Woods

Lake Superior

Claimed

MAINE
(MASS.)

UPPER CANADA

by MASSACHUSETTS
1785)

Lake Michigan

Lake Huron

Lake Champlain

Claimed
by N.Y.
and N.H.

VT.
1791

N.H.

Ottawa

St. Lawrence R.

Also claimed (ceded

by CONNECTICUT

Lake Erie

Lake Ontario

Claimed by
Mass.
(ceded 1786)

NEW YORK

MASS.

CONN. R.I.

Also claimed
(ceded 1786)

(Ceded 1800)

Claimed by Conn.
(awarded Pa. 1782)

Susquehanna R.

Hudson R.

PENNSYLVANIA

N.J.

Illinois R.

Claimed by NEW YORK

Wabash R.

VIRGINIA
(ceded 1784)

Delaware R.

MD.

DEL.

Ohio R.

Potomac R.

VIRGINIA

James R.

(ceded 1782)

Cumberland R.

Roanoke R.

ATLANTIC

Claimed by NORTH CAROLINA
(ceded 1790)

NORTH
CAROLINA

Pee Dee R.

Cape Fear R.

OCEAN

Mississippi R.

Claimed by SOUTH CAROLINA (ceded 1787)

SOUTH
CAROLINA

Savannah R.

Claimed by GEORGIA
(ceded 1802)

Chattahoochee R.

GEORGIA

Altamaha R.

L O U I S I A N A
(CEDED by SPAIN to FRANCE 1800)

Tombigbee R.

Disputed between U.S. and SPAIN
(ceded by SPAIN 1795)
(ceded by GEORGIA 1802)

Flint R.

S P A N I S H   F L O R I D A

St. Johns R.

G U L F   O F   M E X I C O

CLAIMS *and* CESSIONS
of the
ORIGINAL STATES
1776-1802

Thirteen original states
after land cessions

ceded territory

0   50 100 150 200

118

CEDING LAND *to the* NATION

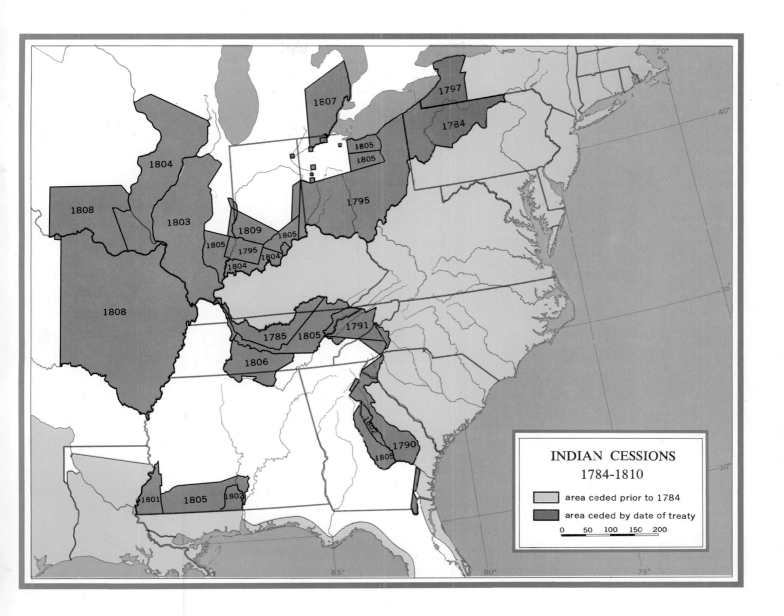

INDIAN CESSIONS
1784-1810

area ceded prior to 1784

area ceded by date of treaty

0   50   100   150   200

At the start of the Revolution seven states insisted that they owned, under colonial charters and grants, lands extending to the Mississippi River (map on opposite page). The other six original states, as early as 1777, demanded that large areas of the west—especially what was secured in the war—should be the common property of the nation. Virginia, which had the biggest claims, flatly refused to relinquish them. Maryland, in angry reprisal, declined to sign the Articles of Confederation. The deadlock was broken by the legislature of New York, which voted in 1780 to cede claims west of its present boundaries to the four-year-old United States. (This cession was formally completed in 1782.) Virginia then grudgingly surrendered its claims north of the Ohio River, but retained sovereignty over Kentucky until 1789. Connecticut similarly held on to the Western Reserve—the northeast corner of Ohio, including present-day Cleveland—after yielding claims within Pennsylvania (West-

moreland County), and west of Lake Erie. Several states reserved tracts for Revolutionary veterans (see page 121) or for private land companies (page 123). But most of the region beyond the Alleghenies became a national public domain—totaling nearly 222 million acres—which Congress could sell to raise funds, apportion among deserving ex-soldiers, and divide into additional states.

The national government also acquired the sole power to negotiate treaties with Indian tribes. The map above shows the progress of such negotiations to 1810, including large cessions of land beyond the Mississippi, within the 1803 Louisiana Purchase. Some Indian cessions were peaceably arranged; others followed armed conflicts. But all were accompanied by payments and solemn promises to the Indians. And, in accordance with the previous English custom, all of them had to be acknowledged in formal, written treaties that were acceptable in the white men's courts.

119

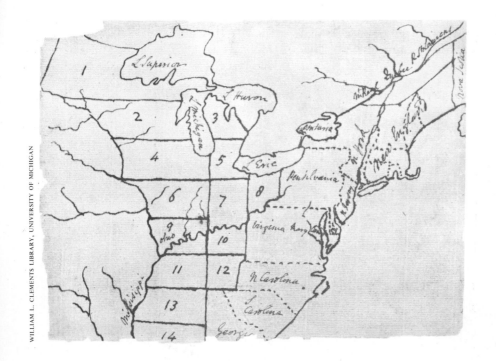

NEW STATES
and
TERRITORIES

The first new states—Vermont, Kentucky, Tennessee, and Ohio—were admitted before the purchase of French Louisiana. The rest of the national domain was consolidated in two Federal "territories," Indiana and Mississippi (opposite page). The basic plan for governing and subdividing these territories—and many more to come—was established by the old Continental Congress. A governor, council, and judges were named for each territory by Congress, later by the President. When a territory attained 20,000 population, it elected a legislature and began practicing local self-government. It also elected one non-voting delegate to the national Congress. When its population grew as large as any of the 13 original states, it could apply to Congress to be-

come a state. Before being admitted, however, it had to agree to obey the United States Constitution, and never to secede from the Union.

Thomas Jefferson, a Virginia congressman in 1784, presented a plan—outlined in the rough sketch above—to slice the Federal lands into 14 new states with an assortment of names which he invented: Cherronesus, Assenesipia, Illinoia, Michigania, Polypotamia, and others. Congress rejected most of his names and his artificial boundary lines. But it adopted one of Jefferson's suggestions—the permanent prohibition of slavery—and applied it specifically, in 1787, to the evolving Northwest Territory (below), out of which eventually came four states and part of a fifth, Minnesota.

CONNECTICUT RESERVE

TERRITORY NORTHWEST OF THE RIVER OHIO 1787-1800

Fort Recovery

INDIANA TERRITORY 1800-1803

TERRITORY NORTHWEST OF THE RIVER OHIO 1800-1803

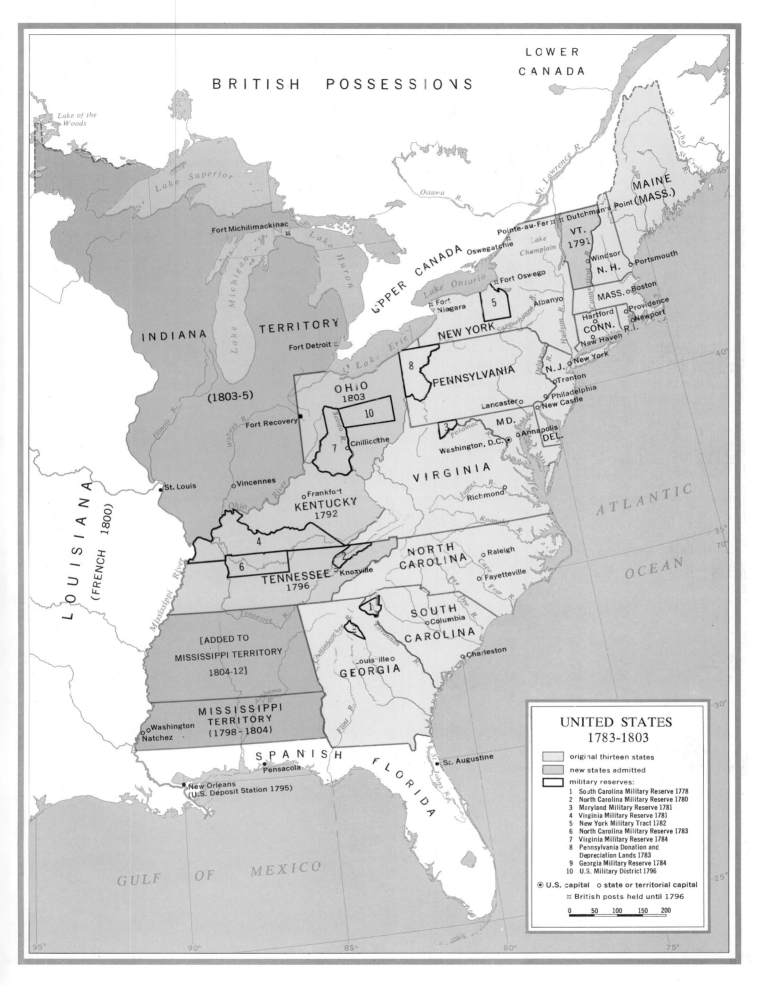

BRITISH POSSESSIONS

LOWER CANADA

Lake of the Woods

INDIANA   TERRITORY

(1803-5)

Fort Michilimackinac

Lake Superior

Lake Michigan

Lake Huron

Fort Detroit

Lak. Erie

OHIO
1803

Fort Recovery

10

Scioto R.

7

Chillicothe

○ Vincennes

● St. Louis

L O U I S I A N A

(FRENCH 1800)

Illinois R.

Wabash R.

○ ○ Frankfort

KENTUCKY
1792

Ohio *River*

4

6

TENNESSEE
1796

○ Knoxville

Mississippi River

Tennessee R.

[ADDED TO
MISSISSIPPI TERRITORY
1804-12]

Alabama R.

MISSISSIPPI
TERRITORY
(1798-1804)

○ ○ Washington
Natchez

S P A N I S H

Chattahoochee R.

Flint R.

GEORGIA

○ Louisville ○

● Pensacola

● New Orleans
(U.S. Deposit Station 1795)

G U L F   O F   M E X I C O

UPPER CANADA

Oswegatchie

St. Lawrence R.

Ottawa R.

Pointe-au-Fer ⊭ ⊭ Dutchman's Point

Lake Champlain

⊭ Fort Oswego

Lake Ontario

⊭ Fort
Niagara

5

NEW YORK

8

PENNSYLVANIA

Susquehanna R.

Albany ○

Hartford ○

New Haven ○

Lancaster ○

3
Potomac R.

Washington, D.C. ⊙

VIRGINIA

MAINE
(MASS.)

VT.
1791

○ Windsor

N. H.

MASS. ○ Boston

○ Portsmouth

CONN.

○ Providence
○ Newport
R.I.

Hudson R.
Delaware R.

N.J. ○

○ Trenton

○ New York

○ Philadelphia
○ New Castle

MD.
○ Annapolis
DEL.

James R.

○ Richmond

Roanoke R.

St. John R.

St. Croix R.

ATLANTIC

OCEAN

NORTH
CAROLINA

○ Raleigh

○ Fayetteville

Cape Fear R.
Pee Dee R.

1

SOUTH
CAROLINA

○ Columbia

○ Charleston

Savannah R.

2

F L O R I D A

● St. Augustine

St. Johns R.

UNITED STATES
1783-1803

☐ original thirteen states

☐ new states admitted

☐ military reserves:
1 South Carolina Military Reserve 1778
2 North Carolina Military Reserve 1780
3 Maryland Military Reserve 1781
4 Virginia Military Reserve 1781
5 New York Military Tract 1782
6 North Carolina Military Reserve 1783
7 Virginia Military Reserve 1784
8 Pennsylvania Donation and
   Depreciation Lands 1783
9 Georgia Military Reserve 1784
10 U.S. Military District 1796

⊙ U.S. capital   ○ state or territorial capital

⊭ British posts held until 1796

0   50 100 150 200

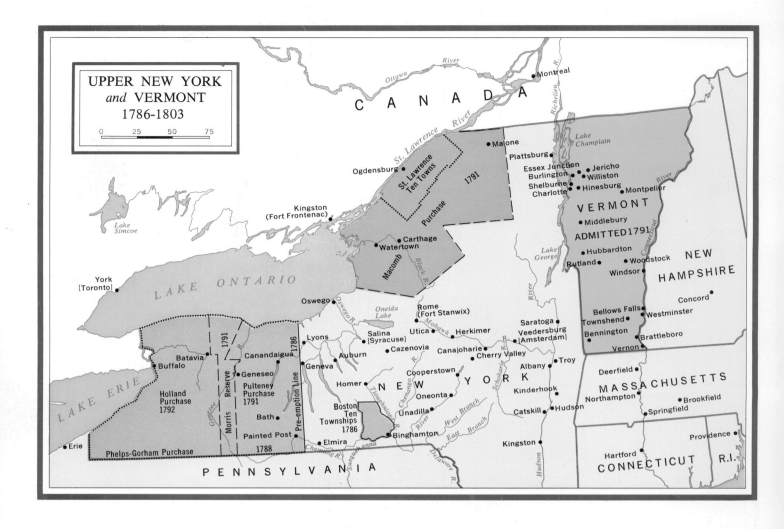

DEVELOPERS *and* SPECULATORS

The overflow of prolific New England, a million restless, land-hungry Yankees, staged the first mass migration toward the West. New York State alone, in the two decades following the Revolutionary War, absorbed 500,000 new settlers and tripled its population. On the map above, the "Pre-emption Line," from Lake Ontario to Pennsylvania, marks the settlement of an old dispute between Massachusetts and New York. Massachusetts surrendered its sovereignty claim in this region in return for the right to sell six million acres west of the Pre-emption Line. This it soon did, for about three cents an acre, to two Massachusetts speculators, Oliver Phelps and Nathaniel Gorham. Phelps and Gorham were unable to pay, and the tract passed, in 1790, to Robert Morris, Philadelphia banker and signer of the Declaration of Independence. Morris failed to make payments, also, and went to a debtors' prison. His holdings were developed into townsites and farms by English capitalists (Pulteney Purchase), Amsterdam investors (Holland Purchase), and a Maryland group including Nathaniel Rochester, for whom a future city was named.

Most of the rest of central New York, west of the Chenango River, was sold to speculators and developers by the New York state government. (One large tract, the Boston Ten Townships, was reserved to Massachusetts, and sold by that state.) North of the Mohawk, Alexander Macomb acquired four million acres, including the St. Lawrence Ten Towns. The new state of Vermont was the product of an earlier speculation. Beginning in 1749 a royal governor of New Hampshire, Benning Wentworth, sold tracts to settlers there, although New York proved its title to the land east of the Connecticut River. Thirty years of local fighting between Yorkers and Green Mountain Boys finally demonstrated, in 1784, that holders of the New Hampshire grants were a determined majority. So New York gave up its claim.

On the southwest frontier (opposite page) speculation was complicated by the presence of numerous, partly civilized Indians—Cherokees, Chickasaws, Choctaws, and Creeks—who refused to move off the land. Nevertheless, the corrupt Georgia legislature, in 1789, and again in 1795, sold 25 million acres to the Yazoo companies (named after the Yazoo River in present-day Mississippi). These sales were so obviously fraudulent that a reform Georgia legislature revoked them in 1796. But the Yazoo speculators pushed their claims in court, and collected $4,282,151 from the United States.

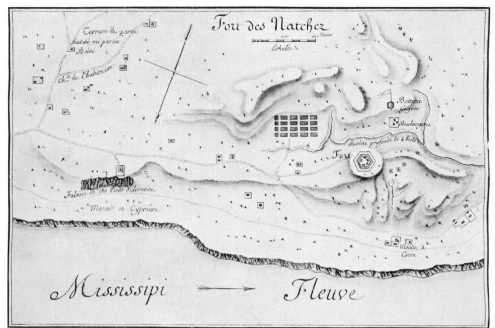

This detailed plan of Spanish Fort Natchez, on the east bank of the Mississippi, in an area claimed by the United States and Spain, was drawn by Georges Henri Victor Collot, a French army officer who journeyed from Pittsburgh to New Orleans on a spying mission in 1796. It is reproduced here from Collot's original drawing, which is in the Bibliotheque Nationale in Paris.

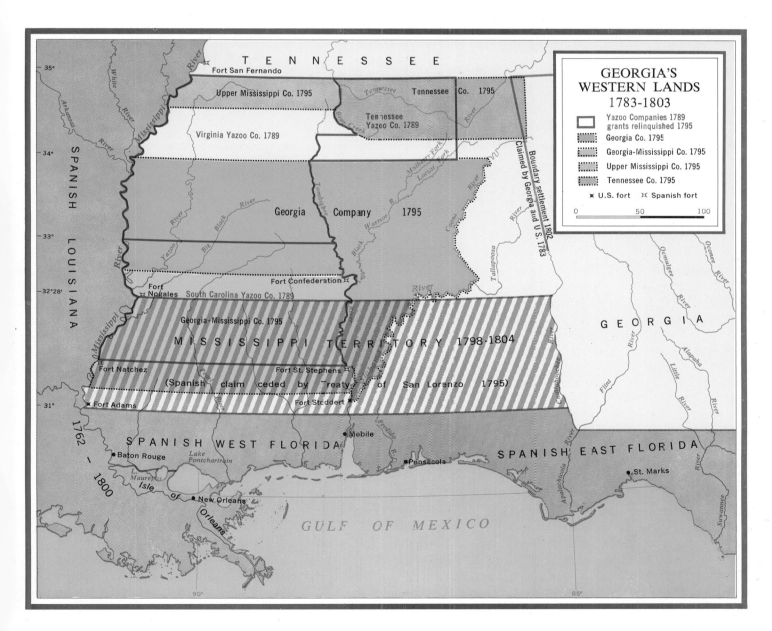

WEST *of the* ALLEGHENY MOUNTAINS

Permanent settlement began in Ohio in April, 1788, when an organized party of Revolutionary veterans, led by General Rufus Putnam, began building huts and laying out lots for a town on the north side of the Ohio River, near the mouth of the Muskingum. They named the place Marietta, in honor of Queen Marie Antoinette of France. These arrivals, mostly New Englanders, included shipwrights and carpenters who built an impressive fort (below) and celebrated the Fourth of July with an outdoor feast of venison, turkey, bear, and a broiled pike, six feet long, which they speared in the Muskingum. At far-off Mount Vernon their old commander felt a twinge of longing to be with them. "If I was a young man, just proposing to begin the world, or if advanced in life and had a family . . . I know of no country where I should rather fix my habitation," Washington wrote to his friend, Richard Henderson.

The Marietta settlers acquired their land from the Ohio Company of Associates, a group of responsible investors who bought 1,500,000 acres in southeast Ohio (map on opposite page) from the United States. Other, less scrupulous, speculators formed the Scioto Company and defrauded 500 French emigrants by selling them land at Gallipolis ("City of Gauls"), which the Ohio Company owned. Log barracks with one small dark room for each family received the unhappy Frenchmen in 1790. Farther west John Cleves Symmes and other New Jersey politicians bought a million acres from the Continental Congress and founded Losantiville, which was soon renamed Cincinnati, after the society of Revolutionary officers. George Rogers Clark and his

veterans received their grant in Indiana, across from Louisville, from Virginia in 1781.

Congress staged five Indian treaties and "extinguished" —as the saying went—Indian claims in much of Ohio. But some tribes refused to sign treaties and murdered settlers, vowing to push them all back across the Ohio River. The Indians inflicted humiliating defeats on the infant U.S. Army, under Generals Harmar and St. Clair. In 1794 General Anthony Wayne, with a force of well-drilled riflemen, decimated Little Turtle's Miami warriors at the Battle of Fallen Timbers. Wayne then forced the neighboring tribes to accept the Treaty of Greenville, which drew a line through north and central Ohio, as the temporary boundary of settlement. In 1796 Congress appointed Ebenezer Zane to cut a new road through the forests of central Ohio.

Kentucky during and after the Revolution tried to break away from Virginia; in 1776 it was all one county, in 1780 it was split into three, in 1789 it became a self-ruling district in preparation for statehood three years later. A secessionist spirit also produced, in 1784, a would-be state which called itself Franklin, in an area which North Carolina ceded to the nation and then tried to take back. Congress would not admit the state of Franklin, and it vanished four years later. Its territory went mostly to Tennessee, where 300 southern frontiersmen founded a chain of fortified towns on the Cumberland River in 1779–80. They named their principal settlement Nashville after a North Carolina general, Francis Nash, who had died from his wounds at the Battle of Germantown, two years before.

The American Pioneer, MARCH, 1842

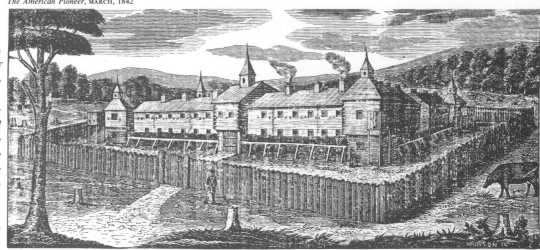

The Campus Martius, right, was a private fort built by the settlers of Marietta, Ohio, to supplement the U.S. Army post at Fort Harmar, across the Muskingum River. Its blockhouses and inner bastions could withstand any Indian attack, while its outer walls of heavy timbers were designed to contain and protect more than 800 people. In normal times one blockhouse served as a church, another as a school. This woodcut view, drawn from the recollections of pioneers, was published in 1842.

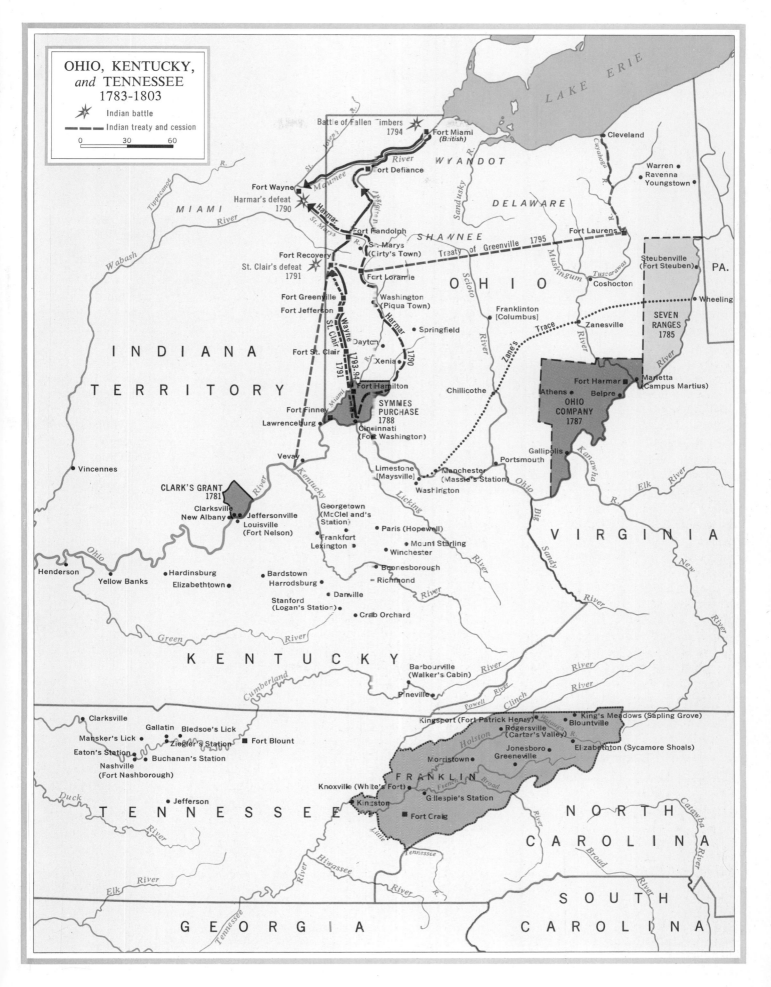

OHIO, KENTUCKY,
and TENNESSEE
1783-1803

★ Indian battle

- - - Indian treaty and cession

0   30   60

LAKE ERIE

Battle of Fallen Timbers
1794
■ Fort Miami
(British)

● Cleveland

Cuyahoga R.

WYANDOT

● Warren
● Ravenna
Youngstown

Maumee River

St. Joseph's R.

■ Fort Defiance

● Fort Wayne
Harmar's defeat
1790

DELAWARE

Sandusky R.

MIAMI

Harmar

St. Marys R.

Tippecanoe R.

■ Fort Randolph

SHAWNEE

● Fort Laurens

Fort Recovery
St. Clair's defeat
1791

St. Marys
(Girty's Town)

Treaty of Greenville 1795

Muskingum R.

Tuscarawas

Steubenville
(Fort Steuben)

PA.

Wabash River

Fort Loramie

O H I O

Scioto

Coshocton

● Wheeling

Fort Greenville
Fort Jefferson

Washington
(Piqua Town)

Franklinton
[Columbus]

Zanesville

SEVEN
RANGES
1785

Zane's Trace

Fort St. Clair

Dayton

Springfield

River

Marietta
(Campus Martius)

Fort Harmar ■

I N D I A N A
T E R R I T O R Y

Wayne
1793-94

Xenia

Chillicothe

Athens
● Belpre

St. Clair
1791

Harmar
1790

OHIO
COMPANY
1787

Fort Hamilton

Fort Finney

SYMMES
PURCHASE
1788

● Gallipolis

Kanawha River

Lawrenceburg

Cincinnati
(Fort Washington)

● Portsmouth

Ohio River

● Vincennes

Vevay

Limestone
[Maysville]

● Manchester
(Massie's Station)

Big Sandy

CLARK'S GRANT
1781

Kentucky River

Washington

V I R G I N I A

Clarksville
New Albany
Jeffersonville
Louisville
(Fort Nelson)

Georgetown
(McClelland's
Station)

Licking River

● Paris (Hopewell)

Elk River

New River

Frankfort
Lexington

● Mount Sterling
● Winchester

Ohio River

● Henderson

● Yellow Banks

● Hardinsburg
Elizabethtown

● Bardstown
Harrodsburg

Boonesborough
Richmond

● Danville

Kentucky River

Green River

Stanford
(Logan's Station)

● Crab Orchard

K E N T U C K Y

Cumberland River

Barbourville
(Walker's Cabin)

River

River

● Clarksville

● Pineville

Powell River

Clinch River

Kingsport (Fort Patrick Henry)

● King's Meadows (Sapling Grove)
● Blountville

● Gallatin
Bledsoe's Lick

Holston River

Rogersville
(Carter's Valley)

● Mansker's Lick

Ziegler's Station

■ Fort Blount

Jonesboro
Greeneville

● Elizabethton (Sycamore Shoals)

Eaton's Station
Buchanan's Station

Nashville
(Fort Nashborough)

● Morristown

F R A N K L I N

Nolichucky River

French Broad River

N O R T H

Knoxville (White's Fort)

Gillespie's Station

● Jefferson

Kingston

■ Fort Craig

Little Tennessee River

C A R O L I N A

Duck River

Tennessee River

Broad River

Catawba River

T E N N E S S E E

Hiwassee River

Elk River

River

G E O R G I A

S O U T H
C A R O L I N A

WESTERN LANDS *and the* SURVEY SYSTEM

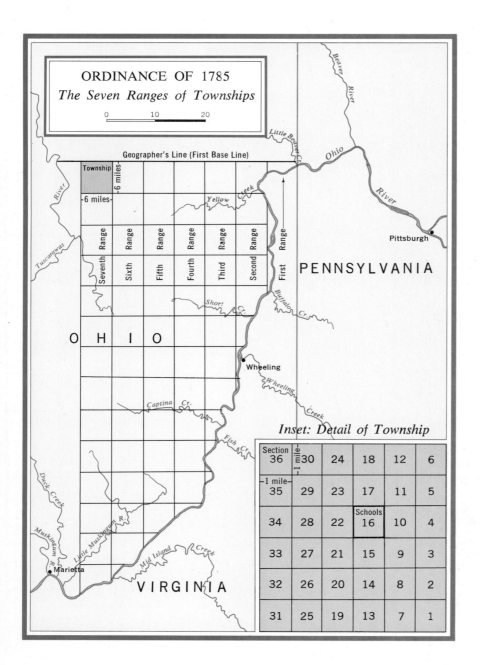

ORDINANCE OF 1785
The Seven Ranges of Townships

0   10   20

Geographer's Line (First Base Line)

Township | -6 miles-

-6 miles-

Seventh Range | Sixth Range | Fifth Range | Fourth Range | Third Range | Second Range | First Range

O H I O

PENNSYLVANIA

Beaver River

Little Beaver Cr.

Ohio River

Pittsburgh

Yellow Creek

Short Cr.

Buffalo Cr.

Wheeling

Wheeling Creek

Captina Cr.

Creek

Fish Cr.

Tuscarawas River

Duck Creek

Muskingum R.

Little Muskingum R.

Mid Island Creek

Marietta

VIRGINIA

Inset: Detail of Township

Section 36	1 mile / 30	24	18	12	6
-1 mile- 35	29	23	17	11	5
34	28	22	Schools 16	10	4
33	27	21	15	9	3
32	26	20	14	8	2
31	25	19	13	7	1

The first survey of the national lands, above, was directed on the spot by Thomas Hutchins, a native of Monmouth County, New Jersey, who was an engineer officer in the British army during the French and Indian War, designed Fort Pitt, and was imprisoned in London in 1779 because he refused to bear arms against his fellow Americans. He escaped to France in 1780 and reached South Carolina in time to join the patriot forces. In 1781 he was appointed Geographer to the United States. The seven ranges of townships which he laid out include today the cities of Steubenville and East Liverpool, and parts or all of several counties. Ohio's virgin soil—Hutchins reported to Congress—was "too rich to produce Wheat . . . but it is well adapted for Indian Corn, Tobacco, Hemp, Flax, Oats &c and . . . abounds with great quantities of Pea Vine, Grass, and nutritious Weeds of which Cattle are very fond."

On September 22, 1785, a crew of surveyors set up their instruments at the spot where the Ohio River leaves Pennsylvania, and began running the first section lines in the United States. The area they completed, before winter and Indian threats ended their work for the season, is outlined in the cartographer's drawing at left. (See also the map of Ohio on previous page.) The dimensions of the new townships (six miles square) and sections (one mile square, equalling 640 acres) were specified by the Continental Congress; they established a pattern which was followed in mapping and selling public lands all the way to the Pacific coast, and down to the present day. Sections, half sections, and quarter sections of land became the basis of farms and ranches; the precise geometrical boundaries between them gave the West its rectilinear roads.

By the law of 1785 the national lands could not be sold or given to settlers until they were surveyed in this manner, with boundaries that followed "meridians and parallels of latitude." The first seven ranges, shown here, added up to about 63 full-sized townships. Of these, nine were reserved for distribution as bounty lands to officers and men of the Continental army. The others were offered at public sale, in lots no smaller than one mile square, at $1 per acre. Before the Constitution went into effect, money received from the sale of such land was divided among the 13 states; after 1789 it went into the Federal treasury.

Within each township itself there were further restrictions. Congress reserved for future national use all sections numbered 8, 11, 26, and 29, and set aside each section 16 to provide funds for the township's schools (inset detail at left). Delegate Rufus King of New York tried to reserve still another section, for the support of churches and ministers. His fellow congressmen voted down this idea, on the grounds that it would "establish" religion, and lead to feuds among various sects competing for Federal funds.

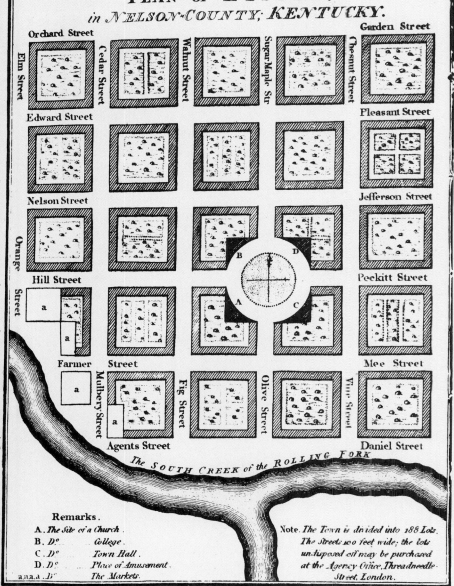

PLAN of LYSTRA,
in NELSON COUNTY, KENTUCKY.

MAP
of
FOUR TOWNSHIPS
in Marengo County
ALABAMA.
Granted to the French Emigrants
by Act of Congress 3rd March 1817,
by
E. PAGUENAUD.

The surveying pattern of regular squares which became standard for public lands was followed also by private developers, as in the overly optimistic plan for Lystra, Kentucky, above. London investors bought 15,000 acres on the Rolling Fork of Kentucky's Salt River, and laid out a town with 188 lots and named streets in 1794. The promoters offered a free lot to the first congressman, senator, and college president who would settle in Lystra, but there seem to have been no takers, for the town never materialized. At right is a similar plan, involving government-owned land in west central Alabama, near the junction of the Black Warrior and Tombigbee rivers. Congress in 1828 set aside four surveyed townships for the free use of French immigrants, brought over by the "Tombeckbee Association," to introduce grape and olive cultivation in a region which was recently taken from the Choctaw Indians.

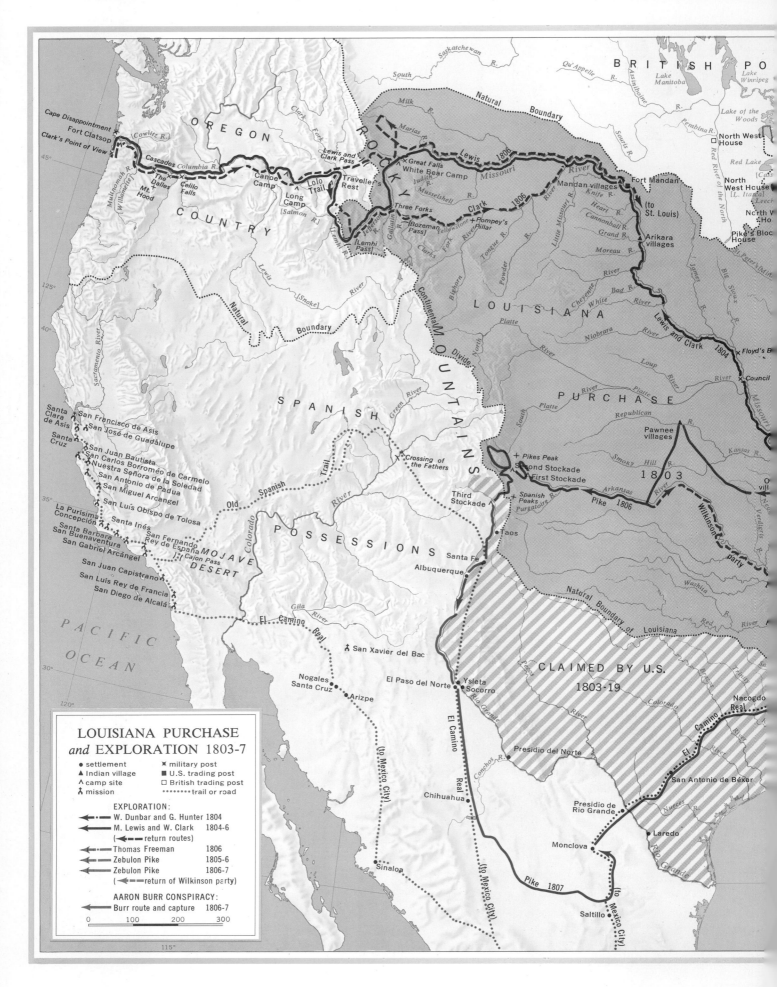

LOUISIANA PURCHASE and EXPLORATION 1803-7

- ● settlement
- ▲ Indian village
- ∧ camp site
- ⚲ mission
- ✳ military post
- ■ U.S. trading post
- □ British trading post
- ·········· trail or road

EXPLORATION:
- W. Dunbar and G. Hunter 1804
- M. Lewis and W. Clark 1804-6
- (◄--- return routes)
- Thomas Freeman 1806
- Zebulon Pike 1805-6
- Zebulon Pike 1806-7
- (◄--- return of Wilkinson party)

AARON BURR CONSPIRACY:
- Burr route and capture 1806-7

0   100   200   300

CLAIMED BY U.S. 1803-19

SPANISH POSSESSIONS

LOUISIANA PURCHASE 1803

OREGON COUNTRY

PACIFIC OCEAN

BRITISH PO...

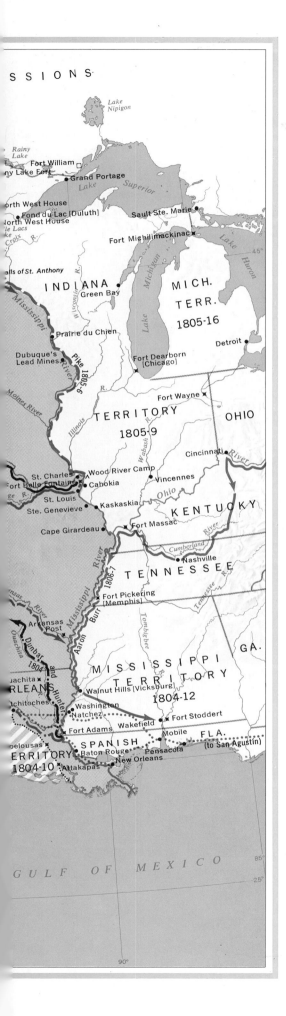

LOUISIANA ACQUIRED

In 1801 Thomas Jefferson expressed the opinion that the United States already possessed enough territory to satisfy its expanding population for a hundred, perhaps for a thousand, generations. He was also committed to reducing the national debt. By 1803, however, he had nearly doubled the area of the country by buying Louisiana territory, and had floated a $13 million bond issue to pay for it.

The key to his reversal was New Orleans, which Jefferson called the "single spot, the possessor of which is our natural and habitual enemy." Western farmers floated their produce down the river network to New Orleans, there to be reloaded on ocean-going vessels for shipment to eastern markets. When Spain (having agreed to return Louisiana to France) canceled the Americans' "right of deposit" at New Orleans in 1802, Jefferson was prepared to go to any length to regain that right. He offered to buy New Orleans. The French countered by offering him all of Louisiana for $15 million. Reluctantly, he agreed.

Louisiana's western boundary was not known in 1803. Jefferson, already intensely curious about the West, sent a number of explorers into the region. Lewis and Clark, who found a route from the Missouri to the Columbia, and Zebulon Pike, who in 1805–6, prior to his trip to the Colorado Rockies, had explored the upper Mississippi, are the best known of these. Farther south, the parties of Thomas Freeman and of William Dunbar and George Hunter were turned back by Spanish forces. Spain's interest extended throughout the Southwest, from the California missions to east Texas. The possibility of carving an empire from this vast area was one element in the mysterious conspiracy of Aaron Burr, who was arrested in Mississippi Territory and charged with treason while leading an "army" of 60 followers toward New Orleans in 1807.

GASS, *Journal,* 1812

This 1812 print shows Clark and some of his men hunting bears.

What made Lewis and Clark's expedition important was not that the men explored new territory, but that they were meticulous amateur scientists. Jefferson ordered Meriwether Lewis, who was his secretary, to collect specimens of plant and animal life, survey soil conditions, look for mineral deposits, keep a record of climate and rainfall, and, of course, map the region. Lewis chose William Clark, an Indian fighter, as co-captain. They set out from St. Louis in May, 1804, reached the Pacific in November, 1805, and after waiting vainly through the winter for a ship, returned overland, arriving back in St. Louis in September, 1806.

They brought back hundreds of specimens (including two bear cubs which Jefferson kept in a pit on the White House lawn) and detailed journals. Lewis died in 1809, and the journals were not published until 1814. Meanwhile, Clark prepared a map of the West. A section of it, reproduced above, shows the mountain wilderness of present-day Idaho (right), traversed by the explorers in getting from the headwaters of the Missouri to the Snake (Lewis River) and the Columbia (left). Clark added to the map information supplied by trappers and others who followed him to the West, and whom he quizzed when they returned to St. Louis.

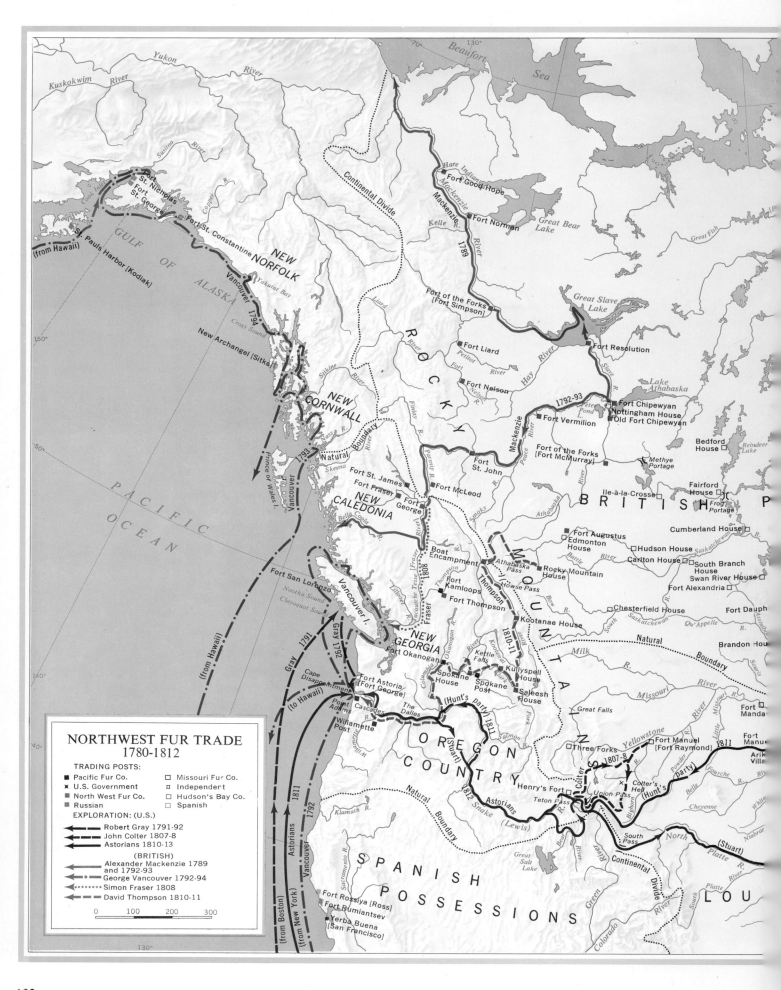

NORTHWEST FUR TRADE
1780-1812

TRADING POSTS:
- ■ Pacific Fur Co.
- ✕ U.S. Government
- ■ North West Fur Co.
- ■ Russian
- □ Missouri Fur Co.
- ⊞ Independent
- □ Hudson's Bay Co.
- □ Spanish

EXPLORATION: (U.S.)
- ⟵ Robert Gray 1791-92
- ⟵ John Colter 1807-8
- ⟵ Astorians 1810-13

(BRITISH)
- ⟵ Alexander Mackenzie 1789 and 1792-93
- ⟵ George Vancouver 1792-94
- ⟵⋯ Simon Fraser 1808
- ⟵ David Thompson 1810-11

0   100   200   300

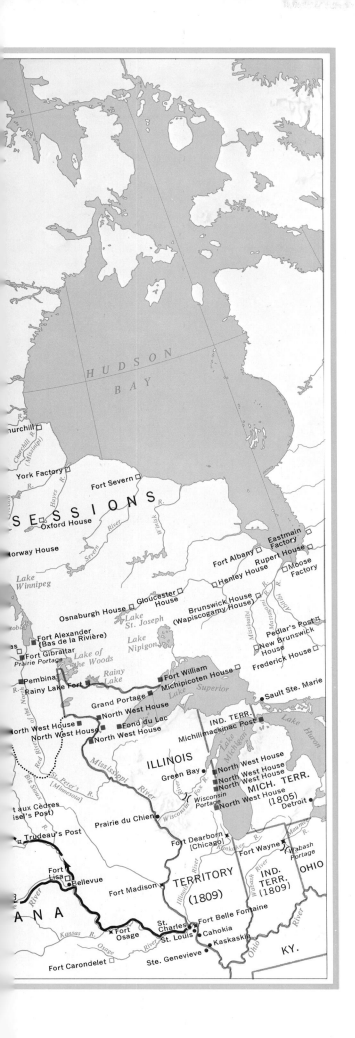

FUR POSTS *to the* PACIFIC COAST

Herds of timid, defenseless sea otters, swimming on their backs, and nursing their young as they swam, attracted the first shiploads of commercial hunters to the Northwest's Pacific coast. The sea otter's deep brown-gold pelt was the costliest in the world, and brought especially high prices in China; it supplied the basis for most of the trade which the Chinese government allowed to foreigners in the 18th and early 19th centuries. Russians from Alaska, Spaniards from Mexico, Britons following Captain Cook, and Yankee skippers from around Cape Horn, collected cargoes of otter skins from California to the Aleutians, and established claims to sovereignty there for their respective nations.

Robert Gray, of Rhode Island and Boston, took his trading ship *Columbia* across the bar at Cape Disappointment on May 11, 1792; his feat (later duplicated by Britain's Vancouver) gave the Northwest's great river its name, and helped, eventually, to make the United States owner of the Oregon Country. England and Spain almost went to war over a fur post at Nootka Sound, on Vancouver Island; the Nootka Convention, which they signed in 1790, opened vast areas north of Puget Sound to British exploitation.

Farther east, fierce competition between the Hudson's Bay Company of London and the North West Company of Montreal depleted central Canada of furs and stimulated a race toward the West. Alexander Mackenzie of the North West Company was the first explorer to reach the Pacific overland (1793), 12 years before Lewis and Clark. He started from Old Fort Chipewyan, on Lake Athabaska, and followed the Peace, Parsnip, Fraser, and Bella Coola rivers. (Four years earlier, in 1789, Mackenzie explored to the Arctic Ocean the northward flowing river which bears his name.) Other North West Company partners, Simon Fraser and David Thompson, pushed across the Canadian Rockies to found posts in present-day British Columbia, Montana, Idaho, and Washington.

Manuel Lisa of the Missouri Fur Company followed Lewis and Clark's trail from St. Louis to central Montana, and sent John Colter on a trading trip through the Wind River and Teton mountains. Wilson Hunt led a party for John Jacob Astor's Pacific Fur Company to the mouth of the Columbia, where he was joined by other Astor employees arriving by sea. Fort Astoria, which they built as a fur post, was doomed by the War of 1812, and was sold to the North West Company. Robert Stuart, returning with reports for Astor, discovered South Pass (with Indian help), and traversed much of the future Oregon Trail, 1812–13.

A ROBUST YOUNG NAVY

Congress awarded this gold medal to Captain Thomas Truxton of the U.S.S. Constellation *for his victory over the powerful French frigate,* La Vengeance, *in West Indian waters, in 1800.*

During the American Revolution, the Navy had acquitted itself with distinction against the British, producing a great hero in John Paul Jones, who terrorized the British coast between 1778 and 1780 in such vessels as the *Ranger* and the *Bonhomme Richard.* After the Treaty of Paris, however, the Navy was allowed to decline until in 1797 it possessed only a handful of revenue cutters. In that year, responding to French depredations against American merchantmen, Congress authorized the construction of three frigates, the *Constitution,* the *United States,* and the *Constellation,* which proved to be the most formidable warships of their era. In 1798 Congress established a separate Department of the Navy and began a still larger program of naval expansion. By 1800, while unable to stop attacks on American shipping on the high seas, the Navy was able to protect American waters fairly effectively.

When he became President, the peace-loving and parsimonious Jefferson severely cut back naval appropriations, which had consumed almost a quarter of the nation's revenues during the Adams administration. He laid up seven of the Navy's 13 frigates, intending to rely upon tiny, 50-foot gunboats to protect the coast. Gunboats were cheap—$10,000 to $14,000 each, compared to $300,000 for a frigate—and easily maintained. Since they were small, the work of building them could be parceled out among dozens of small-town shipyards. This was good politics, but as historian Henry Adams put it, it left the United States "at the mercy of any Power which might choose to rob it."

However, Jefferson's economy drive was disrupted by the Pasha of Tripoli. The North African states of Tripolitania, Tunisia, Algeria, and Morocco had been exacting tribute from the European powers for many years under threat of attacking their merchant vessels in the Mediterranean. After independence, the United States also contributed, paying each of these pirate states between $20,000 and $30,000 a year for what was at best partial immunity against attack. In 1801, after Jefferson had refused to increase these payments, the Pasha declared war on American ships.

The President disliked paying tribute even more than paying for a navy; he dispatched a squadron to the Mediterranean to blockade the port of Tripoli and convoy American merchantmen. The war dragged on, and finally, in 1803, a stronger force commanded by Commodore Edward Preble in the U.S.S. *Constitution* was sent to deal with the problem. Although he lost the spanking new frigate *Philadelphia,* which ran on a reef while pursuing a pirate cruiser off Tripoli and was captured, Preble pressed the enemy hard, bombarding Tripoli five times during the summer of 1804 and causing much damage. Victory came in June, 1805, after almost the entire American Navy had been sent to the Mediterranean. The combined threat of this force—and that of a motley army of Americans, Greeks, and Arabs, organized in Alexandria by an American adventurer, William Eaton, which captured the cities of Bomba and Derna in April, 1805—persuaded the Pasha to make peace.

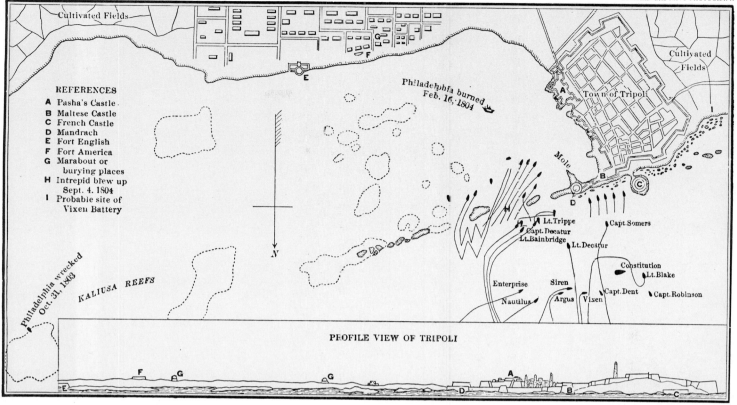

REFERENCES
A Pasha's Castle
B Maltese Castle
C French Castle
D Mandrach
E Fort English
F Fort America
G Marabout or
   burying places
H Intrepid blew up
   Sept. 4. 1804
I Probable site of
   Vixen Battery

Most of the excitement in the Barbary war was concentrated around the port of Tripoli. After the pirates extricated the Philadelphia from the Kaliusa reefs (left, above), they towed her to within the protection of their shore batteries for refitting. On the night of February 16, 1804, Commodore Preble, now blockading the port, sent 25-year-old Lieutenant Stephen Decatur in a captured ketch to destroy her. The pirates, taking the ketch for one of their own, permitted it to come alongside the Philadelphia, whereupon the Americans swept the decks and set fire to the captured frigate, escaping without the loss of a man.

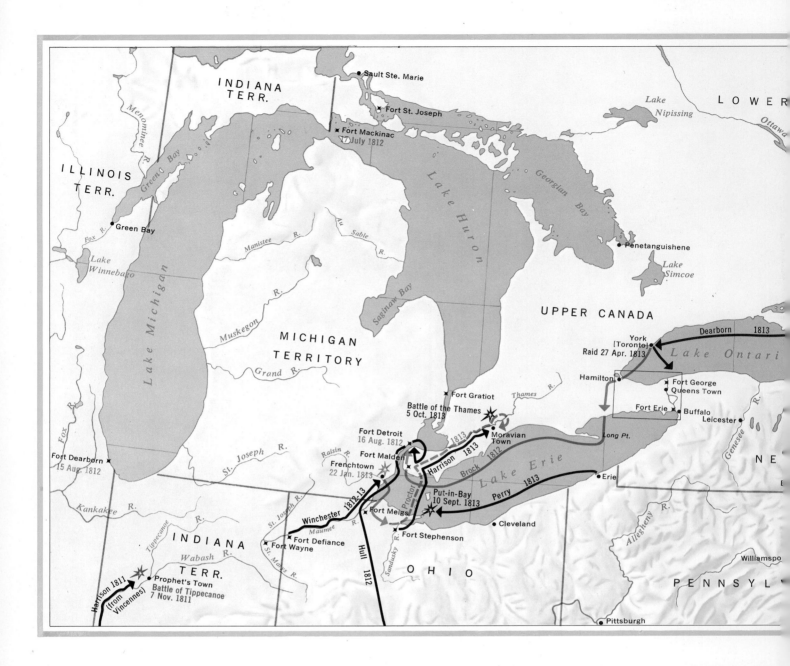

SECOND WAR
with ENGLAND

When the War of 1812 broke out, westerners were eager to attack Canada, hoping to take over rich farmlands north of Lake Erie. In July, 1812, General William Hull, after marching to Detroit, crossed into Canada with 2,200 men, but when Indians threatened his flank he fell back and then meekly surrendered Detroit to General Isaac Brock. Initial American thrusts in the Niagara and Lake Champlain regions also failed, and by August, 1812, the British had taken Forts Mackinac and Dearborn.

In 1813 the tide turned somewhat. At Put-in-Bay a naval force under Oliver Hazard Perry destroyed the British Great Lakes fleet, making Detroit untenable. William Henry Harrison, hero of the 1811 Battle of Tippecanoe, which had scattered members of Tecumseh's Indian confederacy, then moved into Canada, defeating the British at the Battle of the Thames.

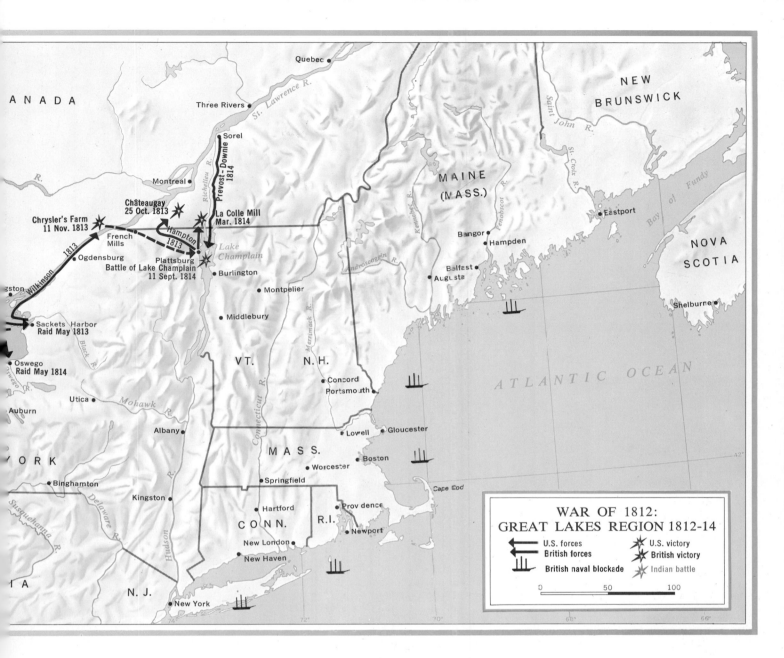

WAR OF 1812: GREAT LAKES REGION 1812-14

⬅ U.S. forces	✦ U.S. victory
⬅ British forces	✦ British victory
⬛ British naval blockade	✦ Indian battle

0   50   100

A force under Henry Dearborn burned York (now Toronto), and moved on, under Winfield Scott, to capture Fort George. The British retreated westward (map at right), but at Stoney Creek they defeated the pursuing Americans, capturing Generals Winder and Chandler. Campaigns in the Montreal-Lake Champlain theater (above) proved similarly indecisive.

The next summer Americans captured Fort Erie (right) and drove north, defeating the enemy at the Chippewa River and fighting a superior force to a draw at Lundy's Lane. But then they fell back, eventually recrossing the Niagara River. That fall the British struck south from the St. Lawrence under Sir George Prevost. However, when his fleet was smashed at the Battle of Lake Champlain by Thomas Macdonough, Prevost abandoned the campaign. The war in the north was a standoff.

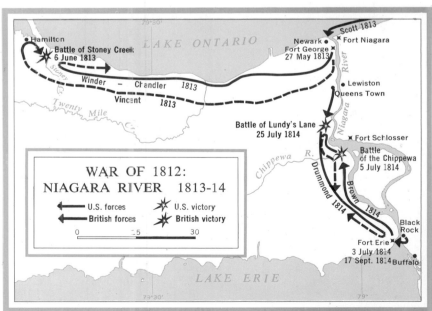

WAR OF 1812: NIAGARA RIVER 1813-14

⬅ U.S. forces	✦ U.S. victory
⬅ British forces	✦ British victory

0   15   30

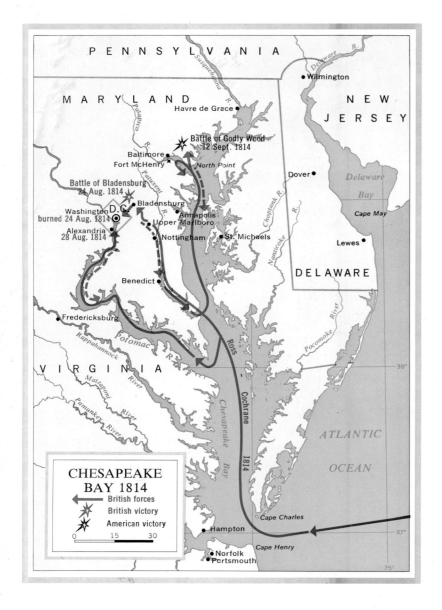

CHESAPEAKE
BAY 1814
← British forces
✶ British victory
✶ American victory
0   15   30

BRITISH FAILURES

In Atlantic waters, sea power gave the British the upper hand throughout the war. With a tight blockade pinning the powerful American frigates in their home ports, the enemy could attack at will along the coast. After Napoleon's exile to Elba temporarily ended the fighting in Europe, Britain increased pressure on the United States. Prevost's Lake Champlain offensive of 1814 (previous page) was part of a three-pronged drive. A second force, under General Robert Ross and Admiral Sir Alexander Cochrane, landed in Maryland and marched on Washington. (A squadron of American gunboats fled up the Patuxent River, there to be blown up to avoid capture.) Troops defending the capital retreated in disorder from Bladensburg, and the British took Washington easily, burning the White House and many public buildings. However, when Cochrane's ships moved against Baltimore, the guns of Fort McHenry held them off, and Ross's troops were badly mauled at Godly Wood. Unable to take Baltimore, the invaders withdrew to Jamaica in the West Indies.

The third phase of the British offensive fared still worse. In Jamaica, Cochrane embarked 7,500 troops under General Sir Edward Pakenham and sailed for New Orleans. On December 14, at the mouth of Lake Borgne, the British overcame a small force of American gunboats. Putting his troops ashore, Pakenham headed them for the Mississippi. A few miles below New Orleans they were met by an American army under Andrew Jackson, famous by now as an Indian fighter (his Tennesseans, retaliating for Indian assaults at Burnt Corn Creek and Fort Mims, had attacked severely at Talladega, Horseshoe Bend, and elsewhere). At Pensacola, Jackson had beaten off a British threat to Mobile and had then hastened to New Orleans. After halting Pakenham's advance elements on December 23, he threw up a formidable defensive line below the city and waited for the main British attack (see pages 140–41).

This British view of the burning of Washington exaggerates the destruction.

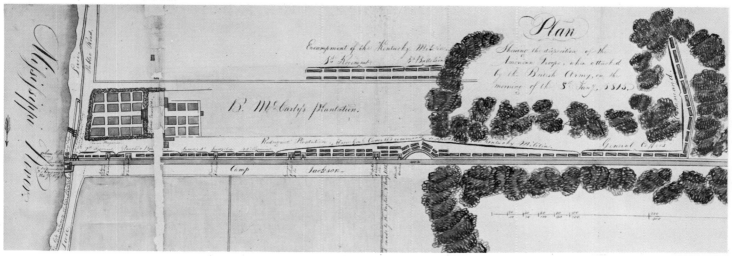

Jackson's defense line below New Orleans is shown above in a contemporary plan.

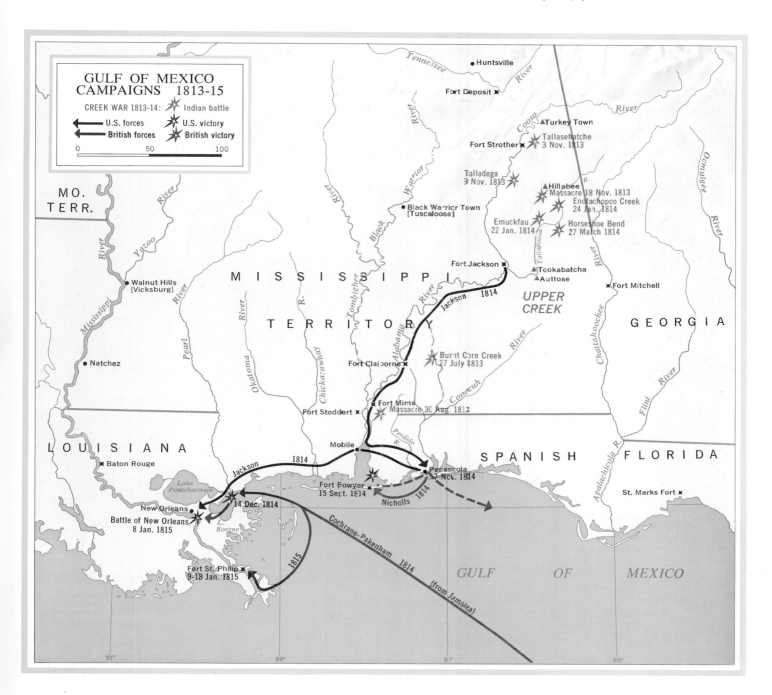

GULF OF MEXICO CAMPAIGNS 1813-15

CREEK WAR 1813-14:

⭐ Indian battle

← U.S. forces   ⭐ U.S. victory

← British forces   ⭐ British victory

0 — 50 — 100

MO. TERR.

Huntsville

Tennessee River

Fort Deposit

Coosa River

Turkey Town

Fort Strother   Tallasehatche 3 Nov. 1813

Talladega 9 Nov. 1813   Hillabee Massacre 18 Nov. 1813

Black Warrior Town [Tuscaloosa]   Enotachopco Creek 24 Jan. 1814

Emuckfau 22 Jan. 1814   Horseshoe Bend 27 March 1814

Walnut Hills [Vicksburg]

Yazoo River

MISSISSIPPI

Fort Jackson   UPPER CREEK

Tookabatcha   Auttose   Fort Mitchell

Jackson 1814

TERRITORY

GEORGIA

Natchez

Pearl River   Okatoma   Chickasawhay R.   Tombigbee River   Black Warrior River   Alabama River

Fort Claiborne   Burnt Corn Creek 27 July 1813

Conecuh River   Chattahoochee River   Flint River

LOUISIANA

Baton Rouge

Fort Stoddert   Fort Mims Massacre 30 Aug. 1813

Jackson 1814

Mobile   Perdido R.   SPANISH   FLORIDA

Lake Pontchartrain

Pensacola 7 Nov. 1814

New Orleans   14 Dec. 1814   Fort Bowyer 15 Sept. 1814   Nicholls 1814   St. Marks Fort

Battle of New Orleans 8 Jan. 1815   L. Borgne

Fort St. Philip 9-18 Jan. 1815   1815

Cochrane-Pakenham 1814 (from Jamaica)   GULF   OF   MEXICO

91°   89°   87°   85°

139

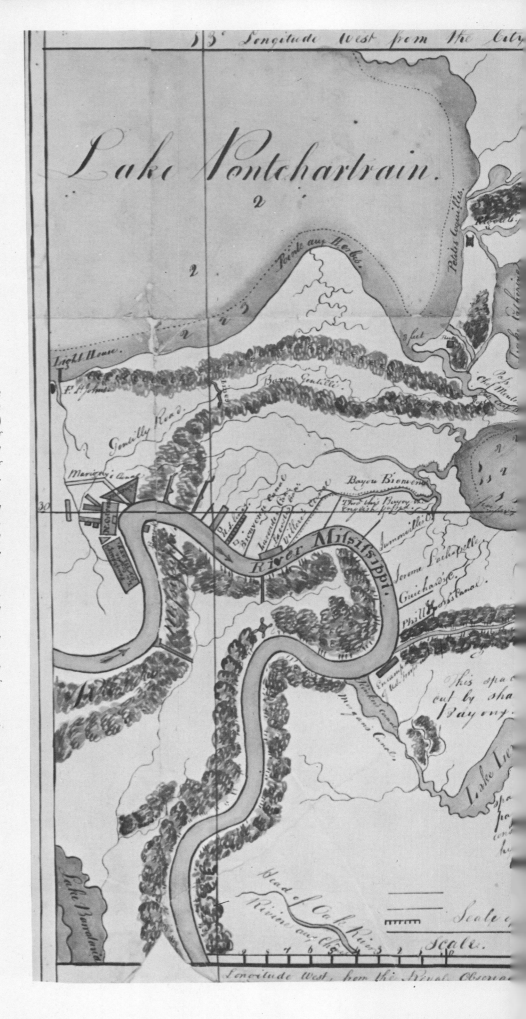

This map drawn by an unknown American shows the twisted, soggy neck of land north of a bend in the Mississippi River (left center) where American defenders won the battle of New Orleans on January 8, 1815. The Royal Navy brought the British invaders by way of the Gulf of Mexico and Lake Borgne (upper right) to within 15 miles of New Orleans' wharves, where 150,000 bales of cotton waited as a rich prize of war. Andrew Jackson's Kentucky and Tennessee riflemen, with local companies of Creoles and Negroes, and pirate cannoneers from Lake Barataria, dug in behind earthworks and logs on the McCarty plantation seven miles below the city. The British charged this strong position (marked "U.S. line" on the map) with magnificent but foolhardy courage. The river on one side, and cypress swamps on the other, funneled the British regulars into a partly flooded field where they were easy targets. More than half the assault force—2,057 officers and men—were casualties; the British commander, Sir Edward Pakenham, was hit three times and bled to death under a live oak tree. American losses were 13 killed and 58 wounded. The battle was the last ever fought between the United States and England. It was also unnecessary: unknown to the participants, the treaty of peace had been signed at Ghent, in French-ruled Belgium, December 24, 1814.

Washington.

Pearl River

Bay of St. Louis

Pass Christian

Pass Maryann

Oyster Bar

Cat Island

South pass.

Pass au pois.

St. Joseph Islands.
Here the U.S. gun boats
were taken 14 Augt 1814.

Malheureous Islands.

Lake Borgne.

Grande Isle.

Longue Isle.

Point Three Bayou

Bayou Point au Chicot

This space has never been accurately surveyed, but is considered a Morass, checkered by Ponds and small Bayous,
the surface of the soil not more than six inches above
the common tide. Bayou point au Chicot has been penetrated by Hunters, who report, that it branches out into a variety channels, and is finally lost in the swamps. This
latter Bayou is the only water course, which has
wood upon its banks, near Chandeleur
Bay.

Part of Chandeleur Bay.

Map
of the seat of the
War in Louisiana
in the years 1814 & 1815.

CHAPTER 5

THE NATIONAL ERA

Historians sometimes refer to the War of 1812 as "the Second War of Independence." They do so not because the British had the remotest chance of reconquering the country, but because, after 1815, Great Britain and all the world realized that the United States had established itself permanently as a free nation. Furthermore, the Americans themselves emerged from the conflict with a heightened sense of national pride and a determination to get on even more rapidly with the task of subduing and civilizing the continent.

Although the years from 1815 to 1860 generated many fierce internal conflicts, culminating in the Civil War, the period was truly a National Era, a time of growth rather than of disruption. During these decades the nation extended its boundaries to the Pacific, partly by diplomacy, partly by war. The rugged western mountains began to yield their harvest of precious metals and furs, the forests of Michigan and Wisconsin their apparently limitless timber. The Indians were driven forever from their hunting grounds east of the Mississippi, and the constricting vise of white civilization began to push them from the western plains and from California. Explorers and hunters located and mapped passes across the mountains; trails were marked out, and tiny islands of settlement were established around mining and logging camps and army posts.

The hectic pace of these developments far exceeded the immediate needs of the people. It resulted from a new attitude of mind, a new social psychology, summed up in the phrase "Manifest Destiny." As late as 1840 Americans had not yet settled a third of the present-day United States. It had taken them about 150 years to advance from Jamestown and Plymouth to the Appalachians; after another three-quarters of a century the frontier ran in a ragged line from Michigan to Missouri and Arkansas. Throughout these long decades the march westward had appeared fraught with peril, the new land something to be won only at the expense of enormous effort and in the face of constant danger from wild animals, Indians, and foreign powers. John Adams expressed the common attitude when he spoke of "conquering" the West from "the trees and rocks and wild beasts." Its possibilities "enflamed" him, but he assumed that the prize would be won only if men were strong and brave and patient.

Suddenly the atmosphere changed. It was as though the Americans, after toiling for generations up a steep slope, had crossed the divide and could see ahead an easy path leading downward to paradise. Almost overnight, they realized that the entire continent, like a ripe fruit, was theirs for the taking. A journalist, John L. O'Sullivan, put their feelings in words. It is, he wrote in 1845, "our *manifest destiny* to overspread the continent allotted by divine Providence for the free development of our yearly multiplying millions." The puny

Appalachians had loomed like Everest before their grandfathers; now Americans dismissed the Rockies as "mere molehills." Before the end of the decade the United States had obtained secure title to the Oregon Country, annexed Texas, and wrested the entire Southwest from Mexico by war.

The men of this dynamic era saw themselves living in magnificent isolation from the broils and intrigues of Europe. At the very time that the Atlantic barrier was fast contracting—by 1850 sailing clippers could cross the ocean in a month, steam-powered vessels in ten days—Americans were luxuriating in the misguided belief that events on the ancestral continent were not their concern. In 1823 President Monroe crystallized popular attitudes in a message to Congress. Mexico and most of South America had recently won their independence, and some of the European Powers were threatening to subdue the rebels by force and return the area to Spain. Monroe announced that the United States would oppose any interference with the "free and independent condition" of the new republics. The age of colonization in the Americas was over. Europe's political system was "essentially different" from the New World's. The United States would not meddle in strictly European affairs and would expect in return that the Powers would not meddle in the Western Hemisphere. Although later generations would make Europe reckon time and again with this bold "Monroe Doctrine," Monroe's government was powerless to enforce it. Its immediate significance was as an expression of the American people's wish to be left, like Voltaire's Candide and Cunégonde, to cultivate their own garden.

Cultivate it they certainly did. Between 1820 and the outbreak of the Civil War, the value of American farm produce rose from about $300 million (in current values) to nearly $1.5 billion. Cotton production zoomed from 209,000 bales in 1815 to 4.5 million bales in 1859. Between 1839 (the first year for which records are available) and 1859, corn production increased from 327 million bushels to 838 million, wheat from 84 million bushels to 173 million. These cold statistics take on life when they are translated into millions of newly plowed acres and tens of thousands of new homesteads in the old Northwest Territory and in the South from Alabama and Mississippi to the wide plains of Texas.

At the same time, manufacturing was taking hold with a rush in New England, in the Middle Atlantic states, and to a lesser extent in the Middle West. By 1860, 1.3 million Americans were earning their living in factories and in handicraft industries. In that year, for example, the nation milled almost 40 million barrels of flour, and wove 845,000 bales of cotton into cloth. Eastern cities, and many in the upper Ohio valley, became veritable hives of industry and commerce in these decades; the town of Lowell, Massachusetts, founded only in 1826, had a population of 32,621 in 1850. In its booming cotton factories, 300,000 spindles turned, and 9,000 power looms wove machine-made thread into cloth for the fast-growing demands of the nation.

Geography interacted with the expansive energies of the American people in other ways. The country's size and varied resources stimulated growth and specialization, but they also posed problems of communication which had widespread economic, social, and political repercussions. In the colonial period each community was to a large extent self contained—trade and commerce were important, but limited in extent. Goods moved from place to place by water—over rivers, along the coast, and across the Atlantic. Each local community had its own craftsmen, merchants, and farmers. A national economy in the modern sense did not exist, and westward expansion decreased the likelihood that one would develop. The cost of moving freight over long distances was prohibitively high except by water, and the rivers of trans-Appalachia flowed from north to south, not from east to west.

Yet during the National Era a genuinely integrated economy did begin to take form; Americans conquered geographical obstacles, building first roads, then canals, and, finally, railroads that linked distant areas and dramatically reduced the cost of transportation. Hard-surfaced roads enabled merchants to move manufactured products across long distances economically, but bulky farm produce demanded more efficient methods. (A team of horses hauling a wagon loaded with grain for a thousand miles would eat up all the grain before it arrived at its destination.) Canals solved this problem because horses towing barges could haul more than 100 times the weight they could transport in wagons. As early as 1830, the nation had over 1,200 miles of canals; by 1840, over 3,000 miles.

Rail transportation proved even more efficient. The iron horse could move heavier loads faster; it could climb mountains, negotiate the roughest terrain, and it was not paralyzed, as canals were, by freezing weather. There were only 23 miles of track in the United States in 1830, but in 1850 there were 9,000 miles and in 1860 over 30,000. These transportation miracles allowed manufacturers in New England to sell their cloth, shoes, and other goods anywhere in the country, and enabled farmers in Illinois and Iowa to raise food for the city dwellers of New England, and even of Europe. The economy boomed, but political and social unity also resulted. The controversy over slavery challenged this unity, but did not destroy it. Indeed, the network of canals and railroads, by tying the Old Northwest to the East, probably prevented the breakup of the Union, for, without it, the Northwest would have been dependent upon use of the Mississippi and would thus have been at the mercy of the seceded South.

the Treaty of Ghent contained no cod-
nsferring territory or redrawing bound-
the peace that it established between Great
tain and the United States reshaped American
borders. In a new atmosphere of friendship the
two countries quickly solved problems that had
vexed their relations ever since the Revolution.
In 1817, in the Rush-Bagot Agreement, they effectively demilitarized the Great Lakes, and the next
year they signed a convention setting the boundary between the United States and Canada from
Lake of the Woods to the Continental Divide at
the 49th parallel. Beyond the Divide the vaguely
defined Oregon Country was to be jointly occupied for ten years. With the border thus at peace,
the Northwest Territory boomed. In 1810 the region north and west of Ohio (see maps at top
right for political changes) had only 31,000 inhabitants. By 1820 its population was above 200,000.

The ending of the War of 1812 also led to the
settlement of outstanding difficulties with Spain.
West Florida had been occupied during the war,
and American pressure on the rest of the peninsula
was increasing fast. With its hold on its Latin
American possessions crumbling, Spain feared
that the United States would seize not only Florida but Spanish Mexico too. To forestall this
possibility, which was increased by the vague-
ness of the Louisiana boundary, Luis de Onís,
the Spanish minister in Washington, agreed to
negotiate a general treaty in 1819 with Secretary
of State John Quincy Adams. No tougher bar-
gainer ever lived than Adams. Besides obtaining
Florida for only $5 million, he forced Onís to cede
a rich section of southwestern Louisiana and to
give up all claims beyond the Rockies north of
the 42nd parallel. Onís even agreed that where
the new line between Louisiana and Mexico followed the Sabine, Red, and Arkansas rivers,
American territory should extend to the west
bank, not merely to midstream. Adams was proud
of this "transcontinental" treaty. "The acquisition
of a definite line of boundary to the [Pacific]
forms a great epoch in our history," he wrote.

*Midshipman Lawrence Kearny of the U.S. Navy drew this
sketch of Pensacola, Florida, after Andrew Jackson captured it—for the second time in four years—in 1818.*

TRANSCONTINENTAL

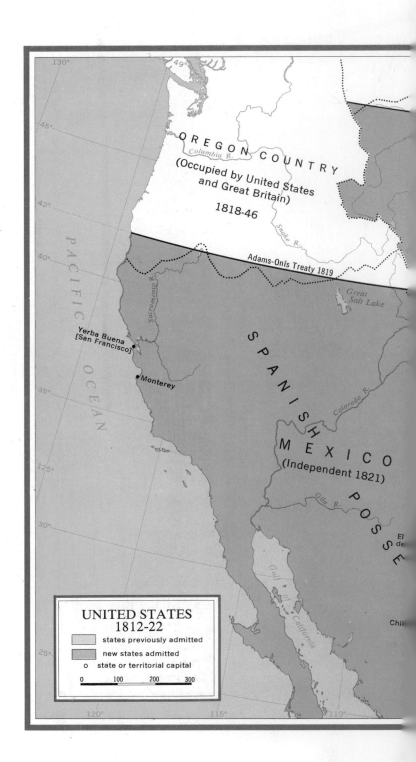

BOUNDARIES

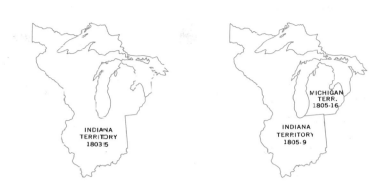

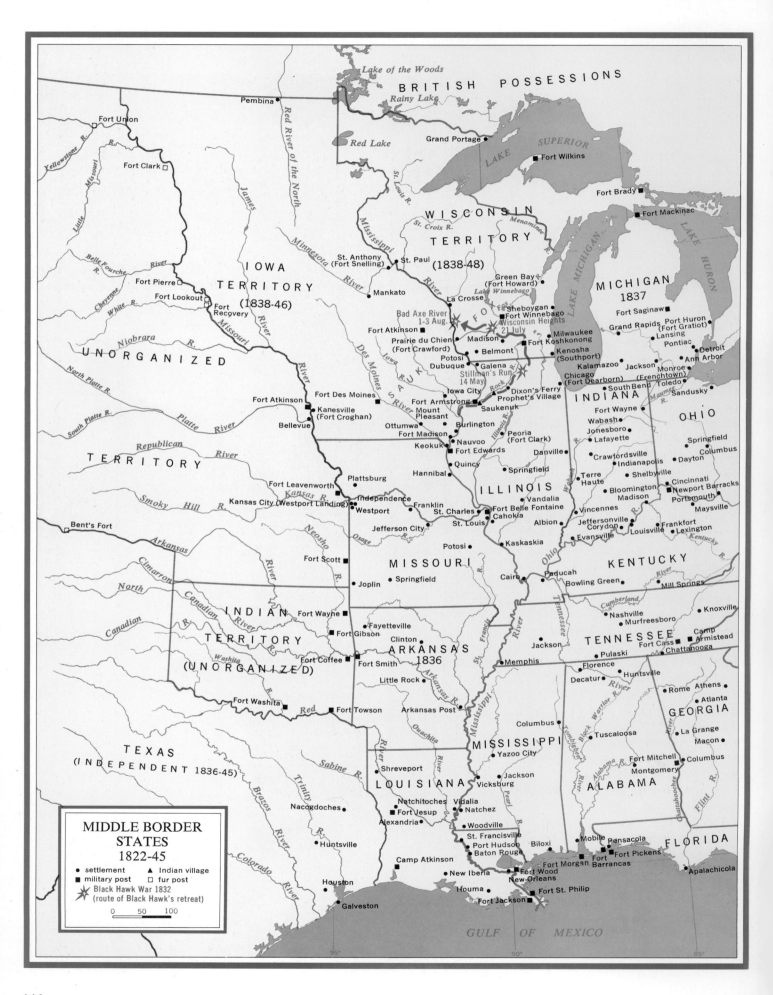

British Possessions

Lake of the Woods
Rainy Lake
Pembina
Fort Union
Red Lake
Grand Portage
Red River of the North
Fort Clark
Yellowstone R.
Little Missouri
Fort Wilkins
LAKE SUPERIOR
James River
St. Louis R.
Fort Brady
Belle Fourche R.
Fort Pierre
Cheyenne R.
White R.
Fort Lookout
Fort Recovery
St. Croix R.
WISCONSIN TERRITORY (1838-48)
Menominee R.
Fort Mackinac
IOWA TERRITORY (1838-46)
Minnesota River
St. Anthony (Fort Snelling)
St. Paul
MICHIGAN 1837
North Platte R.
Niobrara R.
UNORGANIZED
Missouri River
Mankato
Green Bay (Fort Howard)
Fort Saginaw
Lake Winnebago
Grand Rapids
Port Huron (Fort Gratiot)
La Crosse
Lansing
Des Moines River
Bad Axe River 1-3 Aug.
Sheboygan
Fort Winnebago
Wisconsin Heights 21 July
Pontiac
Detroit
Fort Atkinson
Madison
Milwaukee
Fort Koshkonong
Kalamazoo
Jackson
Monroe (Frenchtown)
Ann Arbor
South Platte R.
Prairie du Chien (Fort Crawford)
Belmont
Kenosha (Southport)
Chicago (Fort Dearborn)
South Bend
Toledo
Sandusky
Potosi
Dubuque
Galena
Stillman's Run 14 May
Fort Des Moines
Fort Atkinson
Kanesville (Fort Croghan)
Iowa City
Fort Armstrong
Dixon's Ferry
Prophet's Village
Saukenuk
INDIANA
Fort Wayne
Wabash
OHIO
Republican River
Platte River
Bellevue
Mount Pleasant
Burlington
Jonesboro
Springfield
Smoky Hill R.
TERRITORY
Peoria (Fort Clark)
Lafayette
Columbus
Ottumwa
Fort Madison
Danville
Crawfordsville
Dayton
Fort Leavenworth
Plattsburg
Nauvoo
Indianapolis
Shelbyville
Kansas R.
Keokuk
Fort Edwards
Springfield
Terre Haute
Kansas City (Westport Landing)
Independence
Westport
Hannibal
Quincy
Bloomington
Madison
Cincinnati
Newport Barracks
Portsmouth
Franklin
ILLINOIS
Vandalia
Vincennes
Maysville
Bent's Fort
St. Charles
Fort Belle Fontaine
Cahokia
Albion
Jeffersonville
Corydon
Louisville
Frankfort
Lexington
Arkansas River
Jefferson City
St. Louis
Evansville
Neosho R.
Osage R.
Potosi
Kaskaskia
Ohio R.
KENTUCKY
Kentucky R.
Cimarron R.
North Canadian R.
Fort Scott
MISSOURI
Cairo
Paducah
Cumberland R.
Canadian River
Joplin
Springfield
Bowling Green
Mill Springs
Tennessee R.
INDIAN TERRITORY (UNORGANIZED)
Fort Wayne
Nashville
Knoxville
Fayetteville
Murfreesboro
Camp Armistead
Washita R.
Fort Gibson
Clinton
ARKANSAS 1836
Jackson
TENNESSEE
Fort Cass
Chattanooga
Pulaski
Fort Coffee
Fort Smith
Memphis
Florence
Huntsville
Little Rock
Decatur
Rome
Athens
Fort Washita
Arkansas R.
St. Francis River
Atlanta
GEORGIA
Red River
Fort Towson
Arkansas Post
Columbus
Tuscaloosa
La Grange
Macon
Ouachita R.
MISSISSIPPI
Black Warrior R.
Tombigbee R.
TEXAS (INDEPENDENT 1836-45)
Yazoo City
Fort Mitchell
Columbus
Sabine R.
Shreveport
Jackson
Montgomery
ALABAMA
Alabama R.
Trinity R.
Nacogdoches
LOUISIANA
Vicksburg
Brazos River
Natchitoches
Fort Jesup
Vidalia
Natchez
Pearl R.
Chattahoochee R.
Flint R.
Alexandria
Woodville
Mobile
Pensacola
FLORIDA
Huntsville
St. Francisville
Biloxi
Port Hudson
Baton Rouge
Fort Morgan
Fort Barrancas
Fort Pickens
Colorado River
Camp Atkinson
New Iberia
Fort Wood
Apalachicola
Houston
Houma
New Orleans
Fort Jackson
Fort St. Philip
Galveston
GULF OF MEXICO

MIDDLE BORDER STATES 1822-45

• settlement   ▲ Indian village
■ military post □ fur post
✳ Black Hawk War 1832
   (route of Black Hawk's retreat)

0   50   100

95°   90°   85°

American soldiers on a steamboat, armed with artillery, fire on Black Hawk's fleeing followers, at the junction of the Mississippi and Bad Axe rivers, August 1, 1832. Two days later more Indians were massacred here as they tried to escape to Iowa. This lithograph was made by Henry Lewis, an English-born artist who lived in St. Louis during the Black Hawk War.

SETTLEMENT FRONTIER *and* INDIAN WARS

In the two decades before 1845 more than two million new settlers poured into the former Northwest Territory, which by then was divided into the states of Ohio, Indiana, Michigan, Illinois, and Wisconsin Territory (map on opposite page). The total population of the area, on the eve of the Mexican War, was about 3,500,000. Settlement began in Iowa in 1832; a dozen years later this newest territory had 150,000 people. On the middle and southwest borders a cluster of five new states—Missouri, Arkansas, Louisiana, Mississippi, and Alabama—counted about two million inhabitants in 1845.

In the north a few Indian conflicts only speeded up the pace of settlement. Black Hawk's attempt, in 1832, to repossess ancestral cornfields of the Sauk and Fox tribe in northern Illinois, produced a one-season "war" in which about 1,000 Indians were slaughtered (above). Among militiamen who chased after Black Hawk was Abraham Lincoln, aged 23, who told Congress in an 1848 speech that he did not catch up with "any live, fighting indians . . . but I had a good many bloody struggles with the musquetoes."

In Florida (right) two wars with the Seminoles delayed full-scale settlement for decades. U.S. troops, pursuing runaway slaves, blew up Negro Fort and burned the Seminole village of Fowltown; Andrew Jackson then invaded west Florida—while it belonged to Spain—and captured Pensacola. In the Second Seminole War, which ranged south to Fort Lauderdale, 1,500 American soldiers were killed. The Indian leader Osceola was tricked into captivity, and died in an army prison.

FLORIDA *and* **SEMINOLE WARS** 1817-42

- settlement ▲ Indian village ■ military post
- ✦ First Seminole War 1817-18
- ✸ Second Seminole War 1835-42

0   50   100

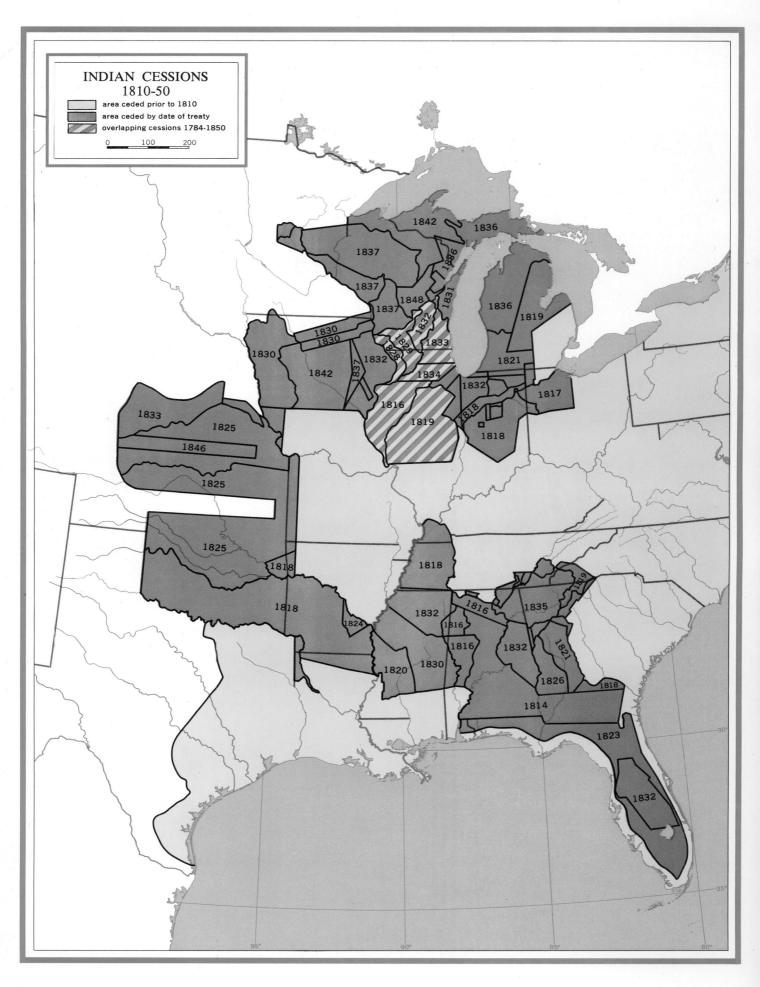

INDIAN CESSIONS
1810-50

area ceded prior to 1810

area ceded by date of treaty

overlapping cessions 1784-1850

0   100   200

REMOVAL
of the
INDIANS

In August, 1830, President Andrew Jackson rode south from his Hermitage home to meet with Chickasaw chieftains at present-day Franklin, Tennessee. Jackson (whose Indian name was, appropriately, Sharp Knife) urged the Indians to abandon all land they occupied within southern states. "Old men!" he admonished. "Lead your children to a land of peace and promise before the Great Spirit shall call you to die. Young chiefs! Forget the prejudices you feel for the soil of your birth. . . ." In any case, the President warned grimly, the Indians would have to go: "You must submit—there is no . . . alternative." Congress had passed, by a 5-vote majority, an Indian Removal Bill sponsored by Jackson's administration.

The extinction of Indian land titles, and the cruel suppression of Indian rights, was most poignant in the South, where five nations named on the map below were bullied by state and Federal governments into mass migrations in the 1830's. Some 50,000 men, women, and children were herded into boats and concentration camps, on their way to barren reservations in the distant Indian Territory. The rich and civilized Cherokees of Georgia, who had converted their language into printed characters, sent their children to college, and lived under a constitution and president, suffered 4,000 deaths from exposure, disease, and harsh treatment on their 1,000-mile-long "Trail of Tears." More than 300 Creeks drowned when an unfit steamboat, assigned to them by the government, blew up in the Mississippi. The expulsion of the southern tribes threw open millions of acres of rich new land for southern planters whose eastern holdings had been depleted by cotton culture.

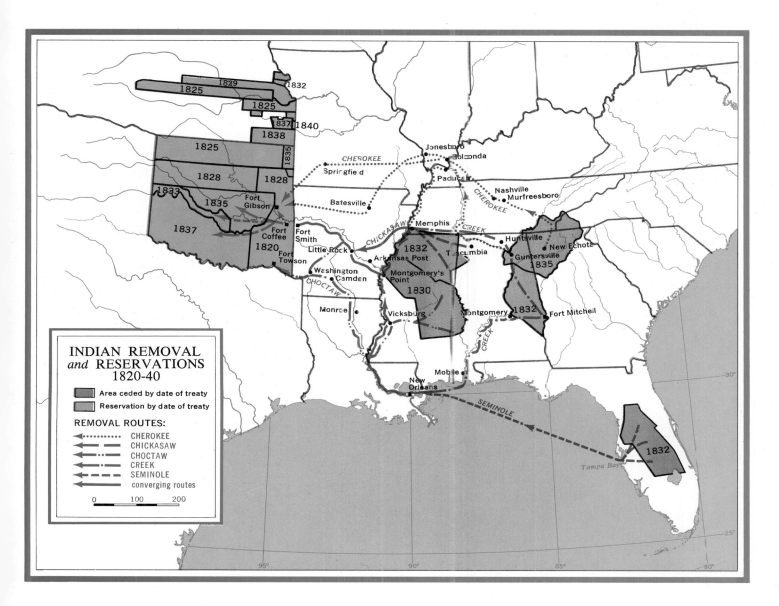

INDIAN REMOVAL *and* RESERVATIONS 1820-40

- ▨ Area ceded by date of treaty
- ▨ Reservation by date of treaty

REMOVAL ROUTES:
- ·········◄ CHEROKEE
- —·—·—◄ CHICKASAW
- —··—··◄ CHOCTAW
- —·—·◄ CREEK
- — — —◄ SEMINOLE
- ——◄ converging routes

0   100   200

ROUTES *of* TRANSPORT *in the* EAST

Except for the post road (now U.S. 1) running from Boston to Savannah, no important intersectional roads existed in colonial times. However, once settlement pushed beyond the Appalachians, good highways became essential. By 1812 there were three main routes westward. One, from New England, ran through Albany and over the Mohawk Turnpike to Lake Erie. From Philadelphia and Baltimore, wagon roads reached west to Pittsburgh. Southerners followed the Great Valley Road and the Nashville and Wilderness roads to central Tennessee and Kentucky. In 1818 the Federal government completed the National Road (now U.S. 40) between Cumberland and Wheeling. Although this route was eventually extended to Vandalia, Illinois, sectional rivalries hampered Federal development—most roads were built by the states or by private turnpike companies which charged tolls.

Canal building began in the 1790's, but none of the canals were as much as 30 miles long until New York began work on the Erie in 1817. The completion of this 363-mile link between Buffalo and the Hudson triggered a canal building boom. Pennsylvania spent $10 million on a project linking Philadelphia and Pittsburgh, mainly by water; Ohio and Indiana built canals between Lake Erie and Marietta, Portsmouth, Cincinnati, and Evansville on the Ohio; Illinois between Chicago and a tributary of the Mississippi. Canal users paid tolls, but in many cases the cost of construction far exceeded the revenues earned; some states were bankrupted by their ill-advised canal investments. But the country benefited immensely. One striking feature revealed by the map at right is the relative scarcity of long-distance transportation facilities in the South, as compared with the North. Although southern rivers carried much traffic, they did not provide the intrasectional connections that had such a stimulating effect on the economy of the North.

A sketch of a once-common scene along the Erie Canal demonstrates the ease with which two horses, plodding along the towpath, could move a heavy grain barge.

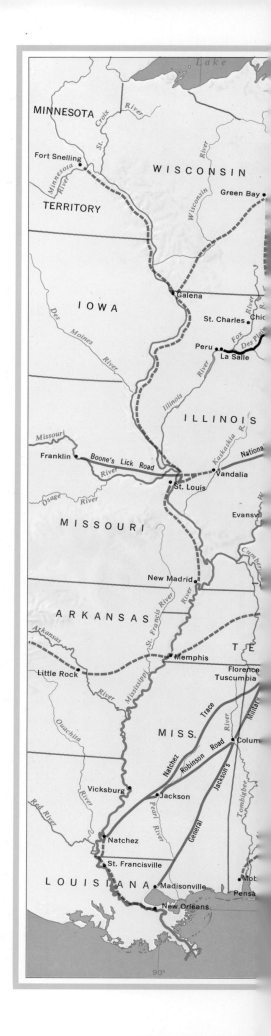

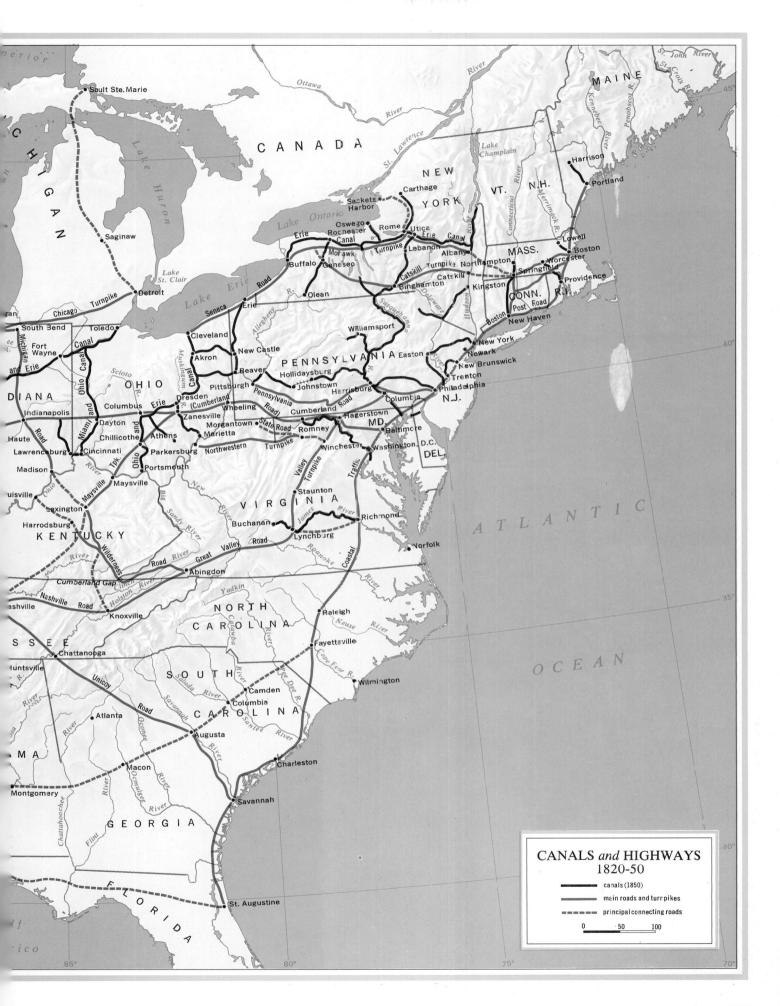

CANALS and HIGHWAYS
1820-50

━━━━━ canals (1850)

━━━━━ main roads and turnpikes

╌╌╌╌╌ principal connecting roads

0   50   100

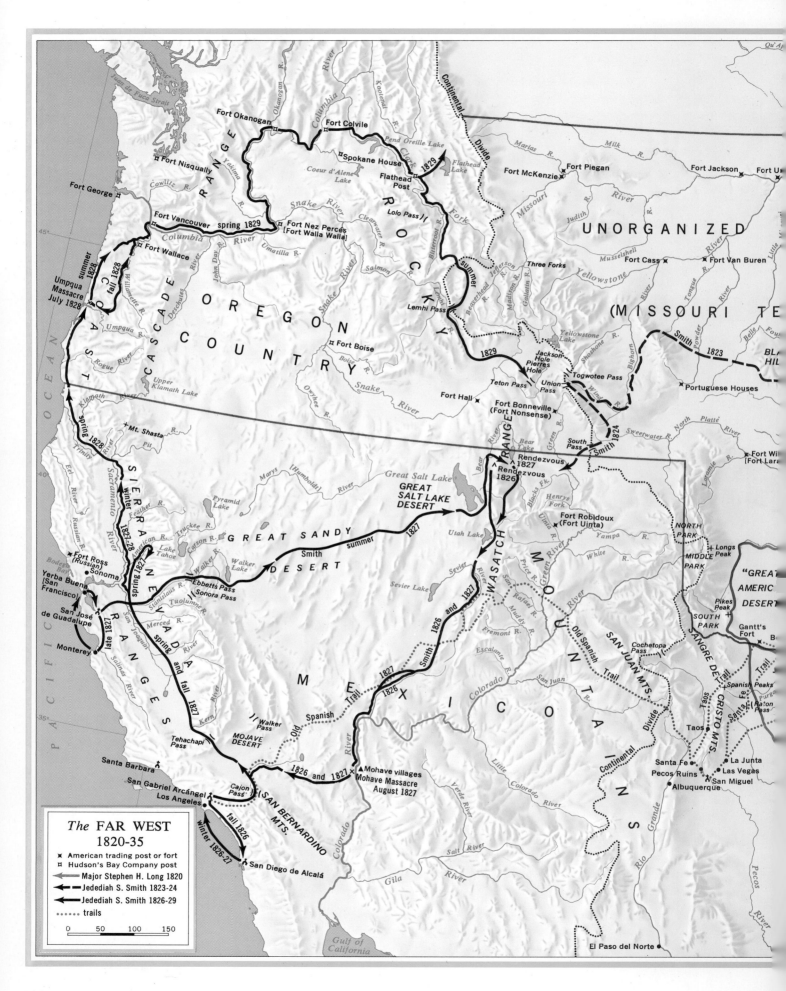

Fort Okanogan
Fort Colvile
Fort Nisqually
Spokane House
Flathead Lake
Fort McKenzie
Fort Piegan
Fort Jackson
Fort U
Continental Divide
1829
Flathead Post
Okanogan
Pend Oreille Lake
Clark Fork
Marias R.
Milk R.
UNORGANIZED
Fort George
Columbia River
Coeur d'Alene Lake
Yakima
Missouri River
Judith
Musselshell R.
Fort Cass
Fort Van Buren
Fort Vancouver spring 1829
Fort Nez Percés [Fort Walla Walla]
Snake River
Clearwater R.
Lolo Pass
Bitterroot R.
summer
Jefferson
Three Forks
Yellowstone
(MISSOURI TE
Fort Wallace
Columbia River
John Day R.
Deschutes R.
Umatilla R.
Salmon
Salmon
Lemhi Pass
Beaverhead
Madison R.
Gallatin R.
Yellowstone Lake
R.
summer 1828
fall 1828
Umpqua Massacre July 1828
OREGON COUNTRY
Umpqua River
Fort Boise
Boise R.
1829
Jackson Hole Pierres Hole
Teton Pass
Togwotee Pass
Bighorn
Smith 1823
BLA HIL
Rogue River
CASCADE RANGE
Upper Klamath Lake
COAST
Fort Hall
Fort Bonneville (Fort Nonsense)
Union Pass
Wind R.
Portuguese Houses
spring 1828
Mt. Shasta
Klamath River
Pit R.
Trinity R.
Snake River
Owyhee R.
RANGE
Bear Lake
South Pass
Smith 1824
Sweetwater R.
North Platte R.
Fort Wi [Fort Lara
Eel River
Russian River
Marys [Humboldt] River
Great Salt Lake
GREAT SALT LAKE DESERT
Rendezvous 1827
Rendezvous 1826
Green River
Fort Robidoux (Fort Uinta)
Yampa R.
NORTH PARK
Longs Peak
SIERRA
winter 1827-28
Pyramid Lake
Utah Lake
Uinta R.
White R.
MIDDLE PARK
Sacramento River
Fort Ross (Russian)
Sonoma
Feather R.
Truckee R.
Carson R.
Lake Tahoe
GREAT SANDY DESERT
summer 1827
Smith
WASATCH
Price R.
"GREAT AMERIC DESERT
Yerba Buena [San Francisco]
guide 1827
American R.
Walker Lake
Walker Lake
Smith summer
Sevier R.
RANGE
San Rafael R.
Muddy R.
Fremont R.
Pikes Peak
SOUTH PARK
Gantt's Fort
San José de Guadalupe
NEVADA
Stanislaus R.
Ebbetts Pass
Sonora Pass
Sevier Lake
MOUNTAINS
Old Spanish Trail
Cochetopa Pass
SAN JUAN MTS.
Monterey
late 1827
Tuolumne R.
Merced R.
Smith 1826 and 1827
Colorado River
SANGRE DE CRISTO MTS.
Spanish Peaks
San Joaquin River
spring and fall 1827
Kern R.
San Juan R.
Santa Fe Trail
Spanish Fe Trail
Raton Pass
Santa Barbara
MEXICO
1827
1826
Smith 1827 1826
Escalante R.
Little Colorado R.
Continental Divide
Taos
La Junta
Tehachapi Pass
Walker Pass
Spanish Trail
MOJAVE DESERT
Old Spanish Trail
Verde River
Santa Fe
Pecos Ruins
Las Vegas
San Miguel
San Gabriel Arcángel
Los Angeles
Cajon Pass
SAN BERNARDINO MTS.
1826 and 1827
Mohave villages
Mohave Massacre August 1827
Colorado River
Albuquerque
fall 1826
Winter 1826-27
San Diego de Alcalá
Gila River
Salt River
Rio Grande
Pecos River
El Paso del Norte

The FAR WEST 1820-35

✗ American trading post or fort
� Hudson's Bay Company post
→ Major Stephen H. Long 1820
➤ Jedediah S. Smith 1823-24
➤ Jedediah S. Smith 1826-29
····· trails

0   50   100   150

Gulf of California

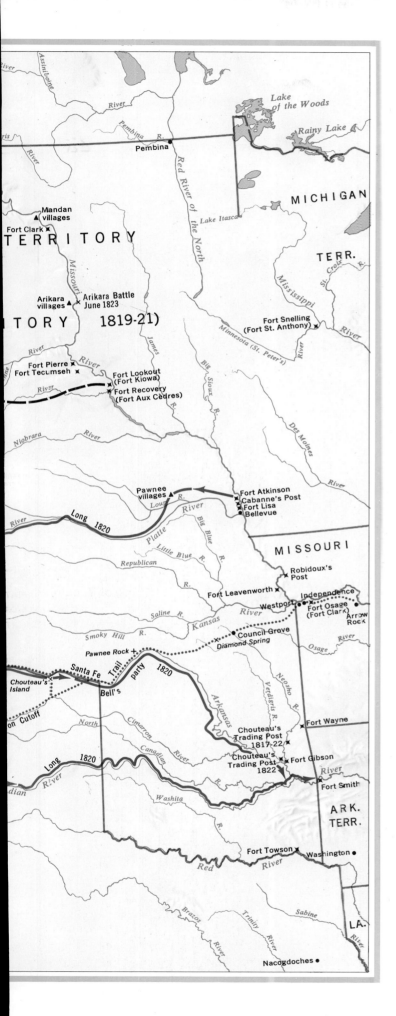

A distant view of the Rockies illustrated Major Long's report.

INVESTIGATING
the WEST

"The whole of this region seems peculiarly adapted as a range for buffalos, wild goats, and other wild game . . . It is . . . of course, uninhabitable by a people depending on agriculture." So reported Major Stephen H. Long, a Dartmouth-educated Army engineer who led an exploring party through present Nebraska and Colorado to the Rocky Mountains in 1820. The published account of Long's expedition included a map on which the words "GREAT AMERICAN DESERT" were printed across the high plains that lie east of Pikes Peak. Major Long thought this treeless expanse would be useful, however, "inasmuch as it is calculated to serve as a barrier against too great an expansion of our population westward."

In 1821 the Hudson's Bay Company absorbed its Canadian rival, the North West Company (see pages 132–33). The resulting monopoly dominated the Columbia River fur trade, and impelled Americans to find new supplies of beaver amid the peaks and streams of the Rockies, and in unexplored areas farther west. Among the men who excelled in this enterprise—and added hugely to geographical knowledge—was Jedediah Strong Smith, a sober, pious upstate New Yorker whose travels ranged from the Bighorn Mountains to Spanish San Diego, across the Great Basin to Great Salt Lake (the first such crossing recorded by white men), and north to the Canadian border. Smith survived Indian battles with the Arikara in South Dakota, the Mojave in Arizona, and the Umpqua in Oregon, and made a fortune from furs. In 1831, at the age of 32, he was killed by Comanches near Santa Fe on what he had planned as his last trading trip. A map he drew of his journeys was roughly copied in the 1840's, but the original has been lost.

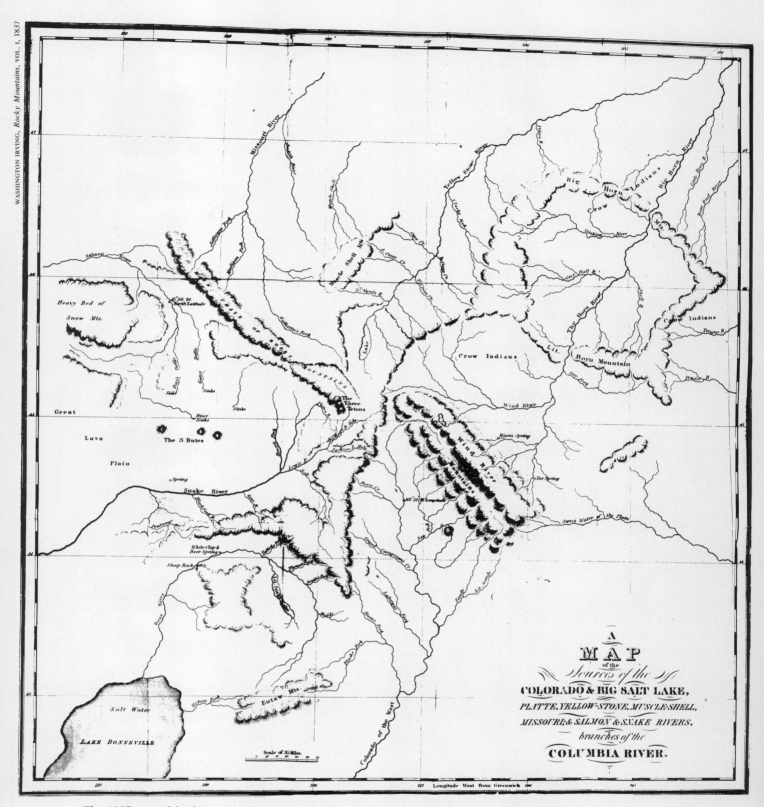

This 1837 map of the fur trappers' country was drawn by Captain Benjamin L. E. de Bonneville, a French-born U.S. Army officer, whose adventures as a western fur trader were described in a book by Washington Irving.

MOUNTAIN MEETING PLACES

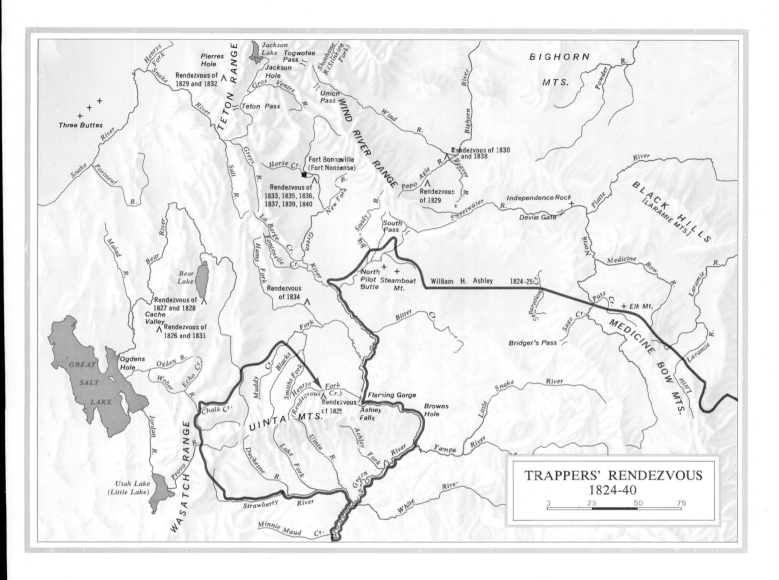

TRAPPERS' RENDEZVOUS 1824-40

Emerging from their neatly built lodges, in the clear, cold waters of western streams, hundreds of thousands of hard-working beavers were lured into traps and drowned by human cunning in the years before 1840. The beaver's luxurious underfur ("muffoon") was equipped with microscopic barbs which made it the ideal ingredient of matted felt used to manufacture men's tall hats, fashionable then in Europe and America. A beaver's pelt weighed about two pounds, and brought $3 a pound at the annual fur marketing fairs—the celebrated trappers' rendezvous—held at scattered mountain meadow locations (above) in what is now the four-state area of Utah, Wyoming, Idaho, and Montana.

The originator of the rendezvous system was General William Henry Ashley, a Virginia-born Missouri politician who made a big fortune in four years of wilderness dealings, and then remained in St. Louis and Washington, where he was a Congressman, financing other fur speculators. Ashley in 1822 published a famous want ad in the *Missouri Gazette* of St. Louis, asking for 100 "Enterprising Young Men" to work in the fur trade. He and his partner Andrew Henry out-

fitted white trappers and guaranteed to buy their catch, along with that of competing Indians, and "free trappers" who equipped themselves. The British Hudson's Bay Company was already sending its brigades as far south as the Great Salt Lake (where Peter Skene Ogden, a Hudson's Bay executive, gave his name to a river and a modern city). Racing to compete with the Hudson's Bay men, Ashley in 1824 opened up a new overland route into western Wyoming, and personally piloted a bullboat which descended the dangerous, unexplored Green River, then circled around to Henrys Fork, where the first rendezvous was held (1825). Ashley returned in 1826 for another rendezvous in Cache Valley west of Bear Lake. Perhaps the most famous rendezvous was held in 1832 at Pierres Hole (named for an Iroquois trapper). Nearly 1,000 whites and Indians attended, and the meeting was climaxed by an all-day gun fight between Gros Ventre Indians on one side, and Flatheads, Nez Perces, and white trappers on the other. A business panic in 1837, and a change in men's fashions to silk hats, instead of beaver felt, brought the picturesque rendezvous to their end.

ACROSS *the* ROCKIES
and the SIERRA NEVADA

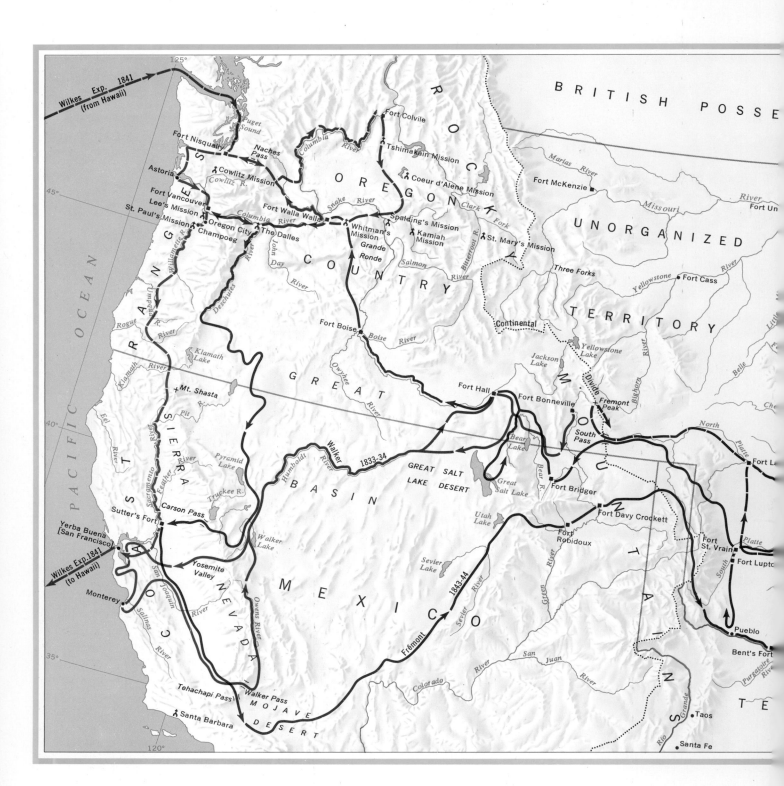

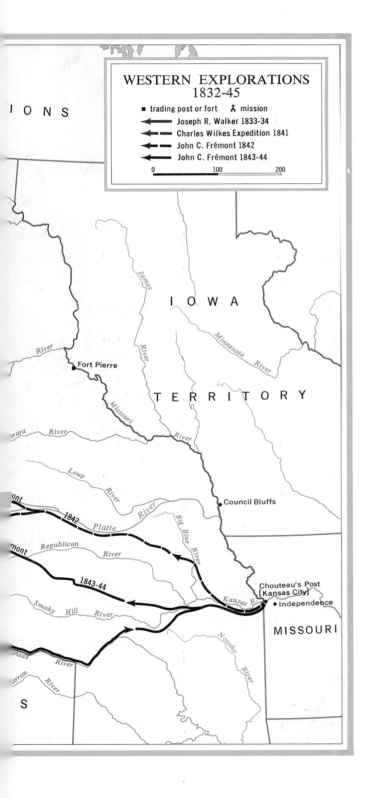

This view of the "Central Chain of the Wind River Mountains," not far from South Pass, was published in Frémont's 1845 report of his two expeditions in 1842–44. It was drawn by Charles Preuss, a German-born cartographer who was official artist with both exploring parties. Preuss liked to make the Rocky Mountain scenery look like the Austrian Alps.

FRÉMONT, First and Second Expeditions 1842-43-44, 1845

WESTERN EXPLORATIONS
1832-45

■ trading post or fort   ⚐ mission
⟵ Joseph R. Walker 1833-34
⟵ Charles Wilkes Expedition 1841
⟵ John C. Frémont 1842
⟵ John C. Frémont 1843-44

0   100   200

I O N S

I O W A

T E R R I T O R Y

Fort Pierre

Council Bluffs

Chouteau's Post
[Kansas City]
• Independence

MISSOURI

On May 2, 1842, Second Lieutenant John Charles Frémont, aged 29, bade good-by to his pretty 17-year-old wife in Washington and started out—at first by railroad, canalboat, and stagecoach—on his explorations of the West. On a steamboat between St. Louis and Independence, Frémont met the mountain man Kit Carson and hired him as a guide. From Chouteau's Post (present-day Kansas City) the first Frémont expedition followed the Kansas, Big Blue, and North Platte rivers in order to chart the Oregon Trail; this route was already being used by wagons as far as Fort Laramie. Pushing on to South Pass, Frémont compared the gradual, upward slope to the summit to "the ascent of the Capitol Hill from the [Pennsylvania] Avenue, in Washington." He used his barometer to measure what he decided was the highest peak in the Rockies, which he and five others climbed. His belief was incorrect: Fremont Peak in the Wind River Range is 13,730 feet above sea level, and there are dozens of higher ones along the Continental Divide.

The second Frémont expedition, in 1843–44, mapped the rest of the Oregon Trail, and also served partly as a spying mission in preparation for the war with Mexico. After examining Great Salt Lake, Frémont followed the emigrants' route to Whitman's Mission (established in 1836) and Fort Walla Walla of the Hudson's Bay Company. At The Dalles on the Columbia River, he turned south through the unexplored area of central Oregon and western Nevada. He camped beside Pyramid Lake, and made a dangerous midwinter crossing of the Sierras (guided by Carson) into the Sacramento Valley of California, where he was not welcome. On his return, he made a wide southern sweep through Mexican territory, across the Mojave Desert, Nevada, Utah, and Colorado. Frémont's reports provided the most popular descriptions yet of the West, and were especially gratifying to his father-in-law, Senator Benton of Missouri, a leading spokesman for western expansion.

A decade before Frémont reached California, Joseph Reddeford Walker, a Virginia-born fur hunter, located the route across the salt flats of Utah, and along the Humboldt River of Nevada, which became the California Trail. Walker crossed the Sierras twice on this trip, near Walker Lake, and farther south through Walker Pass. Lieutenant Charles Wilkes of the Navy preceded Frémont in Oregon and northern California. Wilkes' surveyors mapped this region as part of a six-year, round-the-world, exploring mission which also took in Antarctica and the Hawaiian Islands.

157

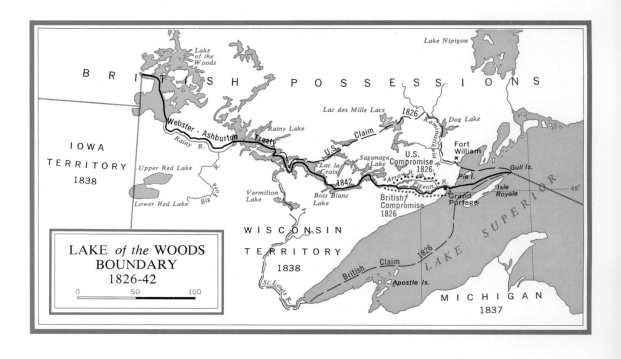

LAKE *of the* WOODS
BOUNDARY
1826-42

0   50   100

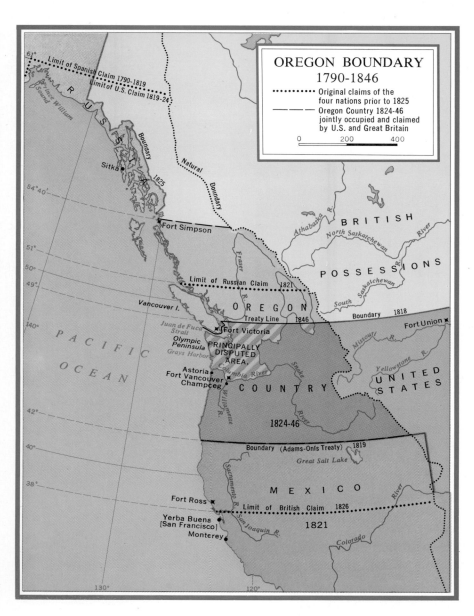

OREGON BOUNDARY
1790-1846

.... Original claims of the
four nations prior to 1825
— — — Oregon Country 1824-46
jointly occupied and claimed
by U.S. and Great Britain

0   200   400

The boundary disputes that arose so frequently in America's early history stemmed chiefly from the fact that statesmen, drawing lines on crude maps, often had little or no information about the regions whose fate they were determining. Typical of these disputes was the argument with Great Britain over the Maine boundary which, because of inadequate geographic knowledge, had not been settled satisfactorily after the Revolution (see pages 114–15). In 1815 the two nations set up a commission to locate the boundary. It got nowhere, and an arbitration effort by the king of the Netherlands (1827–31) was rejected by the United States. The issue became pressing in 1838 when Canadian lumberjacks in the Aroostook valley precipitated a heated, but bloodless, "Aroostook War." In 1842 Secretary of State Daniel Webster and Lord Ashburton, British envoy in Washington, finally worked out a compromise (top of opposite page).

The same Webster-Ashburton Treaty also drew a final line between Lake Superior and Lake of the Woods (above). Ashburton considered this "wild country" of "little importance to either party." He thus abandoned about 6,500 square miles north of the St. Louis River, which, it was later discovered, contained the Mesabi Range, one of the richest deposits of iron ore in the world.

The Oregon Country had been claimed originally by both Spain and Russia, as

SETTLING OLD PROBLEMS

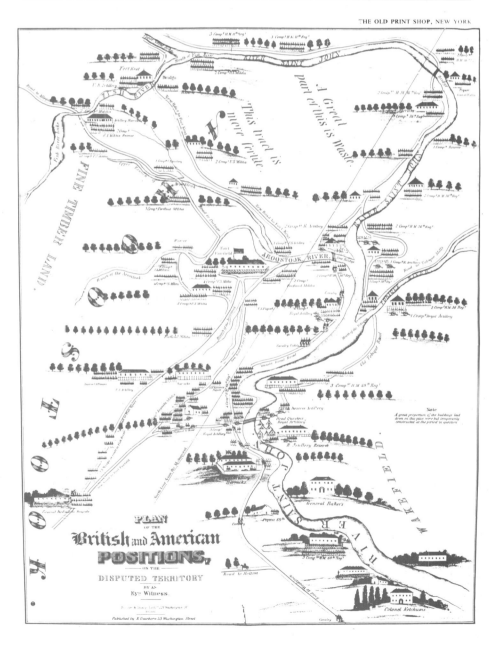

MAINE and BAY OF FUNDY BOUNDARY 1783-1842

0   50   100

well as by Great Britain and the United States. The Adams-Onís Treaty extinguished Spain's interest. Russia had built Fort Ross on the coast north of San Francisco Bay in 1812, but in 1821 she had limited her claim to territory north of the 51st parallel. Three years later, by treaty with the United States, she withdrew to the line of 54° 40′ N. The Anglo-American joint occupation agreement of 1818 was extended indefinitely in 1827, each nation reserving the right to cancel it on one year's notice.

By 1845, however, with 5,000 Americans living in the Willamette valley, compared to 750 Britons, who clustered mainly about Fort Vancouver and Puget Sound, joint occupation had become unpalatable. This was an affront to Manifest Destiny; an "Oregon fever" swept the land. Expansionists demanded the "reoccupation" of all Oregon, and in April, 1845, Congress authorized President Polk to terminate the joint occupation. Actually, the United States had no interest in land north of the 49th parallel, and the British little interest south of it. They compromised on that line in 1846, bending the boundary around Vancouver Island to give the British access, via Juan de Fuca Strait, to Fort Victoria.

Conflict over the "fine timber land," seen in the print at right, turned the Aroostook area into an armed camp. Maine and New Brunswick called up militia units, but war was averted.

PLAN OF THE **British and American POSITIONS,** ON THE DISPUTED TERRITORY BY AN Eye Witness.

159

TEXAS: *the* FIGHT *for* INDEPENDENCE

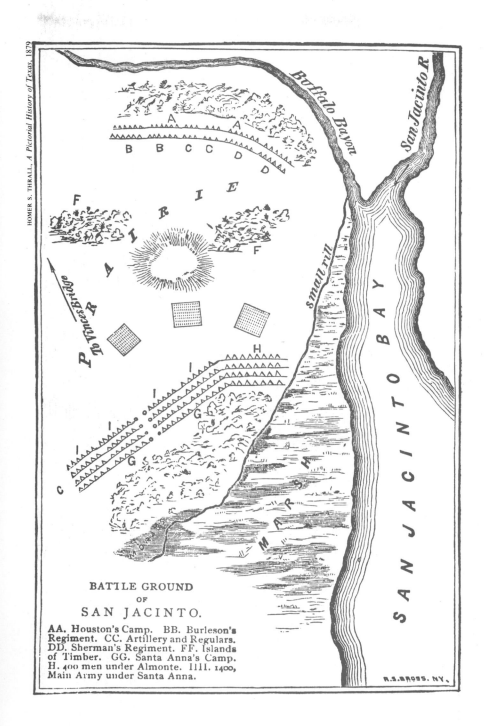

HOMER S. THRALL, *A Pictorial History of Texas,* 1879

BATTLE GROUND
OF
SAN JACINTO.

AA. Houston's Camp. **BB.** Burleson's Regiment. **CC.** Artillery and Regulars. **DD.** Sherman's Regiment. **FF.** Islands of Timber. **GG.** Santa Anna's Camp. **H.** 400 men under Almonte. **IIII.** 1400, Main Army under Santa Anna.

R.S.BROSS. NY,

The first Americans to settle in Texas, led by Stephen A. Austin, founded a colony at San Felipe, on the Brazos River, in 1821. Austin and other *empresarios* obtained large grants from the Mexican government, and the population of the province increased rapidly, from about 1,800 settlers in 1825 to 20,000 in 1830.

Austin tried hard to keep on good terms with the Mexicans, even assisting them in suppressing an "independence movement" organized by Benjamin Edwards in the Nacogdoches area in 1826. But religious and cultural differences, and conflict over slavery, which was illegal in Mexico, prevented true assimilation. The Texans remained fundamentally Americans.

Alarmed by this fact, Mexico banned in 1830 further American colonization in Texas. Trouble followed, and by 1835 the Texans were in full revolt. Mexican generals Santa Anna and Urrea moved quickly to subdue them. After Texans seized San Antonio in December, 1835, Santa Anna recaptured the town, slaughtering the garrison of the Alamo. Urrea wiped out San Patricio's defenders, then executed 300 captives after the Battle of Goliad.

The Texans, commanded by Sam Houston, fell back, but at San Jacinto they turned on Santa Anna, capturing him and routing his army. Texas was soon cleared of Mexican troops; independence had been won. Although Mexico did not recognize the new republic, an informal truce prevailed. It was occasionally broken, as at Mier in 1842, by a boundary dispute—Mexico claiming the Nueces River, and Texas the Rio Grande.

Backed against Buffalo Bayou (upper left), Sam Houston's men at San Jacinto seemed unable to attack. Santa Anna, sure of victory, took up a position below a wooded hill and allowed his men a siesta. When the Texans charged, shouting "Remember the Alamo," more than 1,300 Mexicans were killed or captured in 18 minutes.

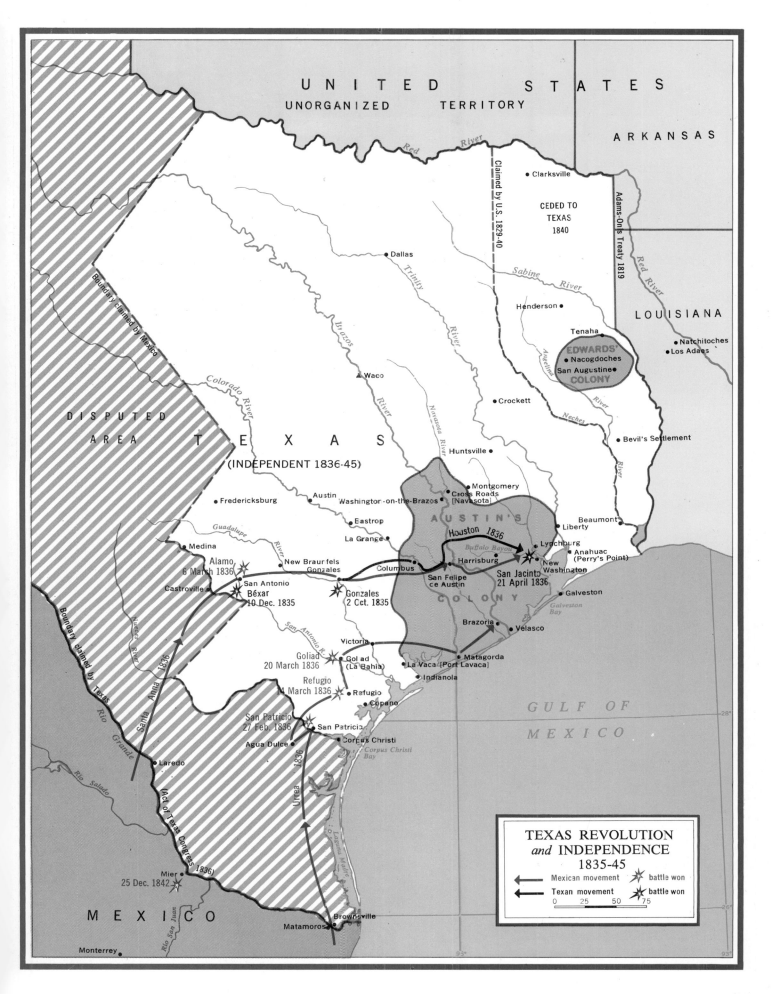

UNITED STATES

UNORGANIZED TERRITORY

ARKANSAS

• Clarksville

CEDED TO
TEXAS
1840

Claimed by U.S. 1829-40

Adams-Onís Treaty 1819

Red River

• Dallas

Sabine River

Henderson •

LOUISIANA

Tenaha •

EDWARDS'
Nacogdoches •
San Augustine •
COLONY

• Natchitoches
• Los Adaes

Trinity River

Brazos River

Navasota River

Angelina River

Neches River

DISPUTED

AREA   T E X A S

• Waco

• Crockett

Huntsville •

• Bevil's Settlement

Boundary claimed by Mexico

Colorado River

(INDEPENDENT 1836-45)

• Montgomery

• Fredericksburg

Austin •

Washington-on-the-Brazos •

Cross Roads
[Navasota]

• Eastrop

AUSTIN'S

Houston 1836

• Liberty

Beaumont •

Guadalupe River

La Grange •

Buffalo Bayou

Lynchburg

• Medina

New Braunfels •

Columbus

Harrisburg •

• Anahuac
(Perry's Point)

Alamo
6 March 1836

Gonzales

San Felipe
ce Austin

San Jacinto
21 April 1836

New
Washington

Castroville •

San Antonio

Béxar
10 Dec. 1835

Gonzales
2 Cct. 1835

COLONY

• Galveston

San Antonio R.

Victoria •

Brazoria •

Galveston
Bay

• Velasco

Boundary claimed by Texas

Nueces River

Goliad
20 March 1836

• Goliad
(La Bahía)

• Matagorda

Refugio
14 March 1836

La Vaca [Port Lavaca]

GULF OF

Santa Anna 1836

• Indianola

San Patricio
27 Feb. 1836

• Refugio

• Copano

San Patricio

MEXICO

Agua Dulce •

• Corpus Christi

Rio Grande

Laredo •

Corpus Christi
Bay

Urrea 1836

(Act of Texas Congress

Rio Salado

28°

TEXAS REVOLUTION
and INDEPENDENCE
1835-45

Mier
25 Dec. 1842

1836)

←—— Mexican movement   ✦ battle won

Rio San Juan

←— Texan movement   ✦ battle won

0   25   50   75

MEXICO

Brownsville •

Matamoros •

26°

Monterrey •

95°   93°

WAR *with* MEXICO

The grand strategy of the Mexican War consisted of three elements: driving the Mexicans south of the Rio Grande and occupying their northern provinces; seizing the sparsely populated California-New Mexico regions; and attacking Mexico City. The map at right shows the campaigns that, conducted over vast distances and aided by American sea power which blockaded Mexican ports and moved men and supplies to key points, achieved these ends.

General Zachary Taylor won the first objective, Winfield Scott the third (see page 164). The conquest of the Southwest commenced with Stephen Watts Kearny's march from Fort Leavenworth to Santa Fe, and from there—followed by Cooke and the Mormon Battalion—to southern California. (From Santa Fe, another column, under Alexander Doniphan, struck south to Chihuahua.)

Meanwhile, American settlers in California, aided by an exploring party under John C. Frémont, staged the "Bear Flag Revolt" at Sonoma. Commodore John Sloat's fleet took Monterey and San Francisco; and combined units, under Commodore Robert Stockton, invaded southern California. Initial American successes were nullified when *Californios* rebelled. At that point Kearny arrived and, after a temporary setback at San Pasqual, joined Stockton's forces at San Diego. Together they defeated the *Californios* at San Gabriel. Despite a brief revolt at Taos, the Southwest was in American hands by February, 1847.

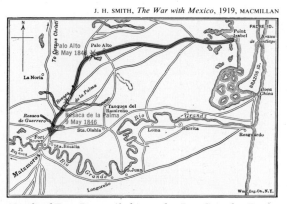

J. H. SMITH, *The War with Mexico*, 1919, MACMILLAN

North of Fort Brown (left), on the Rio Grande, Taylor won victories at Palo Alto and Resaca de la Palma.

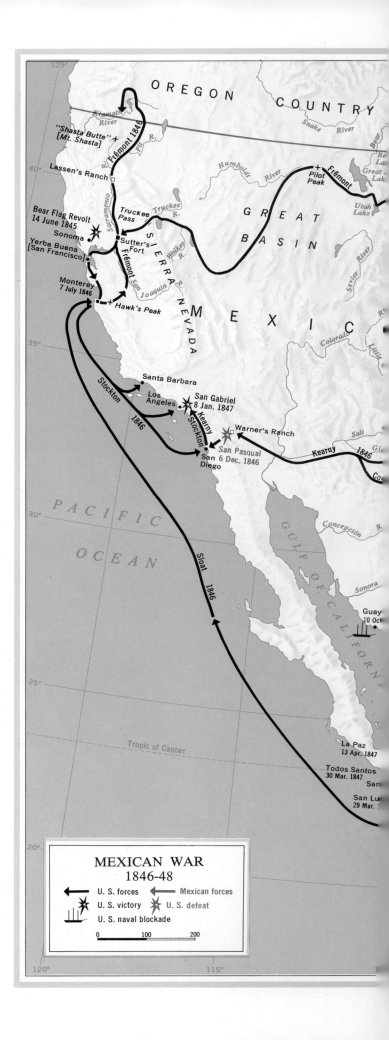

MEXICAN WAR 1846-48

- ← U. S. forces
- ← Mexican forces
- 🟊 U. S. victory
- 🟊 U. S. defeat
- U. S. naval blockade

0   100   200

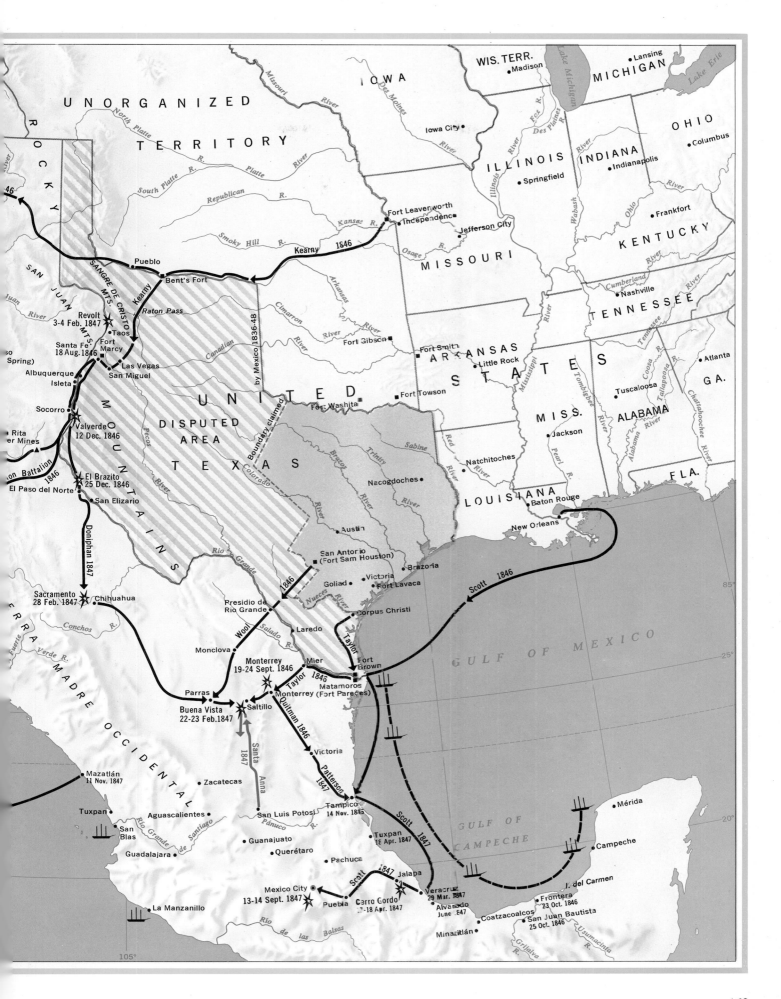

WIS. TERR.
• Lansing
MICHIGAN

IOWA
• Madison
Lake Erie

IOWA
• Iowa City
ILLINOIS
INDIANA
OHIO
• Columbus

UNORGANIZED

TERRITORY

North Platte
South Platte R.
Platte River
Republican R.
Smoky Hill R.
Kansas R.
Fort Leavenworth
Independence
Kearny 1846
Jefferson City
MISSOURI
Springfield
Indianapolis
Frankfort
KENTUCKY

Pueblo
Bent's Fort
Kearny
Raton Pass
Arkansas River
Cimarron River
Fort Gibson
Fort Smith
ARKANSAS
Little Rock
Nashville
TENNESSEE
Atlanta

ROCKY
SAN JUAN
San Juan River
SANGRE DE CRISTO MTS.
Revolt 3-4 Feb. 1847
Taos
Fort Marcy
Santa Fe 18 Aug. 1846
Canadian River
Fort Washita
Fort Towson
STATES
Tuscaloosa
GA.

Spring
Albuquerque
Isleta
Las Vegas
San Miguel
UNITED
Boundary claimed by Mexico 1836-48
MISS.
ALABAMA
Jackson

Socorro
MOUNTAINS
Pecos River
DISPUTED AREA
TEXAS
Sabine River
Red River
Natchitoches
Pearl R.

Rita er Mines
Valverde 12 Dec. 1846
Boundary claimed
Brazos River
Trinity River
Nacogdoches
LOUISIANA
Baton Rouge
FLA.

on Battalion 1846
El Brazito 25 Dec. 1846
El Paso del Norte
San Elizario
Colorado River
Rio Grande
Austin
New Orleans

Doniphan 1847
San Antonio (Fort Sam Houston)
Brazoria
GULF OF MEXICO

Sacramento 28 Feb. 1847
Chihuahua
Presidio de Rio Grande
Wool
Salado R.
1846
Nueces River
Goliad
Victoria
Fort Lavaca
Corpus Christi

Conchos R.
Monclova
Laredo
Taylor
Fort Brown

SIERRA
Fuerte
Verde R.
Monterrey 19-24 Sept. 1846
Mier
Matamoros
Monterrey (Fort Pareces)

MADRE
Parras
Taylor 1846
Saltillo
Buena Vista 22-23 Feb. 1847
Quitman 1846
Santa Anna 1847

OCCIDENTAL
Victoria
Patterson 1847

Mazatlán 11 Nov. 1847
Zacatecas
San Luis Potosí
Tampico 14 Nov. 1846
Scott 1847
GULF OF CAMPECHE
Mérida

Tuxpan
San Blas
Aguascalientes
Pánuco R.
Guanajuato
Querétaro
Tuxpan 18 Apr. 1847
Campeche

Guadalajara
Rio Grande de Santiago
Pachuca
Scott 1847 Jalapa
I. del Carmen

La Manzanillo
Mexico City 13-14 Sept. 1847
Puebla
Cerro Gordo 17-18 Apr. 1847
Veracruz 29 Mar. 1847
Alvarado June 1847
Frontera 23 Oct. 1846
Coatzacoalcos
San Juan Bautista 25 Oct. 1846

Rio de las Balsas
Minatitlán
Usumacinta R.

105°

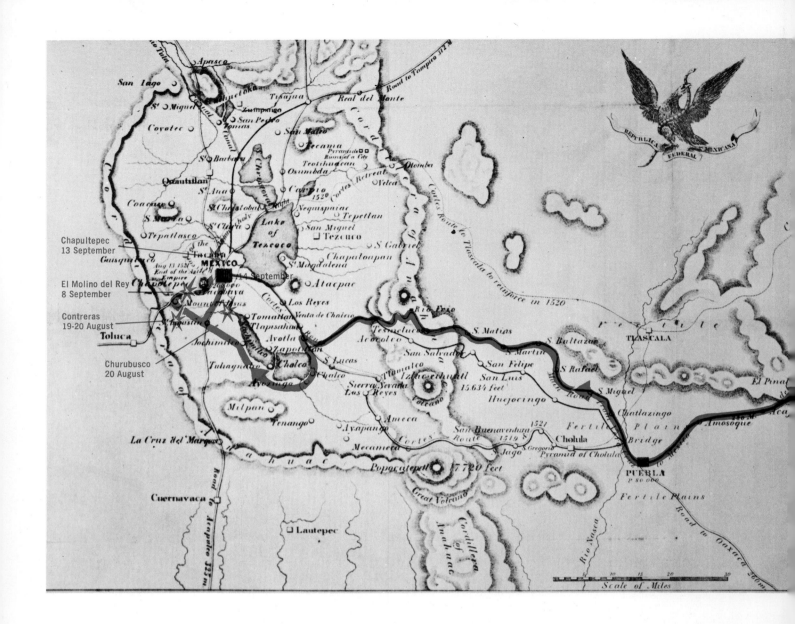

Chapultepec
13 September

El Molino del Rey
8 September

Contreras
19-20 August

Churubusco
20 August

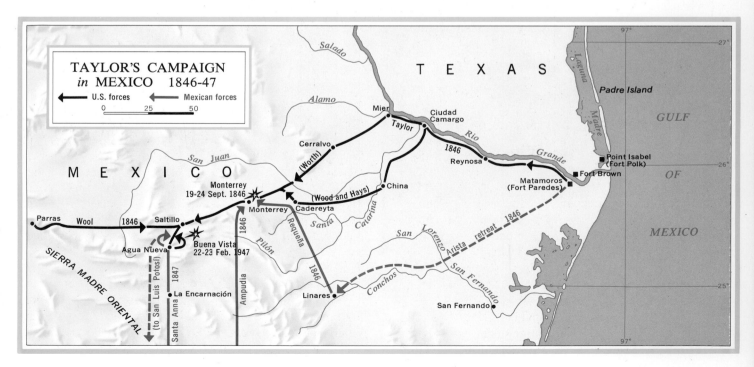

TAYLOR'S CAMPAIGN
in MEXICO 1846-47

U.S. forces ◄—   Mexican forces ◄—

0   25   50

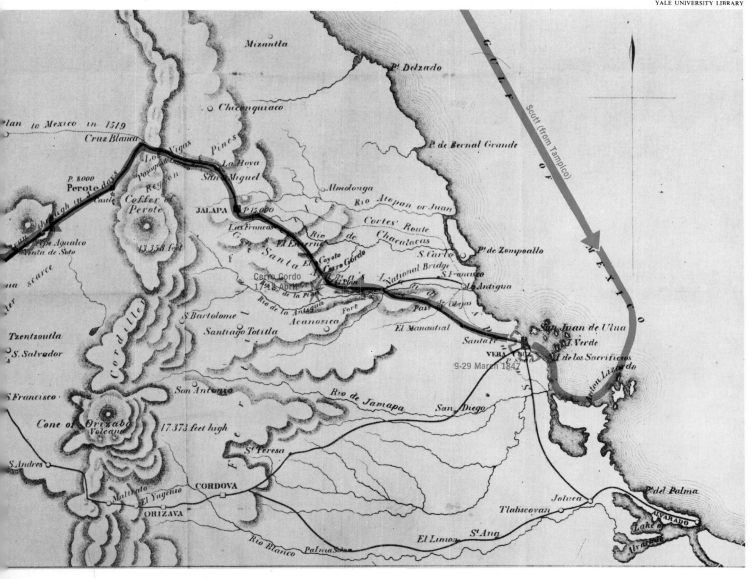

Scott (from Tampico)

Cerro Gordo
17-18 April

9-29 March 1847

THE MAJOR CAMPAIGNS

After occupying Matamoros on May 18, 1846, Zachary Taylor established a base at Ciudad Camargo. In August he launched a two-pronged attack on Monterrey with 6,200 men. One wing, commanded by General William J. Worth, took the western defenses by storm; the other drove the Mexicans into the citadel, where they finally surrendered. After a two-month armistice, Taylor advanced to Saltillo, where he was joined by General John E. Wool, who had invaded Mexico from San Antonio (see page 163). Moving to Agua Nueva, Taylor found himself facing a large Mexican army under Santa Anna. Outnumbered three to one, he fell back to strong positions near Buena Vista. When Santa Anna attacked, Taylor routed him in a bloody battle that ended the campaign in Mexico's northern provinces.

President Polk, suspecting the popular Taylor of political ambitions, put Winfield Scott in charge of the campaign to take Mexico City. Scott, who was an excellent soldier, sailed to Veracruz with 10,000 men, and captured that port city almost without loss after a three-week siege. His advance over the road from the coast to Mexico City (see contemporary map, above) was a model of sound tactics. At Cerro Gordo, near Jalapa, where the road rose steeply toward the mountains, he outflanked and then overwhelmed a Mexican army, taking 3,000 prisoners. Maintaining discipline and treating the populace fairly, he pushed rapidly across country, reaching Puebla in May. After waiting for reinforcements, he marched on the capital, won two hard-fought battles on the outskirts, and smashed his way into the city's last defenses on September 14, 1847, suffering only 1,000 casualties to the Mexicans' 4,000. The war was over.

Besides winning the entire Southwest for the United States, the Mexican War was a training ground for many young officers, including Grant, Lee, Sherman, and "Stonewall" Jackson, who later won distinction in the Civil War.

ORGANIZING *the* NEW TERRITORIES

By the Treaty of Guadalupe Hidalgo, which ended the Mexican War, the United States acquired not only the disputed territory of southern Texas, but all of Mexico north of the Rio Grande and the Gila River—about a million square miles of land. When, in 1853, a small strip south of the Gila was purchased to gain possession of a feasible railroad route, the present-day boundaries of the continental United States were, except for Alaska, complete.

Much of the newly acquired region was—and still is—sparsely populated. Nevertheless, the political subdivision and management of the area caused a variety of problems. The unique American process of state making had been created by the Northwest Ordinance of 1787. By 1848 the process had been completed smoothly in the original Northwest Territory, although, as the territorial maps (top right and on page 145) show, it had involved a number of steps and many realignments of boundaries. Applying it beyond the Missouri proved equally complicated. In the Compromise of 1850, occasioned by conflict over the future of slavery in the Southwest, California became a state without passing through territorial status, and the rest of the Mexican cession was split into Utah and New Mexico territories. Western Texas was added to New Mexico, the Federal government giving Texas $10 million in return to pay debts accumulated during its time as an independent republic.

In 1853 the growing Oregon Territory was subdivided without incident. But in 1854 an attempt to establish a territorial government for the plains country between the Missouri and the Rockies caused another crisis. In 1820 Congress had barred slavery from the region north of latitude 36° 30′ N., Missouri's southern border. Now Senator Stephen A. Douglas of Illinois proposed dividing the section into two territories, Kansas and Nebraska, without specifically outlawing the "peculiar institution." The success of this maneuver was a cause of the Civil War. (See pages 196–97.)

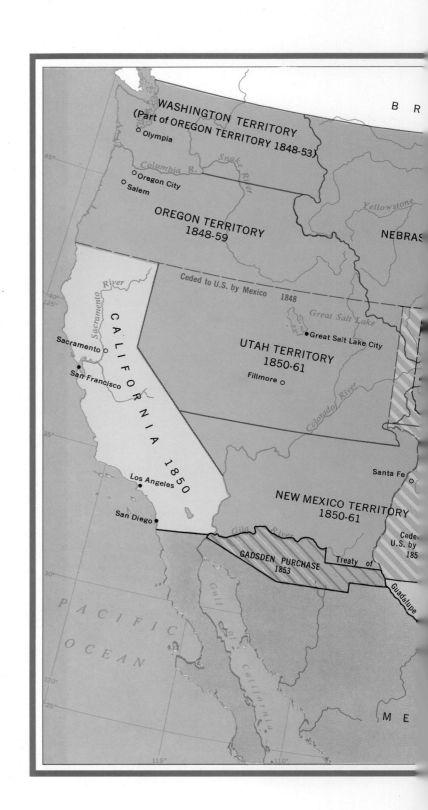

MICHIGAN TERRITORY 1834-36

WISCONSIN TERRITORY 1836-38

MICHIGAN TERRITORY 1836-37

IOWA TERRITORY 1838-46

WISCONSIN TERRITORY 1838-48

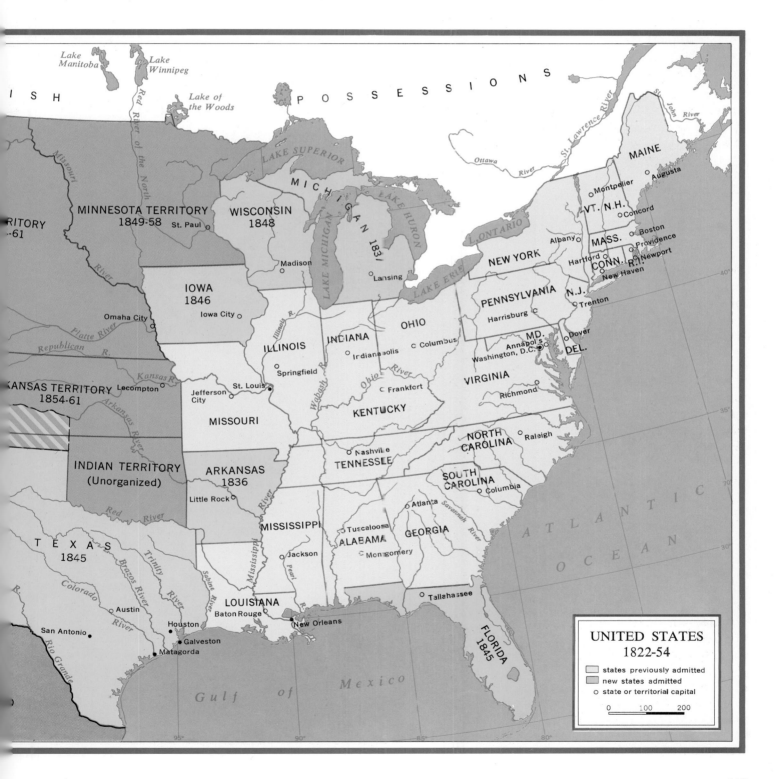

Lake Manitoba
Lake Winnipeg
Lake of the Woods
Red River of the North
ISH
POSSESSIONS
Ottawa River
St. Lawrence River
St. John River

LAKE SUPERIOR
MICHIGAN
LAKE HURON
LAKE MICHIGAN 1837
L. ONTARIO
LAKE ERIE

MAINE
Augusta
Montpelier
VT. N.H.
Concord
Albany MASS. Boston
Hartford Providence
CONN. R.I. Newport
New Haven

MINNESOTA TERRITORY 1849-58
St. Paul

WISCONSIN 1848
Madison
Lansing

Missouri River

RITORY -61

IOWA 1846
Iowa City
Omaha City
Platte River
Republican R.

NEW YORK

PENNSYLVANIA
Harrisburg
N.J.
Trenton

ILLINOIS
Springfield
INDIANA
Indianapolis
OHIO
Columbus

MD.
Annapolis
Washington, D.C.
DEL.
Dover

Kansas R.

KANSAS TERRITORY 1854-61
Lecompton
St. Louis
Jefferson City
MISSOURI

Arkansas River

Illinois R.
Wabash
Ohio River
KENTUCKY
Frankfort

VIRGINIA
Richmond

NORTH CAROLINA
Raleigh

INDIAN TERRITORY (Unorganized)

ARKANSAS 1836
Little Rock

Nashville
TENNESSEE

SOUTH CAROLINA
Columbia

Red River

TEXAS 1845
Austin
San Antonio
Houston
Galveston
Matagorda

Colorado River
Brazos River
Trinity River
Sabine River

Mississippi River

MISSISSIPPI
Jackson
Pearl R.

Tuscaloosa
ALABAMA
Montgomery

Atlanta
GEORGIA
Savannah River

ATLANTIC OCEAN

LOUISIANA
Baton Rouge
New Orleans

Tallahassee

FLORIDA 1845

Rio Grande

Gulf of Mexico

UNITED STATES 1822-54

- states previously admitted
- new states admitted
- o state or territorial capital

0   100   200

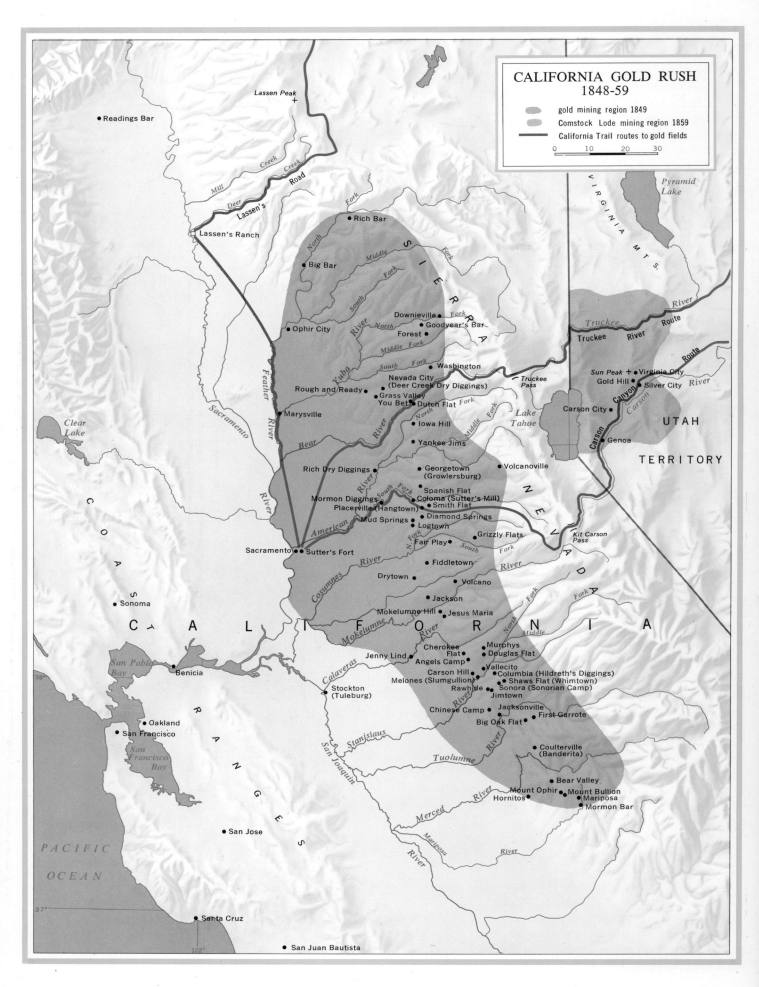

CALIFORNIA GOLD RUSH
1848-59

gold mining region 1849
Comstock Lode mining region 1859
California Trail routes to gold fields

0   10   20   30

Readings Bar

Lassen Peak

Mill Creek   Deer Creek   Road
Lassen's

Lassen's Ranch

North Fork   Middle Fork   SIERRA   Fork
Rich Bar

Big Bar

South Fork   River

Ophir City   Downieville   Goodyear's Bar
Forest
Middle Fork
South Fork   Washington

Feather River   Yuba   Nevada City
(Deer Creek Dry Diggings)
Rough and Ready   Grass Valley   Dutch Flat   Fork
You Bet
Marysville   Bear   River   Iowa Hill
Clear Lake   Yankee Jims

Sacramento   River   Rich Dry Diggings   Georgetown   Volcanoville
(Growlersburg)
River   Spanish Flat
Mormon Diggings   Coloma (Sutter's Mill)
Placerville (Hangtown)   Smith Flat
South Fork   Diamond Springs
Mud Springs   Logtown   NEVADA
American   N. Fork   Grizzly Flats
COAST   Sacramento   Fair Play   South Fork
Sacramento   Sutter's Fort   River
River   Fiddletown
Cosumnes   River
Drytown   Volcano

Sonoma   Jackson

Mokelumne Hill   Jesus Maria
CALIFORNIA
Mokelumne   River   North Fork   Middle

Cherokee   Murphys
Jenny Lind   Flat   Douglas Flat
San Pablo   Angels Camp   Vallecito
Bay   Benicia   Calaveras   Carson Hill   Columbia (Hildreth's Diggings)
Melones (Slumgullion)   Shaws Flat (Whimtown)
Stockton   Rawhide   Sonora (Sonorian Camp)
(Tuleburg)   Jimtown
Oakland   RANGES   Chinese Camp   Jacksonville
San Francisco   Big Oak Flat   First Garrote
San   Stanislaus
Francisco   San Joaquin   Coulterville
Bay   (Banderita)

Bear Valley
Mount Ophir   Mount Bullion
Hornitos   Mariposa
Mormon Bar

San Jose   Tuolumne   River
PACIFIC   River
OCEAN   Merced   River   River

Santa Cruz

San Juan Bautista

VIRGINIA MTS.   Pyramid Lake

Truckee   River   Route
Truckee   River   Route
Route
Truckee Pass   Sun Peak   Virginia City
Gold Hill   Silver City
Lake Tahoe   Carson City   River
Carson Canyon   Carson   UTAH
Genoa
Kit Carson   TERRITORY
Pass

When James W. Marshall stumbled into Sutter's Fort near Sacramento on January 28, 1848, with a white cotton rag stuffed with flakes of pure gold, he inaugurated a new era in the history of the West. He had found the gold in a gravel bed along the American River, and the prospectors who flocked to the region when news of his discovery became known scoured this and every other stream that coursed toward the Pacific from the High Sierras. Actually, these eager searchers were collecting the scrapings of the fabulous Mother Lode. Eons earlier the upheavals that formed the Sierras had exposed a long band of gold-bearing volcanic rock. Countless centuries of erosion had loosed flakes and nuggets of the metal and washed them toward the sea. The heavy gold, collecting in backwaters, cracks, and gravel beds from the Mariposa River to the North Fork of the Feather, provided fortunes for many lucky prospectors. But the bulk of the wealth of the lode could be extracted, in time, only by big corporations possessing adequate capital to dig, transport, and refine large masses of less pure ore.

News of the discovery of gold spread fast. By 1849 prospectors were pouring in by the tens of thousands—farmers from Oregon, peons from Mexico (who gave their home district's name to the town of Sonora), and then hordes from the East and from Europe, who came either by sea round the Horn or across Panama to San Francisco, or overland by way of Carson Pass, Truckee Pass, or the Lassen trail. The influx caused the sleepy port of San Francisco to become a metropolis, made Sacramento and Stockton major commercial centers, and sprinkled a hundred boomtowns across the Mother Lode country, the names of which—Slumgullion, Volcano, Rough and Ready—reflect their rowdy, explosive character.

Thousands of gold seekers, headed for Carson Pass, had plodded past Six-Mile Canyon in Nevada. Some had found small amounts of gold. But in 1859, after the California rush had petered out, a prospector in the canyon revealed a deposit of bluish quartz—the Comstock Lode—which proved to be the richest gold and silver ore in America. Another rush was on. Virginia City became the greatest of all boomtowns; its inhabitants soon extracted $12 million in ore annually. In 20 years the Comstock yielded $306 million.

BOOMTOWNS
in the
MINING REGIONS

News of Marshall's strike led the military governor of California to send Lieutenant William Tecumseh Sherman to investigate. Sherman made these maps, which were sent, along with gold samples, to Washington. When President James Polk spoke enthusiastically of the discovery in his 1848 Annual Message to Congress, the Gold Rush was on.

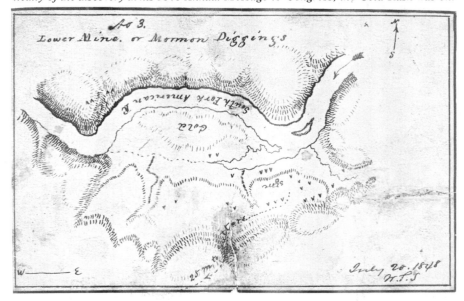

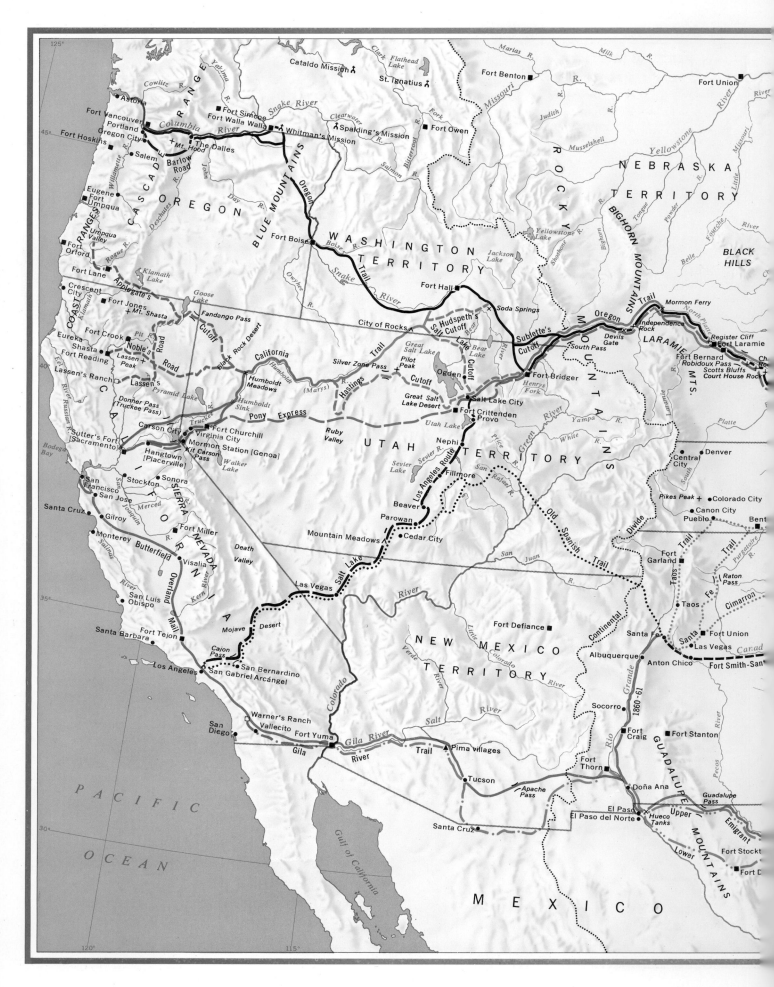

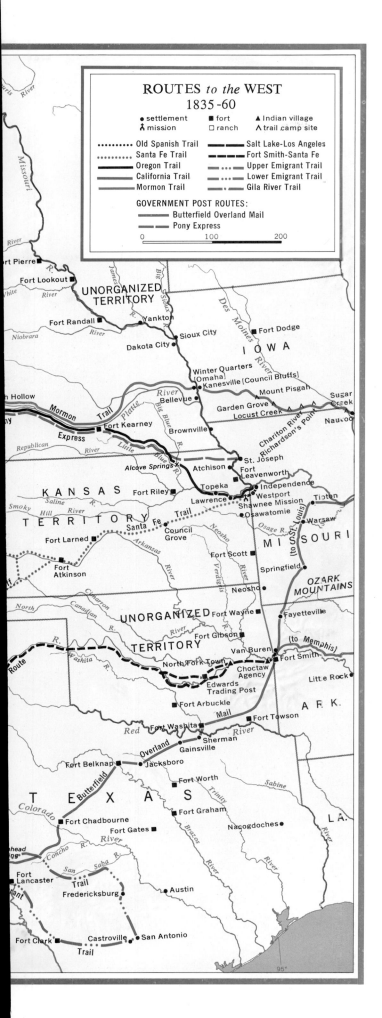

EVOLUTION *of* OVERLAND TRAILS

California's gold rush, and other mining booms elsewhere, caused a crush of westbound traffic on historic trails. At Fort Laramie (below), a principal rest stop on routes to Oregon, Utah, and California, the Army register showed 39,506 men, 2,421 women, 609 children, 23,172 horses, 36,116 oxen, and 9,927 wagons traveling west in the year 1850. It was believed that perhaps 10,000 more emigrants did not register at the fort.

The earliest overland route in the West was the Old Spanish Trail, which was mapped in part in 1776 by the Franciscan missionary Father Escalante. From Sante Fe it curved north into Utah (to avoid hostile Indians and difficult country farther south), and extended eventually to Los Angeles. Mormons from Salt Lake City adopted it for their colonizing trips into southern Nevada.

American traders made regular use of the trail to Santa Fe from 1823 on; the route was surveyed by the government in 1825–27. By the early 1840's the Oregon Trail was an emigrants' road. Branching off from the Oregon Trail near Fort Hall, the California Trail was elaborated with short cuts and side roads during the gold rush years. The Mormon Trail began in Iowa, and paralleled the Oregon Trail through Nebraska. Twin routes in west Texas were called the Upper and Lower Emigrant trails. The Butterfield Overland Mail, with a 2,800-mile route to San Francisco, and the Pony Express from St. Joseph, were a heavy expense to the government, and existed three years and a year and a half, respectively.

O CROSS, *Expedition to Oregon,* 1850

Fort Laramie in 1850 was drawn for a U.S. Army report.

This panoramic view of the Sierra Nevada, near Noble's Pass in northern California, was engraved from an 1854 drawing by F. W. von Egloffstein.

ABOVE: *U.S. Pacific Railroad Survey*, VOL. XI, 1855

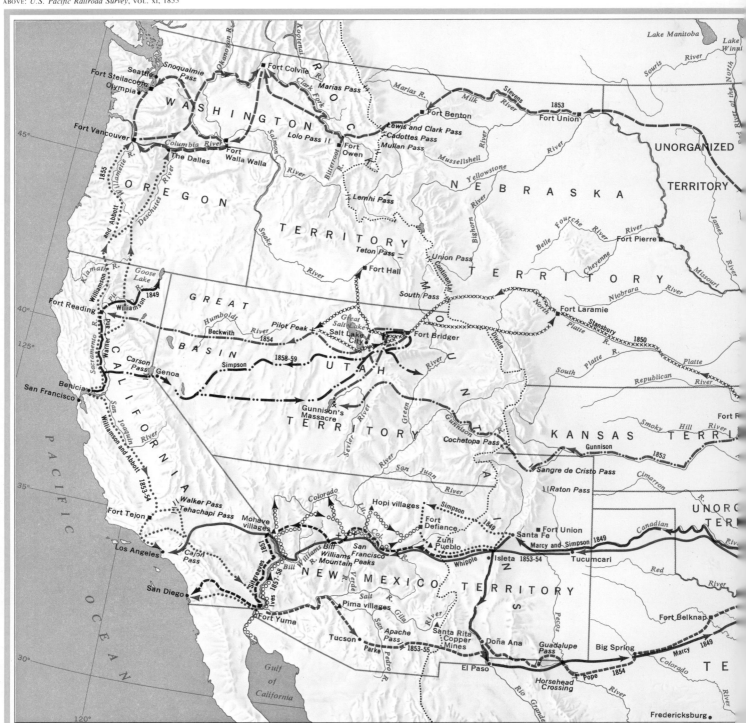

It was published in the report of Lieutenant E. G. Beckwith, who surveyed the central (41st parallel) railroad route as far as the mountains.

GOVERNMENT EXPLORATION
and SURVEYS 1849-60

◄───── Marcy and Simpson 1849
◄•••••• Simpson 1849
◄───── Warner and Williamson 1849
◄xxxxx Stansbury 1850
◄─ ─ ─ Sitgreaves 1851
◄ooooo Ives 1857-58
◄──•─• Simpson 1858-59

PACIFIC RAILROAD SURVEYS

◄───── Stevens 1853-54
◄──•── Gunnison 1853
◄─ ■ ─ Beckwith 1854
◄───── Whipple 1853-54
◄─ ─ ─ Pope 1854
◄─•─•─ Parke 1853-55
◄•••••• Williamson and Abbott 1853-55

0   100   200   300

STUDY *of the* WEST'S TERRAIN

Topography is a word derived from the Greek; it means the describing of places. As a science, topography includes all physical features of the land: mountains, rivers, trails and roads, geological strata, composition and color of the soil; the density (or lack) of forests and other vegetation; effects created by animals; human habitations, if any; along with exact calculations of latitude, longitude, altitude, temperature, contour, and distance. In the 19th century the American West was the world's great theater of topographical studies; the work was done mostly by 72 men who were appointed, between 1838 and 1863, to the elite Corps of Topographical Engineers of the U.S. Army.

The explorations of Long and Frémont (depicted on previous maps) were directed by Army topographers, as were most of the expeditions charted on the map at left. Soon after the Mexican War, Captain Marcy and Lieutenant Simpson opened a new, direct route to Santa Fe; Simpson pushed on into Navaho country. Lieutenants Warner and Williamson, from San Francisco, mapped California's Mother Lode, and crossed the Sierras to remote Goose Lake, where an Indian arrow killed Warner. Captain Stansbury studied Mormon Utah, which soon after was invaded by U.S. troops; Captain Sitgreaves reconnoitered southwestern deserts, on a route now used by the Santa Fe Railroad. In the late 1850's Captain Joseph Ives led a famous ascent of the lower Colorado, and Simpson conducted a scientific tour of the Great Basin and Uinta Mountains. Government plans for a transcontinental railroad led to other ambitious explorations and a series of richly informative reports of possible routes in the north (Stevens), across the central plains (Gunnison—who was killed with seven of his men in a Ute Indian ambush—and Beckwith), and of alternate southern routes (Whipple, Pope, and others).

PEOPLING *the* RISING CITIES

The political expansion of the United States was far more rapid than the actual advance of settlement. The nation had extended to the Pacific in 1848, but in 1860 the only significant centers of population west of the mountains were in Oregon, California, and Mormon Utah. Nevertheless, the human march westward had been impressive; by 1860, the center of population, reflecting the development of the Mississippi Valley, had moved to south central Ohio.

Urban growth accompanied the general expansion. Only 182,000 persons—about .3 per cent of the population—lived in cities of 10,000 or more in 1800. By 1860 over 4.6 million—15 per cent—lived in such centers. The northern states were more densely populated and far more urbanized than the southern. Except for New Orleans, no southern city had 100,000 people in 1860; only seven others south of Tennessee had as many as 10,000. But most of New England, and the region between New York and Washington, were thoroughly urbanized. Even the "agricultural" Middle West had dozens of thriving cities.

The concentration of Negroes in the South had much to do with the section's slow growth. In 1800 one American in five was a Negro, in 1860 less than one in seven. In general, immigrants avoided the slave states. Yet, within the South, the most densely populated areas had the most Negroes; whatever prosperity the area had was built largely on the exploitation of their labor.

The three-part lithograph, below, depicts a panoramic view of San Francisco in 1862. The tower at right is on Russian Hill. Telegraph Hill is the distant knob, at left.

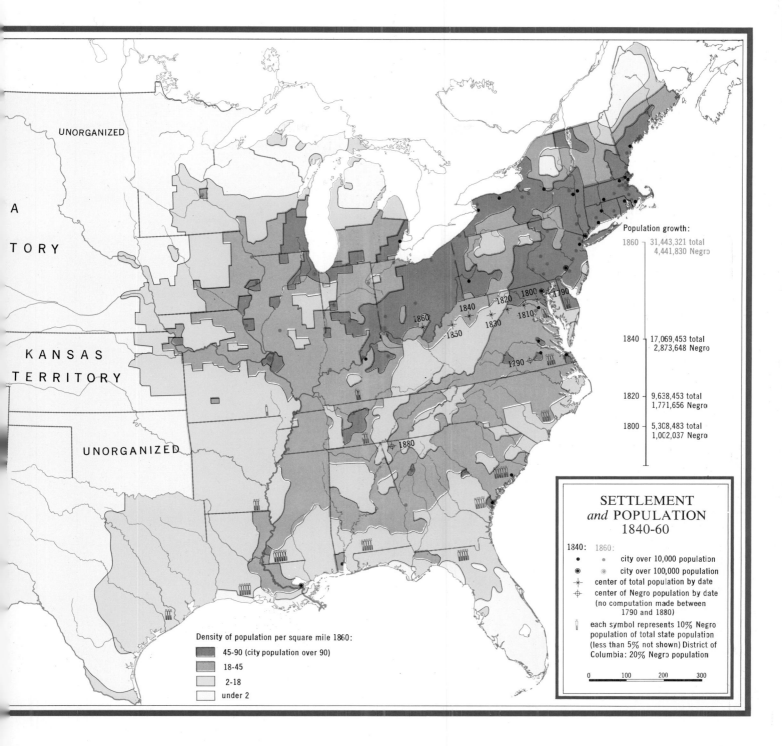

UNORGANIZED

A

TORY

KANSAS
TERRITORY

UNORGANIZED

1790

1880

1860

1850

1840

1830

1820

1810

1800

1790

1790

PHELPS STOKES COLLECTION, NEW YORK PUBLIC LIBRARY

Population growth:

1860   31,443,321 total
     4,441,830 Negro

1840   17,069,453 total
     2,873,648 Negro

1820   9,638,453 total
     1,771,656 Negro

1800   5,308,483 total
     1,002,037 Negro

SETTLEMENT
and POPULATION
1840-60

1840:   1860:

●   ●   city over 10,000 population

◉   ◉   city over 100,000 population

✳   center of total population by date

⊕   center of Negro population by date
     (no computation made between
     1790 and 1880)

     each symbol represents 10% Negro
     population of total state population
     (less than 5% not shown) District of
     Columbia: 20% Negro population

0   100   200   300

Density of population per square mile 1860:

■ 45-90 (city population over 90)

■ 18-45

■ 2-18

□ under 2

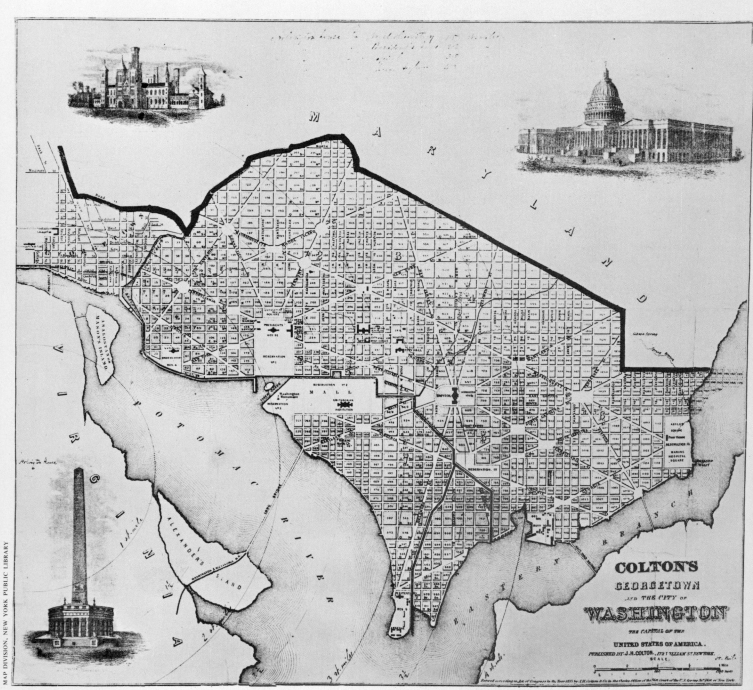

Fifty-one years after it had become the nation's capital, Washington, as shown by this street plan of 1851, had developed along the geometric lines proposed by its designer, Major Pierre Charles L'Enfant, in 1791. The Capitol (center), with great avenues radiating from its plaza, could be seen from almost all parts of the city, whose principal expansion had occurred westwardly along Pennsylvania Avenue to the White House and, beyond it, to Georgetown (at left). The Smithsonian Institution, the Capitol, and the Washington Monument, pictured above and seen also in the 1852 view on the opposite page, were not yet finished and, in both cases, represented artists' versions of what they would look like when they were completed.

CITY VIEWS

A Portfolio of Mid-Nineteenth-Century Prints

"Could I begin life again knowing what I now know," said John Jacob Astor in 1848, "I would buy every foot of land on the Island of Manhattan." Astor could sense a good investment, and he was right again. By the mid-1800's the growth of American cities was a national phenomenon. In the East, the influx of immigrants was bursting the seams of many cities; in the Middle West new towns were blooming into metropolises almost overnight. Many of the cities already had large slums. But most citizens overlooked these portents of future problems. What they saw instead—notable public buildings, handsome homes and churches—is reflected in this collection of mid-century views.

*At mid-century, Boston was sorely in need of growing space, although extensive landfill operations,
beginning in 1803, had already altered the city's original tadpole shape. By 1850, when this view
of the "Athens of America" appeared, land reclaimed from the mud flats of Back Bay had become
the Public Garden (foreground), an adjunct to the 45-acre Common, seen just beyond it. To the*

left of the Common, another project, the leveling of Beacon Hill, had made room near the handsome dome of the State House for many of the city's most prestigious residences. At upper right, the less elegant Fort Hill section was filling with newly arrived Irish immigrant families. At extreme left, the Bunker Hill Monument in Charlestown overlooks bridges spanning the Charles River.

New York in the 1850's was already a teeming metropolis, even though its municipal boundaries were still limited to Manhattan Island. Brooklyn (lower right) was a separate "City of Churches," linked to lower Manhattan by side-wheeier ferries, while Queens (upper right) was a fringe of villages along the East River. Across the Hudson, Jersey City (lower left) was itself a substantial seaport, and Hoboken (left center) was the place where New Yorkers went to play and watch the new game of baseball. In this panoramic bird's-eye view from a point in the harbor just south of the Battery, the perspective is distorted to give a better look at the business district, which barely extended beyond City Hall (the columned, tree-fringed building at center). Broadway, running zigzag north and south, was the scene of the city's original traffic jams; it is shown here thronged with pedestrians, wagons, and omnibuses of three competing lines—the "Red Birds," "Yellow Birds," and "Original Broadways." Central Park is far to the north with its projected circular drives and malls seen in outline (in the 1850's it was still a wilderness of rocks and trees which the city was beginning to clear). Above Canal Street (beyond City Hall) the streets were solidly lined with chocolate-brown stone residences. But in 1859 business took a long jump north to Madison Square (at 23rd Street) where Amos Eno built his luxurious, marble-fronted Fifth Avenue Hotel, with gas chandeliers and private baths in all of its more than 100 suites, and a "perpendicular railway" (elevator) intersecting each of its six floors.

181

Flotillas of river boats and seagoing vessels lined the long, curving water front of New Orleans, the nation's great cotton port, in 1851. Extending northwest from the banks of the Mississippi

*River, broad, tree-lined Canal Street separated the Vieux Carré, with its impressive Cathedral
of St. Louis (right), from the American Quarter, distinguished by its large Greek revival buildings.*

Antebellum Charleston (above) took pride in the refinement of its churches, in its pleasant, riverside promenade, and in the "airy, Oriental appearance" of its homes. St. Louis on the Mississippi (below) was no less dignified, though a busy river trade helped to swell its population fivefold, to 80,000, between the years 1840 and 1850.

MAP OF
THE CITY OF
SAN FRANCISCO.
CALIFORNIA.

COPIED FROM ORIGINALS WITH CORRECTIONS AND ADDITIONS.

1850

AGNEW'S
STEAMBOAT
LANDING

CENTRAL WHARF

RINCON POINT

GOVERNMENT RESERVE

YERBA BUENA
CEMETERY

Washington
Square

Portsmouth
Square

Public Square

Public
Square

BAY ST
FRANCISCO ST
CHESNUT ST
LOMBARD ST
GREENWICH ST
FILBERT ST
UNION ST
VALLEJO ST
BROADWAY
PACIFIC ST
JACKSON ST
WASHINGTON ST
CLAY
SACRAMENTO ST
CALIFORNIA ST
PINE ST
BUSH ST
SUTTER ST
POST ST
GEARY ST
O'FARRELL ST
ELLIS ST
EDDY ST
TURK ST
MARKET
MISSION ST
HOWARD ST
FOLSOM ST
HARRISON ST
BRYANT ST
TOWNSEND ST
BRANNAN ST
FIRST ST
SECOND ST
THIRD ST
FOURTH ST
LARKIN ST

Scale of Mexican Varas.

100 Mexican Varas = 276 English Feet.

View of San Francisco in 1849.
THE LARGE VESSEL AT THE WHARF IS THE "APOLLO" STORE SHIP.

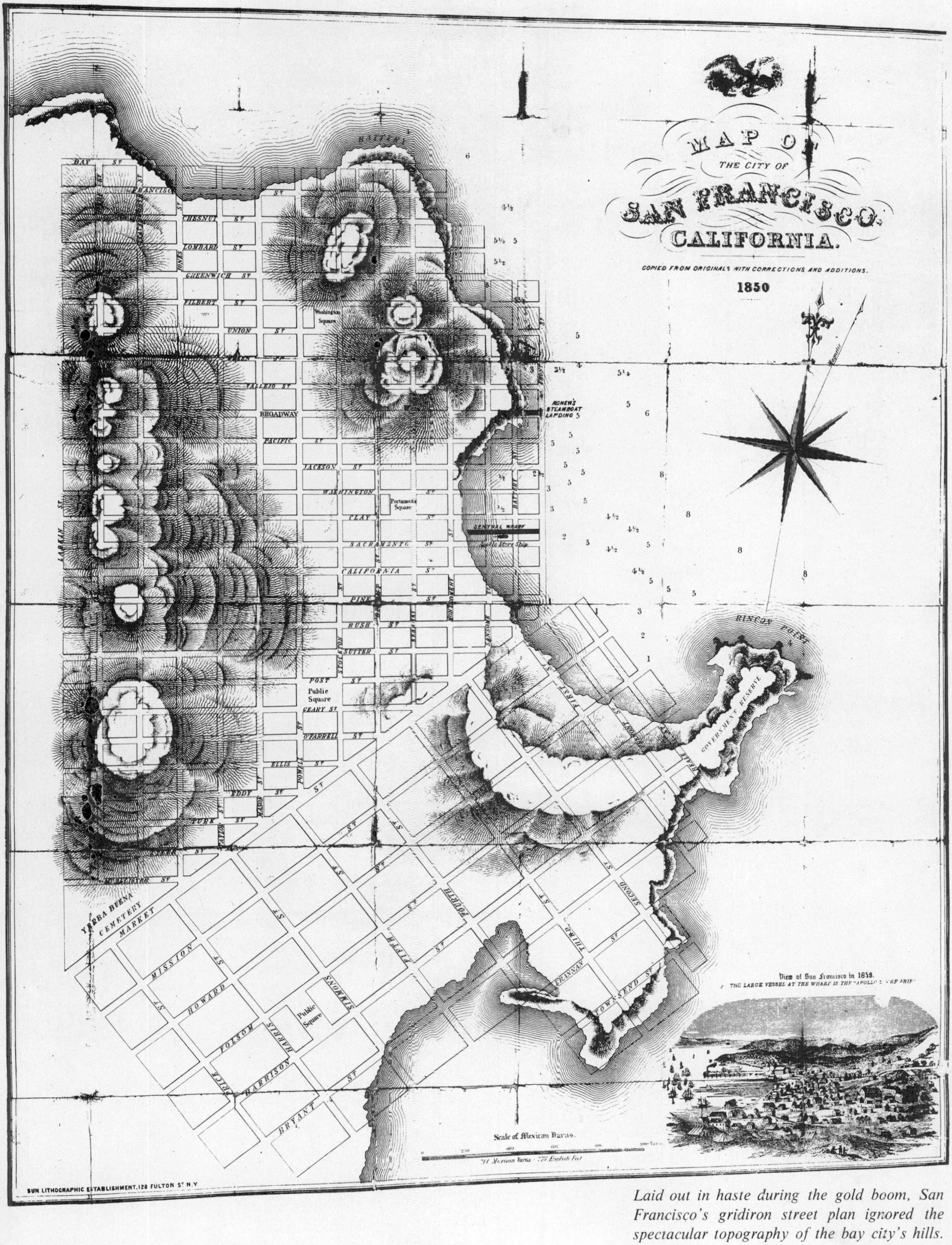

Laid out in haste during the gold boom, San Francisco's gridiron street plan ignored the spectacular topography of the bay city's hills.

In 1860 about four million Americans were of foreign birth, roughly the same as the number of slaves. The use of this comparison is not entirely capricious. Although all Americans (except for the Indians) were of immigrant stock, older settlers tended to look down on newcomers. Immigrants were nearly all poor. Many were totally illiterate, still more spoke no English. Some had habits and customs that established citizens found offensive. Immigration, therefore, posed serious economic and social problems, although, as most intelligent persons realized, the immigrants were also a priceless asset to a rapidly growing country.

From the Revolution until after the Napoleonic Wars, immigration was relatively insignificant. But 500,000 persons entered the country in the 1830's, 1.5 million in the 1840's, and 2.6 million in the 1850's. As the chart at right shows, the bulk of these new Americans came from Ireland, where a potato blight had caused a disastrous famine, and from Germany, where crop failures and unsettled political conditions encouraged many to emigrate to the New World. In 1849 about 267,000 Irish and German immigrants arrived. In 1853, another typical year, 305,000 came.

Most of the Irish settled in eastern cities, where they became day laborers and factory hands. Many Germans also became city dwellers, but they tended to move westward to cities such as Cincinnati and Milwaukee. Other Germans, along with most of the Scandinavian and British newcomers, took up farming on the frontier, which helps explain the heavy concentration of foreign born in the upper Middle West. Before 1860 nearly all Asiatic immigrants were Chinese, who came to the California gold fields. Canadians of French descent who entered the U.S. tended to become workers in the New England mills, while those of British stock mostly took up land on the frontier.

Although a large percentage of the immigrants were Catholics, the United States stayed overwhelmingly Protestant. Most sects had congregations in every section, but certain geographical concentrations were discernible—Congregationalists in New England, for example, and Methodists and Baptists in the Midwest and South. The migration of the Mormons illustrates both the cohesiveness and dedication of the many new sects of the period.

FOREIGN-BORN POPULATION
IMMIGRATION
and RELIGION
1840-60

THE SPREAD *of* FOREIGN POPULATION *and* RELIGION

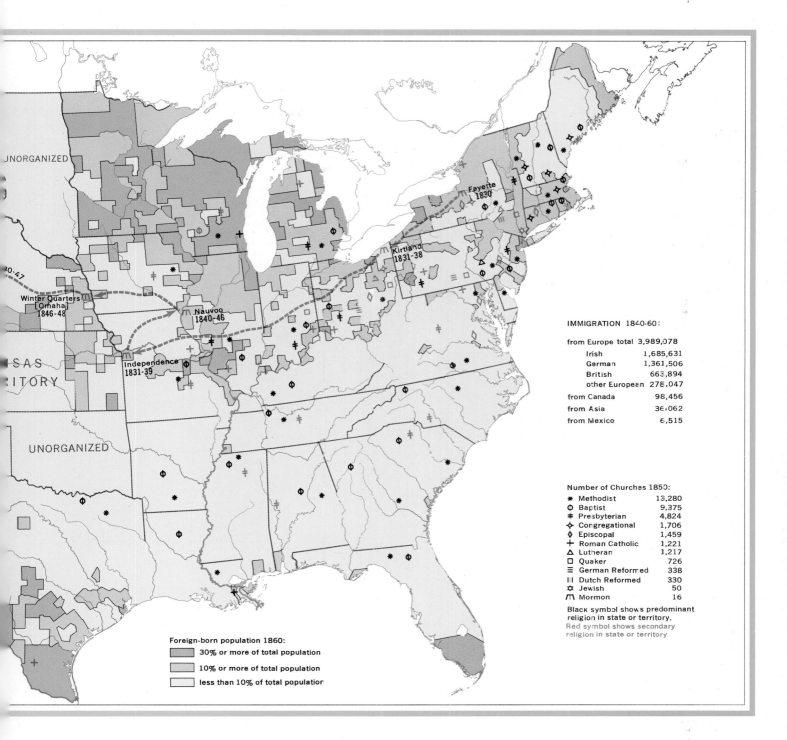

IMMIGRATION 1840-60:

from Europe total 3,989,078

Irish	1,685,631
German	1,361,506
British	663,894
other European	278,047
from Canada	98,456
from Asia	36,062
from Mexico	6,515

Number of Churches 1850:

✳	Methodist	13,280
◯	Baptist	9,375
✤	Presbyterian	4,824
✧	Congregational	1,706
◇	Episcopal	1,459
✛	Roman Catholic	1,221
△	Lutheran	1,217
☐	Quaker	726
☰	German Reformed	338
‖‖	Dutch Reformed	330
✡	Jewish	50
⋒	Mormon	16

Black symbol shows predominant religion in state or territory.
Red symbol shows secondary religion in state or territory

Foreign-born population 1860:

- 30% or more of total population
- 10% or more of total population
- less than 10% of total population

L'Illustration, PARIS, 1849

Most immigrants crossed the ocean in far less comfort than the persons shown in this 1849 illustration. Those willing to risk the crowded, fetid conditions of the steerage on a cargo vessel could purchase their passage from Liverpool to New York for about $15.

An 1848 print shows a McCormick reaper.

MECHANIZED FARMING *and* "KING COTTON"

Two slaves could operate a simple gin with ease.

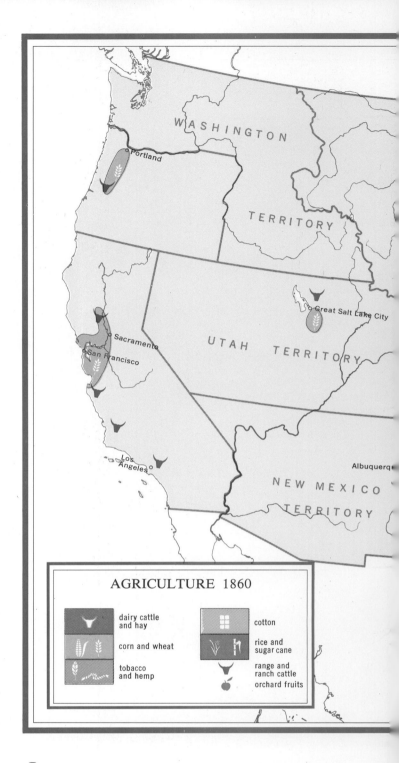

AGRICULTURE 1860

- dairy cattle and hay
- corn and wheat
- tobacco and hemp
- cotton
- rice and sugar cane
- range and ranch cattle orchard fruits

In 1859 the economy of the United States was still over-whelmingly agricultural. In that year the nation's approximately two million farms yielded harvests worth nearly $1.5 billion. Corn production exceeded 838 million bushels, wheat 173 million bushels. About 4.5 million bales of cotton were raised, as well as 66 million bushels of potatoes, some 20 million tons of hay, and large amounts of other farm products for which no accurate records were kept.

As the map shows, some crops were concentrated in particular regions; growing conditions, for example, gave the southern states a monopoly of cotton, rice, and sugar production. Yet even in the heart of the South, corn and wheat were raised, along with cattle and other livestock. About

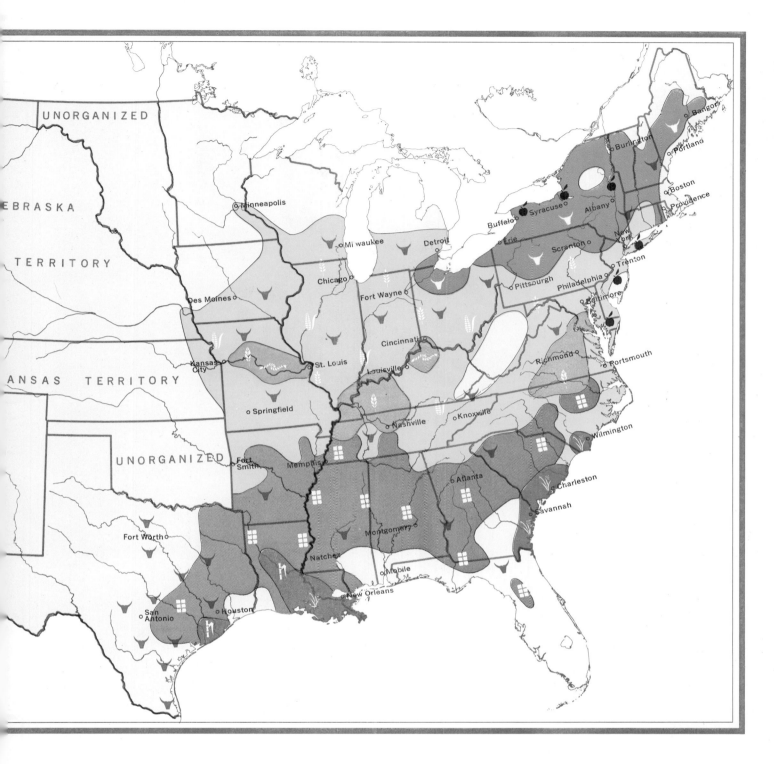

half the arable land on the average southern plantation or farm was devoted to raising food for local consumption. Generally speaking, most parts of the country produced their own meat, dairy products, fruit, and other perishables, for high-speed transportation and mechanical refrigeration had not yet been developed. But agriculture loomed large in American commerce, especially in the export trade. Of the $316 million worth of goods exported in 1860, cotton alone accounted for $192 million, about $150 million of this total going to Great Britain. Their near monopoly of the world's cotton supply led southerners to argue that "Cotton is King." The North, they believed, would yield to any southern demand to save this rich resource. If it did not, the

South, by 1860, felt it could count on foreign backing should it decide to secede from the Union.

Rising demand encouraged farmers to increase output, but labor shortages limited their ability to do so. A solution to the problem was provided by newly invented farm machinery. Steel plows became common; one manufacturer, John Deere, was producing 10,000 plows a year by 1857. With Cyrus H. McCormick's reaper, laborers could harvest 14 times as much wheat as with hand tools. By 1860 McCormick had sold 80,000 reapers. With other manufacturers turning out binders, disc harrows, and other tools, the annual value of farm equipment produced in the United States rose during the fifties from $152 million to $246 million.

Industrialization was nationwide. The mine in Nevada (above) employed heavy machinery as well as horsepower. But the complexities of mechanization are better seen in the view, below, of a Boston sewing machine factory.

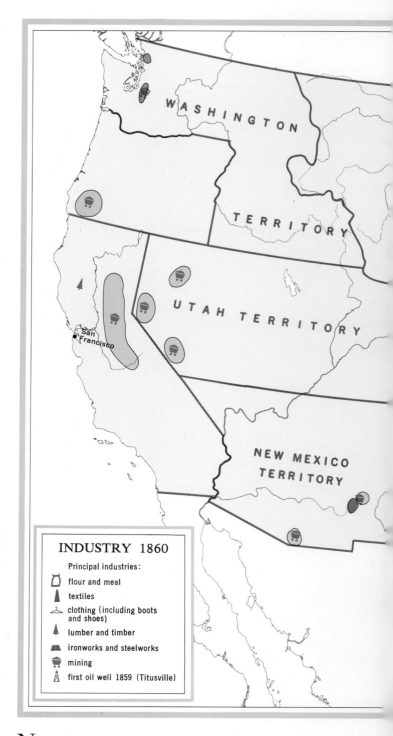

INDUSTRY 1860

Principal industries:

⚱ flour and meal

▲ textiles

⚖ clothing (including boots and shoes)

🌲 lumber and timber

⬛ ironworks and steelworks

⛏ mining

🗼 first oil well 1859 (Titusville)

INDUSTRIAL PROGRESS

Nothing illustrated better the importance of American agriculture in 1860 than the flourishing state of American manufacturing. Of the ten leading industries—flour, cotton textile, lumber, shoe, clothing, iron, leather, woolen goods, liquor, and machinery—all but iron and machinery depended directly on the products of the soil for their existence. Put differently: of the total value of manufactures in 1860 (about $2 billion), well over one half represented the cost of raw materials, most of them the products of burgeoning American farms.

The source of supply of raw materials dictated the location of some industries, such as lumbering, copper and coal mining, and iron production. Most manufacturing, however, was not controlled by that factor so much as by the avail-

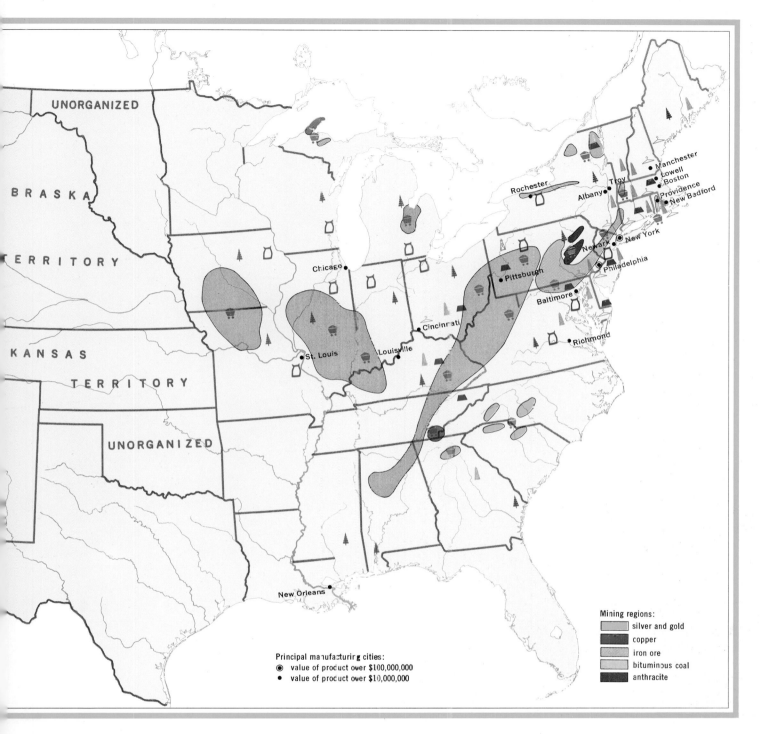

Principal manufacturing cities:
◉ value of product over $100,000,000
• value of product over $10,000,000

Mining regions:
silver and gold
copper
iron ore
bituminous coal
anthracite

ability of capital and labor and the presence of industrial enterprise. Less than 10 per cent of manufacturing was in the South, for instance, principally because slavery absorbed most southern capital and, at the same time, discouraged immigrants (who were the bulk of the industrial labor force by 1860) from settling in the South. Thus the booming American cotton textile industry, using immigrant labor, became centered chiefly in New England, far from the source of the raw material. Of the major industries, only flour milling was widely diffused, and even in this case, great milling centers were already developing in the Middle West, upper New York State, and New York City.

As manufacturing expanded, the cities of America continued their rapid growth. By 1860 New York had about one million inhabitants, Philadelphia half a million, and seven other cities more than 100,000 each. Over 15 per cent of the people lived in urban centers, most of them earning their bread directly or indirectly from non-farm activities. But America was not yet a nation of factories. Few large corporations existed; most manufacturing was carried out in small shops, or even in homes. The typical American remained a farmer, although the situation was changing fast.

One aspect of the change was the rapid spread of the telegraph. Samuel F. B. Morse installed the first line, between Washington and Baltimore, in 1844. Eleven years later, as the map (overleaf) shows, every major center was utilizing the new form of communication, although the South, as in many other ways, lagged behind the rest of the country.

Tariff of Rates by the National Telegraph Lines,

FROM PITTSBURGH, PA.

TO ALL PARTS OF THE UNITED STATES AND THE CANADAS.

Office, South East corner of Wood and Third Streets.

A

Alexandria, Va.; Albany, N.Y.; Auburn; Amsterdam; Erie, Pa.; Ausable Forks; Avon; Ann Arbor, Mich.; Adrian; Algonac; Albion; Akron, Ill.; Aurora; Attica, Ind.; Astoria; Athens, O.; Akron; Ashtabula; Ashland; Appleton, Wis.; Atlanta, Ga.; Augusta; Arrow Rock, Mo.; Allentown, Pa.; Altoona; Amherst; Augusta, Me.; Antogonish, N.S.; Amherst; Annapolis

B

Baltimore, Md.; Bedford, Pa.; Beaver; Beaver Dam; Brownsville; Bethlehem; Berwick; Beach Haven; Bloomsburg; Beach Creek; Bellefonte; Bath; Baton Rouge, La.; Buffalo, N.Y.; Batavia; Brockport; Baldwinsville; Bennington, Vt.; Burlington; Bellows Falls; Brattleboro; Brandon; Burlington, Iowa; Battle Creek, Mich.; Birmingham; Boston, Mass.; Bradford; Belfast, Me.; Bangor; Beloit, Wis.; Belvidere, Ill.; Beardstown; Bristol; Bellefontaine; Beallsville; Bolivar; Bellevue; Bardstown, Ky.; Bridgeport, Conn.; Brantford, C.W.; Berthier; Bogasanville; Brockville; Bytown; Belleville; Boonville, Mo.; Barry; Bend of Petticodiac, N.B.; Bridgetown, N.S.; Bolivar, Tenn.

C

Chambersburg, Pa.; Carlisle; Columbia; Columbus; Clarksville; Catasqua; Chapman; Cheraw, S.C.; Camden; Columbia; Charleston; Columbus, Ga.; Columbia, Ala.; Cantwell's Bridge, Del.; Columbus; Cincinnati; Circleville; Chillicothe; Cuyahoga Falls; Cleveland; Chagrin Falls; Canton; Carlton; Cardington; Canal Fulton; Cambridge; Crawfordsville; Covington; Clinton; Columbus, Miss.; Canton; Clinton; Carrollton; Carmel, N.Y.; Cooperstown; Canandaigua; Cherry Valley; Coxsackie; Catskill; Cold Spring; Caraeadaree; Caldwell; Chester; Chazy; Clinton; Cuylerville; Castleton, Vt.; Chester; Claremont, N.H.; Chicopee; Corwall, C.W.; Chippewa; Clifton House; Chicago; Cairo; Carrollton; Cold Water, Mich.; Constantine; Crown Point; Clarkston; Chelsea; Cairo, Me.; Churchfield; Cape Girardeau, Mo.; Columbia, Tenn.; Clarksville; Cedarburg, Wis.; Charlestown, Va.; Charleston; Covington, Ky.; Cumberland, Md.; Concord, N.H.; Charlestown; Cottingsville; Chatham, N.B.; Chester, N.S.

D

Detroit, Mich.; Dover, Del.; Easton; Debance; Dresden; Delaware; Dover; Dixe; Dundee; Dubuque, Iowa; Davenport; Delhi; Doddville, Wis.; Dundas; Darlington; Dover, N.H.; Danville; Danville, Me.; Dorchester, N.B.; Danby

E

Evansville, Ia.; Eugene; Elkhart; Erie, Pa.; Easton; Elyria, O.; Eaton; Elgin, Ill.; Eastport, Miss.; Elmyra, N.Y.; Elizabethtown; Eastville; Ellsworth, Me.; East Thomaston; East Machias; Eastport; Enfield, N.H.; Essex, Vt.; Eddyville

F

Fredericksburg, Va.; Fanville; Fayetteville, N.C.; Fort Plain; Fredonia; Fort Edwards; Fonda; Fulton; Frankfort, Ky.; Florence, Ala.; Frederick City, Md.; Fort Wayne, Ia.; Fort Atkinson, Wis.; Fou du Lac; Flint, Mich.; Franklin Mills; Fairport; Fremont; Fayette, Mo.; Fort Madison, Iowa; Freemansburg, Pa.; Franklin, Mass.; Fall River; Fitchburg; Fitzwilliam; Fredericton, N.B.

G

Greensburg, Pa.; Gordon; Girard; Georgetown, D.C.; Galena, Ill.; Geneva; Greenville; Gallipolis; Granville; Germantown; Glasgow, Ky.; Gallatin, Tenn.; Gallatin, Miss.; Granada; Grand Gulf; Green Bush, Wis.; Green Bay; Goshen; Goodrich, Mich.; Gilea's Falls, Vt.; Genesee; Germanpee, C.W.; Griffin, Ga.; Gardiner, Me.; Gorham; Greenfield, Mass.; Grand Falls, N.B.

H

Harrisburg, Pa.; Hollidaysburg; Huntingdon; Hazleton; Havre de Grace, Md.; Hannibal, Mo.; Holly Springs, Miss.; Hudson; Hebron; Hamilton; Hamilton, N.C.; Hopkinsville, Ky.; Halifax, N.S.; Herkimer, N.Y.; Hudson; Hornesville; Hamilton; Hatsonville; Hazleton, Wis.; Kensington; Hd'son; Hartford, Conn.; Hallowell, Me.; Hanover, N.H.

I & J

Jersey City, N.J.; Jackson, Mich.; Janesville; Joliet; Janesville, Ill.; Jacksonville; Jersey Shore, Pa.; Irving; Johnstown; Junction; Jasonto; Jacksonburg, Ia.; Jay; Jefferson; Jefferson, Wis.; Janesville; Jefferson City, Mo.; Jamestown; Independence, Ia.; **Indianapolis**; Junction, Mass.

K

Kalamazoo, Mich.; Keokuk, Iowa; Kingston, C.W.; Kaskaski, Miss.; Kingston; Keene; Knderhook; Knoxville; Kanawha, Va.; Kingston; Kenosha, Wis.; Kenosha; Keene, N.H.

L

Lewistown, Pa.; Lancaster; Lewisburg; Lock Haven; Lebanon; Liverpool; Lexington, Mo.; Liberty; Lewistown, Del.; Lexington, Ky.; Lafayette; Logansport; Laporte; Lima; Lakeport; Little Falls; Lockport, N.Y.; Lenox; Lyons; Lockport, Ill.; Lynchburg, Va.; Lowell, Mass.; Lebanon; Lewisburg; Lake Mills; Lexington

M & Mc

Mt. Carbon, Pa.; Meadville; Montrose; March Chunk; Milton; Muncy; M'Ewensburg; Milesburg; M'Ewensville; Montgomville; Mill Hall; Mifflinstown; M'Kee's Falls; Macon, Ga.; Montgomery, Ala.; **Mobile**; Milford, Del.; Morris, Ill.; Mt. Sterling; Morengo; Mt. Carroll; Marietta; Massillon; Milan; Maumee City; Middletown; Mt. Gilead; Mt. Vernon; Medina; Mansfield; M'Connellsville; Morrow; Medina, N.Y.; Mott; Mt. Morris; Monroe, Mich.; Marshall; Mt. Clemens; Michigan City, Ind.; Mt. Carroll; Madison; Milwaukie, Wis.; Monmouth; Milwaukie; Mineral Point; Middlebury, Vt.; Montpelier; Maysville, Ky.; Marion; Macon; **Memphis**, Tenn.; Middletown, Conn.; Meriden; Muscatine; Martinsville, Va.; Malden; Manchester, Me.; Machias, Me.

N

New York City; Norristown, Pa.; New Castle; Northampton; Nazareth; North East; Northumberland; New Buffalo, Mich.; Niles; Newport; New Baltimore; Naperville, Ill.; New Washington; New Lisbon; New Richmond; New Philadelphia; Newark; Niagara Falls, N.Y.; Newburg; Norwich; **Natchez**, Miss.; Northfield, Vt.; Nashua, N.H.; New Glasgow; **New Orleans**, La.; **Nashville**, Tenn.; New Albany; Norwich; Newport, R.I.

O

Ottawa, Ill.; Oswego, N.Y.; Oriskny Falls; Ogdensburg; Oneida; Oxford; Oakville; Oquaqua, Wis.; Oshkosh; Orwell, Vt.; Oshawa, C.W.

P

Philadelphia, Pa.; Port Richmond; Pottstown; Pottsville; Plymouth; Pittstown; Port Clinton; Petersburg, Va.; Point Pleasant; Portsmouth; Princeton, N.J.; Paoli, Ia.; Perrysville; Peru; Plymouth; Pomeroy, O.; Portsmouth; Port Washington; Pikston; Painesville; Papa; Poughkeepsie, N.Y.; Palmyra; Parkskill; Plattsburg; Pike; Port Yan; Port Hope, L.C.; Prescott; Preston, Wis.; Pekin, Ill.; Plattsville; Palmyra; Portsmouth, N.H.; Pittsfield, Mass.; Palmer; **Providence**, R.I.; Palmyra, Ala.; **Portland**, Me.; Port Huron; Pontiac; Paris; Plymouth; Paducah; Peru, N.S.

Q

Quebec, L.C.; Quincadee, C.W.; Quincy

R

Reading, Pa.

Rochester; Richmond, Va.; **Raleigh**; Rock Island, Ill.; Rock Island; Rockford; Rockton; Ripley, O.; Republic; Ravenna; Roscoe; Richmond, Ia.; Rising Sun; Racine, W.T.; Rome, N.Y.; Rochester; Rondout; Rutland, Vt.; Ripley; River Trent, C.W.; River De Loup, L.C.; Randolph, Mass.; Rockland, Me.; Richmond; Richmond, N.B.

S

Sharon, Pa.; Sunbury; Scotia's Grove; Shippensburg; Somerset; Smithland; Smithland, Ky.; Shelbyville; Steubenville, O.; Springfield; Shelbyville; Somerset; Sandusky City; Salem, Ill.; Springfield; St. Charles; South Bend, Ind.; Shelbyville; Southport, Wis.; Shiolsburg; Sheboygan Falls; Schenectady; Syracuse; Saugerties; Saratoga Springs; Silver Creek; Sandy Hill, N.Y.; Sheldon; Sherburne, Vt.; St. Johnsbury; St. Albans; Springfield; St. Catharine's, C.W.; Saganow, Mich.; St. Clair; Sturges; Saline; South Bend; St. John's, N.B.; Sackville; St. Andrew's; St. George; Shediac; Salem, Mass.; Springfield; Savannah, Ga.; Suffolk; Smithfield; Stamford, Conn.; St. Louis, Mo.; St. Joseph; St. Genevieve; St. John; Savanna; St. Stevens, N.S.; Sidney

T

Trenton, N.J.; Tuscumbia, Ala.; Toledo; Troy; Tiffin; Thressa; Tonawand; Toronto, C.W.; Three Rivers; Terre Haute, Ia.; Trumansburg; Truro, N.S.; Tobique; Taunton, Mass.; Thomas, Me.; Trenton, Mich.

U

Uniontown, Pa.; Utica, N.Y.; Urbana, O.; Uticaville; Union, Mo.

V

Vincennes, Ia.; Valparaiso; Versailles, Ky.; **Vicksburg**, Miss.; Vergenes, Vt.

W

Wrightsville; Waterford; Warren; Wilkesbarre, Pa.; Washington; West Greenville; Williamsport; West Chester; Washington, D.C.; **Wheeling**; Winchester; Wellsville; Warren; West Union; Wooster; Woodsfield; Wellington; Westfield; Wilmington; Washington; Waverly; West Troy; Watertown; White Hall; Warrensburg; Waterloo; Water ville; Waukesha, Wis.; Whitewater; Wabash, Ill.; Warsaw; Whitby; Washington, Mich.; Wilmington, N.C.; Woodstock; Waterbury; Windsor; West Randolph; Wells River; Wellsham; Woodbury; Whipple; Warrenton; Woodville; Weston, Mo.; Weymouth, N.S.; Windsor; Wickham; Wilkeston; Warsaw, Ga.; Woodstock, C.W.

X

Xenia, O.

Y

York, Pa.; Youngstown; Ypsilanti, Mich.; Yarmouth; Yanoo City, Miss.

Z

Zanesville, O.

J. D. REID, Sup't. National Telegraph Lines.

Telegraph now in operation between Vera Cruz and the City of Mexico. Morse Patent... all the intermediate cities and towns. A line is contemplated to extend from the City of Mexico to the Pacific 500 miles. There is now in process of construction on the Island of Cuba 1200 miles, House Patent, embracing 51 Stations. Total cost estimated at $8,400,700

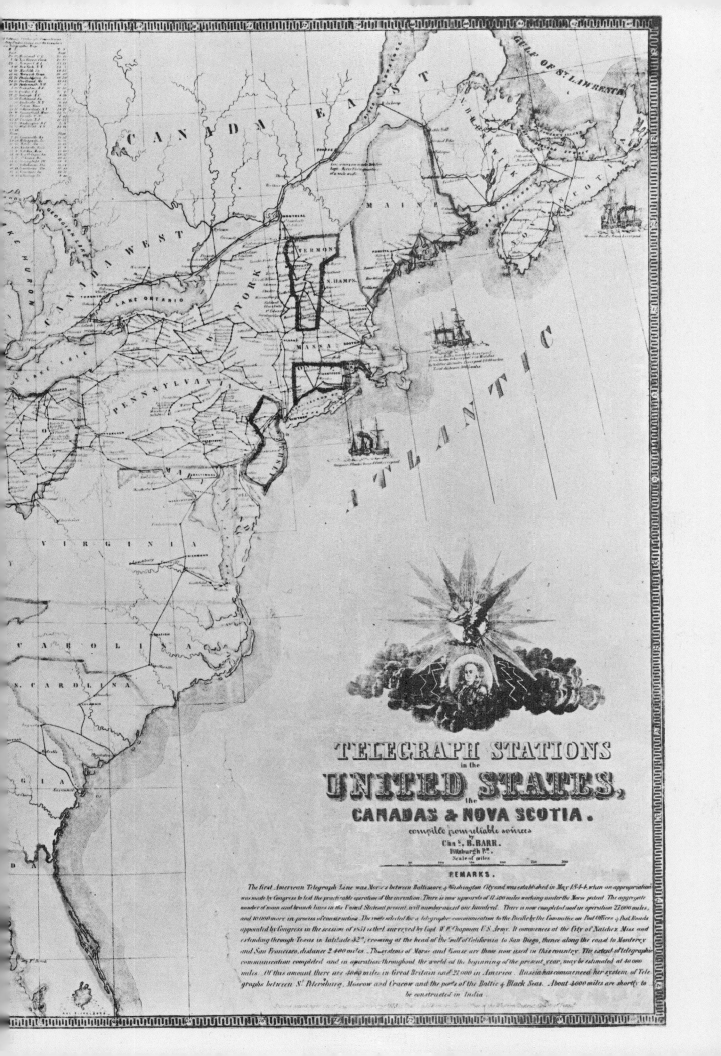

TELEGRAPH STATIONS
in the
UNITED STATES,
the
CANADAS & NOVA SCOTIA.

compiled from reliable sources

by

Chas. B. BARR.

Pittsburgh Pa.

Scale of miles

REMARKS.

The first American Telegraph Line was Morse's between Baltimore & Washington City and was established in May 1844, when an appropriation was made by Congress to test the practicable operation of the invention. There is now upwards of 17,500 miles working under the Morse patent. The aggregate number of main and branch lines in the United States at present, will number about one hundred. There is now completed and in operation 27,000 miles, and 10,000 more in process of construction. The route selected for a telegraphic communication to the Pacific by the Committee on Post Offices & Post Roads appointed by Congress in the session of 1851 is that surveyed by Capt. W.H. Chapman U.S. Army. It commences at the City of Natchez, Miss. and extending through Texas in latitude 32°, crossing at the head of the Gulf of California to San Diego, thence along the coast to Monterey and San Francisco, distance 2,400 miles. The systems of Morse and House are those now used in this country. The extent of telegraphic communication completed and in operation throughout the world at the beginning of the present year, may be estimated at 40,000 miles. Of this amount there are 40,000 miles in Great Britain and 27,000 in America. Russia has commenced her system of Telegraphs between St. Petersburg, Moscow and Cracow and the ports of the Baltic & Black Seas. About 4,000 miles are shortly to be constructed in India.

CHAPTER 6
THE NATION DIVIDED

U p to the close of the war with Mexico, in 1848, telling the story of America by means of maps involves chiefly presenting maps that will show the nation's growth to full continental expanse—from a comparatively narrow strip along the Atlantic seaboard to a vast area that reaches from ocean to ocean. After that the story for a time becomes different.

Until then, the map of the U.S. keeps growing larger, generation after generation, as new regions are acquired and explored. Now it has reached its limit, and the outline stays the same. The changes henceforth are internal. The boundaries that cut the continental expanse into segments become all-important.

It is as if the growing nation had swallowed more than it could digest, so that its primary task had suddenly become consolidation. America had grown into a continental power, but it began to look as if the separate parts that made up this continental domain had not been properly cemented together. Success had attended the great, unceasing drive to expand to the uttermost limits, but there was grave danger that the fusion had been imperfect and that fission would follow.

At the bottom of it all there was the fact that human slavery existed in one part of the nation and was outlawed in the other part. This took place not so much because the men in one part had one idea about the virtues of slavery while the men in the other part had different ideas, as because slavery was profitable in one part and was unprofitable in the other. Over the course of the years, different societies had developed because of this fact. The southern states were ideally adapted to the mass production of the great agricultural staple cotton—for which world demand had increased enormously after cheap new methods of turning the raw fiber into cloth had been devised. To raise cotton in the huge quantities that were now sought by mills in New England, in England, and in France, what would now be called the factory-farm was ideal. The work required gang labor, unskilled but abundant, and the soil and climate in much of the southern part of the United States could grow as much cotton as the world needed, provided the abundance of that gang labor supply remained unchecked. It also developed that in certain parts of the South both rice and sugar could also be produced in this way.

In the North it was different. Gang labor was not adapted to the growing of wheat, corn, livestock, or ordinary garden truck. A farmer in New York, Pennsylvania, or Ohio who undertook to operate an oversized farm with a gang of 100 slaves would go broke in short order. Since slave labor did not seem to be suitable for work in factories, the North quickly discarded the institution; it simply did not pay.

As a result, the southern states developed an economy and a society based on the large plantation and chattel slavery, and in a short time this economy and society developed interests quite unlike those in the North. It was predominantly a rural society, with no large cities and comparatively few small ones. It relied upon world markets, and hence it believed in low tariffs—it exported much of what it produced, and it imported most of what it did not produce. It had little use for government policies that would foster the spread of industry or bind the whole national area together into an economic unit. As long as there was plenty of cheap land and cheap labor, this society could get along very well. It wanted to be let alone with what it had.

In the North, naturally enough, things were just the reverse. An entirely different sort of economy and society developed there. To farmers, businessmen, and workers, the domestic market seemed all-important, and more and more they came to feel that the government ought to protect that market; and out of this feeling, of course, came a belief that substantial tariff barriers were entirely proper. It was also believed that the central government ought to do all it could to foster the spread of internal improvements, so that farmer and manufacturer could be near their markets and could have ready access to raw materials. By sheer force of circumstances people in the North saw themselves as part of a unified nation; far from wanting to be let alone with what they had, they wanted the whole land bound together into a cohesive whole.

So the new nation, which had hardly begun to adjust itself to its new, enlarged boundaries, found that it contained two societies whose people had different wants and different ways of regarding themselves and the country they lived in. Folkways and habits of thought became divergent. A sense of separateness began to develop.

Taken by itself, this might not have been a very serious problem. The two sections continued to be highly interdependent. In the South, men needed the goods brought down from the North, all the way from salt pork to wagons, from sewing machines to ironware; and in the North the people who produced all of those things needed the southern market—and the rapidly growing New England textile industry was, of course, totally reliant on an unbroken supply of southern cotton. The two societies may have had different attitudes, but the forces that bound them together were still stronger than the forces that tended to drive them apart.

. . . except for the institution of slavery itself, and the emotions it produced.

Slavery was the indigestible lump. In a land dedicated to freedom and equality, chattel slavery was a mockery and a cruel anachronism, and increasingly it came to look like a moral wrong that ought to be righted. Unfortunately, it was ever so much easier for people to feel this way in the North, where, after all, slavery did not exist, than in the South, where it not only existed but lay at the very foundation of the whole economic setup. The northerner could come to see slavery as an evil that ought to be abolished; the southerner was much more likely—indeed, he was almost certain—to see it as an evil that had to be lived with. To tear it up by the roots would mean, for the South, an economic upheaval of shattering proportions. As antislavery agitation increased in the North the subject became charged with the deepest emotions. Seeing slavery as a moral wrong, men could believe that the people who upheld slavery were morally wrong; seeing this institution attacked with rising fervor, the southerner could believe that the antislavery agitation was aimed at him personally, that it was an attempt to destroy not merely a human institution (about which, privately, he had grave doubts of his own) but the whole structure of southern society.

To complicate matters still more fatally, population in the North was growing much more rapidly than it was growing in the South. This was inevitable, because the free, developing North offered infinitely more economic opportunities to the average man than did the plantation South, but it upset the balance just when the emotional tension was growing more and more nearly unendurable.

Until approximately the end of the Mexican War, the two sections had been roughly equal in political strength. Neither section could gain full control of the national government without the consent of at least a fair part of the other section, which meant that in the long run the opposing aims of the sections were likely to be compromised. The Democratic Party was largely dominant, and it drew its strength from the South and the Middle West. Under this system, extreme demands from either North or South were not apt to be embodied in national policy.

But after 1848 the balance began to shift at a rather rapid rate. Until then, the South had been able to exercise a somewhat loose control over the central government; but by 1850 a thoughtful southerner was compelled to realize that this probably was not going to go on much longer. Sooner or later the North was bound to be so much more populous that control would pass to its hands. Once that control became solid, southern institutions—not merely slavery, but the entire southern way of life that rested on slavery—were probably doomed.

So for the better part of two decades the story is told in smaller maps, showing how men tried to cope with the approaching change, what they did when the change became imminent, and what came of it all.

MISSOURI COMPROMISE 1820

SECTIONAL STRUGGLE *and* COMPROMISE

For a long time the story of America's effort to handle the emerging crisis is the story of political compromise. It began in 1820, when the need to preserve the balance between the two sections was already visible, and the map at the upper left shows the arrangement made by the famous Missouri Compromise.

In this map, slave states are shown in dark brown. Missouri claimed admission as a state, and it was agreed in Congress that Missouri, where slavery existed, could come in with slavery, but that any states that might thereafter be formed from the territory lying north of Missouri's southern boundary, the line of 36° 30′ N., would come in as free states.

This delicate balance lasted until the end of the Mexican War, when the unorganized territory in the West was suddenly vastly expanded. If the Missouri Compromise line ran west to the Pacific coast the balance would vanish, because obviously many more states could be created north of that line than south of it. In addition, California was demanding admission as a free state, and half of California lay south of the line.

So the Compromise of 1850 was devised, after months of most heated debate in Congress. By this time the emotions generated by the slavery controversy had grown much higher, and when the "free soil" advocates in the North demanded that slavery be outlawed in all of the territory acquired from Mexico, the South began to talk about secession. Only diligent work by such men as Henry Clay, Daniel Webster, and Stephen A. Douglas worked out the compromise.

The map at center shows some of the

COMPROMISE OF 1850

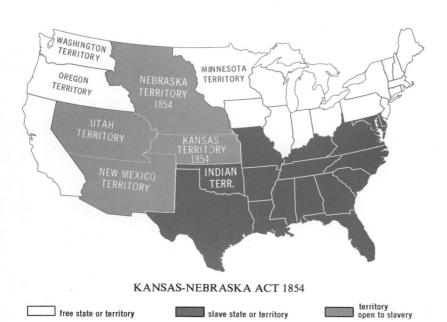

KANSAS-NEBRASKA ACT 1854

☐ free state or territory   ■ slave state or territory   ■ territory open to slavery

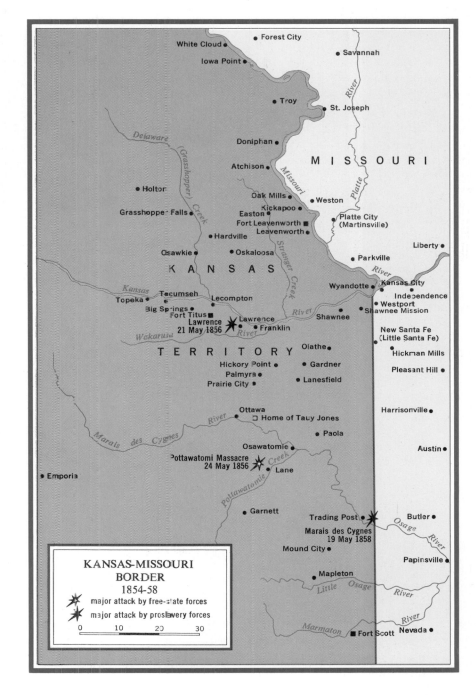

The immediate consequence of the 1854 Kansas-Nebraska Act was much bloodshed in eastern Kansas, where proslavery and antislavery settlers (strongly backed by important people in the North and in the South) came to fighting. The map below shows the area in which the clashes took place; at right is a view of the town of Lawrence, a free-state stronghold in Kansas, after slavery proponents had sacked it in May, 1856.

effects. California was admitted as a free state. The vast Utah and New Mexico territories were allowed to have slavery (although, as a matter of fact, these lands were ill-adapted to slavery, and the institution never took roots) with the proviso that when states were created there, the inhabitants of the territories would decide for themselves whether the states should come in as slave or free. In addition, a tighter fugitive slave law was adopted . . . and an uneasy peace descended on the political scene.

This peace did not last long. In a short time it became necessary to set up territorial governments for the sprawling areas of Kansas and Nebraska—this, largely because it was obviously going to be necessary to build a railroad to the Pacific, and the territory through which the railroad would run must have some sort of governmental organization. The trouble was that southern leaders vigorously opposed this, inasmuch as both Kansas and Nebraska lay north of the Missouri Compromise line and hence would eventually become free states.

Senator Douglas's Kansas-Nebraska Act of 1854 (bottom map, opposite page) was the result. It repealed the Missouri Compromise, opened the new territories to slavery, and provided that the territorial voters themselves would have the right to determine whether the states that would finally be formed should or should not have slavery.

As a temporary makeshift, this averted the impending storm for a time. As a long-range matter, however, it intensified it. On paper (as the map shows), it greatly expanded the slavery area.

KANSAS-MISSOURI
BORDER
1854-58

★ major attack by free-state forces

✴ major attack by proslavery forces

0   10   20   30

SLAVE TRADE *and* ABOLITION

Perhaps one of the nation's problems, as the tormented decade of the 1850's came to an end, was the fact that people looked at the map instead of at reality.

The map at right shows how the slave and free areas were divided at that time. The difficulty is that the map was just a little unreal.

For example, the map shows the two sections, but it means less than it seems to. Slave states and free states were as they are depicted here, and so were the territories; but although all of the territories were legally open to slavery, they were not territories in which slavery could prosper. Slavery was profitable to the slaveowners only in areas where staple crops like cotton, or sugar, or rice could be produced by gang labor, and by 1860 those areas were already included in the southern states. The territories, open to slavery by law, were places where it simply did not pay to use slaves. If the men of that day had been able to discard emotion and use cold intelligence, they would have seen easily enough that New Mexico, the Kansas-Nebraska country, and all the rest of the West was not a region in which slavery could pay its way.

But, meanwhile, the domestic slave trade was most active. From such states as Virginia and Kentucky, where it was less and less a paying business to operate farms with slave labor, the surplus of slaves drained off to the Gulf Coast states.

Most of this trade moved overland. Gangs of slaves were formed in "coffles," ironed and guarded, and marched hundreds of miles into the Deep South for sale to the cotton planters. Northern abolitionists hotly accused Virginians and Kentuckians of conducting breeding farms to supply this trade—which, of course, did nothing to make Virginians and Kentuckians feel more kindly toward their northern brethren.

Some of the slaves went to their destination by sea, from such ports as Norfolk, Charleston and Savannah. The importation of slaves from Africa was illegal, and although some smuggling was done, via Cuba, by 1860 this trade had become unimportant.

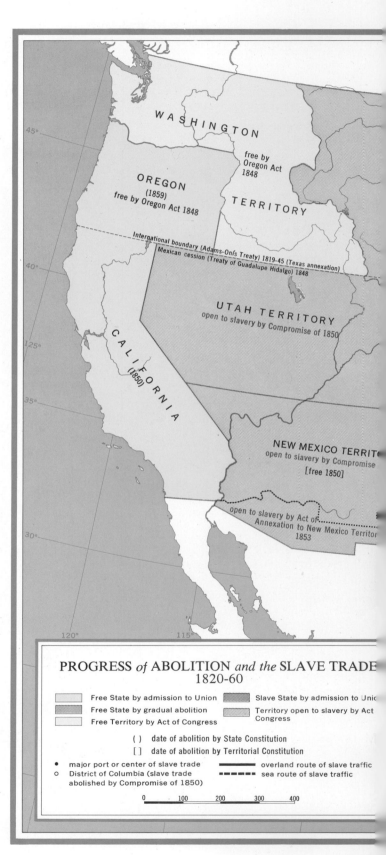

CLARKSON, *History of the Abolition of African Slave Trade*, 1808

The original slave trade from Africa to the United States was unspeakably horrible. The contemporary diagram above depicts how the captives were packed, sardine-like, in a typical slave carrier.

Map labels

WASHINGTON

free by Oregon Act 1848

OREGON (1859) free by Oregon Act 1848

TERRITORY

International boundary (Adams-Onis Treaty) 1819-45 (Texas annexation)
Mexican cession (Treaty of Guadalupe Hidalgo) 1848

UTAH TERRITORY open to slavery by Compromise of 1850

CALIFORNIA (1850)

NEW MEXICO TERRIT[ORY] open to slavery by Compromise [free 1850]

open to slavery by Act of Annexation to New Mexico Territor[y] 1853

PROGRESS *of* ABOLITION *and the* SLAVE TRADE 1820-60

Free State by admission to Union
Free State by gradual abolition
Free Territory by Act of Congress
Slave State by admission to Uni[on]
Territory open to slavery by Act [of] Congress

( ) date of abolition by State Constitution
[ ] date of abolition by Territorial Constitution

• major port or center of slave trade
o District of Columbia (slave trade abolished by Compromise of 1850)
—— overland route of slave traffic
----- sea route of slave traffic

0   100   200   300   400

This roughhewn frontier home, seen in 1857, was the Governor's Mansion at Lecompton, the capital of Kansas Territory.

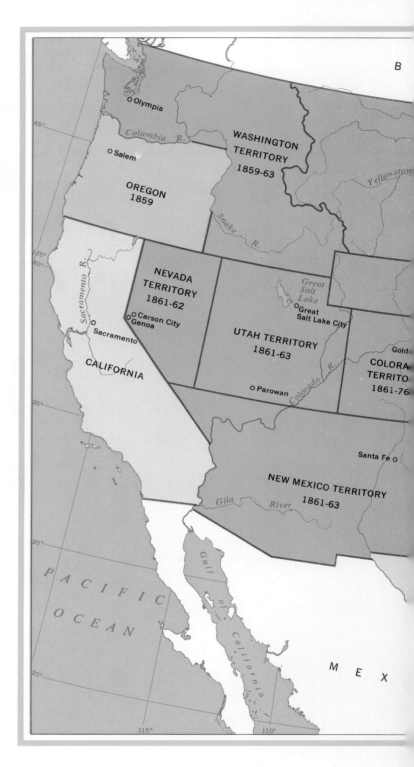

Between 1854 and 1861—that is, between the time of the Kansas-Nebraska Act and the outbreak of the Civil War—the map of the United States looked like this.

It was all one country, running from one ocean to the other, solidly organized and settled east of the Mississippi, less solidly organized and settled west of there. From Lake Superior to the Gulf there was a huge bloc of states, functioning as parts of the American Union. On the map, this was a unit. It was the United States—tied together by economic and spiritual bonds, a recognizable and coherent nation. In point of fact it was torn by anger, suspicion, and fear, but on paper it was the American nation, one and indivisible.

One of the divisive elements in the situation then was the immense stretch of territorial country, shaded in green on this map, running west from the Missouri River. California and Minnesota came in during the 1850's, and so at last did Oregon, with Kansas following once the war began; but most of the rest of this country was empty, or nearly so, awaiting settlers. But the question of what would happen once the settlers arrived was highly disturbing. Would this area be slave or free? If it became slave, the precarious old balance could continue, and northerners who disliked slavery could go on fearing that slavery was by nature expansionist, never satisfied with what it had, but claiming more and more territory. If it became free, on the other hand, the people of the South could see the old balance destroyed forever and could look forward to nothing but an eventual overturn of the foundations of the way of life that looked good to them.

So the complicated set of emotions that led up to the Civil War grew out of this question of whether slavery should or should not exist in enormous reaches of country where hardly anyone at all, free or slave, then lived. It was unreal, in a way, because it tried to grapple with a question that simple geography would finally resolve, but it was dreadfully real in that it went to the heart of emotions that had all Americans deeply stirred.

UNION
in the BALANCE

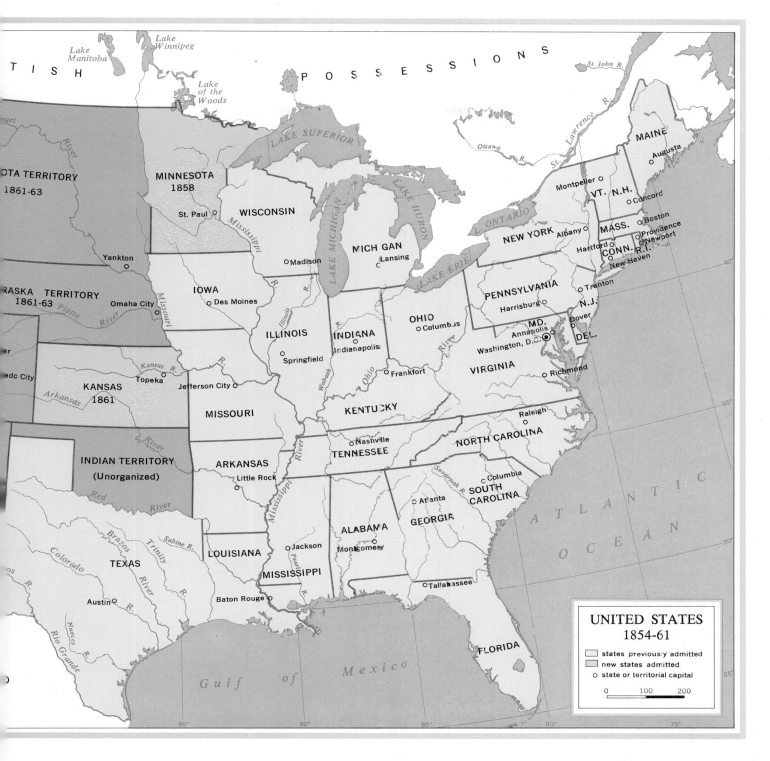

UNITED STATES
1854-61

☐ states previously admitted
☐ new states admitted
○ state or territorial capital

0   100   200

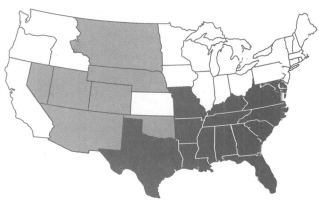

Dividing the American nation in 1861 into free and slave
areas, coloring the areas in which slavery was permitted dark
brown, leaving the areas in which it was not permitted white,
and putting light brown on the region where the question was
still undecided, you get a map like the one on the left. The
northern states were smaller in total geographic area, but
were much bigger in population and resources. The western
territories where no decision had been made were very largely
unsettled, and one of the supreme ironies of American history
is the fact that the argument over slavery in the sparsely populated territories was a moving factor in the cause of war.

THE RAILROADS

One of the things the country talked about most during the 1850's was slavery; one of the things that it did most enthusiastically, and to the most enduring effect, was to build a railroad network. This map, highlighting in red the roads built in the 1850's, shows what had been accomplished by the time the Civil War broke out.

A nation that lives largely by automobiles and airplanes may have a little trouble understanding just what railroads meant in the 1850's. At that time they were lifelines, the all-essential means by which distant areas were tied together, the channels of transportation without which a region could not grow and prosper.

As will be seen by a glance at the map, the decade of the 1850's was a time of frenzied railroad construction. As a matter of course, the greater part of this took place in the North, where there were more goods to be carried. By the end of the decade the northern part of the country had a fairly comprehensive railroad network. There were three trunk lines, connecting the great interior of the nation with the East Coast. These roads branched out through connecting lines to cover such growing states as Ohio, Indiana, and Illinois, with additional branches running off into Iowa, Wisconsin, and Missouri. Nobody quite realized it, but the big east-west trunk lines had already ended the Middle West's dependence on the Mississippi River as a principal artery of traffic. The main economic tie of the western country now was with the East rather than with the southern states.

Development in the South had been equally striking, considering the fact that the South was much less thickly settled and had fewer manufacturing centers. However, there was a subtle difference. Many of the southern railroads were built simply to connect agricultural areas with seaports or river ports. There was only one east-west trunk line—the road that ran east from Memphis to Chattanooga, forking there to send one line on to Richmond and Norfolk and another down through Atlanta to Charleston and Savannah.

What this meant was that by 1861, when the two sections went to war, the North had a railroad network that tied the states together and helped enormously in the conduct of the war; and the South had a series of independent lines that looked like a network on the map but actually were a good deal less than that. In the North the railroads were a framework for industrial and commercial solidarity; in the South they served separate regions, and when war came these contrasting situations helped the North and gravely handicapped the South.

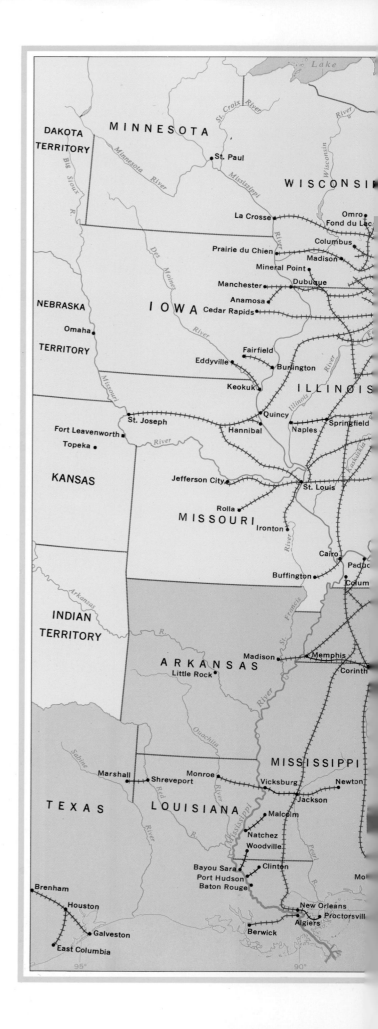

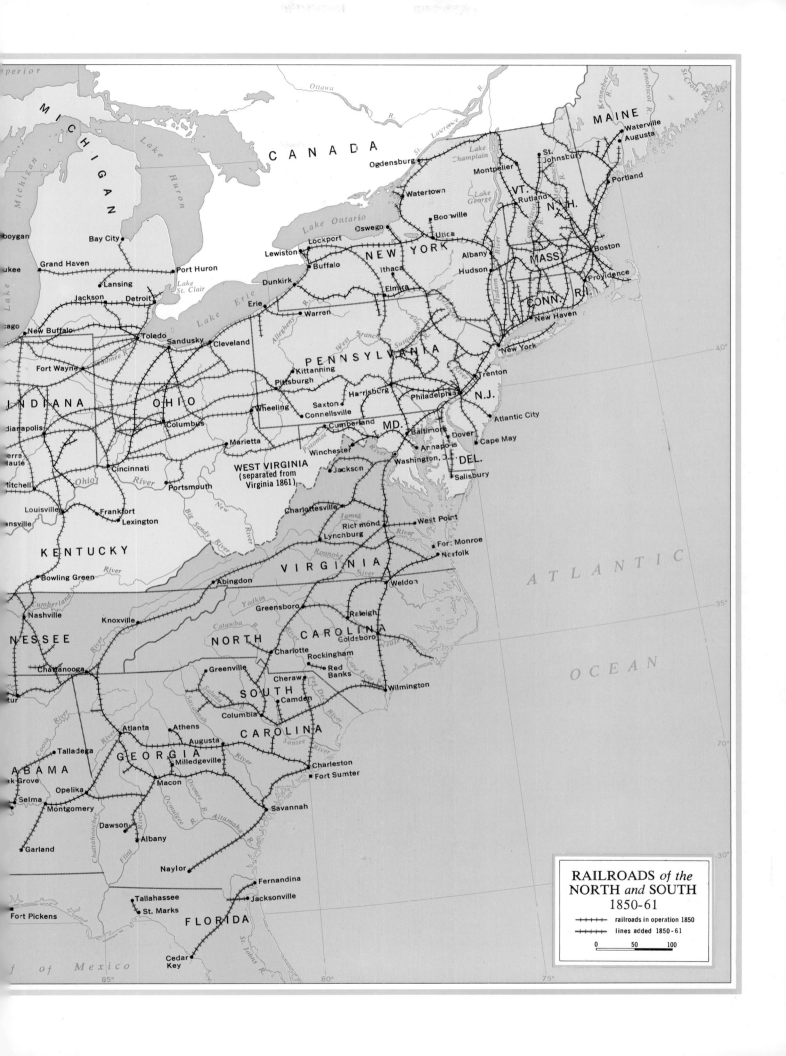

RAILROADS *of the*
NORTH *and* SOUTH
1850-61

railroads in operation 1850

lines added 1850-61

0   50   100

Percentage of slaves in total population (by county) 1860:

■ 50% or over

■ 10-50%

□ under 10%

□ no slaves or unsettled

The Underground Railroad—the system by which slaves running away from servitude were helped across the free states into Canada, where there were no slave-catchers— never actually existed as a central, co-ordinated entity. It simply consisted of a large number of routes across the North in which a fugitive slave could (if his luck was in) find someone to shelter him, feed him, and send him on toward freedom.

There were a good many of these routes, and the map above shows how they ran. The slave's first step was to reach free state country. Then, if he had the right connections or instructions, he could probably find someone who would help him along. Most routes ran up to the Great

Lakes, and if a slave got that far he could usually count on getting someone to stow him aboard a vessel bound for Canada. His travel across the free states was risky, because the fugitive slave law was tolerably well enforced and there was always the danger that local authorities would stop him and send him back south.

When secession came, the southern vote contained few surprises. Seven states seceded before the bombardment of Fort Sumter, and except for a few pockets of Unionist sentiment—most notably in east Tennessee and northern Alabama and Georgia—they were united. After Fort Sumter, Delaware and Maryland rejected secession, and in Kentucky and Missouri a majority held for the Union.

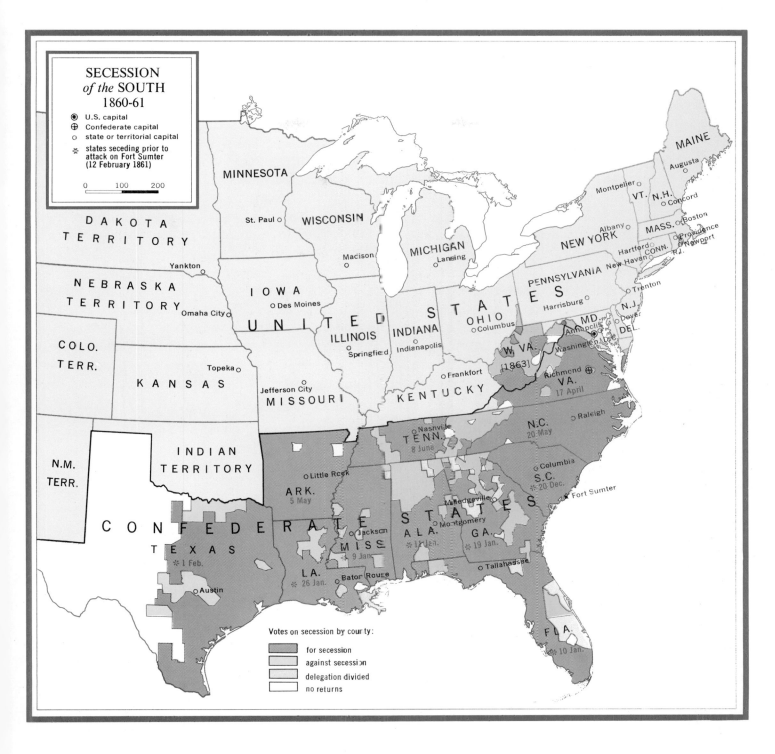

SECESSION
of the SOUTH
1860-61

⊙ U.S. capital
⊕ Confederate capital
○ state or territorial capital
✳ states seceding prior to attack on Fort Sumter (12 February 1861)

0 ———— 100 ———— 200

MINNESOTA

DAKOTA
TERRITORY

St. Paul ○

WISCONSIN

MICHIGAN
Lansing ○

MAINE

Augusta ○

Montpelier ○

VT. N.H.
Concord ○

Yankton ○

NEBRASKA
TERRITORY

IOWA
Des Moines ○

Macison ○

Albany ○

MASS. ○ Boston
Providence

NEW YORK

Hartford CONN. Newport
New Haven R.I.

Omaha City ○

UNITED STATES

PENNSYLVANIA
New York

COLO.
TERR.

KANSAS

Topeka ○

ILLINOIS

Springfiel ○

INDIANA

Indianapolis ○

OHIO

Columbus ○

Harrisburg ○
Trenton ○
N.J.
Dover

MD.
Annapolis ○
Washington DEL.

N.M.
TERR.

Jefferson City ○

MISSOURI

Frankfort ○

KENTUCKY

W. VA.
[1863]

Richmond ⊕
VA.
17 April

INDIAN
TERRITORY

Little Rock ○

Nashville ○
TENN.
8 June

N.C.
20 May

Raleigh ○

C O N F E D E R A T E   S T A T E S

ARK.
5 May

Columbia ○
S.C.
✳ 20 Dec.

Fort Sumter

TEXAS
✳ 1 Feb.

Jackson ○

Milledgeville ○
Montgomery ○

MISS.
✳ 9 Jan.

ALA.
✳ 11 Jan.

GA.
✳ 19 Jan.

Austin ○

LA.
✳ 26 Jan.

Baton Rouge ○

Tallahassee ○

FLA.
✳ 10 Jan.

Votes on secession by county:

for secession
against secession
delegation divided
no returns

SEPARATION
of
GOVERNMENTS

The firing on Fort Sumter, in Charleston Harbor, precipitated the crisis.

THE WAR BEGUN.

Very Exciting News from Charleston.

Important Correspondence Between General Beauregard, Major Anderson and the Southern Secretary of War.

The Summons to Major Anderson to Surrender.

MAJOR ANDERSON'S REFUSAL.

Bombardment of Fort Sumter Commenced.

Terrible Fire from the Secessionists' Batteries.

Brilliant Defence of Maj. Anderson and His Gallant Garrison.

Reckless Bravery of the Confederate States Troops.

SIXTEEN HOURS FIGHTING.

Breaches in the Walls of Fort Sumter.

Several of Major Anderson's Guns Silenced.

THE SCENE

Charleston and Its Defences---Plan of the and Moultrie, Cummings Poin Floating Battery a

lives, and at every shot jump upon the ramparts, observe the effect, and then jump down, cheering.

A party on the Stevens battery are said to have played a game of the hottest fire.

The excitement in the community is indescribable. With the very first boom of the gun thou-

Major Anderson is busy repairing damages received twenty-nine full shots from Stevens tery alone, making the bricks fly from the wa all directions.

It is estimated that from twelve to eig hundred balls and shells were fired durin day. Over one hundred shells took effect i

OPERATIONS.

or, Showing the Position of Forts Sumter
n Battery, Fort Johnson, the
ther Fortifications.

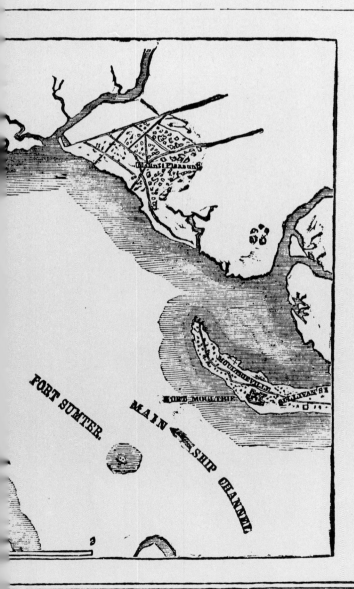

reported that three war vessels are outside

CHARLESTON, April 12—Evening.
firing has ceased for the night, but will be
ed at daylight in the morning, unless an at-
is made to reinforce the fort, which ample
ements have been made to repel.

CHARLESTON AND ITS DEFENCES.

The news of the bombardment of Fort Sumter by the
Confederate forces, which we publish this morning, in-
duces us to give a full description of the scene of operations, embracing the city of Charleston, its harbor and
fortifications. The plans of the forts and batteries, showing the stronghold of Major Anderson and the position of

FORT MOULTRIE.

Fort Moultrie, which first opened its batteries
upon Major Anderson and his command, is one
of the sentinels that guard the principal entrance
to Charleston harbor. It is opposite to and distant from Fort Sumter about one and a half
miles. It is more properly speaking, a huge water battery,
without any guns under cover. Its armament consists of
eleven guns of heavy calibre and several mortars. The
outer and inner walls are of brick, capped with stone and
filled with earth, making a solid wall fifteen or sixteen
feet in thickness. This work has been much strengthened recently, and presents a saucy front to Fort Sumter.
It is now in command of Major Ripley, formerly of the
United States Army, who has under his command several
hundred experienced artillerists.

THE IRON FLOATING BATTERY.

This novel war machine, designed for harbor operations, is now anchored near Sullivan's Island, commanding the barbette guns of Fort Sumter. It is
constructed of palmetto logs, sheathed with plate iron,
and is supposed to be impregnable against shot. It
is embrasured for and mounts four guns of heavy calibre.
It requires sixty men to operate it. The first impression
on seeing this machine is that of immense solidity.
The outer or gun side is covered with six plates of
iron—two of them of the T railroad pattern,
placed horizontally, and the other four bolted
one over the other, in the strongest manner, and
running vertically. The wall of the gun side is
full four feet thick, constructed of that peculiar palmetto
wood so full of fibrous material that sixty four pounders
cannot pierce it. The main deck is wide and roomy.
In nineteen open chambers, on the port side of the deck,
we found a profusion of shot—thirty-four pounders—
while just beyond them is an immense pile of sand bags,
which protect an overhanging roof, under which is to be
placed the hospital. This also protects the magazines
(three in number), under which is the hold proper.
There are six entrances to the hold, which will contain,
if necessary, over three hundred men. It is kept in
place by four heavy wedges, driven down by a species
of ram, which will hold it fast, and prevent any swaying
around by the tide

CUMMING'S POINT IRON BATTERY.

The nearest point of land to Fort Sumter
is Cumming's Point, distance 1,150 yards. On
this point is the celebrated railroad iron battery, an illustration of which we give above.
It consists of a heavy framework of yellow pine logs.
The roof is of the same material over which dovetailed
bars of railroad iron of the T pattern are laid from top to
bottom—all of which is riveted down in the most secure
manner. On the front it presents an angle of about
thirty degrees. There are three portholes, which open
and close with iron shutters of the heaviest description.
When open, the muzzles of the columbiads fill up the
space completely. The recoil of the gun enables the shutters to be closed instantly. It is asserted, on high military authority, that this inclined plane will effectually
resist guns of the heaviest calibre—first, because no shot
can strike it except at an obtuse angle, which would
cause the ball to glance; second, because its power of
resistance is sufficient to withstand the fall of the heaviest

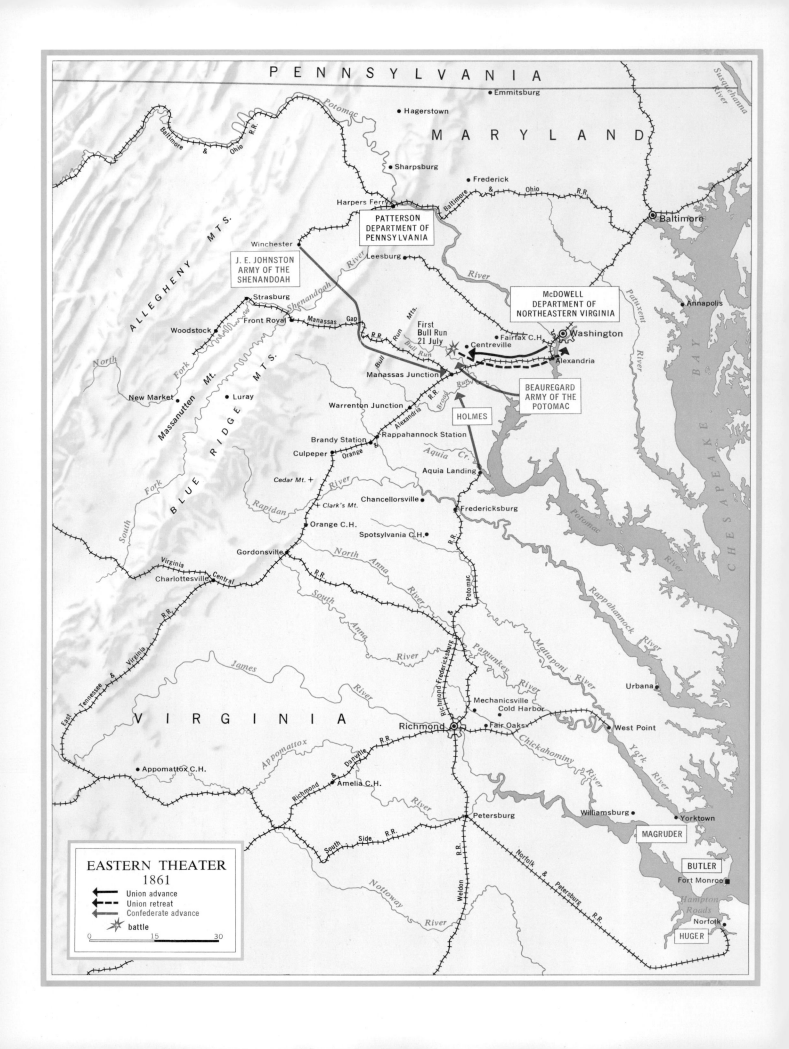

PENNSYLVANIA

MARYLAND

• Emmitsburg

• Hagerstown

Baltimore & Ohio R.R.

• Sharpsburg

• Frederick

Baltimore & Ohio R.R.

◉ Baltimore

Harpers Ferry

**PATTERSON
DEPARTMENT OF
PENNSYLVANIA**

• Winchester

**J. E. JOHNSTON
ARMY OF THE
SHENANDOAH**

• Leesburg

River

• Annapolis

• Strasburg

Shenandoah River

Front Royal

Manassas Gap

**McDOWELL
DEPARTMENT OF
NORTHEASTERN VIRGINIA**

River

Patuxent River

• Woodstock

North Fork

R.R.

Bull Run

First
Bull Run
21 July

• Fairfax C.H.

◎ Washington

Centreville

C H E S A P E A K E

• New Market

Massanutten Mt.

BLUE RIDGE MTS.

• Luray

Manassas Junction

Bull Run

Broad Run

Alexandria

**BEAUREGARD
ARMY OF THE
POTOMAC**

B A Y

Warrenton Junction

Alexandria & R.R.

HOLMES

• Brandy Station

Rappahannock Station

Orange &

Aquia Cr.

• Culpeper

South Fork

Cedar Mt. +

River

Rapidan

• Chancellorsville

Aquia Landing

Potomac

• Orange C.H.

+ Clark's Mt.

• Spotsylvania C.H.

Fredericksburg

Rappahannock River

• Gordonsville

North Anna River

R.R.

• Charlottesville

Virginia Central R.R.

Virginia & Tennessee R.R.

South Anna River

James River

Pamunkey River

Mattaponi River

• Urbana

Richmond Fredericksburg &

• Mechanicsville
Cold Harbor

York River

• West Point

V I R G I N I A

Richmond ◎

• Fair Oaks

Chickahominy River

Appomattox River

Richmond & Danville R.R.

• Amelia C.H.

River

• Williamsburg

• Yorktown

• Appomattox C.H.

South Side R.R.

• Petersburg

Weldon R.R.

Norfolk & Petersburg R.R.

MAGRUDER

BUTLER
Fort Monroe ■

Nottoway River

Hampton Roads

**EASTERN THEATER
1861**

← Union advance
⇠ Union retreat
← Confederate advance
✴ battle

0   15   30

• Norfolk

HUGER

CONTEST *for the* CAPITALS

The first major conflict of the Civil War came in July, 1861, when Union and Confederate armies met along Bull Run creek some 30 miles south and west of Washington. It grew out of an optimistic "on to Richmond" drive by General Irvin McDowell, commander of the Federal Department of Northeastern Virginia.

With 30,000 men, McDowell struck the principal Confederate army, then called the Army of the Potomac (the name was dropped, soon after, and was adopted by the Federals), led by General G. T. Beauregard, who was in position behind Bull Run with 20,000 men. In the Shenandoah Valley with 12,000 more was Beauregard's superior, General J. E. Johnston. Federal plans required General Robert Patterson, who had 15,000 men, to keep Johnston occupied while McDowell crushed Beauregard. The overall situation of the opponents is shown on the opposite page.

McDowell advanced, fought a small preliminary engagement against Beauregard's right on July 18, and brought on a general battle on July 21. Feinting at the Confederate right (below), the Federals moved upstream, crossed Bull Run at Sudley Springs, and moved south to strike Beauregard's main position on Henry House Hill.

For McDowell, all went wrong. Patterson failed to hold Johnston, who joined Beauregard. After an initial success the Federal attack failed, Johnston and Beauregard made a counterstroke, the Federals fell back, and finally McDowell's army recrossed the creek and fled for Washington in a wild rout.

Now Washington, not Richmond, was imperiled, and remained in uneasy security until the war's end (see page 224).

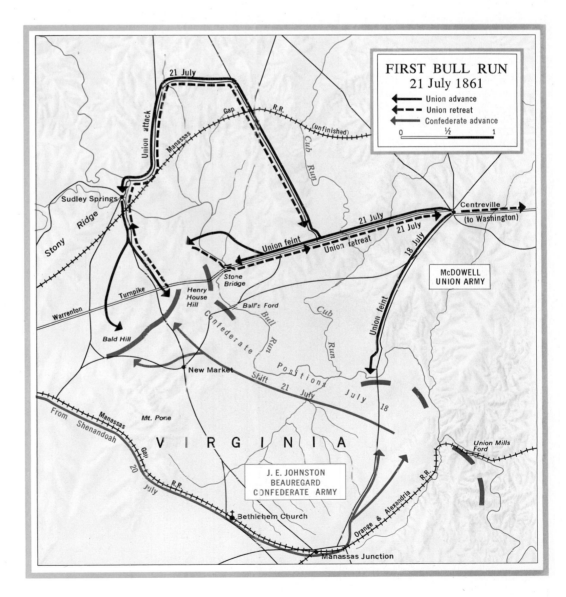

THE WAR *in the* WEST

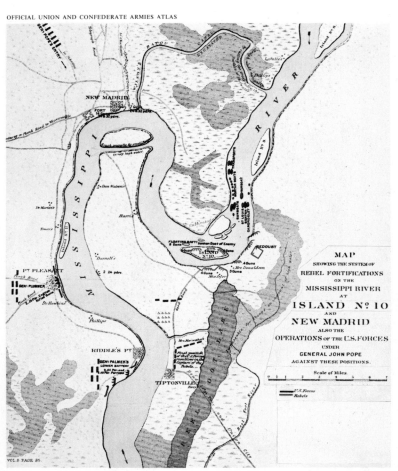

MAP
SHOWING THE SYSTEM OF
REBEL FORTIFICATIONS
ON THE
MISSISSIPPI RIVER
AT
ISLAND Nº 10
AND
NEW MADRID
ALSO THE
OPERATIONS OF THE U.S. FORCES
UNDER
GENERAL JOHN POPE
AGAINST THESE POSITIONS.

Scale of Miles

The advance of Federal forces down the Mississippi River in the spring of 1862 was blocked by a strong Confederate fort on Island No. 10, whose location is shown on the map above. Union gunboats tried unsuccessfully to bombard the fort into submission, then ran past it. General John Pope occupied New Madrid and moved down the west bank of the river, and the Confederates were forced to abandon the fort. The bombardment of Island No. 10 is depicted below, as sketched for Leslie's Weekly.

In the East the Confederacy began the war with a resounding success. In the West the action commenced much later, but once it was under way the Confederacy met a series of reverses.

After occupying Paducah, Kentucky, in the fall of 1861, General Ulysses S. Grant, aided by a fleet under Flag Officer Andrew Foote, advanced in February, 1862, on Confederate Forts Henry and Donelson. These two forts were captured, along with nearly 15,000 Confederate troops, and Grant moved on up the Tennessee River.

The fall of the forts made it impossible for General A. S. Johnston, commanding the principal Confederate army, to remain at Nashville, and he retreated to northern Alabama. He soon joined up with troops from the Deep South under General Braxton Bragg and troops from the Mississippi led by General Beauregard, who had been transferred west. Johnston led his reinforced army up to meet Grant, who in turn was reinforced by Union troops under General Don Carlos Buell, and the Union and Confederate armies fought a bloody engagement at Shiloh April 6–7 (see portfolio of battle maps after page 225). Grant narrowly escaped defeat, but finally drove the Confederates away. Johnston was killed, and Beauregard withdrew the Rebel army to Corinth.

Meanwhile, Federals under General John Pope cleared the upper Mississippi by taking the Confederate strong points at New Madrid and Island No. 10; Admiral David G. Farragut forced open the mouth of the Mississippi, the Federals occupied Baton Rouge and New Orleans; and in May General H. W. Halleck, taking command of the armies of Grant, Buell, and Pope, drove Beauregard out of Corinth and forced him to retreat to Tupelo. Federal gunboats overpowered a Confederate flotilla at Memphis and moved on downstream. Farragut steamed up the river, bombarded Vicksburg without effect, and returned to the lower river. The balance was tipped heavily against the Confederacy.

Leslie's Weekly, APRIL 5, 1862

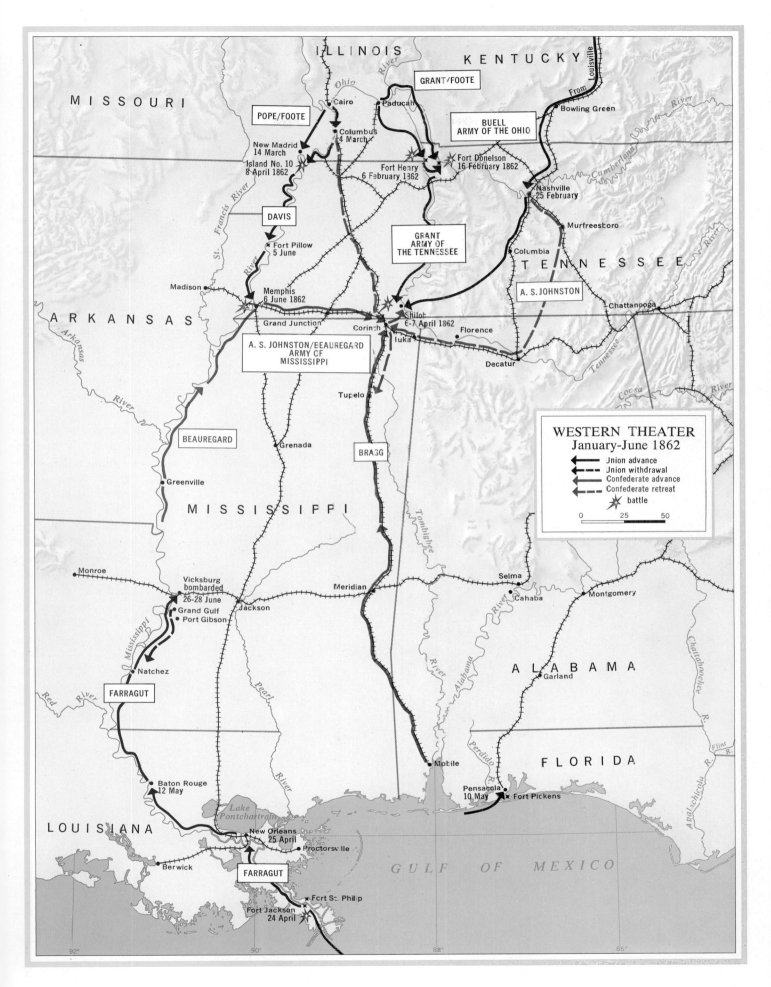

WESTERN THEATER
January–June 1862

Union advance
Union withdrawal
Confederate advance
Confederate retreat
★ battle

0   25   50

CAMPAIGNS *in* VIRGINIA

In the spring of 1862 the Federals tried a new advance on Richmond. General George B. McClellan took the Army of the Potomac down to Fort Monroe, laid siege to York-town, took the place on May 4, and after a fight with General Johnston's rear guard at Williamsburg went on to take position astride the Chickahominy River within a few miles of Richmond. Johnston failed to drive McClellan away in the Battle of Fair Oaks at the end of May, was wounded, and was replaced by General Robert E. Lee.

Then came trouble. In the Shenandoah Valley, Lee had 15,000 men under General T. J. "Stonewall" Jackson, and Jackson proceeded to bewilder the Federals. He fought General James Shields at Kernstown on March 23, moved to the upper end of the valley, went west to beat General John Charles Frémont's Federals at McDowell on May 8,

quickly returned to the valley, moved north, and forced the new Federal commander, General Nathaniel Banks, to retreat to Winchester. There Jackson defeated him on May 25. After feigning an invasion of Maryland, Jackson went back up the valley, beat Frémont again at Cross Keys, and then repulsed Shields at Port Republic and slipped southeast to join Lee at Richmond.

The result was that the Federals, alarmed, withheld troops that were to have joined McClellan. Lee struck McClellan at Mechanicsville on June 26, and after a series of hard fights forced him to retreat to Harrison's Landing, on the James River.

The map opposite traces the engagements of McClellan's unsuccessful Peninsular Campaign of 1862; the one below shows the theater of Jackson's skillful movements.

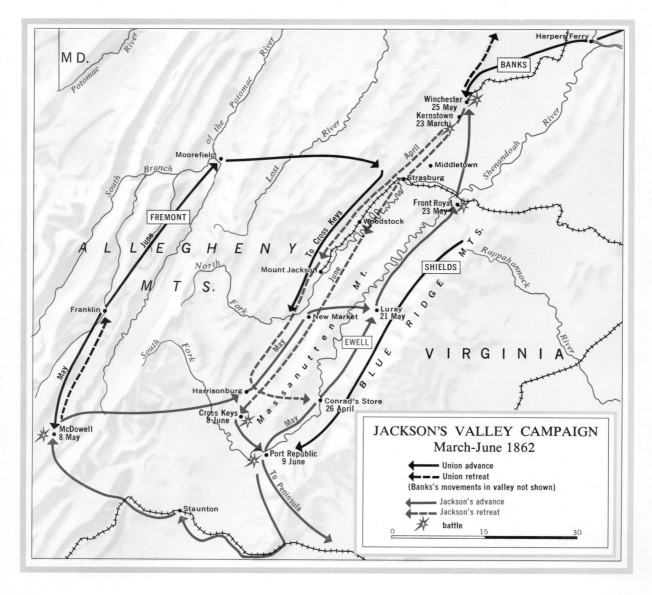

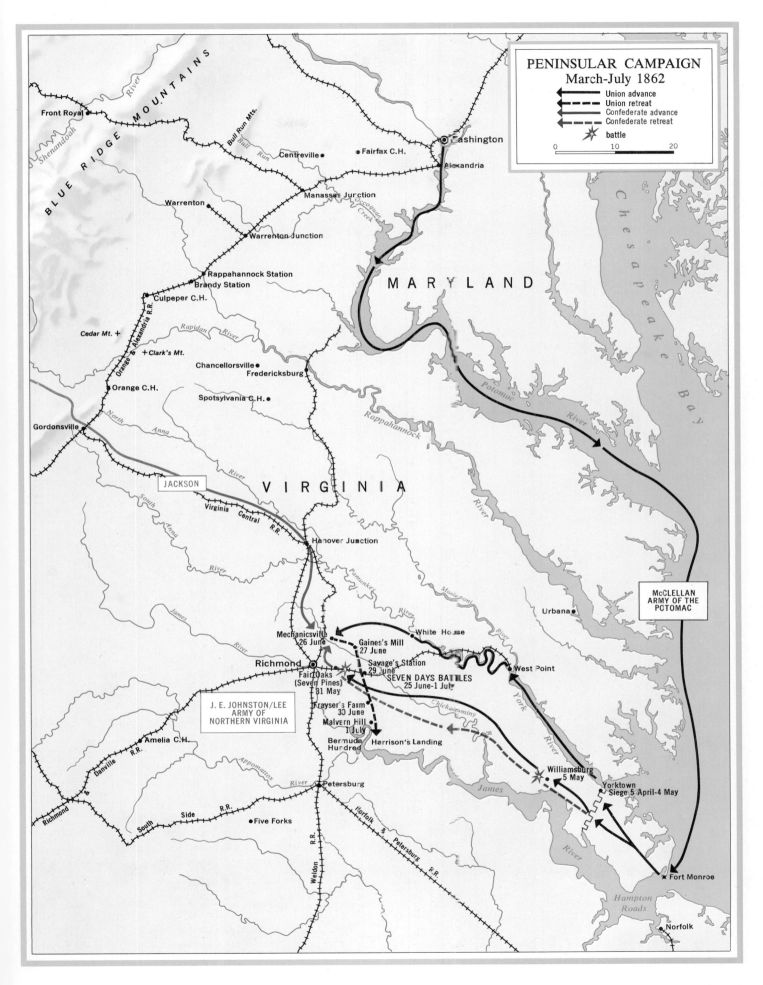

PENINSULAR CAMPAIGN
March–July 1862

Union advance
Union retreat
Confederate advance
Confederate retreat
battle

0   10   20

MARYLAND

Front Royal

BLUE RIDGE MOUNTAINS

Shenandoah River

Bull Run Mts.

Centreville
Fairfax C.H.
Washington
Alexandria

Warrenton

Manassas Junction

Warrenton Junction

Rappahannock Station
Brandy Station
Culpeper C.H.
Cedar Mt.
Clark's Mt.

Rapidan River

Chancellorsville
Fredericksburg
Spotsylvania C.H.

Orange C.H.

North Anna River

Gordonsville

Rappahannock River

Potomac River

Chesapeake Bay

JACKSON

VIRGINIA

Virginia Central R.R.

South Anna River

Hanover Junction

Pamunkey River

Mattaponi River

Urbana

MCCLELLAN
ARMY OF THE
POTOMAC

James River

Mechanicsville
26 June
Gaines's Mill
27 June
White House

Richmond

Savage's Station
29 June
SEVEN DAYS BATTLES
25 June–1 July

West Point

Fair Oaks
(Seven Pines)
31 May

J. E. JOHNSTON/LEE
ARMY OF
NORTHERN VIRGINIA

Frayser's Farm
30 June
Malvern Hill
1 July

Bermuda
Hundred

Harrison's Landing

Chickahominy River

York River

Amelia C.H.

Danville R.R.

Appomattox River

Petersburg

Richmond

Side R.R.

South

Five Forks

Weldon R.R.

Williamsburg
5 May

Yorktown
Siege 5 April–4 May

Norfolk & Petersburg R.R.

James River

Fort Monroe

Hampton
Roads

Norfolk

FIRST DRIVE NORTH

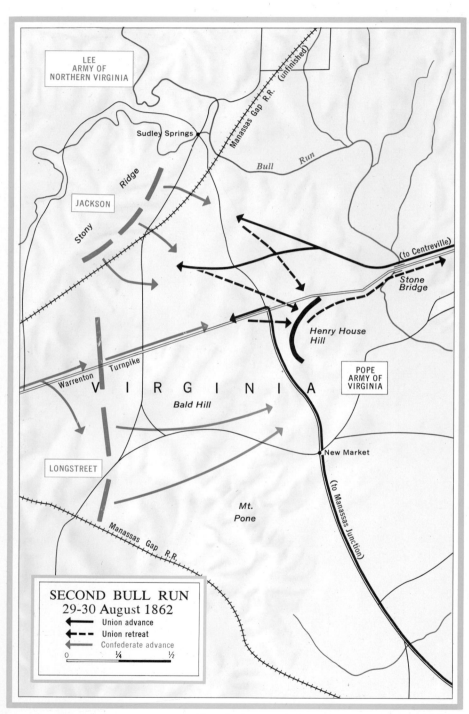

Inside the map:

**LEE
ARMY OF
NORTHERN VIRGINIA**

Sudley Springs

Bull   Run

Manassas Gap R.R. (unfinished)

Ridge

JACKSON

Stony

(to Centreville)

Stone
Bridge

Henry House
Hill

Warrenton   Turnpike

V I R G I N I A

Bald Hill

POPE
ARMY OF
VIRGINIA

LONGSTREET

New Market

(to Manassas Junction)

Mt.
Pone

Manassas Gap R.R.

**SECOND BULL RUN
29-30 August 1862**
→ Union advance
⇢ Union retreat
→ Confederate advance
0   ¼   ½

After Jackson raided Pope's base at Manassas Junction, he withdrew to high ground northwest of the Henry House Hill, where Pope attacked him on August 29. Jackson held his ground, and the next day Longstreet's newly arrived corps, as shown above, struck Pope's left flank and forced him to retreat.

Lee's army had no sooner ended the threat posed by McClellan's advance up the Virginia peninsula than it had to meet a new one. McClellan's army had been beaten, but it had by no means been put out of action; it was still powerful, strongly entrenched hardly a day's march from Richmond, and ready to make a new advance whenever its commander felt able to do so.

Meanwhile, Washington had pulled together the various Federal units that had been operating so ineffectually in the Shenandoah Valley and in northeastern Virginia and had formed a new army, which was called (for the brief time that it existed) the Army of Virginia. This was entrusted to General John Pope, who had won Island No. 10 on the Mississippi and who had a good deal of driving energy. Pope began to move down along the line of the Orange & Alexandria Railroad. Federal strategy now was to have Pope advance on Richmond from the north while McClellan advanced from the south; the southern capital would be caught in a pincers, and Lee's army would be crushed by overwhelming numbers.

Lee met this threat before it took full form. He was aided by the fact that McClellan was reluctant to advance and because close co-operation between two armies as widely separated as his and Pope's was extremely difficult. So Lee was able to detach Stonewall Jackson, with 20,000 men, and send him up to meet Pope, while he remained before Richmond with the rest of his army to guard against a thrust by McClellan.

Jackson met Pope's advance units at Cedar Mountain, beyond the Rapidan River, on August 9, attacked them savagely, and drove the Federals back in retreat. It now seemed to Washington that the plan to apply a pincers was not going to work, and (much against his desire) McClellan was ordered to evacuate his lines at Harrison's Landing and bring his army back up the Potomac.

Lee promptly took the rest of his army up to join Jackson and laid a plan to outflank Pope. Pope, who was beginning to be reinforced by parts of McClellan's army, discovered the threat just in time and retreated to a safer spot behind the Rappahannock, where he waited for the balance of the Army of the Potomac to join him. Once this happened he would be much too strong for Lee to attack.

Realizing this, Lee now executed one of the most brilliant strategic strokes of his career. With half of the army, Jackson marched on a long detour behind the Bull Run Mountains and then came swiftly east and captured Pope's supply base at Manassas Junction. This compelled Pope to make an immediate retreat. As soon as Pope's army moved, Lee followed in Jackson's footsteps with the remainder of his force, while Pope tried desperately to bring Jackson to battle before Lee and his troops arrived.

The battle that resulted took place on August 29 and 30, on the field where the first Battle of Bull Run had been fought. Jackson had his troops on high ground a mile or more from the Henry House Hill, and on the first day he was just able to stand off the Federal assaults. On the second day, Lee arrived with Longstreet's corps and struck Pope in the left flank, beating him soundly and compelling him to retreat. Lee's army followed; there was an indecisive fight at Chantilly, and then Washington ordered Pope back to the capital. Pope was replaced, his Army of Virginia ceased to exist, and McClellan resumed command of the Army of the Potomac.

Lee knew that he was not strong enough to attack Washington, which was heavily fortified, so he maneuvered to compel McClellan to leave the fortifications and fight in the open country. He went north of the Potomac, crossed the ridge of South Mountain, sent Jackson off to capture a Federal garrison at Harpers Ferry, and awaited developments.

McClellan followed fast, although he was unable to save Harpers Ferry from Jackson. In mid-September he broke by the Confederate rear guards at Crampton's Gap and South Mountain more rapidly than Lee had expected, and for a time it seemed that he might destroy the southern army piecemeal. Lee hastily pulled his scattered forces together at Sharpsburg, on Antietam Creek, and there, on September 17, the bloodiest single day's encounter of the whole war took place—the Battle of Antietam.

From dawn to late afternoon the Federals attacked vigorously. Lee managed to beat off these attacks, but at last he had to retreat, with his first northern invasion ending in failure. Tactically a draw, the battle was a decided strategic victory for the North.

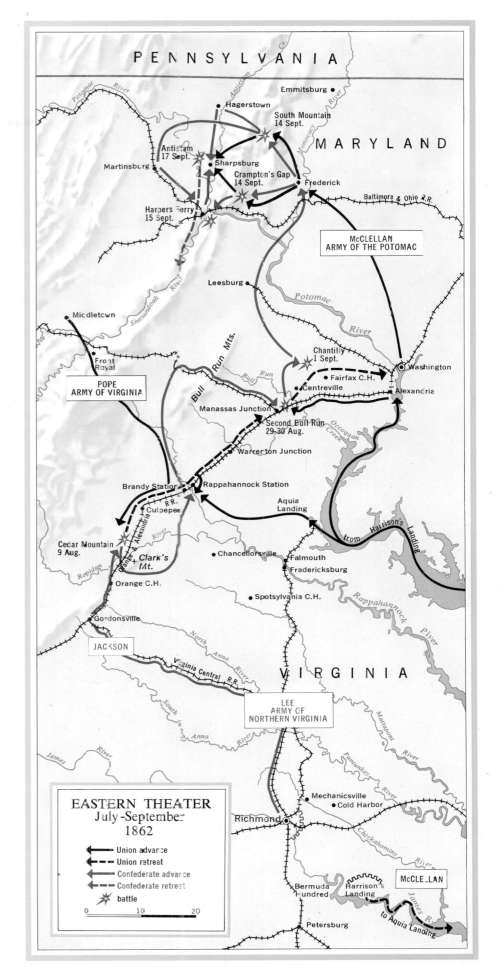

EASTERN THEATER
July–September
1862

→ Union advance
--→ Union retreat
→ Confederate advance
--→ Confederate retreat
✴ battle

0   10   20

MAP OF THE BATTLE OF FREDERICKSBURG, VA., December 13, 1862.

CONFEDERATE HIGH NOON

Burnside's attacks at Fredericksburg were handled with a minimum of skill. As the map at left indicates, he made two main assaults—one on the high ground just west of the city, and the other on Lee's right a few miles to the south. Both assaults failed with immense loss to the Union forces. The map on the opposite page shows how the rival armies moved north from Fredericksburg to Gettysburg.

In the East, the failure of Lee's first invasion of the North was followed by unbroken Confederate successes.

In December the Federal General A. E. Burnside, who had replaced McClellan, attacked Lee's lines at Fredericksburg and met a costly defeat. Joe Hooker took Burnside's place, and in the spring flanked Lee out of Fredericksburg only to meet an equally costly defeat at Chancellorsville—a bitter victory for the South, because Stonewall Jackson was killed. A few weeks later Lee undertook his second northern invasion, moving northwest to the Shenandoah Valley. A cavalry fight at Brandy Station on June 9 showed Hooker where Lee was going, and the Army of the Potomac moved north to meet him. Lee kept on, crossed Maryland and fanned out across eastern Pennsylvania; his cavalry, under Jeb Stuart, swept far to the east, got behind the Federal

army, and was unable to join Lee in time to give him proper scouting and screening. Near the end of June, Washington, distrusting Hooker's ability to meet Lee's thrust, replaced Hooker with General George Gordon Meade.

Moving blindly in Stuart's absence, Lee's army collided with Meade's at Gettysburg on July 1, and during the next three days the two armies fought the climactic battle of the Civil War. Lee won minor successes on the first two days but was unable to drive Meade from his position, and at last was compelled once more to retreat into the Shenandoah Valley. (See battle map in portfolio after page 225.) Lee lost more than 20,000 men in the fierce fighting at Gettysburg, and the result was conclusive: for all his military genius, Lee simply was not strong enough to succeed in a large-scale invasion of the North.

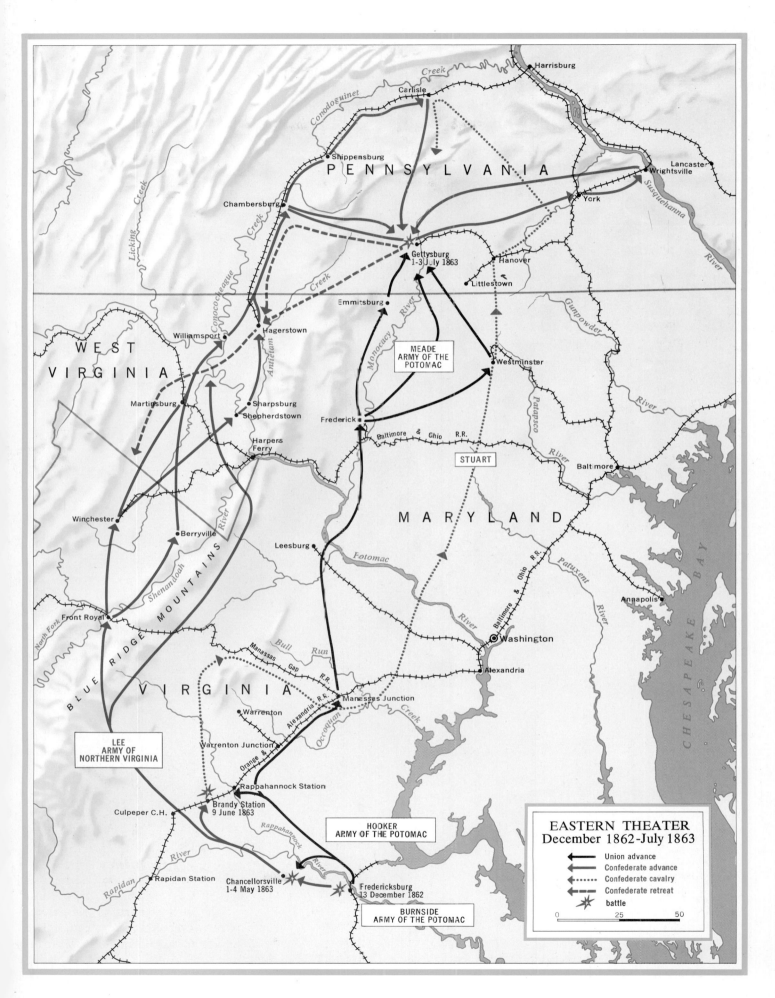

Harrisburg

Creek

Carlisle

P E N N S Y L V A N I A

Shippensburg

Lancaster
Wrightsville

Chambersburg

Conodoguinet

York

Gettysburg
1-3 July 1863

Hanover

Littlestown

Emmitsburg

WEST
VIRGINIA

Williamsport

Hagerstown

Creek

MEADE
ARMY OF THE
POTOMAC

Westminster

Martinsburg

Sharpsburg
Shepherdstown

Frederick

Baltimore & Ohio R.R.

Gunpowder

River

Balt more

Harpers
Ferry

STUART

M A R Y L A N D

Winchester

Berryville

Shenandoah River

Leesburg

Potomac

River

Baltimore & Ohio R.R.

Patapsco River

Annapolis

C
H
E
S
A
P
E
A
K
E

B
A
Y

North Fork

Front Royal

B L U E   R I D G E   M O U N T A I N S

Patuxent River

Washington

LEE
ARMY OF
NORTHERN VIRGINIA

V I R G I N I A

Manassas Gap R.R.

Bull Run

Warrenton

Manassas Junction

Alexandria

Occoquan

Creek

Warrenton Junction

Alexandria R.R.

Orange &

Rappahannock Station

HOOKER
ARMY OF THE POTOMAC

EASTERN THEATER
December 1862-July 1863

Culpeper C.H.

Brandy Station
9 June 1863

Rappahannock

Rapidan Station

Chancellorsville
1-4 May 1863

River

Fredericksburg
13 December 1862

Rapidan

BURNSIDE
ARMY OF THE POTOMAC

←	Union advance
←	Confederate advance
◄····	Confederate cavalry
◄---	Confederate retreat
✳	battle

0   25   50

217

TURNING *the* TIDE *in the* WEST 1862

After the Federal occupation of Corinth, Mississippi, in the spring of 1862 (see pages 210–11), General Halleck was called east to be general-in-chief of Union armies. From Corinth the Army of the Ohio, under Buell, moved east toward Chattanooga, while Grant's Army of the Tennessee, extending toward Memphis, prepared to start south into Mississippi. Bragg, the new Confederate commander, eluding Buell, detoured via Mobile to regroup at Chattanooga, and then marched north into Kentucky, aided by a force led by Edmund Kirby Smith which went north from Knoxville.

Buell had to abandon his own advance and follow Bragg into Kentucky; Grant sent him reinforcements and was tem-

WESTERN THEATER
July 1862–January 1863

→ Union advance
→ Confederate advance
⇢ Confederate retreat
★ battle

0   50   100

porarily immobilized by Confederate units that fought him at Iuka and Corinth in his front; and by autumn the Union situation looked bad. But Bragg was unable to capitalize on his opportunity. Buell brought him to battle at Perryville, Kentucky, on October 8, and although the fight was inconclusive Bragg felt obliged to go back into Tennessee. Buell was replaced by General W. S. Rosecrans, who followed Bragg and attacked him savagely at Murfreesboro at the end of the year, forcing him to retreat to Tullahoma. Both armies were so exhausted by this battle that they spent six months recuperating. Yet the tide had turned; from now on the Confederates in the west were on the defensive.

In November, 1862, Grant struck at Vicksburg, taking one force overland from the Tennessee border and sending another one under William Tecumseh Sherman down the Mississippi by boat. Grant's advance was halted when his supply base at Holly Springs, Mississippi, was destroyed by Confederates. Sherman's troops landed a few miles above Vicksburg but were beaten back at Chickasaw Bayou (below). Grant's hope for the quick seizure of Vicksburg was dashed. The events of the protracted siege that ended in the city's surrender on July 4, 1863, are shown in the portfolio of battle maps following page 225.

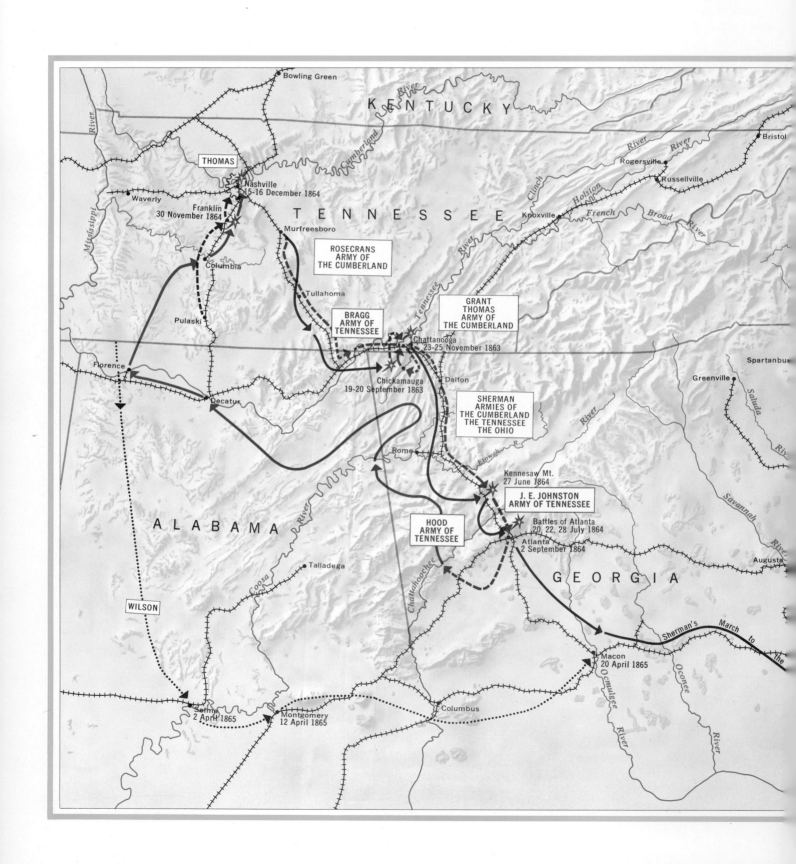

KENTUCKY

Bowling Green

Bristol

THOMAS

Rogersville

Russellville

Waverly

Nashville
15-16 December 1864

TENNESSEE

Franklin
30 November 1864

Knoxville

Murfreesboro

ROSECRANS
ARMY OF
THE CUMBERLAND

Columbia

Tullahoma

GRANT
THOMAS
ARMY OF
THE CUMBERLAND

Pulaski

BRAGG
ARMY OF
TENNESSEE

Chattanooga
23-25 November 1863

Spartanbur

Florence

Chickamauga
19-20 September 1863

Dalton

Greenville

Decatur

SHERMAN
ARMIES OF
THE CUMBERLAND
THE TENNESSEE
THE OHIO

Rome

Kennesaw Mt.
27 June 1864

J. E. JOHNSTON
ARMY OF TENNESSEE

ALABAMA

Talladega

HOOD
ARMY OF
TENNESSEE

Battles of Atlanta
20, 22, 28 July 1864

Atlanta
2 September 1864

Augusta

GEORGIA

WILSON

Macon
20 April 1865

Selma
2 April 1865

Montgomery
12 April 1865

Columbus

Sherman's March to the

FORCE

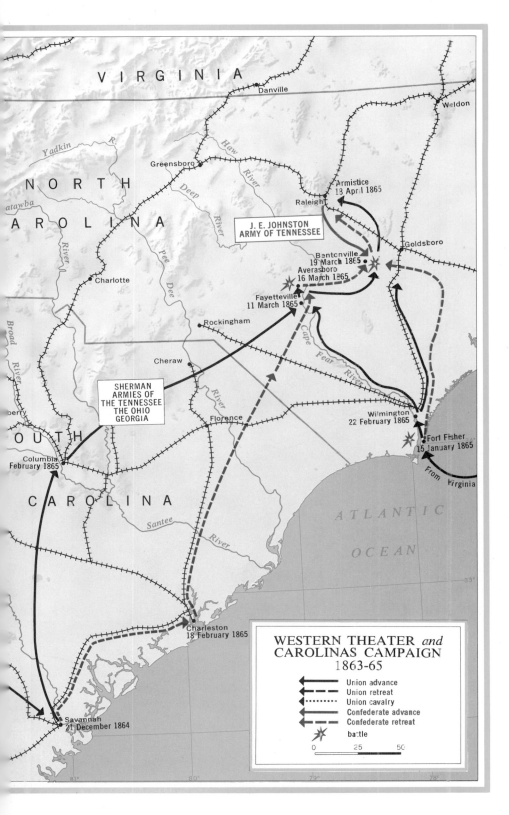

SHERMAN ARMIES OF THE TENNESSEE THE OHIO GEORGIA

J. E. JOHNSTON ARMY OF TENNESSEE

WESTERN THEATER *and* CAROLINAS CAMPAIGN 1863-65

◄———	Union advance
◄- - -	Union retreat
◄·······	Union cavalry
◄———	Confederate advance
◄- - -	Confederate retreat
✶	battle

0   25   50

Starting from Murfreesboro, Tennessee, in June, 1863, Rosecrans drove Bragg back on Chattanooga. Reinforcements reached both sides, and from September through November fierce battles were fought that finally secured the city for the northern armies, now commanded by Grant, Thomas, and Sherman (see portfolio of battle maps). After retreating into Georgia, Bragg was replaced in December by Joseph E. Johnston. Three months later, Sherman assumed command of the principal Federal armies in the West, and in May he marched toward Atlanta.

Johnston delayed him skillfully, and repulsed him at Kennesaw Mountain, but at last had to withdraw into Atlanta, where Richmond removed him and put aggressive John B. Hood in his place. Hood attacked Sherman three times in front of Atlanta, lost each fight, and at the beginning of September had to evacuate this important railroad and munitions center. Sherman moved in, and after a month or more of sparring along his line of supplies he sent part of his troops back to Tennessee and with 60,000 men struck out boldly for Savannah.

On the "march to the sea" Sherman had no real opposition. Hood believed that a hard blow at Tennessee might force Sherman to retreat, so he marched across northern Alabama, causing Union troops to withdraw to Franklin. There, Hood defeated the Federal rear guard in a ruinous victory that cost the southerner more men than he could afford to lose. On December 15 and 16 Thomas struck Hood on the hills south of Nashville, routing him completely and winning one of the decisive victories of the war. Hood's military career came to an end, and only fragments of his army were ever able to get back into action again.

Sherman, meanwhile, moved steadily down across Georgia, creating much havoc as he moved, and late in December he occupied Savannah. After spending a month re-equipping his army, Sherman marched north across the Carolinas, taking Columbia in February. The Confederacy was unable to muster enough of a force to do more than delay him. He went on into North Carolina, established contact with Federal forces on the coast, and after repulsing the Confederate Army of Tennessee, again under Johnston, at Bentonville, signed an armistice with Johnston on April 18.

ROAD *to* APPOMATTOX

The road to Appomattox, where the curtain at last came down on Confederate hopes, began on May 4, 1864, when Grant led Meade's Army of the Potomac across the Rapidan River to engage Lee's Army of Northern Virginia, and ended on April 9, 1865, when Lee surrendered at Appomattox Court House. The map below shows the ground covered by the armies in 11 months of almost continuous fighting.

Terrible battles were fought in The Wilderness and at Spotsylvania Court House. Neither was a Federal victory, yet after each one Grant resumed his advance and Lee had to retreat. Lee rebuffed his attempt to force a way across the North Anna River, and—brought to bay at Cold Harbor on June 3—gave him an extremely costly whipping when Grant tried a massive assault on the Confederate lines. Undismayed, Grant eventually withdrew from his own trenches, sideslipped deftly, crossed the James River, and tried to seize the important railroad center of Petersburg, which was vital to the Confederate defense of Richmond.

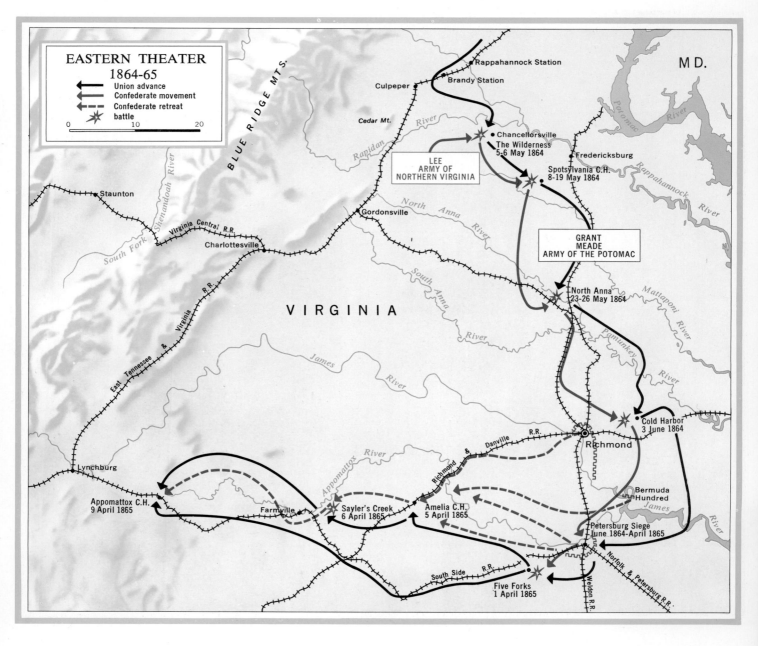

EASTERN THEATER 1864-65
Union advance
Confederate movement
Confederate retreat
battle
0   10   20

Petersburg had been strongly fortified, and the map below shows how the lines had been laid out. Grant's advance guard came up to these lines in the middle of June, carried the outer works, and might have gone on to take the city if the commander of the advance had realized how weakly the place was held. But the opportunity was missed, Lee got his own armies into the works, and the long and bloody siege of Petersburg was begun.

The armies remained in position here until the end of March, 1865. Grant made numerous attempts to break the lines, the most spectacular of which came when a Federal mine was exploded under a key Confederate fort, but Lee's lines always held. Grant kept extending his own lines to his left, so that by mid-summer the Confederate defenses bore little resemblance to the lines shown on the map. But Lee met him at every point, and by fall many people in the North concluded that the case was hopeless and despaired of final victory—so much so that late in August President Lincoln

temporarily believed that his own re-election was impossible.

Yet Grant was winning—slowly, and at enormous cost. Lee was pinned down. In the summer of 1864 he was able to send a detachment under General Jubal Early to cross the Potomac River and threaten Washington, but the thrust against the capital had no weight behind it, and the Federals were able to beat it off. Grant sent a strong force under Phil Sheridan to the Shenandoah Valley, Early was at last disposed of, and when winter came, it was clear that the Confederacy had just about reached the end of the line. Lee's army was badly diminished, and on April 1 Grant broke the southerner's right in the battle of Five Forks and compelled him to leave Petersburg. When Petersburg fell, Richmond also fell, and Lee retreated toward the west. Grant pursued vigorously, sent a column under Sheridan to get in front of Lee, and on April 9, 1865, reached Appomattox and received the surrender of Lee's army. With that surrender the South's last hope flickered out.

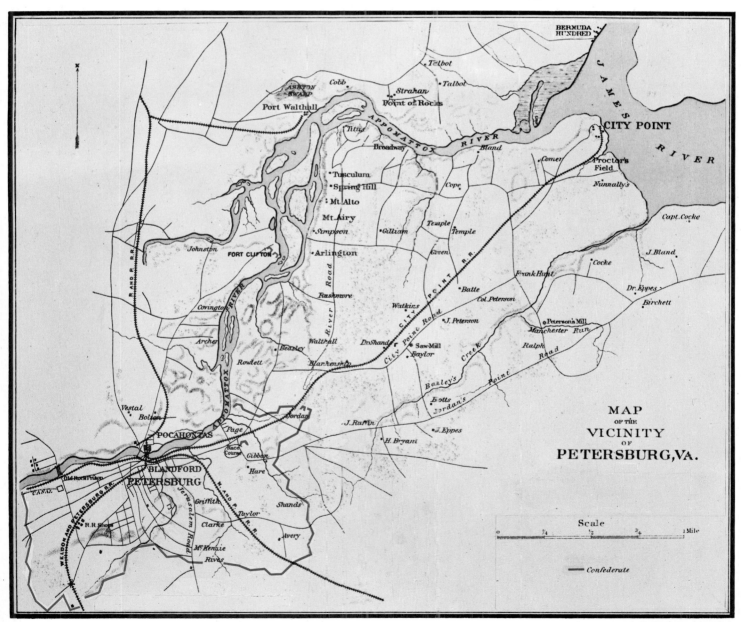

MAP
OF THE
VICINITY
OF
PETERSBURG, VA.

Scale

— Confederate

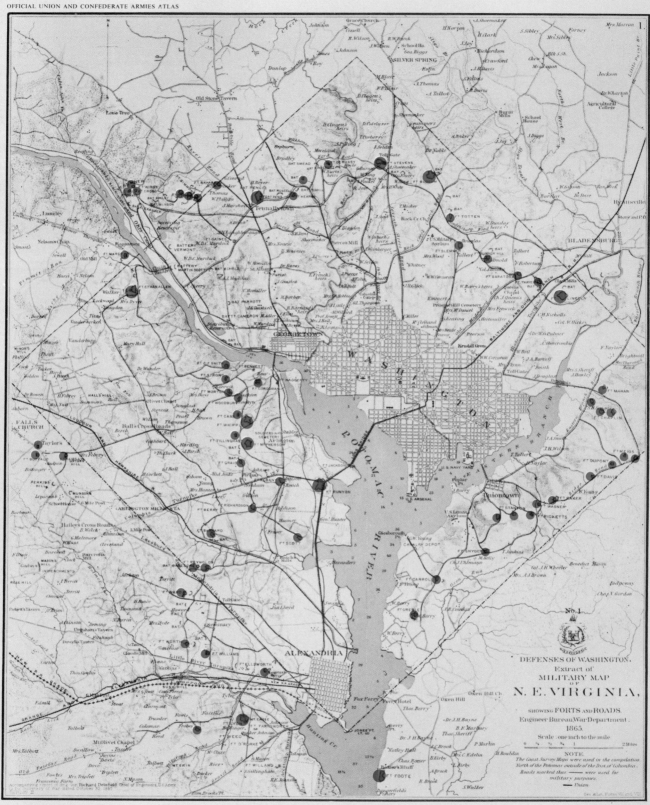

DEFENSES OF WASHINGTON.
Extract of
MILITARY MAP
OF
N. E. VIRGINIA,

SHOWING FORTS AND ROADS.
Engineer Bureau War Department.
1865.
Scale : one inch to the mile

Throughout the war the abiding fear of the northern government was that the Confederates might be able to seize Washington itself. As a result the city became the most strongly fortified place in America, and this contemporary map shows how it was ringed with forts that covered approaches from all directions. Properly manned, these forts were invulnerable. General Jubal Early tapped at Fort Stevens (top center, above) in July, 1864, but made no attempt to storm the works.

BATTLES
of the
CIVIL WAR

A Portfolio of Pictorial Maps

Eight of the major engagements of the Civil War—Shiloh, Antietam, Chancellorsville, Vicksburg, Gettysburg, Chattanooga, The Wilderness-Spotsylvania, and Nashville—are pictured on the following pages. Created originally by David Greenspan for *The American Heritage Picture History of the Civil War,* the three-dimensional maps show not merely how the opposing armies were arrayed on the fields, hills, and roads, and along the rivers, but how each large-scale battle—some of them fought over huge areas—might have looked if an observer had been able to hover high enough above the combat to gain a detailed as well as an over-all view of what was occurring on both sides. From such a vantage point, the problems of terrain and movement become clear. More importantly, these maps serve as reminders that the battles were fought, not by inanimate little blocks on a flat black and white surface, but by living men in a tangle of woods, fields, ridges, and meandering streams.

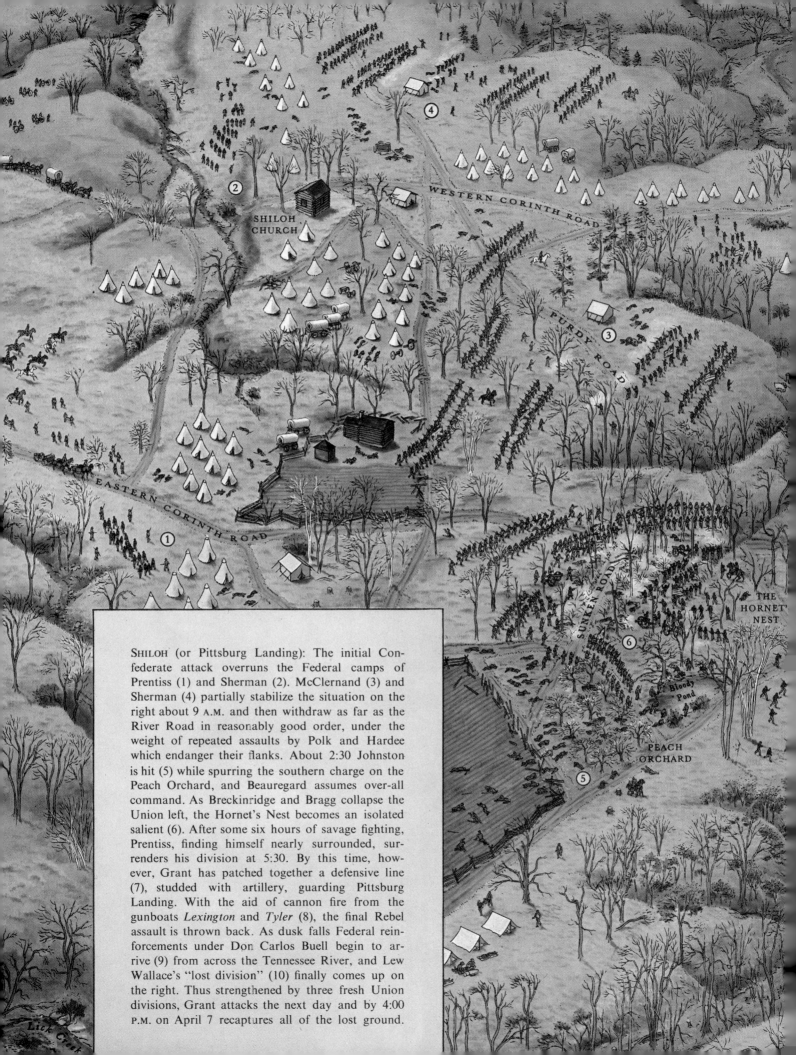

WESTERN CORINTH ROAD

PURDY ROAD

EASTERN CORINTH ROAD

SHILOH
CHURCH

SUNKEN ROAD

THE
HORNET'S
NEST

Bloody
Pond

PEACH
ORCHARD

Lick Creek

SHILOH (or Pittsburg Landing): The initial Confederate attack overruns the Federal camps of Prentiss (1) and Sherman (2). McClernand (3) and Sherman (4) partially stabilize the situation on the right about 9 A.M. and then withdraw as far as the River Road in reasonably good order, under the weight of repeated assaults by Polk and Hardee which endanger their flanks. About 2:30 Johnston is hit (5) while spurring the southern charge on the Peach Orchard, and Beauregard assumes over-all command. As Breckinridge and Bragg collapse the Union left, the Hornet's Nest becomes an isolated salient (6). After some six hours of savage fighting, Prentiss, finding himself nearly surrounded, surrenders his division at 5:30. By this time, however, Grant has patched together a defensive line (7), studded with artillery, guarding Pittsburg Landing. With the aid of cannon fire from the gunboats *Lexington* and *Tyler* (8), the final Rebel assault is thrown back. As dusk falls Federal reinforcements under Don Carlos Buell begin to arrive (9) from across the Tennessee River, and Lew Wallace's "lost division" (10) finally comes up on the right. Thus strengthened by three fresh Union divisions, Grant attacks the next day and by 4:00 P.M. on April 7 recaptures all of the lost ground.

SHILOH

First Day: April 6, 1862

OWL CREEK

RIVER ROAD

CREEK

Pittsburg
Landing

TENNESSEE RIVER

LEXINGTON

TYLER

David Greenspan

ANTIETAM

September 17, 1862

TO POTOMAC RIVER

LEE'S HQ

TO HARPERS FERRY

Sharpsburg

ANTIETAM CREEK

BURNSIDE'S BRIDGE

David Greenspan

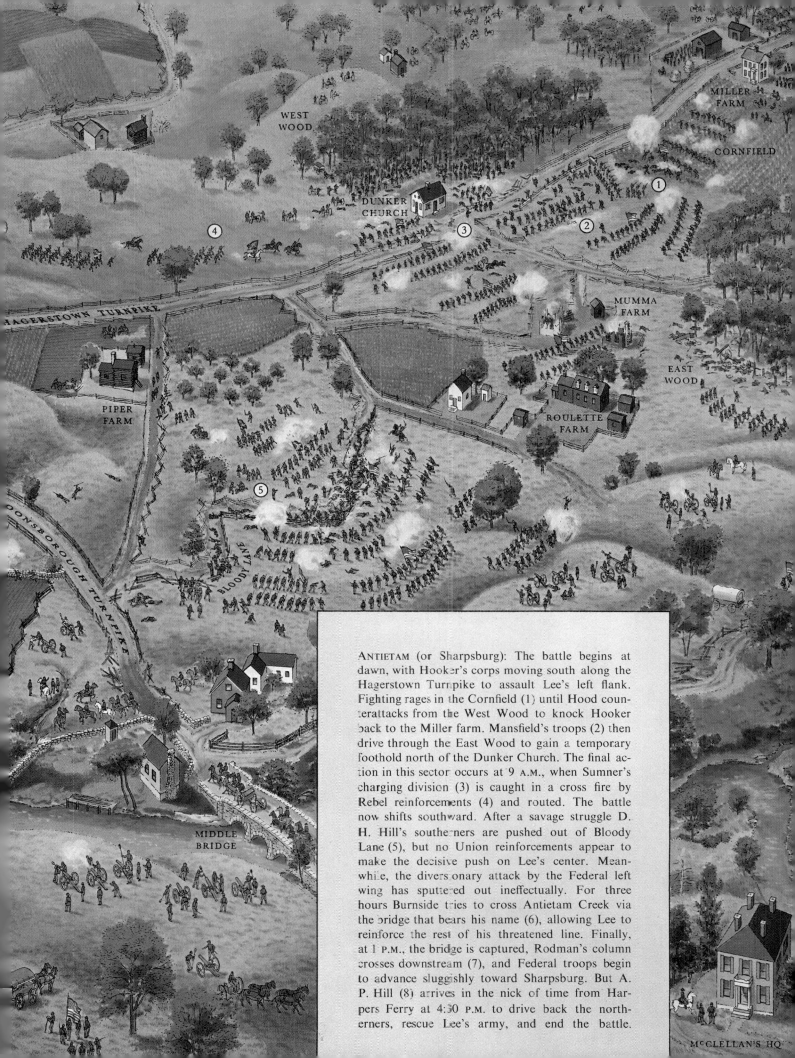

WEST WOOD

MILLER FARM

CORNFIELD

DUNKER CHURCH

①

②

④

③

MUMMA FARM

EAST WOOD

HAGERSTOWN TURNPIKE

PIPER FARM

ROULETTE FARM

⑤

BLOODY LANE

BOONSBOROUGH TURNPIKE

MIDDLE BRIDGE

ANTIETAM (or Sharpsburg): The battle begins at dawn, with Hooker's corps moving south along the Hagerstown Turnpike to assault Lee's left flank. Fighting rages in the Cornfield (1) until Hood counterattacks from the West Wood to knock Hooker back to the Miller farm. Mansfield's troops (2) then drive through the East Wood to gain a temporary foothold north of the Dunker Church. The final action in this sector occurs at 9 A.M., when Sumner's charging division (3) is caught in a cross fire by Rebel reinforcements (4) and routed. The battle now shifts southward. After a savage struggle D. H. Hill's southerners are pushed out of Bloody Lane (5), but no Union reinforcements appear to make the decisive push on Lee's center. Meanwhile, the diversionary attack by the Federal left wing has sputtered out ineffectually. For three hours Burnside tries to cross Antietam Creek via the bridge that bears his name (6), allowing Lee to reinforce the rest of his threatened line. Finally, at 1 P.M., the bridge is captured, Rodman's column crosses downstream (7), and Federal troops begin to advance sluggishly toward Sharpsburg. But A. P. Hill (8) arrives in the nick of time from Harpers Ferry at 4:30 P.M. to drive back the northerners, rescue Lee's army, and end the battle.

McCLELLAN'S HQ.

CHANCELLORSVILLE

Second Day: May 2, 1863

N

ELY'S FORD ROAD

Little Hunting Run

RAPIDAN RIVER

Big Hunting Run

THE WILDERNESS

HAWKINS FARM

④

⑤

WILDERNESS CHURCH

DOWDALL'S TAVERN

TURNPIKE

Scott's Run

③

TALLEY FARM

ORANGE PLANK ROAD

JACKSON'S FLANK MARCH

TO RAPPAHANNOCK RIVER

TO SALEM CHURCH

RIVER ROAD

TURNPIKE

Mott's Run

Chancellorsville

HOOKER'S HQ

ORANGE PLANK ROAD

FAIRVIEW CEMETERY

② ⑦

⑧

AN WERT HOUSE

HAZEL GROVE

⑥

FURNACE ROAD

CATHERINE FURNACE

①

JACKSON'S FLANK MA

CHANCELLORSVILLE: At first light on May 2 Jackson begins a flank march (lower right) across the Union front. Sickles glimpses the tail of this column, moves forward from Hazel Grove, and attacks (1). His minor success convinces Hooker that the Confederates are in full retreat, and that Lee's probing attacks (2) are merely rear-guard actions. Jackson, meanwhile, has gone into position athwart the Union right flank, which faces south along the Turnpike. At 6 P.M. he drives forward (3), routing the XI Corps, his wide battle line overlapping the desperate Union attempts to form (4). The victorious Confederates sweep up the Turnpike, past the Wilderness Church and Dowdall's Tavern. Here remnants of the XI Corps make a last stand (5) and, reinforced with a few guns, delay Jackson's men long enough for the rest of the troops to make good their escape. Sickles falls back to Hazel Grove, where Union guns knock back a Rebel attack (6) threatening this key position. The fire of Hooker's massed artillery at Fairview Cemetery (7) finally halts the southern advance. At 9 P.M. Jackson and his staff, returning from a reconnoitering mission to locate the new Federal positions, are fired on by a nervous Confederate regiment, and Jackson is fatally wounded (8).

David Greenspan

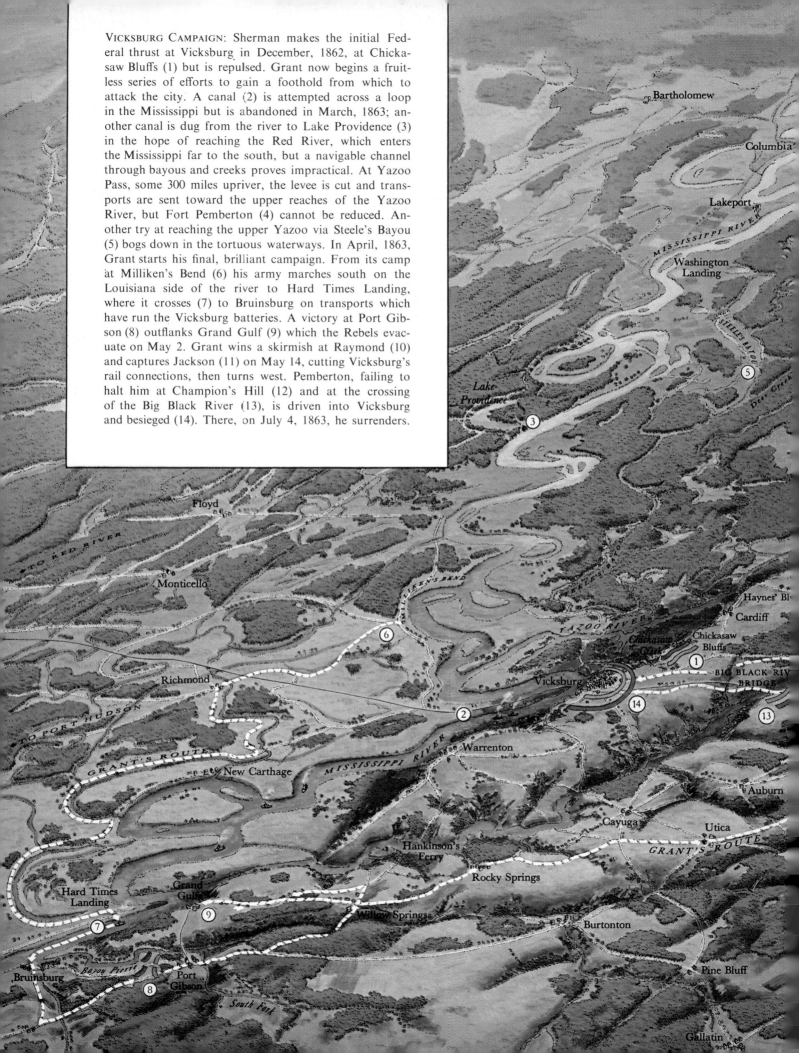

VICKSBURG CAMPAIGN: Sherman makes the initial Federal thrust at Vicksburg in December, 1862, at Chickasaw Bluffs (1) but is repulsed. Grant now begins a fruitless series of efforts to gain a foothold from which to attack the city. A canal (2) is attempted across a loop in the Mississippi but is abandoned in March, 1863; another canal is dug from the river to Lake Providence (3) in the hope of reaching the Red River, which enters the Mississippi far to the south, but a navigable channel through bayous and creeks proves impractical. At Yazoo Pass, some 300 miles upriver, the levee is cut and transports are sent toward the upper reaches of the Yazoo River, but Fort Pemberton (4) cannot be reduced. Another try at reaching the upper Yazoo via Steele's Bayou (5) bogs down in the tortuous waterways. In April, 1863, Grant starts his final, brilliant campaign. From its camp at Milliken's Bend (6) his army marches south on the Louisiana side of the river to Hard Times Landing, where it crosses (7) to Bruinsburg on transports which have run the Vicksburg batteries. A victory at Port Gibson (8) outflanks Grand Gulf (9) which the Rebels evacuate on May 2. Grant wins a skirmish at Raymond (10) and captures Jackson (11) on May 14, cutting Vicksburg's rail connections, then turns west. Pemberton, failing to halt him at Champion's Hill (12) and at the crossing of the Big Black River (13), is driven into Vicksburg and besieged (14). There, on July 4, 1863, he surrenders.

THE CAMPAIGN
AND SIEGE OF VICKSBURG

December, 1862 — July, 1863

David Greenspan

Gettysburg

GETTYSBURG

Second Day: July 2, 1863

ZIEGLER'S GROVE

CULP'S HILL 7

CEMETERY HILL

MEADE'S HQ

8

SEMINARY RIDGE

CODORI HOUSE

CEMETERY RIDGE

6

ROGERS HOUSE

5

TROSTLE FARM

PEACH ORCHARD

WHEAT FIELD

3

WARFIELD HOUSE

EMMITSBURG ROAD

ROSE HOUSE

David Greenspan

GETTYSBURG: The action on the second day opens with a Confederate artillery barrage at 4 P.M. An hour later Hood's Rebel division sweeps in around the Union left flank, overruns Devil's Den (1), and begins the ascent of the undefended Little Round Top, which dominates the entire Federal position. Warren hastens troops to the crest, and they repulse Hood's men after a bitter struggle (2). As the battle shifts steadily northward, Longstreet sends in McLaws, who shatters Sickles' salient (3), embracing the Peach Orchard and the Wheat Field, and advances toward a gap in Meade's line (4). Artillery is rushed forward to hold together the battered Union line until reinforcements arrive. At the Trostle Farm, Barksdale's Mississippians manage to take a Yankee battery (5), but Barksdale is mortally wounded and his brigade wrecked. The Rebels strike at the Union center (6), where they meet stiff resistance, including a doomed counterattack by the 1st Minnesota, and are stopped. At dark Ewell demonstrates against the Federal right, but fails to take the strong position on Culp's Hill (7). In the day's final action Jubal Early gets two Rebel brigades in among the Union batteries on Cemetery Hill (8), but they are not strong enough to resist counterattacks and are driven off.

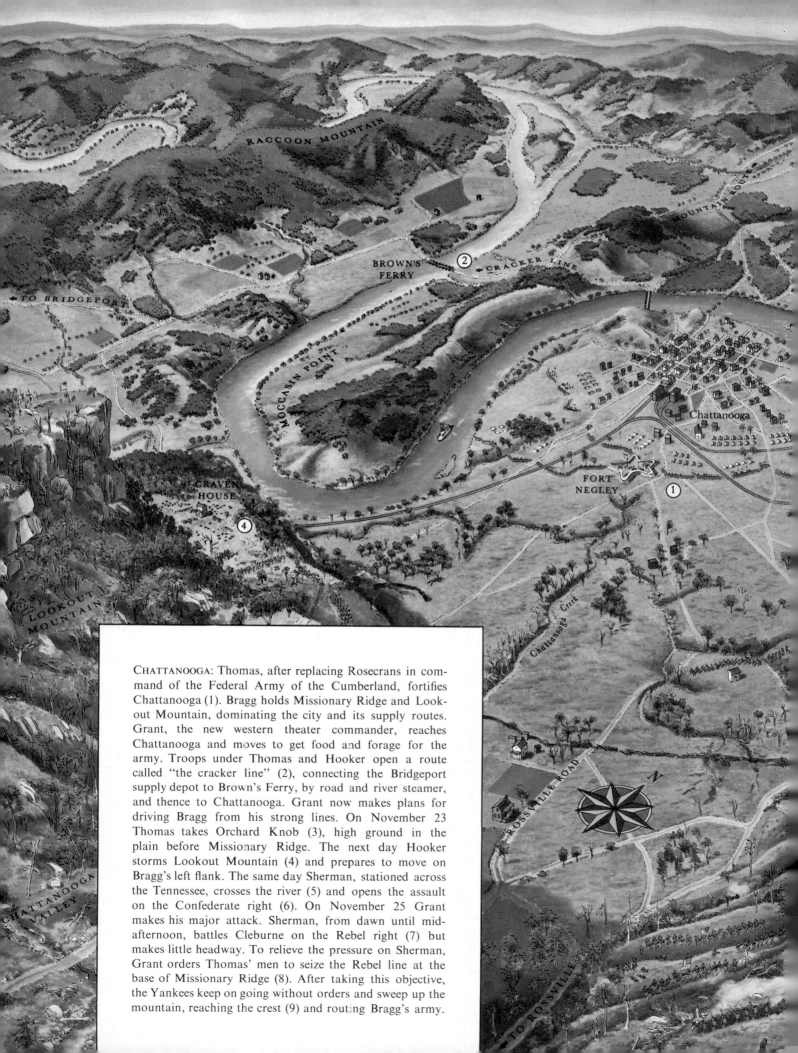

CHATTANOOGA: Thomas, after replacing Rosecrans in command of the Federal Army of the Cumberland, fortifies Chattanooga (1). Bragg holds Missionary Ridge and Lookout Mountain, dominating the city and its supply routes. Grant, the new western theater commander, reaches Chattanooga and moves to get food and forage for the army. Troops under Thomas and Hooker open a route called "the cracker line" (2), connecting the Bridgeport supply depot to Brown's Ferry, by road and river steamer, and thence to Chattanooga. Grant now makes plans for driving Bragg from his strong lines. On November 23 Thomas takes Orchard Knob (3), high ground in the plain before Missionary Ridge. The next day Hooker storms Lookout Mountain (4) and prepares to move on Bragg's left flank. The same day Sherman, stationed across the Tennessee, crosses the river (5) and opens the assault on the Confederate right (6). On November 25 Grant makes his major attack. Sherman, from dawn until midafternoon, battles Cleburne on the Rebel right (7) but makes little headway. To relieve the pressure on Sherman, Grant orders Thomas' men to seize the Rebel line at the base of Missionary Ridge (8). After taking this objective, the Yankees keep on going without orders and sweep up the mountain, reaching the crest (9) and routing Bragg's army.

RAISING THE SIEGE OF CHATTANOOGA

Orchard Knob: November 23, 1863
Lookout Mountain November 24, 1863
Missionary Ridge November 25, 1863

TO KNOXVILLE

Chickamauga Creek

TENNESSEE RIVER

FORT GROSE

WESTERN & ATLANTIC R.R.

CHATTANOOGA & CLEVELAND R.R.

GRANT'S HQ

ORCHARD KNOB

THE TUNNEL

BRAGG'S HQ

MISSIONARY RIDGE

RETREAT TO GEORGIA

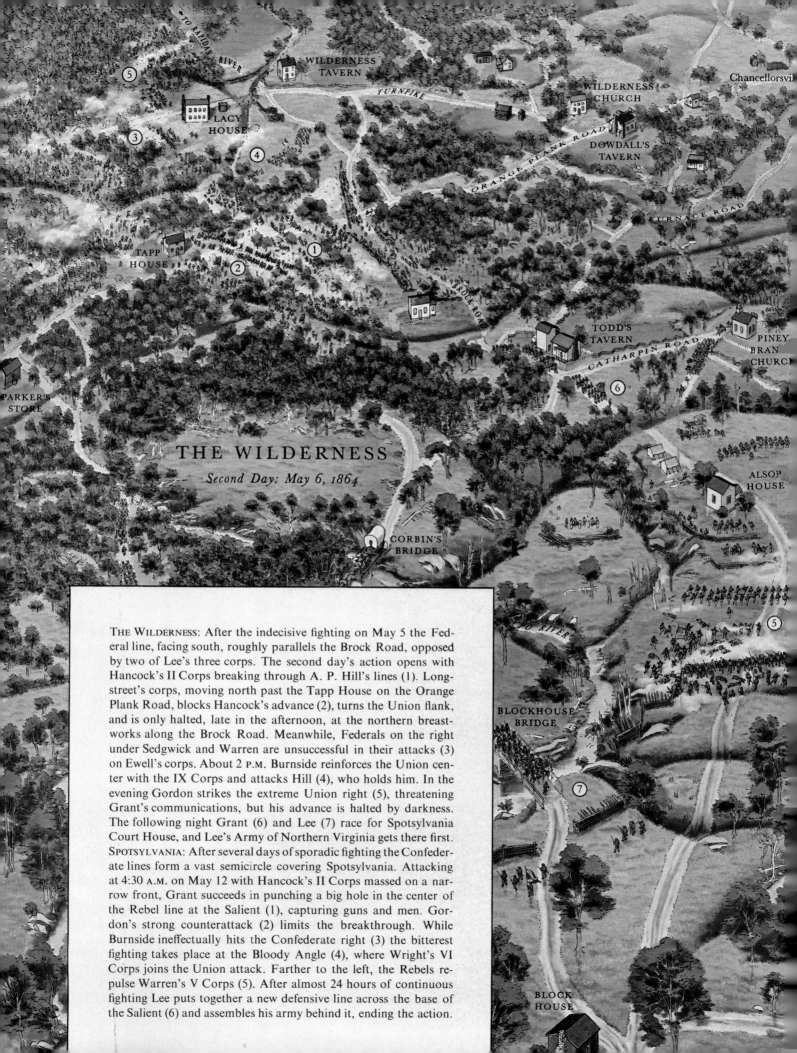

THE WILDERNESS

Second Day: May 6, 1864

THE WILDERNESS: After the indecisive fighting on May 5 the Federal line, facing south, roughly parallels the Brock Road, opposed
by two of Lee's three corps. The second day's action opens with
Hancock's II Corps breaking through A. P. Hill's lines (1). Longstreet's corps, moving north past the Tapp House on the Orange
Plank Road, blocks Hancock's advance (2), turns the Union flank,
and is only halted, late in the afternoon, at the northern breastworks along the Brock Road. Meanwhile, Federals on the right
under Sedgwick and Warren are unsuccessful in their attacks (3)
on Ewell's corps. About 2 P.M. Burnside reinforces the Union center with the IX Corps and attacks Hill (4), who holds him. In the
evening Gordon strikes the extreme Union right (5), threatening
Grant's communications, but his advance is halted by darkness.
The following night Grant (6) and Lee (7) race for Spotsylvania
Court House, and Lee's Army of Northern Virginia gets there first.
SPOTSYLVANIA: After several days of sporadic fighting the Confederate lines form a vast semicircle covering Spotsylvania. Attacking
at 4:30 A.M. on May 12 with Hancock's II Corps massed on a narrow front, Grant succeeds in punching a big hole in the center of
the Rebel line at the Salient (1), capturing guns and men. Gordon's strong counterattack (2) limits the breakthrough. While
Burnside ineffectually hits the Confederate right (3) the bitterest
fighting takes place at the Bloody Angle (4), where Wright's VI
Corps joins the Union attack. Farther to the left, the Rebels repulse Warren's V Corps (5). After almost 24 hours of continuous
fighting Lee puts together a new defensive line across the base of
the Salient (6) and assembles his army behind it, ending the action.

TO RAPPAHANNOCK RIVER

TO FREDERICKSBURG

SALEM CHURCH

TURNPIKE

UNFINISHED RAILROAD

ORANGE PLANK ROAD

SPOTSYLVANIA

Fourth Day: May 12, 1864

N

LANDRUM HOUSE

NI RIVER

SALIENT

④

①

BLOODY ANGLE

McCOOL HOUSE

②

③

HARRISON HOUSE

BROCK ROAD

⑥

TO SPOTSYLVANIA C. H.

NASHVILLE: Thomas advances from his solid entrenchments (1) on December 15 to drive the Rebels back to a position astride the Franklin and Granny White pikes. On December 16 the initial Federal attacks launched against the Rebel right at Overton Hill (2) are unsuccessful, but later that afternoon the storm tactics of McArthur and Couch overwhelm the Confederate left (3). To Hood's rear, dismounted Union cavalry (4) force him to fight a three-sided battle. With his left and center (5) in complete rout, Hood orders a retreat (6) down the Franklin Pike to the south. Several delaying actions were fought later by Forrest's cavalry before the decimated Army of Tennessee reached safety in Mississippi.

NASHVILLE

Second Day: December 16, 1864

Edgefield

CUMBERLAND RIVER

NASHVILLE & CHATTANOOGA R.R.

Nashville

FORT MORTON

FORT CASINO

FORT NEGLEY

Brown's Creek

MONTGOMERY HILL

NASHVILLE & DECATUR R.R.

HILLSBORO PIKE

GRANNY WHITE PIKE

BRADFORD HOUSE

OVERTON HILL

FRANKLIN PIKE

GRANNY WHITE HOUSE

David Greenspon

THE SURRENDER OF LEE.

Grant's Operations Against Lee in Virginia; of Sherman's Operations Against him in North Carolina; of Stoneman's Operations on the Danville and Greensboro Railroad, and of Hancock's Movement from Staunton.

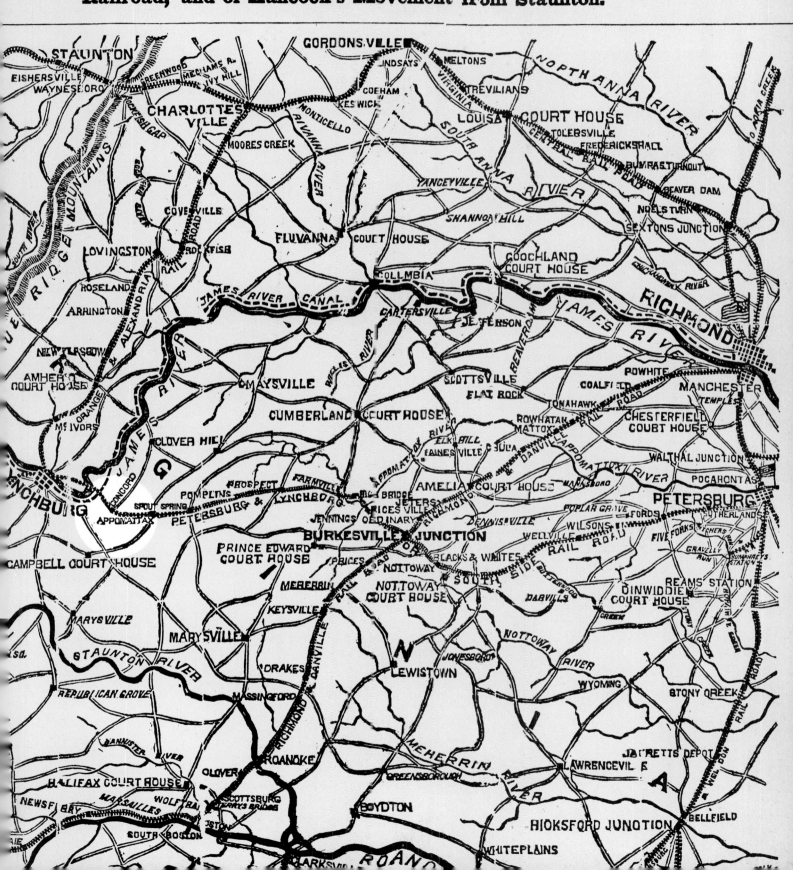

CHAPTER 7
EXPANSION
AND
INTEGRATION

Despite the heavy toll of blood and treasure exacted by the Civil War, the United States emerged from the conflict with an immense store of pent-up energy that almost literally exploded during the next few decades. The war's material damage had been largely confined to the South, and that region recovered from its losses only slowly; it took until nearly 1880 before the states of the former Confederacy had gotten back to where they had been in 1860. Elsewhere, however, the demands of war had strengthened rather than weakened the country. Once peace was restored, men turned with zest to the use of new energies. All earlier growth paled by comparison with the aggressive display of exploitation and development.

The period 1865–1914 uniformly excites superlatives, but whether what happened was superlatively good or superlatively evil is less easy to decide. Much was accomplished, but at fearful cost. Psychologically, men were still convinced that America possessed limitless wealth, that the need to develop quickly the country's resources justified any means employed to do so, and that individual opportunity must inevitably result in social, as well as personal, advancement. In these postwar decades, new technology enormously increased men's power, and men used the power, selfishly and without scruple, sure that the nation as a whole would thereby benefit. Americans became increasingly fascinated with the Darwinian idea that progress was the child of conflict. Belief in the survival of the fittest required, or at least justified, the ruthless destruction of the weak and the inefficient. The western Indians stood in the way of railroad builders, miners, and farmers. Not to thrust them aside would be "mawkish sentimentalism," most Americans decided, and in a generation the job was done, almost totally without regard for the Indians' prior claim to the land or for simple humane values. The Negroes, the Chinese laborers on the West Coast, and the thousands of European immigrants who poured into the country in search of a new start received only slightly more consideration from the dominant majority.

In the same spirit, Americans slashed down ancient forests without planting new seedlings; they all but wiped out the huge buffalo herds (15 million head in 30 years); they extracted precious metals, iron, copper, coal, and petroleum from the earth as fast as they could make shovels fly and drills bore. The land itself became prey to speculators, despoiling corporations, claim jumpers, and crooked politicians.

In dealing with one another the exploiters were equally unrestrained. "Root, hog, or die" seemed to be the national philosophy. Government on all levels was riddled with corruption. Businessmen stole and lied in the name of competition. Stock frauds, favoritism, illegal deals, and false advertising were the order of the day. Wealth accumulated, but men, indeed, decayed. Increasingly, opportunity appeared threatened by entrenched power, equality—even democracy itself—by monopoly, every human value by selfish materialism.

The new national heroes were either retired-generals-become-politicians like U. S. Grant, honest and well-meaning but scarcely aware of the forces controlling American development, or new tycoons who had mastered every acquisitive technique—men like Andrew Carnegie, the steel master, and Cornelius Vanderbilt, the railroad builder. Even the unblushing industrial "robber barons" of the age, the Jay Goulds and Jim Fisks, more often than not received the grudging admiration of the masses, so profound was the respect that riches inspired. When an American of this era "asked what a man was worth," the historian Henry Steele Commager has written, "he meant material worth, and he was impatient of any but the normal yardstick."

Yet this aspect of life in the so-called Gilded Age can easily be overstressed. The conditions that made American individualism dangerous to society operated also to make men co-operate with one another, and the materialism that ran wild produced so much wealth that even those who were exploited improved their lot greatly. A nation dedicated to progress eventually became progressive in a broader sense—committed to spiritual as well as material advance. In essence, when men seized upon science and technology for selfish purposes, they created such a complex society that they could no longer function as complete individualists.

When large corporations battled for control of an industry, they usually ended up by combining into trusts or holding companies, a form of co-operation. Once one giant combine dominated a field, as in the case of Rockefeller's Standard Oil Company, the management of its far-flung activities called for executive teamwork of the highest order. Mass production and mechanization depended for efficiency on specialization, and specialists could not function effectively except by taking into account the work of others.

More efficient methods of production and distribution created in these years a truly integrated economy. Wheat from the fields of Minnesota was ground into flour in Chicago and baked into bread in the great cities of the East. Cattle raised on the plains of Colorado and Wyoming were slaughtered in Kansas City and sold to butchers all over the world. The Mesabi iron ore was converted into steel in Pittsburgh and used to build bridges and railroads from the Far West to Africa. Wool raised in Montana was woven into cloth in Massachusetts, sewn into suits in New York, and sold in every state of the Union. This system was more complex than the finest watch, and, like a watch, it operated accurately only when the parts were fitted together precisely, kept in perfect condition, and carefully regulated. Ruthless competition and the concept

of *laissez faire,* or every man for himself, were unsuited for such an interrelated system.

Furthermore, as Americans learned more about mastering their continent and exploiting its resources, they became impatient with the idea that progress, or evolution, was an immutable process governed by natural laws that could not be modified by human ingenuity. Increased knowledge led them to hope that they could change and direct the flow of events. They also became in a sense more generous; wealth encouraged, first, private philanthropy and, then, the belief that society as a whole had the power, and therefore the responsibility, to improve the lot of its less fortunate members. Government seemed the logical organ for regulating the machinery of society and for directing the common effort toward a better life for all. Government took on more functions; between 1871 and 1900, the number of Federal employees rose from 53,000 to 256,000.

The change in the public's attitude toward government occurred very gradually, and not without controversy. The first major step came in 1887, when a national system of railroad regulation was established under the direction of the Interstate Commerce Commission. The I.C.C. proved ineffective at first, but by 1914 a comprehensive system of rate regulation and general railroad supervision had been worked out. In 1890, in the Sherman Antitrust Act, the Federal government undertook to control the activities of large corporations. At the state level, laws regulating the hours and conditions of labor began to be passed, and efforts were made to improve conditions in the nation's many industrial slums. To deal with the complexities of modern life, it was necessary to know a great deal more about what was actually happening. The government began therefore to gather more statistics and conduct more investigations; and when it did, the evidence collected operated to increase the public demand for still more information, and for new laws. When men tried to use government for the difficult tasks of social regeneration and control, they became alarmed by its inefficiency; hence the drive for civil service reform, the attack on corrupt political machines, and the demand that government be made responsive to public opinion.

All these developments had important international implications. Productive efficiency enabled Americans to invade new markets all over the world. The acquisitive spirit of the Gilded Age did not flag when continental resources had been engrossed; soon Americans were looking greedily toward the Far East and toward Latin America. Imperialism and the emergence of the United States as a world power were the results. Yet here, too, a fundamentally humane spirit eventually took over. The American overseas became a missionary as well as an exploiter, and if, like many missionaries, he often tried too hard to impose his own values on other peoples, he also contributed to their welfare.

CANADA

WASHINGTON
TERRITORY
1863-89

Olympia

Columbia R.

OREGON

Salem

IDAHO
TERRITORY
1868-90

Boise

Snake R.

MONTANA
TERRITORY
1864-89

Virginia City

Bannack

Yellowstone R.

WYOMING
TERRITORY
1868-90

DAKOTA
TERRITORY
1868-82

MINNESOTA

Mississippi R.

WIS.

Missouri R.

Yankton

IOWA

NEBRASKA
1867

Cheyenne

Platte R.

Lincoln
(Lancaster)

Great
Salt Lake

NEVADA
1864

Great Salt
Lake City

Sacramento River

Sacramento

Carson City

CALIFORNIA

UTAH
TERRITORY
1868-96

COLORADO
1876

Golden o   o Denver

Kansas R.

Topeka

KANSAS

MO.

Colorado R.

PACIFIC   OCEAN

ARIZONA
TERRITORY
1866-1912

Tucson

Gila   River

NEW MEXICO
TERRITORY
1863-1912

Santa Fe

Pecos R.

Arkansas R.

INDIAN
TERRITORY
(UNORGANIZED)

ARK.

Red R.

Rio Grande

River

Sabine R.

LA.

TEXAS

Colorado R.

Trinity R.

Brazos R.

Austin

Gulf
of
California

Nueces R.

Gulf of
Mexico

MEXICO

WESTERN
UNITED STATES
1861-76

- [light] states previously admitted
- [dark] new states admitted
- o   state or territorial capital

Abolition of slavery in Territories:
- —— by Act of Congress 1862
- - - by Thirteenth Amendment 1865

0   100   200   300

Lake of
the Woods

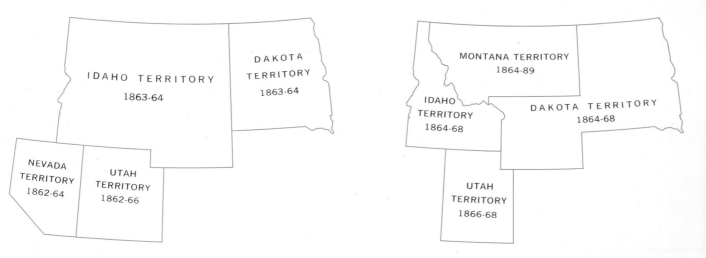

IDAHO TERRITORY
1863-64

DAKOTA
TERRITORY
1863-64

NEVADA
TERRITORY
1862-64

UTAH
TERRITORY
1862-66

MONTANA TERRITORY
1864-89

IDAHO
TERRITORY
1864-68

DAKOTA TERRITORY
1864-68

UTAH
TERRITORY
1866-68

REBUILDING *the* NATION

After the Civil War the process of state making in the West proceeded, if not without incident, in a relatively routine manner. Nevada had been admitted to the Union in 1864, long before its population justified statehood, to swell Lincoln's electoral vote in the crucial election of that year. The admission of Nebraska reflected the normal westward movement of the frontier; that of Colorado, the influx of miners after the discovery of gold and silver in the Pikes Peak area. The rest of the West moved gradually through shifts and complications of territorial alignments, as shown at the bottom of the opposite page.

State rebuilding in the South, however, was far more complex. During the fighting, Lincoln had appointed provisional governors to administer areas controlled by Union troops. He proposed that when 10 per cent of the voters of 1860 in these states had taken a loyalty oath, they could establish civilian governments. Tennessee, Arkansas, and Louisiana did so in 1864, but these were merely puppet regimes, like the one created in the new state of West Virginia, the non-slaveholding counties of Virginia that had refused to secede from the Union in 1861. Andrew Johnson continued this policy after Lincoln's assassination, and by December, 1865, all the southern states had set up governments and elected representatives to Congress.

Congress, however, refused to seat these men. Alarmed by "black codes" that kept former slaves in a subordinate status despite the 13th Amendment, it overrode Presidential vetoes and divided the Confederacy (except for Tennessee) into five districts controlled by the Army. To rid themselves of the military and get back in the Union, the southern states had to adopt new constitutions guaranteeing Negroes the right to vote and otherwise protecting their civil rights. Between 1868 and 1870, after additional legislation had placed elections and voter registration under Federal control, these states reluctantly complied.

The new governments were controlled by white men—northern "carpetbaggers" and southern "scalawags"—and by Negroes. As soon as northern determination to protect Negro rights began to flag, they began to crumble. White terrorist groups, like the notorious Ku Klux Klan and the more respectable "Red Shirt" element in Mississippi, drove Negroes from the polls and soon "Conservative" parties took over. This happened as early as 1869 in Tennessee, but not until after the 1876 presidential election in South Carolina, Louisiana, and Florida. Slavery itself had died quickly, eliminated by state action or by the 13th Amendment in the Border States, and by Johnsonian reconstruction in the rest of the South. But real freedom for the Negro had not resulted.

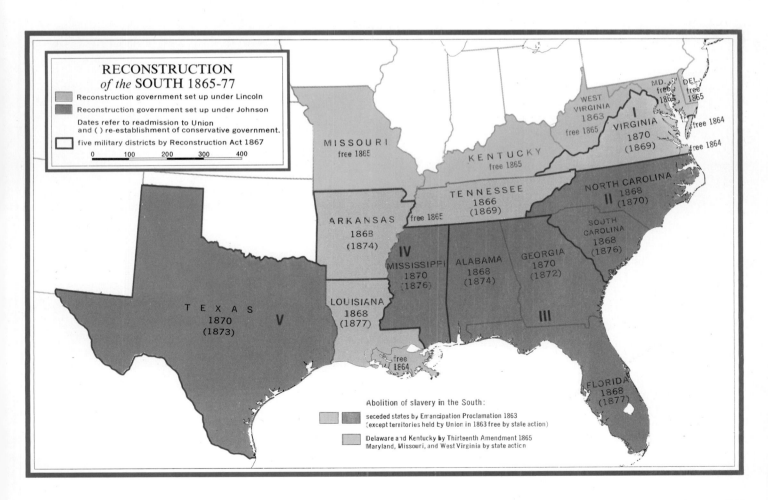

RECONSTRUCTION *of the* SOUTH 1865-77

Reconstruction government set up under Lincoln

Reconstruction government set up under Johnson

Dates refer to readmission to Union and ( ) re-establishment of conservative government.

five military districts by Reconstruction Act 1867

0   100   200   300   400

MISSOURI
free 1865

WEST VIRGINIA 1863
free 1865

MD. free 1864   DEL. free 1865

VIRGINIA 1870 (1869)
free 1864
free 1864

KENTUCKY
free 1865

I

NORTH CAROLINA
II   1868 (1870)

TENNESSEE 1866 (1869)

ARKANSAS 1868 (1874)
free 1865

SOUTH CAROLINA 1868 (1876)

IV

MISSISSIPPI 1870 (1876)

ALABAMA 1868 (1874)

GEORGIA 1870 (1872)

TEXAS 1870 (1873)
V

LOUISIANA 1868 (1877)

III

free 1864

FLORIDA 1868 (1877)

Abolition of slavery in the South:

seceded states by Emancipation Proclamation 1863 (except territories held by Union in 1863 free by state action)

Delaware and Kentucky by Thirteenth Amendment 1865 Maryland, Missouri, and West Virginia by state action

BREAKING INDIAN RESISTANCE

The stampede for Colorado gold touched off an era of Indian wars in the Great Plains and bordering areas. An estimated 100,000 miners and settlers crossed Kansas in 1859, pushed aside the Cheyennes and Arapahos, and deprived them of food by scattering the buffalo herds. In the ensuing conflict, Colonel J. M. Chivington and 750 Colorado militiamen struck a peaceful band of sleeping Cheyennes at Sand Creek (bottom right on map), and ruthlessly slaughtered more than 100 women and children. In retaliation, inflamed Indians burned wagon trains and stage stations.

In Minnesota, the eastern Sioux, hemmed in by the advancing agricultural frontier, staged a terrible uprising in 1862, killing hundreds of settlers and soldiers. They were crushed by the U.S. Army. The western Sioux had more success, for a time, in stopping traffic on the trail which John M. Bozeman opened, in 1863, to the Montana gold regions. Red Cloud's Sioux killed 81 soldiers, including Captain William Fetterman, near Fort Phil Kearny, Wyoming; the government then promised the Sioux perpetual possession of the Dakota Black Hills as a hunting preserve. The promise was broken when gold was discovered in the Black Hills, and a rush of prospectors started another war. A great Indian victory on the Little Bighorn River had no effect on the inevitable outcome—Sitting Bull, one of the Sioux leaders, fled to Canadian exile, and the Sioux were forced onto reservations. Other military operations (including a 1,700-mile chase of Chief Joseph and his Nez Perces), together with the work of hide hunters who exterminated 13 million buffalo between 1867 and 1883, completed the work of discouraging the Indians, and secured the West for permanent settlement.

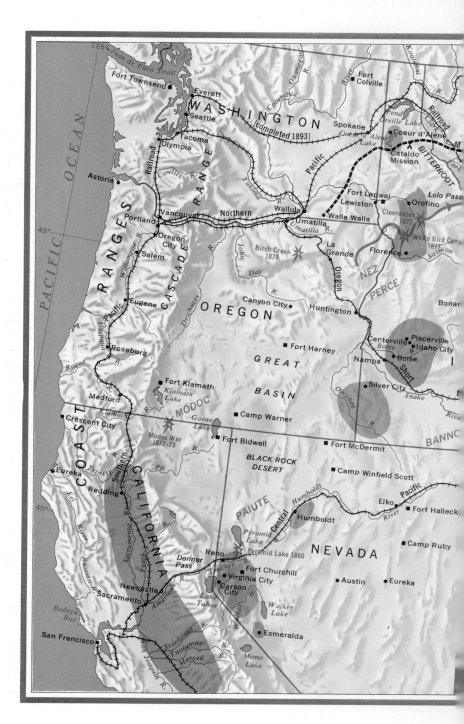

Harper's Weekly, 1876

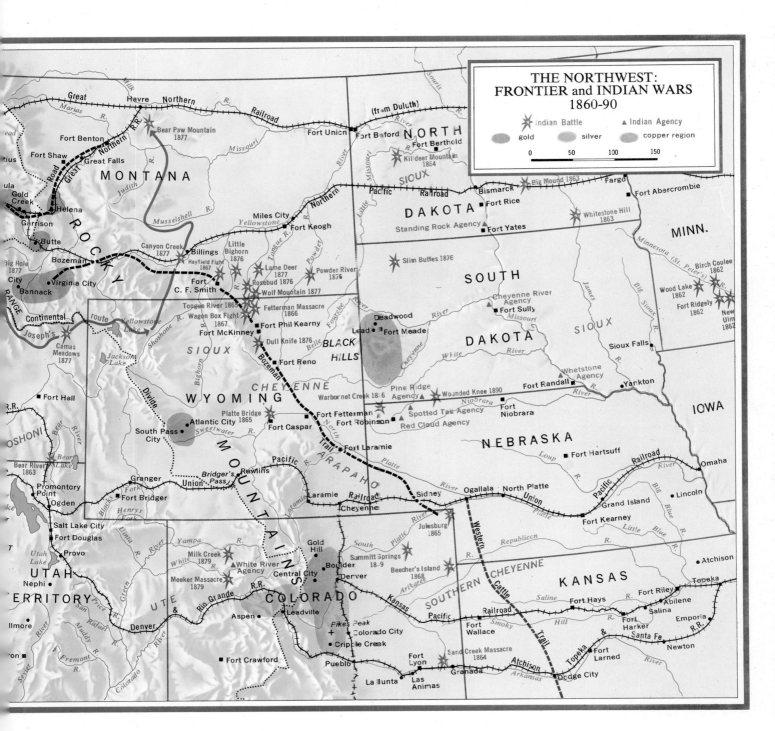

THE NORTHWEST: FRONTIER and INDIAN WARS 1860-90

✶ Indian Battle   ▲ Indian Agency

gold   silver   copper region

0   50   100   150

MONTANA — Great Falls, Fort Benton, Fort Shaw, Helena, Gold Creek, Garrison, Butte, Bozeman, Virginia City, Bannack, Billings, Miles City, Fort Keogh, Canyon Creek 1877, Bear Paw Mountain 1877, Havre, Great Northern Railroad, Northern Pacific Railroad, Little Bighorn 1876, Hayfield Fight 1867, Lame Deer 1877, Rosebud 1876, Wolf Mountain 1877, Powder River 1876, Fort C. F. Smith, Tongue River 1865, Fetterman Massacre 1866, Wagon Box Fight 1867, Big Hole 1877

NORTH DAKOTA — Fort Union, Fort Buford, Fort Berthold, Killdeer Mountain 1864, Bismarck, Fort Rice, Standing Rock Agency, Fort Yates, Big Mound 1863, Fargo, Fort Abercrombie, Whitestone Hill 1863

SOUTH DAKOTA — Slim Buttes 1876, Deadwood, Lead, Fort Meade, Cheyenne River Agency, Fort Sully, Whetstone Agency, Fort Randall, Yankton, Sioux Falls, Pine Ridge Agency, Wounded Knee 1890, Spotted Tail Agency, Red Cloud Agency, Warbonnet Creek 1876

WYOMING — Fort Phil Kearny, Fort McKinney, Dull Knife 1876, Fort Reno, Fort Laramie, Fort Fetterman, Fort Robinson, Platte Bridge 1865, Fort Caspar, Atlantic City, South Pass City, Fort Hall, Rawlins, Granger, Union Pacific Railroad, Laramie, Cheyenne, Fort Bridger, Bridger's Pass, Camas Meadows 1877, Jackson Lake, Yellowstone Lake

NEBRASKA — Fort Niobrara, Fort Hartsuff, Sidney, Ogallala, North Platte, Grand Island, Lincoln, Omaha, Fort Kearney, Julesburg 1865

UTAH TERRITORY — Salt Lake City, Fort Douglas, Provo, Nephi, Promontory Point, Ogden, Bear River 1863

COLORADO — Milk Creek 1879, White River Agency, Meeker Massacre 1879, Central City, Gold Hill, Boulder, Denver, Summit Springs 1869, Beecher's Island 1868, Leadville, Aspen, Pikes Peak, Colorado City, Cripple Creek, Pueblo, Fort Lyon, Sand Creek Massacre 1864, Granada, La Junta, Las Animas, Fort Crawford

KANSAS — Atchison, Topeka, Fort Riley, Abilene, Salina, Emporia, Newton, Santa Fe, Fort Harker, Fort Hays, Fort Wallace, Fort Larned, Dodge City, Kansas Pacific Railroad, Santa Fe R.R., Western Cattle Trail, Atchison Topeka

MINN. — Birch Coulee 1862, Wood Lake 1862, Fort Ridgely 1862, New Ulm 1862

IOWA

Fort Fetterman on the Wyoming plains (left) was a busy post in the 1876 Sioux war. It was named for an officer killed by the Sioux ten years before. At right is an Indian painting of the Little Bighorn battle in Montana, June 25, 1876, when George A. Custer and some 250 cavalrymen were overwhelmed and killed. It was painted by Whitebird, a Sioux, about 1894.

FRONTIER'S END

General William Tecumseh Sherman called Indian fighting "the hardest kind of war"—and Sherman was an authority. After the Civil War, he commanded the Division of the Missouri, in charge of troops who guarded railroad builders, and punished Indians who interfered. After 1869 he commanded the whole U.S. Army, which had 14,000 Indian fighters deployed from Texas to North Dakota, and from Kansas to California. In 25 years—1866 to 1891—the Army fought 1,065 engagements with Indians across an area twice as large as the theater of the Civil War.

Against the hard-riding men in blue uniforms, the mounted Indians of the plains and Southwest were equal foes, on a man to man basis. Most Indians were not good shots, but their horses were usually faster, and their ability to slip down on the far side of a pony, using its body as a shield, and fire under its neck at encircled troops, gave them the edge in surprise attacks. Kiowas and Comanches were skilled in these tactics, and used them for years to keep ranchers out of their buffalo grounds in the Texas Panhandle.

The longest Indian war was fought in the deserts and mountain canyons of Arizona and New Mexico; it began, in fact, in 1598, with the first Pueblo revolt against Spanish rule, and was almost continuous for 300 years. Neither Spain nor Mexico ever subdued the Navahos and Apaches. Arizona was rich in minerals, and New Mexico tempted cattlemen. But there were few attempts at American settlement until the mid-1850's, when Army forts and 1,500 troops were available for protection. In an Army drive during the Civil War —with Colonel Kit Carson among the commanders—664 hostile Indians were killed, and 8,793 were made prisoners. The Navahos and most Apaches then agreed to live on reservations. A few irreconcilables continued to fight—on both sides of the Mexican border—until 1886. Their elusive leader, Geronimo, eventually surrendered and was exiled, at first to Florida, and then to Oklahoma. He lived to ride in the Inauguration Day parade for President Theodore Roosevelt, in 1905.

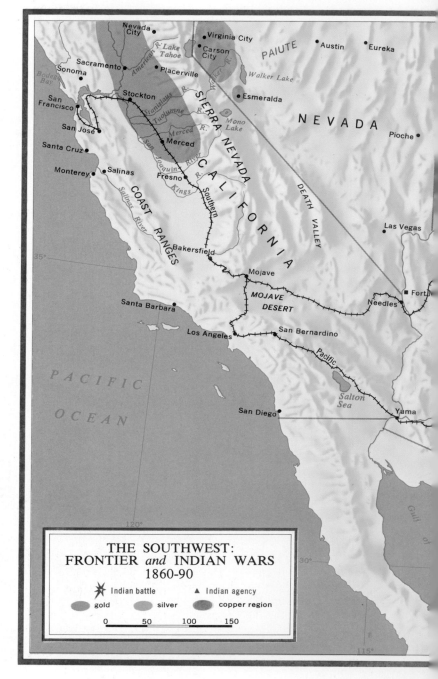

THE SOUTHWEST:
FRONTIER *and* INDIAN WARS
1860-90

✴ Indian battle   ▲ Indian agency

gold   silver   copper region

0   50   100   150

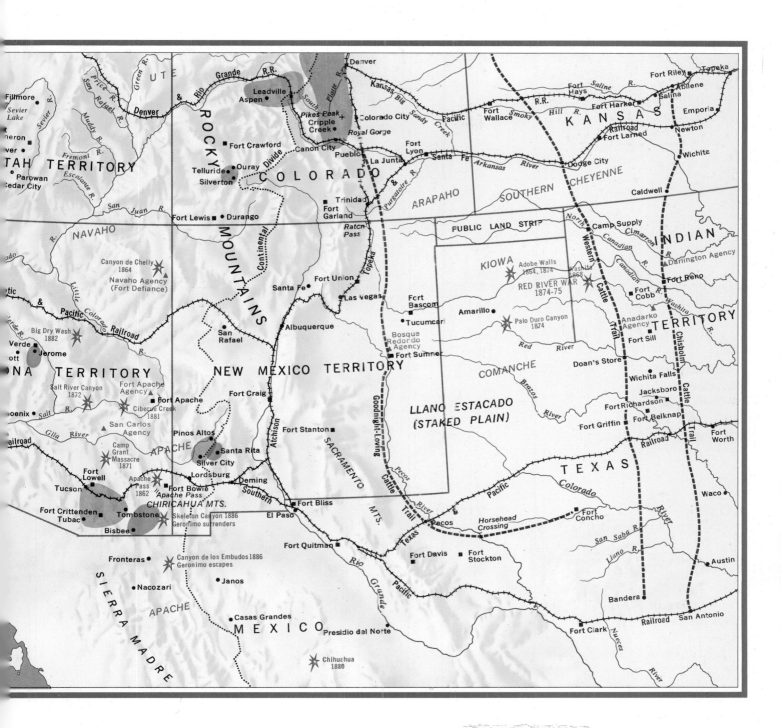

Fort Yuma, left, on the west bank of the lower Colorado, guarded the main crossing from Arizona to California on mail, freight, and emigrant routes. At right is the Mission San Jose de Tumacacori, built by Jesuits in 1696, near Tubac, the first Spanish settlement in Arizona (just above the Mexican border on the map above). Both of these woodcuts were illustrations in J. Ross Browne's 1869 travel account, Adventures in the Apache Country.

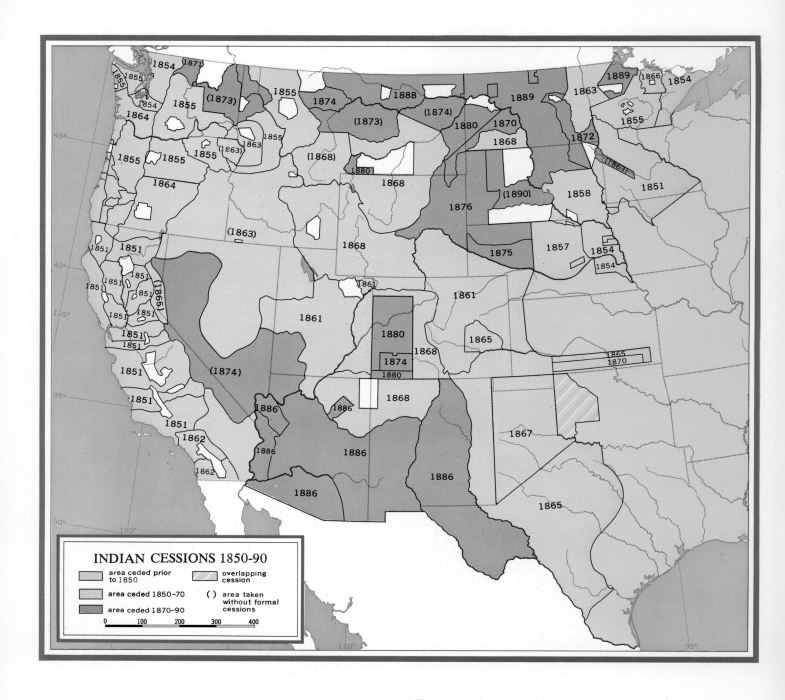

INDIAN CESSIONS 1850-90

area ceded prior to 1850

area ceded 1850-70

area ceded 1870-90

overlapping cession

( ) area taken without formal cessions

0   100   200   300   400

SURRENDERED HUNTING GROUNDS

In 1850 about 250,000 Indians roamed freely over the western half of the United States. Today there are more than half a million Indians, but they own only tiny fragments of the vast country they once inhabited. The tribes lost most of their domain between 1850 and 1890. When whites first began pouring into Oregon and California, the Federal government thought that commissioners might induce the western tribes to migrate—as the eastern tribes had done—to the plains country, which still had little attraction for white men. The western natives refused to move, however; and without the force to evict them, as the government had done in the East, negotiators signed treaties in which tribes retained part of their lands as "reserves," but sold the rest for annuities and other payments.

By this system tribes ceded large tracts of the West to the white man. But other areas were simply seized, and considered ceded. In California, whites expropriated most Indian

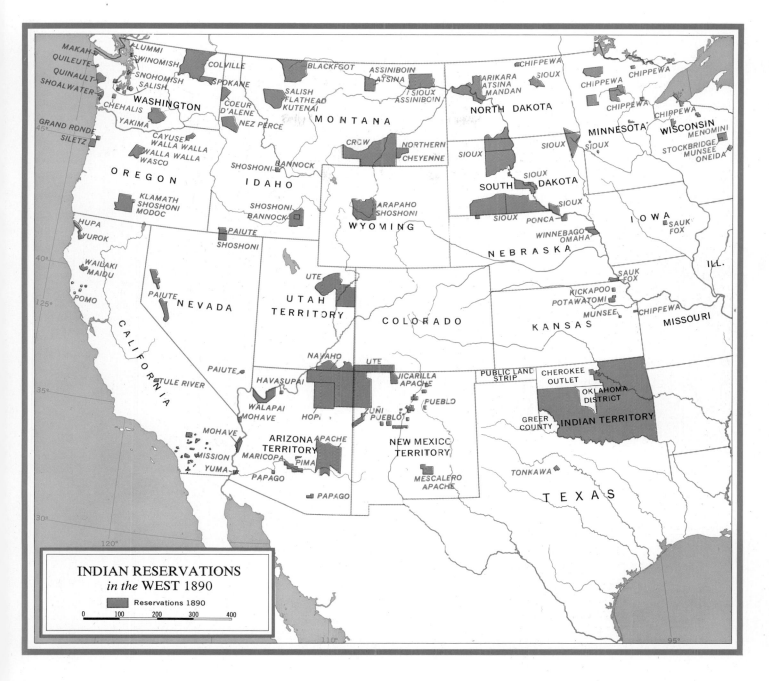

INDIAN RESERVATIONS
in the WEST 1890

Reservations 1890

| 0 | 100 | 200 | 300 | 400 |

lands, killing at least 50,000 natives between 1849 and 1852. When, in other regions, Indians refused to sell, the resulting wars ended inevitably with beaten Indians being forcibly dispossessed and driven onto reservations.

By 1890, the West was dotted with these last holdings of the First Americans. Present-day Oklahoma was filled not only with the tribes that had been removed there from the Southeast in the 1830's, but with survivors of groups that had ended up there, voluntarily or by force, from original homelands from New York to Oregon. Elsewhere, reservations changed in size and shape from time to time. Pressure to wipe out the reservations never ceased. Under the Dawes Severalty Act of 1887, Congress hoped to hasten Indian assimilation by allotting natives individual farms and selling leftover reservation land to whites. The policy failed, but it cost the Indians 90,000,000 more acres. Today, most tribes jealously guard the land still left to them.

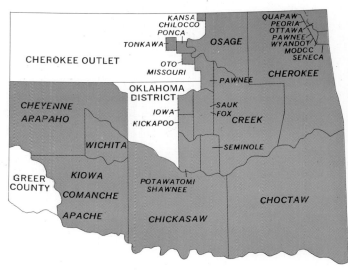

INDIAN TERRITORY 1890

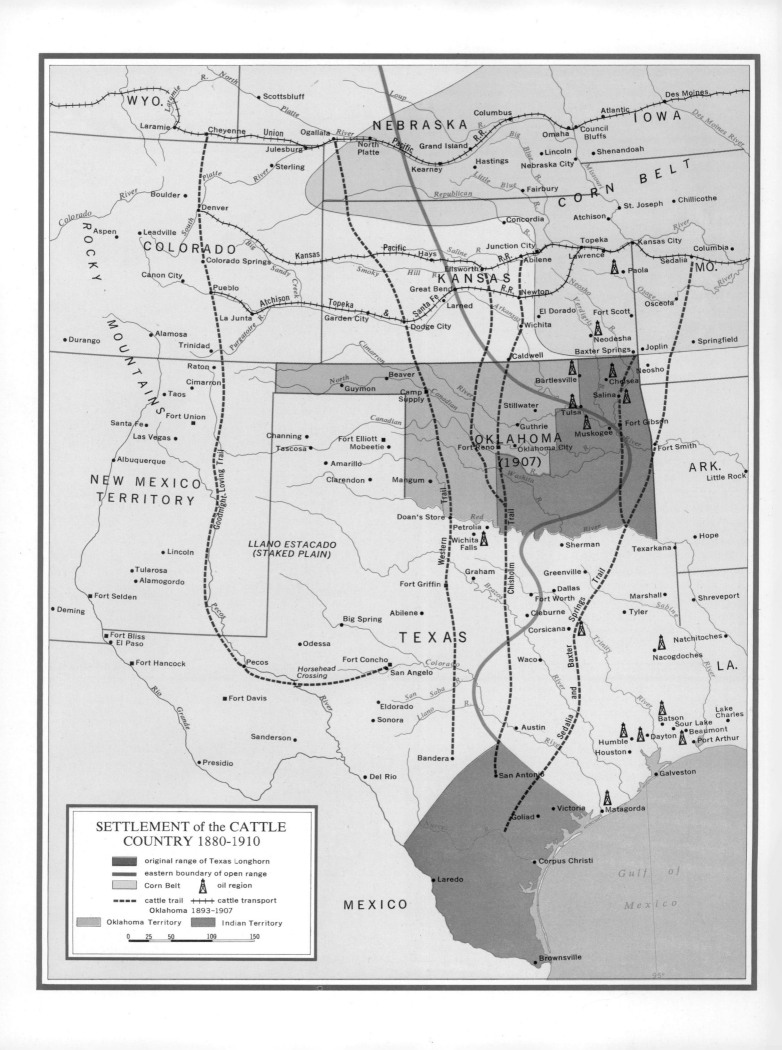

SETTLEMENT of the CATTLE
COUNTRY 1880-1910

original range of Texas Longhorn

eastern boundary of open range

Corn Belt   oil region

cattle trail   ┼┼┼┼ cattle transport
Oklahoma 1893–1907

Oklahoma Territory   Indian Territory

0   25   50   100   150

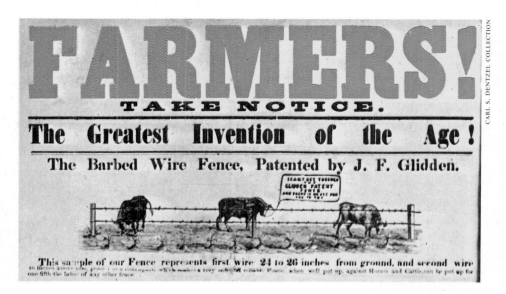

On the Great Plains, where wood was scarce or non-existent, fencing was a problem until 1874, when Joseph F. Glidden invented a practical type of barbed wire. Farmers, trying to keep cattle off their land, welcomed it; but some ranchers used it illegally to prevent rivals from driving livestock across the public lands.

CATTLE TRAILS *and the* OPEN RANGE

Christopher Columbus brought the first cattle to America on his second voyage, in 1493, and later colonists took the animal to every corner of Spain's empire. In Mexico the open country encouraged cattle raisers to allow their herds to range freely. The animals thrived, and in Spanish Texas strays by the thousands eventually roamed all over the area between the Rio Grande and the Nueces. When settlers from the United States reached that country, their own stringy cattle interbred with the Spanish variety, creating the tough, fleet, ferocious Texas longhorn. Neglected during the Civil War, some five million of these animals roamed wild in 1865 in southern Texas. They could be claimed by anyone who took the trouble to round them up, and were worth, locally, three or four dollars a head.

Texas cattle had been shipped to eastern markets before the Civil War; but in 1865, with beeves bringing $40 a head in St. Louis and Chicago, Texans began to round up the herds on a large scale. The nearest rail connection to the east was at Sedalia, Missouri; in 1866 about 250,000 head were driven over the Sedalia Trail, grazing along the way. This route, however, led through wooded country, where the animals were hard to control, and across settled parts of Missouri, where farmers objected to the herds. The next year, inspired by a cattle dealer, Joseph McCoy, drivers began to follow a more westerly route across open country to a new railhead at Abilene, Kansas. This route became known as the Chisholm Trail, after Jesse Chisholm, a half-breed trader who had blazed part of it. As the railroads pushed west to Ellsworth and Dodge City, the trails shifted with them. By the 1880's some four million head of Texas cattle had been shipped east from Kansas yards.

As early as 1866 Charles Goodnight and Oliver Loving had begun driving cattle to Colorado for sale in the mining camps. To avoid hostile Kiowas and Comanches, they took a circuitous route up the valley of the Pecos River into New Mexico Territory before turning north. More than a million cattle, far more than the miners could consume, had plodded over this Goodnight-Loving Trail by 1869. But the drivers soon discovered that hardy longhorns could survive the harsh winters of the northern plains, and that millions of acres of grass—public property—lay open to anyone who wished to graze his cattle. By staking out a 160-acre homestead claim along a stream or around a waterhole, a rancher could obtain exclusive use of all the surrounding country without actually buying it. The cattle roamed freely, but not too far; instinct kept them from drifting out of range of water.

The Panic of 1873 (when falling prices caused shippers to hold cattle at the railheads and find temporary grass for them) hastened the trend to use of the northern range. This, with the building of railroads to shipping points in Texas, spelled the end of the long trail drives. By 1880 about 4.5 million head populated the vast sea of grass between Kansas and the Rockies and north to Montana. Thoroughbred eastern bulls were imported to improve the stock, and as the demand for beef rose, fortunes were made. Associations of ranchers pooled their water rights; easterners and foreigners invested in the business; and, from Texas to Canada, operators dominated princely domains.

But prosperity led to overstocking and depletion of the grass, and the advancing frontier of settlement produced competition for land between ranchers and farmers. Then came the winter of 1886-87, when blizzards killed an estimated 80–90 per cent of the cattle on the northern plains. Thereafter, in one way or another, cattlemen everywhere obtained legal title to their land, fenced it, and sank wells powered by windmills to provide water. The bonanza years were over; the open range was no more. But a new bonanza, petroleum, the "black gold," was soon to give much of the area another, equally dramatic, kind of prosperity.

Harper's Weekly, 1869

At right is an 1869 view of the Union Pacific railroad station at Sherman, Wyoming Territory. The UP, first of the transcontinental lines, received (in addition to large land grants) Federal loans in the form of bonds: $16,000 to $48,000 per mile of track, depending on the difficulty of the terrain. The repayment of the principal and interest, long delayed, was settled by a compromise agreement reached after much wrangling between the railroad company and lawyers of the government.

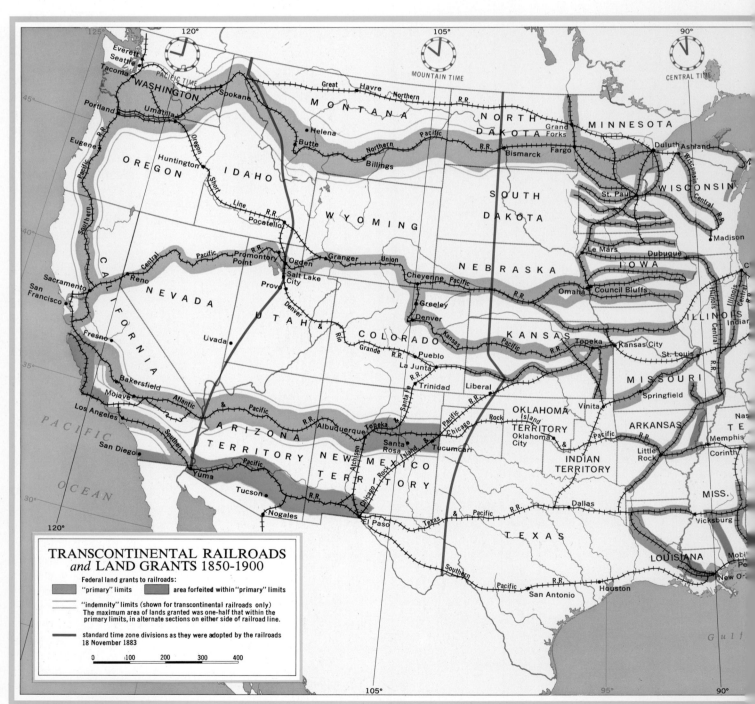

TRANSCONTINENTAL RAILROADS and LAND GRANTS 1850-1900

Federal land grants to railroads:

■ "primary" limits   ■ area forfeited within "primary" limits

"indemnity" limits (shown for transcontinental railroads only)
The maximum area of lands granted was one-half that within the primary limits, in alternate sections on either side of railroad line.

━━━ standard time zone divisions as they were adopted by the railroads 18 November 1883

0   100   200   300   400

RAILROAD
LAND
GRANTS

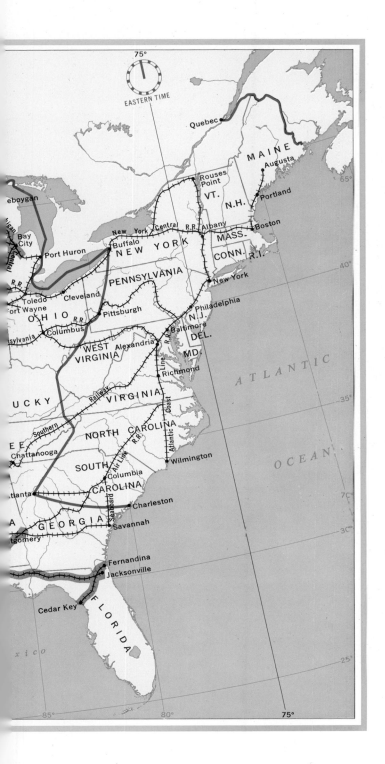

Between 1850 and 1900, American railroad men laid almost 250.000 miles of track, a huge achievement. Finding capital for this construction posed great difficulties, particularly in the West, for private investors hesitated to build in sparsely settled country where they could not hope to earn profits for years. Public construction would have been a logical solution, but in the individualistic Gilded Age, few persons were ready for such a policy. Instead, beginning in 1850, with an allotment to the promoters of the Illinois Central, the Federal government aided private builders by giving them public land—more than 200 million acres in a period of about 20 years.

This land was either sold or used as security for loans by the builders to obtain funds with which to construct the lines. Whether or not this land-grant policy was in the public interest has been long debated. The country gained a much-needed transportation system, but at the price of a great national asset—land. In spending other people's money, railroad men often wasted funds and sometimes diverted large amounts into their own pockets. To protect the value of the grants, homesteaders were barred from public lands in railroad zones, even from the "indemnity" bands that were set aside so that the roads could make up for sites in the "primary" zones already occupied by settlers. Some companies withheld their lands from sale for speculative reasons, thus retarding settlement. The grants speeded railroad expansion considerably, but the existence of prosperous lines like the Great Northern, built across almost empty country near the Canadian border without any subsidy, showed that grants were not necessary, however much they eased the burdens of railroad financiers.

But the picture was not all negative. The bands on the map (left) exaggerate the size of the grants, which actually took the form of a checkerboard. Every other square-mile section remained in the public domain; the railroads never owned as much of such states as Iowa, Minnesota, and Washington as the map suggests. Furthermore, the railroads did not profit inordinately from the sale of their lands. Much of it, running through barren country, was practically worthless. Moreover, as tracks were pushed westward, land values increased rapidly in the territories served. Those sections of the checkerboard still publicly owned were then often worth more than the whole region had been before the railroad grants were made. And whenever a company failed to fulfill its agreement to lay track, its land grants were repossessed. Some 25 million acres thus reverted to the public domain through forfeiture.

Any balanced assessment of the land-grant system must also take into account the role of the railroads as colonizers of the West. To encourage settlement, many lines advertised the virtues of the country widely—in Europe as well as in the United States. They offered cut-rate "land exploration" tickets to prospective settlers and sold land, generally, at fair prices and on easy terms. Some even set up dormitories at the railheads where pioneers could live while getting established. Finally, land-grant roads were required to move mail and troops for the government at reduced rates; many, in fact, argue that, in the long run, the lines got far the worst of the bargain.

Even before the Civil War, expansion-minded Californians had urged that the United States buy Alaska from Russia. Not until 1867, however, did Secretary of State William H. Seward, prodded by fishing interests in Washington Territory, make a firm offer to the Czar's representative; eager to sell their only holdings in America (profits from their fur company had decreased, and Alaska was indefensible against a possible British take-over), the Russians quickly accepted $7,200,000 in exchange for more than 586,400 square miles of peaks, fjords, unmapped plateaus, and scattered islands. But although the purchase price, which came to less than two cents per acre, was certainly right, most Americans regarded Alaska as a white elephant. "Seward's Folly" and "Seward's Icebox" were only two of the derisive names that newspapers assigned to the region, despite the fact that the rich sealing and fishing grounds there guaranteed an eventual profit on the deal. For 17 years, the area was an unorganized territory; governed first by the Army, later by the Navy, and in between by no one at all, Alaska's residents were so neglected that they had to ask the British for help against hostile Indians in 1879. The first American governor was not appointed until 1884, and limited territorial status was not granted until 1912. By that time, "Seward's Folly" had become the locale of dreams of quick and fabulous fortunes.

In 1880, news of gold strikes had brought prospectors to the area around Juneau; six years later, new deposits were discovered in the interior, just west of Fortymile. More miners came to Alaska and began to fan out: some struggled over the Chilkoot Pass into the Canadian Yukon; others worked placer mines at Rampart, Circle, and similar new towns along the rivers; still others began operations on Kodiak Island, around Cook Inlet, and on the Alaska Peninsula. By 1895, Alaska was processing $800,000 worth of gold annually from placer mines and an additional $1,725,000 from lodes. In 1896 (the year that W. A. Dickey named the tallest mountain on the continent after Presidential candidate William McKinley), 1,000 miners were panning for gold along the Yukon River. All this was prelude, however, to the rush resulting from the discovery of gold in the Klondike region of the Canadian Yukon in 1896. When the news spread to the states, an estimated 100,000 hopefuls dropped everything and headed north. Many sailed to St. Michael, then traveled upriver to Canada; others chose the arduous routes beginning at Valdez, Yakutat, Skagway, and Wrangell. Most were totally inexperienced and unprepared for the frigid weather, steep and icy trails, sickness, and starvation that lay ahead of them. Only about 40,000 made it to Dawson, the Klondike boomtown. The others died, returned home, or filtered back into Alaska, making their way eventually to sites of new rushes, such as Nome in 1899 or Fairbanks in 1902. But the Klondike bonanza focused attention on Alaska; the now-obvious riches and tremendous potential of the territory were no longer ignored. The gold rush also led to settlement of the border controversy with Canada, which claimed access to the Pacific through the Panhandle. An international commission supported the U.S. position in 1903, and the boundary was fixed at its present location.

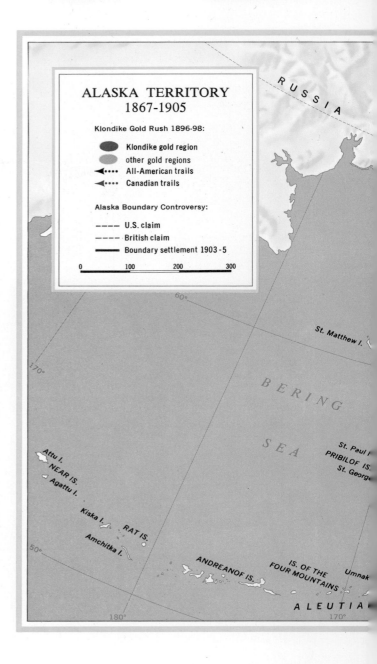

ALASKA TERRITORY
1867-1905

Klondike Gold Rush 1896-98:

⬤ Klondike gold region
⬤ other gold regions
◄···· All-American trails
◄···· Canadian trails

Alaska Boundary Controversy:

----- U.S. claim
----- British claim
—— Boundary settlement 1903-5

0   100   200   300

PURCHASE
from RUSSIA

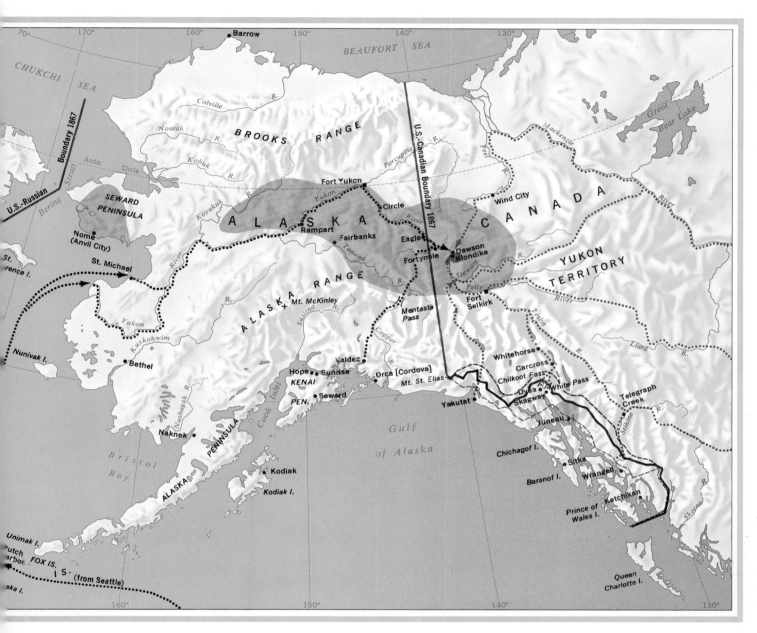

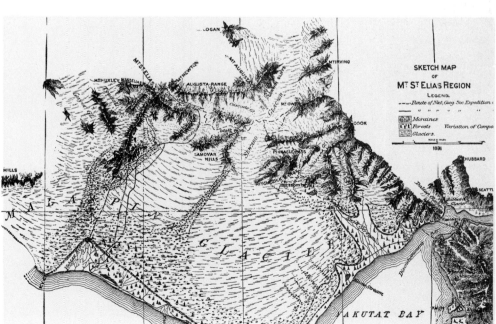

The map at right, of the region around Mount St. Elias, appeared in The Journal of Geology in 1893. It illustrated an article by the geologist Israel C. Russell, who, under the auspices of the National Geographic Society and the United States Geological Survey, had mapped the area and studied the gigantic Malaspina Glacier, which covered more than 1,500 square miles. Although most Americans persisted in thinking of Alaska as a largely unknown wasteland, accurate knowledge of much of the territory was acquired during the 1880's and 1890's by government and private exploring parties. The extent of the major mountain ranges and the courses of the most important rivers were well known by 1900.

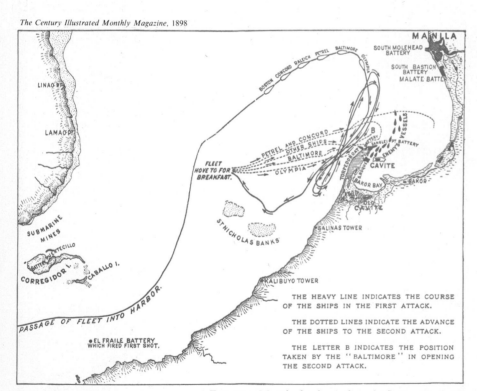

The Century Illustrated Monthly Magazine, 1898

THE HEAVY LINE INDICATES THE COURSE OF THE SHIPS IN THE FIRST ATTACK.

THE DOTTED LINES INDICATE THE ADVANCE OF THE SHIPS TO THE SECOND ATTACK.

THE LETTER B INDICATES THE POSITION TAKEN BY THE "BALTIMORE" IN OPENING THE SECOND ATTACK.

Entering Manila harbor after dark on April 30, Dewey closed to within 5,000 yards of the Spaniards at Cavite. At 5:35 A.M., with the order, "You may fire when you are ready, Gridley," he began the bombardment. After five passes, he withdrew to assess the damage, then closed again. At 12:25, their fleet destroyed, the Spaniards surrendered. Only eight Americans were wounded in the fight.

SPANISH CONFLICT SETTLED *by* WAR

Although the war with Spain was fought to free Cuba, the first fighting took place on the opposite side of the world, in the Philippine Islands. The United States Pacific Fleet, under Commodore George Dewey, was based at Hong Kong. Acting on earlier orders from the Navy Department, Dewey had already prepared to attack, even to the extent of making contacts with Filipino nationalist elements. On April 28, 1898, only hours after receiving notice that war had been declared, he steamed toward Manila on the U.S.S. *Olympia* with five other warships and three supply vessels. After smashing the Spanish fleet on May 1, he remained in Manila harbor, and when troops finally arrived from California in August, he covered their attack on the city.

In Atlantic waters, action was delayed until Admiral Pascual Cervera's fleet, steaming from Spain, had been located. Commodore Winfield Scott Schley's "Flying Squadron" stood by to protect coastal cities against possible attack, while Rear Admiral William T. Sampson, maintaining a blockade of the Cuban coast, sailed east to bombard San Juan, Puerto Rico. On May 12 Cervera was reported in the Caribbean, and both American squadrons

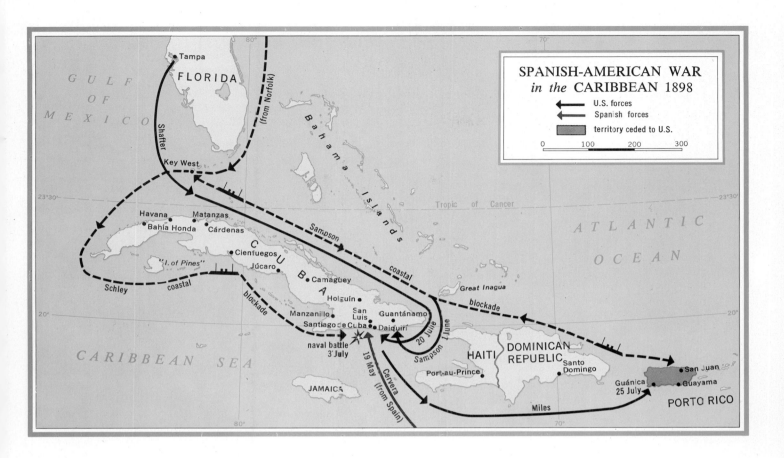

Harper's New Monthly Magazine, 1898

hastened to intercept him. Before they could find him, however, he took shelter behind the harbor defenses of Santiago de Cuba, where, on May 29, American warships finally pinned him down.

On June 14 a 17,000-man invasion army commanded by General William Shafter sailed from Tampa, Florida, to attack Cuba. Landing at Daiquirí, east of Santiago, these troops took Caney and San Juan Hill on July 1. With his fleet in range of American artillery on the heights above Santiago, Cervera was forced to put to sea and face the combined fleets of Sampson and Schley. He did so on July 3, heading west along the coast at top speed. The Americans, led by U.S.S. *Brooklyn* and U.S.S. *Oregon,* their 8- and 13-inch guns blazing, quickly ran down his outclassed vessels. The contest was brief; within four hours the entire Spanish squadron was destroyed. Only one American sailor lost his life in the fight.

Thereafter, Spanish resistance crumbled rapidly. Santiago fell on July 17, while an American force under General Nelson Miles, diverted from the Cuban campaign, invaded Puerto Rico on July 25 and easily overran that island. By August 12 the fighting was over.

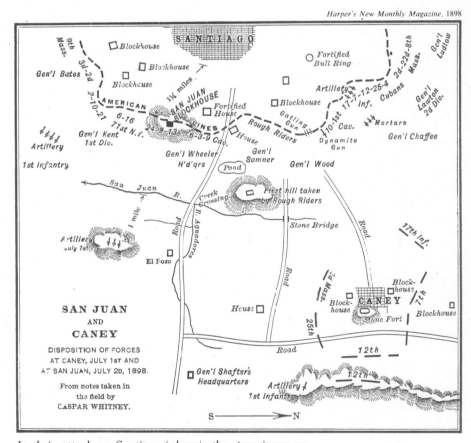

In their attack on Santiago (above), the Americans on July 1 took Caney and stormed the hills guarding the city. The Rough Riders' charge that day, under Theodore Roosevelt, was up Kettle Hill (center). The American lines, after the heights were won, are seen at top.

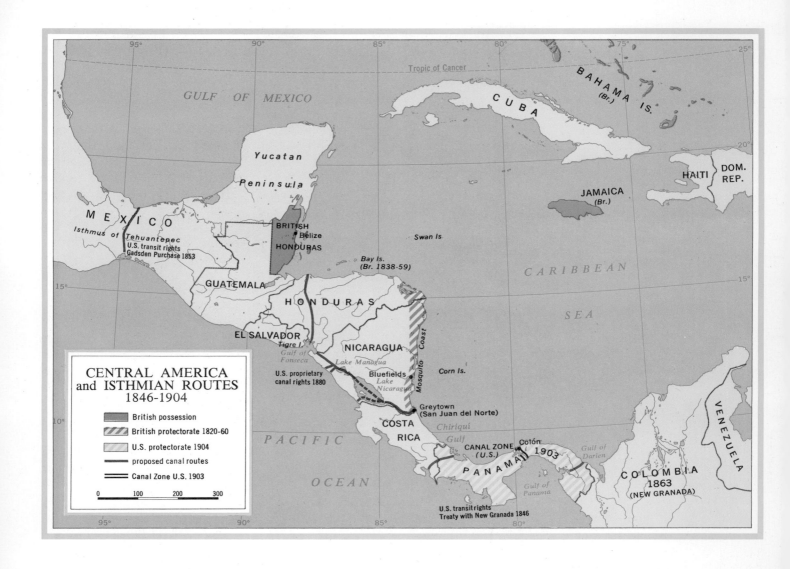

CENTRAL AMERICA
and ISTHMIAN ROUTES
1846-1904

British possession
British protectorate 1820-60
U.S. protectorate 1904
proposed canal routes
Canal Zone U.S. 1903

0   100   200   300

SECURING *the* PANAMA GATEWAY

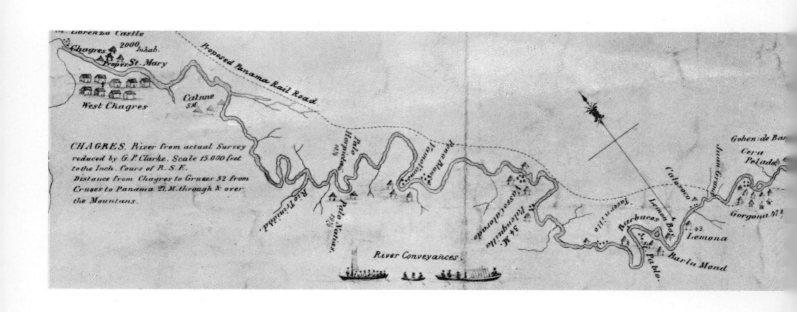

CHAGRES, River from actual Survey
reduced by G.P. Clarke. Scale 15.000 feet
to the Inch. Cours of R.S.E.
Distance from Chagres to Cruses 52 from
Cruses to Panama Ti.M. through & over
the Mountans.

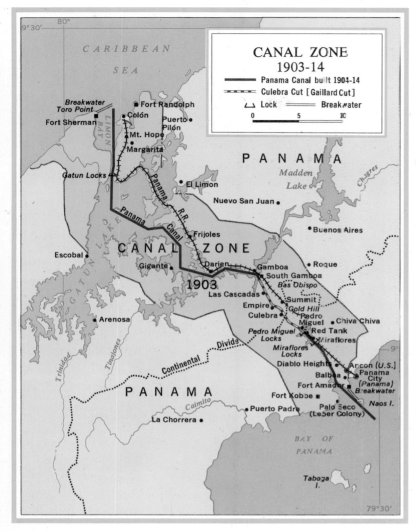

CANAL ZONE
1903-14

— Panama Canal built 1904-14
⊢⊣⊢ Culebra Cut [Gaillard Cut]
⊿ Lock   ═══ Breakwater
0   5   10

The question of whether to build the canal in Panama or in Nicaragua was hotly debated for a long time. The terrain in Panama was more difficult and the climate unhealthier. But the route was 134 miles shorter, and the existence of good harbors and the Panama Railroad were important considerations. The planners took advantage of natural waterways, both Gatun Lake and the Chagres River (seen below in a chart drawn in 1850), to reduce the cost and labor of construction.

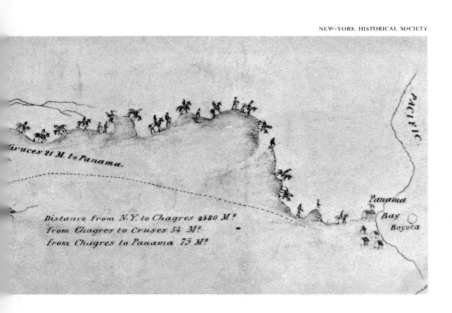

American interest in an interoceanic canal in Central America began in 1846, when Benjamin A. Bidlack, the United States chargé d'affaires in Bogotá, persuaded New Granada to grant Americans the right of transit across the Isthmus of Panama in return for an American promise to protect the area in time of war. Americans were also concerned about British interest, for by 1848 Great Britain had gained control of the Mosquito Coast of Nicaragua, terminus of another prospective canal route. To check the English, the United States agreed, in the Clayton-Bulwer Treaty of 1850, to the neutralization of any future waterway. Both powers promised not to build a canal independently. Rights to another route, across Mexico's Isthmus of Tehuantepec, however, were obtained by the U.S. in the Gadsden Purchase of 1853.

In 1881 a private French company, directed by Ferdinand de Lesseps, builder of the Suez Canal, began work on a canal in Panama, but the task proved too difficult and the company went bankrupt. Between 1889 and 1893 an American company also failed in an effort to cut a waterway through Nicaragua.

After the Spanish-American War, the demand in the United States for an isthmian canal became irresistible, for both strategic and commercial reasons. In 1901 Great Britain agreed to the cancellation of the Clayton-Bulwer Treaty, and in 1903 the United States negotiated a pact with Colombia which gave it a six-mile-wide zone across the Colombian province of Panama for $10 million and an annual rental fee. When the Colombian senate rejected the treaty, holding out for $25 million, local Panamanians, with the enthusiastic support of the United States, revolted, established an independent government, and then signed a treaty granting the United States a zone ten miles wide.

Actual digging of the Panama Canal began only after health officers under Colonel William C. Gorgas had cleaned out the mosquitoes that made yellow fever endemic in the area. Beginning in 1907, construction was under the supervision of General George Washington Goethals. The engineering problems reached staggering proportions. Besides cutting through mountains and building huge locks, Goethals had to supply homes, schools, and other facilities for 30,000 employees and their families. Rockslides, particularly in the area of the Culebra Cut, where the route crossed the continental divide, posed additional difficulties. By the time the canal was opened to traffic in 1914, it had cost approximately $375 million.

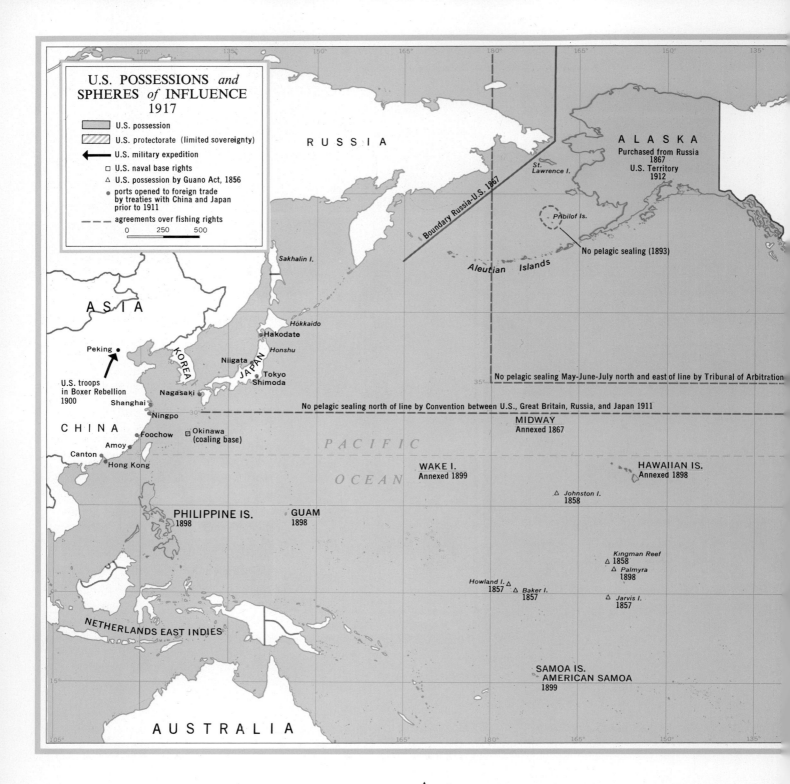

RUSSIA

ALASKA
Purchased from Russia
1867
U.S. Territory
1912

St. Lawrence I.

Boundary Russia-U.S. 1867

Pribilof Is.

No pelagic sealing (1893)

Aleutian Islands

ASIA

Sakhalin I.

Hokkaido
Hakodate
Honshu
Niigata
Tokyo
Shimoda

KOREA

JAPAN

Peking •

U.S. troops
in Boxer Rebellion
1900

Nagasaki

Shanghai

Ningpo

CHINA   Foochow   □ Okinawa
(coaling base)

Amoy

Canton

Hong Kong

No pelagic sealing May-June-July north and east of line by Tribunal of Arbitration

No pelagic sealing north of line by Convention between U.S., Great Britain, Russia, and Japan 1911

MIDWAY
Annexed 1867

PACIFIC

OCEAN

WAKE I.
Annexed 1899

HAWAIIAN IS.
Annexed 1898

△ *Johnston I.*
1858

PHILIPPINE IS.
1898

GUAM
1898

Kingman Reef
△ 1858
△ *Palmyra*
1898

Howland I. △
1857   △ *Baker I.*
1857

△ *Jarvis I.*
1857

NETHERLANDS EAST INDIES

SAMOA IS.
AMERICAN SAMOA
1899

AUSTRALIA

OVERSEAS FRONTIERS

Although the emergence of America as a world power co-incided with the Spanish-American War, the nation had many overseas interests long before 1898. In the Pacific, the China trade and whaling activities scattered Americans over the whole ocean—to Hawaii as early as 1819, to Samoa by 1839. Several uninhabited atolls such as Baker, Johnston, and Jarvis were claimed in the 1850's. In the 1880's, after the purchase of Alaska, a controversy developed over seal fishing in the Bering Sea. The Pribilof Islands were the breeding ground for a valuable herd of pelagic seals. Canadian and, later, Japanese fishermen killed these animals recklessly in international waters, and well-intentioned but

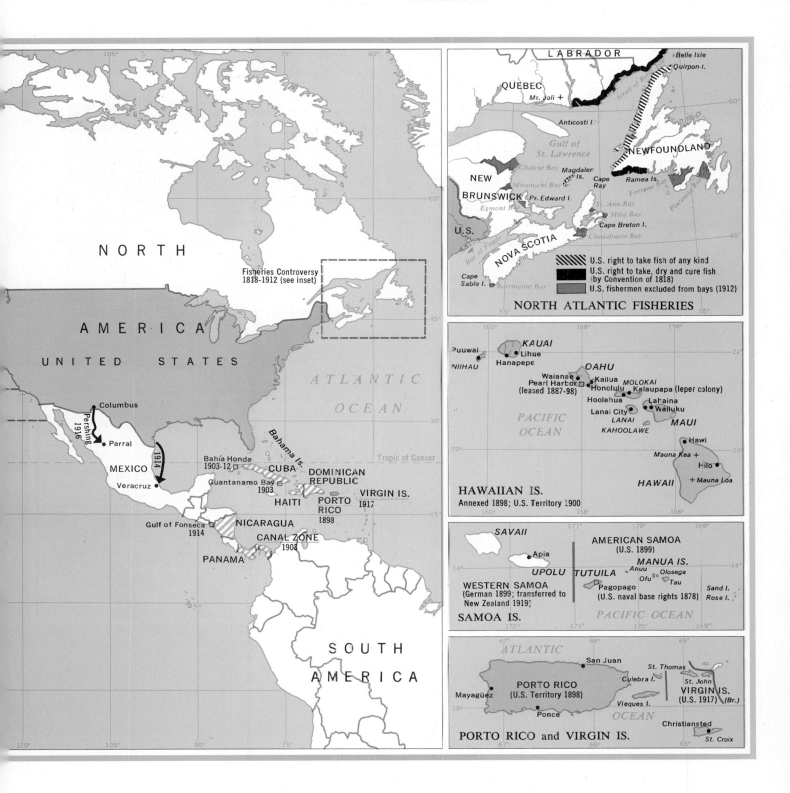

NORTH ATLANTIC FISHERIES

U.S. right to take fish of any kind
U.S. right to take, dry and cure fish (by Convention of 1818)
U.S. fishermen excluded from bays (1912)

HAWAIIAN IS.
Annexed 1898; U.S. Territory 1900

SAMOA IS.

AMERICAN SAMOA (U.S. 1899)
MANUA IS.
WESTERN SAMOA (German 1899; transferred to New Zealand 1919)
TUTUILA (U.S. naval base rights 1878)

PORTO RICO and VIRGIN IS.

PORTO RICO (U.S. Territory 1898)
VIRGIN IS. (U.S. 1917) (Br.)

high-handed efforts of the United States to stop them by seizures outside the three-mile limit caused recurrent crises until 1911, when all the powers concerned agreed to ban pelagic sealing north of the 30th parallel.

Increased American settlement and investment in Hawaii led first to the acquisition of a naval base at Pearl Harbor (1887), then to an American-inspired revolution (1893), and finally (1898) to annexation. In 1879 the United States, Britain, and Germany had set up a tripartite protectorate over the Samoan Islands, and in 1899 the eastern islands were formally annexed. The settlement of the Spanish conflict completed the expansion of the United States in the Pacific by adding the Philippines and Guam to American holdings.

In the Atlantic, Americans were chiefly concerned with the Caribbean region, although the ancient controversy over the Newfoundland fisheries was not finally settled until 1912. Besides outright acquisition of Puerto Rico, the Virgin Islands, and the Canal Zone, protectorates were established over Nicaragua, Haiti, and the Dominican Republic, frequently by the use of armed intervention. While technically not a protectorate, Cuba was also closely controlled; the Platt Amendment to the Cuban Constitution gave the United States the right to intervene to guarantee the island's independence and financial stability.

CONTINENTAL UNITED STATES
1876-1912

	states previously admitted
	new states admitted
o	state or territorial capital

0   100   200   300

Oklahoma rushes onto newly opened Indian lands produced tent cities, like Oklahoma City, seen here in 1889.

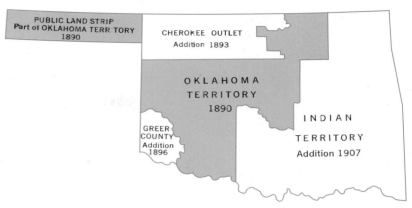

PUBLIC LAND STRIP
Part of OKLAHOMA TERRITORY
1890

CHEROKEE OUTLET
Addition 1893

OKLAHOMA
TERRITORY
1890

GREER
COUNTY
Addition
1896

INDIAN
TERRITORY
Addition 1907

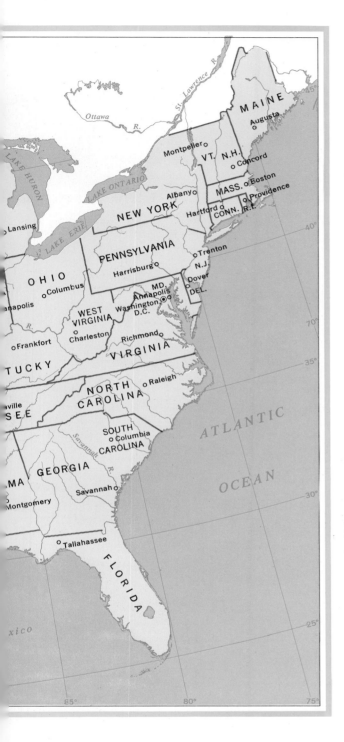

The map at left portrays the last stages of a process that began in 1787 with the enactment of the Northwest Ordinance by the Continental Congress. It represents the final—or, considering Alaska and Hawaii, the penultimate—triumph of a great liberal idea, and of an experiment in practical democracy without parallel in history. The term "United States" has become a name rather than a description, and to a degree this is unfortunate, for it obscures the great difficulties overcome in creating 48 separate independent commonwealths without destroying their unity and individuality. The American method of state making appears all the more admirable when the problems that beset it are fully understood. The furor over the Missouri Compromise and the Compromise of 1850, the blood spilled in pre-Civil War Kansas, the secessionist plots and sordid political maneuvering that characterized so much of the history of this process in America, merely serve to point up its fundamental wisdom.

The last surges of state making produced their full share of controversy. Beginning in the 1870's, the development of railroads and the existence of cheap land caused an immense influx of population into the northern plains and mountains. Only 14,000 people lived in the entire Dakota Territory in 1870; in 1885 there were about 550,000. By 1888 Montana Territory had nearly 140,000 residents, Washington about 350,000, Wyoming about 60,000. All clamored for statehood—Nevada, which had been a state since 1864, had less than 50,000 inhabitants in 1888. Yet because the area was Republican, the Democrats, controlling at least one House of Congress, refused to admit any to full partnership in the Union. When the Republicans finally won control of both Houses, in 1888, they swiftly admitted all to statehood, even dividing Dakota Territory in two to increase their strength in the Senate.

Statehood for Oklahoma came in bizarre fashion. Barred from this Indian Territory by Federal law, white settlers repeatedly "invaded" it, only to be ejected by troops. Finally, in 1889, after Indian land titles had been purchased, Congress opened the central section (see map, above). In a single day 100,000 settlers rushed in to claim 1,920,000 acres of land. In 1893, when the Cherokee Outlet was opened, another 100,000 flooded in overnight.

Arizona and New Mexico became states in 1912, after their citizens had earlier rejected a Congressional offer to admit them as a single state. Arizona's case involved an interesting legal question. It was first refused admittance because its constitution authorized the removal of state judges by popular vote. The Arizonans circumvented Congressional prejudices by eliminating this clause in order to obtain admission and then re-enacting it as soon as statehood had been granted.

FORTY-EIGHT STATES *of the* UNION

In 1890 the Superintendent of the Census pointed out that the United States no longer had a continuous frontier between the settled East and the unsettled West. The significance of this fact, emphasized by the historian Frederick Jackson Turner, was apparent to all. Many pessimists even predicted that there would be a slackening of American growth once the frontier had disappeared. Of course, this did not happen. There was still an enormous amount of underdeveloped land in the United States. Between 1913 and 1918, for example, more raw land was taken up under the Homestead Act than between 1862, when the law was passed, and 1893, when Turner wrote his famous essay that called attention to the frontier's passing.

Yet the expansion of the population between 1900 and 1920 was of a different character than that of earlier periods. The Mountain and Pacific states continued to grow very rapidly, more than doubling in these 20 years; but that vast area was so sparsely populated, to begin with, that its expansion failed to shift the center of population very much—it still remained in western Indiana, far to the east of the Mississippi River. New York and Pennsylvania, alone, increased in total population as much as the entire western third of the nation. The growth of the population in the first decades of the 20th century was essentially a response to industrialization, and thus was particularly large in urban areas. In 1900 there were 38 cities with at least 100,000 residents; in 1920 there were 68. The number of cities in the 10,000 to 100,000 class rose from 402 to 684. Most of these cities, as the map shows, were concentrated in the region north of the Ohio and east of the Mississippi, the industrial heart of the country. By 1920, for the first time in its history, the United States was more an urban than a rural nation.

Industrialization and the resulting urbanization of the United States had a powerful impact on the Negro population. On the eve of the Civil War there were some 340,000 Negroes in the free states, or about 7 per cent of the total Negro population of almost 4.5 million. In 1900 about 10 per cent of all Negroes were residents of the North. By 1920, however, over 1.5 million Negroes, some 15 per cent of the Negro population, were living outside the states of the old Confederacy.

Although the percentage of Negroes in the total population was shrinking, chiefly because of the huge influx of European immigrants, this fact did not account for the decline of the Negro population in the South, for few foreigners settled in that part of the country. Negroes were actually leaving the South in large numbers. In 1920 the Negro population of South Carolina and Mississippi still exceeded 40 per cent, but well over 300,000 Negroes had moved out of those states since 1900. Every other southern state except Florida experienced a similar, if somewhat smaller, loss of Negro citizens. In the same decades, about 115,000 Negroes moved into Pennsylvania, nearly 100,000 into New York, over 90,000 into Illinois, and 85,000 into Ohio. Southern white prejudices helped induce this large migration, but it was mainly the economic opportunities available in the industrial cities that drew the Negroes to the northern part of the country.

THE GROWTH *of*

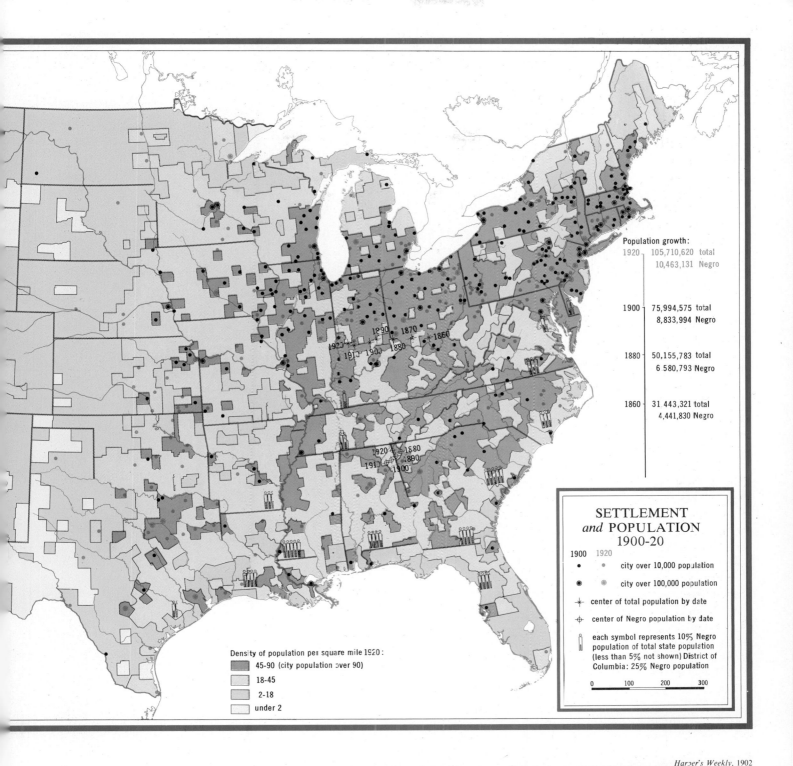

Population growth:
| 1920 | 105,710,620 total |
| | 10,463,131 Negro |

| 1900 | 75,994,575 total |
| | 8,833,994 Negro |

| 1880 | 50,155,783 total |
| | 6,580,793 Negro |

| 1860 | 31,443,321 total |
| | 4,441,830 Negro |

SETTLEMENT
and POPULATION
1900-20

1900   1920

· ● city over 10,000 population

⊙ ⊙ city over 100,000 population

✳ center of total population by date

⊕ center of Negro population by date

each symbol represents 10% Negro
population of total state population
(less than 5% not shown) District of
Columbia: 25% Negro population

0   100   200   300

Density of population per square mile 1920:

45-90 (city population over 90)

18-45

2-18

under 2

URBAN AREAS

Emigrating West in 1902 was cheaper than it had been in covered wagon days.

Industrialization, which so profoundly influenced the population shifts of the post-Civil War decades, had equally monumental effects upon the immigration of foreigners to the United States. In the first place, the factories' insatiable demand for labor attracted newcomers at a constantly increasing rate. In the five-year period of 1910–14, five million foreigners entered the U.S., more than in the 30 years preceding the Civil War, itself a period of relatively great immigration. As early as the first decade of the 20th century, over half of all industrial workers were of foreign birth.

Industrialization also accounted for a change in the sources of immigration—a shift that began in the 1880's. Before that time northern Europe provided a big portion of the new settlers. For example, 350,000 of the 788,000 persons who migrated to America in 1882 came from Great Britain and Germany. Increasingly, thereafter, the flow originated in southern and eastern Europe. In 1907, the all-time peak year of immigration (1.28 million arrivals), only 116,000 came from Great Britain and Germany, while 285,000 Italians and 258,000 Russians entered the country. This change came about mainly because the economy of Europe was in a state of flux. Increased food production in America, Australia, and other "new" areas, combined with improvements in transportation, flooded European markets with cheap grain and meat. Local farmers could not compete. In northern Europe farmers tended to become industrial workers, but in unindustrialized countries like Greece, Italy, and Russia, large numbers of peasants, no longer able to exist on the land, decided to seek new opportunities in America.

The new waves of immigrants produced sharp changes in the strength of various religious groups. The number of Catholics and Jews rose rapidly. By 1920 there were 17.7 million Catholics in the United States, over 7.5 million more than in 1900. In the same period, the number of Methodists increased by only 1.9 million, of Baptists by 1.4 million, of Presbyterians by 620,000. Collectively, however, the Protestants continued to outnumber all other religious groups by a wide margin. Urbanization also affected religion, the wretchedness of life in the slums leading clergymen to become deeply concerned with social problems.

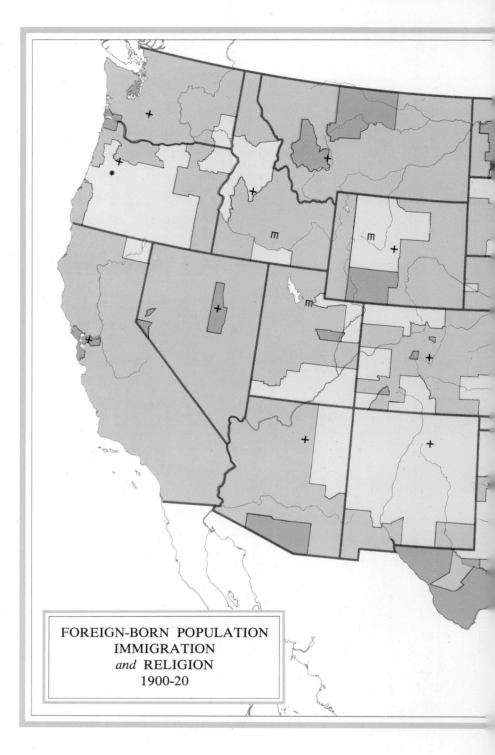

FOREIGN-BORN POPULATION
IMMIGRATION
and RELIGION
1900-20

NEW AMERICANS

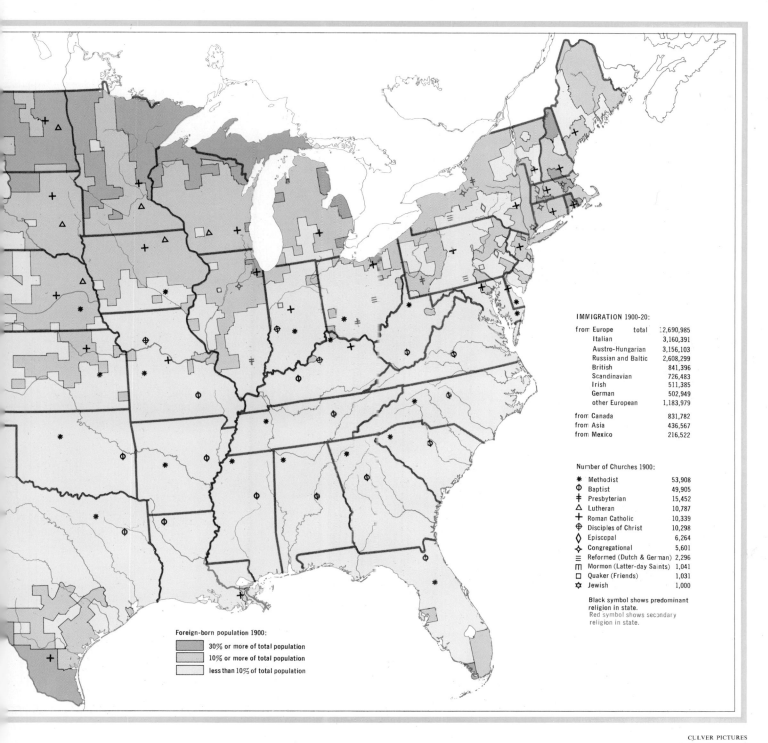

IMMIGRATION 1900-20:

from Europe	total	12,690,985
	Italian	3,160,391
	Austro-Hungarian	3,156,103
	Russian and Baltic	2,608,299
	British	841,396
	Scandinavian	726,483
	Irish	511,385
	German	502,949
	other European	1,183,979
from Canada		831,782
from Asia		436,567
from Mexico		216,522

Number of Churches 1900:

✳	Methodist	53,908
Φ	Baptist	49,905
‡	Presbyterian	15,452
△	Lutheran	10,787
+	Roman Catholic	10,339
⊕	Disciples of Christ	10,298
◇	Episcopal	6,264
✦	Congregational	5,601
≣	Reformed (Dutch & German)	2,296
ⅢⅢ	Mormon (Latter-day Saints)	1,041
☐	Quaker (Friends)	1,031
✡	Jewish	1,000

Black symbol shows predominant religion in state.
Red symbol shows secondary religion in state.

Foreign-born population 1900:

■ 30% or more of total population
▨ 10% or more of total population
☐ less than 10% of total population

Hundreds of thousands of immigrants per year entered the U.S. after being processed at Ellis Island, pictured above in 1891.

In the nation as a whole, agriculture was much less important by 1920 than it had been on the eve of the Civil War. The census of 1920 revealed that, for the first time in American history, over half the population was living in urban areas. Farm products accounted for far less than half the value of all goods produced. Nevertheless, the decline of agriculture was only relative. In 1920 there were three times as many farms (6.5 million), and they produced crops worth more than ten times as much ($16 billion) as compared to 1860. American farmers in 1920 owned about 70 million head of cattle, roughly three times the 1860 total. Cotton production had also tripled, corn production had quadrupled, wheat production had quintupled, tobacco production had expanded even more dramatically. This enormous increase in farm output did not result merely from the opening up of more land. The annual consumption of fertilizers rose between 1860 and 1920 from 164 million tons to 7.1 billion tons; farmers' investments in machinery and other equipment from $246 million to $3.5 billion.

The major influences on agricultural trends during this period were all related to industrialization. Of prime importance was the continuing expansion of American cities. The demands of millions of urban factory workers and white-collar employees led farmers to increase their output rapidly. The upper half of the Mississippi basin, from Indiana to Kansas and north to the Dakotas, became the nation's breadbasket, producing each year tremendous crops of wheat, corn, cattle, and hogs. Farmers in the eastern section of the country, unable to compete in the raising of these staples, shifted to the growing of perishables—milk and other dairy products, vegetables, and fruits. In California, and in the semiarid Mountain States, the use of irrigation made farming possible in dry regions; between 1890 and 1920, the area of irrigated land in the country increased from 3.7 million acres to 14.4 million.

Despite the great demand for agricultural products, farmers were anything but uniformly prosperous in this period. Boom conditions existed during the Civil War; then a long, irregular decline set in, culminating in the depression of 1893–96. Thereafter, prosperity returned, reaching a peak during World War I. The basic difficulty was that farming became increasingly commercial. Many farmers did not even raise all their own food, concentrating instead on one cash crop. This was especially true in parts of the South, where cotton predominated. When, for one reason or another, the cash crop failed, or was in great oversupply, the income of one-crop farmers declined drastically. Often they were at the mercy of sudden shifts in the business cycle that had nothing at all to do with farming.

The cost of farm operation also increased, for farmers had to make heavy investments in machinery and fertilizer to compete. They often had to borrow money to buy such items, and if their income fell off, fixed charges for interest frequently bankrupted them. By 1920, over 2.4 million farms were operated by tenants. Farming in 1920 was a big business, but in some ways a sick one.

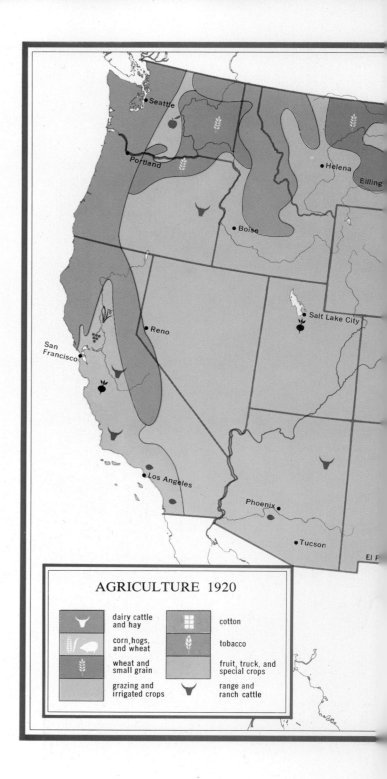

AGRICULTURE 1920

	dairy cattle and hay		cotton
	corn, hogs, and wheat		tobacco
	wheat and small grain		fruit, truck, and special crops
	grazing and irrigated crops		range and ranch cattle

UPS *and* DOWNS

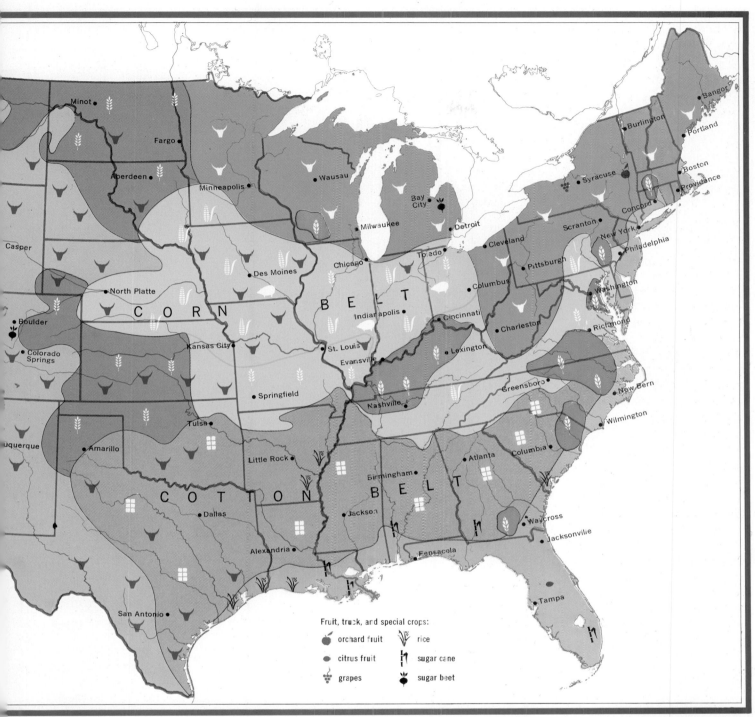

CORN BELT

COTTON BELT

Fruit, truck, and special crops:

🍎 orchard fruit   🌾 rice

🫐 citrus fruit   sugar cane

🍇 grapes   sugar beet

of the FARMER

Have you placed a Sentimental Value on your Horses out of proportion to the work they are able to perform?

BAILOR MOTOR CULTIVATORS

Ads like this one of 1920 speeded the mechanization of farms.

The history of American industry between 1860 and 1920 reveals a pattern of almost continual growth, accompanied by monumental technological changes. The old leaders, such as flour milling, meat packing, and textiles, expanded; some that were slightly less important in 1860, most notably iron and steel, rose to the first rank; and a number of entirely new industries—first petroleum, next electricity, and then automobiles—quickly assumed major importance.

Overall, the volume of manufactured goods more than quintupled between 1860 and 1900, and more than doubled again by the end of World War I. What this meant can be better understood by the following examples of a few industries: flour production amounted to 40 million barrels in 1860, 130 million in 1920; pig iron output jumped from 821,000 tons to 40 million tons, steel from almost nothing to 42 million tons in the same 60 years. In 1900 only about 4,000 automobiles were manufactured, in 1920 over 1.9 million. These two decades also saw the output of electrical energy rise from less than 6 billion kilowatt-hours to over 56 billion. Nonfarm employment increased from 4.3 million persons in 1860 to nearly 31 million in 1920.

Manufacturing remained centered mainly in the northeastern quarter of the nation. The new automobile industry, for example, was concentrated in the Cleveland-Detroit-Chicago area. But some significant geographical shifts took place. One of the most important developments was the tendency of the cotton textile industry to move south to the Carolinas and Georgia. Although few Negroes were employed in southern mills, the abolition of slavery freed capital and entrepreneurial energy, while the poor-white population of the southern hill country provided a copious supply of cheap labor. Especially after 1880, southern production zoomed. Industries dependent upon mineral resources tended naturally to locate near the sources of their raw materials. Birmingham, Alabama, became the "Pittsburgh of the South" because of the rich iron and coal deposits of the region. The petroleum industry, born in Pennsylvania, expanded into Ohio and Indiana, and then to Oklahoma and Texas, as new oil fields were discovered.

The industrial growth of these years transformed American society. By the early 20th century, the billion dollar corporation (U.S. Steel was the first) had become a reality. These impersonal but efficient giants practically forced working men to band together in national unions, for individuals could not hope to bargain on equal terms with such monster organizations. Big corporations affected political life too; their contributions made them powerful in political party councils, while their size and power aroused public fears and led to the passage of restrictive legislation.

The expansion of manufacturing also speeded up the urbanization of America. By 1920, New York, Chicago, and Philadelphia were great metropolitan centers, each with over a million residents, and nine other cities had more than half a million. Yet, most remarkable of all, the industrial age in America was still in its infancy.

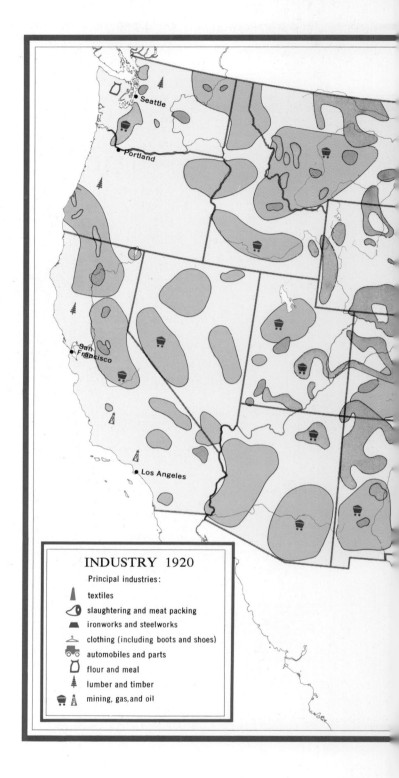

INDUSTRY 1920

Principal industries:

textiles

slaughtering and meat packing

ironworks and steelworks

clothing (including boots and shoes)

automobiles and parts

flour and meal

lumber and timber

mining, gas, and oil

MANUFACTURING

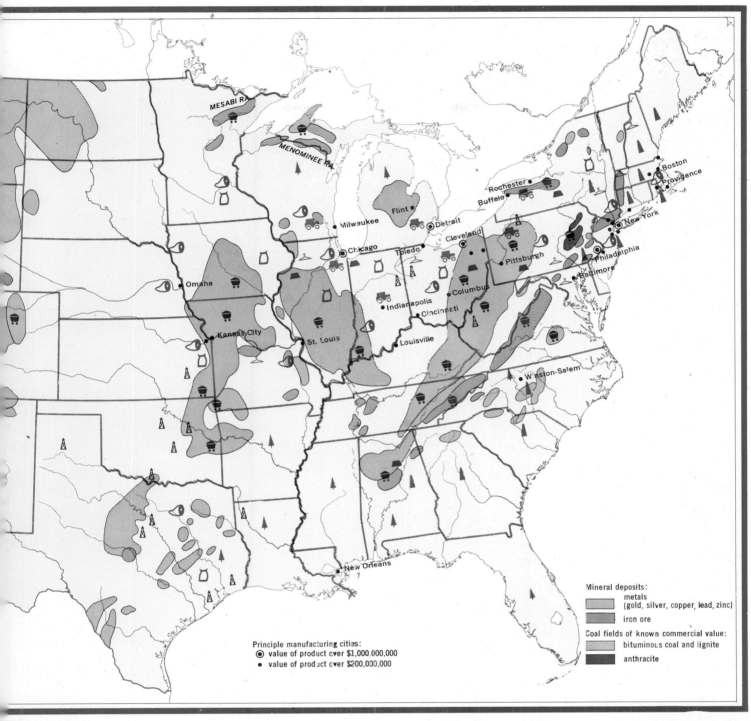

MESABI RA.

MENOMINEE RA.

Omaha

Milwaukee • Flint • Detroit

Chicago • Toledo • Cleveland

Kansas City • St. Louis • Indianapolis • Cincinnati

Columbus • Pittsburgh

Louisville

Winston-Salem

New Orleans

Rochester • Buffalo • Boston • Providence

New York

Philadelphia

Baltimore

Principle manufacturing cities:
⦿ value of product over $1,000,000,000
• value of product over $200,000,000

Mineral deposits:
metals
(gold, silver, copper, lead, zinc)
iron ore

Coal fields of known commercial value:
bituminous coal and lignite
anthracite

and INDUSTRY

In 1904 the horseless buggy was about to change all of America.

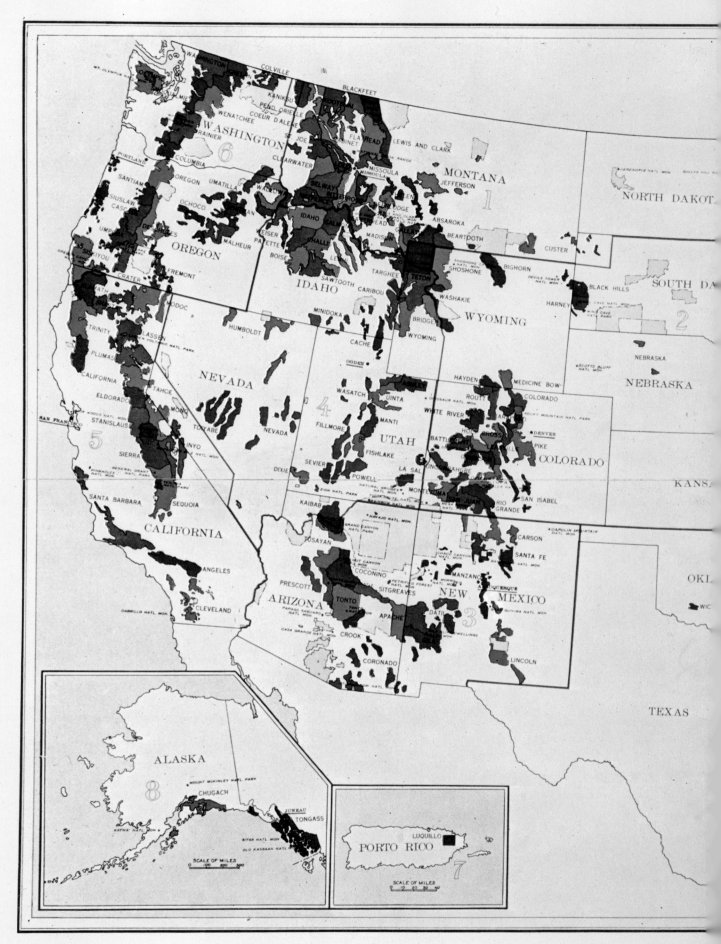

Conservation of the nation's fast-dwindling natural resources made its first headway under Theodore Roosevelt, who established

U. S. DEPARTMENT OF AGRICULTURE
FOREST SERVICE
W. B. GREELEY, FORESTER

NATIONAL FORESTS
NATIONAL PARKS
NATIONAL MONUMENTS
AND
INDIAN RESERVATIONS
1921

SCALE

LEGEND

NATIONAL FORESTS
CORRECTED TO JUNE 30

NATIONAL PARKS

NATIONAL MONUMENTS

INDIAN RESERVATIONS

DISTRICT BOUNDARIES AND NUMBERS

• DISTRICT HEADQUARTERS

he U.S. Forest Service in its present form in 1905. Above is the first official map published showing protected U.S. forests.

CHAPTER 8
A WORLD POWER

For three centuries Americans had gone about the business of nation building, secure in the knowledge that 3,000 miles of ocean lay between them and quarrelsome, strife-torn Europe. The Atlantic barrier (and, to a lesser extent, the Pacific) was to Americans what in the 1930's the Maginot Line was to Frenchmen. Insulation inspired feelings of smug satisfaction; distance bred a sense of perfect security. Not since 1815, outside New Orleans, had foreign troops fought on American soil (and been routed in the most one-sided victory in the nation's military history), and a century later the possibility of such a thing happening again seemed extremely remote.

Because of this historic preoccupation with their own problems, the American people did not don the cloak of world power and influence gracefully, and for many years it rested uneasily upon their shoulders. Many thoughtful Americans were unhappy with the whole idea of colonialism, agreeing with the position taken by Massachusetts' Senator George Frisbie Hoar in the debate over annexing the Philippines in 1898: taking control of "vassal states," said Hoar, was "trampling . . . on our own great Charter, which recognizes alike the liberty and the dignity of individual manhood." Nevertheless, by the turn of the century the United States was a world power whether it liked it or not. It had acquired a tidy little empire—Puerto Rico, Guam, and the Philippines by war with Spain, Alaska by purchase, Hawaii by annexation. It was one of the world's leading industrial powers, and its rate of industrial expansion was such that soon it would outstrip all other nations. As a French diplomat put it, the United States was "seated at the table where the great game is played, and it cannot leave it."

The outbreak of war in Europe in 1914 evoked concern but no particular sense of national danger in the United States. Neither side was clearly "right" or "wrong"; if perhaps the majority of Americans wished the Allies well, a sizable minority sympathized with the Central Powers. There was not even any obvious cause of the war. Colonel House wrote to President Wilson from Europe a month before Sarajevo: "The situation is extraordinary. It is militarism run stark mad." Indeed, it looked to most Americans as if the heavily armed contestants had simply blundered into one another in the dark and started shooting (which was not far from the truth). Regrettable as the bloodletting might be, there was no good reason to interfere.

Only gradually did it become clear that Germany's arrogant militarism truly menaced the traditions and beliefs of western civilization. Yet this realization only set the stage for U.S. intervention; the actual *casus belli* was Germany's tactic of unlimited submarine warfare. In a close parallel to the situation before the War of 1812, American sea-borne commerce was caught between two antagonists desperately flailing at each other. Britain's Royal Navy enmeshed U.S. vessels and goods in its blockade of the Central Powers. The Germans, attempting a counterblockade by means of submarines, also challenged the rights of neutral nations. A torpedo, however, is more dramatic and deadly than a boarding party, and in 1917 the Germans took all wraps off their *Unterseeboot* fleet. Any vessel entering the war zone would be fair game for attack without warning, they announced. America's entry into the Allied ranks was now assured.

The primary problem facing the United States in World War I (and, indeed, in all its wars since then) was logistical—safely transporting fighting men and their equipment across the very seas that guarded the homeland. The challenge was met by U.S. Admiral William S. Sims, who originated the convoy system and exploited his brain child brilliantly. By the early fall of 1918 more than a million doughboys were in the line, and Erich Ludendorff, German chief of staff, wrote: "The Kaiser told me later on, after the failure of [our] July offensive . . . he knew the war could be no longer won."

With hopes high and innocence unstained, Americans marched off to battle "to make the world safe for democracy" and "fit and safe to live in." The Treaty of Versailles, so full of cynicism and bitterness, was hardly calculated to sustain these hopes. Once more America withdrew behind its protecting oceans, intent on its own concerns and eager to return to "normalcy." The dizzy economic spiral of the 1920's and the desperate depression of the 1930's accentuated these responses, pushing the nation deeper into isolationism.

Participation in the 1921 naval disarmament conference, which limited capital-ship construction, and the signing of the Kellogg-Briand Pact (1928), which renounced war as "an instrument of national policy," reflected good intentions but a lack of responsibility. None of the between-wars international agreements had teeth in them, nor did the U.S. armed forces of that period. By 1936 the rising fascist menace could hardly be overlooked. Congress responded by passing neutrality acts that banned loans and the sale of arms to all belligerents, even those fighting fascist aggression.

These acts, however, marked the high-water mark of American isolationism. The danger fascism posed to everything the United States stood for grew distressingly clear. Unlike 1914, there was no question about the identity of the aggressor. In 1939 President Roosevelt warned Congress that "God-fearing democracies cannot safely be indifferent to international lawlessness anywhere." In 1940, after the stunning collapse of France, only the most astigmatic could fail to see the folly of isolationism. "Our duty," warned Walter Lippmann, "is to begin acting at once on the basic assumption that . . . before the snow flies again we may stand alone and isolated, the last great Democracy on earth."

Lippmann's assumption was not unreasonable. England's chances of surviving the Nazi juggernaut looked poor; even if, as Churchill pledged, the Royal Navy would never fall into German hands. America's danger was clear and present. Military technology had made the ocean barrier far less comforting. Hitler's U-boats were capable of driving the U.S. flag from the Atlantic, and the threat from the air could not be ignored. Noting that the Axis might fly 1,500 aircraft to the "bulge" of Brazil from French West Africa virtually overnight, Roosevelt commented: "We have 80 planes that could get there in time to meet them."

Confronted by the frightening efficiency of blitzkrieg warfare, America set about rearming. There was much to be done, however, and Japan's strike at Pearl Harbor found the nation far from ready to fight a global war. Nevertheless, despite the fact that Allied unity required a "Germany first" strategy, within a year of Pearl Harbor the United States was fully engaged in exactly that kind of a war. So immense was its industrial capacity that armored divisions for Europe and carrier task forces for the Pacific were turned out simultaneously. The nation armed its own forces, and turned over to its allies more than $50 billion in lend-lease matériel.

The speed as well as the capacity of this industrial machine amazed friend and foe alike. In September, 1939, the U.S. strategic bomber force consisted of 23 Flying Fortresses; by the end of the war, 12,500 Fortresses, 18,000 Liberators, and 4,200 B-29 Superfortresses—the prototype of which first flew in September, 1942—had been built. The keel of the first *Essex*-class carrier, the key to victory in the Pacific, was laid on April 28, 1941; by August, 1945, 17 of the big flattops were in commission. "Jeep" carriers and destroyer escorts, the weapons that finally defeated the U-boats, were turned out by the score. Although the landing craft needed in huge quantities in both the European and Pacific theaters proved a bottleneck (when this fact complicated planning for D-Day, Churchill grumbled, "The destinies of two great empires . . . seem to be tied up in some God-damned things called LSTs."), enough were produced to mount no less than 128 amphibious assaults in three years.

World War II brought the United States to maturity as a world power. Its fighting men appeared in virtually every war theater, its arms on virtually every battlefield. In 1945 the nation did not turn its back on the world as it had done in 1919; isolationism was a luxury it could no longer afford. As John Kennedy wrote almost two decades later, "We in this country, in this generation, are—by destiny rather than choice—the watchmen on the walls of world freedom."

Central Powers
Allied Powers
Neutral nations
stabilized fronts
maximum Central Powers advance
major battles
A.E.F. supply ports and routes
German submarine war zone 1915

0   100   200

FINLAND

Stockholm

Petrograd (St. Petersburg)

ESTONIA

Novgorod

LIVONIA

Riga

KURLAND

LITHUANIA

Minsk

EAST PRUSSIA

nenberg 1914

Vistula

POLAND

Brest-Litovsk

Eastern Front Dec. 1917

Armistice Line

RUSSIA

Kiev

Kharkov

Dnieper

UKRAINE

Galicia Offensives Aug. 1914 May 1915 July 1915

Brusilov Offensive June 1916

Kerensky Offensive July 1917

Budapest

HUNGARY

Odessa

Sea of Azov

Belgrade

RUMANIA

Rumania defeated November 1916

Bucharest

SERBIA

Serbia defeated October 1915

TE O

inje

Sofia

BULGARIA

BLACK   SEA

Durazzo

ANIA

Constantinople

Gallipoli 1915

GREECE

Aegean Sea

TURKEY

Athens

Cyprus

Crete

EUROPE
at WAR

"One thought that God's curse hung heavy over a degenerate world," wrote Arthur Conan Doyle of the terrible August of 1914 when the Great War began. Thrusting through Belgium, the German Army came perilously close to Paris. The French stand at the Marne halted the flood, and the First Battle of Ypres, a bloody standoff, fixed the pattern for what was to come. During the next three years the best efforts of millions of men and thousands of guns moved the Western Front no more than ten miles in either direction. Each battle had its own distinguishing mark—the 900,000 casualties at Verdun, the horror of mustard gas at Third Ypres—but in sum they achieved little.

The Eastern Front, by contrast, was too vast an arena for stalemate. "Here all Central Europe tore itself to pieces and expired in agony, to rise again, unrecognizable," wrote Winston Churchill. The textbook Battle of Tannenberg, in East Prussia, in which a Russian army had both its flanks turned and was encircled, served as a balm for German distress at the failure on the Marne. The fighting in Galicia and the ill-fated offensives mounted by Brusilov and Kerensky only added fuel to Russia's internal conflagration. The Revolution led to the German-dictated Treaty of Brest-Litovsk.

Italy's duel with Austria was long deadlocked; the constant attrition along the Isonzo River has been sorted for convenience into eleven separate battles. Then the Italian Army simply fell apart, and Caporetto has become a synonym for military rout. Gallipoli is the symbol for a great chance lost. Britain's plan to force the Dardanelles, knocking out Turkey and opening a new Balkan front, was frustrated by inept execution.

Meanwhile, German submarines were draining England of her strength, and the French Army was in open mutiny. By the end of 1917 the Allied Powers lay spent, hanging on until the Yanks arrived.

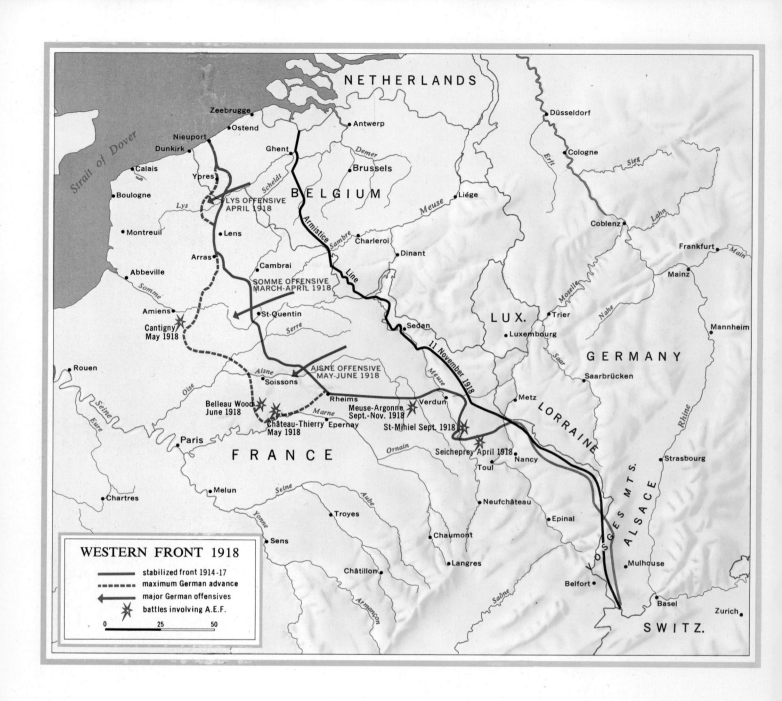

WESTERN FRONT 1918

——— stabilized front 1914-17

- - - - maximum German advance

⟵ major German offensives

✳ battles involving A.E.F.

0   25   50

NETHERLANDS

Düsseldorf

Zeebrugge
Ostend
Nieuport
Dunkirk
Calais
Boulogne
Montreuil
Abbeville
Rouen
Chartres
Melun
Sens
Châtillon

Ghent
Antwerp
Brussels
BELGIUM
Liége
Charleroi
Dinant
Sedan

Ypres
LYS OFFENSIVE
APRIL 1918
Lys
Lens
Arras
Cambrai
St-Quentin
Cantigny
May 1918
Amiens
Somme
Serre

SOMME OFFENSIVE
MARCH-APRIL 1918

Strait of Dover

Demer
Scheldt
Sambre
Armistice Line
Meuse

11 November 1918

LUX.
Luxembourg
Trier

Cologne
Sieg
Erft

Frankfurt
Main
Mainz
Mannheim

GERMANY
Saarbrücken

Metz
LORRAINE
Nancy
Toul
Neufchâteau
Epinal

Coblenz
Lahn
Nahe
Moselle
Saar

Aisne
Soissons
AISNE OFFENSIVE
MAY-JUNE 1918
Rheims
Marne
Epernay
Belleau Wood
June 1918
Château-Thierry
May 1918
Paris
Seine
Eure
Oise

FRANCE
Ornain
Meuse-Argonne
Sept.-Nov. 1918
Verdun
St-Mihiel Sept. 1918
Seicheprey April 1918

Chaumont
Langres
Troyes
Aube
Yonne
Armancon
Saône

VOSGES MTS.
ALSACE
Strasbourg
Rhine
Mulhouse
Epinal
Belfort
Basel
Zurich

SWITZ.

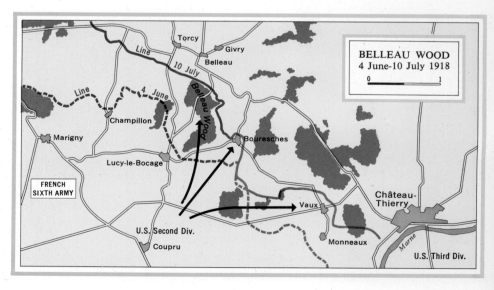

BELLEAU WOOD
4 June-10 July 1918

0   1

Torcy
Givry
Belleau
Line 10 July

Line 4 June
Champillon
Marigny
Lucy-le-Bocage
FRENCH
SIXTH ARMY
U.S. Second Div.
Coupru

Belleau Wood
Bouresches
Vaux
Monneaux

Château-Thierry
Marne
U.S. Third Div.

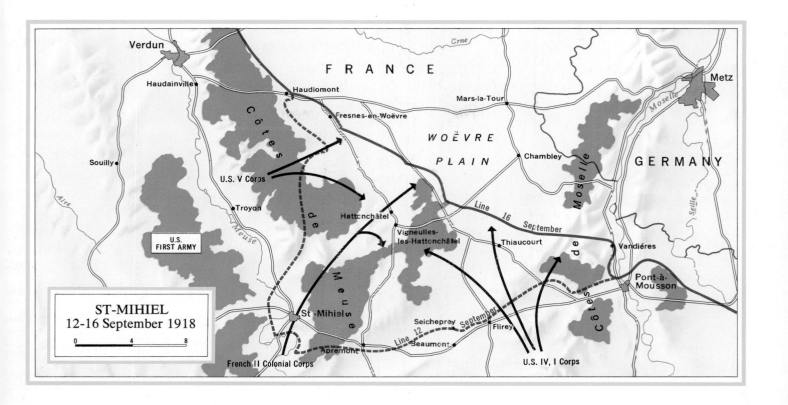

The following map is labeled:

ST-MIHIEL
12–16 September 1918

0   4   8

(Map labels include: Verdun, Haudainville, Souilly, U.S. V Corps, Troyon, U.S. FIRST ARMY, St-Mihiel, French II Colonial Corps, Apremont, Beaumont, Seicheprey, Flirey, Hattonchâtel, Vigneulles-les-Hattonchâtel, Thiaucourt, U.S. IV, I Corps, Haudiomont, Fresnes-en-Woëvre, FRANCE, Mars-la-Tour, WOËVRE PLAIN, Chambley, Vandiéres, Pont-à-Mousson, GERMANY, Metz, Moselle, Aire, Meuse, Seille, Côtes de Meuse, Côtes de Moselle, Line 16 September, Line 12 September)

DOUGHBOYS *on the* WESTERN FRONT

Making use of the extensive railroad network that served them well throughout the war, the Germans rapidly transferred masses of men from the Eastern Front after Russia's collapse. Between November, 1917, and March, 1918, 34 divisions arrived in the trenches in France, with more to come. It was a race against time. Across the Atlantic, on a "bridge of ships" (the convoy system so frustrated German U-boats that not a single troopship was lost en route), came the Americans in droves.

In the Second Battle of the Somme (top map, opposite), the Germans smashed through the British lines for a gain of 14 miles—the greatest advance in the West in three and a half years. A second sledge-hammer blow was struck on the Lys River south of Ypres, a third across the Aisne River. Already the Yanks had been blooded in sharp clashes at Seicheprey and Cantigny; now they were thrown into the battle in division strength to stem the gray tide lapping at the Marne, 50 miles from Paris.

On May 31 a German attempt to throw a bridgehead across the Marne at Château-Thierry was met and driven back by an American machine-gun battalion rushed on ahead of the advancing U.S. 3rd Division. But the French Sixth Army was crumbling under the unceasing pressure, uncovering the road to Paris. Into the breach marched the Marine Brigade of the U.S. 2nd Division. For over a month the Marines were locked in a fierce struggle in Belleau Wood (map, opposite), mangling four German divisions, and tak-

ing casualties of 40 per cent in many units. Finally the wood was cleared, and doughboys drove the enemy out of nearby Vaux. The front had held.

"The Germans were almost through," wrote military historian Hanson Baldwin. "At home war weariness and food shortages and subversion were undermining morale; at the front, the tall strange Western men—the 'Yankees'—were coming fresh and cocky in ever greater numbers." By the end of July, 1918, the American Expeditionary Forces had 29 divisions in France, each twice the size of French and British divisions and four times larger than many depleted German divisions, and new Americans were arriving at the rate of a quarter of a million a month. In August the combined Allied armies under Marshal Foch wrested the initiative from the exhausted enemy. One by one the salients the Germans had won in their spring drives were whittled away.

On August 10 General John "Black Jack" Pershing activated the U.S. First Army, half a million men strong, and prepared the first independent A.E.F. offensive. The St-Mihiel salient (above) dated back to 1914; on September 12, moving up through a dense fog, two U.S. corps struck hard at its flanks and French colonial troops thrust into the salient's tip. Overhead buzzed 1,400 Allied planes, the largest air force yet assembled, commanded by U.S. Colonel Billy Mitchell. In four days the St-Mihiel salient ceased to exist. The bag was some 15,000 prisoners and 257 guns, set against American casualties of 7,000.

WINNING *a* WAR *and* MAKING *a* PEACE

In late September Foch ordered an all-out drive to hold the initiative won in the battles of the salients. A major thrust by the British in the vicinity of Cambrai in Flanders achieved a breakthrough; a simultaneous thrust by the French and Americans in the Meuse River-Argonne Forest sector was equally successful.

More than a million doughboys were staged in secrecy for the Meuse-Argonne offensive (below), largely through the efforts of Colonel George C. Marshall, First Army operations officer. Colonel George Patton led a brigade of tanks, was wounded, and won the Distinguished Service Cross. Every gain had to be wrenched from a tenacious enemy, securely dug in to a depth of ten to twenty miles in the forbidding terrain. After a month of battering, the Americans broke through. By November 1, wrote Hanson Baldwin,

"the heavy lock was smashed, the front unhinged." Much-decorated Douglas MacArthur's 42nd "Rainbow" Division advanced on Sedan. The end was at hand. The German Navy was in revolt and the Kaiser in flight. On November 11, 1918, an armistice was signed at Compiègne, and for the first time in four years the guns fell silent.

The victorious nations, having won a hard war, made a hard peace. The map of Europe was redrawn (opposite). Germany, adjudged solely responsible for the conflict, was saddled with a reparations bill of $33 billion. To American journalist Ray Stannard Baker, the Treaty of Versailles was "a dispensation of retribution with scarcely a parallel in history." In 1929 the last Allied occupation troops were withdrawn. Four years later Adolf Hitler set Germany once more on the road to war.

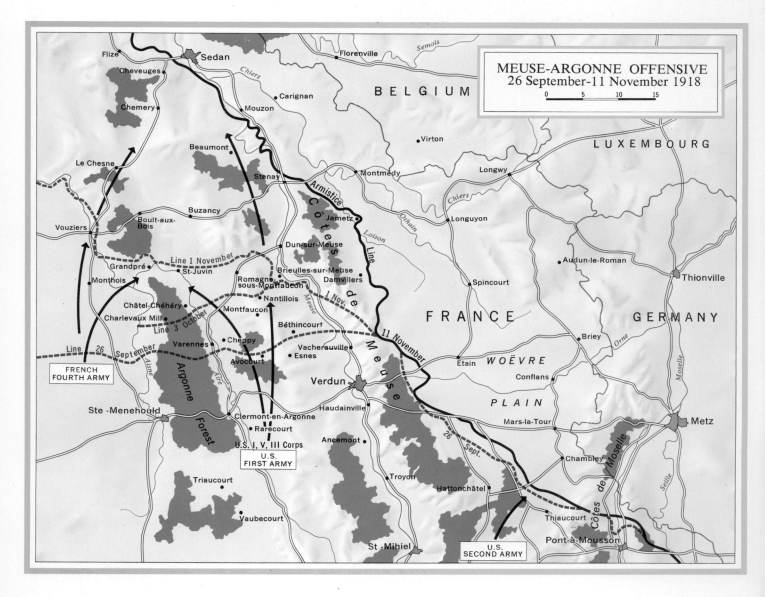

EUROPE
after VERSAILLES
1919

new independent nations
Allied occupation zone

0   100   200

At the end of World War I American aviation, a fledgling at best, nearly expired. When someone asked a barnstormer and former fighter pilot what he considered the most dangerous aspect of flying, he replied, "The hazard of starving to death." Aircraft builder William E. Boeing kept his plant open during the postwar slump by turning to such work as producing interior woodwork, and the pioneering flier Ben Howard frankly admitted that "the thing that really held up aviation's pants for quite a few years was bootlegging." There was no doubt that a special stimulus was needed to keep commercial flying alive, and air mail seemed to offer the best possibility.

At first the Army and the Post Office Department attempted to fly the mail, with not altogether happy results. The inaugural flight of the Washington-Philadelphia-New York service in 1918 ended in humiliation when the pilot got lost, landed in the wilds of Maryland, and had to consign the mail to a train. The New York-Chicago route came to be known to Post Office pilots as the "graveyard run." As the map indicates, progress by 1920 had not been spectacular, but the advocates of air mail persevered. In February, 1921, the mail was flown for the first time from San Francisco to New York, in something over 33 hours.

One of the milestones of American aviation was the Kelly Bill, passed by Congress in 1925 to "encourage commercial aviation and authorize the Postmaster General to contract for air mail service." In the postwar period most flying had been done in surplus military aircraft, but now technical progress (the perfection of a reliable air-cooled engine, the Wright Whirlwind, for one example) and the promise of government contracts stimulated new enthusiasts and new designs. Colonial Air Transport, headed by 26-year-old Juan Trippe, won the mail contract between New York and Boston; the route between Chicago and San Francisco went to Boeing and his partner Edward Hubbard, who put their new Boeing 40 on the job. Another design, Ford's trimotor, was also developed during this period, and carried passengers and freight as well as mail.

Throughout the 1920's a series of spectacular flights kept planes and pilots before the public eye. The military air services particularly sought public attention in hopes of fattening their emaciated budgets. In 1924, for example, the Army reaped a harvest of publicity when one of its pursuit planes "raced the sun" from New York to California, leaving at 4 A.M., picking up an hour in each time zone, and arriving before 6 P.M. But the most spectacular feat was Lindbergh's solo crossing of the Atlantic in 1927. "The Lindbergh flight acted like adrenalin in the blood stream of American aviation," wrote an observer. Within the space of a year U.S. airline routes doubled in mileage; the number of passengers increased four times. In 1929 there were 44 scheduled airlines, nearly 30,000 miles of air mail routes (in 1926 there were 2,800 miles), and more than $400 million in aircraft stocks held by investors. In another year, the foundations of three major transcontinental lines, American, United, and TWA, had been fashioned, and the internationally minded Juan Trippe had his Pan American Airways in operation. The fledgling was now big business.

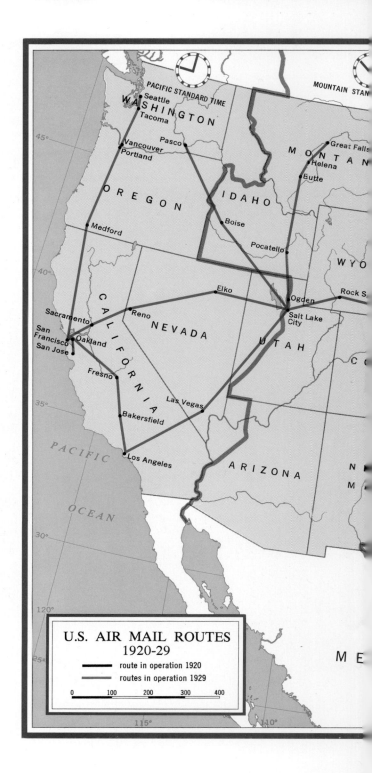

U.S. AIR MAIL ROUTES
1920-29
— route in operation 1920
— routes in operation 1929
0   100   200   300   400

FLYING *the* MAIL

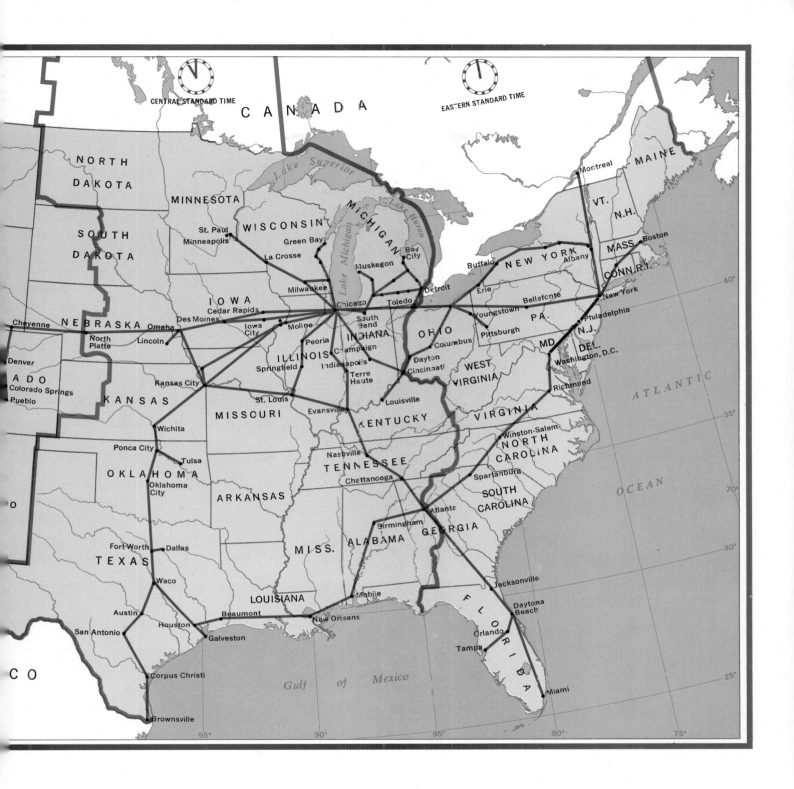

CENTRAL STANDARD TIME

EASTERN STANDARD TIME

At right is an air mail stamp dating from 1926. The first air mail stamps, issued in 1918, cost 24 cents each and were a philatelist's dream. Several sheets were misprinted, and showed a Curtiss Jenny mail plane flying upside down. A block of four of these stamps brought a collector $25,000.

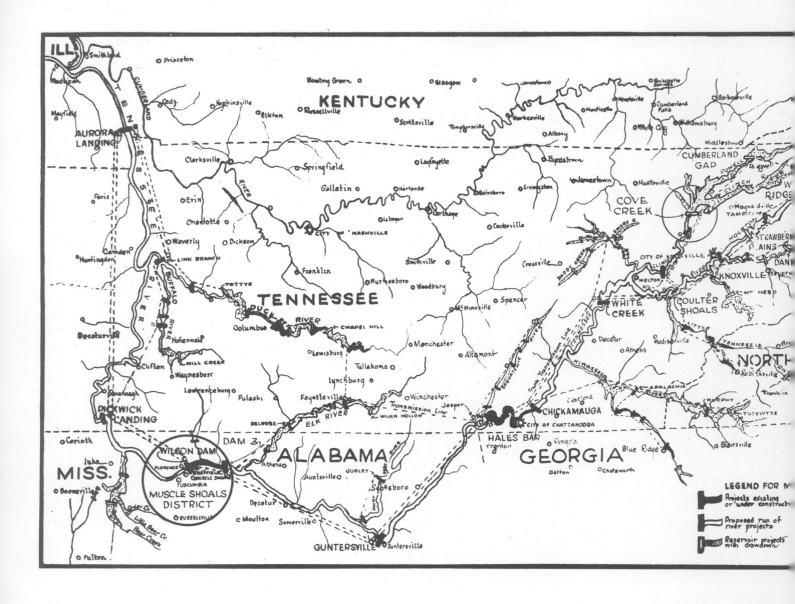

A NEW DEAL *for the* TENNESSEE VALLEY

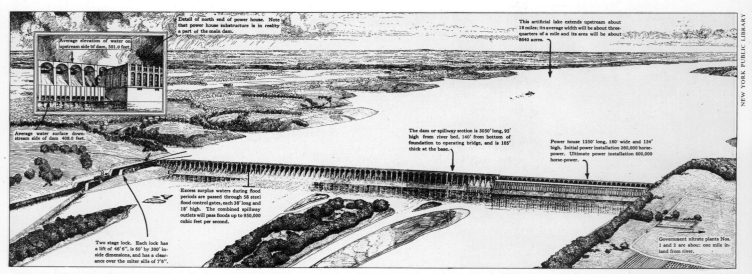

Muscle Shoals Dam (later called Wilson Dam) was being built in 1923 when engineers prepared this prospective view of it for Congress.

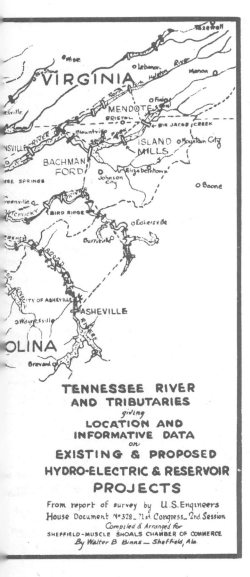

**TENNESSEE RIVER
AND TRIBUTARIES**
giving
**LOCATION AND
INFORMATIVE DATA**
on
**EXISTING & PROPOSED
HYDRO-ELECTRIC & RESERVOIR
PROJECTS**

From report of survey by U.S. Engineers
House Document N°328_71st Congress_2nd Session
Compiled & Arranged for
SHEFFIELD-MUSCLE SHOALS CHAMBER OF COMMERCE
By Walter B. Binns — Sheffield, Ala.

During mobilization for the First World War, the Federal government moved to produce synthetic nitrate for explosives, rather than be dependent on Chilean nitrates. Hydroelectric power best met the needs of the production process, and Muscle Shoals, Alabama, where the Tennessee River falls 130 feet in 40 miles, was selected as the site for the plants and the necessary power dam. The project was completed too late to produce explosives for the war, but it could as easily turn out nitrate fertilizers for agriculture. The result was that Muscle Shoals became the focus of a decade-long debate over the issue of public-versus-private power.

The public power forces, led by Senator George W. Norris of Nebraska, blocked the sale of the Muscle Shoals complex to private industry, but bills authorizing the government to operate the plants and dam were vetoed by Presidents Coolidge and Hoover. In time, Senator Norris developed a comprehensive scheme to develop the entire Tennessee River basin with a series of storage and power dams on the main stream and its tributaries. The 1930 plan at left, based on a survey by the Army's Corps of Engineers, shows the scope of Norris's idea. Wilson Dam at Muscle Shoals and Cove Creek (later Norris) Dam, both circled, were the main centers of controversy. Under the aegis of the government, Norris sought to rehabilitate the Tennessee Valley, one of the poorest regions in the country, by furnishing cheap power, cheap fertilizer, and jobs in industries that would be attracted to the area. The lakes behind the dams would become recreation centers; floods would be controlled; and barren lands would be reforested.

President-elect Franklin D. Roosevelt adopted Norris's plan, and in 1933 the first New Deal Congress created the Tennessee Valley Authority. A showcase of regional development, TVA eventually embraced the network of dams and hydroelectric and steam power plants shown below, producing some four million kilowatts of electricity and dramatically raising the standard of living in more than 40,000 square miles of the United States.

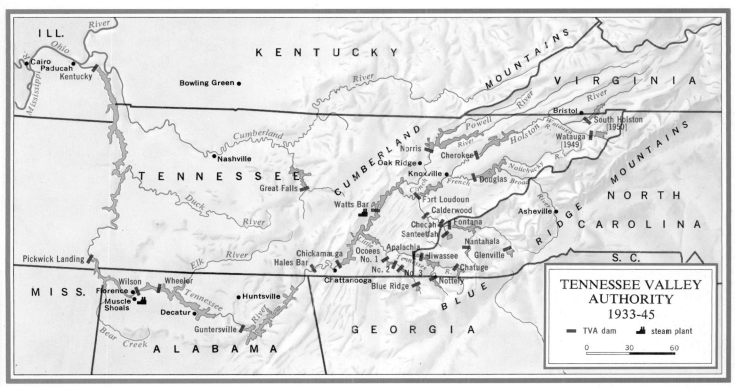

**TENNESSEE VALLEY
AUTHORITY
1933-45**

▬ TVA dam   ⚒ steam plant

0   30   60

ARCTIC OCEAN

ICELAND
British occupied 1940
• Reykjavik

Pechenga (Petsamo)
• Murma

ATLANTIC OCEAN

Faeroe Is. (Danish) British occ. 1940

Lofoten Is.
• Narvik

Allied landings April-May 1940

Namsos
Trondheim •
Andalsnes

Line 5 December 19...
1940 U.S.S.R.

NORWAY 1940

SWEDEN

• Tornio

FINLAND 1941

• Oulu
• Kajaani
• Nurmes

Kc Pen

Shetland Is. Bergen •
Scapa Flow
Orkney Is.
Stavanger •
Oslo •

• Vaasa

• Turku

Helsinki (Viipuri)

Gulf of Bothnia

Gulf of Finland

• Vyborg
• Le ing

Lake Ladoga
Lake Peipus
• Nov

Tikh

Lake Ilmen

UNITED KINGDOM

Aberdeen •
Glasgow •
Edinburgh •
GREAT
NO. IRELAND
Belfast •
Dublin •
IRELAND
Liverpool •
Manchester •

OCEAN

Birmingham •
Bristol •
London •
Plymouth •
Southampton •

Stockholm •

DENMARK 1940
Aalborg •

BALTIC SEA

ESTONIA
Tallinn •

Riga LATVIA

• Kiel
Copenhagen •

LITHUANIA

Königsberg

MEMEL TERR. 1939

Danzig

• Kaunas
• Vilna

• Smolen

NORTH SEA

NETHERLANDS 1940
Amsterdam •
Rotterdam •

• Lübeck
• Hamburg

EAST PRUSSIA

• Grodno

• Minsk

BRITAIN 1940
Coventry •

• Bremen

• Stettin

Posen •

• Bialystok

British evacuation May-June 1940

BELGIUM 1940
Dunkirk
Brussels •

GERMANY

• Berlin

POLAND 1939

Warsaw •

• Pinsk

RHINELAND occ.1936

Essen •
Cologne •
• Kassel

• Leipzig
• Dresden

Oder

• Breslau

Lodz •

Brest-Litovsk •

Brest •
Le Havre •
Paris •

LUX. 1940

• Frankfurt

Lublin •

Cherni

FRANCE 1940

Strasbourg •

• Stuttgart

SUDETENLAND 1938
Prague 1938
Pilsen •

CZECHOSLOVAKIA 1939

Cracow •

Zhitomir • Kiev

Nantes •
Loire
Seine

Elbe
Rhine

Lvov •
• Tarnopol

Bay of Biscay

Bordeaux •

Vichy •
VICHY FRANCE 1940 unoccupied

Bern •
SWITZ.
Lyons •

Munich •

Vienna •

AUSTRIA 1938
Innsbruck •

• Bratislava

Budapest •
• Graz

HUNGARY 1940 • Oradea

BESSARABIA 1940 U.S.S.R.

Toulouse •

Garonne
Rhône

• Milan Venice •

Trieste •
Zagreb •

Szeged •
• Subotica

RUMANIA 1940 • Ploesti

PORTUGAL
Lisbon •

Marseilles •
Toulon •

• Genoa

Zadar (It.)

YUGOSLAVIA 1941

Belgrade •

• Silistra

Florence •

Po

Bucharest •

SPAIN
• Madrid

Corsica (Fr.)

Rome •

ITALY

ADRIATIC SEA

Split •

Sarajevo •
Nis •

Danube

Ruse •

BULGARIA 1941

• Var
• Burg

Balearic Is. (Sp.)

Sardinia

Naples •

Durazzo •
Taranto •

Tirana •

Skoplje •

Sofia •

Plovdiv •

Istanbu

Tagus

Strait of Gibraltar
Tangier •
Gibraltar (Br.)
French Fleet sunk 3 July 1940

SP. MOROCCO

ALBANIA 1939
Valona •

Kavalla •

Salonika •

• Sm

Rabat •

Oran •

Algiers •

TYRRHENIAN SEA

Palermo •
Sicily

MEDITERRANEAN

Bizerte •

Messina •
Catania •

British air strike 11 Nov. 1941

Ioannina •
Missolonghi •

GREECE 1941

AEGEAN SEA

Dardanelles

Patras •
Athens •

MOROCCO 1940

ALGERIA 1940

TUNISIA 1940

Tunis •

SEA

Malta (Br.)

Battle of Cape Matapan 27 March 1941

IONIAN SEA

• Cape Matapan

Crete (Gr.)

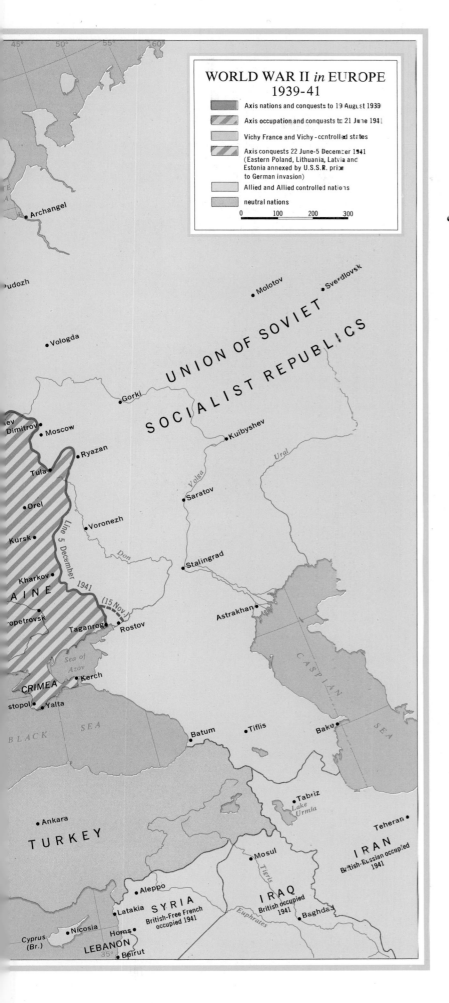

WORLD WAR II *in* EUROPE
1939-41

Axis nations and conquests to 19 August 1939

Axis occupation and conquests to 21 June 1941

Vichy France and Vichy-controlled states

Axis conquests 22 June-5 December 1941
(Eastern Poland, Lithuania, Latvia and
Estonia annexed by U.S.S.R. prior
to German invasion)

Allied and Allied controlled nations

neutral nations

0   100   200   300

BLITZKRIEG
in EUROPE

"Upon the careless and imprudent world . . . Hitler, casting aside concealment, sprang forward armed to the teeth," exclaimed Winston Churchill in 1935. In the following four years, through bluff, blackmail, and diplomacy, Germany's *Führer* militarized the Rhineland and absorbed Austria and Czechoslovakia. Then, contemptuous of his enemies, he convulsed Europe in total war.

On September 1, 1939, German troops swarmed into Poland. Demoralized by the speed of the attack, the Poles were beaten in a month. Even though Great Britain and France declared war and mobilized for battle, there followed a winter of inactivity. This so-called Phony War ended in April, 1940: Denmark fell in 24 hours; Norway, despite amphibious counterstrokes by the British and French, also capitulated. On May 10 German armored spearheads swept westward, teaching a stunned world the meaning of blitzkrieg—lightning war. The Low Countries were rapidly overrun; more shocking was the outcome of the Battle of France. The French Army, unbroken in four years of fighting in World War I, was shattered as an effective force in six weeks. The British rescued their army heroically at Dunkirk and stood alone against Hitler in the West.

When his air force failed in the Battle of Britain, rendering an invasion of the British Isles impossible, the *Führer* once more turned east. After his Italian partner Mussolini ("this whipped jackal," Churchill called him) bungled an offensive in the Balkans, German forces soon brought the area under the Axis heel. British troops who had come to the aid of Greece were forced to retreat; and when Nazi paratroops took the island of Crete only the Royal Navy maintained a precarious equilibrium in the Mediterranean by disabling the Italian fleet at Taranto and off Cape Matapan.

Hitler's greatest gamble, however, was Operation Barbarossa, the invasion of Russia. Jumping off on June 22, 1941, German panzers and motorized infantry swept all before them, inflicting some two million casualties. But on December 8, 1941, with Moscow tantalizingly out of reach and the German legions gripped fast by the fierce Russian winter, Hitler suspended the offensive; blitzkrieg in Europe had turned to stalemate.

ATLANTIC LIFELINE

One of the longest and hardest battles of the war was fought to control the waters between the U.S. and Europe. America had to transport her fighting men and their equipment to the war theaters, as well as supply great masses of food and matériel to the Allies. Great Britain, for example, needed to import simply to live. Before the war her imports averaged 50 million tons annually; in 1942 German submarines cut the figure to 23 million.

The Allies were badly unprepared for the battle. Convoy escorts were too few and their crews too green. Land-based air cover was limited, especially on the North Atlantic run. Not until late in 1943 did the Portuguese dictator Salazar allow the Allies to fly patrols out of the Azores. Bases in the Western Hemisphere, leased from the British in a 1940 destroyers-for-bases deal, proved useful—once the shortage of ships and planes was overcome.

The U-boats had the upper hand until well into 1943. Hunting in wolf packs and using saturation tactics, their toll of merchantmen and tankers climbed steadily to a peak of nearly 800,000 tons in June, 1942. The heavily trafficked North Atlantic route, so lengthy that British convoy escorts took over in mid-ocean from their American and Canadian counterparts, was a favorite hunting ground, as was the long passage around Africa, necessitated by Axis interdiction of the Mediterranean-Suez Canal lifeline. Freighters went down before the eyes of Florida bathers, and night after night burning tankers flamed off the Jersey shore. Vessels loading oil and ores in Caribbean ports were torpedoed at their moorings. But perhaps the greatest ordeal was the run through polar waters to Russia with lend-lease arms. In July, 1942, a Murmansk convoy lost 24 of its 37 ships.

In the spring of 1943 the tide began to turn. From 108 sinkings in March, Allied losses declined steadily. The use of radar and sonar was perfected, more destroyers and destroyer escorts became available, and small "jeep" carriers began to furnish air cover for convoys. The British made a concerted effort in the Bay of Biscay to catch submarines entering and leaving their bases on the coast of France. In May parity was reached: 41 ship sinkings against 41 U-boat killings. The Battle of the Atlantic was on the way to being won.

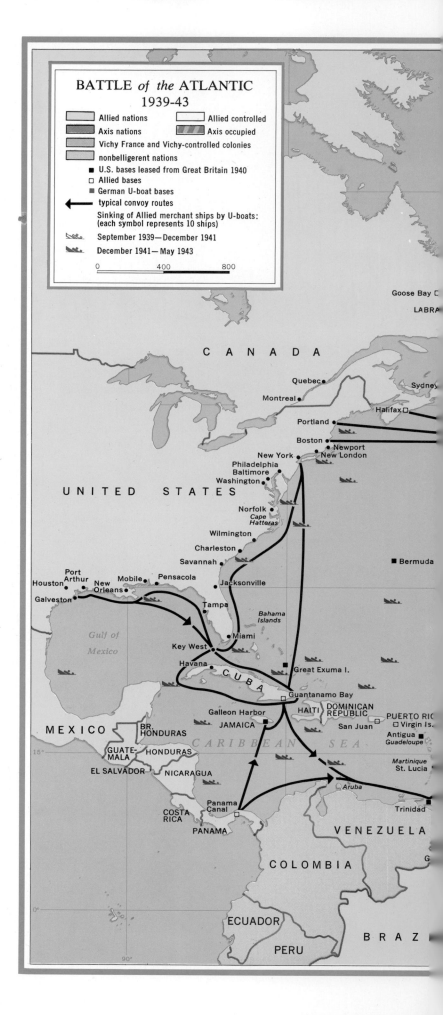

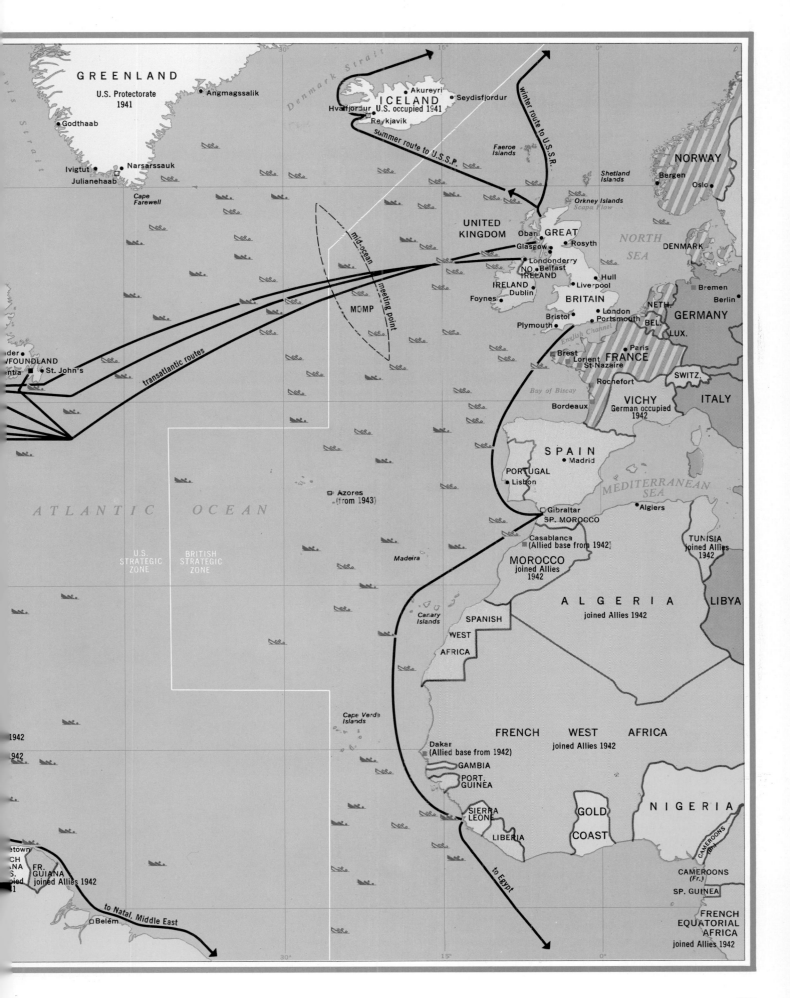

GREENLAND
U.S. Protectorate
1941
• Angmagssalik

• Godthaab

Ivigtut □ • Narsarssauk
Julianehaab

Cape Farewell

Denmark Strait

ICELAND
U.S. occupied 1941
• Akureyri
Hvalfjordur • Seydisfjordur
• Reykjavik

winter route to U.S.S.R.

summer route to U.S.S.R.

Faeroe Islands

NORWAY
• Bergen
Oslo ■

Shetland Islands

Orkney Islands
Scapa Flow

NORTH SEA

DENMARK

UNITED KINGDOM
Oban • GREAT
Glasgow • • Rosyth
• Londonderry
NO. • Belfast
IRELAND
IRELAND • Hull
• Liverpool
Foynes • Dublin
BRITAIN
• London
Bristol • Portsmouth
Plymouth • • Portsmouth

BEL.
NETH.
Bremen ■
Berlin ■
GERMANY
LUX.

mid-ocean
meeting point
MOMP

English Channel

Brest • • Paris
Lorient FRANCE
St-Nazaire
SWITZ.
Rochefort

transatlantic routes

NEWFOUNDLAND
ntia □ • St. John's
der •

Bay of Biscay
Bordeaux •
VICHY
German occupied
1942
ITALY

SPAIN
• Madrid

ATLANTIC   OCEAN

PORTUGAL
• Lisbon

MEDITERRANEAN SEA

□ Azores
(from 1943)

□ Gibraltar
SP. MOROCCO

• Algiers

U.S.
STRATEGIC
ZONE
BRITISH
STRATEGIC
ZONE

Madeira

Casablanca ■
(Allied base from 1942)

MOROCCO
joined Allies
1942

TUNISIA
joined Allies
1942

A L G E R I A
joined Allies 1942

LIBYA

Canary Islands

SPANISH
WEST
AFRICA

Cape Verde Islands

Dakar □
(Allied base from 1942)

F R E N C H   W E S T   A F R I C A
joined Allies 1942

GAMBIA
PORT.
GUINEA
SIERRA
LEONE
LIBERIA

GOLD
COAST

N I G E R I A

CAMEROONS
(Br.)

CAMEROONS
(Fr.)

1942

1942

etown
CH
NA
S.
FR.
GUIANA
joined Allies 1942
pied
1

to Egypt

SP. GUINEA

FRENCH
EQUATORIAL
AFRICA
joined Allies 1942

to Natal, Middle East
□ Belém

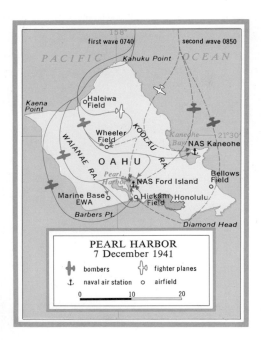

PEARL HARBOR
7 December 1941

bombers   fighter planes
naval air station   airfield

0   10   20

JAPAN STRIKES

The message from Hawaii on December 7, 1941—AIR RAID PEARL HARBOR. THIS IS NO DRILL—reflected American disbelief at Japan's audacity. By crippling the U.S. Pacific Fleet with a carrier-borne air strike (above), General Tojo's military junta intended to insure no interference in assembling the Greater East Asia Co-Prosperity Sphere. Indeed, the conquests (right) came more easily than Hitler's in Europe. Seizure of Hong Kong, Singapore, and the Philippines eliminated the major Allied strong points. The Netherlands East Indies, with oil resources necessary to Japan's war machine, fell on schedule; an outgunned ABDA (American, British, Dutch, Australian) fleet was disposed of in engagements shown at lower left on map. Capture of northern New Guinea, Rabaul, and the Solomons secured the southern flank of the Sphere; Burma, Malaya, and the Russo-Japanese Neutrality Pact guarded the western flank; the Gilbert, Marshall, Caroline, and Marianas island groups furnished a defense-in-depth in the Central Pacific. By August, 1942, the Rising Sun ensign flew over a vast empire, but the Battles of the Coral Sea and Midway (see next page) indicated that high tide had been reached.

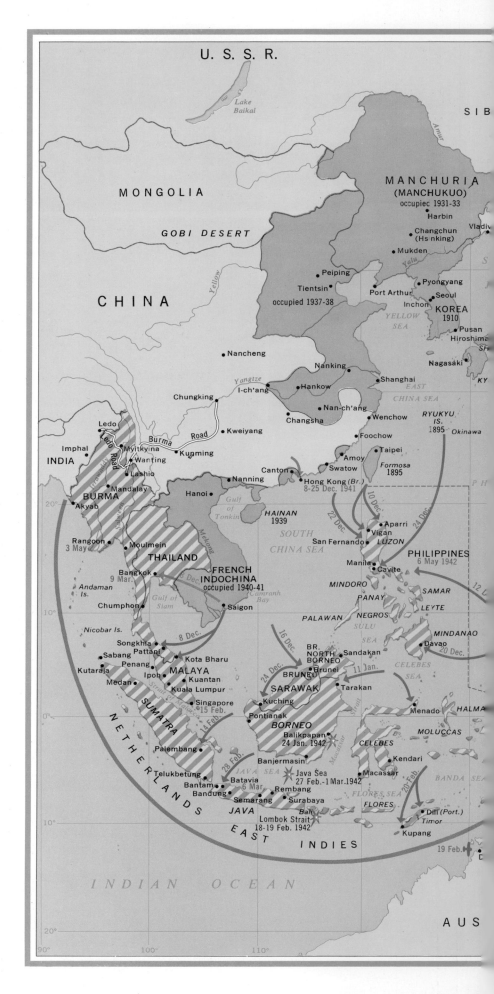

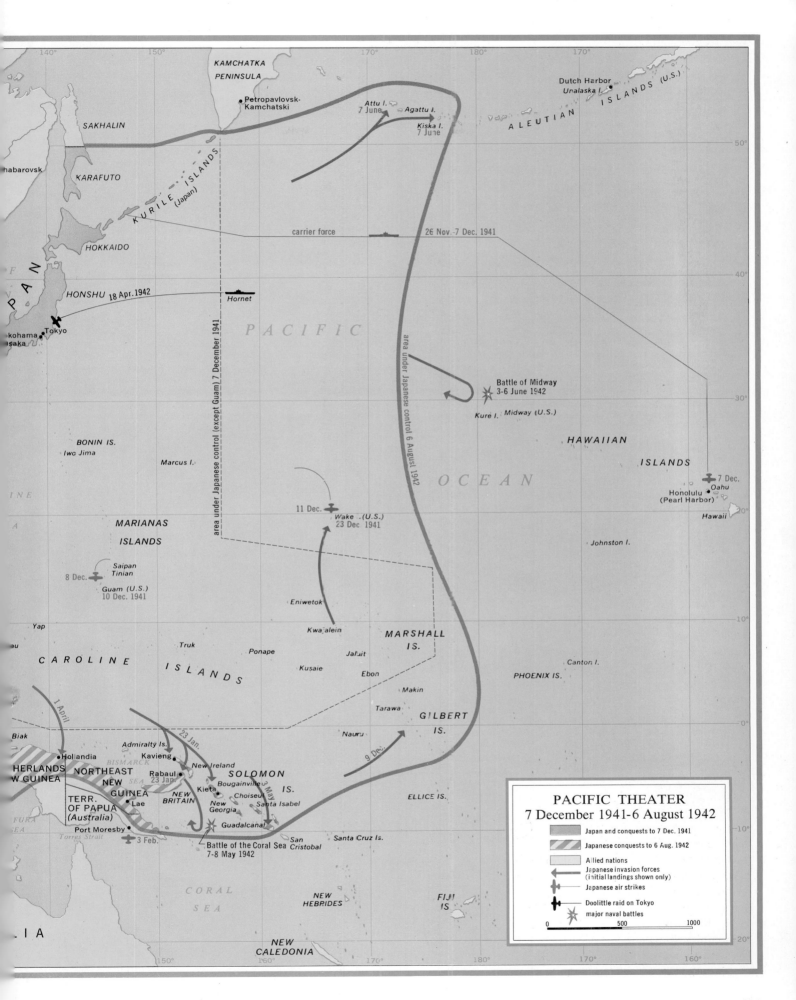

KAMCHATKA
PENINSULA

Dutch Harbor
Unalaska I.

ALEUTIAN   ISLANDS (U.S.)

Petropavlovsk-
Kamchatski

SAKHALIN

Attu I.
7 June   Agattu I.

Kiska I.
7 June

KARAFUTO

KURILE ISLANDS
(Japan)

carrier force   26 Nov.-7 Dec. 1941

HOKKAIDO

HONSHU 18 Apr. 1942

Hornet

PACIFIC

ohama Tokyo

saka

Battle of Midway
3-6 June 1942

Kure I. Midway (U.S.)

HAWAIIAN

BONIN IS.
Iwo Jima

ISLANDS

Marcus I.

OCEAN

7 Dec.
Oahu
Honolulu
(Pearl Harbor)

11 Dec.

Wake .(U.S.)
23 Dec. 1941

Hawaii

Johnston I.

MARIANAS
ISLANDS

8 Dec.   Saipan
Tinian

Guam (U.S.)
10 Dec. 1941

Eniwetok

Yap

Kwajalein

MARSHALL
IS.

CAROLINE   ISLANDS

Truk

Ponape

Jaluit

Canton I.

Kusaie

Ebon

PHOENIX IS.

Makin

1 April

Tarawa

Biak

Nauru

GILBERT
IS.

Hollandia
Admiralty Is.

HERLANDS
W GUINEA

Kavieng

23 Jan.

NORTHEAST
NEW

New Ireland

Rabaul
23 Jan

SOLOMON

ELLICE IS.

GUINEA

NEW
BRITAIN

Kieta

Bougainville

IS.

TERR.
OF PAPUA
(Australia)

Lae

Choiseul

New
Georgia

Santa Isabel

9 Dec.

Port Moresby

Guadalcanal

3 Feb.

Battle of the Coral Sea
7-8 May 1942

San
Cristobal

Santa Cruz Is.

CORAL

SEA

NEW
HEBRIDES

FIJI
IS.

PACIFIC THEATER
7 December 1941-6 August 1942

Japan and conquests to 7 Dec. 1941

Japanese conquests to 6 Aug. 1942

Allied nations

Japanese invasion forces
(initial landings shown only)

Japanese air strikes

Doolittle raid on Tokyo

major naval battles

0   500   1000

I A

NEW
CALEDONIA

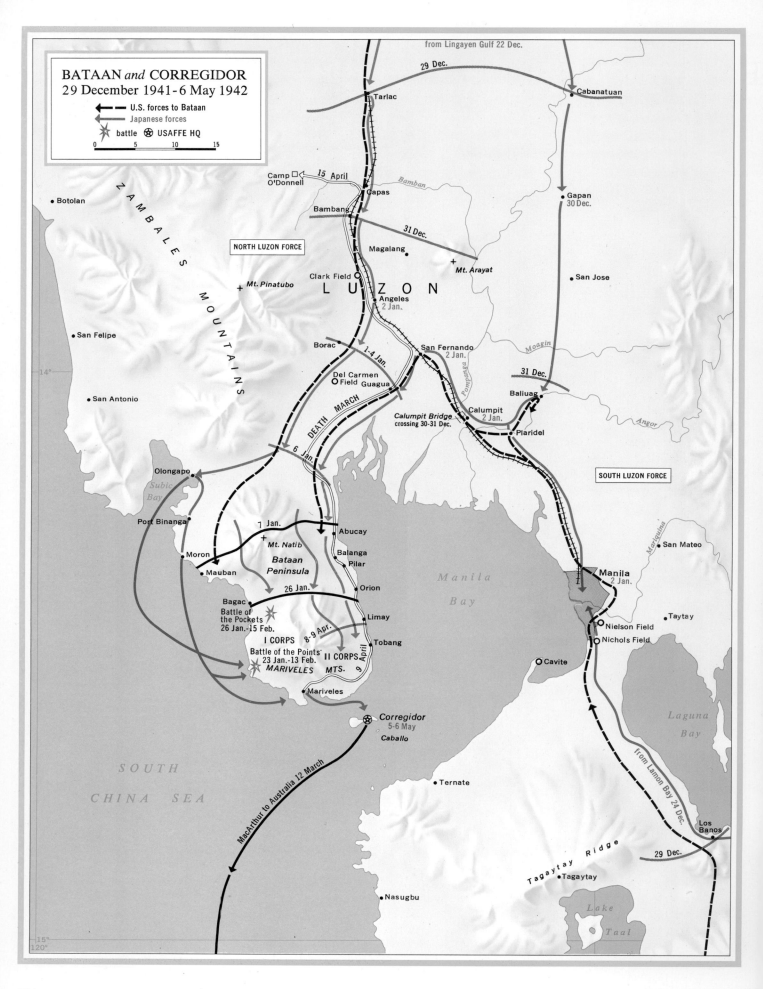

BATAAN *and* CORREGIDOR
29 December 1941 - 6 May 1942

U.S. forces to Bataan
Japanese forces
★ battle ✪ USAFFE HQ

0   5   10   15

BATAAN DEFENSE *to* MIDWAY

The defense of Luzon in the Philippines—the gradual withdrawal of American and Filipino troops to the Bataan Peninsula—is shown on the opposite page. After surrender, some 10,000 men died on the grim Death March to imprisonment. The day after Corregidor fell, the Battle of the Coral Sea (the first naval clash fought entirely by carrier planes) began. Admiral Fletcher suffered a tactical defeat (carrier *Lexington*, tanker *Neosho*, and destroyer *Sims* lost, against the sinking of the light carrier *Shoho*), but won a strategic victory. Japan's Port Moresby invasion force was turned back, and her two new carriers (*Shokaku* and *Zuikaku*) were denied to the Midway operation because of damage or pilot losses. The attempt to lure the U.S. Pacific Fleet into a finish fight at Midway led to Japanese disaster. After initial air attacks had failed to halt Vice Admiral Nagumo's carriers (below, bottom), U.S. dive bombers caught them with their planes on deck and destroyed the *Soryu, Akagi,* and *Kaga,* later also sinking the *Hiryu* to avenge the *Yorktown,* a U.S. loss.

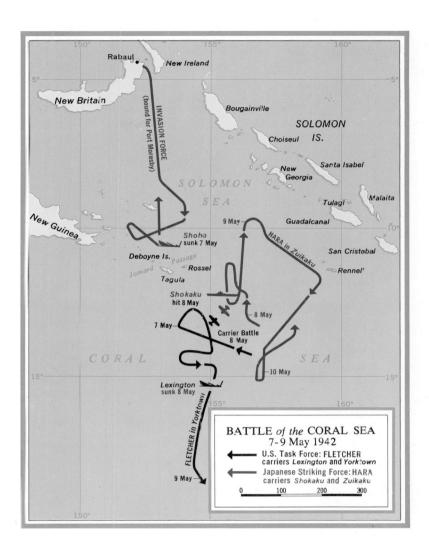

BATTLE *of the* CORAL SEA
7-9 May 1942

U.S. Task Force: FLETCHER carriers *Lexington* and *Yorktown*
Japanese Striking Force: HARA carriers *Shokaku* and *Zuikaku*

0   100   200   300

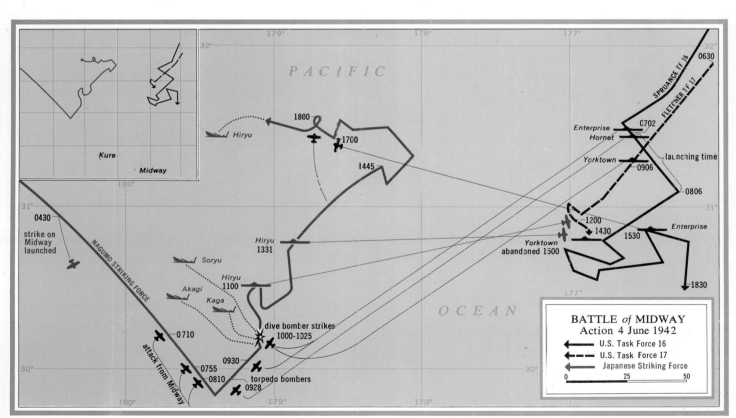

BATTLE *of* MIDWAY
Action 4 June 1942

U.S. Task Force 16
U.S. Task Force 17
Japanese Striking Force

0   25   50

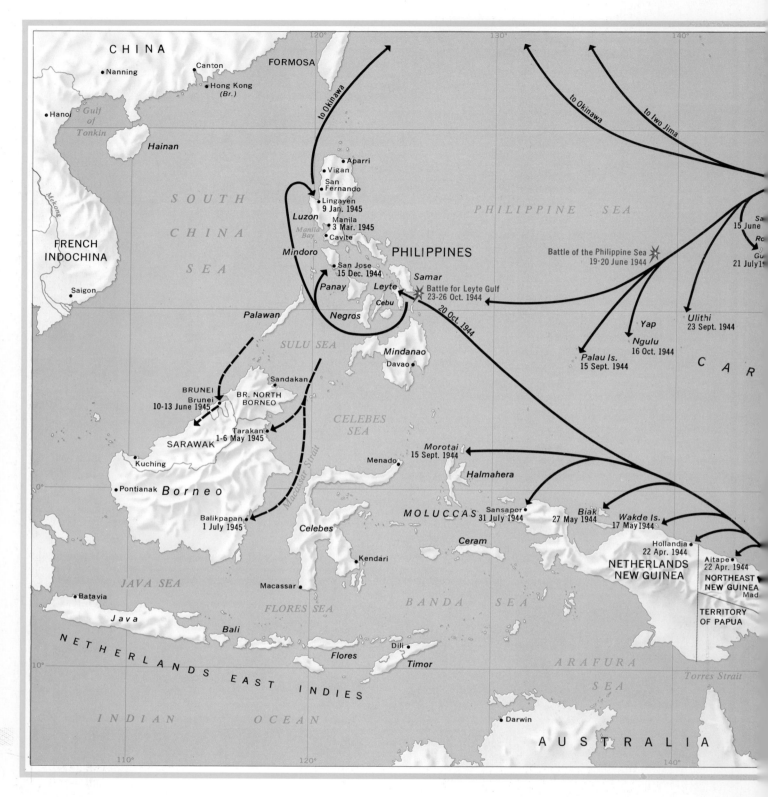

ISLAND HOPPING

American strategy in rolling back Japan was a fluid application of double envelopment. The first step, at Guadalcanal (lower right), was taken to counter a threat to the U.S.-Australian lifeline. After a bitter six-month struggle, the Japanese were expelled, and a flexible island-hopping campaign was begun. Admiral William Halsey directed amphibious assaults "up the ladder" in the Solomons; a second prong under General Douglas MacArthur advanced on New Guinea and New Britain. The objective was Rabaul, linchpin of Japan's South Pacific defenses.

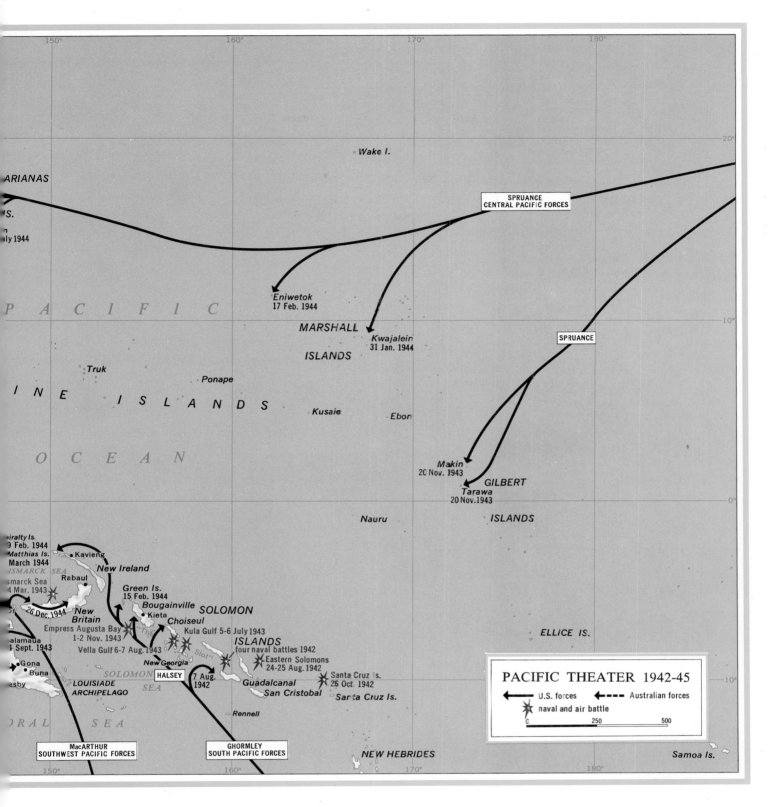

By early 1944 air strikes had rendered Rabaul impotent, and its 100,000-man garrison was left to wither.

In the meantime, a second double envelopment was under way. MacArthur leapfrogged his U.S. and Australian forces along the New Guinea coast, supported by land-based aircraft. To the north amphibious forces and carrier air power under Admiral Chester Nimitz took seven-league strides across the Central Pacific. The Gilberts and Marshalls were taken, the fortress of Truk (center) was neutralized and bypassed, and, in June, 1944, the Marianas were invaded. This triggered the Battle of the Philippine Sea, crippling Japan's carrier arm, and brought the home islands within range of Marianas-based Superfortresses. MacArthur's insistence on the liberation of the Philippines won out over the bypass strategists; his invasion, following the seizure of Palau, resulted in the final destruction of the Japanese Navy in the fight for Leyte Gulf. As MacArthur completed the conquest of the Philippines and prepared for the invasion of Japan (scheduled for November, 1945), Australians reconquered oil centers on Borneo (left).

Much of the fighting at Guadalcanal (below) involved control of the sea and air to keep open the long, tenuous supply lines of both sides. Two carrier actions—in the eastern Solomons and the Santa Cruz Islands (previous page)—were part of the campaign. The Japanese made four major attempts to break the Marines' hold on Henderson Field; all failed narrowly. Of the sea actions shown, the naval Battle of Guadalcanal in mid-November was the most important, for it wrecked the last and largest Japanese offensive. After that, the Army's XIV Corps mopped up.

The conquest of the Central Pacific atolls represented a different sort of warfare. Here the battles were often very sharp, but usually short. The Japanese resisted fanatically to the end, then killed themselves; bloody Tarawa (right) set the pattern.

In the Battle for Leyte Gulf (opposite), the Northern Force lured Halsey away to get at the Leyte beachhead. Highlights of the action, involving 282 warships, were the last battleship duel in history (in Surigao Strait) and the repulse of the powerful Center Force off Samar by six "jeep" carriers and their escorts. The loss of four carriers, three battleships, ten cruisers, and nine destroyers marked the end of the Japanese Navy.

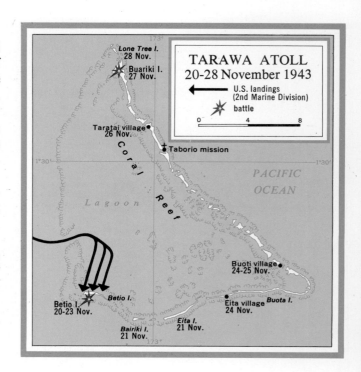

BLOODY RECONQUEST

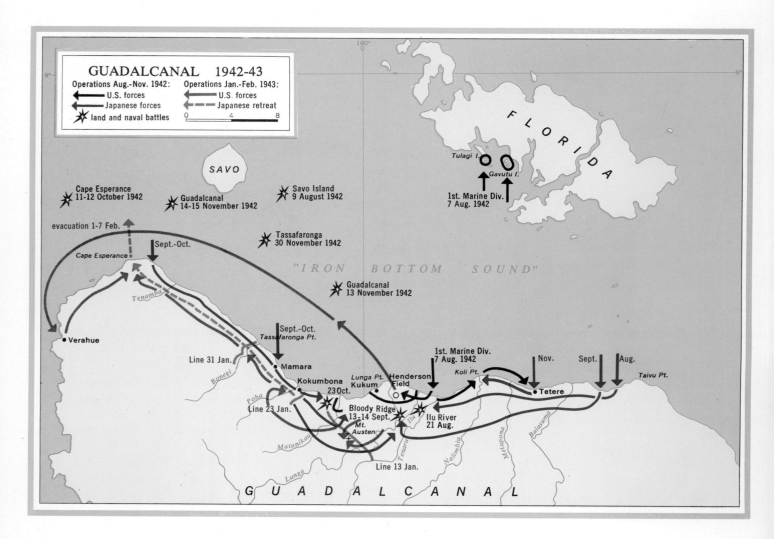

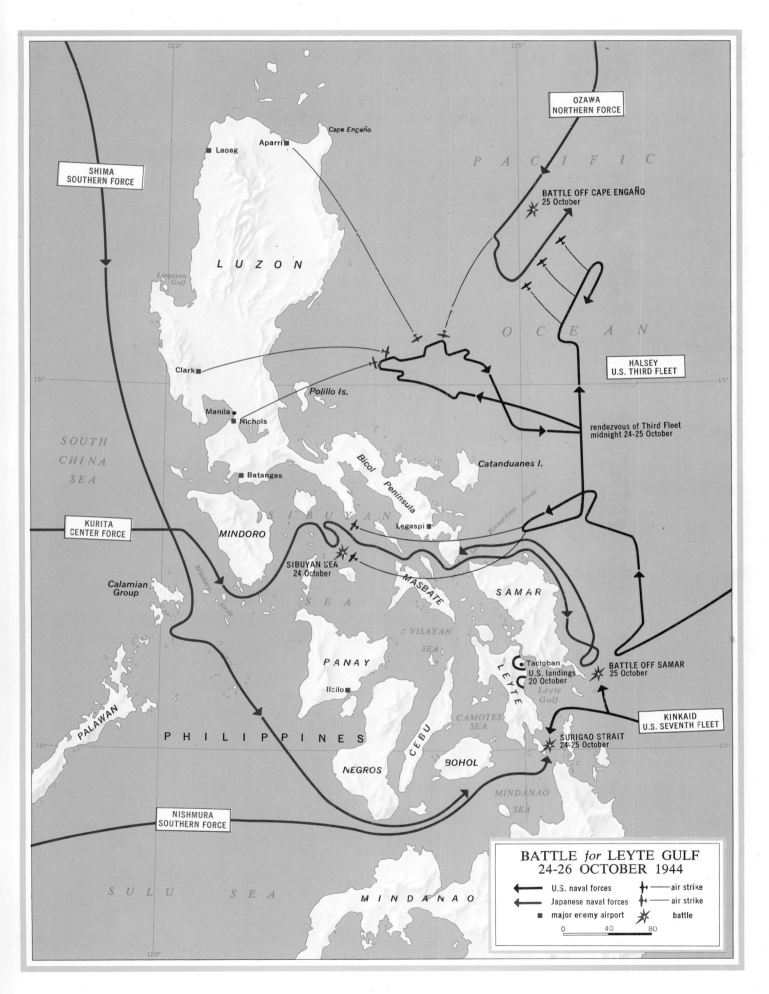

SHIMA
SOUTHERN FORCE

Cape Encaño

■ Laoag

Aparri ■

L U Z O N

Lingayen Gulf

Clark ■

Manila ■
■ Nichols

Polillo Is.

■ Batangas

S O U T H
C H I N A
S E A

KURITA
CENTER FORCE

Bicol Peninsula

Legaspi ■

Catanduanes I.

S I B U Y A N

Calamian
Group

MINDORO

Mindoro Strait

SIBUYAN SEA
24 October

S E A

MASBATE

San Bernardino Strait

S A M A R

Visayan Sea

PALAWAN

P H I L I P P I N E S

P A N A Y

Iloilo ■

N E G R O S

CEBU

Camotes Sea

BOHOL

Tacloban
U.S. landings
20 October

Leyte Gulf

L E Y T E

SURIGAO STRAIT
24-25 October

NISHMURA
SOUTHERN FORCE

Mindanao Sea

S U L U   S E A

M I N D A N A O

OZAWA
NORTHERN FORCE

P A C I F I C

BATTLE OFF CAPE ENGAÑO
25 October

O C E A N

HALSEY
U.S. THIRD FLEET

rendezvous of Third Fleet
midnight 24-25 October

BATTLE OFF SAMAR
25 October

KINKAID
U.S. SEVENTH FLEET

BATTLE *for* LEYTE GULF
24–26 OCTOBER 1944

← U.S. naval forces	✈ air strike
← Japanese naval forces	✈ air strike
■ major enemy airport	✶ battle

0   40   80

The North African desert war, wrote one of its historians, "was fought like a polo game in an empty arena." From 1940 to 1942 the British waged a seesaw war with the Italians and Germans in the narrow, 1,400-mile-long coastal strip between Alexandria and Tripoli. Although the only important road on this barren battlefield was the coastal highway, it was ideal terrain for armor—"a tactician's paradise and a quartermaster's hell," a German general remarked. At stake were the Suez Canal and control of the Mediterranean and the oil fields of the Middle East.

By September, 1942, Field Marshal Erwin Rommel, "the Desert Fox," had driven his Afrika Korps deep into Egypt, but he was at the end of his supply tether. General Bernard Montgomery patiently built up an overwhelming force of men and equipment (via the Cape of Good Hope convoy route), broke Rommel's army in the Battle of El Alamein, and set off westward in pursuit. On November 8 the Anglo-American Operation Torch, under Dwight Eisenhower, put Allied troops ashore in Algeria and French Morocco to open a new theater of operations at Rommel's rear. Vichy France controlled the area, and after much intrigue and diplomatic maneuvering—and sharp fighting—Casablanca, Oran, and Algiers were in Allied hands.

Tunisia now became the cockpit. Rommel had no defensive position behind which to reorganize short of the Mareth

Line; if Eisenhower's troops could take Tunis and Bizerte before Hitler could reinforce the area, Rommel would be hemmed in without a supply port. The Torch army tried hard, thrusting forward with amphibious landings and air drops. But the Germans poured troops into Tunisia by sea and air at the rate of 1,500 a day, and adverse weather turned inadequate roads into quagmires. Although a British spearhead managed to reach within 12 miles of Tunis, the Allies lost the race to cut off the Nazis.

By February, 1943, Rommel had the remnants of his Afrika Korps in contact with the Fifth Panzer Army in Tunisia. Well aware that time was as much an enemy as were the Allies, he attempted to split Eisenhower's force while Montgomery was still held at the Mareth Line. The veteran German armored divisions piled into the green and ill-organized American forces at Kasserine Pass (right), made substantial gains, but could not break clear. "These lessons were dearly bought," Eisenhower said of the G.I.s' experiences, "but they were valuable." Allied strength built up slowly, and when Montgomery's Eighth Army cracked the Mareth Line in March, the outcome was assured. His health broken, Rommel was recalled to Germany. The defensive perimeter shrank steadily until May, 1943, when the Axis forces gave up the fight. The Allies took 275,000 prisoners and secured all of Africa.

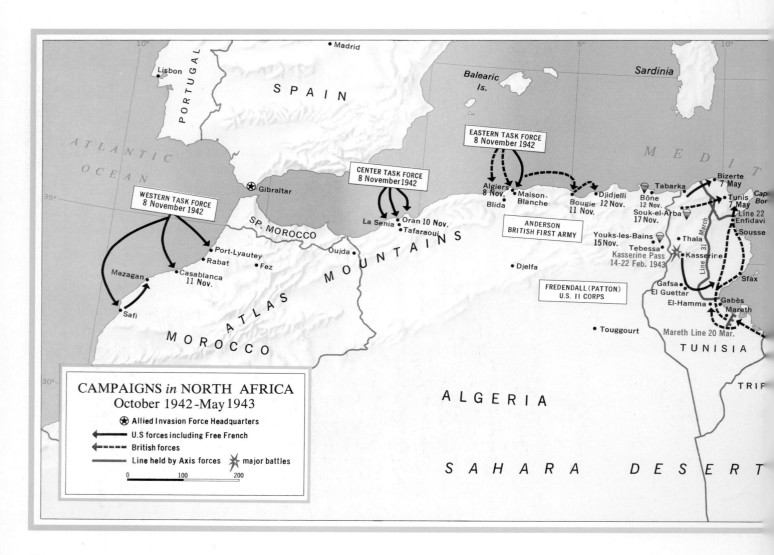

CAMPAIGNS *in* NORTH AFRICA
October 1942–May 1943
⊛ Allied Invasion Force Headquarters
← U.S forces including Free French
⬅--- British forces
— Line held by Axis forces ✳ major battles
0   100   200

DESERT WAR

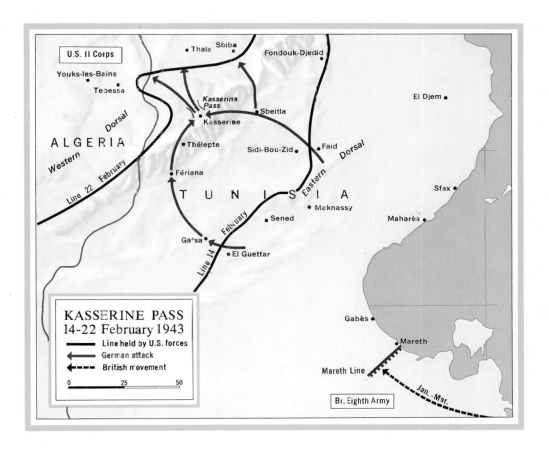

KASSERINE PASS
14-22 February 1943

	Line held by U.S. forces
	German attack
	British movement

0   25   50

U.S. II Corps

Br. Eighth Army

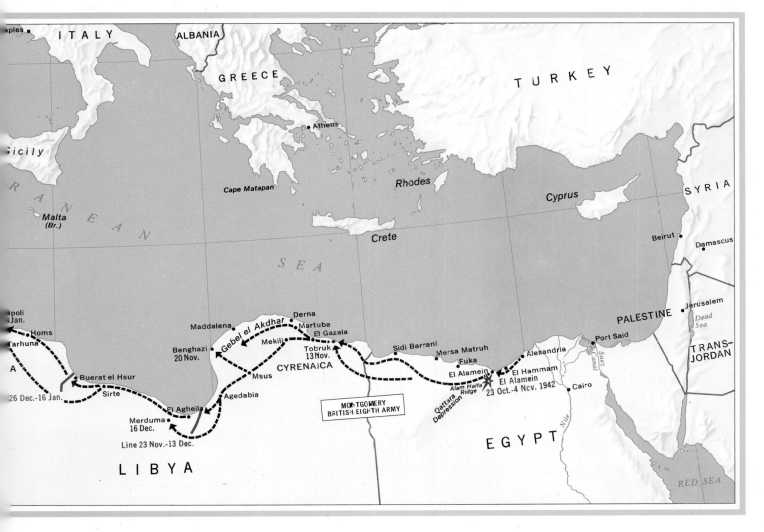

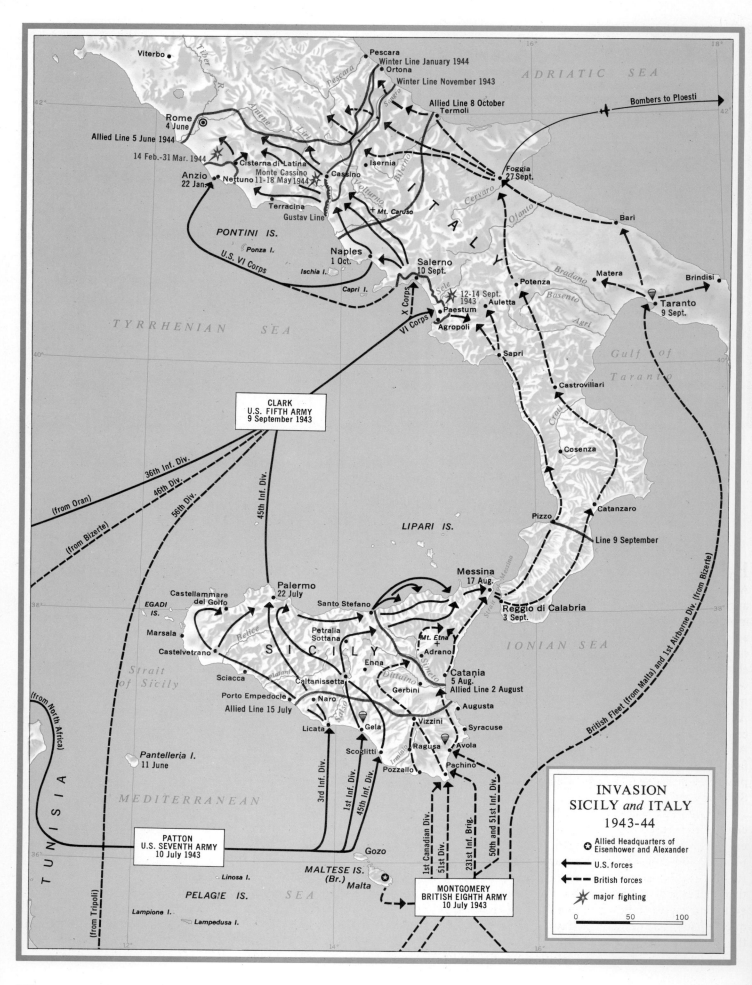

Viterbo

Pescara
Winter Line January 1944
Ortona
Winter Line November 1943

ADRIATIC SEA

Rome
4 June

Allied Line 8 October
Termoli

Bombers to Ploesti

Allied Line 5 June 1944

14 Feb.-31 Mar. 1944

Cisterna di Latina
Monte Cassino
Anzio   Nettuno 11-18 May 1944
22 Jan.

Cassino
Isernia

Foggia
27 Sept.

Bari

Terracina
Gustav Line

+Mt. Caruso

ITALY

PONTINI IS.

Ponza I.
U.S. VI CORPS

Matera

Brindisi

Naples
1 Oct.

Ischia I.

Salerno
10 Sept.

Potenza

Taranto
9 Sept.

Capri I.

12-14 Sept.
1943
Paestum

Sele
Auletta

X Corps

VI Corps

Agropoli

TYRRHENIAN   SEA

Sapri

Gulf of
Taranto

Castrovillari

CLARK
U.S. FIFTH ARMY
9 September 1943

Cosenza

36th Inf. Div.

46th Div.

(from Oran)

56th Div.

45th Inf. Div.

Pizzo

Catanzaro

Line 9 September

(from Bizerte)

LIPARI IS.

Messina
17 Aug.

EGADI
IS.

Castellammare
del Golfo

Palermo
22 July

Santo Stefano

Reggio di Calabria
3 Sept.

British Fleet (from Malta) and 1st Airborne Div. (from Bizerte)

Marsala

Belice

SICILY

Petralia
Sottana

Mt. Etna
+
Adrano

IONIAN SEA

Castelvetrano

Enna

Catania
5 Aug.
Allied Line 2 August

Strait
of
Sicily

Sciacca

Caltanissetta

Gerbini

Porto Empedocle
Allied Line 15 July

Naro

Vizzini

Augusta

Pantelleria I.
11 June

Licata

Gela

Syracuse

Scoglitti

Ragusa

Avola

Pozzallo

Pachino

MEDITERRANEAN

PATTON
U.S. SEVENTH ARMY
10 July 1943

(from North Africa)

TUNISIA

3rd Inf. Div.

1st Inf. Div.
45th Inf. Div.

1st Canadian Div.

51st Div.

231st Inf. Brig.

50th and 51st Inf. Div.

Gozo

(from Tripoli)

MALTESE IS.
(Br.)
Malta

Linosa I.

PELAGIE IS.

SEA

Lampione I.

Lampedusa I.

MONTGOMERY
BRITISH EIGHTH ARMY
10 July 1943

INVASION
SICILY and ITALY
1943-44

✪ Allied Headquarters of
Eisenhower and Alexander

⟶ U.S. forces

⇢ British forces

✸ major fighting

0   50   100

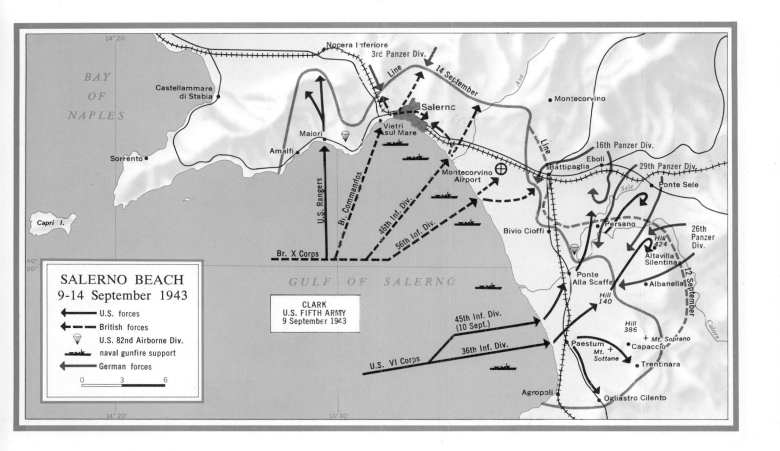

CLARK
U.S. FIFTH ARMY
9 September 1943

ALLIED DRIVE NORTH

By early 1943 there were rumbles of divided strategy in the Anglo-American coalition. The British chiefs of staff looked askance at a cross-Channel invasion until the odds were more strongly in the Allies' favor. They advocated further advances in the Mediterranean theater—in Churchillian rhetoric, "the soft underbelly of Europe." The American chiefs, particularly General George Marshall, saw northwestern Europe as the one proper and direct route to Germany, and they wanted an invasion in 1943. The stubborn Axis resistance in Tunisia, however, made it clear that not enough men and equipment could be released from North Africa in time to mount an invasion before September, too late in the season. The return to France would have to be postponed for a year, and the decision was made to invade Sicily instead.

On July 10 an assault force of 160,000 British and American troops secured beachheads on the island. As Montgomery's Eighth Army fought ahead, the U.S. Seventh Army, prodded and driven by its commander, George Patton, hurried across the island and took Palermo. The two armies then descended on Messina, but the Germans evaded them and got away to Italy with three crack divisions. The conquest of Sicily, achieved in 39 days, secured once and for all the Mediterranean passage.

Disgusted with Mussolini's bumbling and posturing, the Italian people deposed him on July 25; on September 8, after intrigues to match those of the Torch landings, Italy surrendered; the next day the Allies landed at Taranto and Salerno. It was hoped that a quick Italian campaign would entrap sizable elements of the German Army and furnish a base from which to bomb the southeastern quadrant of Hitler's empire. However, the Salerno landing (above) was a sobering experience. Panzer counterattacks nearly drove the invaders into the sea, and two battalions of U.S. paratroopers had to be dropped onto the beachhead as reinforcements. Eventually, the Allied forces linked up and took Naples, but the enemy had gained time to dig in.

Fighting dragged on through the winter in terrain ideal for defense. The major Allied conquest was the complex of airfields at Foggia (upper right, opposite). Soon the U.S. 15th Air Force was established in Italy, with the oil fields at Ploesti in Rumania one of its prime targets. In January, 1944, the Allies landed by sea at Anzio, behind the Germans, but were held to their beachhead. Not until May 25, four months later, could the U.S. Fifth Army reduce the Monte Cassino strongpoint and link up with the Anzio force. Rome fell on June 4, but the campaign endured for another year, with all hope gone for a quick victory. Italy became simply a theater of attrition that helped to grind down Hitler's *Wehrmacht*.

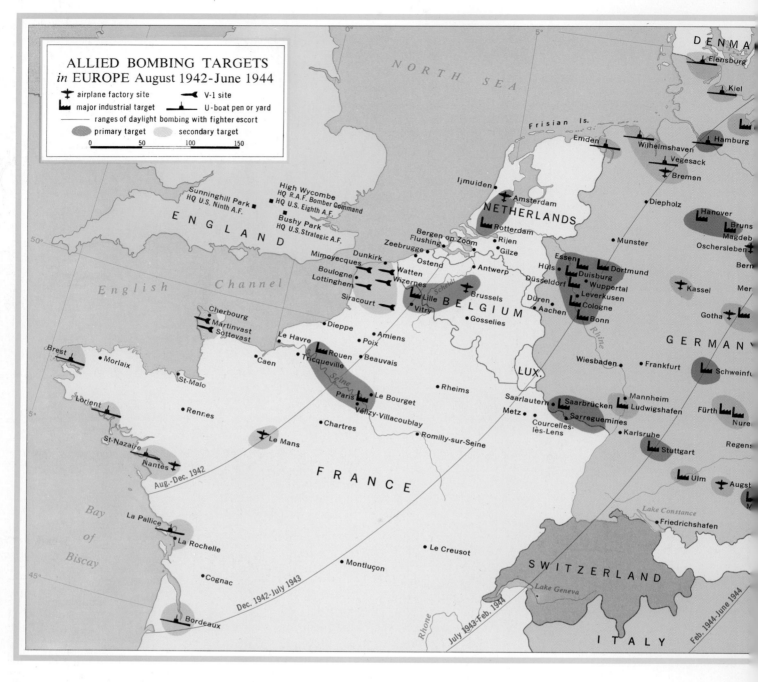

ALLIED BOMBING TARGETS
in EUROPE August 1942–June 1944

- ✈ airplane factory site
- ◣ major industrial target
- ⤙ V-1 site
- ⚓ U-boat pen or yard
- —— ranges of daylight bombing with fighter escort
- ⬮ primary target
- ⬭ secondary target

0   50   100   150

NORTH SEA

DENMA
⚓ Flensburg
⚓ Kiel

Frisian Is.

Ijmuiden

✈ Amsterdam
NETHERLANDS
◣ Rotterdam
Bergen op Zoom
Flushing • Rijen
Zeebrugge • Gilze
Dunkirk • Ostend
Watten Antwerp

Emden ⚓
Wilhelmshaven ⚓
✈ Vegesack
• Bremen
• Diepholz
• Munster

◣ Hanover   Bruns
Magdeb
Oschersleben
Bern

High Wycombe
HQ R.A.F. Bomber Command
Sunninghill Park ■   HQ U.S. Eighth A.F.
HQ U.S. Ninth A.F.   Bushy Park
HQ U.S. Strategic A.F.

ENGLAND

50°

English Channel

Mimoyecques ⤙
Boulogne ⤙
Lottinghem ⤙
Siracourt ✈

Wizernes ⤙
Scheldt
Lille ◣ BELGIUM
Vitry
Gosselies
Brussels

Essen ◣ Dortmund
Hüls • Duisburg
Düsseldorf • Wuppertal
• Kassel ✈
Leverkusen
Düren • Cologne
Aachen • Bonn
Rhine

GERMANY

Gotha ✈   Mer

Wiesbaden • Frankfurt   Schweinfurt ◣

Cherbourg •
Martinvast ✈
Sottevast ✈

Brest ⚓   • Morlaix

Le Havre
Caen •
Rouen
Tricqueville ✈
Seine
Paris • Le Bourget ◣
Vélizy-Villacoublay

• Dieppe
Amiens
Poix
• Beauvais

LUX.

Saarlautern
Metz •
Courcelles-
lès-Lens •

Saarbrücken ◣
Sarreguemines
Karlsruhe

Mannheim
Ludwigshafen

• Frankfurt
Fürth ◣
Nure

Stuttgart ◣

5°

Lorient ⚓
• Rennes

St-Malo
Chartres •

• Rheims

Romilly-sur-Seine

Ulm ◣   Augsb ✈

St-Nazaire ⚓
Nantes ✈
Aug.–Dec. 1942

Le Mans

FRANCE

Regens

Bay

La Pallice ⚓
La Rochelle

of

Dec. 1942–July 1943

• Le Creusot
• Montluçon

SWITZERLAND

Lake Constance
• Friedrichshafen

Biscay

45°

• Cognac

Bordeaux ◣

Rhone
Lake Geneva

July 1943–Feb. 1944

ITALY

Feb. 1944–June 1944

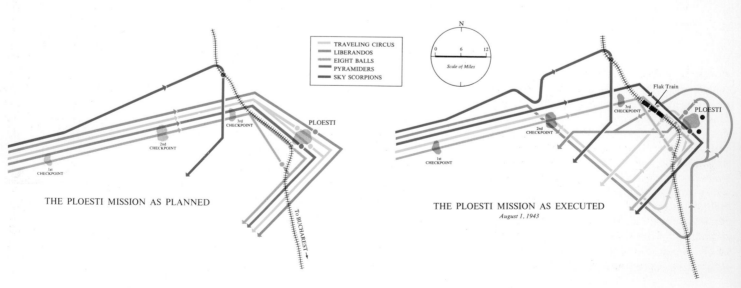

- TRAVELING CIRCUS
- LIBERANDOS
- EIGHT BALLS
- PYRAMIDERS
- SKY SCORPIONS

N

0   6   12
Scale of Miles

1st CHECKPOINT
2nd CHECKPOINT
3rd CHECKPOINT
PLOESTI
To BUCHAREST

THE PLOESTI MISSION AS PLANNED

1st CHECKPOINT
2nd CHECKPOINT
3rd CHECKPOINT
Flak Train
PLOESTI

THE PLOESTI MISSION AS EXECUTED
August 1, 1943

304

TARGET GERMANY

The United States was unique in its use of strategic air power in the Second World War. The Germans—and the Russians—saw the air arm as primarily a tactical, or battlefield, weapon. The *Luftwaffe* never developed an effective strategic bomber, and the Battle of Britain and the blitz of British cities, both strategic air efforts, were failures. Although Britain's Royal Air Force possessed superior bombers and was firmly wedded to a strategic air offensive, it struck only under the cover of darkness, using area, or saturation, bombing aimed as much at German civilians as at German factories.

The U.S. Army Air Force, on the other hand, entered the war committed to high-altitude daylight precision bombing. This was a far more accurate method of striking the German war machine, and was more humane as well. "We should never allow the history of this war to convict us of throwing the strategic bomber at the man in the street," insisted A.A.F. General Ira Eaker. In August, 1942, from bases in England, the U.S. 8th Air Force began raids on the Continent. Its build-up was slow, due in part to a diversion of strength to support the Torch landings in North Africa, and not until January, 1943, did the first American bombs fall on Germany itself. After that, the A.A.F. became increasingly effective. Its Flying Fortresses and Liberators complemented the nighttime efforts of the R.A.F.; together, the two forces nearly wiped out Hamburg with six successive raids in the summer of 1943.

The *Luftwaffe* reacted vigorously to these round-the-clock attacks, and the fall months brought daylight bombing to a crisis. In one week in October, 153 U.S. heavy bombers were shot down, climaxed by the loss of 65 planes in a raid on the German ball-bearing industry at Schweinfurt. But the antidote was at hand. As the range lines on the map indicate, the combat radius of escort fighters was being extended all through 1943, due primarily to the use of gasoline drop-tanks. In December, the P-51 Mustang put in its appearance over Germany. This remarkable fighter had a combat radius of over 450 miles on internal tanks alone—later raised to 850 miles with drop-tanks.

During the so-called Big Week in February, 1944, the air war turned firmly in the Allies' favor. A concerted joint effort by the R.A.F. Bomber Command, the 8th Air Force, and the 15th Air Force in Italy set back Nazi fighter plane production by two months. In addition, at least 450 enemy fighters were shot down. By D-Day, in June, the campaign had heavily damaged German industry, interdicted *Wehrmacht* communications in France (where U.S. and British tactical air forces were particularly effective), and left the *Luftwaffe* a shambles. Serious damage was also done to the launching sites of Hitler's new secret weapon, the V-1 pilotless bomb. The R.A.F. had already set back the V-1 program (and development of the V-2 ballistic rocket, as well) with an attack on the research center at Peenemünde (upper right) in August, 1943.

While strategic bombing played an important role before D-Day, the most effective raids—and three-quarters of the bomb tonnage—hit the Third Reich after the invasion. Especially potent was the offensive against Hitler's oil resources. The refineries at Ploesti and the synthetic-oil installations in Germany were attacked repeatedly, and by September, 1944, German oil output was down 75 per cent—a crippling blow to both the *Luftwaffe* and the *Wehrmacht*.

Producing a third of Hitler's fuel, the refinery complex at Ploesti, Rumania, was perhaps the most attractive target in Europe; it was certainly the best defended. On August 1, 1943, five U.S. bomber groups of Liberators, based in North Africa, raided Ploesti from treetop height. As diagramed at left, the plan went awry when the two lead groups of bombers took a wrong turn, then approached the target on a collision course with the trailing groups. The result was chaos, a savage battle with hundreds of antiaircraft guns, and the loss of one-third of the planes. Damage to the refineries was limited, and output was soon back to normal.

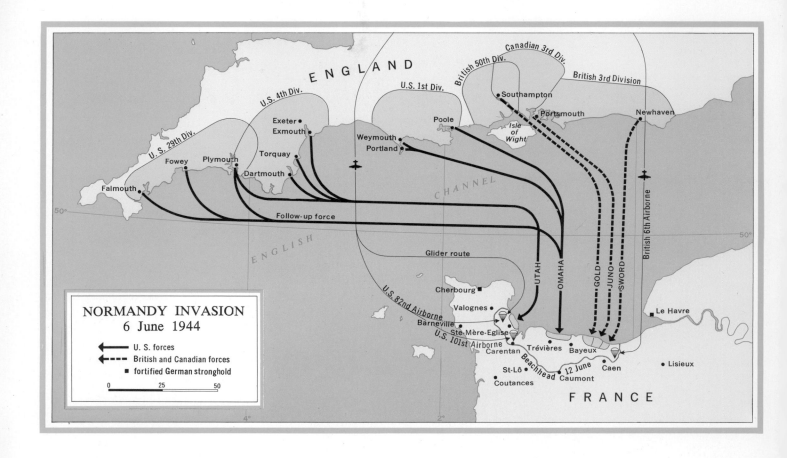

NORMANDY INVASION
6 June 1944

⬅ U. S. forces
⬅ British and Canadian forces
■ fortified German stronghold

0   25   50

There was no way to conceal from the Germans the build-up for the invasion of France. But tactical surprise —the precise time and place of the cross-Channel attack— was possible to achieve, and in this the Allies were entirely successful. By various ruses they persuaded Hitler to believe what he wanted to believe: that the assault on the Continent would take place across the narrowest part of the Channel in the Calais area (top center, opposite). The *Führer* had built his strongest defenses there.

The so-called Atlantic Wall was commanded by Field Marshal Rommel, who wanted to fight the decisive battle on the beaches, using fixed defenses and local reserves. He opposed the plan of his commander, Gerd von Rundstedt, to defend the coast lightly and counterattack with mobile armored reserves; having experienced the weight of Allied air power in North Africa, Rommel doubted that such reserves could actually achieve mobility. Neither German plan was fully implemented, and the Atlantic Wall was far from finished by June of 1944.

Crossing in heavy weather, the 5,000-ship invasion armada took position off Normandy undetected. The actual heralds of invasion (above) were airborne troops, who secured key points behind and flanking the beaches. At Utah Beach the landings were lightly opposed; those in the British zone met more resistance but made solid gains on D-Day. But at Omaha, where the defenses most closely reflected Rommel's strategy, the invaders were nearly thrown back into the sea. A week of hard ground fighting, aided by air and naval support, linked up and deepened the beach-

head. In a little over three weeks the Allies landed one million men; using artificial harbors and breakwaters, they supplied this host without benefit of a deepwater port.

In late July the defensive ring was cracked at St-Lô (map opposite), and General Patton's U.S. Third Army exploded through Avranches, swinging into Brittany, then left to encircle the German armies in Normandy. Montgomery's British and Canadian units could not quite close a trap in the Falaise area, but the rout was on. Moving on a broad front, often supplied by air, the Allies drove hard for the Seine in a second encirclement attempt. Once more, the Fifth and Seventh Panzer armies escaped annihilation, but they were grievously battered; the Fifth crossed the Seine with but 24 of its tanks. By August 25, Paris was liberated by the French 2nd Armored Division, and the newly landed Anvil forces in southern France were at Grenoble.

The pursuit to the German border continued, but with gradually decreasing momentum. Supply became critical. "My men can eat their belts," Patton said, "but my tanks gotta have gas." The key port of Antwerp was taken early in September, but its approaches were not cleared until November 28. There were also serious strategic differences between Supreme Commander Eisenhower, who wanted a broad-front advance to engage the maximum enemy forces, and Montgomery, who sought a single "dagger thrust" in the north to envelop the industrial Ruhr (Essen-Düsseldorf area). No significant breakthrough could be made, however. By December, the Allies were at the line shown—the West Wall—reorganizing for the final thrust into Germany.

OPERATION OVERLORD

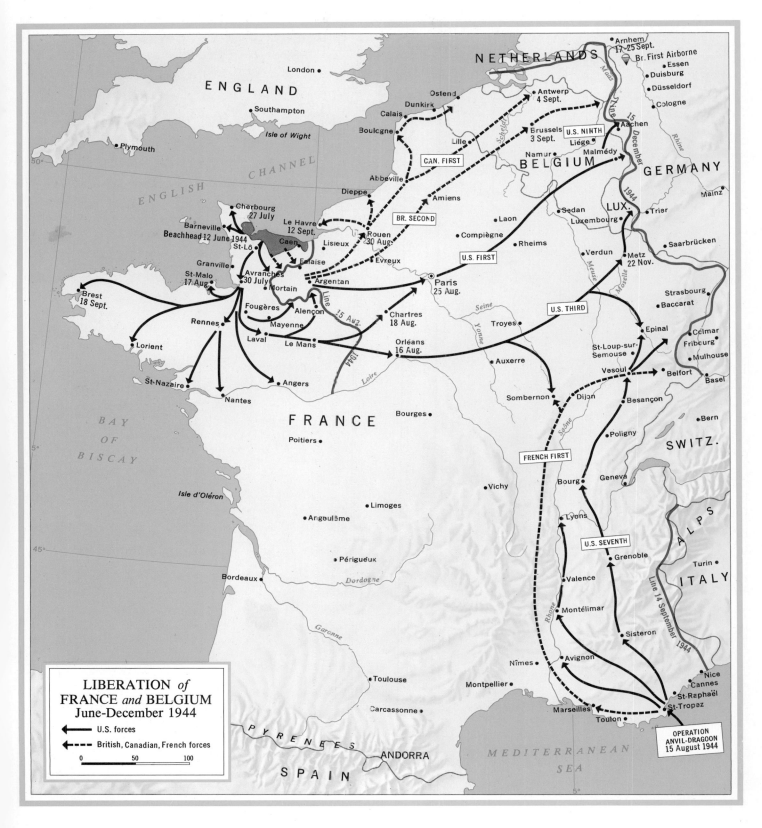

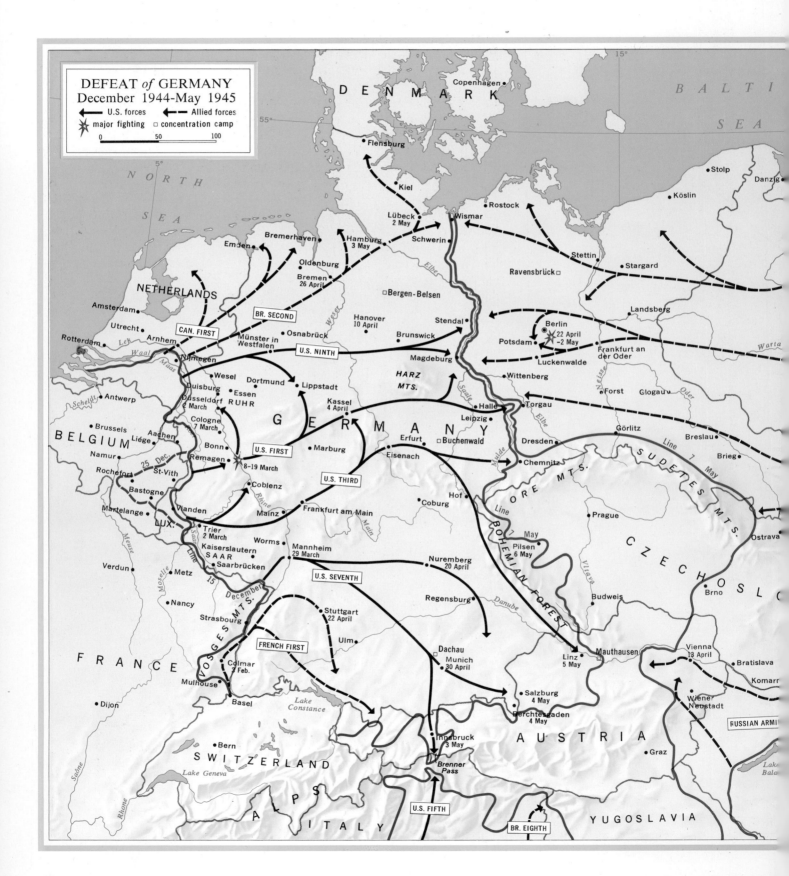

DEFEAT *of* GERMANY
December 1944-May 1945

← U.S. forces ⇠ Allied forces
✸ major fighting ▫ concentration camp

0   50   100

at the ELBE

Allied preparations for breaching the West Wall were jolted by a surprise German counterattack through the Ardennes forest (below), aimed at Antwerp and the isolation of Eisenhower's northern wing. Good progress was made through the thin U.S. First Army front, but vigorous resistance (particularly at Bastogne), counterattacks, fuel shortages, and Allied air strikes eroded the gains. Hitler's stroke set back Eisenhower's offensive by six weeks, but it consumed the last German reserves. The situation on the Eastern Front was equally critical. The subsequent Nazi death throes are traced at left.

The Rhineland campaign (the reduction of the West Wall and the drive to the Rhine) commenced on February 8, 1945. A month later a Rhine bridge at Remagen was seized intact. By March 24, Patton had won two more bridgeheads, near Coblenz and Mainz. The campaign cost the Nazis some 300,000 casualties. Meanwhile, the Red army reached the Oder, and Allied bombing severed Germany's remaining industrial arteries. The last campaigns began.

Eisenhower put the main weight of his thrust behind Omar Bradley's 12th Army Group (First and Third U.S. armies). The Ruhr was surrounded, and on April 18 yielded 317,000 prisoners. Hurrying on, followed by infantry to mop up, armored spearheads fanned out against fragmentary resistance. In Italy the Allies at last broke out of the mountains and drove northward for a linkup with the U.S. Seventh Army at the Brenner Pass. While Hitler busied himself with the defense of Berlin, Eisenhower pulled up his troops at the Elbe (well inside the Russian occupation zone agreed upon at the Yalta Conference) and acted to smother a rumored last stand of fanatic Nazis in the so-called National Redoubt around Berchtesgaden (lower center). On April 30 Hitler killed himself; a week later the holocaust ended. The Thousand Year Reich had lasted twelve years and four months.

END *of an* EMPIRE

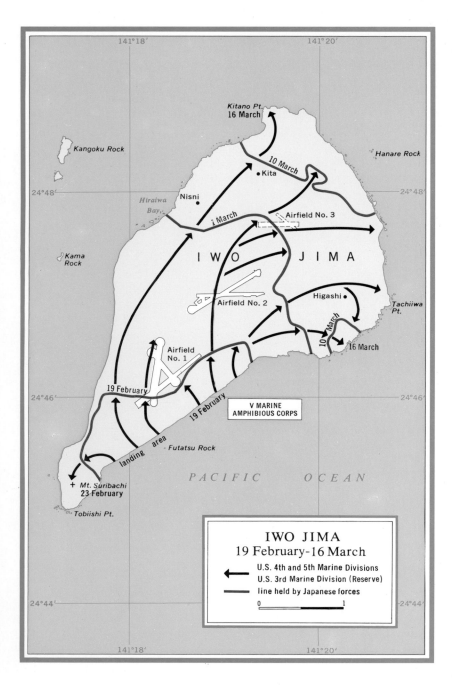

IWO JIMA
19 February-16 March

← U.S. 4th and 5th Marine Divisions
← U.S. 3rd Marine Division (Reserve)
— line held by Japanese forces

0 ————————— 1

The closing campaigns in the Pacific had two goals: to accelerate the bombing of the Japanese home islands, and to seize springboards for their invasion. Superfortresses from the Marianas began raiding Japan in November, 1944, but many damaged bombers went down for want of a sanctuary on the long return flight. The capture of Iwo Jima in the Volcano group would solve this problem, and would also furnish a base for escort fighters. Despite saturation air bombing and naval shelling before the assault, the seizure of Iwo Jima cost the U.S. 24,900 casualties. (By the end of the war, almost the same number of airmen were able to land safely on the island.) The B-29 campaign now quickly gained momentum. Abandoning the strategy of daylight precision bombing used in Europe, the Americans turned to night raids with incendiaries. One by one, Japan's tinderbox cities were set in flames.

In the battle for Okinawa in the Ryukyus (opposite, lower center), Japanese troops reached new heights of fanaticism. Thousands killed themselves rather than surrender. At sea, kamikaze suicide pilots sank 15 U.S. vessels and damaged over 200. During the ensuing build-up for the final invasion, submarines and mine-laying B-29's brought Japan to the brink of starvation, and carrier plane attacks and naval shelling added to the pressure. The atomic bombing of Hiroshima and Nagasaki and Russia's entry into the war were final blows. Japan's surrender, on August 15, ended at last the six-year agony of World War II.

The sketch at right was made on the Okinawa beachhead. The Japanese chose to defend interior positions rather than the beaches; 110,000 Japanese were killed, along with more than 12,500 U.S. soldiers and Marines.

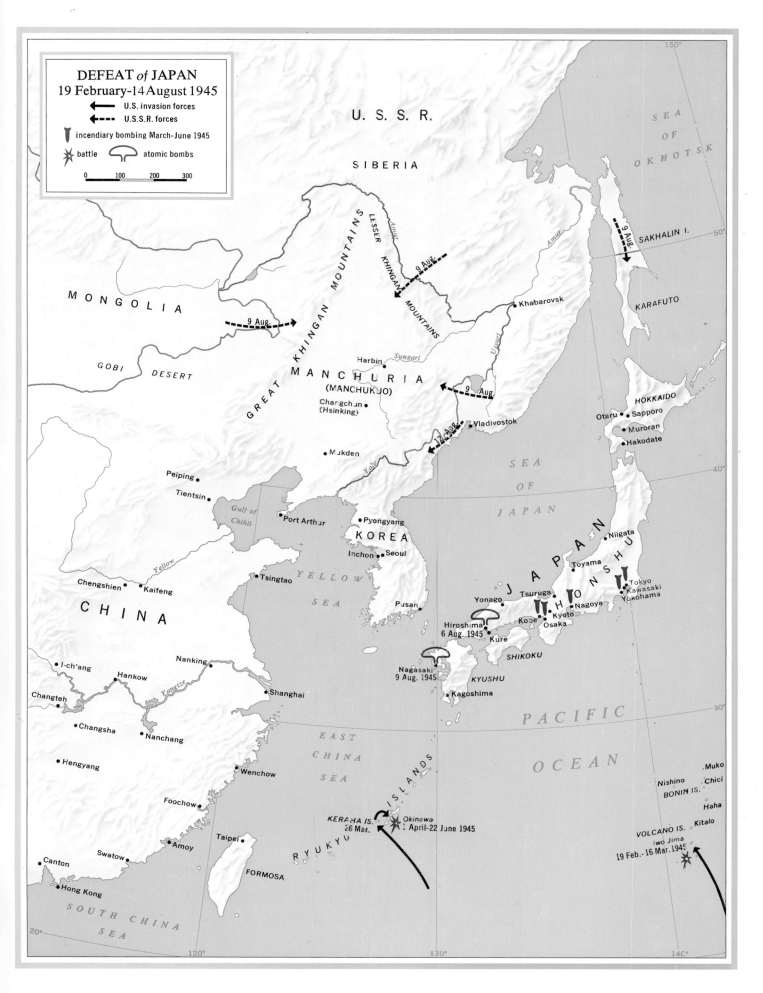

DEFEAT *of* JAPAN
19 February–14 August 1945

⬅ U.S. invasion forces
⬅--- U.S.S.R. forces
▼ incendiary bombing March–June 1945
✳ battle   ⛱ atomic bombs

0   100   200   300

U. S. S. R.

SIBERIA

SEA
OF
OKHOTSK

MONGOLIA

GOBI   DESERT

GREAT KHINGAN MOUNTAINS

LESSER KHINGAN MOUNTAINS

Amur

9 Aug.

SAKHALIN I.

9 Aug.

KARAFUTO

• Khabarovsk

Harbin •

Sungari

MANCHURIA
(MANCHUKUO)

9 Aug.

HOKKAIDO

Changchun •
(Hsinking)

Otaru • Sapporo
• Muroran
• Hakodate

12 Aug.

• Vladivostok

• Mukden

Yellow

SEA
OF
JAPAN

Peiping •

Tientsin •

Gulf of
Chihli

Port Arthur •

• Pyongyang

KOREA

Inchon • • Seoul

Chengshien • • Kaifeng

• Tsingtao

YELLOW
SEA

Pusan •

Niigata •

J A P A N

Toyama •

Yonago •
Tsuruga • H O N S H U Tokyo
Kobe •   Kyoto • Nagoya Kawasaki
  Osaka •   Yokohama

CHINA

Hiroshima •
6 Aug. 1945   Kure •

SHIKOKU

• I-ch'ang

Nanking •

Hankow •
Yangtze

Changteh •

• Shanghai

Nagasaki •
9 Aug. 1945

KYUSHU

• Kagoshima

• Changsha

Nanchang •

EAST
CHINA
SEA

PACIFIC

OCEAN

30°

• Hengyang

Wenchow •

Foochow •

RYUKYU ISLANDS

MUKO •

Nishino •   Chici •
BONIN IS.

Haha •

Taipei •

FORMOSA

KERAMA IS.
26 Mar.

Okinawa
1 April–22 June 1945

VOLCANO IS. Kitalo •
Iwo Jima
19 Feb.–16 Mar. 1945

Amoy •

• Swatow

• Canton

• Hong Kong

SOUTH CHINA
SEA

20°

120°

130°

140°

CHAPTER 9

THE WORLD — DIVIDED YET UNITED

War often makes strange bedfellows, and victory frequently creates as many problems as it solves. Both these rather trite generalizations apply in full measure to the Second World War. One of the reasons why the western democracies failed to combat effectively the rise of fascism in the twenties and thirties was the fact that men like Mussolini and Hitler were bitter foes of communism, which to many persons seemed a far more dangerous threat to western institutions. Germany and Italy, the argument ran, were a bulwark against Soviet Russia; perhaps their warlike posturing would culminate in a fascist-communist struggle in which both forms of totalitarianism would eventually be destroyed.

In America, Pearl Harbor put an end to this kind of reasoning. The Soviets were now allies, not enemies; the dreadful Marshal Stalin was transmuted into the pipe-smoking "Uncle Joe," a grandfatherly type fond of dogs and small children; the Russian people appeared a nation of patriots, heroically fighting for freedom. American newspapers, magazines, and movies, together with political leaders of both parties, joined in praising the Russians and picturing them as working diligently to destroy the Axis powers and create a better world.

During the war, with their very existence as a nation at stake, the Russians did co-operate effectively with the democracies, even agreeing to join in the establishment of the United Nations. While they demanded the right to veto important U.N. decisions, they were no more insistent upon this power than was the United States. Stalin also made stiff territorial demands, especially in eastern Europe, but these seemed reasonable enough in the light of Hitler's unprovoked invasion and the fact that all the area was currently under Nazi control. At the Yalta Conference (1945) Roosevelt and Churchill agreed to allow Stalin to take over eastern Poland and to exact heavy reparations from Germany.

After victory, however, it quickly became apparent that Russia intended to dominate all eastern Europe without regard for the wishes of local populations, and to extend its influence everywhere it could, by subversion or by force. Besides clamping down what Winston Churchill called an "iron curtain" between the West and those parts of eastern Europe which its troops controlled, and rigidly suppressing all elements in those areas that opposed communist rule, the Russians were soon aiding local communist-led revolutionaries in Greece. They demanded territorial concessions from Turkey with a view to dominating the strategic Turkish Straits, and sponsored a separatist movement in Azerbaijan, the northern province of Iran.

These actions naturally alarmed Russia's wartime allies. The burden of countering them fell principally on American shoulders, for alone among the democracies the United States had emerged from the war physically unscathed and with a flourishing economy.

The chief architect of American policy was the Russian expert George F. Kennan. The way to deal with Soviet expansionism, Kennan argued, was by "long-term, patient but firm and vigilant containment." To every Russian pressure the United States should apply a counter pressure. This would involve building up American military strength, which had been sharply reduced after the end of the war, and supplying military and economic aid to noncommunist nations all over the world. Eventually this "containment policy" would convince the Russians that aggression did not pay; then true peace might result.

Of course, containment meant abandoning America's traditional isolationism. The issue was hotly debated. A small minority argued that containment was not enough. Believing a showdown between communism and capitalism inevitable, the minority proposed what Secretary of State John Foster Dulles later called "massive retaliation"—all-out war to check Soviet aggression, free the "enslaved" peoples of eastern Europe, and (extremists suggested) eradicate communism from the earth. Others considered reason a more potent weapon than force; they wished to rely on diplomacy, and particularly upon the U.N., to settle all disagreements with the communists. But almost no one adopted the old isolationist stance. It was obvious that the U.S. could no longer turn its back on the rest of the world. The containment policy was accepted primarily because it was a compromise between two forms of internationalism.

The new policy involved maintaining large contingents of American troops in Europe and in other regions, and outlaying enormous sums of money. In 1945 the United States had spent about $2 billion on foreign aid; in 1947 it spent $6.5 billion, in 1948 nearly $10 billion. Altogether, between 1945 and 1963, expenditures on military and economic assistance to foreign nations amounted to more than $100 billion, all in addition to the billions spent on American defense. At the same time the country signed treaties (with nations as geographically, culturally, and politically disparate as Australia, Turkey, and Brazil) which committed it to defend half the world against attack. The cold war with communism sometimes erupted into real war—the nation suffered 137,000 casualties in Korea, and thousands more in Vietnam. At times it threatened to flare into the nuclear holocaust that all men feared.

However, the divisive aspects of the cold war tended to obscure the fact that it was largely a product of the growing unity of world civilization. It made the contending powers internationally minded perforce, but, more than that, it existed on a global scale only because events in every region now directly affected those in many other regions. Furthermore, the implications of the new internationalism transcended the conflict between communism and democracy. That conflict, it was true, was responsible for the presence of thousands of American troops in Europe and Asia, and for the flood of dollars poured out in defense of allies all over the world. It did not, however, account entirely, or even in major part, for the outward thrust of America. In the postwar decades the communications revolution and the rapid integration of the world's economy brought Americans to dozens of countries on peaceful missions of an astonishing variety. By 1958 the development of the jet airplane enabled men to span oceans in hours, while the increasing complexity of life forced them to specialize more, and thus to depend more on other men in other regions. World trade flourished as never before. American exports rose from $4 billion in 1940 to $26.4 billion in 1964. Imports increased from $2.6 billion to $18.6 billion in the same period. By 1963 American investments abroad amounted to more than $40.6 billion, foreign investments in the United States to about $8 billion. These figures explain why businessmen of all nations became world travelers on an immense scale, but they also provide insights into such apparently unrelated phenomena as the increased interest in foreign language teaching in the schools, and the flocking of American students to foreign universities—more than 13,000 a year by the early sixties. The Peace Corps, designed to provide American technological guidance to the developing nations, was not unrelated to the cold war competition for allies, but it also reflected a wide understanding that the well-being and prosperity of American civilization depended heavily upon other countries having a decent standard of living, stable social institutions, and well-educated populations.

Scientific advances brought men closer together in other ways. Seen close up, the conquest of space was a product of the cold war and of the hot war that preceded it. Advances in rocketry made during World War II by the Germans were taken over and developed by both Russian and western scientists. While producing weapons of awesome power like the intercontinental ballistic missiles, their work also had unlimited nonmilitary implications. Weather satellites circling the globe changed the science of meteorology; the "Early Bird" satellite permitted live intercontinental television broadcasting. Although Russo-American rivalry and suspicion prevented the pooling of knowledge in this area, the psychological effect of men orbiting the earth, and of space vessels penetrating to the moon and the planets, seemed certain, in the long run, to make men more conscious of their common humanity, just as the immense destructive power of nuclear weapons has operated to make nations try harder to settle their differences without resorting to war. In short, scientific knowledge and economic efficiency have heightened many world tensions, but they have also unified the world and its peoples. As never before in history, the fate of the United States is intimately connected with that of every other nation.

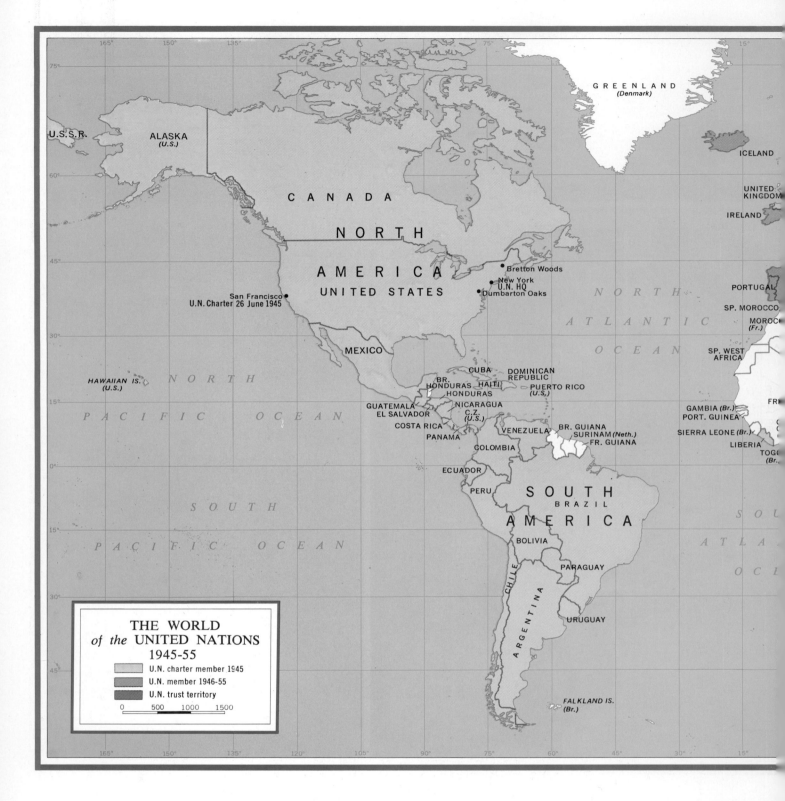

THE WORLD
of the UNITED NATIONS
1945-55

U.N. charter member 1945
U.N. member 1946-55
U.N. trust territory

0   500   1000   1500

POSTWAR HOPES

Although Woodrow Wilson's League of Nations, founded after World War I to provide collective security for all nations, was a dismal failure, Allied statesmen during the Second World War were determined to create a more effective institution for maintaining peace once victory was won. In August, 1941, Roosevelt and Churchill, meeting off Newfoundland on the cruiser *Augusta,* laid the groundwork by drafting the Atlantic Charter, a high-minded if vague statement of war aims. In 1944, representatives of 44 nations, gathered at Bretton Woods, New Hampshire, established an

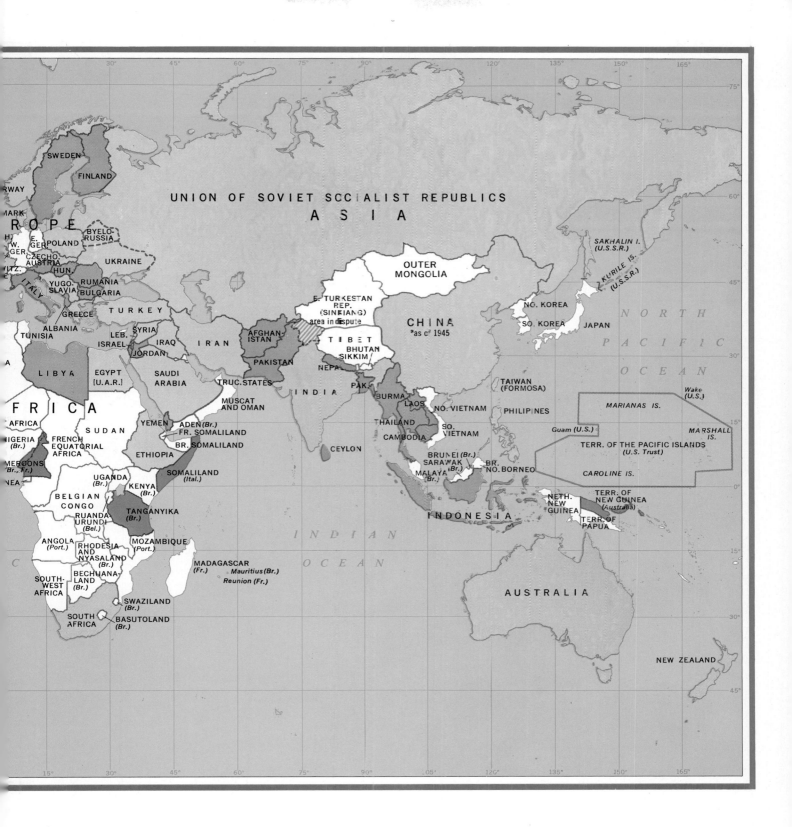

International Bank for Reconstruction and Development to finance the work of rebuilding the war-shattered world. That same year, at Dumbarton Oaks, in Washington, D.C., the United States, Great Britain, Russia, and China drew up a tentative charter for a world organization and summoned a great conference, to be held the following spring at San Francisco, to create the United Nations organization.

The U.N. Charter, signed by 50 nations on June 26, 1945, set up a General Assembly in which each country had one vote, and a Security Council, supposedly the real seat of power, consisting of five permanent members—the United States, Russia, Great Britain, France, and China—and six others selected for two-year terms. A variety of administrative bodies, supervised by a Secretary General, were also created, including an Economic and Social Council and a Trusteeship Council, the latter authorized to supervise former Axis colonies in Africa and Asia. In 1952 the U.N. settled in permanent quarters in New York; by 1955 it had 76 members, as wartime neutrals, newly created states, and minor members of the Axis coalition were admitted.

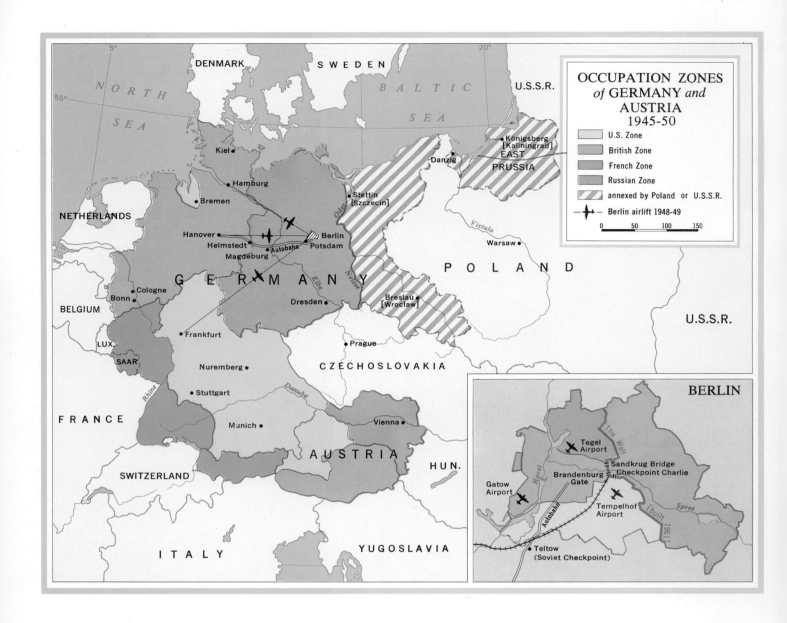

THE COLD WAR

Victory in World War II proved a prelude to further conflict, partly because of the ideological clash between democracy and communism, and partly because of the difficulty of deciding what to do with Germany. The Germans had been crushed in 1918, yet two decades later they had unleashed the most powerful military assault in history. The Allies were determined that this must not happen again. One suggestion was to destroy Germany utterly as an industrial power, turning over peripheral areas to surrounding nations and dividing the remainder into two countries of a "primarily agricultural and pastoral . . . character." This was rejected as too drastic, but at the Potsdam Conference in the summer of 1945, the United States, Great Britain, and Russia agreed to give all of Germany east of the Oder and Neisse rivers to a reconstituted Poland (Russia got a small part of East Prussia), and to divide the rest of Germany and Austria into occupation zones controlled by themselves and by France. In a fateful decision, they also divided the capital cities of Berlin and Vienna into four zones.

Joint control of Austria was terminated in 1955, the powers agreeing to make it a "permanently" neutral coun-

Europe 1945-55 map

try. Too much was at stake to dispose of Germany so easily. Two Germanies quickly emerged: East Germany, a Russian satellite, and West Germany, a democracy occupied by the West until 1955, and thereafter independent. Berlin was a constant source of tension. In June, 1948, the Russians closed land access routes to that city from West Germany. The United States responded by flying in huge quantities of freight on a round-the-clock basis, from Hamburg, Hanover, and Frankfurt. At its peak this "Berlin Airlift" supplied West Berliners with almost 5,000 tons of goods daily, and in May, 1949, the Russians gave up their blockade.

As time passed, West Berlin became a funnel through which thousands of East Germans escaped to the West. Determined to stop this traffic, Russia erected a concrete and barbed wire wall across the city in 1961. The flow ceased, but Russian prestige suffered heavily.

Outside Germany, the Russians, besides establishing a chain of satellite states along their western border, encouraged communist movements eagerly. To combat them, the United States, in 1946, extended $400 million in military and economic aid to Greece and Turkey, announcing

(by the Truman Doctrine) that it would support all free peoples resisting subjugation. Then, in 1948, the Marshall Plan was enacted. To help restore the "normal economic health" on which political stability is based, the U.S. contributed over $13 billion to a co-operative European reconstruction program. The Marshall Plan envisaged the participation of communist nations, but Russia refused to join. Instead, she welded her satellites into an economic union, converted by the Warsaw Pact of 1955 into a military alliance. But the Marshall Plan was a brilliant success. The European economy was soon booming. The seizure of Czechoslovakia by local communists in 1948, when that nation was preparing to accept Marshall Plan aid, marked the last significant expansion of communism in Europe.

To counteract the Russian military threat, the United States and the western European nations, together with Canada and Iceland, founded the North Atlantic Treaty Organization in 1949. Greece, Turkey, and West Germany later became members. The first commander of its international army was General Dwight Eisenhower, who served from 1951 until he resigned to run for President.

Some 171,000 communist troops gave up during the Korean War, using passes like this one that had been dropped to them by plane.

HOT WAR
in KOREA

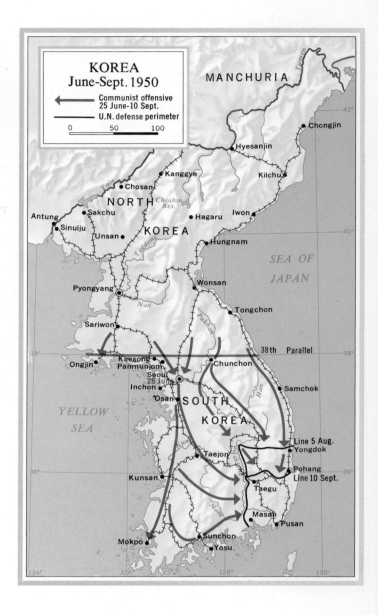

After the defeat of Japan, Russia and the United States divided Japan's province of Korea along the 38th parallel, Russia controlling the northern section, America the southern, the intention being to combine the two eventually into an independent republic. However, the powers could not agree on how to do this, and by 1948 two governments were functioning, a communist-dominated Democratic People's Republic, and the Republic of Korea, supported by the United States and the U.N. Both Russia and the United States withdrew their troops from the peninsula.

On June 25, 1950, without warning, a powerful North Korean army struck across the 38th parallel, sending South Korean forces reeling before it. Acting in the name of the U.N., which had official responsibility for Korea, President Truman ordered American forces into the fight. The North Korean drive was gradually slowed and, by August, after the defenders had been squeezed into a narrow perimeter around the port of Pusan, stopped. Then, on September 15, the U.N. commander, General Douglas MacArthur, launched an amphibious assault on the port of Inchon, on Korea's west coast, some 50 miles south of the 38th par-

allel. The success of these landings and of a counterattack launched simultaneously from the Pusan beachhead, threw the North Koreans into confusion. They fell back rapidly, suffering heavy losses in men and supplies. By October, the United Nations army (eventually troops of 16 nations were represented, although the United States and South Korea supplied about 90 per cent of the total) had pushed the invaders back across the 38th parallel.

The United States had entered the war only to expel the North Koreans from South Korea. But now, with U.N. approval, Truman ordered MacArthur to advance all the way to the Yalu River, the boundary between North Korea and Communist Chinese Manchuria. As MacArthur drove northward, believing that the job would be finished before Christmas, the Chinese began to infiltrate "volunteers" to bolster the retreating North Koreans, and to threaten all-out intervention unless the U.N. troops withdrew. MacArthur dismissed these warnings, but on November 26, 33 Chinese divisions suddenly attacked, smashing through the center of the United Nations line.

Overnight a triumphant advance became a disorderly

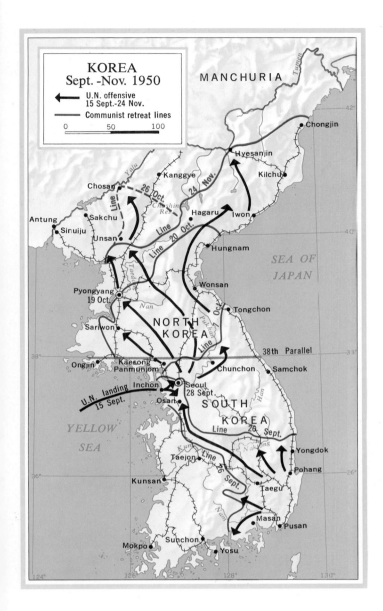

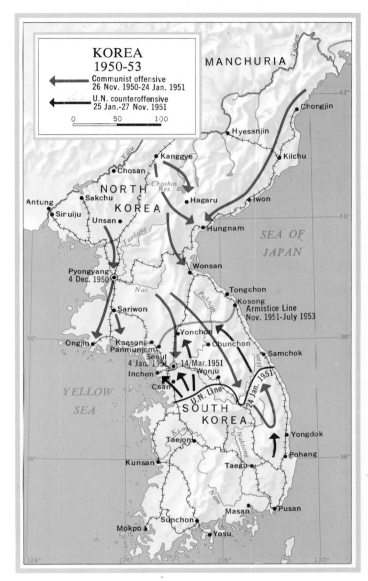

rout. Annihilation threatened the U.N. troops, cut off in rugged, frozen country by superior forces. Although suffering heavy losses, they fought their way out of the Chinese trap, however, and fell back more or less in order south of the 38th parallel. Inchon and the South Korean capital of Seoul passed again into communist hands, but by late January, 1951, MacArthur was able to check the invaders and resume the offensive. Amid bitter fighting the front was once more pushed northward into North Korea. By this time, the term "38th parallel" had become famous, or infamous, all over the world.

By the spring of 1951 the front ran in a wavy line from Panmunjom, on the parallel above Inchon, to a point on the Sea of Japan a few miles farther north. General MacArthur, unable to advance much farther, wished to bomb communist bases in what he called China's "privileged sanctuary" north of the Yalu River. But President Truman refused to permit air attacks on China, which might well have led to a new world war. When MacArthur tried to rally Congressional and public support in the United States for his strategy, Truman, after warning him to desist, replaced

him as commander with General Matthew B. Ridgway.

At last, in June, 1951, the communists agreed to discuss an armistice. Talks began at Kaesong in July, but were soon broken off. They were resumed in October at Panmunjom, but little progress was made. Agreement on a truce was hampered by the fact that many Chinese and North Korean prisoners did not want to return to their homelands, and the U.N. negotiators were unwilling to compel them to do so. After a year of fruitless discussion, the United States broke off the talks in October, 1952. The fighting continued inconclusively, while public opposition to the war mounted in America. After the 1952 election, President-elect Eisenhower paid a visit to the front, and in April, 1953, the truce talks were resumed. An armistice was finally signed on July 27. It established a demilitarized zone along the battle line, which ran from Panmunjom to Kosong, on the Sea of Japan. A Supervisory Commission of neutrals was set up to enforce the cease-fire, and prisoners refusing repatriation were turned over to another neutral committee. Korea remained divided, but the U.N. had successfully demonstrated its power to act against aggressors.

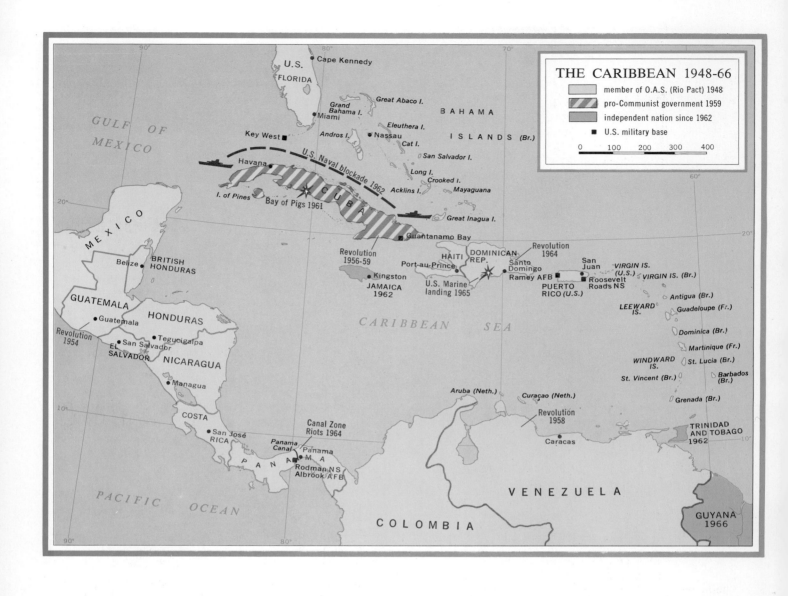

THE CARIBBEAN 1948-66

- member of O.A.S. (Rio Pact) 1948
- pro-Communist government 1959
- independent nation since 1962
- U.S. military base

0 100 200 300 400

AREAS *of* CRISES

The economic and ideological conflicts of the cold war were waged in every corner of the globe. Indeed, so pervasive did American interests become and so widespread were the effects of any local conflict, that the years after 1945 assumed the aspect of one continual crisis. In the Caribbean region, poverty and social instability increased the danger of communist subversion. To combat this threat, the United States and 19 Latin American nations signed, in 1947, the Rio Pact, a hemispheric defensive alliance, and the next year created the Organization of American States, a kind of regional U.N., but without the U.N.'s Great Power veto. However, anti-American sentiment in Latin America grew steadily, the feeling being that the United States cared more about checking communism than helping to improve economic conditions. When a pro-communist government won power in Guatemala in 1954, the U.S., acting unilaterally, sponsored a revolution that overthrew it. But in 1958 a radical regime took over Venezuela, imposing heavy exactions on foreign oil companies.

In 1959 the revolutionary Fidel Castro deposed the Cuban dictator Fulgencio Batista. Although the United States sought Castro's friendship, he soon gravitated into

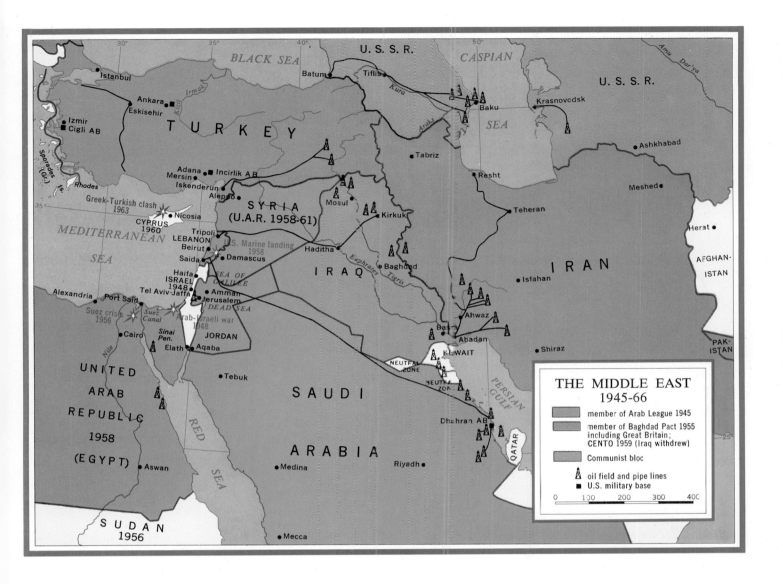

THE MIDDLE EAST
1945-66

member of Arab League 1945

member of Baghdad Pact 1955
including Great Britain;
CENTO 1959 (Iraq withdrew)

Communist bloc

⚑ oil field and pipe lines

■ U.S. military base

0   100   200   300   400

the communist orbit, making Cuba a base for subversive elements seeking power in other Latin American countries. In 1961 the United States tried to depose Castro by organizing an invasion by Cuban exiles from a base in Guatemala. The resulting "Bay of Pigs affair" was a fiasco; the invaders were routed, America's reputation was tarnished, and Castro became even more openly procommunist. However, when Russia began to install bases for atomic missiles in Cuba, President Kennedy clamped a naval blockade on the island, threatened nuclear war if the missiles were used, and forced Russia to withdraw them. His firmness, together with increased economic aid, helped somewhat to improve Latin American relations. Nevertheless, as the use of American Marines to restore order in the Dominican Republic in 1965 showed, America's fear of communist take-overs continued to hamper friendly relations with the nations south of the Rio Grande.

American involvement in the Middle East was influenced by the area's immense oil resources (60 per cent of the world's reserves), and by broad strategic considerations related to the cold war. Middle Eastern tensions were further complicated by the medieval character of Arab society and by the conflict between the Arab League (founded in 1945) and the Jewish state of Israel. Egypt's Gamal Abdel Nasser sought to assume leadership of the Arab world and to take over the Suez Canal from Britain. His willingness to accept Russian aid in achieving these ambitions brought Egypt into conflict with the western powers. Nasser refused to adhere to the Baghdad Pact of 1955, an American effort to establish a Middle East anticommunist alliance. When the United States withdrew promised support for his great Aswan Dam irrigation project, Nasser accepted Russian aid and also (1956) seized the Suez Canal. Britain, France, and Israel then attacked Egypt. However, Russian threats and American disapproval forced them to withdraw, leaving Nasser master of Suez. Nevertheless, the United States managed to maintain a balance of power in the Middle East. When pro-Nasser elements tried to take over Lebanon in 1958, 14,000 Marines were sent in, and the pro-American government was saved. Yet the Middle East remained troubled. A 1963 clash between Turkey and Greece over Cyprus was typical of the difficulties the United States faced in the area, for both Greece and Turkey were American allies, and both were firmly anticommunist.

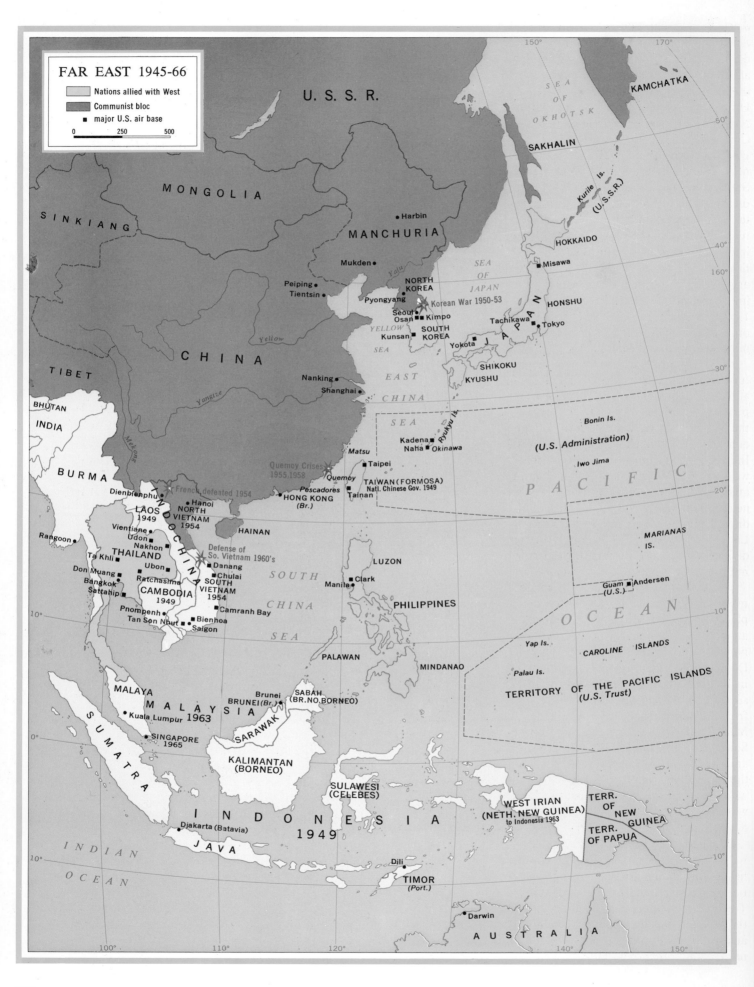

FAR EAST 1945-66

Nations allied with West
Communist bloc
■ major U.S. air base

0 250 500

U.S.S.R.

KAMCHATKA

SEA OF OKHOTSK

SAKHALIN

Kurile Is. (U.S.S.R.)

SINKIANG

MONGOLIA

HOKKAIDO

• Harbin

MANCHURIA

Mukden •

Misawa ■

SEA OF JAPAN

HONSHU

Peiping • NORTH KOREA

JAPAN

Tientsin • Pyongyang

Korean War 1950-53

Tachikawa •

Seoul • • Tokyo

Yalu

Osan ■ ■ Kimpo

SOUTH KOREA

Kunsan ■

Yokota ■

CHINA

SHIKOKU

KYUSHU

Yellow

TIBET

Nanking •

Shanghai •

EAST CHINA SEA

30°

BHUTAN

Bonin Is.

INDIA

Yangtze

Kadena ■ Ryukyu Is.

Naha • • Okinawa

(U.S. Administration)

Iwo Jima

BURMA

Mekong

Matsu •

Quemoy Crises 1955,1958

Quemoy

■ Taipei

TAIWAN (FORMOSA)

Natl. Chinese Gov. 1949

Dienbienphu • INDOCHINA

French defeated 1954

Pescadores •

HONG KONG (Br.)

Tainan •

PACIFIC

20°

• Hanoi

LAOS 1949 NORTH VIETNAM 1954

Rangoon •

Vientiane • Udon ■

Nakhon ■

HAINAN

MARIANAS IS.

Defense of So. Vietnam 1960's

Ta Khli ■ THAILAND

Ubon ■

Don Muang ■ Ratchasima ■

Bangkok • SOUTH VIETNAM 1954

Sattahip • CAMBODIA 1949

Danang ■

Chulai ■

SOUTH CHINA SEA

LUZON

Manila • ■ Clark

Guam • Andersen ■ (U.S.)

OCEAN

10°

PHILIPPINES

Pnompenh • Camranh Bay •

Tan Son Nhut ■ Bienhoa ■

Saigon •

Yap Is. •

CAROLINE ISLANDS

PALAWAN

MINDANAO

Palau Is. •

TERRITORY OF THE PACIFIC ISLANDS (U.S. Trust)

10°

MALAYA

Brunei •

BRUNEI (Br.)

SABAH (BR.NO.BORNEO)

M A L A Y S I A

• Kuala Lumpur 1963

SARAWAK

SINGAPORE 1965

SUMATRA

KALIMANTAN (BORNEO)

0°

SULAWESI (CELEBES)

WEST IRIAN (NETH. NEW GUINEA) to Indonesia 1963

TERR. OF NEW GUINEA

I N D O N E S I A

TERR. OF PAPUA

INDIAN OCEAN

• Djakarta (Batavia)

1949

JAVA

10°

• Dili

TIMOR (Port.)

• Darwin

A U S T R A L I A

100°   110°   120°   140°   150°

Just as Russian power has influenced American actions in Europe and the Middle East, so the power of Red China has affected American policy in every part of the Orient. During World War II the United States had naturally supported the Nationalist regime of Chiang Kai-shek in China. When Chiang's government collapsed before the onslaughts of the Chinese communists in 1949, the United States continued to support it in its refuge on the island of Taiwan, much to the irritation of the communists. Then the Korean War established Red China as an implacable enemy. Meaningless American threats to "unleash" Chiang's Nationalist army against the mainland did nothing to improve relations. In 1955 and again in 1958 Red Chinese shelling of Quemoy and other Nationalist-held islands just off the mainland produced serious crises.

American problems in the Far East were further exacerbated by the nationalist and anticolonial feelings of nearly all Asiatic peoples. After the war, patriot forces in the Netherlands East Indies won their independence, establishing the Republic of Indonesia. In French Indochina, rebels won a shattering victory at Dienbienphu, after which a 19-nation conference at Geneva prepared the way for French withdrawal and the division of Indochina into Laos, Cambodia, and Vietnam, the latter divided along the 17th parallel into communist and pro-western regimes.

While favoring Asiatic independence movements in principle, the United States placed the frustration of Red China above all other considerations. In South Vietnam it backed the unpopular Ngo Dinh Diem simply because he was anticommunist. When rebel (Viet Cong) guerrillas, supported by men and supplies brought from North Vietnam over the Ho Chi Minh Trail, won control of much of rural South Vietnam, the U.S. threw air power and the Seventh Fleet into the battle, and then increasing numbers of troops, but without achieving decisive results. Diem was assassinated, but his successors failed to win much popular support.

By early 1966 about 250,000 Americans were fighting in Vietnam. Casualties were heavy. But offers to end the war by negotiation were rejected by the communists. The United States remained committed to the struggle, but how long it would last, and what the ultimate outcome would be, no one could then predict.

CONFLICT *in the* FAR EAST

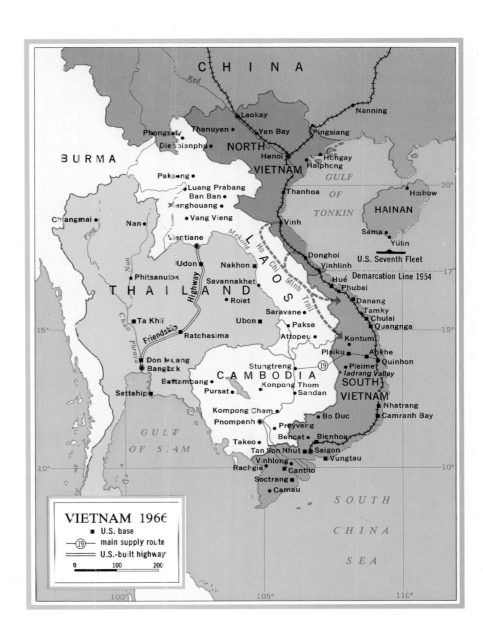

VIETNAM 1966

■ U.S. base

⑲ main supply route

= U.S.-built highway

0   100   200

323

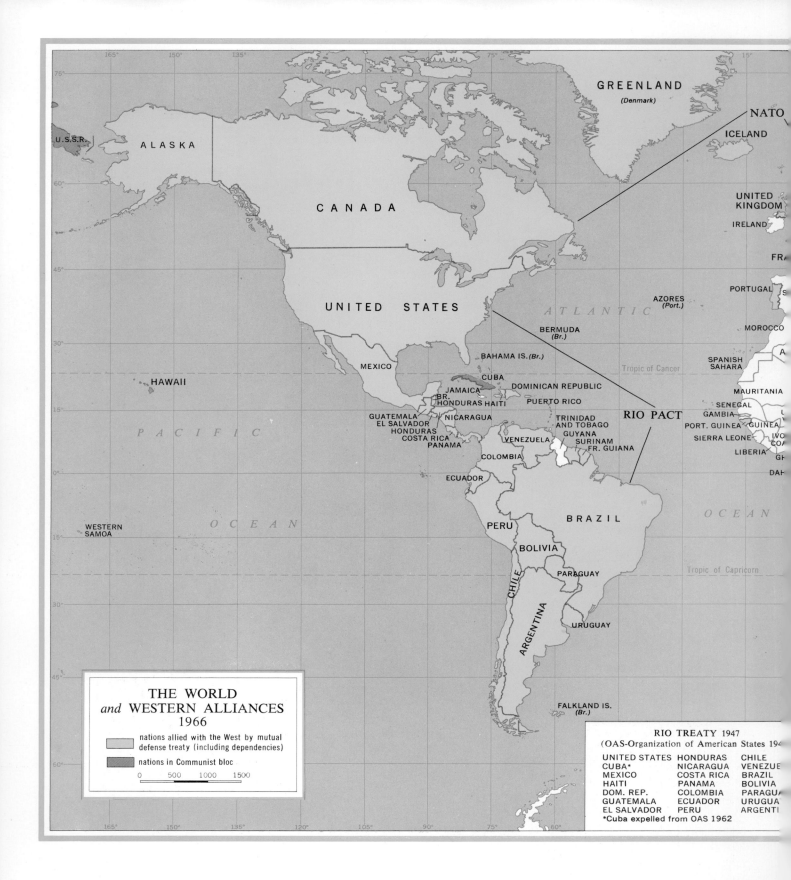

THE WORLD and WESTERN ALLIANCES 1966

☐ nations allied with the West by mutual defense treaty (including dependencies)

■ nations in Communist bloc

0   500   1000   1500

RIO TREATY 1947
(OAS-Organization of American States 194

UNITED STATES	HONDURAS	CHILE
CUBA*	NICARAGUA	VENEZUE
MEXICO	COSTA RICA	BRAZIL
HAITI	PANAMA	BOLIVIA
DOM. REP.	COLOMBIA	PARAGUA
GUATEMALA	ECUADOR	URUGUA
EL SALVADOR	PERU	ARGENTI

*Cuba expelled from OAS 1962

COMMITMENTS *to* FREEDOM

That American isolationism is dead has become a truism; the merest glance at the above map reveals the extent of America's world commitments as of 1966. The various interlocking alliances were in part by-products of the cold war between democracy and communism. The Rio Treaty was designed to combat communist subversion in the Western

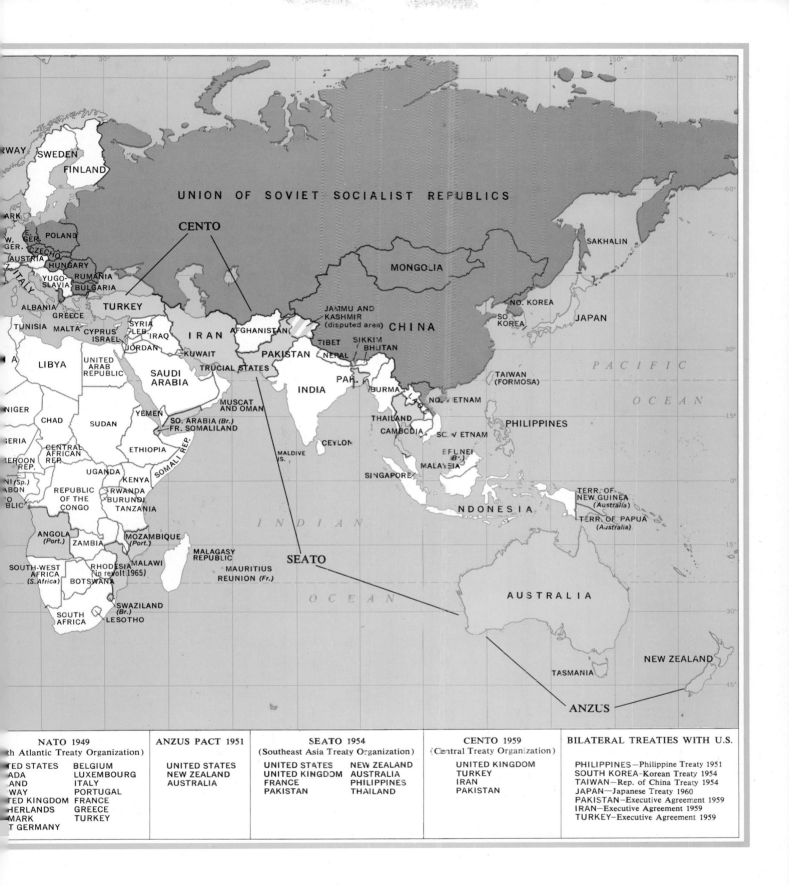

NATO 1949 (th Atlantic Treaty Organization)		ANZUS PACT 1951	SEATO 1954 (Southeast Asia Treaty Organization)		CENTO 1959 (Central Treaty Organization)	BILATERAL TREATIES WITH U.S.
TED STATES	BELGIUM	UNITED STATES	UNITED STATES	NEW ZEALAND	UNITED KINGDOM	PHILIPPINES—Philippine Treaty 1951
ADA	LUXEMBOURG	NEW ZEALAND	UNITED KINGDOM	AUSTRALIA	TURKEY	SOUTH KOREA-Korean Treaty 1954
AND	ITALY	AUSTRALIA	FRANCE	PHILIPPINES	IRAN	TAIWAN—Rep. of China Treaty 1954
WAY	PORTUGAL		PAKISTAN	THAILAND	PAKISTAN	JAPAN—Japanese Treaty 1960
TED KINGDOM	FRANCE					PAKISTAN—Executive Agreement 1959
HERLANDS	GREECE					IRAN—Executive Agreement 1959
MARK	TURKEY					TURKEY—Executive Agreement 1959
T GERMANY						

Hemisphere, NATO to guarantee Western Europe against Russian invasion. SEATO was the response to communist successes in Indochina, CENTO an effort to block Russian penetration of the Arab world. The Anzus Pact and the bilateral treaties with the Asiatic nations were also responses to the need for military co-operation in the postwar world.

Yet, in historical perspective, these alliances will probably seem more significant as indications of the growing interdependence of all nations. Internal disagreements may weaken NATO, the OAS, and the communist bloc as well, but the need for all nations to accommodate themselves to one another is likely to increase steadily.

SECURITY
of the
NATION

Efforts to make the United States militarily secure have rested, since the end of World War II, on increasingly complex global networks of air, naval, and ground troop bases, missile tracking and firing sites, radar warning lines, and sophisticated computer systems that, among other things, have speeded up world-wide command and control of numerous elements of defense and retaliation. Integrated with the commitments to defend other nations in every part of the world, these networks have entailed close co-operation among industry, science, and the military, and have required the annual expenditure of tens of billions of dollars.

Initially, after World War II, American defense relied primarily on the deterrent power of the intercontinental bombers of the Strategic Air Command (SAC), with headquarters at Omaha. The threat of these nuclear bomb-carrying planes, based by treaty in many friendly countries, would, it was believed, deter any enemy from attacking the U.S. In the 1950's, lines of radar stations (the Pinetree, Mid-Canada, and DEW—Distant Early Warning—lines) were erected across North America to guard the northern air approaches to the continent. On the flanks, the warning system was extended across the northern Atlantic and Pacific by the use of radar-equipped picket ships and planes that flew out of Argentia, Newfoundland, and Alaska. The space age development of rockets and missiles led to new systems, whose heart by 1966 was a greatly expanded headquarters of the U.S.-Canadian North American Air Defense Command (NORAD), located in chambers of concrete and shockproof steel within a granitic mountain near Colorado Springs. Supplementing the aircraft-watching DEW Line were the Ballistic Missile Early Warning System (BMEWS), whose radar screens at Clear in Alaska, Thule in Greenland, and Flyingdales Moor in England could detect the launching of missiles by an enemy 3,000 miles away; the U.S. Naval Space Surveillance System (SPASUR) across the southern U.S.; the Air Force's Spacetrack installations on Shemya Island in the Aleutians and at Moorestown, New Jersey; and a contiguous radar coverage maintained around the entire United States by the Air Force.

The warning systems in 1966 could alert civil defense and antiaircraft missile and aviation interceptor units, as well as set in motion the retaliatory blows of SAC planes (now at some 42 bases around the world) and intercontinental missiles and atomic missile-firing submarines. But still in the offing were antimissile missiles (the Nike-X) and defenses against weapons in space.

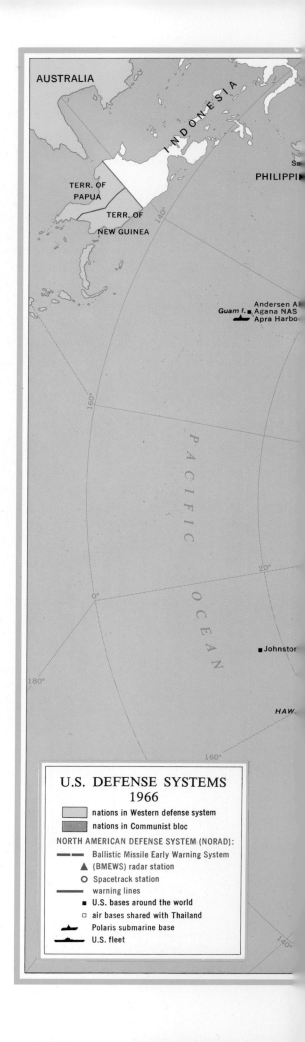

**U.S. DEFENSE SYSTEMS
1966**

- nations in Western defense system
- nations in Communist bloc

NORTH AMERICAN DEFENSE SYSTEM (NORAD):
- ▬ ▬ Ballistic Missile Early Warning System
- ▲ (BMEWS) radar station
- O Spacetrack station
- ▬ warning lines
- ■ U.S. bases around the world
- □ air bases shared with Thailand
- Polaris submarine base
- U.S. fleet

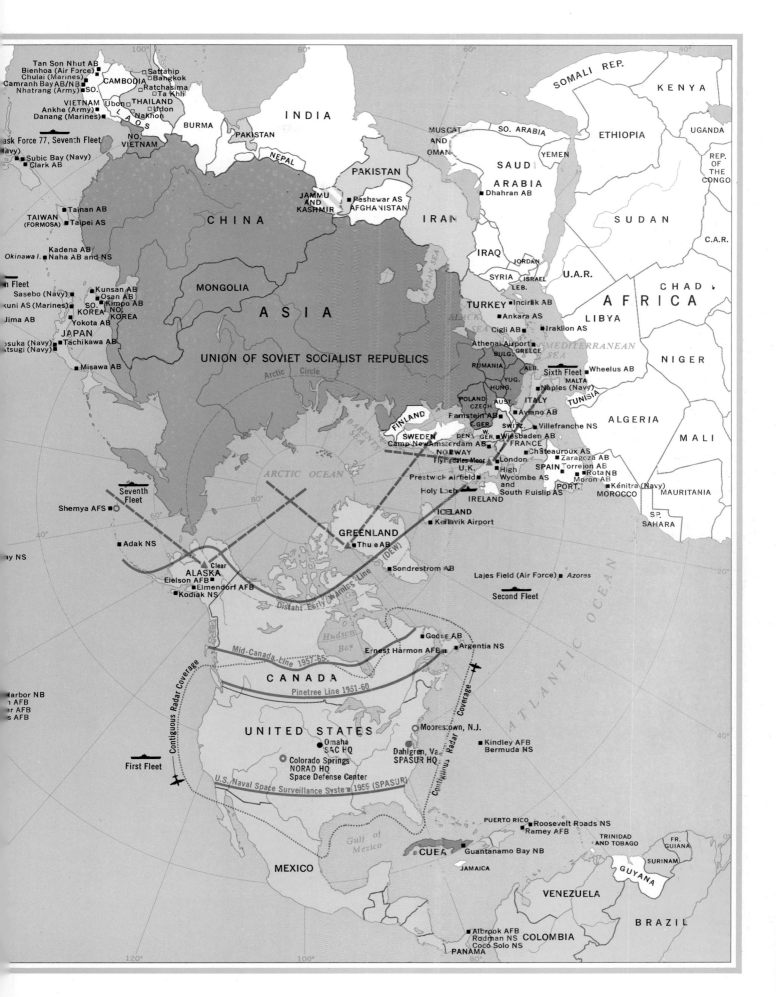

Tan Son Nhut AB
Bienhoa (Air Force)
Chulai (Marines)
Camranh Bay AB/NB
Nhatrang (Army)
CAMBODIA
SO.
VIETNAM
Ubon
Ankhe (Army)
Danang (Marines)
LAOS
Nakhon
NO.
VIETNAM
BURMA

Sattahip
Bangkok
Ratchasima
Ta Khli
THAILAND
Udon

ask Force 77, Seventh Fleet
Navy)

Subic Bay (Navy)
Clark AB

TAIWAN
(FORMOSA)
Tainan AB
Taipei AS

Kadena AB
Okinawa I.
Naha AB and NS

Fleet
Sasebo (Navy)
Kunsan AB
kuni AS (Marines)
Jima AB
JAPAN
suka (Navy)
tsugi (Navy)

Osan AB
SO.
KOREA
Kimpo AB
NO.
KOREA
Yokota AB
Tachikawa AB

Misawa AB

INDIA
PAKISTAN
NEPAL

CHINA

MONGOLIA

ASIA

UNION OF SOVIET SOCIALIST REPUBLICS

Arctic   Circle

JAMMU
AND
KASHMIR
Peshawar AS
AFGHANISTAN

IRAN

IRAQ

SYRIA
LEB.
JORDAN
ISRAEL

MUSCAT
AND
OMAN
SO. ARABIA
YEMEN

SAUDI
ARABIA
Dhahran AB

SOMALI REP.

KENYA

ETHIOPIA
UGANDA

SUDAN

REP.
OF
THE
CONGO
C.A.R.

U.A.R.

AFRICA

CHAD

LIBYA

NIGER

TURKEY
Incirlik AB
Ankara AS
Cigli AB
Iraklion AS

Athenai Airport
GREECE
BULG.
RUMANIA
YUG.
HUNG.
POLAND
CZECH
AUST.
ITALY
Kaiserslautern AB
E. GER.
W.
GER.
SWITZ.

BLACK SEA

MEDITERRANEAN
SEA

Sixth Fleet
Wheelus AB
MALTA
Naples (Navy)
Aviano AB
Villefranche NS
Châteauroux AS
Zaragoza AB
SPAIN
Torrejon AB
Rota NB
Moron AB
Kénitra (Navy)
MOROCCO
MAURITANIA
SP.
SAHARA
PORT.

ALGERIA

MALI

TUNISIA

FINLAND

SWEDEN
NORWAY
Camp New Amsterdam AB
FRANCE
Fly dales Moor
London
U.K.
High
Wycombe AS
and
South Ruislip AS
Prestwick airfield
Holy Loch
IRELAND

ICELAND
Keflavik Airport

ARCTIC OCEAN

BARENTS SEA

GREENLAND
Thule AB
(DEW)
Sondrestrom AB

Seventh
Fleet
Shemya AFS

Adak NS

ay NS

Clear
ALASKA
Eielson AFB
Elmendorf AFB
Kodiak NS

Distant Early Warning Line

Lajes Field (Air Force)   Azores

Second Fleet

Hudson
Bay

Goose AB
Ernest Harmon AFB
Argentia NS

Mid-Canada Line 1957-65

CANADA

Pinetree Line 1951-60

ATLANTIC OCEAN

Harbor NB
AFB
er AFB
s AFB

First Fleet

Contiguous Radar Coverage

UNITED STATES

Omaha
SAC HQ

Colorado Springs
NORAD HQ
Space Defense Center

U.S. Naval Space Surveillance Syste 1959 (SPASUR)

Moores town, N.J.

Dahlgren, Va.
SPASUR HQ

Kindley AFB
Bermuda NS

Continuous Radar Coverage

Gulf of
Mexico

MEXICO

CUBA
Guantanamo Bay NB
JAMAICA

PUERTO RICO
Roosevelt Roads NS
Ramey AFB

TRINIDAD
AND TOBAGO

FR.
GUIANA

GUYANA
SURINAM

VENEZUELA

Albrook AFB
Rodman NS
Coco Solo NS
PANAMA
COLOMBIA

BRAZIL

327

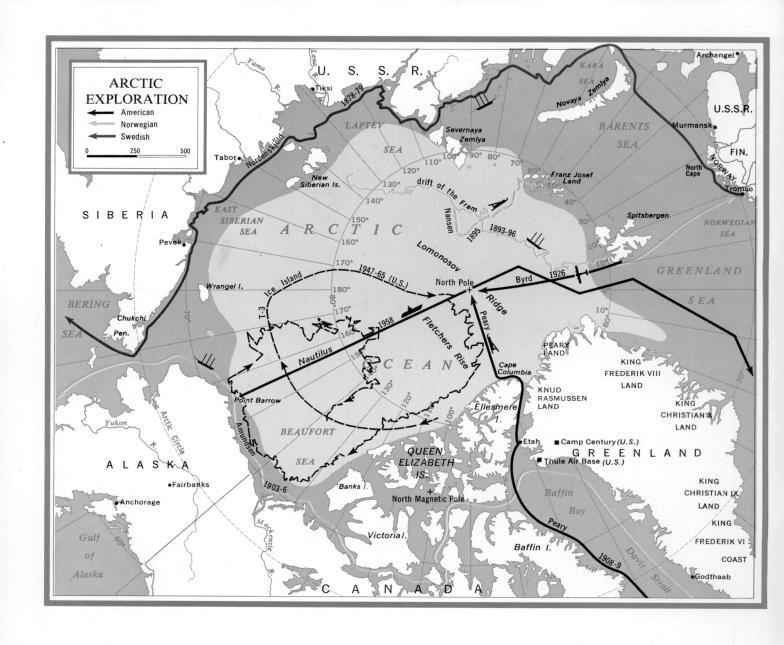

EXPLORING
the
POLAR REGIONS

In 1946 a U.S. Navy expedition of 4,700 men under Admiral Richard E. Byrd landed in Antarctica. Testing new equipment under polar conditions, exploring unknown areas, and mapping from the air some 60 per cent of the continent's coastline, the mission, called Operation Highjump, inaugurated (with a British scientific group) a postwar era of accelerated interest in the polar regions.

The Arctic had lured explorers since the 16th century, when Europeans had first tried to find a sea route to the Orient through the ice floes and uncharted islands of the North. In 1879 Baron Nils A. E. Nordenskjöld of Sweden, following a northeasterly route above Siberia, reached the Pacific via the Arctic. A northwest passage, the elusive goal of many seamen, was finally discovered by Roald Amundsen of Norway in 1906. Intending to be the first to reach the North Pole itself, Fridtjof Nansen, in the 1890's, allowed his ship, the *Fram,* to become icebound off New Siberian Island; the drifting ice, he thought, would carry it toward the Pole. When he realized he would bypass his goal, he left the ship and trudged across the ice. He failed

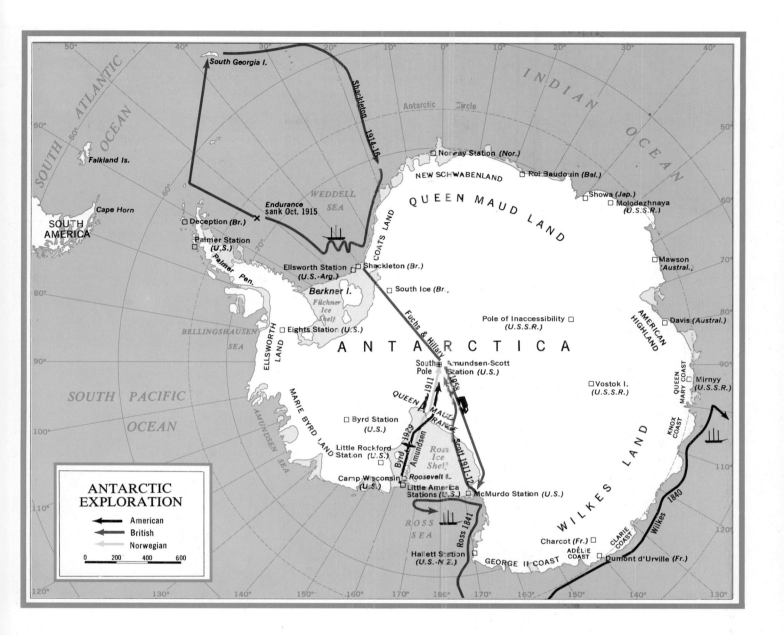

ANTARCTIC
EXPLORATION

→ American
→ British
→ Norwegian

0   200   400   600

to reach the Pole, but survived miraculously to tell about his attempt. It was an American, Admiral Robert E. Peary, who made it to the Pole first, in 1909; in 1926, Richard E. Byrd and Floyd Bennett, his pilot, took off from Spitsbergen in a plane mounted on skis and became the first men to fly over the North Pole.

Today, radar stations and defense installations of both the United States and Russia dot many parts of the Arctic, testifying to the strategic importance of the region. Man's knowledge of the area has increased tremendously through the use of such innovations as laboratories on drifting ice islands. (One of them, T-3, has been closely watched since 1947.) In 1958 the U.S. atomic submarine *Nautilus* sailed submerged across the Arctic and past the Pole, and today even civilians fly casually across the once unattainable area in planes following the polar route to Europe.

The Antarctic, however, is still remote to all but scientists and military explorers. The map bears the names of many men whose willingness to risk death for knowledge or adventure brought them to the region: Lieutenant Charles

Wilkes of the United States Navy, whose exploring expedition, 1838–42, proved that the Antarctic was a continent; Sir James Clark Ross, who discovered the sea and ice shelf now named for him; Robert Scott of England, who journeyed to the South Pole in 1912, only to discover there a note from Amundsen who had preceded him by a few weeks; Sir Ernest Shackleton, who made several trips to the Antarctic, including one in 1915 during which his ship, the *Endurance*, was sunk by ice, forcing him to continue by foot and in a small boat to South Georgia Island; and many others. In 1929 Richard Byrd, who was to lead several expeditions to the southern continent, duplicated his North Pole feat by becoming the first to fly over the South Pole.

Antarctic exploration reached a peak during the International Geophysical Year, 1957–58, when 50 bases, manned by scientists of 12 nations, were established there. The year was climaxed by the first crossing of the continent, by Vivian Fuchs and Edmund Hillary. Several nations now claim portions of Antarctica, which man may some day be able to make habitable for large numbers of people.

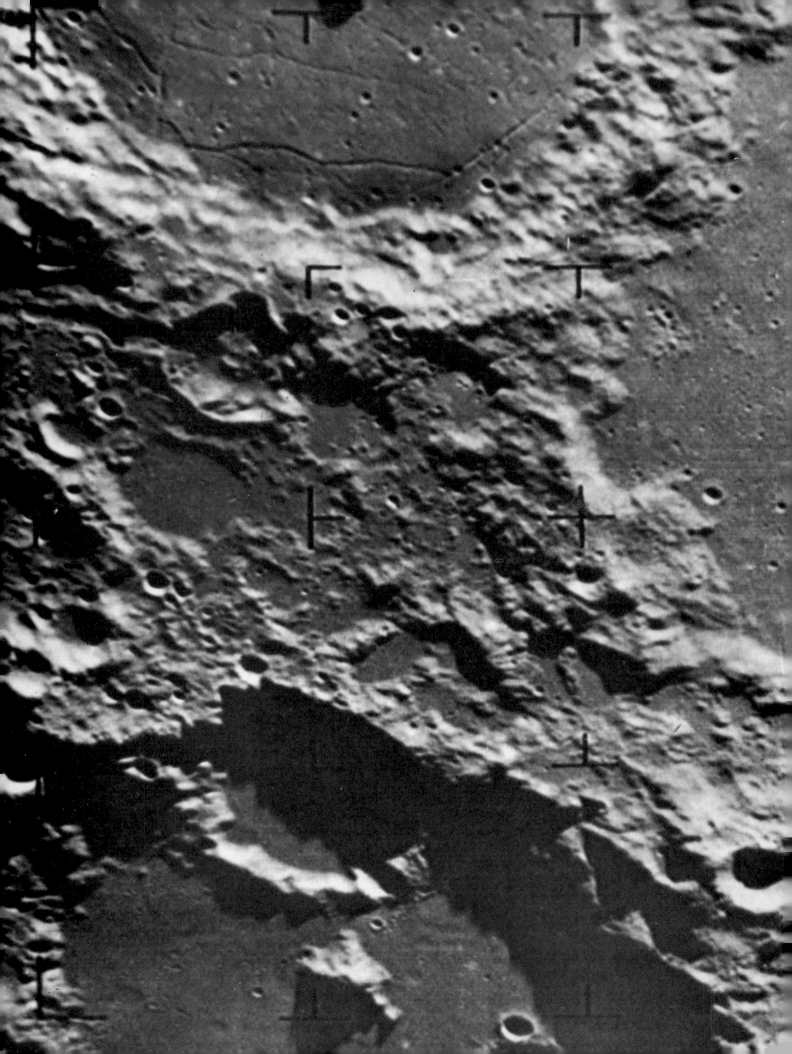

A new chapter in history began on October 4, 1957, when the Soviet satellite, Sputnik I, orbited the earth. On January 31, 1958, the United States sent aloft its own first satellite, Explorer I. After that, the rapidity of the conquest of space made it clear that man was truly on the threshold of reaching the moon and planets. These photos— in effect, exploratory maps—were made by U.S. spacecraft: at left, the topography of 18,000 square miles of the moon was pictured at a distance of 775 miles by Ranger IX, about to impact on March 24, 1965; above are 25,500 square miles of the surface of Mars viewed from only 6,000 miles away by Mariner IV on July 14, 1965.

TO *the* MOON *and* PLANETS

POPULATION
EXPLOSION

By 1941, at the end of a long depression, the population of the United States seemed to be stabilizing itself. During each decade from 1890 to 1930, the country had grown by about 15 million inhabitants, but in the thirties the increase had dropped sharply to under 9 million. Immigration had been reduced to a trickle by restrictive legislation, and Americans, hard-pressed financially, were having fewer children. Between 1929 and 1941 the size of the average family dropped from 4.03 persons to 3.7.

However, with the return of prosperity and the outbreak of World War II, a reversal of this trend occurred. The rate of population increase, under a million a year in the 1930's,

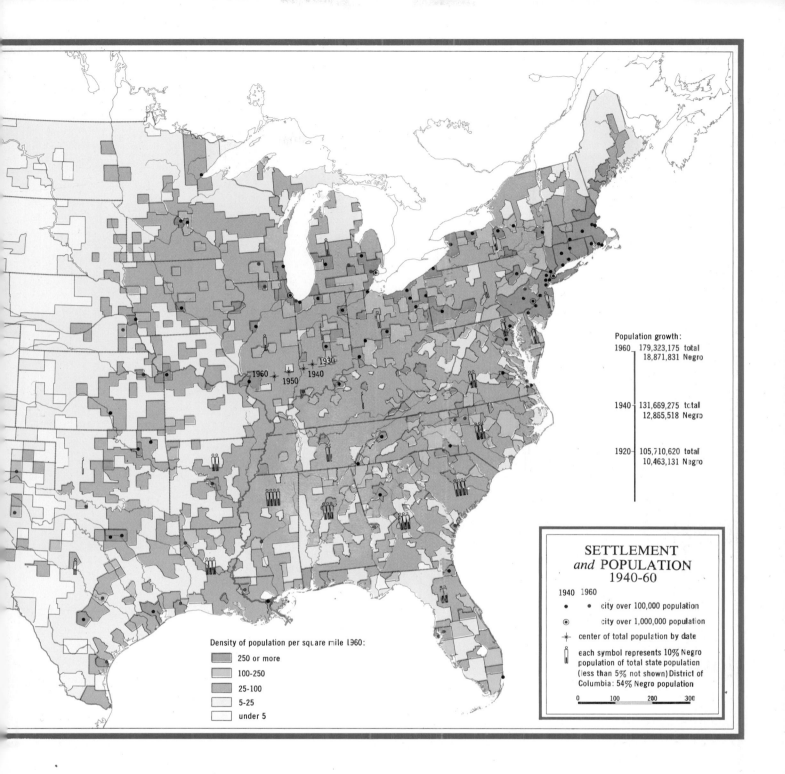

Population growth:
1960	179,323,175 total
	18,871,831 Negro
1940	131,669,275 total
	12,865,518 Negro
1920	105,710,620 total
	10,463,131 Negro

SETTLEMENT
and POPULATION
1940-60

1940 1960

•   • city over 100,000 population

⊙   ⊙ city over 1,000,000 population

✦ center of total population by date

each symbol represents 10% Negro
population of total state population
(less than 5% not shown) District of
Columbia: 54% Negro population

0   100   200   300

Density of population per square mile 1960:

- ▓ 250 or more
- ▒ 100-250
- ▓ 25-100
- ░ 5-25
- □ under 5

jumped to 3 million a year in 1946 and continued at this rate into the mid-sixties. The per cent increase of the population in the 1950's was 18.5, the highest since the first decade of the century. By the sixties, demographers were talking ominously of the "population explosion" and predicting that by the year 2000 the nation would have at least 280 million people, perhaps as many as 360 million.

Rapid growth meant further urbanization. In the Northeast, cities grew so large that they began to overlap one another: the area between Boston and Washington became a vast megalopolis, posing a whole series of problems for urban planners, municipal officials, and plain citizens seeking fresh air and greenery. According to the 1960 census, more than two-thirds of the American people were living in urban communities. However, urbanization was not, as in earlier periods, largely confined to the eastern part of the nation. The West experienced a fantastic boom. California alone grew from 6.9 million people to nearly 16 million between 1940 and 1960. Los Angeles, with over 2.4 million inhabitants, was the third largest city in the land. This migration caused the geographical center of population to resume its westward march, which had almost stopped after 1910. By 1960 it was in south-central Illinois, about 75 miles east of St. Louis (50 miles if Hawaii and Alaska are included).

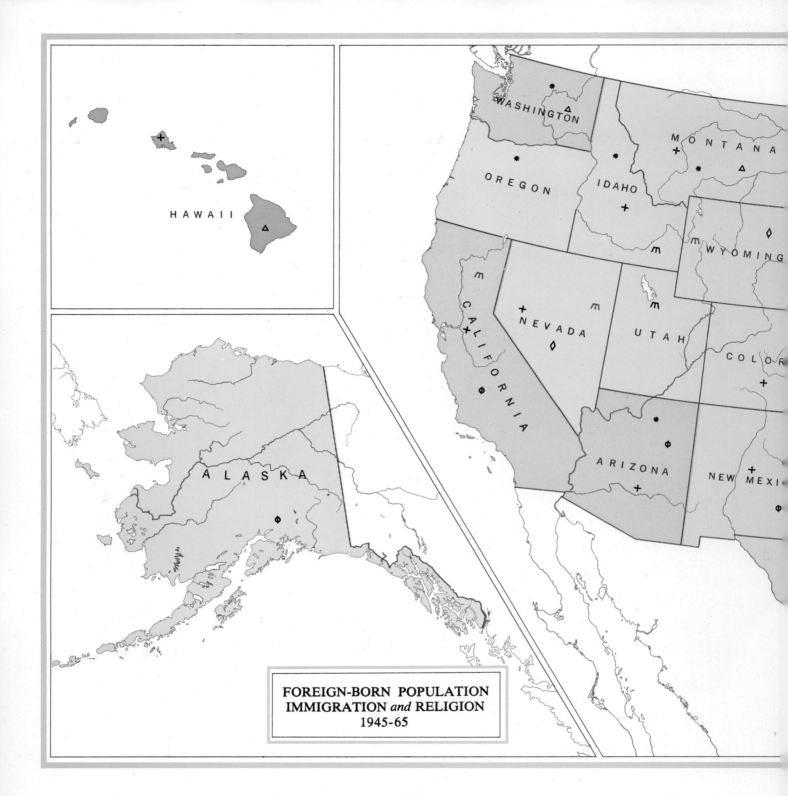

FOREIGN-BORN POPULATION
IMMIGRATION *and* RELIGION
1945-65

RESTRICTION *of* NEWCOMERS

When the influx of immigrants, checked during the First World War, resumed with a rush in 1920, sentiment quickly developed for passing restrictive legislation. A series of laws in the 1920's reduced the flow from 805,000 in 1921 to well below 100,000 a year in the thirties and early forties. These laws set a total limit on annual immigration, and assigned quotas based on nationality, the theory being that persons of some countries would make more desirable citizens than those of certain others. The system heavily favored persons from northern and western Europe. Ireland, with a popula-

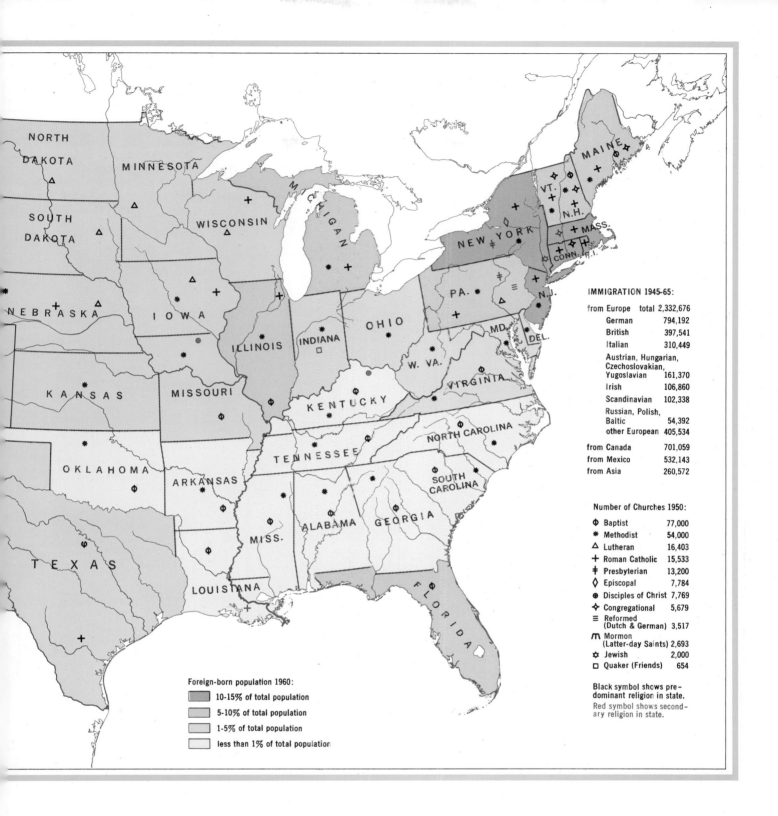

IMMIGRATION 1945-65:

from Europe	total	2,332,676
German		794,192
British		397,541
Italian		310,449
Austrian, Hungarian, Czechoslovakian, Yugoslavian		161,370
Irish		106,860
Scandinavian		102,338
Russian, Polish, Baltic		54,392
other European		405,534
from Canada		701,059
from Mexico		532,143
from Asia		260,572

Number of Churches 1950:

Φ	Baptist	77,000
✳	Methodist	54,000
△	Lutheran	16,403
+	Roman Catholic	15,533
‡	Presbyterian	13,200
◇	Episcopal	7,784
⊕	Disciples of Christ	7,769
✧	Congregational	5,679
≡	Reformed (Dutch & German)	3,517
⋔	Mormon (Latter-day Saints)	2,693
✡	Jewish	2,000
□	Quaker (Friends)	654

Black symbol shows predominant religion in state.
Red symbol shows secondary religion in state.

Foreign-born population 1960:

■ 10-15% of total population
▨ 5-10% of total population
▧ 1-5% of total population
□ less than 1% of total population

tion of under 3 million in 1960, had an annual quota of over 17,000, while Yugoslavia, with 18.5 million people, had a quota of under 1,000. Thus, many countries did not fill their allotments, while tens of thousands of persons from other lands waited for years to obtain admittance.

After World War II, pressure for easing these restrictions led to the admission of displaced persons and other refugees —about 680,000 in all since 1948—and finally, in 1966, to the abolition of the insulting national origins system. However, a limitation on total immigration from countries out-side the Western Hemisphere was retained. Only 800,000 persons had been admitted between 1931 and 1945, but 4.4 million entered between 1945 and 1965. Nevertheless, the foreign-born population declined sharply, from 14.2 million in 1930 to 9.7 million in 1960.

By 1963 the churches of the United States could claim over 120 million members. The Roman Catholics remained the largest single group, with nearly 45 million communicants, but the many Protestant sects retained their collective lead, with more than 66 million members.

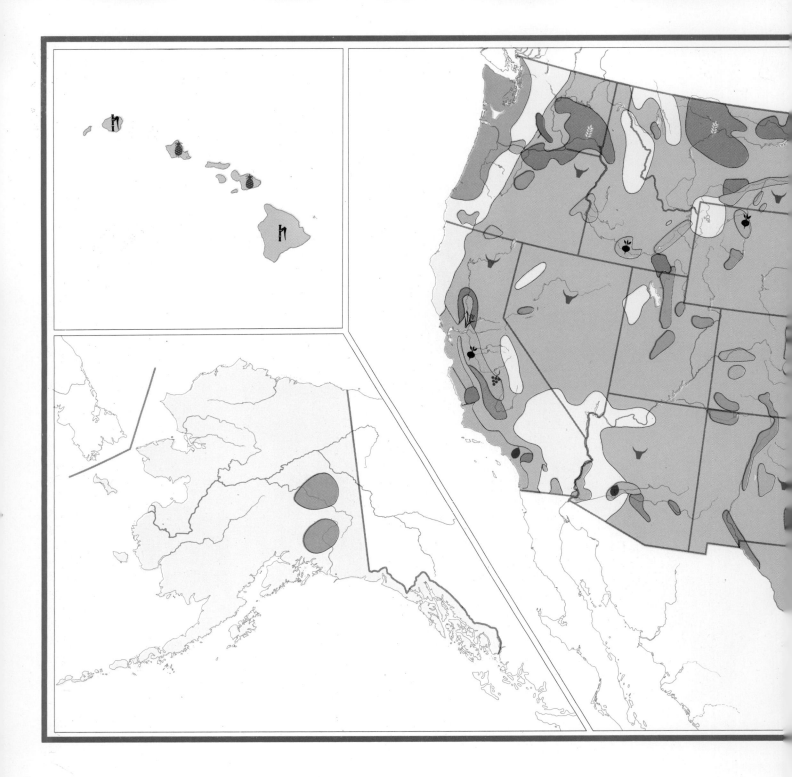

THE NEW AGRICULTURE

No startling geographical shifts occurred in American agriculture between 1920 and 1960, yet in that period farming underwent the most revolutionary changes of its entire history. The number of farms declined precipitously from 6.5 million to under 4 million, and farm employment dropped from 13.4 million to 7 million persons. During World War II, at least 2 million farmers abandoned the land.

In spite of this decline, agricultural production zoomed—from an index (1947–49 = 100) of 70 to 124. Although the government imposed rigorous quotas on the amount of land cultivated, corn production increased from 3 billion bushels to 4.3 billion, wheat from 843 million bushels to 1.3 billion.

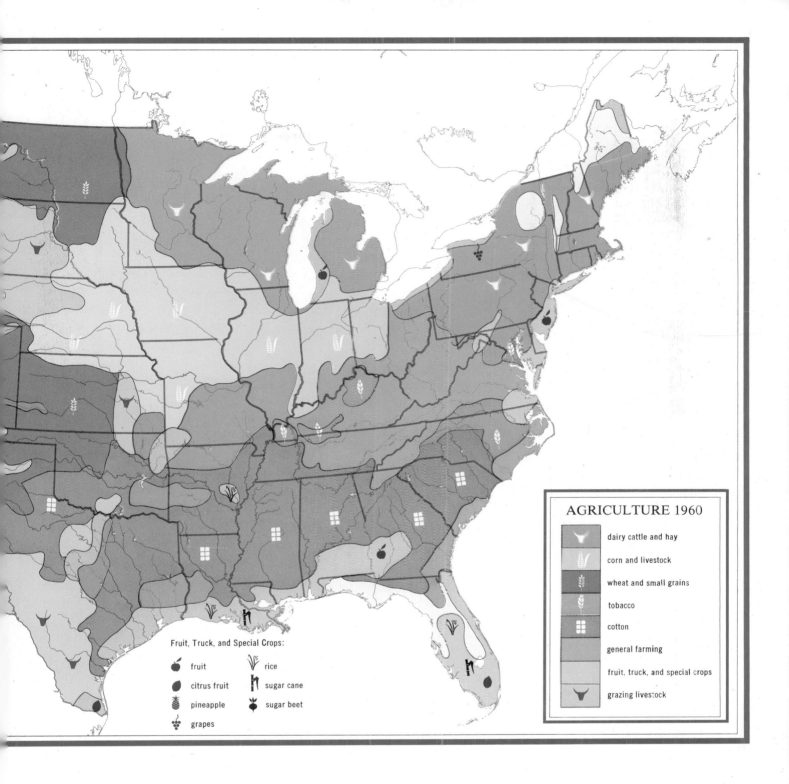

AGRICULTURE 1960

- dairy cattle and hay
- corn and livestock
- wheat and small grains
- tobacco
- cotton
- general farming
- fruit, truck, and special crops
- grazing livestock

Fruit, Truck, and Special Crops:

- fruit
- citrus fruit
- pineapple
- grapes
- rice
- sugar cane
- sugar beet

In 1920 cotton farmers harvested 13 million bales from 34 million acres; in 1960 they harvested 14.2 million bales from a mere 15 million acres.

This enormous increase in agricultural efficiency was the result of technological and scientific revolutions. Farmers increased their already large use of machinery. The consumption of fertilizers almost quadrupled, and the number of acres in dry regions made fertile through irrigation more than doubled. New weed killers and insecticides cut down drastically on crop losses, and scientific breeding, better feeds, and antibiotics produced healthier and meatier livestock. Economists estimate that gross farm output per man-hour of labor rose from an index (1947–49 = 100) of 49 in 1920 to an amazing 213 in 1960, an increase that makes the efficiency of American industrial production almost pale into insignificance. Indeed, it might be said that American farms were becoming food factories; they were larger in size on the average, despite the rise in land values, and were organized on highly efficient lines.

However, efficiency did not always produce prosperity. Farmers suffered heavily in the twenties and throughout the depression. Since then, government price supports and crop quotas have alleviated many of their difficulties, but their share of the national income has declined steadily.

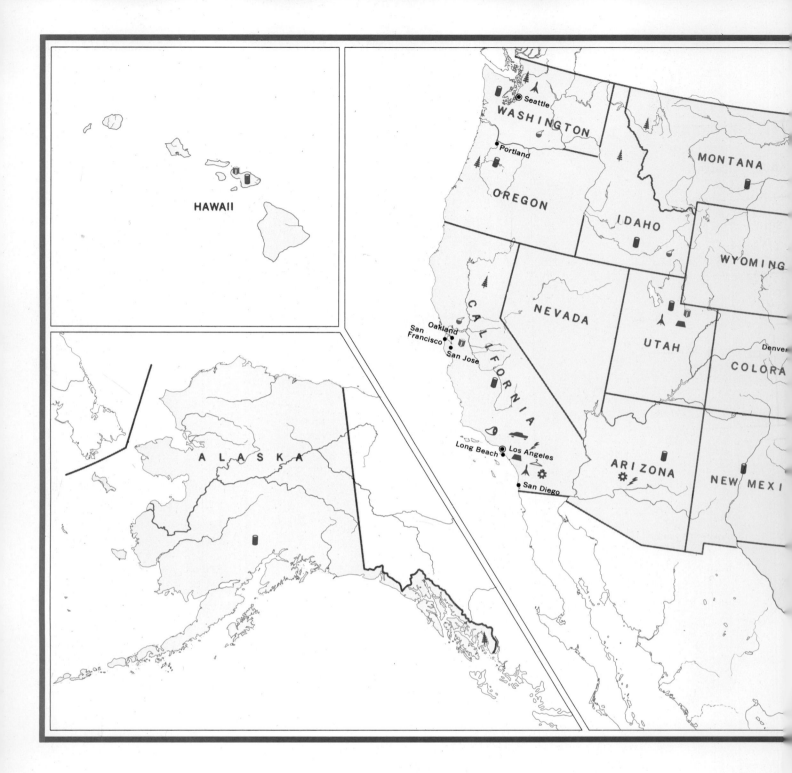

AN INDUSTRIAL NATION

Between 1920 and 1960 American industry passed through three distinct phases. The first, the decade of the twenties, was a time of great prosperity, marked by the flourishing of the automobile industry and the rise of chemical manufacturing and the radio and motion-picture businesses to major rank. The second phase was that of the great depression of the thirties, years of stagnation, when new investment—continually from $2–$3 billion a year during the late twenties—fell to as little as half a billion a year. At the low point, 1932, steel production was down to 13.5 million tons from 56 million and automobile sales suffered a proportionate decline. Then, with the outbreak of World War II, industry em-

INDUSTRY 1960

Principal industries:

- ✿ metal products and machinery
- ⬛ ironworks and steelworks
- ⚙ aircraft and missiles
- 🚗 motor vehicles and parts
- 📖 printing and publishing
- 👔 clothing
- 🔺 textiles
- ⚗ chemicals and allied products
- 🌲 lumber and wood products
- 🥩 slaughtering and meat packing
- 🛢 food processing
- ⚡ electronic components

Principal manufacturing cities:
- ◉ value of manufactures over $1,000,000,000
- • value of manufactures over $100,000,000

barked upon the greatest expansive spurt of all time, one that actually accelerated when the war ended. After 1949, automobile sales averaged well over 5 million a year, and steel production was close to 90 million tons. By 1960 the index of manufacturing production had risen 63 per cent over the level of 1949, which itself was nearly double the level of 1939.

Electronics, aircraft production, and a new space industry triggered the postwar boom. While these industries were scattered all over the country, from Florida to Washington State and from California to New England, their greatest concentration was in the Far West. If the Northeast re-

mained the most important manufacturing section, its virtual monopoly was fast disappearing. The newer industries reflected trends that were transforming all manufacturing: use of automatic machinery, emphasis on skilled labor and scientific research, and an increasing role played by the Federal government both as a designer and a purchaser of manufactured products.

America continued to become more urbanized, being about 70 per cent so by 1960. Even the Far West was dotted by metropolitan centers, from the Los Angeles area, with over 6 million residents, through San Francisco, San Diego, Houston, and Seattle, to Denver, with nearly a million.

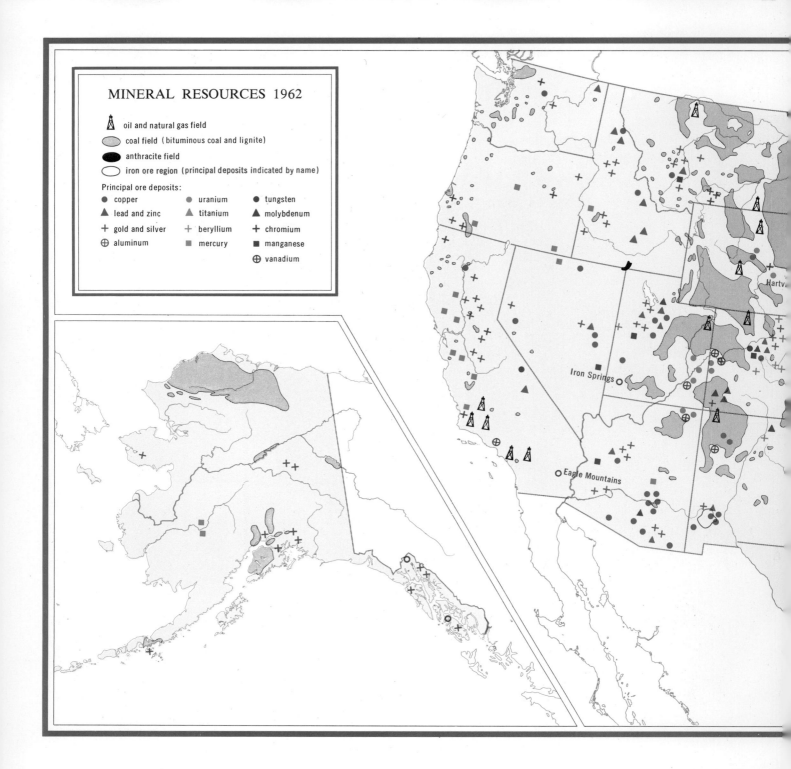

Hartv

Iron Springs ○

○ Eagle Mountains

RICHES *from the* GROUND

The wealth and power of the United States rest, to a large extent, on the amount and variety of its mineral resources. Despite years of thoughtless extraction, these natural bounties continue to provide enormous wealth—in 1962 the total approached $19 billion.

Petroleum is by far the most valuable mineral in the nation; in 1962, 2.6 billion barrels, worth over $7.7 billion, were extracted, principally in Texas, Louisiana, Oklahoma, and California. Annual coal production, which exceeded 100 million tons as early as 1883 and about 500 million tons regularly after about 1910, still tops 400 million tons. Although there have been no major gold strikes since the rush

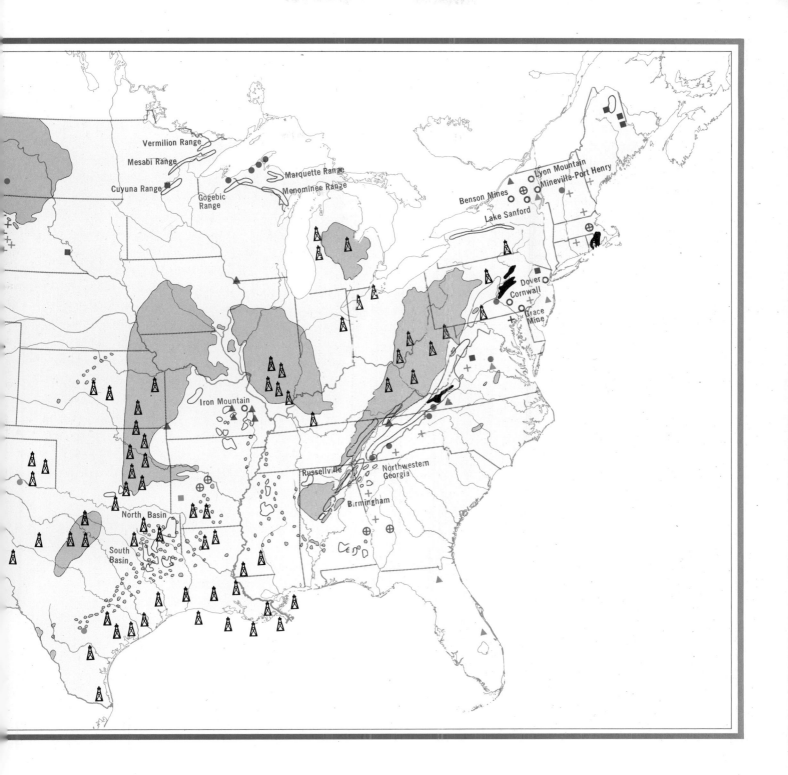

to Alaska in the late 1890's, the all-time high in gold production came in 1940, and output still exceeds 1.5 million ounces a year. The United States also produces about a quarter of the world's copper, 14 per cent of its iron ore, and large amounts of aluminum, uranium, zinc, lead, and many other metals. Yet none of these minerals approaches in value the worth of the different kinds of stone, or even of the sand and gravel, which is quarried in various parts of the nation each year.

The continuing growth of mineral production, despite the huge amounts taken from the earth over the last 100 years, has stemmed from several factors. Demands for new materials, like uranium, tungsten, and molybdenum, have expanded enormously. Advances in geology have made easier the finding of new deposits. New mining methods have been developed. The technique of offshore drilling, for instance, has opened up vast new oil fields in the Gulf of Mexico. Miners have also reduced labor costs sharply. Although coal production is down only 20 per cent since 1919, the current labor force in the industry is now less than 10 per cent of what it was in 1919. Finally, new refining techniques have made possible the mining of low-grade deposits of many kinds that could not have been extracted profitably in earlier times.

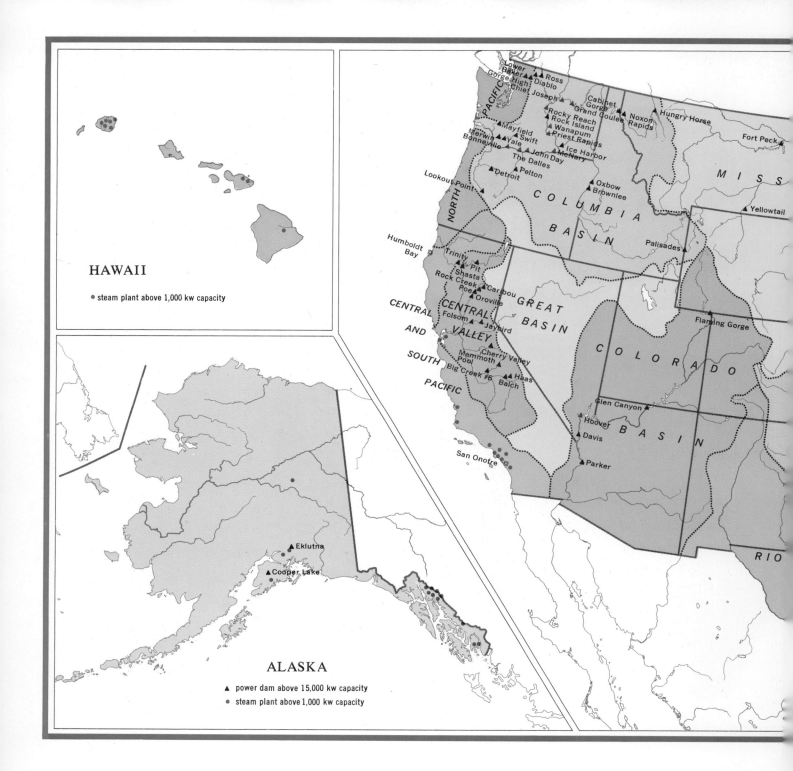

HAWAII

● steam plant above 1,000 kw capacity

ALASKA

▲ power dam above 15,000 kw capacity
● steam plant above 1,000 kw capacity

EXPANDING POWER PRODUCTION

Production of electric power in the United States totaled around five billion kilowatt-hours when the 20th century began. Sixty-five years later it was more than one trillion kilowatt-hours, an increase of better than 20,000 per cent, and it was estimated the demand in 1980 would be for 2.7 trillion kw-hrs. To meet the tremendous need for energy, new and expanding power plants were sown thickly across the map in 1966. The most spectacular were hydroelectric projects, many built on rivers famous in western history. Hoover Dam on the Colorado, at the border of Nevada and Arizona; Bonneville, The Dalles, John Day, and McNary between Oregon and Washington; and Priest Rapids, Wana-

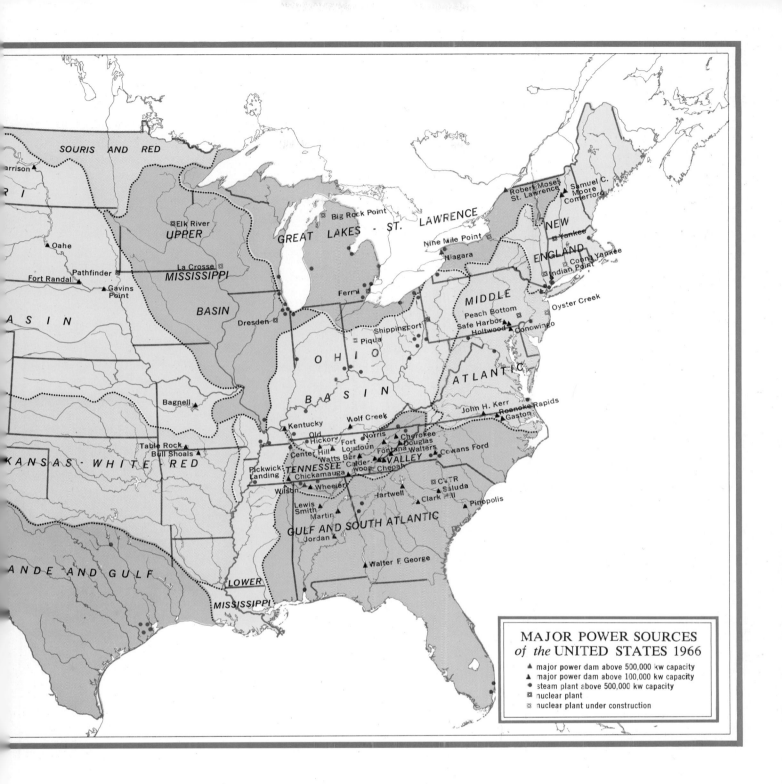

MAJOR POWER SOURCES
of the UNITED STATES 1966

▲ major power dam above 500,000 kw capacity
▲ major power dam above 100,000 kw capacity
● steam plant above 500,000 kw capacity
⊠ nuclear plant
⊠ nuclear plant under construction

pum, Rocky Reach, Chief Joseph, and Grand Coulee, farther up the Columbia River, are among the 25 largest hydroelectric generating plants in the world, with an ultimate capacity of one to more than five million kilowatts. The Niagara plant of the New York State Power Authority also falls in this category.

Regional power administrations and authorities (in the Tennessee Valley, Columbia Basin, Central Valley of California, and elsewhere) regulate the public production of power and its distribution through private utilities, or by municipalities and local co-operatives. Yet all hydroelectric sources combined account for less than 20 per cent of the

nation's production. More than 50 per cent is still created by burning coal in generating plants, more than 20 per cent by burning gas, and around 5 per cent by burning oil. A much smaller fraction comes from the newest and, potentially, an important source: nuclear reactors. In nuclear power plants the heat created by atomic fission is transmitted to steam generators by pressurized water (the most commonly used element), liquid metals, or gases. The first U.S. nuclear power plant began operating in 1957 at Shippingport, near Pittsburgh, Pennsylvania. In 1966 there were 21 others, finished or being constructed, including one at Punta Huegra, Puerto Rico, not shown on the map above.

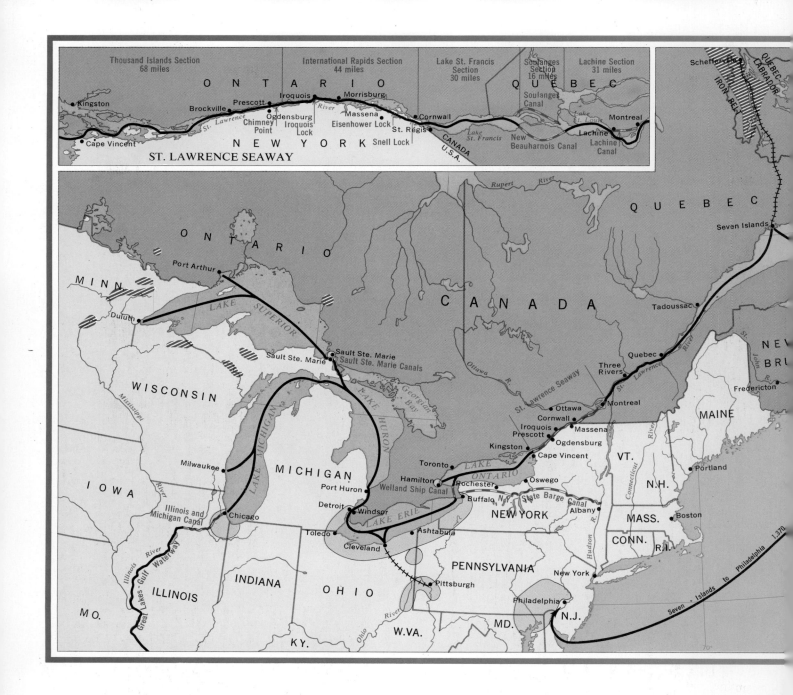

Inset map labels (St. Lawrence Seaway):

Thousand Islands Section 68 miles — International Rapids Section 44 miles — Lake St. Francis Section 30 miles — Soulanges Section 16 miles — Lachine Section 31 miles

ONTARIO — QUEBEC — NEW YORK — CANADA — U.S.A.

Kingston • — Cape Vincent • — Brockville • — Prescott • — Chimney Point — Ogdensburg — Iroquois Lock — Iroquois • — Morrisburg • — Massena • — Eisenhower Lock — Snell Lock — St. Régis • — Cornwall • — St. Lawrence River — Soulanges Canal — New Beauharnois Canal — Lake St. Louis — Lake St. Francis — Lachine • — Lachine Canal — Montreal •

ST. LAWRENCE SEAWAY

Schefferville • — QUEBEC — LABRADOR — IRON BELT

Main map labels:

MINN — ONTARIO — CANADA — QUEBEC — Seven Islands • — Rupert River — Port Arthur • — Duluth • — LAKE SUPERIOR — Tadoussac • — Sault Ste. Marie • — Sault Ste. Marie Canals — WISCONSIN — Ottawa River — Georgian Bay — LAKE HURON — Quebec • — NEW BRU — Three Rivers • — Fredericton • — St. Lawrence Seaway — MICHIGAN — LAKE MICHIGAN — Milwaukee • — Ottawa • — Cornwall • — Massena • — Montreal • — MAINE — Iroquois • — Prescott • — Ogdensburg • — IOWA — Mississippi River — Chicago • — Port Huron • — Detroit • — Kingston • — Cape Vincent • — VT. — Portland • — Toronto • — LAKE ONTARIO — Hamilton • — Rochester • — Oswego • — N.H. — Illinois and Michigan Canal — Windsor • — Welland Ship Canal — Buffalo, N.Y. • — State Barge Canal — Albany • — Boston • — MASS. — Toledo • — LAKE ERIE — NEW YORK — CONN. — R.I. — Illinois River — Cleveland • — Ashtabula • — Hudson River — Illinois-Gulf Waterway — Great Lakes-Gulf Waterway — ILLINOIS — INDIANA — OHIO — PENNSYLVANIA — New York • — Pittsburgh • — Philadelphia • — N.J. — MO. — KY. — W.VA. — MD. — Ohio River — Seven Islands to Philadelphia 1,370

SEACOAST *to the* NORTH

The diagram at right shows how an ocean-going ship is lifted more than 600 feet above sea level during its 2,342-mile journey from the Atlantic Ocean to the western end of Lake Superior. The biggest lift (326 feet) is provided by the eight locks of the Welland Canal, opened in 1932 between Lakes Ontario and Erie. But it was the newer locks and channels (bypassing rapids) of the St. Lawrence Seaway stretch, between Montreal (Lachine Section) and Lake Ontario, that opened the length of the route to deepwater ships.

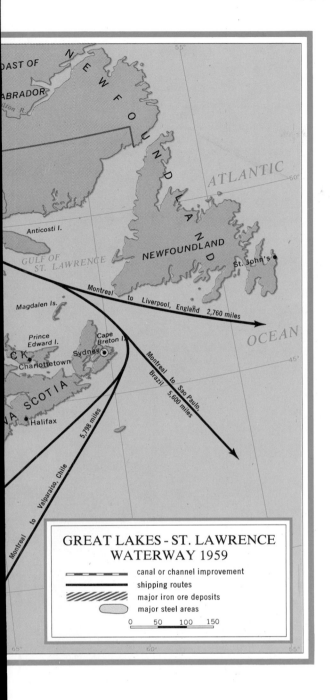

GREAT LAKES - ST. LAWRENCE WATERWAY 1959

- canal or channel improvement
- shipping routes
- major iron ore deposits
- major steel areas

0   50   100   150

Until the development of the railroads in the mid-19th century, the majority of goods transported in the United States was moved by water. While the railroads and, later, trucks and airplanes came to dominate the shipment of most kinds of goods, water transportation has remained important, especially where bulky products like coal and iron ore are concerned. In 1955 over 770 million tons of goods were transported by water in the United States.

The Great Lakes, an immense natural waterway some 2,350 miles in length, have always carried a large proportion of shipping—nearly 194 million tons in 1955. The construction of the St. Lawrence Seaway, completed in 1959, was undertaken to increase this important traffic. Between Lake Ontario and Montreal, the St. Lawrence River falls more than 200 feet, producing a series of unnavigable rapids and shoals. In the 19th century, Canada constructed a system of canals and locks bypassing these natural obstructions, but only small vessels could negotiate the narrow passes. The Seaway Project, a joint enterprise of Canada and the United States, took five years to reach completion and cost some $500 million, but it opened the entire St. Lawrence basin to ocean-going vessels that were capable of carrying up to 25,000 tons of cargo. This made it possible for middle western producers of grain, lumber, automobiles, and many other types of goods, to ship direct to European markets without the expense of transshipment at coastal ports, and for steel manufacturers to tap the rich ore deposits of Labrador at the very time when the Lake Superior deposits were beginning to be exhausted.

The Moses-Saunders power dam, located at Barnhart Island east of Massena, New York, capable of producing about 1.8 million kilowatts of electricity, was a valuable by-product of the Seaway. This new source of power led to the construction of important aluminum plants in the area and also provided economical power for dozens of neighboring communities. In addition, the project has led to a recreational boom, the new lakes that formed behind the various dams attracting boating enthusiasts, fishermen, and other vacationers in large numbers.

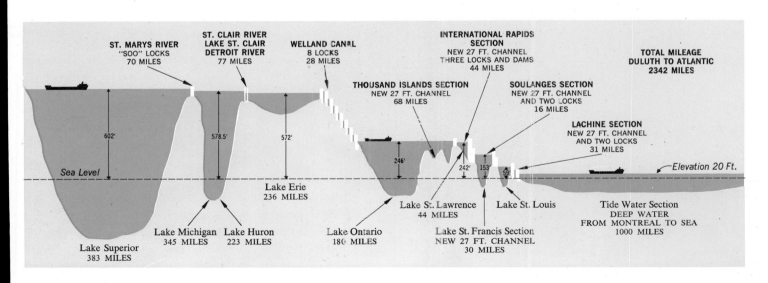

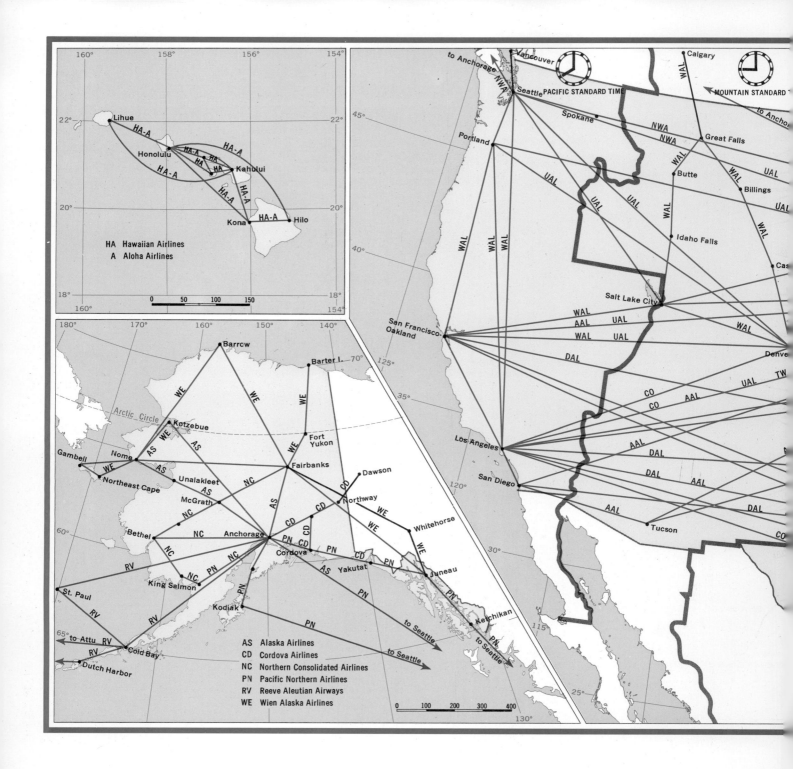

HA Hawaiian Airlines
A   Aloha Airlines

AS Alaska Airlines
CD Cordova Airlines
NC Northern Consolidated Airlines
PN Pacific Northern Airlines
RV Reeve Aleutian Airways
WE Wien Alaska Airlines

JET AGE
TRANSPORTATION

Three major air systems (TWA, United, and American) and numerous minor airlines were operating regularly in the U.S. by the early 1930's. But domestic commercial aviation truly came of age in 1936 with the introduction of the Douglas DC-3, which combined speed, safety, and operational economy. After World War II, domestic air traffic boomed. Airports expanded again and again; new routes crisscrossed the nation; and a succession of new planes like the Constellation, the DC-7, and then jets, were introduced to handle the increasing traffic. By 1965 there were 49 certified airlines in the U.S., carrying 85 million passengers and more than one billion ton-miles of freight per year.

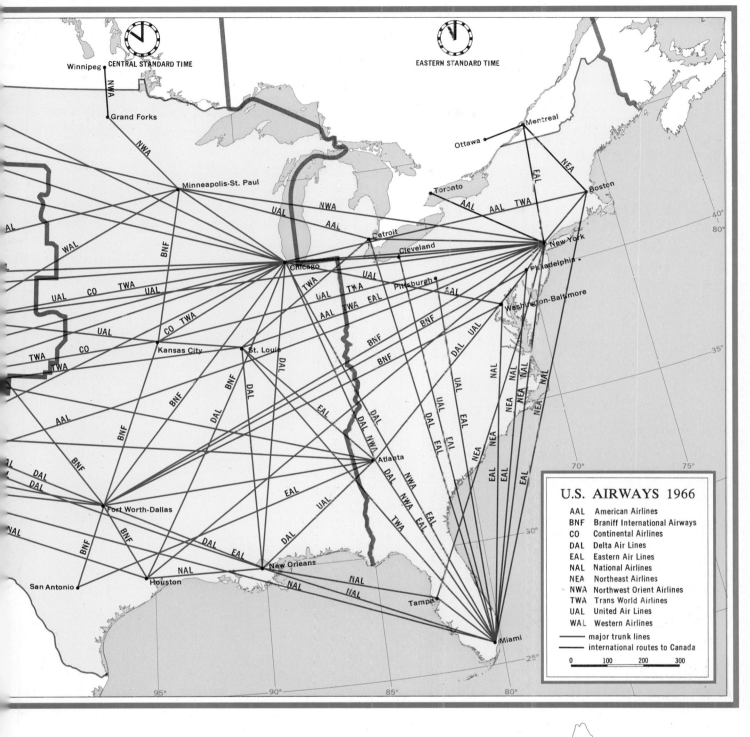

CENTRAL STANDARD TIME

EASTERN STANDARD TIME

Winnipeg

Grand Forks

Minneapolis-St. Paul

Chicago

Detroit

Cleveland

Pittsburgh

Kansas City

St. Louis

Atlanta

Fort Worth-Dallas

San Antonio

Houston

New Orleans

Tampa

Miami

Ottawa

Montreal

Toronto

Boston

New York

Philadelphia

Washington-Baltimore

U.S. AIRWAYS 1966

AAL	American Airlines
BNF	Braniff International Airways
CO	Continental Airlines
DAL	Delta Air Lines
EAL	Eastern Air Lines
NAL	National Airlines
NEA	Northeast Airlines
NWA	Northwest Orient Airlines
TWA	Trans World Airlines
UAL	United Air Lines
WAL	Western Airlines

—— major trunk lines

—— international routes to Canada

0   100   200   300

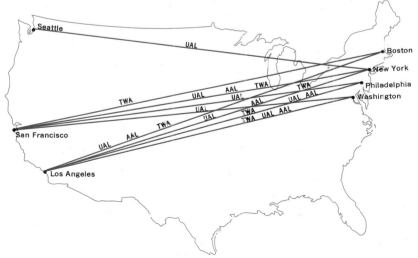

Seattle

Boston

New York

Philadelphia

Washington

San Francisco

Los Angeles

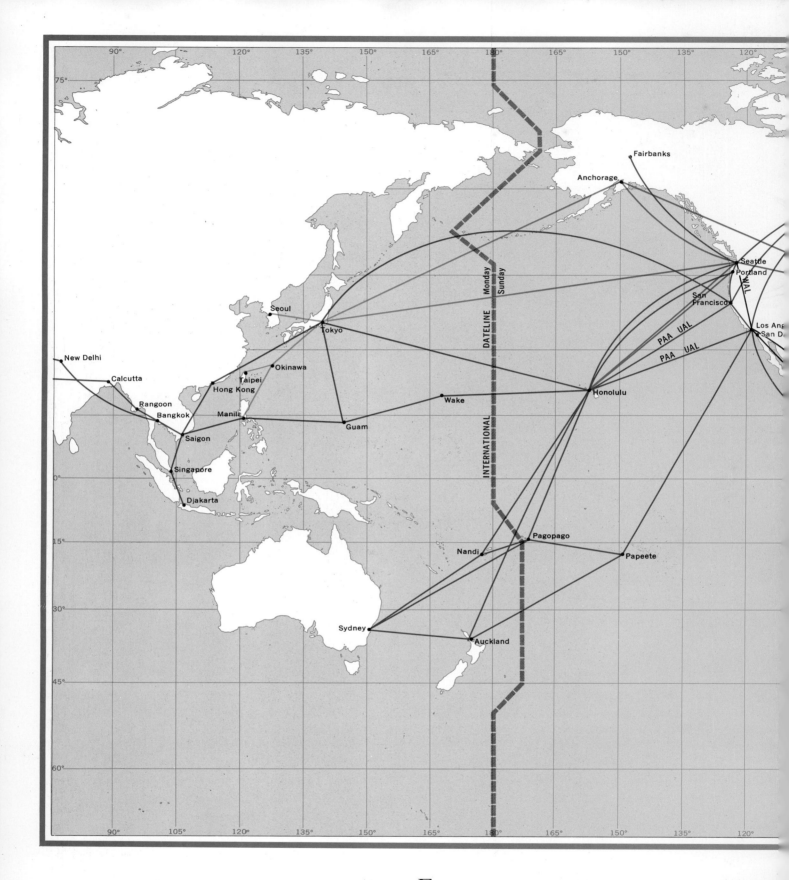

SPANNING
the GLOBE

From a modest birth in July, 1927 (carrying mail between Key West and Cuba), Pan American Airways grew rapidly: by the early 1930's its Fokker amphibians and Sikorsky flying boats were serving South America; by 1937 its Clippers were carrying passengers across the Pacific to Manila and Hong Kong. World War II accelerated the development of

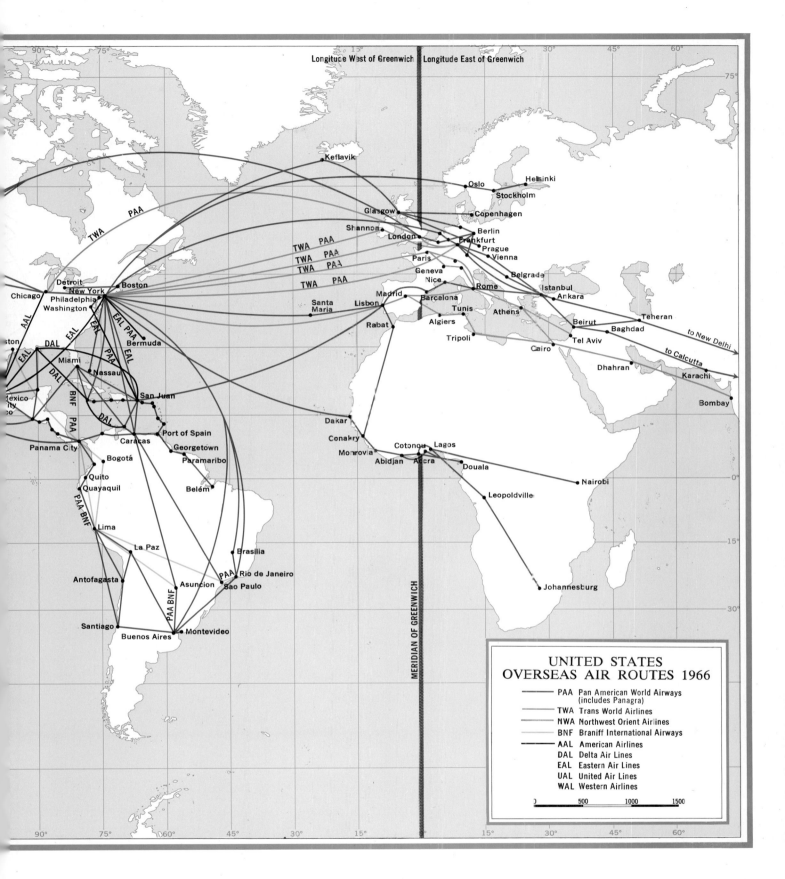

UNITED STATES
OVERSEAS AIR ROUTES 1966

PAA	Pan American World Airways (includes Panagra)
TWA	Trans World Airlines
NWA	Northwest Orient Airlines
BNF	Braniff International Airways
AAL	American Airlines
DAL	Delta Air Lines
EAL	Eastern Air Lines
UAL	United Air Lines
WAL	Western Airlines

0   500   1000   1500

intercontinental air travel, and in the postwar years international commercial aviation became highly competitive big business. The grid above, showing only the routes of scheduled U.S. airlines, omits a dense pattern of international routes of foreign carriers, many of them serving American cities. Yet American-made aircraft were used by the lines of most countries, and U.S. flag carriers, like Pan Am, TWA, and Northwest, carried a large share of the traffic. In 1965, for instance, 49 per cent of that traffic was flown by American lines. International passenger service, still expanding, may only be in its infancy. Ahead lies supersonic (New York to Paris in two and one-half hours) air travel.

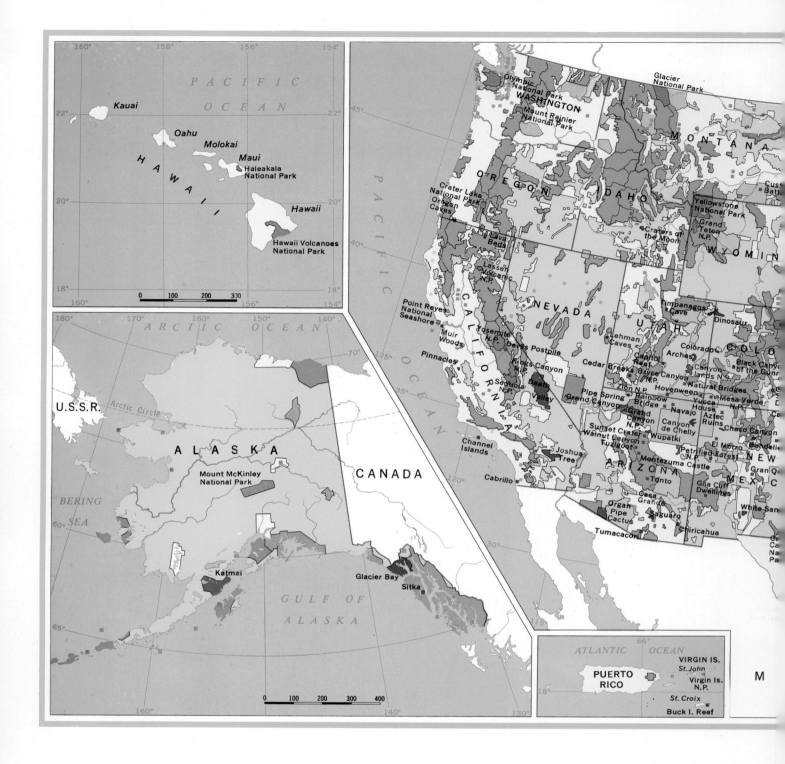

THE PUBLIC DOMAIN

In the years since the founding of the U.S., the Federal government has had a total public domain of about 1.8 billion acres, equal to four-fifths of the nation's present land area. Under a variety of laws it has sold or given away more than a billion acres. Over 247 million acres, for instance, were acquired by private owners under the Homestead Act. Other land was given to veterans, builders of wagon roads, canals, and railroads, and new states (Alaska, almost entirely public domain when it became a state in 1959, is in process of receiving 103 million of its total 375 million acres).

By 1965, the U.S. still owned about 773 million acres, or about one-third of the nation's area. The largest part, some

PUBLIC LANDS
of the
UNITED STATES
1965

National Parks, Seashores and Monuments are named

- National Park or Seashore
- National Monument
- Indian Reservation
- National Wildlife Refuge
- National Forest
- Public Land

0   100   200   300

489 million acres dispersed in fragmented patterns mostly in the western states and Alaska (shown in yellow), is administered by the Bureau of Land Management and is classified for different uses, including watershed protection, livestock grazing, mineral development, and recreation. The rest of the public land comprises national forests, national parks and monuments, wildlife refuges, military reservations, and recreation areas. Indian reservations, included on this map, are owned by the tribes, but are administered under the supervision of the Bureau of Indian Affairs.

Despite the large amount of land still owned by the government, little of it is available for private purchase. Some of the land, like that in the national parks, is maintained for the use of all the people. Other areas, like the national forests, are protected by laws designed to conserve natural resources. Portions may be utilized by timber companies, stockmen, and mineral prospectors, but other parts are reserved for such uses as recreation and the preservation of wildlife. Nevertheless, some land may still be bought by private citizens. Occasionally, the Bureau of Land Management offers land for sale under the Small Tract Act (5 acres or less) or other land laws, like the Desert Land Act which requires the purchaser to develop irrigation facilities. And homesteading is still possible in Alaska.

351

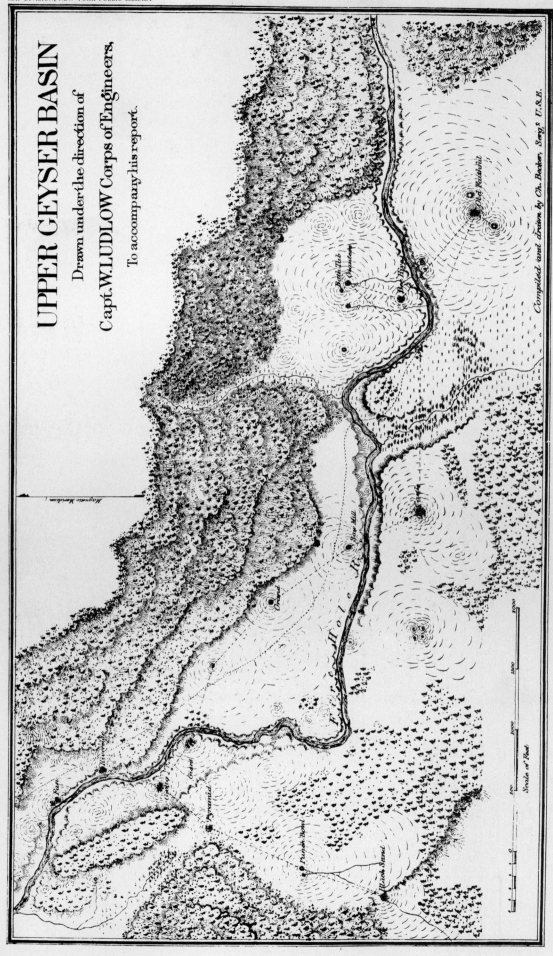

UPPER GEYSER BASIN

Drawn under the direction of
Capt. W. LUDLOW Corps of Engineers,
To accompany his report.

Compiled and drawn by Ch. Becker, Serg.t U.S.E.

Magnetic Meridian

Old Faithful

Scale of Feet

Despite its natural wonders, Yellowstone Park was one of the last parts of the West to be explored. Trappers had generally bypassed the region, because snows were deep there, save from June to September, the time when beaver hunting was at its poorest and mountain men were at their rendezvous. Drawn by persistent rumors of the strange phenomena, however, three groups probed the region from 1869 to 1871, and their vivid reports led to the establishment of the park by Congress. Immediately thereafter, many public and private exploration parties combed the area thoroughly. One of them, led by Captain William Ludlow of the Army's Corps of Engineers, made a reconnaissance in 1875, and the next year issued a report with maps, including the one at the left depicting Old Faithful and the other geysers lining the park's Firehole River.

NATIONAL PARKS
of the
UNITED STATES

A Portfolio of Pictorial Maps

In the 1960's the Federal government turned its attention to the mounting recreation needs of the nation's rapidly swelling population. A Land and Water Conservation Fund Act, passed in 1964 and administered by a Bureau of Outdoor Recreation, helped states and localities finance new recreation areas and facilities. A national Wilderness Act became law; new national recreation areas were created in many parts of the country; and national systems of protected wild rivers and scenic trails were projected. These measures all served to focus interest anew on the brightest gems in the nation's recreation system—the national parks. Begun in 1872 with the creation of Yellowstone Park, the system by 1966 encompassed 32 great parks, from Alaska to the Virgin Islands, visited by some 122 million people. On the following pages are pictorial maps, drawn originally by David Greenspan for *The American Heritage Book of Natural Wonders,* of seven of the most popular national parks.

ATLANTIC OCEAN

FRENCHMAN BAY

EASTERN BAY

WESTERN BAY

BLUE HILL BAY

TO BANGOR

RT 3

RT 102

RT 186

Lamoine

Salsbury Cove

Town Hill

MOUNT DESERT ISLAND

BAR HARBOR

PARK HEADQUARTERS

Anemone Cave

Cadillac Mtn 1,532

Eagle Lake

Sargent Mtn

The Bubbles

Jordan Pond

Sand Beach

Somesville

RT 198

SOMES SOUND

BARTLETT ISLAND

Echo Lake

Long Pond

Beech Mtn

Bernard Mtn

Seal Harbor

OCEAN DRIVE

Northeast Harbor

Center

Seal Cove Pond

Southwest Harbor

ISLESFORD HISTORIC MUSEUM

Seal Cove

Manset

RT 102

GREAT CRANBERRY ISLAND

Bernard

McKinley

▲ CAMPGROUND
△ PICNIC GROUND
■ PARK ENTRANCE

Greenspan

ACADIA
NATIONAL PARK

ter Harbor

SCHOODIC PENINSULA

Schoodic
Head

der Hole

tter
iff

N

LITTLE
CRANBERRY
ISLAND

BAKER
ISLAND

ISLE
AU HAUT

Isle
Au Haut

Jerusalem
Mtn

Long
Pond

N

ATLANTIC
OCEAN

Established in 1919 with the name Lafayette National Park (it was renamed in 1929), Acadia is a delightful preserve of woods, lakes, granite cliffs, and island-dotted waters on the coast of Maine. It encompasses more than 30,000 acres on Mount Desert Island and Schoodic Point on the mainland, and was the first national park east of the Mississippi River.

In a way, the U.S. national park system stems from a state park. Californians, fearful over the threatened despoliation of Yosemite Valley and a grove of majestic sequoia trees, both of which were federally owned, prevailed on President Lincoln in 1864 to transfer the areas to California, which promised to protect them. The two sites, a ten-square-mile strip of Yosemite and a square mile of big trees (the Mariposa Grove), became a state park. It was the first time that any government in the world had set aside public lands for the preservation of their beauty. In 1890, chiefly through the efforts of John Muir, an area circling Yosemite Valley became a national park, and in 1906 California relinquished the valley to the Federal government so that it might become the hub of the present-day Yosemite National Park.

Yellowstone, the first of the national parks, originated as an idea of one man, a Montana attorney named Cornelius Hedges, who was a member of a party exploring the area's wonders in 1870. It was still public domain, which could be claimed, and around a campfire one night, when the explorers were discussing how to divide the region among themselves, Hedges proposed that they abandon plans for private acquisition and work, instead, to secure government protection of the area for the enjoyment of all the American people. Others gave the suggestion effective support, and in March, 1872, President Grant signed a bill creating the park of more than two million acres.

The idea of establishing other national parks, however, did not win approval until 1890. In that year, Yosemite, Sequoia, and General Grant parks were created, all in California. Under Theodore Roosevelt, interest increased, and an Antiquities Act of 1906 provided an opportunity to establish as national monuments areas with historic relics or natural wonders. Making use of that law, President Roosevelt proclaimed a total of 1.4 million acres of public land as national monuments; some of them, including Arizona's Grand Canyon and Petrified Forest and Alaska's Mount McKinley, later became national parks.

The National Park Service itself dates from 1916. Under its administration the nation since then has preserved and maintained the great parks like those seen in this portfolio, as well as a vast system of national historic, military, and battlefield parks, national monuments, seashores, parkways, recreational areas, and cemeteries, and national historic sites and memorials.

355

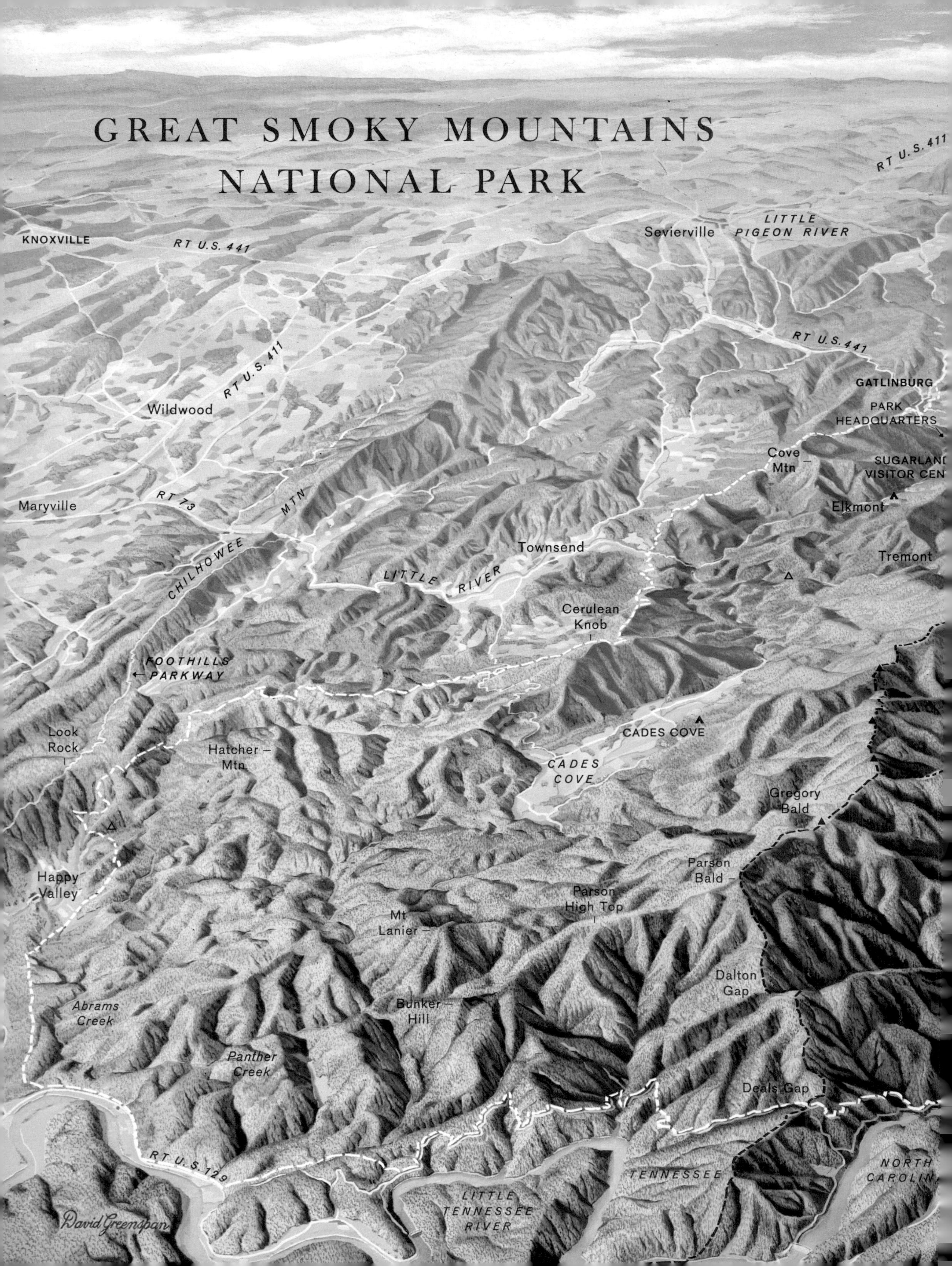

GREAT SMOKY MOUNTAINS
NATIONAL PARK

KNOXVILLE

RT U.S. 441

RT U.S. 411

Wildwood

Maryville

RT 73

CHILHOWEE MTN

FOOTHILLS
PARKWAY

Look
Rock

Hatcher—
Mtn

Happy
Valley

Abrams
Creek

Panther
Creek

David Greenspan

RT U.S. 129

Sevierville

LITTLE
PIGEON RIVER

RT U.S. 411

RT U.S. 441

GATLINBURG

PARK
HEADQUARTERS

Cove
Mtn

SUGARLAND
VISITOR CEN

Elkmont

Tremont

Townsend

LITTLE   RIVER

Cerulean
Knob

CADES COVE

CADES
COVE

Gregory
Bald

Parson
Bald—

Parson
High Top

Mt
Lanier—

Dalton
Gap

Bunker—
Hill

Deals Gap

TENNESSEE

NORTH
CAROLIN

LITTLE
TENNESSEE
RIVER

TEN THOUSAND ISLANDS

Everglades

TAMIAMI TRAIL

EDGE OF MANGROVES

← TO KEY WE

Duck Rock

CHATHAM RIVER

GULF OF MEXICO

LOSTMANS RIVER

Big Lostmans Bay

BROAD RIVER

PONCE DE LEON BAY

SHARK RIVER

Maho Hamn

WHITEWATER BAY

Pauro Pon

N W Cape

Mangrove Trail

WEST LAKE

Middle Cape

Lake Ingraham

CAPE SABLE

Bear Lake

Cool Bay

East Cape

FLAMINGO AREA

JOE KEMP KEY

OYSTER KEYS

SANDY KEY

FLORIDA BAY

N

▲ CAMPGROUND
△ PICNIC GROUND
■ ENTRANCE STATION

David Greenspan

← TO KEY WE

RT U.S 41

LOOP ROAD

TAMIAMI CANAL

TO MIAMI →

SEVEN
MILE
ROAD

RT 27

EDGE OF PINELAND

OPEN EVERGLADES

Homestead

LONG PINE KEY

Pineland
Trail

Pa-hay-okee
Overlook

Florida
City

PARK
HEADQUARTERS

ROYAL PALM
AREA

Gumbo-Limbo →
Trail

Anhinga
Wildlife
Trail

RT U.S.1

hbert Lake
Rookery

EAGLE
KEY

NEST
KEYS

BLACKWATER
SOUND

Key
Largo

COWPENS

Tavernier

EVERGLADES
NATIONAL PARK

FLORIDA KEYS

T. U.S 1

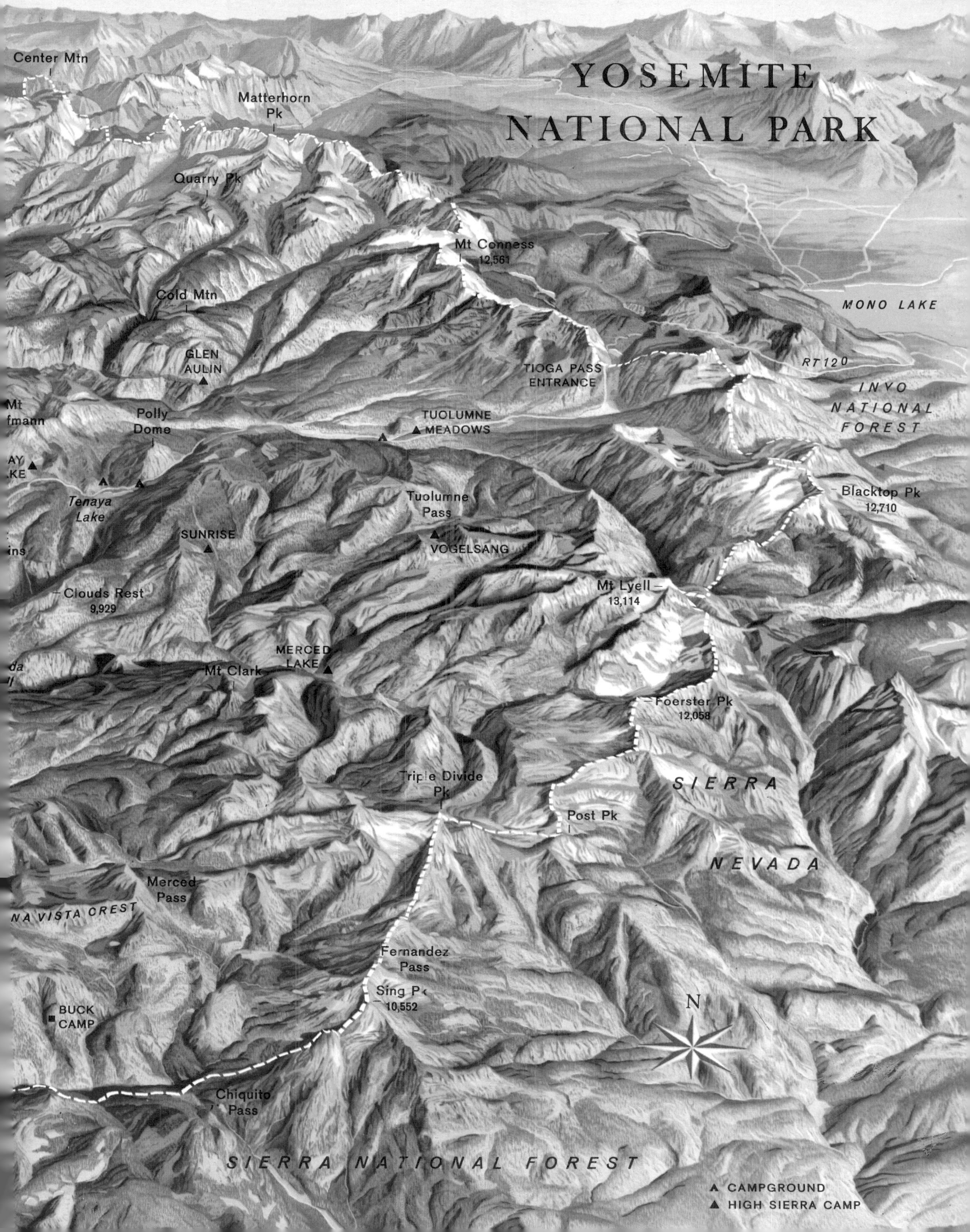

YOSEMITE
NATIONAL PARK

Center Mtn

Matterhorn
Pk

Quarry Pk

Mt Conness
12,561

MONO LAKE

Cold Mtn

RT 120

GLEN
AULIN

TIOGA PASS
ENTRANCE

INYO
NATIONAL
FOREST

Mt
fmann

Polly
Dome

TUOLUMNE
MEADOWS

AY
KE

Tenaya
Lake

Tuolumne
Pass

Blacktop Pk
12,710

SUNRISE

ins

VOGELSANG

Mt Lyell
13,114

Clouds Rest
9,929

da

Mt Clark

MERCED
LAKE

Foerster Pk
12,058

Triple Divide
Pk

SIERRA

Post Pk

NEVADA

Merced
Pass

NA VISTA CREST

Fernandez
Pass

N

Sing P
10,552

BUCK
CAMP

Chiquito
Pass

SIERRA NATIONAL FOREST

▲ CAMPGROUND
▲ HIGH SIERRA CAMP

Mt
Sinyala

HAVASUPAI
INDIAN
RESERVATION

HAVASU CREEK

AZTEC
AMPHITHEATER

COCONINO PLATEAU

Havasupai
Pt

Walapai
Pt

Shiva
Temple

Mescalero
Pt

Pt
Sublime

HERMITS
REST

COLORADO RIVER

Isis
Temple

Buddha
Temple

Hopi Pt

A.T. & S.F.R.R.

GRAND CANYON
VILLAGE
PARK
HEADQUARTERS

Yavapai Pt
7,000

Mather Pt

RT 64

TO WILLIAMS RT U.S. 180

BRIGHT ANGEL CANYC

Yaki
Pt

SOUTH RIM

Wotans
Throne

Cape Royal
7,876

Grandview
Pt

Vishnu
Temple

Ju
Tem

Horseshoe
Mesa

GRANITE GORGE

EAST RIM DRIVE

Apollo
Templ

Solomon
Temple

TUSAYAN
MUSEUM

Desert View
7,450

N

Comanche
Pt

RT 64

TO CAMERON

David Greenspan

GRAND CANYON
NATIONAL MONUMENT

Kanab
Creek →

JUMP UP CANYON

FOSSIL
BAY

Great Thumb
Pt

Steamboat
Mtn

POWELL PLATEAU

GRAND CANYON
NATIONAL PARK

Holy Grail
Temple

The Dragon

KAIBAB PLATEAU

RT 67   TO JACOB LAKE →

KAIBAB NATIONAL FOREST

NORTH RIM

GRAND CANYON
LODGE

Pt
Imperial
8,801

WALHALLA PLATEAU

Atoko Pt

Gunther
Castle

MARBLE
GORGE

NANKOWEAP
MESA

Chuar
Butte

Temple
Butte

LAVA CREEK

Cape
Solitude
6,150

CAMPGROUND
ENTRANCE STATION

PAINTED DESERT

Little
Colorado
River

TO BOZEMAN →

YELLOWSTONE RIVER   RT U.S. 89

GALLATIN

Specimen
Creek

Electric Pk
10,992

Gardiner
NORTH ENTRANCE

SUPERINTENDENT'S
OFFICE

GALLATIN
RANGE

Golden
Gate

MAMMOTH
HOT SPRINGS

GALLATIN
NATIONAL
FOREST

RIVER

Sheepeater
Cliff

Mt Holmes

Obsidian Cliff

Roaring Mtn

Hebgen
Lake

Norris

Virginia Cascades

RT U.S. 20

NORRIS
GEYSER BASIN

CENTRAL
PLATEAU

West
Yellowstone

National
Park Mtn

WEST ENTRANCE

MADISON RIVER

Madison
Jct

Gibbon Falls

LOWER
GEYSER BASIN

Fountain Paintpot

MONTANA
IDAHO

MADISON
PLATEAU

MIDWAY
GEYSER BASIN

Great Fountain Geyser

UPPER
GEYSER BASIN

Morning Glory Pool

TARGHEE
NATIONAL
FOREST

CONTINENTAL

Old Faithful Geyser

Paintpo

Lone Star Geyser

West Thumb

DIVIDE

Shoshone
Lake

WYOMING

N

SHOSHONE
GEYSER BASIN

Lewis
Lake

PITCHSTONE
PLATEAU

Lewis Falls

RED M

Bechler   Cave Falls

SOUTH ENTRANCE

RTS U.S. 89 287

David Greenspan

GRAND TETON
NATIONAL PARK

YELLOWSTONE
NATIONAL PARK

Hellroaring
Pk

Petrified
Tree

Tower Jct

Mt Washburn
10,243

nraven Pass

Inspiration
NYON Pt

Artist Pt
Yellowstone Falls

AYDEN
LLEY   Mud
Volcano

Natural
Bridge

Fishing
Bridge

Lake

Steamboat
Pt

*Slough
Creek*

Soda
Butte

Lamar

Fossil Forest

*MIRROR
PLATEAU*

Pelican
Cone

Lake Butte

Abiathar Pk
10,928

NORTHEAST ENTRANCE

MONTANA

WYOMING

RT U.S. 212

*Cache
Creek*

ABSAROKA

Pollux Pk
11,067

Hoodoo
Basin

LAMAR RIVER

RANGE

Avalanche Pk
10,566

Sylvan Lake

Sylvan Pass

EAST
ENTRANCE

Eagle Pk
11,353

GRAND CANYON

YELLOWSTONE
LAKE

The
Promontory

YELLOWSTONE

heridan
0,308

*HEART LAKE
GEYSER BASIN*

*Heart
Lake*

*TWO OCEAN
PLATEAU*

RIVER

The
Trident

KE RIVER

THOROFARE

*Bridger
Lake*

*TETON
NATIONAL
FOREST*

▲ CAMPGROUND

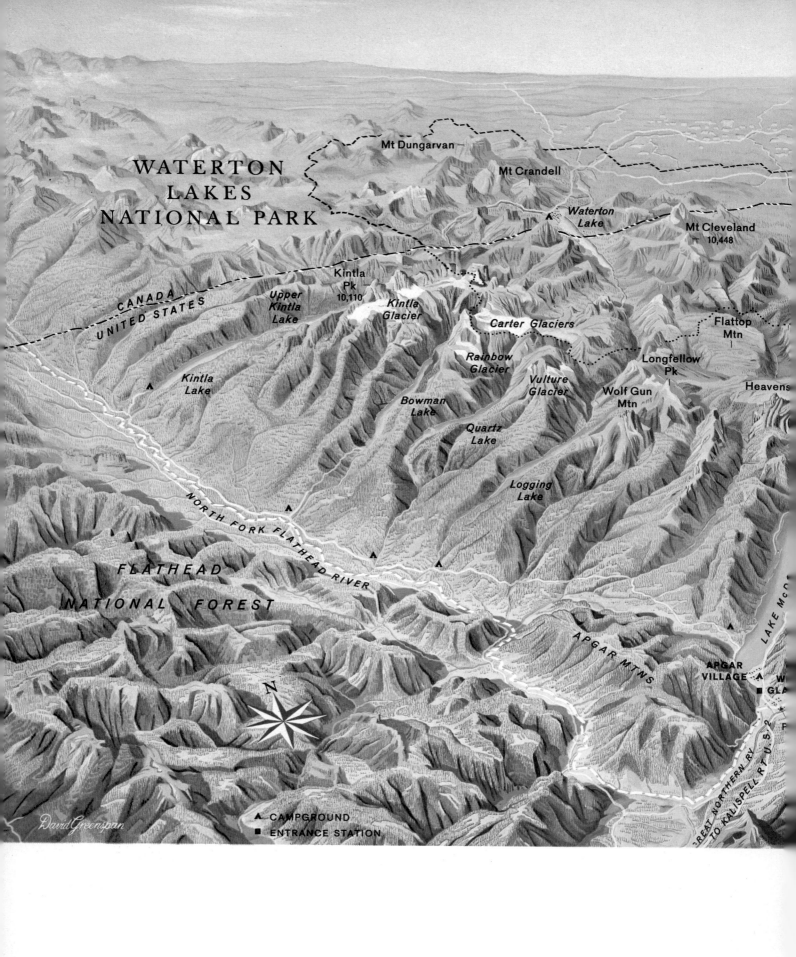

WATERTON
LAKES
NATIONAL PARK

Mt Dungarvan

Mt Crandell

Waterton
Lake

Mt Cleveland
10,448

CANADA
UNITED STATES

Upper
Kintla
Lake

Kintla
Pk
10,110

Kintla
Glacier

Carter Glaciers

Flattop
Mtn

Rainbow
Glacier

Longfellow
Pk

Kintla
Lake

Vulture
Glacier

Wolf Gun
Mtn

Heavens

Bowman
Lake

Quartz
Lake

NORTH FORK FLATHEAD RIVER

Logging
Lake

FLATHEAD

NATIONAL FOREST

APGAR MTNS

LAKE McD

APGAR
VILLAGE

W
GLA

N

GREAT NORTHERN RY
TO KALISPELL RT U.S. 2

David Greenspan

▲ CAMPGROUND
■ ENTRANCE STATION

Chief Mtn

Babb

GLACIER
NATIONAL PARK

Lower St Mary
Lake

Mt
Grinnell

Lake
Sherburne

Swiftcurrent

Many
Glacier

Going-to-
the-Sun
Mtn

RT U.S. 89

BLACKFEET HIGHWAY

Grinnell
Glacier

St Mary
Lake

TO BROWNING

Logan
Pass

Lower
Two Medicine
Lake

East
Glacier
Park

Mt Jackson

Mt Logan

CONTINENTAL DIVIDE

Rising Wolf
Mtn

Hidden
Lake

Mt Stimson
10,165

nsight
Mtn

Sperry
Glacier

Two Medicine
Lake

Harrison
Glacier

Mt Pinchot

RT U.S. 2

Summit
Mtn

Mt
St. Nicholas
9,380

Mt Doody

Statuary
Mtn

Marias
Pass

Summit

Harrison
Lake

Mt Grant

MIDDLE FORK FLATHEAD RIVER

FLATHEAD RANGE

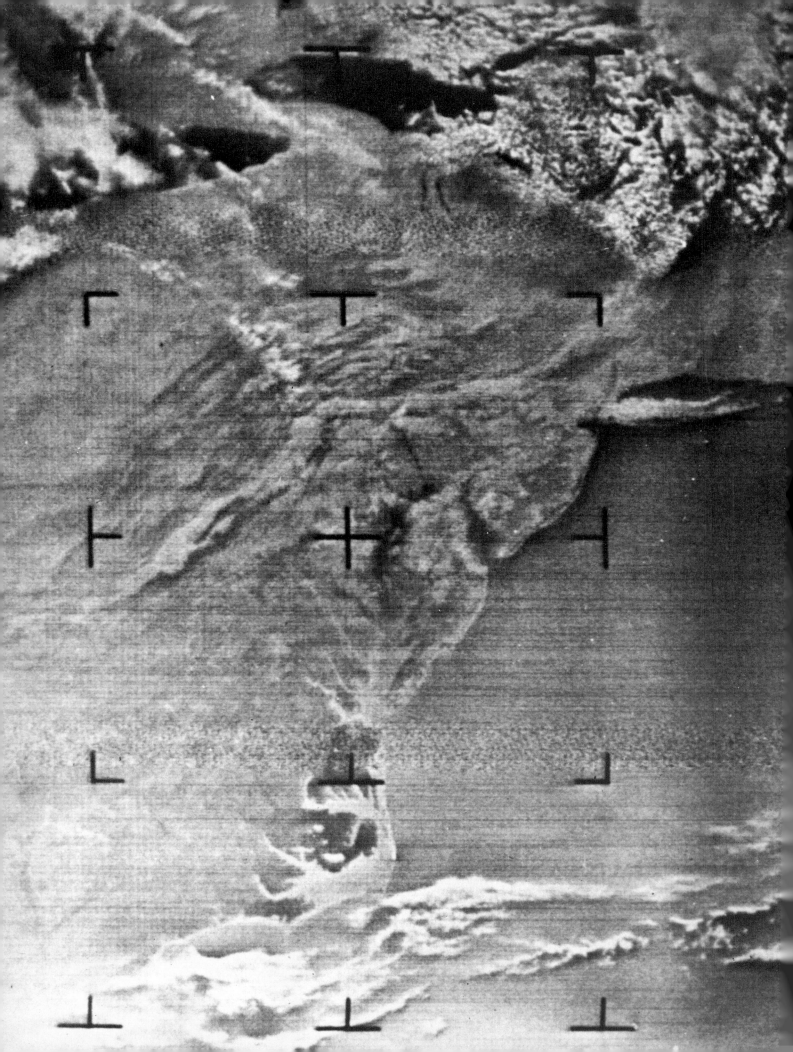

Acknowledgments

The editors are grateful to the following individuals and institutions for their assistance and counsel in the preparation of this atlas, and for their co-operation in making available documentary and pictorial material in their collections:

Academy of American Franciscan History, Washington, D.C.: Rev. Fintan Warren, O.F.M.

American Museum of Natural History, New York: Gordon F. Ekholm, Curator of Mexican Archaeology; Maureen Mahon

Atomic Energy Commission, Washington, D.C.: James D. Lyman, Public Information Officer

Atomic Industrial Forum, New York

British Information Service, New York

British Overseas Airways Corporation, New York: Ray Onslow

Civil Aeronautics Board, Washington, D.C.: Jack Yohe

Frederick J. Dockstader, Director, Museum of the American Indian, Heye Foundation, New York

Federal Power Commission: Martin Inwald, New York; John Stout, Washington, D.C.

German Tourist Information Office, New York

Library of Congress, Washington, D.C.: Charles Harrington, Walter W. Ristow

National Aeronautics and Space Administration, Washington, D.C.: Julian Scheer, Brig. Gen. Harris Hull, Ralph Gesell

National Archives, Washington, D.C.: Charlotte Ashby, Herman Friis, Barbara Jones, Josephine Motylewski, Dr. A. P. Muntz

New-York Historical Society: Shirley Beresford, Thomas J. Dunnings, Jr., Rachel Minick

New York Public Library: Gerard L. Alexander, Chief of Map Division; Maud D. Cole; Wilson G. Duprey; Edward M. Gardner; Romana Javitz; Lewis M. Stark; Norwood B. Vail

North American Air Defense Command, Colorado: Lt. Col. C. J. Matthiessen, Acting Director of Public Information

Old Print Shop, New York: Harry Shaw Newman, Dorothea C. Shipley, Constance R. Van Schaack

Erwin Raisz, Lecturer in Cartography, Harvard University, Cambridge

St. Lawrence Seaway Authority, Ottawa

Smithsonian Institution, Washington, D.C.: Margaret C. Blaker, Peter Welch

Tennessee Valley Authority, Knoxville: Gilbert Stewart, Jr.

United Nations Information Office, New York

U.S. Air Force, Washington, D.C.: Col. C. V. Glines, Chief, Magazine and Book Branch

U.S. Army, Washington, D.C.

U.S. Department of the Interior, Washington, D.C.: Bureau of Commercial Fisheries, John B. Skerry; Bureau of Indian Affairs; Bureau of Land Management; Bureau of Mines; Geological Survey, Arch C. Gerlach, Chief of National Atlas Project

U.S. Navy, Washington, D.C.

William L. Clements Library, University of Michigan, Ann Arbor: Nathaniel N. Shipton

Hannah M. Wormington, Curator, Department of Archaeology, Denver Museum of Natural History

Yale University Library, New Haven: Archibald Hanna

Special acknowledgment is made for permission to use information and map data from the following works:

Atlas of the Historical Geography of the United States by Charles O. Paullin. © 1932 by Carnegie Institution of Washington; published jointly by Carnegie Institution of Washington and the American Geographical Society of New York.

Colonial Virginia, Vol. I, by Richard L. Morton. © 1960 by The Virginia Historical Society; published for The Virginia Historical Society by The University of North Carolina Press, Chapel Hill.

Early Man in the New World by Kenneth Macgowan and Joseph A. Hester, Jr. © 1962 by Kenneth Macgowan and the American Museum of Natural History; published in co-operation with the American Museum of Natural History by Doubleday and Company, Inc., New York.

A Guide to the Military Posts of the United States 1789-1895 by Francis Paul Prucha. © 1964 by The State Historical Society of Wisconsin; published by The State Historical Society of Wisconsin, Madison.

History of United States Naval Operations in World War II, 15 Vols., by Samuel Eliot Morison. © 1948, 1949, 1950, 1951, 1953, 1954, 1956, 1957, 1958, 1959, 1960 by Samuel Eliot Morison; published by Little, Brown and Company, Boston. The base map of Tarawa Atoll, page 298, was derived from the map on page 176 of Vol. VII.

The West Point Atlas of American Wars, Vols. I and II, edited by Col. Vincent J. Esposito. © 1959 by Frederick A. Praeger, Inc.; published by Frederick A. Praeger, Inc., New York.

Grateful acknowledgment is also given to George B. Hartzog, Director of the National Park Service, and to John O. Littleton, Chief of the National Survey of Historic Sites and Buildings, for making available unpublished theme studies of the National Survey of Historic Sites and Buildings.

Through the courtesy of the American Geographical Society, the base for the world maps in this book was derived from the Society's World Map on the Miller Cylindrical Projection, Scale 1:30,000,000.

The Atlantic Coast and the eastern United States, from Canada to South Carolina, including such features as Cape Cod, Long Island, Chesapeake Bay, and Lakes Ontario, Erie, and Huron—all of them once the objects of earth-bound explorers groping to uncover the geographical secrets of a New World—are seen (opposite) in a single photograph taken at a 430-mile altitude by a U.S. weather satellite.

NASA

Index

Italic page numbers indicate text references.
Bold page numbers indicate illustrations.

Charlevaux Mill, France, 282
Charlotte, N.C., 79, 80, 102, 103, 203
Charlotte, Vt., 122
Charlotte, Fort, S.C., 102, 103
Charlotte Harbor, Fla., 35, 147
Charlottesville, Va., 79, 80, 86, 103, 203, 208, 222
Charlottetown, P.E.I., Canada, 89, 345
Chartres, France, 280, 304, 307
Chartres, Fort de, Ill., 53
Châteaugay, Canada, battle (1813), 137 top
Châteauroux Air Station, France, 327
Château-Thierry, France, battle (1918), 280 bottom, *281*
Châtel-Chéhéry, France, 282
Chatfield Farm, Battle of Bemis Heights, 108
Chatham, Earl of. *See* Pitt, William.
Chatham River, Everglades National Park, 358
Châtillon, France, 280
Chattahoochee River, 35, 49, 56, 62, 79, 114, 118, 121, 139, 146, 151, 163, 203, 211, 218, 220
Chattanooga, Tenn., 146, 151, 203, 211, 218, 236–37, 255, 285, 287, 339; (battle 1863) 220, *221*, 236–37
Chattanooga and Cleveland R.R., 236–37
Chattanooga Creek, Siege of Chattanooga, 236
Chattanooga Valley, Tenn., 236
Chatuge Dam, N.C., 287
Chaudière River, Que., Canada, 37, 60, 61 top, 64, 72, 96, 159
Chaumont, France, 278, 280
Chautauqua Lake, N.Y., (Lac Chautauqua) 67; 79
Chautauqua Portage, N.Y., 53
Chavín de Huántar, Peru, 21 center
Cheat River, 69 bottom
Cheboygan, Mich., 255
Chebucto, N.S., Canada, 37
Chebucto Bay, N.S., Canada, 64
Checkpoint Charlie, Berlin, Germany, 316
Chedabucto Bay, N.S., Canada, 263 inset
Chehalis Indians, 23 D-1, *24;* (reservation, Wash.) 251
Chelmsford, Mass., 43, 59 bottom
Chelsea, Mass., 95 left
Chelsea, Okla., 252
Chemehuevi Indians, 23 E-2, *24*
Chemery, France, 282
Chemical industry, 338–39
Chemin des Dames, France, battle (1917), 278
Chemnitz, Germany, 308
Chemung, N.Y., 101
Chemung River, 122
Chenango River, 101, 122
Chengshien, China, 311
Cheoah, N.C., 357
Cheoah Dam, N.C., 287, 343
Cheppy, France, 282
Chequamegon, Fort, Wis., 53
Cheraw, S.C., 79, 80, 102, 103, 203
Cherbourg, France, 278, 304, 306, 307
Chernigov, U.S.S.R., 288
Cherokee, N.C., 357

Cherokee Dam, Tenn., 287, 343
Cherokee Indians, 23 E-5, *24,* 56, 78–79, *122;* (removal of) 149
Cherokee Outlet, Okla., 251, 265
"Cherronesus," Northwest Territory, *120*
Cherry Valley, N.Y., 47, 98, 101, 122
Cherry Valley Dam, Calif., 342
Chesapeake Bay, 41, 47, 48, 49, 56, 79, 80, 99, 103, *112,* 138, 208, 213, 217
Chesapeake and Ohio Canal National Monument, Md., 351
Chester, Ill., 204
Chester, Pa., 47, 99. *See also* Upland.
Chesterfield House, Alta., Canada, 132
Chestnut Ridge, Pa., 69 bottom
Cheticamp, N.S., Canada, 89
Cheveuges, France, 282
Cheyenne, Wyo., 244, 247, 252, 254, 264, 285
Cheyenne Indians, 23 E-3, *24,* 247, 249, *264;* (reservation, Okla. and Mont.) 251
Cheyenne River, 128, 132, 146, 152–53, 156–57, 170, 172, 247
Cheyenne River Indian Agency, S.D., 247
Chiaha, Tenn., 34
Chiang Kai-shek, *323*
Chibcha culture, 21 center; (language group) 25
Chicaca, Miss., 34
Chicacoan, Va., 48
Chicago, Ill., 146, 150, 189, 191, 203, 204, 254, 271, *272,* 273, 285, 339, 344, 347, 349. *See also* Ange Guardien; Dearborn, Fort.
Chicago, Lake, 17 bottom
Chicago Portage, Ill., 53
Chicago, Rock Island and Pacific R.R., 254
Chicago Turnpike, 150–51
Chichagof Island, Alaska, 257
Chichén Itzá, Mexico, 20 left
Chickahominy Indians, 23 E-5, *24*
Chickahominy River, 41, 48, 208, *212,* 213, 215
Chickamauga, Ga., battle (1863), 220
Chickamauga Creek, Battle of Chattanooga, 237
Chickamauga Dam, Tenn., 287, 343
Chickasaw Bayou, Miss., *219*
Chickasaw Bluffs, Siege of Vicksburg, 232
Chickasaw Indians, 23 E-4, *24,* 56, 78, *122;* (removal of) 149; (reservation, Okla.) 251
Chickasaw Old Fields, Ala., 78
Chickasaw Trail, 78
Chickasawhay River, 139
Chief Joseph, Nez Perce chief, 246–47
Chief Joseph Dam, Wash., 342
Chief Mountain, Glacier National Park, 363
Chiers River, France, 282
Chihli, Gulf of, China, 311
Chihuahua, Mexico, 50, 128, 144, *162,* 163; (battle 1880) 249
Chilcotin Indians, 23 C-2, *24*
Chile, 314, 324
Chilhowee Mountain, Tenn., 356
Chilkoot Pass, Yukon, Canada, 257
Chillicothe, Mo., 252
Chillicothe, Ohio, 79, 121, 125, 151
Chilocco Indian Reservation, Okla., 251

Chiltoe Mountain, Great Smoky Mountains National Park, 357
Chimney Point, N.Y., 344 inset
Chimney Rock, Nebr., 170
Chimney Tops, Great Smoky Mountains National Park, 357
Chimú culture, 21 center
China, 93, *133,* 258, 262, 292, 296, 311, 322, 323, 325, 327
China, Mexico, 164
China, Republic of, Treaty (1954), 325. *See also* Taiwan.
Chinese Camp, Calif., 168
Chinigué, Pa. *See* Logstown.
Chinook Indians, 23 D-1, *24*
Chinquapin, Yosemite National Park, 360
Chipewyan, Fort, Alta., Canada, 132
Chipewyan, Old Fort, Alta., Canada, 132
Chipewyan Indians, 23 C-3, *24*
Chippewa Indians, (reservations, Kans., Minn., N.D., Wis.) 251. *See also* Ojibwa Indians.
Chippewa River, Canada, battle (1814) 137 bottom
Chiquita Pass, Yosemite National Park, 361
Chiricahua Mountains, Ariz., 249
Chirikov, Alexei, 51
Chiriquí culture, 21 center
Chiriquí Gulf, Panama, 260
Chisholm, Jesse, *253*
Chisholm Cattle Trail, 249, 252, *253*
Chiswell, Fort, Va., 77, 79, 80
Chiswell, John, *78*
Chitimacha Indians, 23 F-4, *24*
Chiva Chiva, Canal Zone, Panama, 261
Chivington, J. M., *246*
Choctaw Indian Agency, Okla., 171
Choctaw Indians, 23 F-4, *24,* 56, *122, 127;* (removal of) 149; (reservation, Okla.) 251
Choiseul Island, Solomon Is., 293, 295 top, 297
Cholula, Mexico, 20 left, 34 inset
Chongjin, North Korea, 318, 319
Chontal Indians, 23 G-4, *24*
Choptank River, 48, 138
Chosan, North Korea, 318, 319
Choshin Reservoir, North Korea, 318, 319
Chouteau's Island, Kans., 153
Chouteau's Post, Mo., 157
Chouteau's Trading Post, Okla. (1817–22, 1822) 153
Chowan River, 103
Christanna, Fort, Va., 49
Christiania, Norway, 278
Christina, Fort, Del., 46, 48
Chromium deposits, 340–41
Chrysler's Farm, Ont., Canada, battle (1813), 137 top
Chuar Butte, Grand Canyon National Park, 367
Chukchi Peninsula, U.S.S.R., 328
Chukchi Sea, 256–57
Chulai, South Vietnam, 322, 323, 327
Chumash Indians, 23 E-1, *24*
Chumphon, Thailand, 292
Chunchon, South Korea, 318, 319

Colville River, 257
Comanche Indians, 23 F-3, *24, 26, 153, 248, 249, 253;* (reservation, Okla.) 251
Comanche Point, Grand Canyon National Park, 366
Combahee River, 61 bottom, 63
Comerford Dam, Vt., 343
Comfort, Point, Va., 41
Compiègne, France, **282,** 307
Compostela, Mexico, 50
Compromise of 1850, *166,* 196, 198
Comstock Lode, 168, *169*
Conakry, Guinea, 349
Concentration camps, 308–9
Concepcion, Fla., 61 bottom
Concepción River, Mexico, 162
Concho, Fort, Tex., 249, 252
Concho Indians, 23 F-3, *24*
Concho River, Tex., 171
Conchos River, Mexico, 34, 50, 128, 163, 164
Concord, Conn., 271
Concord, Mass., 43, 59 bottom; (battle 1775) 94 right, *95*
Concord, N.H., 80, 122, 137 top, 145, 167, 201, 205, 265. *See also* Rumford.
Concord River, 59 bottom, 94 right
Concordia, Kans., 252
Condé, Fort, Ala. *See* Mobile.
Conecuh River, 139
Conemaugh River, 69 bottom
Conestoga Indians. *See* Susquehanna Indians.
Conewango, Pa., 101
Conewango Creek, 69 bottom, 79, 101
Confederate Army:
  of Mississippi, 211, 218
  of Northern Virginia, 213, 214, 215, 217, 222, *238*
  of the Potomac, 208
  of the Shenandoah, 208
  of Tennessee, 218, 220–21, *240*
  Department of East Tennessee, 218
Confederate states, secession (1860–61), 205
Confederation, Fort, Ala., 123
Conflans, France, 282
Congo, Republic of the, 325, 327. *See also* Belgian Congo.
Congo Republic, 325. *See also* French Equatorial Africa.
Congo River, Africa, 93
Congregational Church, 87, 186–87, 268–69, 334–35
Connecticut, (colony from 1635) 42 bottom, 43, 46, 47, *58,* 59, 76, 77, 80, 86, 89, 94 left; (state of, 1776) 98, 114, 116, *117,* 118, *119,* 121, 122, 137 top, 145, 151, 167, 199, 201, 203, 204; (after 1860) 205, 255, 265, 335, 339, 344, 351. *See also* New Netherland.
Connecticut Company, grant to (1662), 42 bottom
Connecticut Reserve, Ohio, 120 bottom left
Connecticut River, 37, 42 bottom, 43, *44,* 47, 56, 59, 60, 61 top, 64, 69 top, 72, 77, 94 left, 96, 118, 121, 122, 137 top, 151, 159, 203, 344. *See also* Varsche River.
Connecticut Yankee nuclear plant, Conn., 343

Connellsville, Pa., 203
Conness, Mount, Yosemite National Park, 361
Conococheague Creek, 69 bottom, 217
Conodoguinet Creek, 69 bottom, 217
Conowingo Dam, Md., 343
Conrad's Store, Va., 212
Conservation program, U.S., *274*
Constance, Lake, Europe, 304, 308
Constantinople, Turkey, 135, 279, 283. *See also* Istanbul.
Constellation and *La Vengeance,* engagement (1800) **134**
Constitution, U.S., ratification, 116, **117**
Conti, Fort, N.Y., 56
Continental Airlines, 346–47
Continental Congress, *120;* (and township system) *126*
Continental Divide, 128, 132, *144,* 152, 156, 170, 172, 247, 249, 362–63, 364–65
Contoocook River, 43
Convention of 1818, 145
Convoy routes (World War II), 290–91
Cook, James, 51, *133*
Cook Inlet, Alaska, 51, 132, *256*
Cooke, Philip St. George, *162*
Cooke-Mormon Battalion (1846), 162–63
Cool Bay, Everglades National Park, 358
Coolidge, Calvin, *287*
Cooper Lake Dam, Alaska, 342
Cooper's Ferry, N.J., 47
Cooperstown, N.Y., 122
Coos Indians, 23 D-1, *24*
Coosa River, 78–79, 123, 139, 151, 163, 203, 211, 218, 220
Copán, Honduras, 20 left
Copano, Tex., 161
Copenhagen, Denmark, 278, 283, 288, 308, 349
Copper, (mining) 190–91, *242,* 247, 248–49, 272–73; (ore deposits) 340–41
Copper River, 132, 257
Coral Sea, 297; (battle 1942), *292, 293,* 295 top
Corazones, Mexico, 34
Corbin's Bridge, Battle of the Wilderness, 238
Cordilleran Cap, Canada, 16
Cordova, Alaska, 346. *See also* Orca.
Cordova Airlines, 346
Corinth, Miss., 202, 254; (battle 1862) *210,* 211, 218
Corn Belt, 252, 271
Corn crops, *143,* 188–89, 270–71, 336–37
Corn Islands, Caribbean Sea, 260
Cornfield, Battle of Antietam, 229
Cornstalk, Shawnee chief, *78*
Cornwall, Ont., Canada, 344
Cornwall, Pa., iron ore region, 341
Cornwallis, Lord Charles, 97, 102, 103, *106, 112*
Coronado, Francisco Vásquez de, *26,* 34
Corpus Christi, Tex., 161, 163, 252, 285
Corpus Christi Bay, Tex., 161
Corregidor Island, Philippines, battle (1942), 294, *295*
Corsica, island, France, 135, 278, 283, 288, 317

Corsicana, Tex., 252
Corte-Real, Gaspar, 33
Cortés, Hernán, *15, 29,* 34 inset, *35*
Cortlandt Manor, N.Y., 47
Corydon, Ind., 145, 146
Coryel's Ferry, Pa., 99
Cosby, Tenn., 357
Cosenza, Italy, 302
Coshocton, Ohio, 125
Costa Rica, 260, 290, 314, 320, 324
Costanoan Indians, 23 E-1, *24*
Cosumnes River (and North and South forks), 168
Côtes de Meuse, France, 281, 282
Côtes de Moselle, France, 281, 282
Cotonou, Dahomey, 349
Cotton, (industry) *143;* (crops) 188–89, 270–71, 336–37
Cotton gin, **188**
Couch, Darius, *240*
Coulon de Villiers, Sieur de, 64
Coulterville, Calif., 168
Council Bluff, Nebr., 128
Council Bluffs, Iowa, 157, 173, 252, 254. *See also* Kanesville.
Council for New England, grant (1620), 40
Council Grove, Kans., 153, 171
Coupru, France, 280 bottom
Courcelles-les-Lens, France, 304
Court House Rock, Nebr., 170
Coutances, France, 306
Cove Mountain, Great Smoky Mountains National Park, 356
Coventry, England, 288
Cowans Ford Dam, N.C., 343
Cowlitz Indians, 23 D-2, *24*
Cowlitz Mission, Wash., 156
Cowlitz River, 128, 152, 156, 170, 246
Cowpens, Everglades National Park, 359
Cowpens, S.C., battle (1781), 103, *105,* 110–11
Coyoacán, Mexico, 20 right
Crab Orchard, Ky., 79, 125
Cracker Line, Battle of Chattanooga, 236
Cracow, Poland, 283, 288, 309
Craig, Fort, N.M., 170, 249
Craig, Fort, Tenn., 125
Crampton's Gap, Md., battle (1862), 215
Crandell, Mount, Waterton Lakes National Park, 362
Crater Lake National Park, Ore., 350. *See also* (Ice Age) Mazama, Mount.
Craters of the Moon National Monument, Idaho, 350
Crati River, Italy, 302
Craven House, Battle of Chattanooga, 236
Crawford, Fort, Colo., 247, 249
Crawford, Fort, Wis. *See* Prairie du Chien.
Crawfordsville, Ind., 146
Cree Indians, 23 C-3, *24*
Creek Indians, 23 F-5, *24,* 56, 61 bottom, *122;* (removal of) 149; (reservation, Okla.) 251
Creek War (1813–14), 139
Cresaps, Fort, Md., 69 bottom
Crescent City, Calif., 170, 246

part of proper name or full title.

Fort Albany, Ont., Canada, 62, 133
Fort Apache Indian Agency, Ariz., 249
Fort Fraser, B.C., Canada, 132
Fort Frederica National Monument, Ga., 351
Fort Good Hope, N.W.T., Canada, 132
Fort Jefferson National Monument, Fla., 351
Fort Lauderdale, Fla., 147
Fort Liard, N.W.T., Canada, 132; (complex, archaeological site) *18*, 19
Fort Loudoun Dam, Tenn., 287, 343
Fort Matanzas National Monument, Fla., 351
Fort McHenry National Monument, Md., 351
Fort McMurray, Alta., Canada. *See* Forks, Fort of the, Alta.
Fort Nelson, B.C., Canada, 132
Fort Nelson River, Canada, 132
Fort Norman, N.W.T., Canada, 132
Fort Peck Dam, Mont., 342
Fort Pulaski National Monument, Ga., 351
Fort Randall Dam, S.D., 343
Fort Randolph, Canal Zone, Panama, 261
Fort Resolution, N.W.T., Canada, 132
Fort Rock Cave, Ore., *18*, 19
Fort St. James, B.C., Canada, 132
Fort St. John, B.C., Canada, 132
Fort Scott, Kans., 146, 171, 173, 197
Fort Selkirk, Yukon, Canada, 257
Fort Sherman, Canal Zone, Panama, 261
Fort Simpson, N.W.T., Canada. *See* Forks, Fort of the, N.W.T.
Fort Smith, Ark., 146, 149, 153, 163, 171, 173, 189, 252
Fort Union National Monument, N.M., 350
Fort Vermilion, Alta., Canada, 132
Fort Wayne, Ind., 125, 129, 133, 136, 146, 151, 189, 203, 255. *See also* Miami, Fort.
Fort Worth, Tex., 171, 189, 249, 252, 285, 339, 347
Fort Yukon, Alaska, 257, 346
Fortune Bay, Newf., Canada, 263 inset
Forty Fort, Pa., 101
Fossil Bay, Grand Canyon National Park, 367
Fossil Forest, Yellowstone National Park, 365
Foster, John, map by (1677), **44–45**
Fougères, France, 307
Fountain Paintpot, Yellowstone National Park, 364
Four Mountains, Islands of the, Aleutian Is., 256
Fowey, England, 306
Fowltown, Ga., battle (1817), 147
Fox Indians. *See* Sauk and Fox Indians.
Fox Islands, Aleutian Is., 257
Foynes, Ireland, 291
Fram, Nansen's ship, 328
France, 33, *67*, 83, *90*, 92–93, *115*, 135; (after 1914) 278, 280, *281*, 282, 283; (after 1939) *277*, 288, *289*, 291, 304, 306, 307, 308; (after 1945) 314–15, 316, 317, 324–25, 327
Francis I, King of France, *36*
Frankfort, Ky., 121, 125, 145, 146, 163, 167, 199, 201, 203, 205, 218, 265
Frankfurt am Main, Germany, 280, 288, 304,

308, 316, 349
Frankfurt an der Oder, Germany, 308
Franklin, Kans., 197
Franklin, Mo., 146, 150
Franklin, Pa., 204. *See also* Machault, Fort; Venango, Fort; Venango.
Franklin, Tenn., *149*, 218; (battle 1864) 220, *221*
Franklin, W. Va., 212
Franklin, Benjamin, *9, 55, 81, 91*, 114, *115*
Franklin, State of, *124*, 125
Franklin Pike, Battle of Nashville, 240
Franklinton, Ohio, 125
Frankstown, Pa., 69 bottom, 79
Frankstown Branch, of Juniata River, 69 bottom
Franz Josef Land Islands, U.S.S.R., 328
Fraser, Simon, 98, *108*, 132, *133*
Fraser River, Canada, 133, 158 bottom. *See also* Tacoutche Tesse River.
Frayser's Farm, Va., 213
Fredendall, Lloyd R., 300
Frederica, Ga., 49
Frederica, Fort, Ga., 62, 63. *See also* Frederica.
Frederick, Md., 49, 80, 208, 215, 217
Frederick, Fort, Maine, 73
Frederick, Fort, N.B., Canada, 89
Frederick House, Ont., Canada, 133
Fredericksburg, Tex., 161, 171, 172
Fredericksburg, Va., 49, 79, 80, 138, 208, 213, 215, 222; (battle 1862) 217
Fredericton, N.B., Canada, 159, 344
Free Soil Party, *196*
Freeman, Thomas, 128–29
Freeman Cottage, Battle of Bemis Heights, 109
Freeman Farm, N.Y., battle (1777), *98*, 108–9
Freetown, Mass., 43
Frémont, John Charles, 156–57, 162–63, *173*, 212
Fremont Peak, Wyo., 156, *157*
Fremont River, 152, 247, 249
French Army:
  First Army, 307, 308
  Fourth Army, 282
  Sixth Army, 280 bottom, *281*
  2nd Armored Division, *306*
French Broad River, 79, 80, 125, 220, 287
French Creek, 67, 79, 101
French Creek Portage, Pa., 53
French Equatorial Africa, 291, 315. *See also* Central African Republic; Chad; Congo Republic; Gabon.
French Guiana, 92, 291, 324, 327
French Huguenots, *35, 55*, 87
French and Indian War, (1754–63) 67–75
French Indochina, 258, 292, 296. *See also* Cambodia; Laos; North and South Vietnam.
French Lick, Tenn., 78
French Mills, N.Y., 137 top
French Shore, Newf., Canada, 89
French Somaliland, 315, 325
French West Africa, 291, 314–15. *See also* Dahomey; Guinea; Ivory Coast; Mali;

Mauritania; Niger; Senegal; Upper Volta.
Frenchman Bay, Maine, 354
Frenchtown, Mich., battle (1813), 136
Fresnes-en-Wöevre, France, 281
Fresno, Calif., 248, 254, 284
Fribourg, Germany, 307
Friedrichshafen, Germany, 304
Friends, Society of. *See* Quaker Church.
Friendship Highway, Thailand, 323
Friesenhahn Cave, Tex., *18*, 19
Frightful Cave, Mexico, *18*, 19
Frijoles, Canal Zone, Panama, 261
Frisian Islands, North Sea, 304
Frobisher, Sir Martin, 33, *55*
Frog Portage, Sask., Canada, 132
Front Royal, Va., 208, 213, 215, 217; (battle 1862) 212
Frontenac, Fort, Ont., Canada, 47, 53, 56, 60, 61 top, 62, 64, 69 top, 72
Frontenac, Lac, 37, 47, 53, 56, 60, 61 top, 62, 64, 69 top, 72
Frontenac, Louis de Buade, Comte de Palluau et de, 60
Frontera, Mexico, 163
Fronteras, Mexico, 50, 249
Fruit crops, 188–89, 270–71, 336–37
Fuchs, Sir Vivian, 329
Fuka, Egypt, 301
Fundy, Bay of, Canada, 76, 89, 137 top, 159, 263 inset. *See also* Baie Françoise.
Fur trade, (colonial) *37, 46, 51, 52, 55, 57, 78, 82*, 83, 88; (West, after 1780) 132–33, *142, 153*, 155
Furnace Road, (Battle of Chancellorsville) 231; (Battle of the Wilderness) 238
Fürth, Germany, 304
Futatsu Rock, Iwo Jima, 310

G

Gabarus, Baie de, N.S., Canada, 73
Gabès, Tunisia, 300, 301 top
Gabès, Gulf of, Tunisia, 301 top
Gabon, 325. *See also* French Equatorial Africa.
Gadsden, Fort, Fla., 147
Gadsden Purchase (1853), 166, 260, *261*
Gafsa, Tunisia, 300, 301 top
Gaillard Cut, Panama Canal. *See* Culebra Cut.
Gaine's Battle, Fla. (1836), 147
Gaines's Mill, Va., 213
Gainsville, Tex., 171
Galena, Ill., 146, 150
Galicia Offensives (1914–15), 279
Galilee, Sea of, Israel, 321
Gallatin, Miss., 232
Gallatin, Tenn., 125
Gallatin National Forest, Mont., 364
Gallatin Range, 364
Gallatin River, 128, 152, 364
Galleon Harbor, Jamaica, 290
Gallipoli, Turkey, battle (1915), 279

Gozo Island, Maltese Is., 302
Grace Mine, Pa., iron ore region, 341
Graham, Tex., 252
Graham, Fort, Tex., 171
Graham Cave, Mo., *18,* 19
Grain, colonial trade, 83. *See also* Agriculture.
Gran Quivira National Monument, N.M., 350
Granada, Colo., 247
Granby, Fort, S.C., 102
Grand Bahama Island, Bahama Is., 320
Grand Bank, Atlantic Ocean, *36,* 37, 89
Grand Canyon, Ariz., 34, 50; (National Monument and National Park) 350, *355, 366–67*
Grand Canyon, Yellowstone National Park, 365
Grand Canyon of the Tuolumne, Yosemite National Park, 360
Grand Coulee Dam, Wash., 342
Grand Falls, Canada, 159
Grand Forks, N.D., 254, 347
Grand Gulf, Miss., 211, 232
Grand Haven, Mich., 203
Grand Island, La., 199
Grand Island, Nebr., 247, 252
Grand Island, N.Y., 70
Grand Junction, Tenn., 211, 218
Grand Lake, Maine, 159
Grand Manan Island, N.B., Canada, 159
Grand Portage, Minn., 53, 129, 133, 146, 158 top; (National Monument) 351
Grand Pré, N.S., Canada, 60, 61 top, 62, 64, 73
Grand Rapids, Mich., 146, 339
Grand River, Mich., 136
Grand River, S.D., 128
Grand Ronde Indian Reservation, Ore., 251
Grand Teton National Park, Wyo., 350
Grande Baie, Canada, 37, 60, 61 top, 62, 64, 73
Grande Rivière, Canada, 37, 53, 56, 60, 61 top, 62, 64, 69 top, 72
Grande Ronde, Ore., 156
Grande-Terre Island, Guadeloupe Is., 82
Grandpré, France, 282
Grandview Point, Grand Canyon National Park, 366
Granger, Wyo., 247, 254
Granite Gorge, Grand Canyon National Park, 366
Granny White House, Battle of Nashville, 240
Granny White Pike, Battle of Nashville, 240
Grant, Mount, Glacier National Park, 363
Grant, Ulysses S., *165, 210,* 211, 218, *219,* 220, 221, 222, *223,* 226, 232–33, 236, 237, 238, *243, 355*
Grant Village, Yellowstone National Park, 364
Granville, France, 307
Granville, Fort, Pa., 69 bottom
Granville Proprietary, N.C., 49
Grape crops, 270–71, 336–37
Grass Valley, Calif., 168
Grasse, François, Comte de, 103, *112*

Grasshopper Creek. *See* Delaware Creek.
Grasshopper Falls, Kans., 197
Gratiot, Fort, Mich., 136, 146
Gravesend, N.Y., 46 inset, 97
Gray, Robert, 13?, *133*
Grays Harbor, Wash., 158 bottom
Graz, Austria, 288, 308
Great Abaco Island, Bahama Is., 320
Great American Desert, 152–53
Great Basin, *153,* 156, 162, 172, *173,* 246
Great Bay, The, N.Y., 42 bottom, 46, 59 top
Great Bear Lake, N.W.T., Canada, 132, 257
Great Bend, Kans., 252
Great Britain, *115, 133, 158,* 278, 288, 291, 317. *See also* England; Scotland.
Great Carrying Place, Maine, 96
Great Chazy River, 70
Great Cranberry Island, Maine, 354–55
Great Egg Harbor River, 99
Great Exuma Island, Bahama Is., 290
Great Falls, Mont., 128, 247, 284, 346
Great Falls Dam, Tenn., 287
Great Falls of the Missouri, Mont., 132
Great Fish River, Canada, 132–33
Great Fountain Geyser, Yellowstone National Park, 364
Great Harbor, Mass. *See* Edgartown.
Great Head, Maine, 354
Great Inagua Island, Bahama Is., 259, 320
Great Khingan Mountains, Manchuria, 311
Great Lakes, *52, 115, 144,* 344, *345;* (Ice Age) *14,* 17 bottom; (War of 1812) 136–37
Great Lakes-St. Lawrence Basin, 343
Great Lakes-St. Lawrence Waterway, 344–45, *345*
Great Meadow Fort, Vt., 64
Great Meadows, Pa., battle (1754), 67
Great Northern R.R., 246–47. 254, *255*
Great Plains, *246, 253*
Great Redoubt, Battle of Bemis Heights, 109
Great Salt Lake, Utah, 132, 144, 152, *153,* 155, 156, 158 bottom, 162, 166, 170, 172, 200, 244, 247, 264; (Ice Age) *14,* 17 top
Great Salt Lake City, Utah. *See* Salt Lake City.
Great Salt Lake Desert, Utah, 152, 156, 170, 247; (Ice Age) 17 top
Great Sand Dunes National Monument, Colo., 350
Great Sand Dunes National Monument, Ind., 351
Great Sandy Desert, 152
Great Slave Lake, N.W.T., Canada, 132
Great Smoky Mountains National Park, Tenn.-N.C., 351, 356–57
Great Swamp Fight, R.I., (1675), *58, 59* bottom
Great Thumb Point, Grand Canyon National Park, 367
Great Trading Path, 79, 80
Great Trail, 79, 80
Great Valley Road, 80, *150,* 151
Greater East Asia Co-Prosperity Sphere, *292*
Greece, 279, 283, 288, *289,* 301, *312,* 315, 317, 325, 327
Greeley, Colo., 254

Green Bank, Atlantic Ocean, 89
Green Bay, Wis., 129, 133, 136, 146, 150, 285. *See also* Baie Verte, Wis.
Green Bay, Lake Michigan, Wis., 136
Green Islands, Solomon Is., 297
Green Mountain Boys, *122*
Green Mountains, 70, 72, 96
Green River, tributary of Colorado River, 128, 132, 152, 155, 156, 162–63, 170, 172, 247, 249
Green River, Ky., 78–79, 100, 125, 218
Green River Road, Battle of Cowpens, 110
Greenbrier River, 67, 77, 79
Greene, Nathanael, *91,* 103, *104, 106*
Greeneville, Tenn., 125
Greenland, *22, 29,* 33, 92, 291, 314, 324, 327, 328
Greenland Cap, Greenland, 16
Greenland Sea, 328
Greensboro, N.C., 203, 271, 339
Greenville, Miss., 211, 233
Greenville, S.C., 203, 220
Greenville, Tex., 252
Greenville, Treaty of (1795), *124,* 125
Greenwich, Conn., 42 bottom, 43, 47
Greenwood Lake, 97
Greer County, Okla., 251, 265
Gregory Bald, Great Smoky Mountains National Park, 356
Grenada, Miss., 211, 218
Grenada Island, Windward Is., 82, 320
Grenadines, archipelago, Windward Is., 82
Grenoble, France, *306,* 307
Grey Islands, Newf., Canada, 89
Greys River, 155
Greytown, Nicaragua, 260
Griffin, Fort, Tex., 249, 252
Grijalva River, Mexico, 20 left, 163
Grinnell, Mount, Glacier National Park, 363
Grinnell Glacier, Glacier National Park, 363
Grizzly Flats, Calif., 168
Grodno, Poland, 288
Gros Ventre Indians, *24, 155. See also* Atsina Indians.
Gros Ventre River, 155
Grose, Fort, Battle of Chattanooga, 237
Groseilliers, Médart Chouart, Sieur des, 36
Groton, Conn., 42 bottom, 43
Groton, Mass., 43, 59
Growlersburg, Calif. *See* Georgetown.
Guachoya, Ark., 34
Guadalajara, Mexico, 163
Guadalcanal Island, Solomon Is., 293, 295 top; (campaigns 1942–43) *296,* 297, 298
Guadalupe Hidalgo, Treaty of (1848), 166–67, 198
Guadalupe Mountains, 170
Guadalupe Pass, Tex., 170, 172
Guadalupe River, 161
Guadeloupe Islands, Leeward Is., 82, 290, 320
Guagua, Luzon I., Philippines, 294
Guale Indians, 23 F-5, *24*
Guam Island, Marianas Is., 262, *263, 276,* 296, 315, 322, 326, 348
Guanajuato, Mexico, 163
Guánica, Puerto Rico, 259

Júcaro, Cuba, 259
Judaism, 87, 186–87, 268–69, 334–35
Judith River, 128, 152, 170, 247
Julesburg, Colo., 252; (battle 1865) 247
Julianehaab, Greenland, 291
Jump Up Canyon, Ariz., 367
Junction City, Kans., 252
Juneau, Alaska, 257, 346
Juniata River, 67, 69 bottom, 79
Junín, Lake, Peru, 21 center
Juno Beach, Normandy invasion (1944), 306
Juno Temple, Grand Canyon National Park, 366
Jupiter, Fort, Fla., 147
Jutland Peninsula, Denmark, 278

K

Kaatskill, N.Y., 46
Kabah, Mexico, 20 left
Kadena Air Base, Okinawa I., Ryukyu Is., 327
Kaena Point, Oahu I., Hawaiian Is., 292 left
Kaesong, South Korea, 318, 319
Kaga, Japanese aircraft carrier, 295 bottom
Kagoshima, Kyushu I., Japan, 311
Kahoolawe Island, Hawaiian Is., 263 inset
Kahuku Point, Oahu I., Hawaiian Is., 292 left
Kahului, Maui I., Hawaiian Is., 346
Kaibab National Forest, Ariz., 367
Kaibab Plateau, Grand Canyon National Park, 367
Kaifeng, China, 311
Kaigani (Blood) Indians, 23 C-3, 24
Kailua, Oahu I., Hawaiian Is., 263 inset
Kaiserslautern, Germany, 308
Kajaani, Finland, 288
Kalamazoo, Mich., 146
Kalapuya Indians, 23 D-2, 24
Kalaupapa leper colony, Molokai I., Hawaiian Is., 263 inset
Kalimantan, Indonesia, 322
Kaliningrad, U.S.S.R., 316. See also Königsberg.
Kalispel Indians, 23 C-2, 24
Kama Rock, Iwo Jima, 310
Kamchatka Peninsula, Russia, 51; (U.S.S.R.) 293, 322
Kamiah Mission, Idaho, 156
Kamikaze raids, 310
Kaminaljuyú, Guatemala, 20 left
Kaministikwia River, Canada, 158 top
Kaministiquia, Fort, Ont., Canada, 53, 56, 62
Kamloops, Fort, B.C., Canada, 132
Kanab Creek, Ariz., 367
Kanawha River, 67, 77, 79, 100, 125
Kaneohe Bay, Oahu I., Hawaiian Is., 292 left
Kaneohe Naval Air Station, Oahu I., Hawaiian Is., 292 left
Kanesville, Iowa, 146, 171

Kanggye, North Korea, 318, 319
Kangoku Rock, Iwo Jima, 310
Kankakee River, 78, 100, 133, 136, 150–51
Kansa Indians, 23 E-4; 24; (reservation, Okla.) 251 inset
Kansas, 52; (Territory, organized 1854) 166–67, 170–71, 172–73, 174–75, 186–87, 188–89, 190–91, 196 bottom, 197, 199, 204; (admitted 1861) 201; 202, 205, 244, 246, 247, 249, 251, 252, 254, 264, 285, 335, 339, 351. See also Louisiana Province; Louisiana Purchase; Missouri (Territory).
Kansas City, Kans., 243, 271, 285. See also Shawnee Mission; Wyandotte.
Kansas City, Mo., 146, 189, 197, 243, 252, 254, 273, 339, 347. See also Chouteau's Post.
Kansas-Nebraska Act (1854), 166, 196, 197, 199
Kansas Pacific R.R., 247, 249, 252, 254
Kansas River, 128–29, 132–33, 145, 146, 153, 157, 163, 167, 197, 201, 244, 264
Kara Sea, U.S.S.R., 328
Karachi, Pakistan, 349
Karafuto, Sakhalin I., Japan, 293, 311
Karankawa Indians, 23 F-4, 24
Karlsruhe, Germany, 304
Karok Indians, 23 D-1, 24
Kaska Indians, 23 B-2, 24
Kaskaskia, Ill., 53, 62, 90, 100, 129, 133, 145, 146
Kaskaskia Indians, 23 E-4, 24
Kaskaskia River, 100, 150, 202
Kassel, Germany, 288, 304, 308
Kasserine Pass, Tunisia, battle (1943), 300, 301 top
Katmai National Monument, Alaska, 350
Kauai Island, Hawaiian Is., 263 inset, 350
Kaunas, Lithuania, 283, 288
Kavalla, Greece, 288
Kavieng, New Ireland, Bismarck Arch., 293, 297
Kawaiisu Indians, 23 E-2, 24
Kawasaki, Honshu I., Japan, 311
Kayoderosseras Patent, N.Y., 47
Kayuk Complex, Alaska, 18, 19
Kearney, Nebr., 252. See also Kearney, Fort.
Kearney, Fort, Nebr., 171, 247
Kearny, Lawrence, drawing by, 144
Kearny, Stephen Watts, 162–63
Kecoughtan, Va., 41, 48
Keele River, Canada, 132
Keene, N.H., 80
Keet Seel, Ariz., 22
Keewatin Cap, Canada, 16
Keflavik, Iceland, 327, 349
Keith's Division Line, East-West Jersey (1687), 47
Kekionga, Ind., 78
Kellogg-Briand Pact (1928), 277
Kelly Bill (1925), 284
Kenai Peninsula, Alaska, 257
Kendari, Celebes I., Netherlands East Indies, 292, 296
Kénitra Naval Training Command, Morocco, 327

Kennan, George F., 313
Kennebec River, 37, 41, 56, 60, 61 top, 64, 72, 89, 96, 114, 137 top, 151, 159, 203. See also Sagadahoc River.
Kennebunk, Maine, 43
Kennedy, John Fitzgerald, 277, 321
Kennesaw Mountain, Ga., battle (1864), 220, 221
Kenosha, Wis., 146
Kent, Fort, Maine, 159
Kent Island, Md., 48
Kent County, Del., 47
Kenté, Ont., Canada, 37
Kentucky, (District of Va. 1776–92) 101, 116, 119; (admitted 1792) 120, 121; 125, 129, 145, 146, 150–51, 163, 167, 173, 199, 201, 202–3, 204; (after 1860) 205, 211, 218, 220, 245, 254–55, 264–65, 285, 287, 335, 339, 351. See also Appalachia; Transylvania; Virginia.
Kentucky Dam, Ky., 287, 343
Kentucky River, 67, 77, 78–79, 80, 100, 125, 218
Kenya, 315, 325, 327
Keogh, Fort, Mont., 247
Keokuk, Iowa, 146, 202
Keowee, S.C., 79
Keraha Islands, Ryukyu Is., 311
Kerch, U.S.S.R., 289
Kerensky Offensive (1917), 279
Keres language group, 24, 25
Kern River, 152, 170
Kernstown, Va., battle (1862), 212
Ketchikan, Alaska, 257, 346
Kettle Creek, S.C., battle (1779), 102
Kettle Falls, Alta., Canada, 132
Keuka Lake, N.Y., 101
Keweenaw, Lake, 17 bottom
Key Largo, Fla., 359
Key West, Fla., 259, 290, 320
Key West Barracks, Key West, Fla., 147
Khabarovsk, U.S.S.R., 293, 311
Kharkov, Russia, 279; (U.S.S.R.) 283, 289
Khingan Mountains (Great Khingan and Lesser Khingan), Manchuria, 311
Kiatuthlana, Ariz., 22
Kichai Indians, 23 F-4, 24
Kickapoo, Kans., 197
Kickapoo Indians, 23 D-4, 24; (reservation, Kans., Okla.) 251
Kiel, Germany, 288, 304, 308, 316
Kieta, Bougainville I., 293, 297
Kiev, Russia, 279; (U.S.S.R.) 283, 288
Kievits Hook, Conn., 46
Kilchu, North Korea, 318, 319
Killdeer Mountain, N.D., battle (1864), 247
Kimpo, South Korea, 322
Kinderhook, N.Y., 46, 122
Kindley Air Force Base, Bermuda, 327
King, Fort, Fla., 147
King, Rufus, 126
King Christian IX Land, Greenland, 328
King Christian X Land, Greenland, 328
King Frederik VI Coast, Greenland, 328
King Frederik VIII Land, Greenland, 328
King George's War (1744–48), 64, 65

King Philip, Wampanoag chief, *58*
King Philip's War (1675–76), *58, 59* bottom
King Salmon, Alaska, 346
King Street, Battle of Trenton, 106
King William's War (1689–97), 60, **60**
Kingman Reef, Pacific Ocean, 262
Kings Canyon National Park, Calif., 350
King's Meadows, Tenn., 125
Kings Mountain, S.C., battle (1780), 102, **104**
Kings River, 248
Kingsport, Tenn., 125. *See also* Patrick Henry, Fort.
Kingston, Ga., 218
Kingston, Jamaica, 320
Kingston, N.J., 97, 99
Kingston, N.Y., 47, 80, 98, 101, 122, 137 top, 151
Kingston, Ont., Canada, 122, 137 top, 344. *See also* Frontenac, Fort.
Kingston, R.I., 43. *See also* Narraganset Fort.
Kingston, Tenn., 125
Kinishba, Ariz., 22
Kinkaid, Thomas C., 299
Kino, Eusebio Francisco, 50, *51*
Kintla Glacier, Glacier National Park, 362
Kintla Lake, Glacier National Park, 362
Kintla Peak, Glacier National Park, 362
Kiowa, Fort, S.D. *See* Lookout, Fort.
Kiowa Apache Indians, 23 E-3, *24*
Kiowa Indians, 23 E-3, *24, 248,* 249, *253;* (language group) 25; (reservation, Okla.) 251
Kip's Bay, N.Y., 97
Kirkuk, Iraq, 321
Kirtland, Ohio, 187
Kiska Island, Aleutian Is., 256, 293
Kiskiminetas River, 69 bottom
Kissimmee, Lake, Fla., 147
Kissimmee River, 147
Kit Carson Pass, Calif., 168, 170
Kita, Iwo Jima, 310
Kitano Point, Iwo Jima, 310
Kittanning, Pa., 67
Kittanning, Fort, Pa., 101. *See also* Kittanning.
Kittery, Maine, 42 top, 43
Kittery Point, Maine, *64*
Kizil Irmak River, Turkey, 321
Klamath, Fort, Ore., 246
Klamath Indians, 23 D-2, *24;* (reservation, Ore.) 251
Klamath Lakes. *See* Upper Klamath Lake.
Klamath River, 132, 152, 156, 162, 172, 246
Klikitat Indians, 23 D-2, *24*
Klondike, Yukon, Canada, 257
Klondike gold rush (1896–98), 257
Knife River, 128
Knox, Henry, *91, 106*
Knyphausen, Baron Wilhelm von, *106*
Knox Coast, Antarctica, 329
Knoxville, Tenn., 121, 125, 146, 151, 189, 199, 203, 218, 220, 287, 356
Knud Rasmussen Land, Greenland, 328
Kobbe, Fort, Canal Zone, Panama, 261
Kobe, Honshu I., Japan, 311

Kobuk River, 257
Kodiak, Alaska, 257, 346; (naval station) 327. *See also* St. Pauls Harbor.
Kogruk Complex, Alaska, *18, 19*
Kokumbona, Guadalcanal I., 298
Kola Peninsula, U.S.S.R., 288–89
Koli Point, Guadalcanal I., 298
Komarno, Hungary, 308
Kompong Cham, Cambodia, 323
Kona, Hawaii I., Hawaiian Is., 346
Königsberg, Germany, 288, 309, 316
Konpong Thom, Cambodia, 323
Kontum, South Vietnam, 323
Koolau Range, Oahu I., Hawaiian Is., 292 left
Kootenae House, Alta., Canada, 132
Kootenai River, Canada-U.S., 132, 152, 172, 246
Korea, 262, 292, 311, 318, 319. *See also* North Korea; South Korea.
Korean Treaty (1954), 325
Korean War (1950–53), *313,* 318–19, 322
Koshkonong, Fort, Wis., 146
Köslin, Germany, 308
Kosong, North Korea, 319 right
Kota Bharu, Malaya, 292
Kotzebue, Alaska, 346
Koyukon Indians, 23 A-1, *24*
Koyukuk River, 257
Krasnovodsk, U.S.S.R., 321
Ku Klux Klan, *245*
Kuala Lumpur, Malaya, 292; (Malaysia) 322
Kuang-chou-wan, China, 258
Kuantan, Malaya, 292
Kuching, Sarawak, 292, 296
Kuibyshev, U.S.S.R., 289
Kukum, Guadalcanal I., 298
Kula Gulf, Solomon Is., battle (1943), 297
Kullyspell House, Idaho, 132
Kum River, South Korea, 318, 319
Kunming, China, 292
Kunsan, South Korea, 318, 319; (air base) 322, 327
Kupang, Timor, 292
Kura River, U.S.S.R., 321
Kure, Honshu I., Japan, 292, 311
Kure Island, Hawaiian Is., 293, 295 bottom: inset
Kurile Islands, Japan, 293; (U.S.S.R.) 315, 322
Kurita, Takeo, 299
Kurland, 279. *See also* Latvia.
Kursk, U.S.S.R., 289
Kusaie Island, Caroline Is., 293, 297
Kuskokwim River, Alaska, 132, 257
Kuskuski, Pa., 67, 79
Kutaraja, Sumatra, Netherlands East Indies, 292
Kutchin Indians, 23 A-2, *24*
Kutenai Indians, 23 C-2, *24;* (language group) 25; (reservation, Mont.) 251
Kutno, Poland, 309
Kuwait, 321, 325
Kwajalein Atoll, Marshall Is., 293, 297
Kwakiutl Indians, 23, C-1, *24*
Kweiyang, China, 292
Kyoto, Honshu I., Japan, 311
Kyushu Island, Japan, 292, 311, 322

La Bahía, Tex., 50
La Barge Creek, 155
La Baye, Fort, Wis., 53
La Butte, Fort, N.D., 53
La Chorrera, Panama, 261
La Colle Mill, Canada, battle (1814), 137 top
La Crosse, Wis., 146, 202, 285
La Crosse nuclear plant, Wis., 343
La Encarnación, Mexico, 164
La Galette, Fort, N.Y., 47, 53, 69 top, 72
La Grande, Ore., 246
La Grange, Ga., 146
La Grange, Tex., 161
La Harpe, Bernard de, 53
La Have, N.S., Canada, 37
La Have Bank, Atlantic Ocean, 89
La Jolla Site, Calif., *18, 19*
La Jonquière, Jacques, Marquis de, 64
La Junta, Colo., 152, 247, 249, 252, 254
La Junta, N.M., 152
La Luzerne, Anne César, Chevalier de, 114, *115*
La Manzanillo, Mexico, 163
La Pallice, France, 278, 304
La Paz, Mexico, 50, 162
La Paz, Peru, 349
La Plata, South America, 92
La Plata range, Colo., **10–11**
La Pointe de St-Esprit, Wis., 36
La Prairie, Que., Canada, 60, *61,* 70
La Prairie Portage, Man., Canada, 133
La Présentation, N.Y. *See* La Galette, Fort, N.Y., 53.
La Purisima Concepción, Calif., 128
La Reine, Fort, Man., Canada, 53
La Roche-en-Ardenne, Belgium, 309
La Rochelle, France, 304
La Salle, Ill., 150
La Salle, Robert Cavelier, Sieur de, *52,* 53
La Senia, Algeria, 300
La Tolita, Ecuador, 21 center
La Tourette, Fort, Ont., Canada, 53, 56, 62
La Vaca, Tex., 161
La Venta, Mexico, 20 left
La Vérendrye, Sieur de, and sons, *52,* 53
Labrador Cap, Ice Age, 16
Labrador Peninsula, Canada, 76, 89, 263, 290–91, 345
Lac au Claies, Ont., Canada, 72
Lac des Bois, Minn. *See* Lake of the Woods.
Lac des Mille Lacs, Ont., Canada, 158 top
Lac la Croix, Minn., 158 top
Lacandon Maya Indians, 23, G-4
Lachine, Que., Canada, 37, 53, 56, 60, 61 top, 64, 69 top, 70, 72, 344 inset
Lachine Canal, Que., Canada, 344 inset
Lachine Section, St. Lawrence Seaway, 344 inset
Lacy House, Battle of the Wilderness, 238
Ladoga, Lake, U.S.S.R., 288
Lae, Northeast New Guinea, 293, 297
Lafayette, Ind., 146. *See also* Ouiatanon, Fort.
Lafayette, Marie du Motier, Marquis de, 103
Lafayette National Park, Maine, *355*
Lagos, Nigeria, 349

Mawhood, Charles, *106*
Mawson Station, Antarctica, 329
May, Cape, N.J., 46, 47, 49, 138
May Lake, Yosemite National Park, 361
Maya Indians, *15*, 20 left, 23 G-4; (language group) 25
Mayaguana Island, Bahama Is., 320
Mayagüez, Puerto Rico, 263 inset
Mayapán, Mexico, 20 left
Maycock's Plantation, Va., 41
Mayenne, France, 307
Mayfield Dam, Wash., 342
Maysville, Ky. *See* Limestone.
Maysville Turnpike, 151
Mazagan, Morocco, 300
Mazama, Mount, Ore., 19
Mazatlán, Mexico, 163
Meade, Fort, S.D., 247
Meade, George Gordon, *216*, 217, 222, 234, *235*
Meat, colonial trade, 83
Meat packing industry, 272–73, 338–39
Mecca, Saudi Arabia, 321
Mechanicsville, Va., 208, 215; (battle 1862) *212, 213*
Mecklenburg, W. Va., 79
Medan, Sumatra, Netherlands East Indies, 292
Medfield, Mass., 43, 59 bottom
Medford, Mass., 42 top, 43, 59 bottom, 95
Medford, Ore., 246, 284
Medicine Bow Mountains, 155
Medicine Bow River, 155
Medina, Saudi Arabia, 321
Medina, Tex., 161
Mediterranean Sea, 135, 278–79, 283, 288–89, 291, 300–301, 302, 307, 317, 321, 327
Meeker Massacre, Colo. (1879), 247
Megantic, Lake, Canada, 96
Meherrin River, 79
Meigs, Fort, Ohio, 136
Méjico. *See* Mexico City.
Mekong River, Southeast Asia, 93, 292, 296, 322, 323
Mellon, Fort, Fla., battle (1837), 147
Melones, Calif., 168. *See also* Slumgullion.
Melun, France, 280
Melville, Lake, Newf., Canada, 89
Memel, Lithuania, 283, 288
Memphis, Tenn., 146, 149, 150, 173, 189, 199, 202, 218, 254, 339; (battle 1862) *210, 211. See also* Assomption, Fort L'; Pickering, Fort; Prudhomme, Fort; San Fernando, Fort.
Memphremagog, Lake, Vt., 69 top, 72
Menado, Celebes I., Netherlands East Indies, 292, 296
Mendocino, Cape, Calif., *51*
Mendon, Mass., 43, 59 bottom
Mendoza, Juan Domínguez de, 50
Mennonite Church, *46*, 87
Menominee Range, Mich., iron ore region, 273, 341
Menominee River, 136, 146, 202–3
Menomini Indians, 23 D-4; *24;* (reservation, Wis.) 251

Menotomy, Mass. *See* Arlington.
Mentasta Pass, Alaska, 257
Merced, Calif., 248
Merced Grove, Yosemite National Park, 360
Merced Lake, Yosemite National Park, 361
Merced Pass, Yosemite National Park, 361
Merced River, 152, 168, 170, 246, 248, 360–61; (South Fork) 360
Mercer, Fort, N.J., 99
Mercer, Hugh, *106*
Mercereau, John, *Flying Machine*, 81
Mercur Peak, Yosemite National Park, 360
Mercury deposits, 340–41
Merdum, Libya, 301
Mérida, Mexico, 163
Meridian, Miss., 211
Merrimack River, 42 top, 43, *44*, 59 bottom, 60, 61 top, 64, 69 top, 72, 96, 137 top, 151, 203
Merry Mount, Mass. *See* Mount Wollaston.
Mersa Matruh, Egypt, 301
Merseburg, Germany, 304
Mersin, Turkey, 321
Merwin Dam, Wash., 342
Mesa Verde National Park, Colo., 22, 350
Mesabi Range, Minn., iron ore region, *115, 158, 243,* 273, 341
Mescalero Apache Indians, 23 E-3, *24;* (reservation, N.M.) 251
Mescalero Point, Grand Canyon National Park, 366
Meshed, Iran, 321
Messina, Sicily, 288, 302, *303*
Messina, Strait of, 302
Metals, (industry) 338–39; (mining regions) 190–91, *242,* 246–47, 248–49; (ore deposits) 340–41
Metapona River, Guadalcanal I., 298
Methodist Church, 87, 186–87, 268–69, 334–35
Methye Portage, Sask., Canada, 132
Mettawee River, 70
Metz, Germany, 280, 281, 282; (France) 304, 307, 308
Meuse-Argonne Offensive, France (1918), 280, 282
Meuse River, France, 280, 281, 282, 307, 308, 309
Mexican War (1846–48), 162–65
Mexico, 20; (conquest of, 1519–21) 34; (independent, 1821) 144–45, 152–53, 156, 158 bottom; (Texas Revolution and Mexican War, 1835–48) 161, 162–63, 164, *165;* (after 1848) 166–67, 170–71, 248–49, 260; (U.S. expedition, 1916) 263; (after 1945) 314, 320, 324, 327. *See also* New Spain; Spanish possessions.
Mexico, Gulf of, 20 left, 33, 34, 50, *52,* 53, 139, *140,* 146, 147, 161, 163, 164, 202–3, 211, 259, 260, 320, *341*
Mexico City, Mexico, 34, **35**, 50, 349; (battles 1847) 163, **164–65.** *See also* Tenochtitlán.
Miami, Fla., 285, 290, 320, 339, 347, 349. *See also* Dallas, Fort.
Miami, Fort, Ind., 53, 62, 67, 78, 100
Miami, Fort, Mich., 53

Miami, Fort, Ohio, (Battle of Fallen Timbers, 1794) 125
Miami Indians, 23 E-5, *24,* 56, 67, 78, 125
Miami and Ohio Canal, 151
Miami River, 53, 67, 79, 100, 125, 151
Micanopy, Fla., 147
Miccosukee, Lake, Fla., 147
Michigan, (Territory, organized 1805) 129, 133, 136, 145, 153, 167 top, 196; (admitted 1837) 167; 146, 150–51, 158, 163, 199, 201, 202–3, 204; (after 1860) 205, 254–55, 264–65, 285, 335, 339, 344, 351. *See also* Indiana (Territory); Louisiana Province (French); Quebec (colony).
Michigan, Lake, *52,* 76, 78, 100, 114, 118, 121, 129, 133, 136, 145, 146, 150–51, 163, 167, 201, 203, 264, 285, 344. *See also* Illinois, Lac des.
Michigan Central R.R., 255
Michigan City, Ind., 151
Michigan Road, 151
"Michigania," Northwest Territory, *120*
Michilimackinac, Fort, Mackinac I., Mich., (after 1780) 121, 129; (fur post) 133. *See also* Mackinac, Fort.
Michilimackinac, Fort, (now Mackinaw City) Mich., (1715–80) 53, *55,* 62
Michipicoten House, Ont., Canada, 133
Micmac Indians, 23 C-6, *24,* 56
Mid Island Creek, 126
Mid-Canada Line, defense system (1957–65), *326,* 327
Middle Atlantic Basin, 343
Middle Bridge, Battle of Antietam, 229
Middle Park, Colo., 152
Middle Passage, colonial trade route, *82,* 83
Middle Plantation, Va., 48
Middleborough, Mass., 43, 59 bottom
Middlebury, Vt., 122, 137 top
Middletown, Conn., 42 bottom, 43, 59 bottom
Middletown, N.J., 47
Middletown, Va., 212, 215
Midway Geyser Basin, Yellowstone National Park, 364
Midway Island, Pacific Ocean, 262; (battle of, 1942) *292,* 293, 295 bottom
Midway Naval Station, Midway I., 327
Midwout, N.Y., 46 inset
Mier, Mexico, 163, 164; (battle 1842) *160,* 161
Mifflin, Fort, Pa., 99
Milan, Italy, 283, 288
Miles, Nelson A., 259
Miles City, Mont., 247
Milford, Conn., 42 bottom, 43
Milk Creek, Colo., battle (1879), 247
Milk River, of Missouri R., 128, 132, 152, 170, 172, 247
Mill Creek, Calif., 168
Mill Creek, N.Y., Battle of Bemis Heights, 109
Mill Springs, Ky., 146
Mille Lacs Lake, Minn., 129
Milledgeville, Ga., 203, 205
Miller, Fort, Calif., 170

St-Jacques, Fort, Que., Canada. *See* Rupert House.

St-Jean, Fort, N.B., Canada, 73

St-Jean, Fort, Que., Canada. *See* St. John, Fort.

St-Jean, Lac, Que., Canada. *See* St. John, Lake.

St. John, N.B., Canada, 159. *See also* Frederick, Fort, N.B.; St-Jean, Fort, N.B.

St. John, Fort, Que., Canada, (Fort St-Jean) 37, 69 top, 70, 72; 96, 98

St. John, Lake, Que., Canada, (Lac St-Jean) 37, 56, 60, 61 top, 64, 72; 89

St. John Island, Virgin Is., 82, 263 inset, 350 inset

St. John River, Maine, 37, 56, 60, 61 top, 62, 64, 73, 76, 89, 96, 114, 118, 121, 137 top, 151, 159, 167, 201, 344

St. John's, Newf., Canada, 37, 62, 89, 291, 345

St. Johns River, Fla., 35, 49, 61 bottom, 62, 63, 94 left, 118, 121, 147, 203

St. Johnsbury, Vt., 203

St. Joseph, Fla., 147

St. Joseph, Mo., 171, 197, 202, 252. *See also* Robidoux's Post.

St. Joseph, Fort, Mich., 53, 56, 78, 100

St. Joseph, Fort, Ont., Canada, 136

St. Joseph, Lake, Ont., Canada, 133

St. Joseph River, Mich., 78–79, 100, 136

St. Joseph River, of Maumee R., 67, 78–79, 100, 125, 136

St-Juvin, France, 282

St. Kitts Island, Leeward Is., 82

St-Laurent, Fleuve. *See* St. Lawrence River.

St. Lawrence, Gulf of, Canada, *38, 76, 89,* 263 inset, 344–45. *See also* Grande Baie.

St. Lawrence Island, Alaska, 257, 262

St. Lawrence River, Canada, (Fleuve St-Laurent) 37, 40, 47, 53, 56, 60, 61 top, 62, 64, 69 top, 72–73; *17, 36, 61,* 70, 76, 89, 94 left, 96, 98, 118, 121, 122, 137 top, 145, 151, 159, 167, 201, 203, 265, 344, *345*

St. Lawrence Seaway, 344–45

St. Lawrence Ten Towns, N.Y., 122

St. Leger, Barry, 98

St-Lô, France, 306, 307

St. Louis, Mo., *100,* 121, 129, *130–31,* 133, 145, 146, 150, 167, 173, **184,** 189, 191, 199, 202, 254, 271, 273, 285, *333,* 339, 347

Saint-Louis, Senegal, 92

St-Louis, Fort, Ala., 53

St-Louis, Fort, Ont., Canada. *See* Moose Factory.

St-Louis, Fort, Tex., 50, *51, 52,* 53

St. Louis, Lake, St. Lawrence R., Canada, 344 inset

St. Louis River, 146, 158 top

Saint-Loup-sur-Semouse, France, 307

St. Lucia Island, Windward Is., 82, 290, 320

St-Malo, France, 33, 304, 307

St. Marks, Fla., (San Marcos) 61 bottom, 62; 114, 123, 147, 203

St. Marks Fort, Ala., 139

St. Martin Island, Leeward Is., 82

St. Mary Lake, Glacier National Park, 363

Saint Marys, Md., 48, 49

St. Marys, Ohio, 125

St. Mary's Mission, Mont., 156

St. Marys River, Fla., 49, 56, 61 bottom, 63, 76, 94 left, 114, 147

St. Marys River, of Maumee R., 67, 78–79, 100, 125, 136

St. Matthew Island, Alaska, 256

St. Matthias Islands, Bismarck Arch., 297

St-Maurice River, Canada, (St-Maurice R.) 60, 61 top, 64, 72; 96

St. Michael, Alaska, 257

St. Michaels, Md., 138

St-Mihiel, France, (battle 1918) 280, 281; *282*

St-Nazaire, France, 278, 291, 304, 307

St. Nicholas, Fort, Alaska, 132

St. Nicholas, Mount, Glacier National Park, 363

St-Nicolas, Fort, Wis., *52, 53*

St. Paul, Minn., 146, 167, 173, 201, 202, 205, 254, 264, 285, 347

St. Paul Island, Alaska, 256

St. Pauls Harbor, Alaska, 132

St. Paul's Mission, Ore., 156

St. Peter, Lake, Canada, 96

St. Peter's River, 128–29, 133

St. Petersburg, Russia. *See* Petrograd.

St. Philip, Fort, La., 139, 146, 211

St-Pierre, Fort, Minn., 53

St. Pierre Bank, Atlantic Ocean, 37, 89

St. Pierre Island, St. Pierre and Miquelon islands, Atlantic Ocean, (Isle St-Pierre) 37, 62, 76, *77;* 89

St-Quentin, France, 280

St-Raphaël, France, 307

St. Régis, Que., Canada, 344 inset

St-Sacrement, Lac, N.Y., 37, 43, 47, 69 top

St. Simons, Fort, Ga., 63

St. Simons Island, Ga., 49, 61 bottom

St. Stephen, N.B., Canada, 159

St. Stephens, Fort, Ala., 123

St. Thomas Island, Virgin Is., 82, 263 inset

St-Tropez, France, 307

St. Vincent Island, Windward Is., 82, 320

St-Vith, Belgium, 308, 309

St. Vrain, Fort, Colo., 156

Ste-Anne, Fort, Vt., 37, 47

Ste-Croix, Fleuve, N.B., Canada, 73

Ste-Croix, Fort, Wis., 53

Ste. Genevieve, Mo., (Ste-Geneviève) 53; 129, 133

Sainte-Hélène, Jacques Lemoyne, Sieur de, 60

Ste-Marie, N.Y., 37

Ste-Marie, Que., Canada, 36–37

Ste-Menehould, France, 282

Ste-Mère-Eglise, France, 306

Ste-Thérèse, Que., Canada, 37

Saipan Island, Marianas Is., 293, 296

Sakchu, North Korea, 318, 319

Sakhalin Island, U.S.S.R.-Japan, 262, 293, 311; (to U.S.S.R. after 1945) 315, 322, 325

Sakonnet River, 59 bottom

Salado River, Mexico, 161, 163, 164

Salamaua, Northeast New Guinea, 297

Salazar, Antonio de Oliveira, *290*

Saleesh House, Mont., 132

Salem, Ind., 204

Salem, Mass., 42 top, 43, 59 bottom, 69 top, 72, 80, 89

Salem, N.C., 79, 80, 86, 102, 103

Salem, N.J., 47. *See also* Varkinskill.

Salem, Ore., 166, 170, 200, 244, 246, 264

Salem Church, Battle of Spotsylvania, 239

Salem River. *See* Varkins Kill.

Salerno, Italy, battle (1943), 302, 303

Salerno, Gulf of, Italy, 303

Salina, Kans., 247, 249

Salina, N.Y., 122

Salina, Okla., 252. *See also* Chouteau's Trading Post (1817–22).

Salinan Indians, 23 E-1, *24*

Salinas, Calif., 248

Salinas River, 152, 156, 170, 248

Saline River, 153, 247, 249, 252

Salisbury, Md., 203

Salisbury, Mass., 43, 59 bottom

Salisbury, N.C., 79, 80, 103, 199

Salish Indians, 23 C-2, *24;* (language group) 25; (reservations, Mont., Wash.) 251

Salmon City, Idaho, 247

Salmon Falls, N.H., 60

Salmon Falls River, 43

Salmon River, 128, 132, 152, 156, 170, 172, 246

Salonika, Greece, 288

Salsbury Cove, Maine, 354

Salso River, Sicily, 302

Salt Lake City, Utah, (Great Salt Lake City) 166, 170, 172, 186, 188, 200, 244; (after 1868) 247, 254, 264, 270, 284, 346

Salt Lake Cutoff, California Trail, 170

Salt River, Ariz., 22, 152, 162–63, 170, 172, 248–49

Salt River, Idaho, 155

Salt River, Ky., 78–79

Salt River Canyon, Ariz., battle (1872), 249

Saltillo, Mexico, 34, 50, 128, 163, 164, *165*

Salton Sea, Calif., 248

Saluda Dam, S.C., 343

Saluda River, 49, 79, 102, 103, 151, 203, 220

Salum, Egypt, 135

Salween River, Southeast Asia, 292

Salzburg, Austria, 308

Sam Houston, Fort, Tex. *See* San Antonio, Tex.

Sama, Hainan I., China, 323

Samar Island, Philippines, 258, 292, 296; (battle off, 1944) *298, 299*

Sambre River, France, 280

Samchok, South Korea, 318, 319

Samoa Islands, Pacific Ocean, 262, 263 inset, 297

Samoset, Pemaquid Indian, *58*

Sampson, William T., *258,* 259

Samuel C. Moore Dam, N.H., 343

San Agustín, Fla. *See* St. Augustine

San Angelo, Tex., 252

San Antonio, Fla., 35

San Antonio, Luzon I., Philippines, 294

San Antonio, Tex., (missions) 50, 53; (San Antonio de Béxar) 128, 145; (Béxar, battle 1835) *160,* 161; (after 1846) 163, 167, 171, 189, 249, 252, 254, 271, 285, 347, 349

San Antonio de Padua, Calif., 51, 128

PACIFIC OCEAN

PACIFIC OCEAN

Principal Islands of
HAWAII

Kauai I.
Niihau I.
Oahu I.
Molokai I.
Maui I.
Hawaii I.

100   200

BERING SEA

ALEUTIAN ISLANDS
Volcanic Chain

ALASKA PEN.

KODIAK I.

KENAI PEN.

Nunivak I.

St.Lawrence I.

Seward Pen.

Bering Strait

ARCTIC PLAIN

BROOKS RANGE

YUKON FLATS

Yukon R.

ALASKA RANGE

Chichagof I.

Baranof I.

Prince of Wales I.

ALASKA

200   400

PUERTO RICO and
VIRGIN ISLANDS

CORDILLERA CENTRAL

St.Thomas I.
St.John
St.Croix I.

100